CONSTANT PAINE

Ratuchi

Anthu MBiz

1·12·08.

First published in 2008
Copyright © David Bull, 2008

Published by HAGIOLOGY PUBLISHING
170 Westbury Road
Bristol BS9 3AH

ISBN 978-0-9534474-7-3

Designed and typeset by Elizabeth Porter, www.porterlizz-design.com, Bristol
Printed and bound in Great Britain by Haynes Publishing, Yeovil

CONSTANT PAINE

From Southampton Legend
to South African Ambassador

DAVID BULL

in association with

and

Daily Echo

Picture Credits

As ever, the *Southern Daily Echo* has been a major source of illustrations. For reasons explained in the preface, I cannot be entirely sure of the copyright of some images, but the photos known, or thought, to be from the *Echo* appear at pages xi, 33, 39, 41, 46, 49, 52 (both), 55, 56, 58, 59, 60 (both), 65, 68, 69, 73, 74, 75, 80, 89, 91, 92, 96, 97, 99, 102, 103, 104, 106, 107, 111 (left), 112, 115, 117, 118, 119, 121 (both), 124, 127, 129, 133 (top), 134, 138 (both), 175, 185, 186, 187, 188, 191, 192 (both), 195, 201, 202, 203, 207, 211, 212, 215, 222, 223, 224, 229, 232, 234, 237, 240, 241, 242, 251, 253, 257 (all), 259, 263 (both), 264 (both), 266, 283 (all), 311 (bottom two), 337, 371, 401(all), 402, 403 (all), 404, back cover (left).

Other images of known copyright are from the following professional sources:

Getty Images: 152, 153, 158, 161, 172, 174, 179, 180, 331.
Gloucestershire Echo: 347, 362.
Hereford Times: 278, 280, 281, 285, 291, 297 (top right and both below), 299, 311 (top right), 319, 320.
Mirrorpix: 167 (bottom), 173, 239, 297 (top left), 310, 339.
PA Photos: 125, 139, 146, 159, 163, 166, 167 (top), 189.
Solent News: 311 (top left).
E.A Sollars/Winchester City Council: 16, 17, 20, 25, 26, 30, 44.

John Philpott kindly provided two of his studio shots: 168, 333. Other photos, several of them taken especially for this book, have come from the private collections of Terry Paine, 226, 228, 356, 368, 388, 391, 392, 394 (bottom), 397 (both), 398 (both), 405 (left), 406 (bottom), back cover (right); Dave Adlem, 10 (pub); Norman Bainbridge, 111 (right); 405 (right); Arun Banerjee, 305; Jim Brown, 377; Mark Buckland, 359; Paul Evans, 381; Paul Godfrey (Cheltenham Town FC), 345, 346; Carolyn Gordon, back flap; Gerry Gurr, 209; Kevin Hill, 213; Rob Holley, 194; Colin Holmes/John Pennicott, 19; Bryan Horsnell, 328; Cladge Howard, 22; Derek Igglesden, 12, 400; Barry Lambert, 380; Dave Lewis, 354; Roy Lunniss, 123; Cathy MacLeod, 394 (top); Wes Maughan, 78; Trevor Paine, 7,8; Geoff Parker, 364; Ron Parrott, 300; Mary Penfold, 217, 218, 365; John Sillett, 307.

The remaining images are mostly from Duncan Holley's collection, but a few have come, along with most of the programmes used, from Gary Chalk. The programme collections of Paul Godfrey, Bryan Horsnell and Mike Swain have also been tapped.

CONSTANT PAINE

was launched at a celebration of the career of

TERRY PAINE MBE

held at

St Mary's Stadium

by courtesy of Southampton FC

on

23 November 2008

an occasion sponsored principally by

Kevin Stevens of Bright Grey

Copies of this book are presented, with special thanks, to:

To the sponsors of this launch, especially Kevin Stevens, as the principal sponsor.
Paul Bennett, as organiser of the launch.
John Beames of Wilkins Kennedy, as sponsor of the follow-up evening
at the Winchester Discovery Centre, in honour of Terry Paine.
Hagiology Publishing's associates, in the production of this and other books,
at Southampton FC and the Southern Daily Echo.
Gary Chalk, Duncan Holley and Dave Juson, as Hagiology Publishing's
ever-dependable providers of statistics, illustrations and so much support.
Mary Bates, in memory of the late Ted Bates.
Mick Channon, for his foreword.
Mike Swain, for help and support in every way.
Terry Paine, so constant in his support of this book – and so patient with it.

Subscribers

1 Mike Zanelli, Shirley.
2 Brian White, Rownhams.
3 Jonathan Tubb, Bishops Waltham.
4 Ross Taylor, Andover.
5 B Saunders, Bassett Green.
6 Steve Rogers, Romsey.
7 R Penfold, Lyndhurst.
8 A.M. Quigley, Merley.
9 T Marshall, Millbrook.
10 L Joyner-Smith, Millbrook.
11 John Lovelock, Shirley.
12 Tony Kerley, Eastleigh.
13 Cliff Hibberd, WSC P9.
14 Malcolm Hewson, Winchester.
15 Alan Gosling, Woking.
16 Mark Fickling, Rownhams.
17 Pete Ford, Lordshill.
18 Gordon Chambers, Dibden Purlieu.
19 L.N.E Coombes, Blackfield.
20 Malcolm Chamberlain, New Milton.
21 M.J Bennett, Andover.
22 Richard Buckingham-Smith, Eastleigh.
23 Terence Bruty, Whitchurch.
24 Ken Barnett, Hedge End.
25 S Shelton, Kidderminster.
26 Nigel McAllen, New Milton.
27 Don McAllen, Pennington.
28 Stephen Cheffy, Crawley.
29 Graham Watford, Locks Heath.
30 David Stelling, Basingstoke.
31 Nicholas Mansbridge, Romsey.
32 David Thomas, Chandlers Ford.
33 Nigel Burgess, Hoddesden.
34 Raymond Mursell, Bishops Waltham.
35 Ted Tarbart, Shanklin, IoW.
36 David Earley, Southampton.
37 Marion Lebourne, Aldermoor.
38 David Dennis, Southampton.
39 Lucy & Carlo van Leeuwen, Southampton.
40 Dick Collins, Winchester.
41 K Harrison, Fordingbridge.
42 Mark & Carol Judd, Andover.
43 Martin Wartski, Poole.
44 Tony Butt, Gurnard, IoW.
45 Malcolm Wing, Eastleigh.
46 Phil Rawlings, Fair Oak.
47 John Warren, Hitchin.
48 Brian Smith, Birmingham.
49 J.E Prowting-Brown, Jarrow.
50 Richard Derwent, Southampton.
51 Clive Derwent, Southampton.
52 I Hunt, Woolston.
53 Mark Wood, Newbury.
54 Tony Borowiec, Totton.
55 Dave Webster, Fair Oak.
56 Ken Griffin, Bassett.
57 Norman Gannaway, Lymington.
58 David Hutchinson, Chandlers Ford.
59 Michael Bowring, Calmore.
60 David Randall, Thornhill.
61 Denis Croll, Totton.
62 Peter Humphries, Barrow-in-Furness.
63 Roger Hawkins, Botley.
64 Bob Weeks, Coventry.
65 James Grimes, New Milton.
66 Martin Murray, Sompting.
67 Nicholas & Michael Weston, Lyndhurst.
68 Brian Barendt, Bartley.
69 Dave Brindley, Gosport.
70 Graham Comfort, Twickenham.
71 Michael Roberts, Leicester.
72 Hein Ferreira, Shanklin.
73 Malcolm Lewis, West End.
74 Gavin Chase, Warsash.
75 Jim Whitfield, Bitterne.
76 Glen Williams, Locks Heath.
77 Michael Hull, Itchen.
78 Norman Hull, Northampton.
79 Bob Manning, Guanghzou, China.
80 Dave Holmes, Caversham.
81 Brian Dawkins, Romsey.
82 William McCoo, Lenzie.
83 Thomas McCoo, Renfrew.
84 Nick Brice, Lordswood.
85 Trevor Brice, North Baddesley.
86 Dick Leach, Caversham.
87 Bryan Horsnell, Tilehurst.
88 Gary Wilkins, Lordshill.
89 Dennis Robinson, Salisbury.
90 Malcolm Clarke, Eastleigh.

91 Geoff Martin, Itchen.
92 Roy Martin, Thornhill Park.
93 Mick Butt, Elstead.
94 Russell Francis Loughlin, Southampton.
95 Don Miller, County Mayo.
96 Clive Gordon Hevicon, Totton.
97 Andy Beaney, Southampton.
98 Tony Howard, Hartington.
99 Maurice O'Connor, Bassett.
100 John O'Connor, Everton.
101 Malcolm Plumbley, Hamworth Park.
102 Steve Few, Alton.
103 Mike Jones, Cowes.
104 Rod Widger, Whitwell.
105 Tony Widger, Poole.
106 Ron Beeson, Chandlers Ford.
107 Robert Terris, Bartley.
108 David Stephens, Hamble.
109 Ron Grassie, Bursledon.
110 Derek Powell, Rownhams.
111 John Grapes, Southampton.
112 Terry Webb, Southampton.
113 Andrew Murray, Lordswood.
114 Ian Payne, Midanbury.
115 Gary Crease, Glen Vine, IoM.
116 Robin Griffiths, Burnham-on-Sea.
117 Dave Gwilliam, Ledbury.
118 Gary Rogers, West End.
119 H.G. Davies, Aberystwyth.
120 Lee Shutler, Margate.
121 Gerald Powell, Hereford.
122 Barry Markham, Hythe.
123 Mick Graham, West End.
124 Richard Burkin, Hereford.
125 Keith Hall, Leominster.
126 Mike & Heather Hayter, Bishopstoke.
127 Bill Beaney, Southampton.
128 Cliff Huxford, Fair Oak.
129 Tony Godfrey, Oakley.
130 Wesley Maughan, Hamworth Park.
131 Norman Dean, Totton.
132 Peter Vine, Curdridge.
133 Peter Harley, Midanbury.
134 Michael Ellard, Lordswood.
135 John Christie, Chandlers Ford.
136 Harry Penk, Ashurst.
137 Bryn Elliott, Bassett.
138 Ken Jones, Chandlers Ford.
139 Ken Wimshurst, Malaga, Spain.
140 Mick Stickler, Warsash.

141 Colin Holmes, Bishops Waltham.
142 Ken Maxted, Bournemouth.
143 Dave Adlem, Bristol.
144 Barrie Bedford, Bristol.
145 Bill & Ros Ellerington, Southampton.
146 Eric Nottingham, Hereford.
147 Ron Parrott, Hereford.
148 Paul Godfrey, Cheltenham.
149 Trevor Paine, Winchester.
150 Norman Bennett, Andover.
151 Gordon Bennett, Andover.
152 Phil Bumstead, Winchester.
153 Bob Collins, Headbourne Worthy.
154 Denny Marchant, Winchester.
155 Les Elms, Winchester.
156 Keith Guppy, Eastleigh.
157 Tony Miles, Lincoln.
158 Cladge Howard, Southampton.
159 Derek Igglesden, Winchester.
160 Roy Igglesden, Warsash.
161 Gary Igglesden, Winchester.
162 John Johnson, Chandlers Ford.
163 Bert Mace, Winchester.
164 Fred Norris, Winchester.
165 Robin North, Chilbolton.
166 Alan Richmond, Winchester.
167 Richard Peacock, Winchester.
168 Raymond Pennicott, Southampton.
169 John Philpott, Chandlers Ford.
170 Frank Grayer, Southampton.
171 Bill Postle, Midhurst.
172 Ron Gale, Winchester.
173 Steve Postle, Bishopstoke.
174 Jim Postle, Wantage.
175 Rod Kent, Oakley.
176 Henry Spearman, Fleet.
177 Roy Walker, Ringwood.
178 John Walls, Southampton.
179 Mark Adams, Southampton.
180 John Young, Southampton.
181 Eileen Bennett, Shirley.
182 Aidan Hamilton, Marseille, France.
183 Michael Earls, Southampton.
184 Fred, Northam.
185 Roger Fry, Hamble Le Rice.
186 Rob Holley, Southampton.
187 Arun Banerjee, Crook.
188 Robert Wright, Melksham.
189 Nick Powell, Enfield.
190 Ann Chalk, Eastleigh.

Contents

Foreword

by Mick Channon

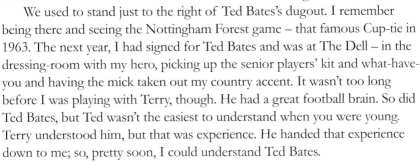

Terry Paine was my hero.

Although we lived on Salisbury Plain, my dad was a Hampshire Hog. His brothers and sisters lived in the area around Southampton, the Droxford area, Locks Heath and those areas. So the Saints were the obvious team to go and watch.

We used to stand just to the right of Ted Bates's dugout. I remember being there and seeing the Nottingham Forest game – that famous Cup-tie in 1963. The next year, I had signed for Ted Bates and was at The Dell – in the dressing-room with my hero, picking up the senior players' kit and what-have-you and having the mick taken out my country accent. It wasn't too long before I was playing with Terry, though. He had a great football brain. So did Ted Bates, but Ted wasn't the easiest to understand when you were young. Terry understood him, but that was experience. He handed that experience down to me; so, pretty soon, I could understand Ted Bates.

And we found that Painie and I had a very good understanding. Terry knew what was going to happen and I knew what he was going to do: it was whether I was quick enough to get on the end of it, sometimes. He was a loose cannon and probably I was, as well. You couldn't tell us what to do, but it just so happened that he and I clicked and we were responsible for a lot of goals for Southampton – even when we got into the First Division and played that fantastic system, 1-9-1, in which I was the '1'.

His delivery was so good; that's what made him such a great player. He was so accurate. And it's not like today, when you've got plastic footballs: you still had those big, heavy balls; and on those pitches! But Painie could deliver, whether it was a beautiful summer's day or a ploughed field and blowing a gale. *That's* how good he was. He was the greatest player I ever played with.

He was so sharp. He was street-wise. He was cute – *anything* to gain any sort of advantage, whether it was taking a quick free-kick or a quick throw-in; or intimidating the referee or intimidating the opposition. He played to get his opponents mad, so that they would lose their cool and give something away. One way or another, he had a great knack of getting up people's noses. But, basically, they didn't like him because he was good.

For the same reason – because he was so good and for so long – the fans loved him. So I think it is appropriate that Terry did this book with people who are fans of his. Who else would you want to do your book?

Preface

I'm not quite sure how it happened. Terry Paine and I were ostensibly sitting next to each other at the launch of *Dell Diamond* in 1998, but neither of us spent much time at the table: I had to get every player present to sign a blow-up of Ron Davies's stunning caricature of Ted Bates, for presentation to Ted, while Terry is never happy at a dinner until he has spoken to everyone in the room.

Yet, somewhere along the way, we seem to have had a conversation in which we agreed that I would write his biography. By midnight, he was telling me that it was a case of 'not if, but when'.

Fair enough, but I'm afraid the 'when' has turned out to be an awful lot later than intended. One reason for that is that I seriously under-estimated what would be involved in researching the career of somebody who went on to play and manage in so many places after leaving Southampton in 1974 and who has lived in South Africa, a brief interlude at Coventry City apart, since 1984.

More importantly, though, other books on the Saints' history, most of which had not been thought of in 1998, found their way onto the Hagiology production line. As it is my responsibility, within the Hagiology collective, to edit each of our books, that repeatedly meant pushing *Constant Paine* onto the back-burner.

One of the consequences of my editorial role is that nobody has edited *my* contributions. I was determined to put that right and, although nobody can be held accountable for having edited this biography, several experts have read some or all of it and commented upon the content. Those who have read sections are Duncan Holley (the Southampton chapters), Richard Prime (Hereford), Paul Godfrey (Cheltenham) and Peter Harvey (South Africa). Mike Swain, my adviser on the England chapters, ended up reading nearly every chapter, as did Ron Allison.

I am so grateful to each and every one of them, especially for correcting factual errors but also for those suggestions that I have been able to heed. I couldn't take all of their ideas on board, quite simply because there were matters on which they differed – though I am glad to say that Terry Paine has consistently agreed with my approach. Among the debating points raised by my readers, four should be mentioned here.

First, there is the question of how one should spell the diminutive of Terry's surname: 'Painie' (as in 'Cloughie') or 'Painey' (as in ''Bally')? There can be no 'correct' answer. So, despite the impassioned objections of one reader, I have opted for 'Painie'. I have been consistent in using the 'ie' ending for other players, save that 'Bally' seems to be established and 'Chaddy' is what it says on David Chadwick's business card.

Secondly, there is the issue of how much you need to know about Terry's team-mates: where they came from; how they fared when playing with him; and where they went. I had contradictory advice, even from the same reader, who wanted to know more about player 'X', but had no interest in 'Y'. I cannot know your prejudices and priorities in this regard, I'm afraid. Again, there cannot be a 'correct' answer, can there?

Thirdly, I ran into the chronological v thematic debate. I am not imaginative or daring enough to attempt a biography which doesn't maintain a substantial degree of chronological order. But a biography is not a diary and some deviations from the chronology are surely necessary.

Take the three chapters I have devoted to Terry's England career. It would have been cumbersome to weave into the relevant chapters the details of how he won his 19 caps; and to relegate them to an appendix would have been to diminish them. I have opted to locate them in Chapters 11-13, between Southampton's winning promotion, in Chapter 10, to Division I and starting life, in Chapter 14, in the top flight.

If that arrangement doesn't appeal to you, please skip Chapters 11-13 – and the other thematic chapters (19 and 23), as well – and keep to the chronological road.

Finally, I was surprised to be asked by two readers: 'where's the gossip?' Why was there so much on formations and tactics, they wondered, and so little on Terry's private life or what he thought about the off-the-field behaviour of others?

Well, contrary to the impression created by many a recent autobiography of a footballer – doubtless encouraged by a publisher pandering to what is perceived to be a scandal-hungry readership – the former footballers I've interviewed have consistently wanted to talk about how the game is, and should be, played, as opposed to how a team-mate was, but shouldn't have been, laid.

So, if it's gossip you're after, this biography is not for you. Terry Paine may have been forever willing to pose for domestic photos, but he kept the details of his private life to himself. As Perry Suckling put it, quite out of the blue in answer to a question about joining Terry at Supersport United,

He's very much a *football man.* I never talked to him about his political views or his social life or things like that. For a start, I didn't know if he was married: he never really spoke about his himself. But he was a great man to speak to about the runs of forwards, about the distribution of goalkeepers, about the high-line of the back four – pressing the field and things – where to win the ball: what parts of the third.

Exactly! And, even within his own home, his partner, Hilly Goffe-Wood, explains, Terry has no wish to gossip about other people: 'He never has a bad word to say about anybody. I'll come home and I'll criticise somebody and, half the time, he doesn't listen: he doesn't get involved in anything too *personal*.'

It is fair to say that Terry Paine is a person who engages his brain – thinking about football – rather than his tongue, wagging about human frailties. This biography reflects that preference.

A football biographer has essentially three kinds of sources to pursue: the published word, mainly in the form of press reports, plus match-day programmes, and maybe a few magazine articles and even books, mainly the biographies of the subject's contemporaries; the unpublished word, in the form of Board minutes or maybe other 'historical' documents; and interviews. And once the text has been assembled from those sources, there is the question of how to illustrate it, mainly with photographs, but perhaps with a few cartoons, plus the odd front cover or line-up from a match-day programme.

I need to explain my exploitation of each of those four kinds of source, in turn. First, the press reports. My principal source was, as ever, the *Southern Daily Echo* and its Saturday edition, under its various names. I shall almost always refer to it as the *Echo,* whether I am drawing upon a weekday or weekend edition. The *Echo* reports – initially by 'Observer'; later by Brian Hayward – of every game that Terry Paine played for Southampton have, of course, been read by Duncan Holley and Gary Chalk, as the main source for *In That Number*, their indispensable chronicle of the Saints' post-war endeavours. A battered copy was always at my side. Dave Juson kindly checked the original reports, not only to compile this book's statistical appendix, with occasional inputs from Gary, but also to draw to my attention various Paine-related highlights. In addition, I had access to Ted Bates's scrapbooks of *Echo* (and a few other) cuttings, while Jez Gale, at the *Echo* library, produced an impressive file of Paine clippings. Beyond that, Dave and Gary each checked specific match reports, on request.

Where a report on a Southampton game appeared in the national press, the identity of the newspaper is not always obvious. That is what comes of drawing upon players' cuttings, from which the name of the 'paper has been cropped. There will consequently be a degree of anonymity about some of the reports cited in the pages that follow.

Ian Henderson kindly arranged access to the bound volumes of the *Hampshire Chronicle* and *Hampshire Observer,* stored at the *Chronicle*'s old offices. That gave me a huge start on Terry's career with Winchester City, subsequently supplemented by access to players' cuttings, mainly those of Terry and John Mace, and by recourse to folders and microfilm in Winchester's Local Studies Library.

The carefully-arranged scrapbook and comprehensive programme collection of Ron Parrott, the Hereford United historian, meant that I could sit in his front room and discover nearly all I needed to know about Terry's three seasons at Hereford – with the subsequent back-up of Ron's meticulous *Complete Record* of the club and of the generous, conscientious replies, from Richard Prime at the *Hereford Times*, to my follow-up questions. And if it's scandal that you want, Malcolm Whyatt kindly allowed me access to his book of cuttings on the persistent campaign, by himself and others, against John Sillett, the Hereford manager who took his friend, Terry Paine, to Edgar Street.

Access to the Cheltenham press reports was initially easy: Sue Robbins, at the *Gloucestershire Echo* library, assiduously helped me to locate them. Follow-ups were more difficult, because copies of this newspaper were latterly unavailable in Cheltenham, other than on microfilm at the Reference Library. That's a stressful form of technology for a reader with worn disks in his neck, as my osteopath will confirm. So trips to the National Newspaper Library, in Colindale, were necessary, for a less strenuous read of the originals. Paul Godfrey, the secretary at Cheltenham Town FC generously gave me access to his programme collection.

Please note: all references, in the Cheltenham chapters, to the *Echo*, are to the *Gloucestershire Echo*.

The ever-resourceful Mike Swain – who must by now feel that he has been brought into this world to be my unpaid research assistant – presented me, unsolicited, with an invaluable notebook, containing his hand-written summaries of every representative game Terry played. It draws not only upon his programme collection but upon sources such as *Charles Buchan Football Monthly* and the *FA News*, his collections of which Mike had scoured for details of Terry Paine's contributions to the international cause. Aidan Hamilton kindly translated newspaper reports of England games that he had traced, for me, in libraries in Lisbon, Prague and Rio. And I consulted, mainly on Terry's international matches, two British nationals – *The Times* and the *Mirror* – selected for the practical reason that each is easily accessible, OnLine, at Colindale. I am grateful to Tom Steele for introducing me, so late in life, to the bountiful resources of Colindale.

In respect of South Africa, Trevor, Terry's brother, provided a bunch of cuttings that Terry had sent him, mainly from *The Citizen*. Newspaper reports on Terry's first visit to South Africa in 1979 have been summarised by Peter Raath in *Soccer Through The Years 1862-2002,* his massive history of that country's football. He advised me of the impossible task of checking reports and records in South African newspapers, even were I to spend much longer in the country than I did. I settled for talking to him from time to time and for doing some background reading, in the form of the scholarly texts of Peter Alegi (who responded generously to my further enquiries) and Douglas Booth, as supplemented by consulting Mary Simons.

For Terry's brief stay at Coventry City, I relied upon the club historian, Jim Brown, drawing both upon his *Complete Record* and upon his generosity in private exchanges. And for his even shorter stay in Kuwait, I ploughed through every issue, during Terry's time in the country, of the *Kuwait Times,* which is stored on microfilm at Colindale.

I have alluded to my dependence upon several libraries. I was also helped by David Barber at the FA library and, with regard to the election of Councillor Paine, by David Hollingworth in Southampton.

Secondly, the unseen sources. I have acknowledged in previous prefaces the efforts of Brian Truscott, Malcolm Taylor, Cynthia Dowsett and Barry Fox that enabled me to act upon Guy Askham's permission to read the minutes of Southampton FC's Board. Paul Godfrey kindly made available the Cheltenham minutes, but the Hereford minutes were destroyed in a fire, so I had to rely upon the recall of two former-chairmen, Frank Miles and Peter Hill. Bryan Horsnell kindly checked what the Reading FC minutes said about the applications, in 1977, for the club's managerial vacancy.

Staff at the County Records Office in Winchester helped me with unpublished documents: correspondence and other papers on the history of King George's Field; and the scorebooks of the Winchester and District Cricket Association. John Walls Jr kindly supplied copies of correspondence between his father and Ted Bates.

Next, the interviews. I conducted over 200 of these with people listed at the end of this preface. For various reasons, I failed to interview everybody I would have liked, especially in South Africa, but also in Coventry. Three ex-players, whose 'side' I'd hoped to hear of stories told about them by others, declined the right of reply: both John Flood and Steve Middleton were friendly when I rang them, but did not wish to go on the record, while Bobby Charlton had a colleague ring back to say that he was 'not an appropriate person to talk about Terry Paine.' He must get so many requests for help, so I was grateful for the courtesy of a reply. The pity is that he would have been an especially appropriate witness, as it was he who took Terry on a life-changing visit to South Africa and who later became involved in an ambassadorial dispute with Terry, of which his side remains unheard.

Nearly all of the interviews drawn upon in this book were conducted especially for the purpose. I have also drawn here and there, however, upon my transcripts of interviews for *Dell Diamond,* as these included plenty of discussion of Terry Paine. It would be tedious to distinguish which persons named below were interviewed for which book – or, indeed, for both.

Most of the interviews were face-to-face, although half a dozen were conducted over the 'phone and one by a lengthy – and addictive – exchange of e-mails. Peter Harvey kindly provided a transcript of an interview he'd done in South Africa on my behalf. Rebecca Coats also transcribed for me.

Unless I've forgotten anybody – profuse apologies if I have – the people interviewed were:

Terry's family: Carol Paine, Pat Paine, Thelma Paine, Trevor Paine and Hilly Goffe-Wood.

People who featured in his life in Winchester, in one or more capacity – as neighbours on the Highcliffe estate; as footballers at Highcliffe Corinthians or Winchester City; as cricketers; or as work-mates at BR Eastleigh: John Beames, Norman Bennett, Phil Bumstead, Bob Collins, Dick Collins, Jean Day, Rosalind Ellerington, Les Elms, Roy Fisher, Jim Flux, Reg Grace, Jimmy Gray, Keith Guppy, Colin Holmes, Bruce Howard, Cladge Howard, Brian Hunt, Derek Igglesden, Roy Igglesden, John Johnson, John Mace, Don Marks, Peter Marston, Norman Morris, Fred Norris, Robin North, Richard Peacock, John Pennicott, John Philpott, Bill Postle, Fred Snell, Henry Spearman, Colin Thorne, Roy Walker, John Walls, Steve White and John Young.

Those who played with him, managed him or were otherwise involved with him at the following clubs:

Southampton: Ray Ames, Mary Bates, Ted Bates, Bill Beaney, Roy Beazley, Paul Bennett, Peter Brown, David Burnside, David Chadwick, Mick Channon, Bob Charles, Lew Chatterley, Martin Chivers, John Christie, Brian Clifton, Ron Thomas Davies, Ron Tudor Davies, Eric Day, Norman Dean, Pat Earles, Michael Earls, Mike Ellard, Bill Ellerington, Bryn Elliott, Hugh Fisher, Brian Flood, Campbell Forsyth, Roger Fry, Jimmy Gabriel, Paul Gilchrist, Tony Godfrey, Steve Guppy, Gerry Gurr, Tommy Hare, Joe Harley, Bernard Harrison, Tony Heaney, Denis Hollywood, Nick Holmes, Cliff Huxford, Ernie Jones, Ken Jones, Michael Judd, George Kirby, Joe Kirkup, Tony Knapp, Bob McCarthy, John McGrath, Ally Macleod, Lawrie McMenemy, Eric Martin, Wesley Maughan, Jimmy Melia, John Mortimore, Tommy Mulgrew, George O'Brien, Gerry O'Brien, Brian O'Neil, John Page, Pat Parker, David Paton, David Peach, Harry Penk,

Denis Pring, Ron Reynolds, Terry Simpson, Jim Steele, Mick Stickler, John Sydenham, Don Taylor, David Thompson, Tommy Traynor, Ian Turner, Peter Vine, David Walker, John Walker, Ian White, Stuart Williams and Ken Wimshurst.

Hereford United: Colin Addison, Tony Byrne, Roy Carter, Steve Davey, Bob Dixon, Steve Emery, Tony Ford, John Galley, Peter Hill, Tommy Hughes, Peter Isaac, John Layton, Dixie McNeil, Frank Miles, Andrew Reed, Kevin Sheedy, John Sillett, Roger Townley, Peter Trevivian, Malcolm Whyatt.

Cheltenham Town (*or local pub football*): Tim Bayliffe, Mark Buckland, Billy Burke, Jasper Cook, John Davies, Dave Lewis, Geoff Parker, Tony Passey and Roger Thorndale.

Crook Town: Arun Banerjee.

Coventry City: Lee Hurst and Steve Ogrizovic.

People involved with him, in football or TV, in South Africa: Billy Anderson, Neil Andrews, Gary Bailey, Mike Barfoot, Rodger Butt, John Clingen, Geraldine Evans, Paul Evans, Tony Ford, Peter Harvey, Mario Lacueva, Eddie Lewis, Jacqui McCord, Shane MacGregor, Thomas Madigage, Thomas Mlambo, Ken Sadler and Perry Suckling.

Team-mates for England: Jimmy Armfield, Alan Ball, Gerry Byrne, Ian Callaghan, Jack Charlton, George Cohen, John Connelly, George Eastham, Jimmy Greaves, Roger Hunt, Norman Hunter, Geoff Hurst, Bobby Smith, Peter Thompson and Ray Wilson.

Several of those England team-mates discussed playing against Terry, as did the following: Ray Bean, Wally Bragg, Gerry Cakebread, Allan Clarke, Pat Crerand, Syd Farrimond, Peter Grummitt, Ron Harris, Gordon Jones, Frank Lampard, Denis Law, Roy Lunniss, Mike Madge, Brian Pitson, Ray Reeves, Graham Ricketts, Mike Summerbee, Ron Tindall and Bob Wilson.

I interviewed two referees – Jim Finney and Denis Howell – *a handful of football journalists* – Ron Allison; Billy Cooper, Derek Goddard, John Hannam, Clive Joyce, Chris Moore, Richard Prime, Peter Raath, Graham Russell and Laurie Teague – and *a few of Terry's associates from business (including horses) and politics*: Toby Balding, Clive Deacon, Penny Kimberley, Mary Penfold and Alan Reynard.

Many interviewees were traced with the help of somebody else mentioned above. Bob Britten, Steve Chaytor, Roger Davies, Pete Ford, Norman Gannaway, Andy Hemington, Kevin Hoskin, Michael Manuel, Tony Rees and Jean Thomasson also helped me to find an interviewee or two.

Most of the face-to-face interviews were conducted in the interviewee's own home, so often in an elegant conservatory – I swear the PFA has a deal with Anglia or Everest – but, alternatively in a hotel lobby, pub or golf club. One or two came to me and I met a few in the homes of other people – Mike and Sarah Barfoot; Roy and Sheila Beazley; Dave Juson; and John and Mary Mortimore – who kindly made a room available.

Travelling up and down the country, not to mention South Africa and the USA, to meet interviewees, I needed only once to check into B&B, thanks to the hospitality of Mike and Sarah Barfoot; Gerald Cohen; Ron and Chris Davies; Geoff and Anne Fimister; Nick and Carolyn Holmes; Norman and Barbara Hull; John and Kay Lenaghan; Nicky and Linda Nickson; Liz Pitman; Ron Parrott; Ann Stanyer and Andrew Hull; Graham Thompson and Brenda Toward; Roy and Sheila Williams; and, most especially, Terry Paine and Hilly Goffe-Wood.

Fourthly, the illustrations. My sources, where known, are acknowledged in the picture credits at page iv. Where photos have been loaned by ex-players, the copyright is not always clear. I trust that any copyright-holders, whose rights I may consequently have infringed, will contact me.

As ever, I have relied mainly upon the *Southern Daily Echo,* to whose Stewart Dunn and Ian Murray I am grateful for permission to reproduce so many photos. Dave Juson helped me to retrieve some of these, but my main debt, in this regard, is to Jez Gale, the *Echo* archivist, who was unstinting in his help. Richard Prime kindly provided several photos from the *Hereford Times*. Although Ian Means and Mark Halliwell did their best to help, the cupboard was mainly bare at the *Gloucestershire Echo.* So I have relied also upon Paul Godfrey's programmes for illustrations of Terry's time at Cheltenham.

The Winchester photos are from the *Hampshire Chronicle* and are mainly the work of E.A (Bob) Sollars. These are now held by the Winchester City Council's Museum Services, where Karen Parker and Pru Hatton so diligently helped me to find what I was looking for and more.

The England photos have been supplied mainly by the three agencies identified in the picture credits. Although geared to the demands of bigger fry than Hagiology Publishing, Mel Knight at Mirrorpix, Kezia Storr (and a predecessor or two) at PA Photos and Barrie Underwood at Getty Images have all been unbelievably patient with my requests for a few photos each.

I have otherwise drawn upon private collections listed in the credits, including John Philpott's studio shots. My main debt, as ever, is to Duncan Holley, first for creating a special Paine file within his vast collection of

Saints photos and then for finding additional photos that I needed – unless they were held by Gary Chalk, who has promptly come up with the goods a few times.

Duncan scanned most of the Southampton photos that were not scanned by the *Echo* or the designer. Peter Harvey scanned a mass of photos for me in Johannesburg, while Sue Fowler, Kevin Hoskin and Jon White each scanned for me in England.

The 'Oz' cartoons of Terry's Southampton career are reproduced by kind permission of the late Don Osmond, while Peter Manders kindly supplied the Hereford cartoon.

You will notice a variation in the quality of the photos. That is mainly explained by my being unable to obtain the originals of a dozen or so images, so that I have had to rely upon scans from magazines or newspapers. This has meant using them in the book in a grainier version than I would have wanted, or I have had to reduce the size, so that the inferior quality is less glaring. That explains, for instance, why the picture of Ron Davies's historic afternoon at Old Trafford in 1969 is so tiny.

The taking, storage and retrieval of football photographs has changed considerably of late, so historians of the club's recent endeavours will not have these problems. As it is, we have done our best with what we have been able to trace and I thank those newspapers, agencies and individuals who have done their best to help me illustrate this book.

In selecting from the mass of material, I will have omitted to use some gems from interviews I conducted: apologies to those whose transcript I failed to feed in at the appropriate moment. I fear that there will also be some inaccuracies of recall in accounts plucked from the memories of ex-players. When asking anybody to describe what happened 40-odd years ago – and, in some cases, before that – I have invariably had the relevant record books with me. That meant that I could often challenge, on the spot, any statement that was contradicted by the records. When I have failed to nail down contradictions on site, I have subsequently tried to trace the origins of the specious. I won't always have succeeded in putting the record straight.

I am grateful to all of those who have put up with my pernickety attempts to be accurate. My biggest debt is to Terry Paine, not only for helping with so many quests for accuracy, but for being so patient when I was otherwise engaged and not asking him anything at all. As I say, the 'when' to which he boldly referred in 1998 has been much delayed.

As the book reached its final stages, I was grateful to Barrie Bedford and Bill Postle for sending out invitations to the book launch at St Mary's

Stadium, being organised by Paul Bennett, and the 'Evening with Terry Paine,' being organised at the Winchester Discovery Centre by Nick Coates.

That relieved me to focus on the design of the book at the elbow of designer, Liz Porter, as creative and forbearing as ever, and edging – in this, her third, book for Hagiology Publishing – towards understanding the language of football. Two football fans were waiting for what Liz has crafted: Sam Coles, to produce an index; and Andy Hayward, a Saints fan, to print it.

To print it, that is to say, some seven years after the projected 'when'. I have explained why publication has been so delayed, but I cannot stress enough how understanding Terry Paine has been. I refer not only to his good-natured patience, but to his authorising me, in effect, to tell the story my way, even when I was reporting negative views of him.

Only once did he suggest that an adverse comment was 'over-the-top'. I agreed: in fact, it was downright offensive. My solution was not to remove, but to paraphrase, the criticism. I would like to think that I have not abused, at any point, the editorial freedom that Terry had afforded me, as I necessarily selected from the plethora of comments and opinions I had transcribed.

I hope, in sum, that my selection of material has been fair to a private person who was willing for his story to be made public, while at the same time reporting, with an appropriate degree of candour, what I judged you might want to know about this Winchester lad, who became a Southampton legend and a South African ambassador.

David Bull
Bristol
November 2008

Chapter 1

Ambassador

I never imagined that I would get up one morning and find an ambassador at my breakfast table, nonchalantly chatting on the 'phone to a midlands radio station – even as he awaited an official car from the BBC – about an international scandal of which he'd been a victim the week before.

It was July 2000 and my overnight guest was Terence Lionel Paine MBE. He had stopped by to update me for this biography, but he had hotter business to attend to. He had recently arrived from Zurich, where he had been an ambassador for the South African World Cup 2006 bid. The bid had been thwarted when New Zealand's Charles Dempsey had abstained, thereby handing Germany the tournament – contrary, it was being said, to how the Oceania representative should have cast his vote. Which is why the British media – so fortunate to have an aggrieved Paine in their midst – were chasing him, eager to learn more of his ambassadorial indignation.

The continent of Africa had had two contenders in the early stages of the Zurich voting, but Morocco was soon eliminated. The South African bid was backed by other African nations, to the extent that the four ex-players on ambassadorial duty in Zurich included Roger Milla, the Cameroon star of the 1990 World Cup Finals in Italy, and the Ghanaian, Abedi Pelé, who had been African Player of the Year three seasons running (1991-93). The other two were both South Africa-based Englishmen. Gary Bailey had been born in Ipswich in 1958, when his father, Roy, was the goalkeeper at Portman Road. But Roy Bailey had gone to work in South African football in 1965, eventually becoming national coach and seeing his son return 'home' to keep goal for Manchester United and England.

Gary Bailey was now working in Johannesburg, on the same TV sports-channel as the fourth man, Terry Paine. But while Bailey had come to South Africa as a child, Paine was quite the late arrival, brought there by football (well, by Bobby Charlton, to be precise) when he was already 40.

That had been quite a journey for somebody with a background that had a special fascination for me, in that it was remarkably similar, in its first few years, to my own: we had each been born in 1939 on an inter-war council estate, not far north of Southampton (Winchester in his case, Salisbury in mine). Of our subsequent journeys, Terry's is the one worth writing about it. But I am pleased to say that my alternative route had brought me to a point, when the two of us met in our late 50s, where our conversation led us to the conclusion that I should write the story of Terry's journey from Winchester to Johannesburg.

I had, of course, no idea of our shared origins when I first saw Terry Paine at the Recreation Ground, Aldershot, on what I later discovered to be his 18th birthday, in March 1957. It was his second game for Southampton and I can picture him now, cutting in from the left wing at the far end from where I was standing, to score his first goal for the club.

Five weeks earlier, the 17 year-old had been playing for Winchester City. His progress from 16 February to 23 March 1957 is, by any standards, meteoric. Consider the calendar below.

Sat	16 Feb	His final game for Winchester City's first team, at home to Newport (IoW) in the Hampshire League, Division I.
Mon	18 Feb	Scored the winner as the Southampton Youth team beat Bristol Rovers 2-1 at The Dell, in an FA Youth Cup Fourth Round replay.
Sat	23 Feb	His only 'youth' cap – for England National Association of Boys Clubs v Scotland at Roker Park.
Mon	25 Feb	Signed pro forms for Southampton.
Sat	02 Mar	**Debut for Southampton 'A'**, in which he scored twice against Cowes Reserves.
Wed	06 Mar	Scored the opening goal as the young Saints beat Spurs 6-0 at The Dell in the quarter-final of the Youth Cup.
Sat	09 Mar	**Debut for Southampton Reserves** v Bristol Rovers, in which he set up the opening goal in a 4-0 win.
Sat	16 Mar	**First-team debut for Southampton** v Brentford, a 3-3 draw at The Dell.
Sat	23 Mar	Away debut – and first goal – at Aldershot, a 1-1 draw on his 18th birthday.

Three features of this remarkable five-week spell deserve comment:

Speed of progress   Note how the teenager made debuts for the Saints at three levels on successive Saturdays.

Demands upon him   The nine games shown do not say it all: if Terry had not been representing the NABC in Sunderland on 23 February, he would have had a conflict between Winchester City's visit to Alton Town in the Russell Cotes Cup and playing for Hampshire Youth v Devon.

His flexibility   Although each of his three debuts for Southampton was at outside-left, where he had played most of his football for Winchester City, he played on the right wing for the Youth team.

All of which poses the question as to what had happened, over the previous 18 years, to result in Terry's playing professional football for Southampton.

Chapter 2

Corinthian

WINCHESTER. The finest country in the world has nothing finer… this historic city, capital of England before London… Here is every kind of thing belonging to our past: the old houses and hospitals, the castle and the gateway, the ancient cross, the quaint passages and crooked ways, the cloister and the green, the great walls and the winding streets, the serenity that comes from trees and meadows and river, our oldest great school and our greatest medieval church … does it not seem that this Winchester is the epitome of England from [King] Alfred until now?… If Hampshire had no other history but Winchester, it would be enough. It is the unequalled town…

Arthur Mee (ed.), *The King's England: Hampshire with the Isle of Wight.*

So there you have it. Hampshire's county town, as described by Arthur Mee in his 1939 edition – the very year of Terry Paine's birth – had allegedly succeeded in conserving 'every kind of thing belonging to our past.'

But not quite everything: during the 1930s, in this, as in so many British towns and cities, families living in housing deemed incapable of conservation ('slums', in a word) – or at least of improvement to a standard that included an inside toilet and running water – were being rehoused from central locations to council estates on the periphery.

Such was the Highcliffe estate where Terry was born and grew up – and was still living until he married in 1963. Alec and Ena Paine had originally moved to 40 Portal Road with their two sons, Roy (born 1929) and Tony (1932). A fourth son, Trevor, arrived in 1946 and the family duly relocated to No.47, one of the larger houses in the road – potentially four bedrooms if you were willing to forgo a 'front room', traditionally preserved, in those days, for taking Sunday tea with visitors or for even rarer excuses to have guests.

The Paines were lucky to have that option of a downstairs bedroom. The new council housing was something of a trade-off: you still stood a good chance of being overcrowded, but you probably had a substantial back garden and fields beyond. Indeed, these three features do much to account, by my reckoning, for three aspects of his childhood that Terry recalls with feeling: the privation; the sharing community; and the space to play.

Cue violins? I hope that's not how the previous paragraph comes across, though maybe you share my reservations about football biographies that routinely romanticise the impoverished, over-crowded conditions in which the rags-to-riches hero grew up. If what follows strikes you as being of that ilk, then I will have failed to do justice to the balanced way in which Terry talks about his Highcliffe upbringing: people should not have to lead such under-resourced lives, he argues – but what resources they enjoyed in their gardens, fields and community spirit! I just hope that my relaying of his sentiments – addressing, in turn, those three issues of privation, community and play – convey the sincerity of what he felt.

First, the privation. Terry's pre-school years spanned pretty much the duration of the Second World War, when the population endured what the historian, Peter Hennessy, has called 'institutional privation', with everyone, even the King, having a ration book. As he neared the end of his first year at primary school – All Saints', just a short walk away, through the cut opposite No.47 – the war in Europe ended. There soon followed a General Election campaign, in which the nation's war-hero, Winston Churchill, warned the electorate that voting out his Conservatives would bring in 'some form of Gestapo' at Westminster. The people were not impressed: amid widespread elation – perhaps especially among its card-carrying members like Alec Paine – the Labour Party won.

The incoming Chancellor, Hugh Dalton, had predicted that a Labour victory would be achievable only 'with the votes of the football crowds.' As those crowds came teeming back to the terraces with the resumption of League football, the Labour Government of 1945-51 presided over the 'austerity years' – characterised by shortages of essentials and rationing, even of bread which had escaped it during the War – while attempting, in its 'Welfare State' measures, to redistribute the limited post-war cake. Yet even as a restless Highcliffe teenager endured secondary education from 1950, social scientists were beginning to question the redistributive impact of the under-funded welfare overhaul. Full employment notwithstanding – Alec Paine had a secure job with the newly-nationalised British Rail – it remained possible for a manual worker with a family to be living in what would come to be labelled 'relative deprivation' or, later, 'family poverty'.

Yet 'it wasn't poverty,' Terry insists. 'No way was it poverty, but it wasn't easy. There wasn't much to be had.' Even as a first-team regular, Terry would still be sharing a bed with his younger brother. This meant that he would arrive second but then command more than his share of the blankets and the other improvised bed-covers – notably army coats – that were badly needed in the winter, when the bedrooms were 'absolutely freezing', Trevor recalls. 'There was no central heating. We had a back boiler with the open fire. I don't even think we had an immersion in those days. Sunday was bath day, so the fire was lit and the water was heated and we all had our baths.' Terry's signing pro in 1957 would be a blessing for them all: he could get a bath or shower at The Dell and could afford to retire from the Sunday rota at No.47. 'That was a luxury for them,' he chortles: 'extra water!'

Being able, by the Spring of 1957, to heat up enough water once a week for the entire household to have a bath was not perhaps among the indicators of progress that Prime Minister Harold Macmillan had in mind when he ventured to Bedford Town's football ground in the July to tell us that 'some of our people have never had it so good.' But so it was for the Paines of Highcliffe.

Secondly, the family belonged to two kinds of 'community', both of them facilitated by the large back garden: the *geographical* community of shared produce; and a *hobby-related* community in which Alec, assisted by Trevor, was active.

Terry Paine is passionate in his recall of the informal trading and exchange that gave so many Highcliffe families a degree of self-sufficiency. The estate was, he reckons, 'a market garden: everybody grew something that you could exchange with somebody else.' His dad's garden kept the family in new potatoes and runner beans, but Alec's speciality was 'those lovely big crysanth's. He'd take a bunch to Micky Marsh up the road, when he wanted some of his special radishes – winter radishes, which are long and magnificent, not the summer radishes, the short global ones. You always had something to trade: six eggs for four lettuces, say.'

Alec could, indeed, offer eggs, having reared the birds. When he was breeding chicks, they would get the warmest spot in the house at night: after emptying the ashes from the tray under the fire, he would bed the chicks in there for the night. Young Trevor may have been freezing, upstairs, as Terry monopolised the army coats, but at least the chicks were warm. The boiler needed fuel, though, and one of the essentials you couldn't get by trading was logs. So, even as the week's great treat – the Saturday morning cinema for kids – awaited him, Terry had to put his back into it:

> Saturday blooming mornings, before I could go to pictures, I had to take the wheelbarrow down to the sawmills and pay nine-pence [4.75p] for a load of logs. And then you had to push them home. So that was my job: logs! And the queue used to be a mile long.

The Paines could, however, trade their peelings. At the northern edge of the Bar End fields that separated the estate from the Winchester by-pass, there were substantial allotments, with several sties in which some of the locals kept pigs. One of them, Mr Dominey, welcomed the Paines' swill – which guaranteed them a leg of pork come Christmas.

If any family had more than they could barter, they would expect to off-load it in the local – the *Heart in Hand*. Geographically, it was on the corner of the estate but it was, Terry insists, 'the centre of the community. It was a community centre – as simple as that.'

Alec's other 'community' was of pigeon-fanciers. He raced his pigeons and was '*good*' at it, Trevor claims: 'he won certificates – all the time, not just locally, but nationally as well.' And he encouraged younger pigeon enthusiasts, like Trevor's school-mate, John Beames, among whose fondest memories of Highcliffe is being among pigeons – his own; at Alec Paine's

Trevor, Alec and Ena Paine
in their back garden,
among the pigeons.

A first prize, won on a
cross-channel flight.

lofts; or amidst all the baskets of birds at Winchester railway station on the eve of a race. Trevor's regular role was to rubber-ring the birds, put them into their baskets and take them to the station on a Friday, to be sent to wherever they would be flying from: perhaps on the 'North Road', which extended up to Newcastle; perhaps on the 'South Road', across the Channel, maybe all the way to Spain.

Terry, always the competitor, was annoyed when his dad's clock failed and his time-recording was thus delayed. So, once he was earning enough as a footballer, he was determined to buy him a decent clock – although his first big splash from those earnings would be on a washing machine: farewell to 'all that scrubbing' for his mum. Having it so good, indeed.

Otherwise, he was not involved with the pigeons – although, once he had wheels, he would occasionally transport them by car, just for short practice flights from, say, Sutton Scotney or Basingstoke. He remembers a Humber Sprite coming in handy for that.

And then, as a local celebrity, he would be at his dad's command to present prizes. He could do so with a genuine admiration for the unwritten code of conduct in that racing community. Thus, he recalls what would happen if bad weather caused a 'crash' and a pigeon dropped into some-body else's loft: the loft-holder would check the ring and send the bird home by train. 'It was a remarkable society.'

His mum was a winner, too. Her sport was darts and she and Mrs Bell, from No 60, were the leading pair in the Ladies' team at the *Heart in Hand* and a star-turn in the local league.

Finally, and most significantly, there was the space to play. Yet, for a lot of the time, Terry had nobody to play with: what was the use of having

Mesdames Paine (*front left*) and Bell (*next to her*) on a Highcliffe ladies' outing.

three brothers if none of them was anywhere near you in age? Actually, he had a choice of spaces. There was the road. You might occasionally see the odd motorbike and sidecar, but car-owners were virtually unheard of. Winchester City director, Henry Parsons, who lived round the corner in Milland Road, was a notable exception, until the sensational arrival (of which more later) of some American cars. So when Terry could find a few lads to play with, Portal Road was free for them to scuff a tennis ball along the gutters in the hallowed tradition of street-games of football. Bill Postle, who lived at No 51, insists that darkness was no obstacle: the 'very impressive lamp posts were excellent for floodlit football.' Terry jokes that games in the road 'gave you a bit of competition,' but he preferred to practise with a full-size leather football that he could kick around, invariably alone, on the Bar End fields.

These were no ordinary fields. They included the Bar End Sports Ground, which the City of Winchester had purchased in October 1938 for £4,350, with the aid of a grant from the King George's Fields Foundation. To say that this development was cutting-edge might be an exaggeration, but the National Fitness Exhibition in Newcastle, in 1939, displayed the drawings of its pavilions and playing fields.

And the Foundation certainly expected to see quick results for its investment. On 23 March 1939 – the very day of Terry's birth – the Town Clerk received a letter from the grant-body, asking when work would begin. This coincided with the arrival of the building firm's signed contract for 'erecting two pavilions and a convenience.' A star is born: now find him somewhere to play!

By the time the budding star was old enough to kick a full-sized football around on King George's Field – the name was mandated by the Foundation and is carved in stone on the gateposts, even though the locals insist on calling it 'King George V Playing Fields' – he was too choosy for that: his sights were set on the King Alfred's College pitches next door. His primary school – All Saints', handily situated at the top of the cut almost opposite his house – was allowed to play matches on the College's pitches, but entry was barred to individuals. This was where Terry wanted to practise, though, especially when the caretaker/groundsman had put the nets up. Which meant that he needed to break in and chance the wrath of this terrifying custodian: 'Jumbo' Kneller was 'a *huge* man,' who 'frightened the life' out of the young trespasser. But not so much that he didn't 'cheek him' and risk the price of being caught: 'many a time, he's put my head in a bucket of water and nearly drowned me.'

His walk to the fields would take him down Vale Road, where he would collect a football – either from the Norrises or their neighbours, the Gregorys. He couldn't be expected to have his own ball. As Fred Norris,

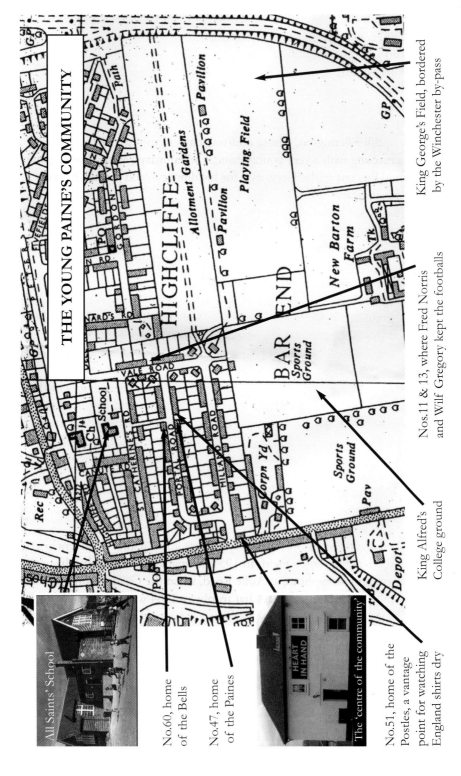

THE YOUNG PAINE'S COMMUNITY

All Saints' School

No.60, home
of the Bells

No.47, home
of the Paines

'The 'centre of the community'

No.51, home of the
Postles, a vantage
point for watching
England shirts dry

King Alfred's
College ground

Nos.11 & 13, where Fred Norris
and Wilf Gregory kept the footballs

King George's Field, bordered
by the Winchester by-pass

reminds us, footballs were 'expensive items' – not just to buy but to maintain: Fred recalls going to *Crosby's* in Southgate Street to get his ball blown up and re-laced with the 'special tools' that this required. If you ever tried to lace a leather football, you'll know what he means. Fred played for Highcliffe Corinthians – or 'Corries' – a side managed by Wilf Gregory, the estate's 'general factotum, who organised everything.'

Wilf's daughter, Rosalind, would marry the Southampton and England full-back, Bill Ellerington, whose courting days, in the late 1940s, included many a meeting with a very young Paine. On Saturdays, after a home game, Bill would bus out to the Gregorys' for his dinner – 'and practically every time I got up there, there was little Terry Paine stood against the table, in his short trousers.' The youngster was less impressed with the England international: he can remember him smoking a cigar. If he recalls correctly, the occasion was Christmas but, even so, Terry 'was always told professional footballers never smoked. So that was the first thing that hit me.'

All Saints' would annually compete with Stanmore to be Winchester's top primary school. The prestige of an All Saints' v Stanmore final at Winchester City's Airlie Road ground was such that luminaries could be attracted from The Dell to referee it. Terry recalls Ted Bates, then still playing for the Saints, coming to officiate – this was probably 1950, when, if his memory serves, Stanmore won 4-0. Not that Terry was unduly impressed at the time: 'I'd never heard of him. I didn't know who Ted Bates was. I never watched Southampton Football Club before I played.' It seems that some of Bates's team-mates may have performed the honours in other years – the name of George Curtis is one that crops up. One way or another, then, the mountain was coming to Mohammed. Ellerington, Bates and maybe Curtis, too: Southampton's early post-war heroes were coming to Highcliffe, yet Terry had yet to see the Saints play – or, indeed, to venture the 12 miles to Southampton for any reason at all.

His experience of being a football fan was almost entirely confined to watching the Corinthians, who played their home games on an enclosed area of the King George's Field. In 1953, he managed to get himself into the presentation photo, at Airlie Road, when the Corries won the Northbrook Cup. They retained that trophy in 1954 when, for good measure, they won the Winchester and District League and beat Camper and Nicholsons 3-1 to win the Hampshire Junior 'A' Cup. Terry 'can remember going – in a double-decker, sat upstairs – all the way to Fratton Park' to watch that 'A' Final. In that same season, though, he had his first glimpse of the professional game, a Corries' outing to Highbury. Arsenal were entertaining Sunderland – although the prime entertainer was the visitors' Len Shackleton in a 4-1 away win.

Corinthians captain Derek Igglesden receives the Northbrook Cup in 1953.
Jazza Nicholls's mother, an ardent fan complete with rosette, gets pride of place among the
Corries supporters, but 14 year-old Terry Paine squeezes in between
her and Igglesden, to catch the photographer's attention.

By now, Terry was at secondary school. He has his own take on the
allocation to Secondary Modern Schools of the four in five children who
had failed to pass the 11+ exam – the passport, for Winchester boys, to a
Grammar School education at Peter Symonds. 'The thickoes went to St
Thomas,' he explains. 'Those in between that and Peter Symonds went to
Danemark.' So if you went to Danemark, like Terry, did that mean you were
thick, but smart, I wondered? Terry roars at my classification: 'that's
probably right, yeah: street-wise!' None of which meant a lot once boys
from the two schools were redrafted to a spanking new school on the
Romsey Road in January 1953.

The county's first post-war secondary school, it was heralded by the
Hampshire Chronicle as a MILESTONE IN CITY'S EDUCATIONAL
HISTORY, with its 'magnificent' location offering panoramic views of the
city Mee had extolled. But no amount of new building, however splendidly
situated, could hide the fact that Sec Mods were hardly equipped to provide
their 11+ rejects with an education suited to their 'age, ability and aptitude',
as mandated by the 1944 Education Act. That said, Terry had the good
fortune to find a new mentor at Romsey Road, a teacher who would
passionately commit to developing his particular ability and aptitude. The
Head of PE was Henry Spearman, a self-confessed 'fitness fanatic' who
acquired two acolytes from the amalgamation.

One was Colin Holmes, a lad five days younger than Terry, who had been at St Thomas. Tall for his age and 'so physically strong', he was 'the tower of strength' in Spearman's football team and 'a helluva good boxer,' too: 'Colin was the one who you thought would have made it. He was *so* strong.'

But, then, big lads have such an advantage at that age over good little 'uns, like Colin's class-mate, Terry Paine. Forty-odd years on, Spearman enthusiastically recalled his smaller protégé:

> I *did* like the boy. I was smitten by his *personality*. He was full of life – vivacious from the eyes: the sparkling eyes and the rosy cheeks and the curly hair. Very lightweight, but what skill! He really had skill and he had this lovely turn of pace. Not over a long distance, but at the footballer's distance, I'd term it. And he had amazing *trickery*. He could go by players, beat players, rather like Stanley Matthews in a way, with his own skill. He was so small that he made idiots of school defences. And he used to knock those goals in.

Bob Collins, a year below Terry, recollects both his smallness and his cockiness: 'he was so confident that he could beat everybody – and, to be fair, he beat *most*. He always wanted the ball. He wasn't over-keen on going and getting the ball or passing the ball when he had it. But when he had it, he was wonderful.'

Spearman urged his inclusion in the Mid-Hants District team but this recommendation proved premature: 'being so lightweight, he really got pegged into the mud and they hit him. His physical equipment at that time wasn't quite up to District level and he really had a rough time. He was all upset, really tearful.' But his mentor urged patience: 'I said to him, in the gym, "Terry, you wait, my lad, until it's speed and skill at 18. You'll be back!" And, of course, I'm pleased to say I was so right.' Aren't we all?

If working with Spearman – both on the field and in the school gym – helped to develop his game, the schoolboy Paine still had three uses for his local fields: he would continue to practise solo, breaking into the King Alfred's facilities as and when; there were Sunday morning kick-abouts; and, finally, he would turn up – from about the age of 12, Fred Norris reckons – for the Corries' practice sessions.

Sunday mornings at Bar End brought footballers of all ages from all parts of the city and beyond. Corinthians 'Nicky' Nickson and Derek Igglesden would come down, by motorbike, from Oliver's Battery. Nicky, some 16 years older than Terry, claims that 'you couldn't miss the kid, because he was always out of his class for his age-group: he could just go round some of those guys as if they weren't there – even then, when you're talking about five, six, seven years' difference.' That could be an exaggerated recall, given that Terry reckons you'd be lucky, once the morning's numbers grew to 20-or-more-a-side, to get more than three touches an hour.

Maybe so, but Bob Collins counters that, as newcomers arrived, 'you didn't know who was on whose side. That was probably half the reason Terry kept the ball. And he was good enough to keep it for a time.' Whatever, Nickson had a better chance to observe Terry's 'little shimmy' when he joined the Corinthians at practice: 'he reminded me of Stan Matthews in some of his mannerisms, the way he kind of weaved his body. He didn't just run straight at you. You didn't know till he was gone.'

Never mind these Matthews-like touches: Nickson, who had been on Preston's books as a teenager, was keen to teach Terry – such 'a quick learner' – some of the tricks he had seen his North End contemporary, Tom Finney, perform. One was bringing his right foot up over the ball – a little 'jump' that Nicky reverently demonstrated to me, 60-odd years later. He concluded, though, that Terry's body-swerve was such that he did not need that Finneyism in his repertoire. That said, he admired the way Terry practised shooting to the goalkeeper's left, 'like Tommy Finney used to do,' combating the tendency of right-footed forwards to shoot across right-handed 'keepers, thus going to their stronger side. 'It took a lot of practice,' Nicky recalls, 'because you had to hit it just right to get it in that bottom left-hand corner.'

And then there were his corner-kicks: even at 13 or 14, Terry 'could take a beautiful corner,' Nicky reckons. 'I used to show him how to do that and so did Jazza [Arthur Nicholls, a Corries inside-forward, who lived in Portal Road] and one or two others.' Others like John Johnson, who would later play with Terry at Winchester City, and Fred Norris.

Hanging out with the Corinthians afforded Terry a strange social life. Norris and Norman Morris – each of them seven years older than Terry – had a series of American cars. Norman could recall an Oldsmobile; a Buick; a '38 Packard, which had an overdrive; and a Canadian Ford. Highcliffe had seen nothing like it: one neighbour asked him not to park his car on the street as it was obscuring his light. Terry was a welcome passenger, whether they were racing their cars on the Winchester by-pass or venturing as far west as Totton: 'we didn't have a lot of money,' Norman recalled, 'but we saw a lot of life – well, except for Terry.' The caveat is a reference to their pub-stops. Terry was still under-age and too small to pretend otherwise: he had to sit outside and be served lemonade and crisps. But he had established a pattern, whereby his friends and associates would tend to be somewhat older than he.

In the summer of 1953, he had a chance – one of the few, it seems, during his early teens – to take advantage of his size. Queen Elizabeth II was crowned on Tuesday 2 June and there were street parties across the land on Saturday 6 June – which also happened to be Derby Day. Terry entered his road's fancy-dress parade as the newly-knighted champion jockey, Gordon Richards, who rode his first Derby winner, that afternoon, at his 28th attempt. Not for the last time, Terry had backed a winner – although his costume was good enough only for third prize.

It is not clear exactly when he graduated with the Corinthians from hanger-on to team-member: the *Hampshire Chronicle*'s reports on Winchester and District League matches were limited to a list of scorers. It seems that he had a game or two at the end of the 1953-54 season, when the Corries were, as already noted, winning everything and had a fixture pile-up – although, echoing Henry Spearman's reflections on his protégé, Fred Norris felt that the 15 year-old Paine was inadequately built for this level of competition: 'he was so *small*! When he had a Corinthians shirt on with the long sleeves, if it rained and he got wet-through, it was heavy.' We do know that, at the end of the next season, Terry Paine, recently turned 16, was playing – and scoring his first recorded goal – for the Corinthians in their 7-0 win over Bar End United. But he was already practising with bigger fry. He'd been given permission, by Winchester City's manager, Harry Osman, a pre-war Southampton winger, to attend their training sessions.

This meant running across town to Airlie Road. But so keen was he that he gained a reputation for being the first there, so that later arrivals would find him already practising on his own. He had to work his way into the group sessions, like the kick-ins. The way inside-left John Young remembers it, these would take place at the bottom of the Airlie Road slope, where the floodlights 'sent out an arc of light':

> I remember how a young lad would come along. And the ball would go out of that arc of light into the darkness, up the slope slightly, and he'd run off, like a jack-rabbit, and bring it back, give it back to us and we'd continue kicking in. And, after a while, we felt so sorry for the lad that we'd say 'go on, nipper, have a kick yourself.' This sort of grew and grew and, in the end, he was kicking in with all of us at training sessions. That was one of my first contacts with Terry.

Young was commuting from Southampton, but those evenings at Airlie Road would also have been the first contact with Terry Paine for any Winchester-based player who was familiar neither with the Corries nor the Sunday morning free-for-alls. 'Not being part of the Bar End scene,' wing-half Phil Bumstead had 'never heard of him or seen him before,' but retains an image, from those 1954-55 training evenings, of him shooting-in: 'I can see him now, just shouting to Keith Guppy or Reg Grace, in goal: "where d'you want it? Top left or top right?" He could put a ball just anywhere.'

First-team 'keeper Guppy confirms how accurate Terry's shooting was and recalls how, 'after training, he always used to come up and he used to say "how did I do?" He was always concerned – had he done enough?' Guppy relished being consulted and 'took him under my wing.' But how, I wondered, could Terry hit the ball as hard as they were telling me, when he was only 15? 'It's timing,' Keith explained. 'It's not the strength. It's the timing.'

Harry Osman had obviously liked what he saw. Come the start of the 1955-56 season, Terry was a Winchester City player and eligible to feature in the *Chronicle*'s line-ups and match reports. Which is how we know that 'T.L. Paine... played an intelligent game' at outside-left for the second-string 'Blues' in the pre-season trial match against the first-team 'Stripes' and 'capped a good display by scoring a well-judged goal.' 'Ben Winton', the Winchester City columnist in the Southampton *Football Echo*, agreed: 'it was obvious, even after only a few taps of the ball... that he has natural ability.'

Other admirers of the newcomer's performance included his marker, John Mace, City's veteran right-back, 10 years Terry's senior. He liked the way the youngster was prepared to cut inside him and 'let fly: he really could

Wearing his Blues shirt for the warm-up for Winchester City's 1955-56 season, Terry Paine (*left*) lines up with John Johnson (*centre*) and Bruce Howard.

hit it with his right foot.' He acknowledges that he 'gave him too much room' to display that art but, despite complaints from team-mates that the new kid was 'running rings' round him, Mace was not going to 'hit him' and maybe 'kick a bit of football out of him: you can – can't you? – when they're that young.'

Cosseted or not, Terry had done enough to satisfy the selectors. City's manager was also the landlord of the *Wykeham Arms,* which doubled as the club's official headquarters. So, on Monday evenings, the man responsible for the Reserves would report to HQ to help pick the two teams for the coming Saturday. For that 1955-56 season, goalkeeper Grace was the player-manager, whose duties included a weekly selection meeting at Osman's pub.

Over and above the two managers, Terry would acquire plenty of mentors at this 'lovely club: a load of them all thought about you, all cared about you.' The interest in him of first-teamers Mace and Guppy – a one-time Dell trialist as a centre-forward and later a 'keeper on West Brom's books – has already been noted. Brian Hunt had been on the Saints' books in the early 1950s and both of the Howard brothers had been at The Dell: Bruce, now captaining City's Reserves, had played a couple of games for the Saints first team in 1941, while the younger Cladge, the first-choice outside-right, had been a member of the Southampton 'B' team that had won every trophy in sight in 1946 – as had centre-forward Roy Fisher, who would arrive at Airlie Road in the 1956 close season, in time to enjoy a few first-team games with Terry. Among the Reserves, the novice could count on his left-wing partner, John Young, while centre-half John Philpott, a former Saints 'A' player, would take a keen interest in Terry's temperament, having himself fallen out with the management at The Dell, a misfortune he shared with Robin North, who would join the City in Terry's final season with them.

John Philpott

In other words, Terry was setting out on an 18-month journey through the City's ranks in which he would not only be guided by older players, but in which he would be able to count upon some of those veterans, as and when the question arose of his perhaps up-grading, to give him the benefit of their wisdom as to what that might take – especially at The Dell.

Chapter 3

Citizen Paine

T. Paine (as he was now being called, as the *Chronicle* inched towards informality) duly made his debut for the Reserves, the Saturday after the trial match, against Portsmouth Civil Service in the Hampshire League, Division II.

Quickly making the No.11 shirt his own, he was soon breaking the *Chronicle*'s formality barrier: 'one bright spot' in a 'dull' 6-0 home defeat by Newport Reserves on 3 September 'was the promising play of young Terry Paine.' The *Echo*'s reporter agreed: trailing 3-0 as half-time approached, the City at last managed a shot – by 'Paine, their tiny outside-left, who up to this time had been playing very much a lone game in attack.' Which rather invites the question: how could such a small 16 year-old be standing out like this so soon? And on his 'wrong' wing, what's more.

His chance to play on his more 'natural' wing came the following month, when Chris Williams, the regular outside-right, was injured. Wearing No.7 at Totton, Terry scored both goals in a 4-2 defeat. That was for one game only: he reverted to outside-left and scored in a 3-3 draw, a month later, with British Railways Eastleigh in the Hants Intermediate Cup.

He could well have been playing for the opposition. His father was a charge-hand welder at BR's Eastleigh sheds, where his Uncle Bert also worked. Terry reckons that his dad 'insisted that I followed him when I left school' at 15. He had to wait until he was 16 before he could start his apprenticeship. So he marked time as the Wagon Shop's office boy until he was eligible to learn his trade as a Body Shop coach-builder. Terry admits to being 'useless' but he had opportunities to enjoy himself, both in and out of the Shop.

For a start, his job of putting the floors down in the bare shells as they came into the Body Shop placed him right at the Shop entrance, a vantage point from which he was able, as John Walls Jr of the Finishing Shop recalls, to 'shout out to people as they went through – always a bit of banter.' And when he was not cheeking his elders, he could impress them at football, whether in the lunch-time kick-abouts or in the end-of-season knock-out competition between the Shops.

If, like Terry, you lived too far from the sheds to go home for lunch, you could get your sandwiches down you and head for the football pitch, across the road, for what would sometimes be a 20-a-side game – of the kind on which Terry had been brought up, of course – though more often eight-or-so-a-side. Again, it needed a mentor with a ball. Step forward John Walls Sr, John's father, who worked on wheel lathes in the Wagon Shop. His Shop-mate, Colin Thorne, recalled that 'eventually the ball split and we all paid so much – two shillings [10p] each, or something – and he went and bought a new one.' Terry chortles at the notion that he'd have been able to chip in his share:

> Two shillings? Christ! I couldn't afford that. I got £1.10s [£1.50] a week, when I started and I used to give Mum a pound of that. Come Wednesday, I was skint and Mum and I used to have a big argument. She probably had about eight shillings [40p] left and I wanted 20p of it. So a big argument on the Thursday: who was going to have it?

Come the light evenings, the Shops would have their annual football knock-out. Terry represented the Body Shop when they won the Inter-Shop Cup in 1956. We have photographic evidence of that, but it seems that he had previously played for them when they beat the 1954 winners, the Loco Offices team, to reach the 1955 Final. The Body Shop's goalkeeper, John Pennicott, has vague memories of that triumph of the 'workers' over the

The Body Shop team that won the Inter-Shop Cup in 1956.
The players featured in the text are
1 John Pennicott; 2 Colin Holmes; and 3 Terry Paine

'nobs', while Richard Peacock, from the Offices, remembers it as 'the first occasion I met Terry Paine and he walked all over us.'

Although the Body Shop had more grown men to choose from than most, it fielded not only the teenage Paine but his former Romsey Road class-mate, Colin Holmes, at centre-half. As already noted, Colin's strong physique was enabling him to progress faster than his slip of a work-mate. He had signed amateur forms for Southampton in January 1956, while Terry continued to be a regular at No.11 for Winchester's Reserves, where his slight frame had to overcome two obstacles: some hulking full-backs and some heavy grounds.

The *Hampshire Observer* had reflected, in its report on his debut, that the teenage winger was 'going to come up against some pretty hefty backs, men probably half his size again and years older.' But if Terry's size was likely to be 'a disadvantage when it comes to "mixing it",' the *Observer* envisaged that it could 'be an asset when speed and manoeuvrability are required.' Grace, his player-manager, was likewise

> a little concerned about his *welfare* on the pitch, because he did tend to be a cocky little devil and he was very tricky, and there were certain older full-backs in that league who weren't too happy about being made to look a bit silly by a lad of his age.

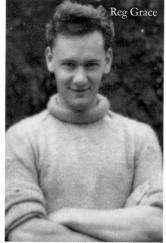

Reg Grace

Young, his inside-left, and Pete Marston, playing behind him at left-half, both felt that Terry might help his cause if he settled for beating his full-back just the once: 'these old full-backs don't like to be beaten twice,' Marston counselled him, 'they're going to cart you over the line.' But Grace's 'fear that he was going to get chopped down' and injured was not realised: 'I guess he was too quick for them.' For Philpott, it was a question of balance: 'he just had that balance – something that one person in 10,000 has got. Tremendous balance!'

That may have helped him evade lumbering opponents, but how could such a slight young lad get that heavy ball across? It was all about 'weight distribution,' Philpott suggests, 'coupled with balance.' Whatever the explanation, Marston marvelled at Terry's ability. Nine years his senior, he recalls how lesser players had to hit that old leather ball 'so hard: you couldn't float them like he used to – well, I couldn't. He was a natural, wasn't he?'

It seems to be agreed that the Airlie Road pitch was not one of Hampshire's worst surfaces, overall: the problem was the way it sloped. There were other slopes in the Hampshire League and Philpott was impressed by his young team-mate's ability to cope with some of the uphill grinds and yet still show off his array of attributes:

> he could cross the ball; he could slot in, through the inside-forward position, and score magical goals; he was two-footed; and he knew exactly what he was going to do with the ball as it was coming towards him.

The Airlie Road surface sloped not just from goal to goal, though, but also towards the left corner as you kicked downhill. So even if he had the strength to battle uphill, there was always going to be a problem, for the other half of the game, for an outside-left: 'once he got down in that corner,' Robin North explains, he wasn't likely 'to get out of there and get a cross in. Get isolated in there and the full-back, and everybody else, would just smother you.' Which is why North was so impressed by the way Terry avoided that corner: 'as soon as he got to the half-way line, he started cutting in and, of course, that was favouring his right foot.'

That description tells you that Terry was comfortable coming deep to collect the ball to feet. It was still an expectation of a wing 'pair' in the 1950s that the inside-forward would play the ball out to his winger, often angled inside the full-back, giving the winger a flying start on his marker. It is clear that Terry could ably work the flank with his inside-left – John Young in the Reserves and, as we shall see in the next chapter, Roy Walker in the first team. But the expectation that a winger might drop back to receive from his full-back had been raised, surely, by Alf Ramsey's impudent reflection, on his England debut, that Stanley Matthews's desire 'to have the ball hit straight at him' was how football 'should be played between winger and full-back.'

Terry's ability to do that would be confirmed when he made the City's first team and dropped back to collect from left-back Norman Bennett. A former winger himself, Bennett approved of Terry's willingness 'to come off his full-back and find a bit of space. He wasn't afraid to take them on.' This didn't sit so well, though, with the 'traditional' school, as represented for instance, by Reserves wing-half Phil Bumstead, who didn't like the way Terry would 'wait there and want the ball. He didn't want to run for anything. He was very strong-willed about that. That's being kind to him: he was a pain in the arse, really.'

Self-assurance and a strong will were not sufficient to keep him in the side for the home game on 10 December, however. Terry was omitted because, 'with his small build,' the *Chronicle* explained, 'he is not suited to heavy conditions.' He had no need to take it personally: Cladge Howard was rested, for the same reason, from his regular first-team spot on the right wing. If an experienced 28 year-old needed protecting against the mud, it rather suggested that this might hold for a slight 16 year-old. That logic flew out of the window, however, when the first team headed, three weeks later, for their New Year's Eve fixture on Alton Town's notoriously heavy Anstey Park pitch.

It was a makeshift side that set out from Winchester. One of the absentees, inside-left Roy Walker, explains that family men were allowed to opt out of a 'holiday' game at Christmas and Easter. Reserves full-back, Don Marks, home from National Service, was surprised to find his club 'struggling like mad to get 11 out that day,' to the extent that he made the team. It got worse: when the team-bus reached the point on the Worthy Road where outside-left, Ian Carsley, was to be picked up, he was not there. Somebody ran down to his home and found him unfit to travel. There was only one thing for it: back-track in search of Terry Paine. They found him and played him. He 'showed up well' in a 9-1 defeat.

Mr Lewington presents Keith Alderman with a signed photo album.
The numbers indicate personnel who feature in the text:
1 Director, Henry Parsons; 2 Cladge Howard; 3 Hunt; 4 Snell; 5 Paine;
6 Harry Osman; 7 Bruce Howard; 8 Guppy; 9 Marks; 10 Mace.

That verdict by the *Hampshire Chronicle* might equally have been applied to his achieving such a prominent position in the post-match photograph – a knack that Terry would retain throughout his career. The occasion was a visit by the team to Alton's Treloar Hospital, where Mr Lewington, the club chairman and Head Teacher at All Saints', presented Keith Alderman, a 10 year-old City fan, with an album containing signed photos of the team.

Then, despite Carsley's emigrating to Canada soon afterwards, Terry was back in the Reserves for the rest of the season, his highlights – to judge from the *Chronicle* – being a January visit to the Isle of Wight, where he 'found the orange ball, which Newport are now using, well to his liking,' followed by a run of six goals in seven games. He finished the season as the Reserves' top-scorer away from home.

He had certainly done enough to live down a nickname, which stemmed from his wing-partnership with John Young. This was, remember, 1956 when we still talked of a 'wing-pair': Alf Ramsey's Wingless Wonderland was 10 years away. The regular left-wing pair for City's Reserves was Young and Paine. So when Edmund Hockridge burst into the Top 20 singles hits, in February 1956, with *Young and Foolish*, it was perhaps inevitable, in the manner of dressing-room drollery, that Terry would become known as 'Foolish'. 'He took it all in good part,' Young recalls. 'But it soon died down: you couldn't really call him "foolish" for very long.'

The season over, Terry was free to resume his one-man practice sessions on his local fields, although it was, of course, time for the 'summer game' to be played there. Although Henry Spearman, 'a fanatic cricketer,' encouraged his protégés to bowl at him in the gym, cricket was not an organised sport at Romsey Road. So Terry's experience of it as a team-game mainly consisted of umpteen-a-side matches, a bit like Sunday morning football, down the fields with an improvised wicket.

But then, when Terry was 15, Wilf Gregory, the man with the football, took in a lodger with a cricket ball. And a cricket *team*, to boot: Les Elms captained YMCA (Winchester), essentially a team from Littleton, a village on the far side of town, which included Keith Guppy, City's goalkeeper. Elms soon befriended Terry: 'he had an infectious sort of nature. You couldn't help but like the lad.' Like the rest of Terry's Highcliffe mates, Les was seven years his senior. That was a consequence, Elms reckons, of how 'precocious' Terry was: 'he could mix with the older ones because, with his natural talent and his personality, he was way above his years.'

The YMCA played their home games on their fields at Weeke, quite a hike across town from Highcliffe, by public transport, carrying your cricket bag. Les's walk to the bus took him past Terry's gate, where he recalls stopping to chat about a sport of which his young friend had, as I say, no meaningful experience. One day, he wondered whether Terry might like to try his hand:

> He was uncertain. He was a little bit lacking in confidence, because it was a new venture. I arranged to take him down to the King George Playing Fields and bowl at him for an hour or so, one evening. You didn't have to be bowling at him long before you realised that he was really quite talented.'

On the strength of that trial, Terry was offered a game. He accepted, subject to being able to find anything that might pass as a suitable kit: 'have you got any plimsolls,' Les remembers pleading, '*anything* white?' John Hooker, a senior member of the side, undertook to find him some whites and Terry duly turned out looking like a cricketer. Elms decided that his protégé should bat third-wicket down and was not disappointed: 'he went in and made the place his own.'

You can get some idea of his batting contribution from the scores posted in the local press in that summer of 1956. On 19 May, he was second-highest scorer with 35, as YMCA rattled up 166-8 against Greatbridge's 58. And on 7 July, he was third highest on 17 as their 106 eclipsed Easton and Martyr Worthy's 35. Low scores were not their opponents' prerogative, however. The day after their romp at Easton, YMCA were skittled out for 17 by King Alfred Old Boys. And then there was his fielding. 'He was a *wonderful* fielder,' in the opinion of Les Elms, whose successor as captain converted him to a wicket-keeper: 'he'd never done it before – he could just *do* it.' He might as readily have become a bowler, Elms reckons:

> We had some very good bowlers, but I feel we would have made a bowler out of him if he'd been playing for a longer period of time. He was only with us for a couple of years… but he was a natural sportsman. I've met a few of them and it doesn't matter what shape of ball you put in front of them, they're master of it. He proved it in golf, didn't he?

There was always a question, though, about Terry's commitment to the summer game. Elms would continue to bowl to him down the fields, occasionally of an evening, and the two of them would bus across town; but this was never going to be a sport to which Terry was dedicated in the way that he was to football. As his mentor puts it, 'in the middle of summer, he'd be thinking of football again. I can assure you that, if he'd been *that* dedicated at cricket, he would have been a county cricketer.'

The YMCA (Winchester) cricket team, August 1956
The numbered personnel feature in the text:
1 Keith Guppy; 2 Les Elms; 3 Terry Paine; 4 John Hooker

In that summer of 1956, Terry did continue, though, to play cricket into August – we have a photo that says so – but his priority was a busy footballing calendar, starting with trials at Portsmouth and Arsenal, at the latter of which he was accompanied by Colin Holmes. Another mentor, Don Marks – the Winchester City reserve who was, inevitably, seven years their senior – drove them up in his Ford Prefect. He recalls Tom Whittaker, the Arsenal manager, sitting in a chair on the half-way line: 'afterwards, he spoke to all the lads. He said to Terry "you're a bit small, but come and see us in a year." I can remember him saying that.' But it seems as though Terry should have received some follow-up paperwork. Jack Crayston, Arsenal's Assistant Manager, would leave soon after these trials to manage Doncaster Rovers, the capacity in which he would next meet Paine in 1959. As Terry recollects, that was when Crayston told him that a secretarial oversight at Highbury had led to his not being sent the necessary forms to sign for Arsenal.

It would have been more appropriate, though, for him to join Portsmouth, where his father had been brought up: young Alec had been a 'mudlark', diving into the water when people threw money off the pier. But there was perhaps little chance of Terry's being picked up by a club whose manager, Eddie Lever, seems to have been a remarkably poor judge of a

young forward's potential. Around this time, he not only rejected Bill
Ellerington's recommendation of Scottish soldier, George O'Brien, but
also turned down Roger Hunt, who was playing non-league football in
Lancashire for Fred Worrall, one of Pompey's 1939 Cup-winners.

John Mace

I mention this for the benefit of
readers from the 'what if?' school of
football fandom, who will be able to
imagine Terry Paine inheriting Peter Harris's
No.7 shirt and jinking down the wing at
Fratton Park to cross to such a goal-hungry
pair as O'Brien and Hunt. The reality in
August 1956, however, was that Terry was
again wearing a blue No.11 shirt for
Winchester's pre-season game and John
Mace was again facing him in the first-team
stripes. Whether the manager really gave his
veteran full-back licence to 'hit him as hard
as you like', this time around, is disputed but
Mace was certainly less accommodating than
in 1955. Yet Paine nevertheless convinced
the *Chronicle* that he was 'a strong contender for a place in the first-team this
season – unless Portsmouth or Arsenal… snap him up.'

That evaluation was four months premature, but it will by now be
apparent to you that Terry had made quite an impression at the *Chronicle*.
Ironically, one of its sports staff had seen very little of the new lad on his
doorstep. Ron Allison, who would come to follow Terry's professional
career closely as a reporter with the BBC, first in Southampton and later in
London, was at the *Chronicle* until 1957, but was mainly editing the accounts
coming in from reporters who were watching Terry in the Reserves.

Eventually, a colleague took him along to see for himself. He could see
what the fuss was about: 'all I say is that, if *anybody* had seen Terry on a
football pitch, that little lad, you'd have said "that lad's going to play for
England one day." You couldn't but be taken by him.'

As the 1956-57 season got under way, Terry's champion at the *Chronicle*
continued to lobby for his promotion. Thus, the Reserves' second game of
the season, a defeat by Southampton 'A', 'clearly established that City's
young left-winger is well worth a place in the 1st XI.' What's more, he had
demonstrated that against the most accomplished full-back he had yet
encountered or would meet for a while yet: Bill Ellerington. As a reminder,

though, of how far Terry was still behind his Body Shop-mate, Colin Holmes was alongside Ellerington at centre-half, having made his debut for Saints Reserves earlier that week.

As the City's Reserves slumped to the bottom of their division, Paine's performances would relieve the gloom for the *Chronicle*. His 'sparkling display' was deemed 'the only bright feature' of a 4-2 defeat by Cowes Reserves in September, not least for the way he beat four men to score the City's second. And he was the only forward pardoned as the team 'went to pieces' to lose 5-2 to Blackfield and Langley a month later. For an Intermediate Cup-tie against the same opponents, the following week, an 'experiment' was announced: Terry would play on the right wing, where he had performed for the Hampshire Youth team in mid-week.

And it was in that position that he got back into the first team, after almost a year's break, for the game at Andover on 22 December. The *Chronicle* reported that he had been 'selected in place of Howard [who was] not at his best on heavy grounds.' So, a year after both men had been rested for that reason, the 17 year-old was now considered more capable of coping than the 29 year-old.

The explanation could lie in the fact that the teenager was filling out: enthusing about his progress two weeks later, under a cross-head of PAINE HAS MADE THE GRADE, the *Echo*'s 'Ben Winton' described him as 'a stockier, more experienced Terry Paine,' who had scored both in that Andover game and the next match against Bournemouth Gasworks and had 'brought new life to the City's first team attack.'

A prescient Ben Winton could 'only hope the City could hang on to him for a little longer.' As the man from the *Echo* saw it, Terry had 'clearly demonstrated' in these two games 'his potentialities as a winger':

> Combining a natural gift for the game with a calm, unruffled approach to everything he does on the field, Paine has become a player to be reckoned with. Against Bournemouth Gasworks, … Paine was repeatedly to be found in the right place at the right time – either starting a move or centring with some extremely accurate passes, considering the state of the ground.

This assessment of his showing over two games is the more remarkable, in that Terry had reverted, for the visit of the Gasworks, to outside-left, the position that he would retain for the rest of his stay at Winchester. A work-mate of Cladge Howard would come to introduce him, over the years, as the outside-right who confined Terry Paine to the other wing. But Howard modestly counts his blessings that his young team-mate 'had two good feet' and was capable of playing on the left, because Cladge 'wouldn't have had a chance,' otherwise, of holding his place: for him, Terry had by now become 'a brilliant player. He was just a natural winger. It didn't matter which side it was.' Which is why, when he looks back, Howard is simply 'so *proud* of being on the field with him and playing with him.'

And yet the *Hampshire Observer* felt that the new boy on the left still had something to learn from the modest man on the right. Raving about Terry's 'superb performance' against the Gasworks, their reporter continued:

> Frequently beating much bigger opponents, his positional play and accurate placing of the ball made him a constant menace to the Gasworks defence. He is a much more mature player than he was a year ago and will do even better if he can acquire some of the aggressiveness of C. Howard…
> in the tackle.

In only his third first-team game, then, Terry's not tackling back had become an issue. Not that this was going to impede his meteoric progress over the next two months. The *Chronicle* was now describing him as 'established' in the City's first team.

How wrong could they be?

Chapter 4

Changing Stripes

Established? The young winger being hailed as a 'discovery' was on the verge of swapping the red-and-white stripes of Winchester City for the red-and-white stripes of Southampton.

He had in fact been wearing the latter on amateur terms, off-and-on since September, as the Youth team made its way through the rounds of the FA Youth Cup. They would survive in that competition until April but, for the moment, Winchester City were on a Cup run of their own.

If you are too young to remember the FA Amateur Cup, you may find it difficult to comprehend what a glamorous competition it could be for a club like Winchester City – a break from the local fare of the Hampshire League, with the 'giant-killing' prospect of being able to topple a team or two from the Home Counties set of the Athenian, or Isthmian, League.

Which is why the *Hampshire Observer* found 'the atmosphere charged with excitement,' when Southall of the Athenian League came to Airlie Road on 12 January for a First Round Proper tie. The City had already won their way through four Qualifying Rounds to reach this stage for the first time in their history. Terry Paine, returning after a Saturday off for a National Association of Boys Clubs (NABC) trial in Ludlow – the furthest north he'd ever ventured – was partnered on the left-wing by Roy Walker. Their time together would be short, so they needed to gel quickly. Schoolteacher Walker – Terry called him 'Schoolie' – feels they did:

> I never played with a winger as good as he was. He had a quick brain. He was an instinctive footballer. It was almost as if he'd always played. He was intelligent for a lad that age. He knew where to give you the ball – and I think I did. We did play together well – everybody said so at the time.

The *Chronicle* certainly thought so and was soon calling their pairing 'the best left-wing partnership in the League.' So it was appropriate that the one 'sparkling move' that an 'indifferent' City forward line produced in a 2-1 win over Southall was, for the *Observer,* 'a neat Walker-Paine move [which] ended with the latter sending in a grand drive,' the ball being deflected past the 'keeper for the decisive second goal.

That set up a Second Round home-tie against Hayes, the Athenian League leaders. 'During the 73 years they have been in existence,' the *Echo* solemnly declared, 'Winchester City Football Club have probably never

The Winchester players, in their change-strip, meet the Mayor, Cllr Paul Woodhouse,
who is accompanied by Mr Lewington, the chairman, and captain Fred Snell.
The six players in shot are (*left to right*) Guppy, Mace, Walker, Macklin, Jeffery and Bennett.
A seventh player, peeping into the picture, is thought to be Terry Paine.
He would soon learn better than to be caught out of the frame.

before had to contend, in competitive football, with such tough opposition.'
Which explains why the Mayor turned up to meet the teams, before a record
crowd of 3,430. The *Chronicle* thrilled to Paine's 'spectacular run down the
middle' and the *Observer* to his 'beautifully accurate' distribution; and it was
from one of his crosses that Hayes conceded the penalty from which the
City scored a late consolation in a 2-1 defeat.

Terry Paine's first and last Amateur Cup campaign was over. But, as I
say, there were still Youth Cup-ties to be played. Although the competition
was in its fifth year, this was the first time Southampton had entered.
Which is hardly surprising, as they had never previously assembled a Youth
team as such. That they did so in 1956 owed a lot to serendipity. If it was
Ted Bates's modest way to exaggerate the part played by luck in his
managerial achievements, there is no gainsaying that he enjoyed several
lucky breaks in 1956.

First, he had a visit from former Wales international, Ernie Jones, who
had been a Saints team-mate from 1949 to 1951. Ernie's second coming to
Southampton in 1956, following a post-Dell career at Bristol City and Rhyl,
coincided with an offer by Charles Henwood, of CPC Engineering, to
make a contribution to the club. Jones brought not only his football
knowledge but engineering skills: he had helped to design and erect Rhyl's

floodlights. Bates, the master-broker, brilliantly exploited this coincidence of ambitions and aptitude: Henwood would become his 'Youth Organiser', unpaid, of course; Jones would have paid employment at CPC; in his spare time, he could coach the club's inaugural Youth team, on an expenses-only basis; CPC could sponsor them – paying their expenses and dressing them in CPC-emblazoned shirts – and the nucleus of the side could also play for CPC.

I say 'nucleus' because it is important to note that this successful Youth side was not playing together regularly. While half of them were turning out for CPC, albeit divided between two of Henwood's sides, the others were playing in the Hampshire League, whether for Saints 'A' or, like Terry, for another club – centre-forward Wes Maughan for Cowes and reserve goalkeeper Tony Godfrey for Basingstoke. All of them were part-timers. How Jones envied Manchester United, where Youth players were on the ground-staff.

But, then, *everybody* had cause to envy United, as it dawned on them that Matt Busby had stolen a march on them and 'cornered' young talent from far and wide, Duncan Edwards from the West Midlands and Bobby Charlton from Northumberland being, of course, the prime examples. Before the introduction of the Youth Cup in 1952, his scouts had been finding Busby more 'Babes' than he could find games for.

Ernie Jones

Jones's lads didn't even train on a pitch together, save on Sunday mornings. That became possible when Mr Barber, the club chairman, made available an area of his estate at Rownhams, which engineer Jones was deployed to turn into a training ground, complete with changing rooms. On Tuesday and Thursday evenings, they would train at The Dell, but not on the pitch; they had to make do with the carpark.

All credit, then to Ernie – though it seems to be agreed that he never got enough of that – for getting this assortment to gel. Inside-right Terry Simpson feels the defence who – save for Holmes, from Winchester – had played together for Southampton Schoolboys (along with Simpson and outside-left Sydenham), were an under-rated 'unit', while the forward-line comprised a variety of talents. He was what Jones called 'the leg-merchant'. But somebody had to play this role in such a line: Maughan and Sydenham were speed-merchants, while

CONSTANT PAINE

Simpson reckoned that 'Painie was pure *class* as a crosser of the ball and [inside-left] Peter Vine was phenomenal. Everybody complemented everybody else.'

The novices had been making good progress, knocking out the Youth teams of two First Division clubs – Cardiff City and Portsmouth – to set up a Fourth Round tie, away to Bristol Rovers. Colin Holmes arrived in Bristol – or, to be more accurate, a sports ground in Kingswood, across the Gloucestershire border from Bristol – fresh from appearing in a TV experiment the previous weekend. The FA and the BBC had agreed that the Youth international against Luxembourg would be played under West Ham's floodlights on the Saturday evening and televised live (well, all bar the first 15 minutes of the second-half).

The viewers saw England win 7-1, with Jimmy Greaves scoring four and missing a penalty. For Terry Paine, though, the important thing was to be able to watch his work-mate on the telly. A TV set was a symbol of the 'having it so good' society that had yet to reach 47 Portal Road; so, after they had played in Winchester's 3-0 defeat by Basingstoke that afternoon, John Mace took Terry home to watch the game on his set.

After that excitement, the Youth Cup-tie in Kingswood was a distinctly modest affair, as you may judge not only from the venue, but from the fact that Second Division Rovers could run only to a crudely-typed programme.

It was nevertheless one of the tougher ties of the Saints' run. A 1-1 draw meant a replay at The Dell. The young Saints won 2-1, in an encounter that the Rovers' manager, Bert Tann, rated 'a better game than many I have

```
       THE FOOTBALL ASSOCIATION YOUTH CHALLENGE CUP COMPETITION - 4TH ROUND
                         BRISTOL ROVERS v. SOUTHAMPTON
   WED. 6TH FEBRUARY, 1957.                              KICK-OFF: 2.45 p.m.
     R.                          BRISTOL ROVERS                        L.
                                    LUNDEN
               BEAN                                PITSON

          RICKETTS               MADGE                DAVERIDGE
          (Capt.)

               JONES                         ALLEN
     ADAMS                      SHEFFIELD                          BAKER
     Ref: Mr. G. Walker (Glos.)     0      Linesmen: Mr. S.T. Rummins
                                                     Mr. M. Coggins
     SYDENHAM                      MAUGHAM                          PAINE
               VINE                          SIMPSON

          SCURR               .  HOLMES             HARLEY
               STICKLER                      GLASSPOOL
                                FLOOD
     L.                                                            R.
                             SOUTHAMPTON
                    RED AND WHITE VERTICAL STRIPES
```

seen in the Second Division as far as speed, technique and tactics were concerned.' He had just given a debut in that division to his Youth-team captain, Graham Ricketts, who remembers the replay as 'very competitive... there were so many good players in the 22 that were on that pitch.' But, then, that was the point of the competition: as the FA saw it, it would 'give talented school leavers finding it hard to break immediately into senior football the ideal breeding ground for the footballers of the future.'

Fine words, indeed, but we all know that this 'ideal' will not be realised for so many of the promising teenagers who compete at this level. So it is noteworthy that 12 of the lads who lined up for that Rovers v Saints tie would play in the Football League. Check it out: the entire Southampton forward line would win a first-team place; and so would half-backs Holmes and Scurr. Four of their opponents – Baker, Hamilton, Jones and Ricketts – would go on to play for Rovers, while Sheffield would have a nomadic career away from Eastville.

I mention those stats as a way of locating the teenage Paine in his peer-group of budding professionals. Right-half Joe Harley admired both Paine and Vine for their two-footedness, yet felt that 'there were no stars, really. There was nobody that really stood out, because everybody was on a level. I think that's what made us such a good side.' Colin Shindler devoted an entire book to the subsequent careers of the lads who played in the 1964

With Walker replacing Glasspool, the team lines up in CPC-sponsored shirts, between Ted Bates (*left*) and Ernie Jones, for the replay against Bristol Rovers. Back row (*left to right*): Walker, Scurr, Harley, Flood, Holmes, Stickler. Front: Paine, Simpson, Maughan, Vine, Sydenham.

semi-final of this competition – when Manchester United beat their City neighbours 8-4 over two legs – on the grounds that 17 of the 22 players would make it into League football. The title of his book, *George Best and 21 Others,* may be a little insulting to the likes of Aston, Doyle, Pardoe and Rimmer, who were among the also-rans. By the same token, though, my brief reflections on this 1957 tie could be headed *Terry Paine and 21 Others* – with perhaps only John Sydenham having any cause to remind us that he, too, was there.

Yet the point remains that Terry was not standing out in 1957. Having succeeded in the NABC trials, he was about to represent England Boys Clubs v Scotland but, unlike three of his team-mates – Holmes, Vine and Sydenham – he would never win a Youth cap. Indeed, he would never get so much as a trial, the way Simpson did, let alone be a 'travelling reserve', as goalkeeper Brian Flood had been for that Luxembourg match. That said, 'Nomad' found his run on to Maughan's through-pass and 15-yard winner 'really exhilarating'. The Bristol press likewise applauded this 'brilliant shot' and ranked Paine with Holmes and Sydenham as the pick of the Saints side.

The Rovers defenders were certainly impressed with the opposing wingers, especially Sydenham. Centre-half Mike Madge recollects that John was 'the danger-man: he was absolutely brilliant,' while right-back Ray Bean 'can distinctly remember reading the report,' on the game at Kingswood, 'that said "Sydenham rang rings around Bean"'. Having tantalised Bean, Siddie swapped wings with Paine and left an impression on Brian Pitson, the left-back, who 'can remember John Sydenham more than Terry Paine' from that first game. Come the replay, though, Pitson 'was more aware of Terry Paine… I'm afraid I got a bit of a roasting the first half. He gave me a complete run-around.' Looking back at his youthful encounter with two wingers who would total more than 1200 first-team games for the Saints, Pitson reflects that 'they were talented. Terry Paine was a lot cleverer footballer, but John Sydenham was really quick.'

So, having been compared for some time with the stronger Holmes, Terry had now reached the stage where the winger's repertoire – was he fast or was he clever? – had become the issue. And long would it remain so – albeit accompanied increasingly by another question about the winger's job description that the *Hampshire Chronicle* had already raised: does he tackle back?

Those two games with Bristol Rovers sandwiched what would turn out to be Terry's last game for Winchester City – a 4-4 draw with Newport on 16 February. Centre-forward Roy Fisher, having played semi-pro for Salisbury, had had to sit out the Amateur Cup-run, so he'd hardly played with the young winger, who so impressed him in this game: 'Terry stood out – absolutely marvellous. He was outstanding. I remember that game, and

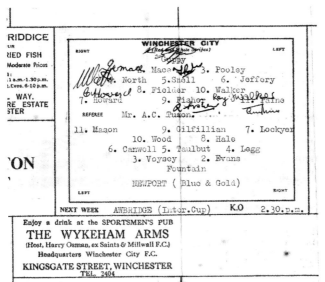

RIDDICE
UR
RIED FISH
Moderate Prices
I:
.1 a.m.-1.30 p.m.
L.Eves. 6-10 p.m.

- WAY.
RE ESTATE
STER

'ON
,

WINCHESTER CITY
(Red and White Stripes)
RIGHT   LEFT

Mace   3. Pooley
4. North   5. Snell   6. Jeffery
7. Howard   8. Fielder 10. Walker
            9. Fisher   11. Paine

REFEREE   Mr. A.C. Tuson.

11. Mason   9. Gilfillian   7. Lockyer
        10. Wood   8. Hale
    6. Canwell 5. Taulbut   4. Legg
        3. Voysey   2. Evans
            Fountain

        NEWPORT (Blue & Gold)

LEFT   RIGHT

NEXT WEEK   AWBRIDGE (Inter.Cup)   K.O   2.30.p.m.

Enjoy a drink at the SPORTSMEN'S PUB
THE WYKEHAM ARMS
(Host, Harry Osman, ex Saints & Millwall F.C.)
Headquarters Winchester City F.C.
KINGSGATE STREET, WINCHESTER
TEL. 2404

The line-up for Terry's last game for Winchester City, signed by the eight players who have contributed to this biography. Note the advert' for the *Wykeham Arms*, which strangely fails to mention that Harry Osman was managing the City. The blank boxes on this centre-fold reflect the lowly status of the club that could not sell its advertising space.

have done over the years, for the performance of Terry Paine: positioning, speed, ball control – brilliant! He was *way* above.'

The *Chronicle* again enthused about the Walker-Paine partnership: 'Time after time, Walker sent Paine away with accurate passes, and on several occasions the young winger left a trail of three or four defenders sprawling behind him as he weaved his way through the Newport lines.' As another measure of Terry's development, the other wing was 'nowhere near as effective, as usual on the heavy ground' – though Howard did plough into the area to score from what the *Echo* considered 'a clever cross-shot from Paine.'

The following Saturday, Terry was at Roker Park – a well-nigh Arctic adventure for a lad who'd barely been out of Hampshire – for the NABC meeting with Scotland. He was expected back, of course, for training on Tuesday. 'Where's Painie?' Walker enquired when Terry didn't show. Young was equally puzzled. They had missed the news: Terry had turned pro for Southampton on the Monday.

There are two versions of why Ted Bates moved to give professional terms to Paine and Holmes. Both of them could be true – more or less.

It is beyond dispute that John Walls, the work-mate with the football who featured in the previous chapter, played a part in recommending Terry to Bates. Colin Thorne, who'd had a spell at The Dell and was now playing for the Wagon Shop, remembered Walls as something of a local talent-spotter, who had tipped off Bates about prospects in the Body Shop and elsewhere; and a series of letters from Ted to John, in the summer of 1960, is evidence of how seriously Bates took those tip-offs. One of those letters, reproduced at the start of Chapter 6, acknowledges Walls's role in bringing Paine to the Saints.

Back in 1956-57, Thorne reckoned Holmes, 'a more solid player than Terry,' to be the better bet: 'everything he did was correct – and more forceful.' But according to his son, John Jr, Walls was pushing Terry's case. John Jr recalls the evening when his father was late home for tea, having taken his protégé to meet Bates. I suspect this was the occasion of Terry's signing *amateur* forms in the summer of 1956, after he had been for those trials at Portsmouth and Arsenal, the latter accompanied by Holmes, who had signed long before and had been playing for Saints 'A'. Wes Maughan remembers turning up for a trial at The Dell at that time and meeting another new boy, Terry Paine, who told him of his recent trial at Arsenal.

That said, it could be that Walls needed to remind Ted Bates, in February 1957, that the two Arsenal trialists had been invited back to Highbury for a second look, so he had better get a move on and offer them professional terms. It seems to be agreed that there was now a degree of panic and that both Paine and Holmes were summoned to The Dell.

The other explanation is that Harry Osman tipped off his former team-mate that Chelsea were watching his young 'discovery'. There is a consensus that a Chelsea scout – Fred Snell thought it was their former 'keeper, Harry Medhurst – was making enquiries after one of the Cup-ties, probably the Southall game. The Chelsea manager, Ted Drake, was, of course, a former City player and one of his first signings, on taking over at Stamford Bridge in 1952, was Winchester's Alan Rule.

Rule never made the grade there, yet Snell felt Terry should have followed him to Chelsea – and told him so. But Terry had had six months to weigh up life with the Saints and, as noted in Chapter 2, there were plenty of former Dell boys at Airlie Road who could have advised him. Having walked out, in anger, on Jimmy Easson – the coach who had arrived at The Dell from Pompey in 1950 – John Philpott knew that a young player would need the right attitude, as well as ability.

When Terry first asked him whether he believed he might hack it at Southampton, John wondered whether he had the necessary temperament. The more he saw of him, though, the more convinced he became that 'that was one thing he had in great abundance.'

So when Ted Bates and Bill Ellerington eventually got Paine and Holmes into the manager's office, and Bates told them they could leave when they'd committed to Southampton, it couldn't have been entirely a novel idea to Terry. Indeed, the alternative question was: why had Bates waited so long? Subsequent evidence of his managerial style suggests two possible reasons.

First, even as he travelled far and wide in search of players, young and old, he tended to take it for granted that local youngsters were his for the asking: that's Martin Chivers's explanation for why Ted left it so late to sign him in 1963. And secondly, he was too tight: why pay a young lad to play, while he was happy to perform for nothing? Soon after his hand was forced with Paine and Holmes, he would find himself in a similar situation with Terry Simpson. More of that in a moment; meanwhile, we surely have sufficient evidence that dawdling over Terry Paine was typical Ted Bates.

Not that Southampton got Terry for nothing. In its end-of-season report, the *Chronicle* noted that Winchester City had been compensated for 'the departure of young T.Paine… a loss which should not be under-estimated':

> A cheque for £25 has been received from Southampton Football Club in appreciation of the City's efforts on their behalf, no doubt a gesture over the development of Paine.

Oddly, Terry's parents never get a mention in this matter of his signing pro. What we do know, from an interview with Terry and his dad, for a railway magazine in 1964, is that Alec Paine was not enamoured of the idea. 'Dad wasn't at all keen,' Terry revealed. 'He felt there was more security about a job with BR. But he didn't stand in my way.' Even though Terry would have won five caps by the time he was interviewed, Alec was not minded to exploit hindsight: 'I still reckon it was a gamble. Terry would have been just as good a railwayman as he's proved to be a footballer.'

That line must surely have been manufactured for the benefit of the magazine's specialist readers: much as he enjoyed his job in the Body Shop, Terry reckons he was 'useless'. Anyhow, his football contract was part-time at first, though it was arranged that the young apprentice's indentures would be transferred to CPC. Not that Terry ever played for Mr Henwood: having got him on the payroll, Ted Bates was suddenly in a hurry to get his money's worth. Terry went straight into the 'A' team – at outside-left for the game against Cowes Reserves on 2 March.

That was something of a demotion, in that he was back in the Hampshire League's Second Division. Taking the step-down in his stride, he scored twice. Then it was back to the Youth Cup in midweek, a 6-0 trouncing of Spurs. The Southampton director, Rex Stranger, was so impressed that he presented the victors with a *Wagon Wheel* each. If you were a youngster in the 1950s, you will surely recall those huge chocolate biscuits with a marshmallow filling. A treat? Maybe – but hardly so if you'd just taken Tottenham's Youth team to the cleaners. Full-back Mick Stickler thought Stranger's gesture 'was a little bit mean.'

CONSTANT PAINE

Ted Bates had a bigger reward in mind for two of his forwards: the right-wing pair of Paine and Simpson were promoted to the Reserves for the visit, on the Saturday, of Bristol Rovers. Paine would, however, be on the left-wing, his Winchester City position; only in the Youth team had he been a regular on the right.

His wing partner for the Reserves was Johnny Walker, a disenchanted inside-forward who was on the transfer list, after having to deputise for much of the season on the left wing. Walker was smitten by the two young debutants. Come the close season, he would act as a go-between in the attempt by his former club, Wolverhampton Wanderers, to sign Simpson. As with the Arsenal threat in Paine's case, Ted Bates hurried to sign Simpson on.

Meanwhile, Walker had more immediate business with Terry Paine. He still loves to recall how he hastened to inform Ted Bates 'what a wonderful player this lad's going to be.' The manager took his point: when Walker returned to first-team action at home to Brentford the next Saturday, Paine was alongside him. The way Walker then serviced his protégé in a 3-3 draw greatly impressed 'Defender' of the Portsmouth *Evening News*, as 'exactly the right sort of pass rolled out to [Paine] repeatedly and he responded by putting over a series of accurate crosses as good as any seen at The Dell this season.' 'Defender' surmised that the 'success' of his 'daring experiment' with his teenage winger 'was probably greater than… Ted Bates had anticipated.'

The experiment had been announced in time for the *Echo* to head-line it in its Friday football coverage – which also included, ironically, the news that John Sydenham, who had 'created such an impression' in the Youth team's trouncing of Spurs, would be going to France and Germany, later in the month, as 'travelling reserve' to the England Youth team. It was as if Ted Bates had spotted something – Walker-assisted or not – in Terry Paine that had passed the international selectors by. It is not as if they were utterly unaware of him: the England Youth coach – George Curtis, a former team-mate of Ted Bates, whom you may recall from Chapter 2 – had seen his 'capital goal', the *Echo* reported, that knocked out Bristol Rovers.

Joe Harley, the player who felt the Youth team had no stars, was 'quite surprised' by Paine's call-up, 'because I didn't think he stood out that much.' No matter that Terry would 'mature as a player and just get better and better,' his promotion, from a bunch of Hampshire youngsters shaping to take on the Busby Babes, was a bit sudden.

The news of a first-team debut for 'a British Railways apprentice' even made it into the *Daily Mirror* on the morning of the game. Gerry Cakebread, the Brentford goalkeeper, recalls that the visitors had seen this publicity. But the photo of Terry cutting in on Cakebread's goal, chased by two defenders,

DAILY MIRROR, Saturday, March 16, 1957

Saints try boy from Railways

TERRY PAINE, 17, a British Railways apprentice, gets his League chance for Southampton today — one week after playing his first reserve game.

Paine, normally an outside right, plays on the left wing in place of Johnny Hoskins against Brentford.

He has been one of the stars in Southampton's colts' team that has reached the semi-final of the F.A. Youth Cup for the first time this season.

might suggest that they were not sufficiently forewarned. The photographic evidence of Wally Bragg's stride makes it easy to see why Terry has repeatedly referred to his marker, over the years, as a 'lumbering full-back'. Reminded of that evaluation 40-odd seasons later, Bragg felt that he should have prevented Terry turning inside him the way he had been able to do in the Hampshire League:

> The one principle that was always stressed to us was to get the winger down the line. The more he cuts in the more dangerous he is. If he's cutting in, he's putting you out of the game. *And* he's drawing the centre-half, who doesn't know whether to leave the centre-forward. He's put in two minds: 'Shall I stay or shall I go?'

Debutant Paine leaves his 'lumbering' opponents in his wake, as he cuts in against Brentford.

The *Echo* was impressed with that tendency to 'cut in from the wing when the occasion arose,' and reflected that he could become 'a scoring winger.' Terry proved the point in his next two games. The first was at Aldershot on 23 March, his 18th birthday. His parents didn't go but sent him a telegram, with the surname misspelled by the Post Office. He clinched a 1-1 draw, when he scored his first Saints goal, beating his full-back and cutting in to shoot right-footed. Goalkeeper John Christie, watching this from the other end, thought the way Terry came off his wing and 'just stuffed it in was absolutely magnificent. I just stood there and clapped. I couldn't do anything else. It was fantastic.' A second goal followed, three days later, in a 4-2 win at Reading – where, for good measure, Terry also played a part in goals by Roper and Walker.

Each performance brought rave reviews from the *Echo*. His display at Aldershot was 'one of the best individual efforts that a Saints' player has produced this season' and 'Observer' considered it 'fairly certain that a good deal more will be heard of Paine.' He also enjoyed his 'excellent performance' at Elm Park, which got the nationals going as well. Under the headline of TERRY WAS A TERROR, Ross Hall was excited about the way 'Terry the Terror took over' against Reading and 'combined the soccer wisdom of a veteran with the enthusiasm of youth.' Which was tame compared with the gauntlet thrown down by the *Mail*'s Jack Wood: 'you can throw me in Southampton Docks if Terry Paine doesn't become a headline name before he's much older.'

The *Chronicle* was not amused by the hype: 'while hoping that Paine will, in fact, go on to achieve great things,' their reporter suggested that 'Southampton Water is quite an appropriate spot for several of the national sports reporters, whose lack of knowledge of the games about which they write is only equalled by their lack of ability to express themselves.' To

The 'ruddy faced country boy' who was an instant hit with national reporters and their headline-writers.

support his case, he cited other labels already being touted by the nationals – not only 'Terry the Terror' but also 'the ruddy faced country boy'. His manager was unfazed: 'Ted Bates insists,' Wood reported, 'that this fresh-faced, well-built lad is a much better outside-right.'

For the moment, his only chance to prove that would be in a two-legged Youth Cup semi-final against Manchester United. As already intimated, Matt Busby's scouting tentacles had stretched across the British Isles to yield him such a monopoly of young talent that his 'Babes' had yet to be beaten in this five season-old competition.

In the first leg at The Dell, the young Saints took an early lead through Wesley Maughan's 'gem of a header' from Paine's 'perfect centre'. But they did little else to warrant the *Echo*'s superlatives and went to Old Trafford trailing 5-2.

Tony Godfrey, who'd taken over in goal from the injured Flood, for the quarter-final, was everybody's Man-of-the-Match in this away leg, although Maughan grabbed the headlines with his two goals. The reporters were not quite sure how Paine 'bustled' in one of his side's three goals, but he confesses to punching it in. Such sleight of hand may have helped to secure a 3-2 win on the night, but it could not prevent a 7-5 aggregate defeat.

Still, it did burst the Busby bubble and it was a memorable moment for the young visitors when the United manager came to the dressing room to congratulate them – even if a cynical Peter Vine feels that 'Busby couldn't understand that a bunch of yokels had beaten his star players.' The Southampton lads were 'like a team of ragamuffins,' Terry Simpson suggests – an image perhaps exaggerated by his recollection of Paine and Holmes arriving for evening training in their railway overalls. And home-grown ragamuffins at that: as Ernie Jones liked to remark, the 'only foreigner' in his team was Wes Maughan, 'from the Isle of Wight.' That's if you discount the other imports from across Hampshire: Paine and Holmes from Winchester; and Godfrey from Basingstoke.

While Maughan and Godfrey both took to Terry, some of the locals weren't so sure. Vine 'quite liked him,' although he found him something of a 'rustic' compared with the Sotonians: 'we were sharper, but he was shrewder. He was a crafty little bastard.' Overall, he was the least assimilating of the immigrants, Harley suggests: 'He didn't get on awfully well with the local lads. It wasn't that we were cliquey, but Terry used to go off on his own a bit.' Yet he suspects that Terry's 'single-minded' attitude may actually have helped him to 'get by. Maybe if he'd been one of the lads, he wouldn't have done so well.'

The replacement of Flood by Godfrey raised to eight the number who would go on to play League football for Southampton. Godfrey would have to wait a while, though: the only member of that Youth team who was about to join Paine in the first team was John Sydenham. When he came in for the last game of the season on the left-wing – a 3-0 home win over Newport County – Terry and he 'stole the show', as 'Observer' saw it. Although the two of them were permitted to swap wings in the second-half, as they had at Youth level, the left-footed Sydenham was wearing No.11, while Paine was now at No.7. He would still be in that number, 17 years later.

Indeed, the next several chapters are the story of how Terry Paine became a fixture for the Saints, making more appearances than the rest of his semi-final team-mates put together. Four of those peers – Simpson, Godfrey, Maughan and Vine – would get their debuts, in that order, in 1958-59. It is a measure of Paine's progress that Vine's first League game would be Terry's 90th.

In fact, it would be Vine's *only* league appearance. Yet everybody involved with the Youth team will assure you that he was its outstanding player. Ernie Jones 'had sleepless nights over that lad. He was perfect. He had *everything*.' Bill Ellerington talks of 'throwing a life away. Two great feet. In fact, I thought he was as good, or better, a passer of the ball than any of the pros.'

Terry Simpson can think of only two footballers he has seen kick a ball as well as, or better than, Peter Vine. Ellerington himself is one; Bobby Charlton is the other. In fact, for all-round skill, Simpson puts Vine on a par with Charlton. Terry Paine impressed Simpson, as we have seen, but Vine was 'Number One'. As Joe Harley puts it, 'it didn't matter which foot Peter kicked with, left or right. Terry Paine had two good feet, but Peter Vine was the best two-footed player I've ever seen.'

Although he regrets that 'Peter wasted it,' Harley feels that most of the players, himself included, were there 'for the love of the game. There wasn't that *ambition* to play then. You played for the love of the game – and that was it.'

The 'laid-back' Holmes personified that attitude: 'I was never really that bothered, to be honest. I was quite happy to play and enjoy it, but I was not ambitious. Terry had that streak – that determination.' Colin feels that his own early success and his class-mate's urge to 'catch up' may even 'have spurred him on a bit. I think he really wanted to prove himself and he shot through, then. I was pleased for him.' And so was Peter Vine: 'He pushed himself and did us proud. He was so confident. That's what drove him on and made him a good player.'

That confidence in his own ability is a recurrent theme of his team-mates' assessments. 'Nothing fazed him on a football field,' Maughan soon found. 'He felt he was The King, even in those Youth days.' Meeting Terry at their joint trial, Wes instantly warmed to this 'confident, mischievous kind of guy, with a good sense of humour,' even though 'he would try to drop you in it.' And he envied the way in which Terry's 'supreme confidence and cockiness' propelled his career: 'when he walked out onto a football field, he felt he could beat anybody and that was always a good thing.'

That all begs the question of how the rather less cocky Sydenham soon followed Paine into the first team. Maughan reasons that John had 'a fair amount of confidence, but he was quite special, because he had that turn of speed, which Terry didn't have. I think John knew that that electric pace was one of his greatest assets – and he used it well.' There's no getting away from it: team-mates and opponents alike were in awe of the teenage Sydenham's raw speed. It was as if it was a more quantifiable factor, at this stage of their development, than Paine's two-footed skills. 'But as he moved out of Youth-team level,' Maughan argues, it was soon more apparent that

'Terry was so good on the ball – in a Matthews-style of being able to take it up to somebody, drop his shoulder and beat players.'

Even if he had had Paine's drive to succeed, Vine was almost 21 months his junior and could hardly have been expected to make his debut ahead of him. Goodness knows, there were those who thought it crazy enough to be bringing in Terry, a week before his 18th birthday.

Walker may have seen 'a wonderful player' in the making, but it was not universally obvious that Ted Bates needed to replace either of his wingers: outside-left John Hoskins, who was becoming 26 as that 1956-57 season ended; or John Flood, still only 24 but with 120 League games to his name, on the right. Hoskins, who had made the step-up from Winchester City to Southampton in 1952, had another 73 League games left in him. So Sydenham would have to spend most of the next two seasons in the Reserves. But Flood was obliged to cede his No 7 shirt to Paine. After just two more League games the following season, he would be on his way to Bournemouth.

Which is why Paine's accelerated promotion raised eyebrows both at Airlie Road and The Dell. It was less than three weeks since Roy Walker had spotted his absence from the Winchester dressing room, yet Terry was now playing in the Football League. Roy remembers meeting up with Brian Hunt, on the morning of Terry's debut, to travel to an away game: the question was whether, having survived the Hampshire League full-backs, Terry had the physique to cope in Division III.

However much he might fear for Terry's welfare, Hunt was 'delighted' for him. He knew, from personal experience, what it was like to be a

Brian Hunt

youngster at The Dell, in a long queue behind a Reserve team stuffed with old pros. But there had been a change of manager since his days in waiting:

> Terry was very lucky, having the manager he had, because age didn't matter to Ted. It was wonderful. Prior to that, the club had an idea that you had to be a certain age to play in the first team and it was all very regimented. It was very, very difficult for young players to break into the first team. I was absolutely amazed when Terry came through so soon. He was a very good player but he had an awful lot to learn when he came to Southampton and went into the first team.

Two Southampton first-teamers who could see why Ted Bates brought Paine through at Flood's expense were goalkeeper John Christie and centre-half Pat Parker, each a regular in the defence that conceded fewer goals in that 1956-57 season – 52 – than any other side in the entire Football League. Neither of them questioned Flood's ability. He was 'a good winger,' says Christie. 'On occasions, he was very good. He got the ball over and we scored quite a lot of goals from that.' But, after what he witnessed at Aldershot, Christie felt that 'there was no question at all' that Terry would soon be taking over on the right wing, where he had watched him play for the Youth team.

Parker, who had been paying less attention to the Youth team's Cup-run, still marvels at Terry's performance at Aldershot: 'You couldn't believe that this young lad had such ability against senior players: his coolness; his confidence, in being able to take on a full-back and beat him.' Even so, Pat 'wouldn't like to say that Terry was that much better than John Flood at that stage.' But having got the team to defend better – they had let in 81 the previous season – Bates was beginning to assemble a side that would *attack* its way out of the division. And 'if you're rebuilding a team,' Parker reasons, 'you'd take Terry in place of John.'

If that sounds fair enough at this distance, the seeming consensus is that Flood was not amused. Getting a few games with John in the Reserves in that 1957-58 season, Simpson was privy to 'an underlying comment that Painie was in the side because Ted liked him a bit too much – but, saying that, he was a bloody good player. And, as it turned out, who was right? Ted was, wasn't he?'

Indeed. But, then, the second-string dressing room must be an unparalleled crucible for festering resentment of managerial decisions. Brian, one of Flood's younger brothers – the one who had kept goal for the Youth team and who joined John in the Reserves a few times that season – considers that John was entitled to feel

> a little bit of resentment. You're bound to, aren't you? You're the established pro, there, and you get these youngsters come along. There again, I think Terry deserved to be in there. Terry was class... The first time I met him was, I think, a trial for Hampshire Youth. He turned up – at Victory Road Transport in Romsey – and I didn't know him from Adam. You could see it – in 10 minutes, a quarter-of-an-hour – that he had it. He was a really top-class winger. His dribbling on the ball was quick. His crossing was perfect. He was a born winger, I think.

Born to be great? Really? Was he not already having to work hard to prove himself, against accusations that he had been promoted too soon?

It was beginning to look as though he might need a thick skin.

Chapter 5

Rising Star

Terry Paine was here to stay. The No.7 shirt was indisputably his. As far as Ted Bates was concerned, that is, whatever the mutterings were in the dressing room as to his premature preferment.

Which meant that two wingers – Dickie Dowsett and Eric Day – could be let go in the summer of 1957. Dowsett had been scoring from either flank for the Reserves, when Paine came flashing past him. He would become a free-scoring inside-forward, at Bournemouth and then Crystal Palace.

Day's departure was quite another story. Thanks to the War, Eric was 25 before he played his first 'official' game for Southampton in November 1945. And yet he would chalk up over 400 appearances, with 158 goals, to put him third in the club's all-time list of scorers (although four players – Paine included – would subsequently overtake him).

Eric had had to bide his time – just as Terry would – playing on the left until a vacancy arose on the right. Once he had made the No.7 shirt his own, however, he had retained it until the start of the 1953-54 season,

whereupon he metamorphosed into a prolific goal-scoring centre-forward. On becoming manager in September 1955, Ted Bates had initially kept his old team-mate at No.9, but had moved him back to the right wing towards the end of that season.

Eric Day had to serve a Dell apprenticeship – as Terry Paine later would – crossing from the left.

In his last four appearances, in the spring of 1957, Day was at No.7 with Paine at No.11. He had featured infrequently that season, while the Board repeatedly debated, and rejected, his request to go part-time. Disappointed with the way he had been treated, one of the club's most loyal servants departed for non-league football in June 1957.

One of the team-mates who had obliged Day to linger on the left had been Don Roper, although the versatile Roper could – and did – play all along the forward line. Having gone to Arsenal in 1947, as what their manager described as a 'two-footed powerful winger', 'The Don' had come home to Southampton, midway through the 1956-57 season, essentially to play as an inside-forward – and a 'bloody good' one at that, according to Peter Vine, a potential heir to his position.

All of which left Terry with only two competitors for the No.7 shirt: Peter Brown and John Flood. Brown considered that Flood and he were 'similar: we both used to like getting down the wing and cutting across.' That required him to be able to score with his left foot – which he felt he could use 'reasonably well'. And he rated himself as 'quick' – quick enough for a winger – although he preferred to operate at inside-forward, a position in which he reckoned to score 'a few goals' – prolifically so for the Reserves in 1956-57. He was a 'bit upset' when that didn't earn him promotion in that role: he wasn't expecting to displace Flood.

But then, there was a new winger around, arriving so suddenly that Brown hadn't seen him coming. It became evident to him in 1957-58, however, that the new kid was here to stay – 'he was so *fit*, wasn't he? He never seemed to get many knocks' – and, after making only one appearance all season, he left for Wrexham. The disgruntled Flood would get two games and be off to Bournemouth.

In contrast, John Hoskins, the other winger whose place was threatened by one of Ted's Teenies, had a fine season, missing only five League games and scoring 18 goals along the way. When he pulled a thigh muscle in October, Paine returned to outside-left, again partnering Walker, who had been ever-present. But, two weeks later, Johnny was playing his last game for Southampton. When Terry Paine came into the dressing room and realised that his mentor had departed for Reading, leaving Tommy Mulgrew in charge of the No.10 shirt, it was his introduction to the brutal reality of the game's here-today-gone-tomorrow pragmatism:

> In those days, I hadn't realised what the game was all about: to find out, when I came in, that the guy I'd been stripping next to had gone was something I found very hard to understand at the time. You think 'Christ! How can *they* go?' You know, you didn't really understand the world of a professional footballer.

Yet until the introduction of 'transfer windows', that would, of course, be how the market functioned. It would be a rare player who would announce, like Len Wilkins, that his 275th game in April would be his last before he emigrated to Canada – so that he received a standing ovation, just walking to the centre-circle to toss up, to say nothing of the prolonged cheering as he left the pitch.

While far from matching Hoskins's strike-rate, Paine initially lived up to the predictions of becoming a goal-scoring winger, with three goals in the first seven games, one of them – a 'cool volley' at Walsall – exciting Ted Bates in his next 'Team Manager's Notes'. Then he averaged a goal a game in December, but could manage only three more in the New Year. Not that that mattered when centre-forward Derek Reeves was on fire, with 14 goals in the last 14 games, to bring his season's League tally to 31.

Roper, operating mainly as Paine's right-wing partner, contributed 18 goals and the side finished with 112. It was the first time the club had reached treble figures, but it was good enough only for sixth place, thanks to the 72 goals conceded. The side didn't incur many embarrassing defeats, but the goals were going in regularly at both ends.

Goalkeeper John Christie was only too glad not to be facing Terry Paine. Although he would develop a reputation as a lazy trainer, Terry was not averse to going back for extra practice of an afternoon, *with a ball*. Christie 'can always remember' such an occasion, when he asked Terry to practise with him: 'I wanted to use Terry – for my own benefit, just to see what his reaction would be – because he was such a good player on the ball. I would make a position for him and say "what would you do now, nipper?"'

John would keep changing his position and be impressed by the way his young team-mate adjusted accordingly his use of the ball:

> He could chip it or pull it back. If you gave him the space at the near post, he would just smash it in at the near post. Anybody who played up front could rest assured that he would get the ball where he wanted it.

As noted in the previous chapter, Pat Parker had taken an instant liking, like Christie, to the confident young newcomer. He enjoyed having Paine and Sydenham about the place, dressed to kill in what he remembers as being 'very tight, expensive-looking Italian suits.' And then there was Terry's freedom of speech, as he shattered the convention that a youngster would wait to be spoken to by the senior professionals. This is hardly surprising if you consider how he had long been adopted as an equal by his elders. Parker was not complaining. Nor was Bryn Elliott, 14 years' Terry's senior: he just wishes he'd 'been like him and so confident.' And Bryn couldn't help but take to Terry, anyhow, because 'he always laughed at my jokes.'

The smartly-dressed young wingers board the team-bus

Coming sixth in the table served a purpose. This was the season when the sides finishing in the top half of each of the Third Division's regional sections would form a nationwide Third Division for 1958-59. One of the sides that missed the cut was Aldershot. When Terry returned to the Recreation Ground on Christmas Day 1957, the scene of his first Saints goal nine months before, he scored in a 5-1 win. He did so again in the 2-2 'return' at The Dell the following day. The Saints have never played their Hampshire neighbours since.

The 1958-59 season would be a busy one for Paine, who would be the only ever-present player. As noted in the previous chapter, four team-mates from the 1957 Youth team would get their first start, as Ted Bates fidgeted with his line-ups.

There was a notable debutant, too, on the terraces, for the first home game of the season. Jack Channon had taken his nine year-old son, Michael, from their home on Salisbury Plain – pretty much equi-distant between Southampton and Swindon – to watch the two sides at The Dell. Mick later recalled that experience in his autobiography – how Ken Birch scored from the spot and all. In fact, it was John Page who took the penalty – and missed!

Birch, signed from Everton in March of that year, did manage three goals from right-half before Ted Bates pulled the plug on this misguided signing. His young outside-right objected that Birch used to 'launch' the ball:

'he just couldn't keep it on the ground. My neck! I had neck-ache. Every time he kicked it, you had to look up for it.'

Bates's alternatives at No.4 were Brian Clifton and Terry Simpson. Clifton had come up through Hampshire Schools and the Hampshire League (with Whitchurch United) to make his debut the previous season, while Simpson was one of those four graduates from the 1957 Youth team who would now make their debut. Another one of the four, Tony Godfrey, was threatening John Christie for the goalkeeping jersey, but Christie had seen off several contenders for it since his debut in 1951. When Woking came to The Dell for a First Round FA Cup-tie in November, Birch and Christie were still in possession.

The visitors fielded three Amateur international forwards, including Charlie Mortimore, the older brother of John, who had been likewise capped on his way to becoming a Chelsea centre-half. John would come to occupy all manner of positions at Southampton, some of which will cause him to feature later in this book. The other two were more immediately involved in the Terry Paine story. Roy Littlejohn would join Southampton later that season and get a few games in the Reserves at outside-right, never becoming one of the more serious contenders – on parade in Chapter 19 – for Paine's shirt, while it could be argued that outside-left Reg Stratton had denied Terry an England Youth cap.

A few months younger than Terry, he was already in Woking's Isthmian League side when he played against Luxembourg in the same England Youth team as Colin Holmes in February 1957 – the televised game discussed in the previous chapter – by which time Terry had just broken into Winchester City's first team. Although a few of Paine's Youth team-mates had been noticed by the selectors, Stratton assumes that the League he was playing in, with all those chances to catch the eye in the London suburbs, gave him a headstart over the provincial Paine.

But it was Terry's turn, that November afternoon in 1958, to turn it on, scoring Saints' third goal, following a solo run in which he beat three men. A 4-1 win set up a Second Round tie at Loftus Road, with Godfrey and Simpson coming in for Christie and Birch. But when the Third Round brought Blackpool, starring Stanley Matthews, to The Dell, the two older players returned, as did Tommy Traynor for Barry Hillier and Reeves for Clifton. It still rankles with Simpson that the manager 'went for experience. That's what he told me… A big game – everybody wants to play against Matthews and I sat in the stand.'

In a change that went against that bias, Sydenham came in for Hoskins. The hard surface – a sprinkling of snow covered the frozen pitch – might have suited his speed, if only he had had the right footwear. As it was, he had to rummage in a cupboard for a pair of rubber boots. His problem was that one or two sizes fitted all – hard luck if you took a size 5 like him! Blackpool were better equipped and Jimmy Armfield recalls how their goalkeeper, George Farm, 'wore a track-suit. In those days, things were less sophisticated. So, for a goalkeeper to wear a track-suit was a bit unusual.'

With Armfield in close attendance and Livesey coming late to assist,
Paine goes flying over the unusually-attired Farm.

Blackpool 'had to pull a few stops out,' Armfield recalls, 'because Southampton had one or two good players: I remember these two young wingers.' Although he cannot recollect that the visitors 'were ever really in trouble,' their hosts were on the verge of achieving a 1-1 draw when an 88th-minute corner from Matthews – who 'had all the right gear on,' Sydenham enviously recollects – set up a winner for Blackpool, leaving Ted Bates to concentrate, as the cliché goes, on getting out of Division Three. The state of the boot cupboard was but a minor reminder of the ramshackle outfit he had inherited. His bigger problem was timing the infusion of young blood into an ageing team.

Peter Vine argues – not on his own behalf, he insists – that, having accelerated Paine, and nursed Sydenham, into the first team, Bates had become too cautious: Simpson deserved better; and Harley should surely have been given a chance. That said, Bates did introduce, this season, another youngster who would have a huge impact – if not in the hoped-for way – on promotion hopes. The murky tale of how Charlie Livesey arrived at The Dell in 1956 involved a deal between Herbert Blagrave, the Southampton FC President; and Jimmy Thompson, the celebrated Chelsea scout.

Mr Blagrave was a horse-racing man, with stables at Beckhampton, for whom Thompson used to place bets. Chelsea had rejected Livesey, so Thompson was free to bring him to The Dell as a favour to Blagrave. This also fulfilled a promise he'd made to a judge in a London court, when young Livesey found himself in the dock. The story that Thompson assured the judge that he'd found a good home for him in Southampton may sound far-fetched, yet I was told it not only by Charlie but by John Corbett, who had been a director at the time and who later succeeded Blagrave as President.

The delinquent Livesey was placed in digs with Tony Godfrey and Denis Pring, who were amazed by his life-style. 'He was a good-looking fellow,' Denis recalls. 'He was smart and he liked himself a little bit.' And there were people who liked him enough to keep him out late: 'he'd be out to three o'clock in the morning before a game,' Godfrey recollects, 'no thought about going to bed or anything like that.'

Derek Reeves, who was unhappy with playing inside-right to Livesey

This was very far removed from the priorities of Paine, the prudent professional. But Terry was fascinated by such 'a wide boy – a different kind

Charlie Livesey, whose life-style shocked his young team-mates.

of person to any I'd ever met' – and took him home to tea in Highcliffe. A year older than Paine, Livesey was developing more slowly. His break came in August 1958.

Carrying on where he'd left off in the May, Reeves started the season with four goals in a 6-1 win at Mansfield. But he broke his toe in the next game and Livesey was in. He didn't impress; but just as he was thinking he'd blown his chance, Charlie popped in six goals in successive home wins over Hull City and Halifax Town.

And so, with Reeves fit and ready to reclaim his No.9 shirt, Ted Bates had a dilemma of the kind managers are alleged to love: how to accommodate two rampant goalscorers? Well, he could move one of them to inside-forward. It was invariably Reeves who went to No.8. He was not happy with the arrangement. Although the Board knew this, it nevertheless agreed, in March, to Ted Bates's suggestion that Livesey be paid at the top rate, along with Paine: there was still a maximum wage but that didn't mean everyone was on it.

Come the end of the season, though, there was a change of mind: Livesey could be sold. Ted Drake now wanted him at Stamford Bridge. His market-research being well-advanced, Bates was in a position to complete an unimaginably good exchange-deal. If it would prove a triumph not just for his shrewd handling of the sums, it also relied on quite a lot of luck and the judgment of Bill Ellerington.

Ellerington has claimed – modestly, if correctly in most cases, surely – that '*nobody* finds a player. There are always people watching. Anybody who claims to have "discovered" a player is lying.' That said, Bill is reckoned – not least by Terry Paine, as we shall see later – to have been a superb judge of talent; and his principal role in Ted Bates's close-season deals in 1959 is not disputed. In his final two seasons as a player under George Roughton, while Bates was coaching the Reserves, Ellerington was playing only occasionally for the first team and was doing a spot of scouting, a role he would develop – in tandem with being player-coach to the 'A' team – once his old-team mate had succeeded Roughton.

Any talent-spotter could have a fruitful day out in the late 1950s, watching Chelsea's Reserves. Which was how Ellerington became an admirer of Cliff Huxford, a 22 year-old wing-half, whom he recommended to Bates as a 'destructive' defender. Drake agreed to pay £12,000 plus Huxford for Livesey. Terry, who had enjoyed playing with Charlie, even if he was 'never quite as good a finisher as he looked,' rates this 'one of the shrewdest signings that Ted ever made.'

So now Bates, with £12,000 in spare change, was in the market for an attacking wing-half and goal-scoring inside-forward – preferably one alongside whom Reeves would feel comfortable. Grimsby's Dick Conner came to wear the No.4 shirt, while Ellerington had lined up a No.8. In fact, he had already recommended this young Scot after watching him for Roughton. Dunfermline's George O'Brien had been doing his National Service at RAMC, Crookham – with Livesey, ironically – when Bill took a shine to him. But Roughton did not bite, which is how Ellerington came to recommend O'Brien to Eddie Lever at Portsmouth – again in vain, as you may recall from Chapter 3.

It was Raich Carter who eventually brought O'Brien south – as far as Leeds. In two-and-a-bit seasons, he managed to score only six times in 44 starts for Carter and his successor, Bill Lambton. Ellerington still fancied him but it needed two lucky twists to bring O'Brien to the south coast.

Cardiff's Ron Hewitt, the Wales international who had played in the 1958 World Cup finals, topped Bates's shopping list. Only when Hewitt opted to return 'home' to Wrexham, instead, did Bates make O'Brien his target. And he was helped by an upheaval at Elland Road. A new manager, Jack Taylor, was willing to offload his Scottish inside-forward, without waiting to take a good look at him. George had a champion in the Leeds boardroom in the chairman, Sam Boulton, but Taylor contrived to sell him to Bates while his chairman wasn't around.

This major episode in the managerial career of Ted Bates merited fuller coverage in his biography than would be justified here. Yet, because of the way Bates's summer signings reshaped the prospects for Terry Paine, I have tried to demonstrate the mixture of scouting skills and serendipity that enabled him to complete a three-for-one deal that even he thought 'amazing'. Not that the dealing stopped there: he signed six other players that summer, one of whom was an outside-right. Despite his ambitious claims, discussed in Chapter 19, Bernard Harrison was never going to wrest the No.7 shirt from Terry Paine.

To make room for this influx, Ted Bates released 14 players. They included Don Roper, John Hoskins and John Christie. Terry feels that he had benefited from partnering Roper, an 'elder statesman' to whom he had been able to take his problems. But he was now 20 and would jolly well have to look after himself – although O'Brien, his elder by three-and-a-half years, recalls that he coached Terry in how to improve his autograph: 'I just showed him how to make the "T" bigger to cover "Terry" and the "P" bigger to cover "Paine".' He would also form a brutal alliance with Terry in the sarcasm stakes, from which nobody, it seems, would be exempt.

Paine's biting humour, continuing far beyond his relationship with O'Brien, is a recurring feature of his story. For the moment, though, what was happening on the pitch was the story, as Paine and O'Brien clicked in a most successful side. On the other flank, with the departure of Hoskins, would be Sydenham, the two young wingers becoming a formidable threat – surely the most feared in the division. As Gerry Cakebread, standing between Brentford's posts, remembers it,

> whenever you played them, … you always got stretched defensively. You always went on the field knowing you had to contain Paine and Sydenham, because they were setting things up all the time for them… They always seemed to have a lot of width. It makes it very difficult to defend and

cover: if you get people playing wide, it stretches the defence. It's often lost in the lower levels of football, because players tend to home-in on the goal and don't keep their width.

Ted Bates, with his pair of contrasting wingers who 'stretched' Third Division defences in 1959-60.

Denis Pring, an inside-forward whose brief League career was effectively ended by the signing of George O'Brien, remembers how '*exciting*' the two young wingers soon became. Although less than two years older than Pring, Paine – encouraged, as I say, by O'Brien – was already lording it over him. Denis lapped it up, though: 'Terry was a good mickey-taker. It was never ultra-serious, if there's such a description. It was silly fun – he was always messing about, doing things. I *loved* it.'

With Christie transferred to Walsall, Pring's digs-mate, Tony Godfrey, looked established in goal. But an injury in September cost him his place and he would be out of contention for almost 18 months. His initial replacement would be Bob Charles, a local lad who had represented England at Schoolboy and Youth levels. Another 'young 'un', then, to be the butt of the Paine humour but, like Pring, Charles found Terry 'a good lad. He was good to me: he helped me along. I couldn't fault anything with him.'

While Maughan and Simpson each got a game or two in that promotion season, the final two debutants from the 1957 Youth team also featured: Dave Scurr would get a couple more games, in Division II, but this would be the only first-team opportunity for Colin Holmes, Paine's class-mate and work-mate who, as we saw, had been way ahead of him – size does matter – in their teenage years. In other words, youth was getting its occasional chance, but only Paine and Sydenham were regulars, while two Youth-team graduates shared the goalkeeper's jersey until March.

CONSTANT PAINE

The 11 main players of 1959-60, nine of whom would make 42 League appearances or more.
Back row (*left to right*): Conner, Traynor, Charles, Page, Davies, Huxford.
Front: Paine, O'Brien, Reeves, Mulgrew, Sydenham.

So, in this remarkably stable season, the main eleven, over the 46 League games, would be Charles (24 appearances); Davies (46), Traynor (43); Conner (45), Page (45), Huxford (46); Paine (46), O'Brien (42), Reeves (46), Mulgrew (33) and Sydenham (45). Every member of the side has been introduced already, save for the ever-present right-back. Ron Thomas Davies – not to be confused with Ron Tudor Davies, whose sensational contribution to our story begins in Chapter 14 – had arrived from Cardiff, towards the end of Paine's first full season, to fill the breach left by the emigrant Wilkins.

To say that Bates's summer dealings had produced a side that picked itself would seem to be an under-statement. It was a nice blend, age-wise. Mulgrew, at 30, was the eldest; Sydenham, at 19, the youngest. Three other regulars were over 25, yet Bates decided that 22 year-old Huxford – with but six League games to his name – would be his captain. The Board's Management Committee doubted the wisdom of this, with Colonel Meyrick expressing the hope that 20 year-old Paine – already a veteran of 99 League appearances – could be encouraged to give the rookie captain the backing he needed. The manager was persuaded to make the appointment provisional, but it never came up for review. And far from finding Paine supportive, Huxford would feel himself undermined by him.

This was the first of several instances, in the first half of the season, when the Board questioned the manager's judgment. It began after six games. The side had already scored 15 goals (with Reeves and O'Brien on four each) but, by dint of conceding 13, were lying only ninth. You might have thought questions would be asked about the defence, but the chairman had calculated that the Saints would be leading the table had Reeves not missed so many chances. Ted Bates defended his centre-forward, as being 'one of the key members if [the team] were to get promotion. The Board should remember that with a dry lively ball, the forwards will miss more goals than they will score.'

And Reeves might be especially liable. The point, John Sydenham explains, is that

> Derek actually wasn't a good finisher, but he was always in there. You never saw anybody *miss* as many chances as Derek Reeves, but he was always in there, where it counted. Miss or not, he scored loads of goals, rebounds off knees, any part of his body. He just had that knack of being in the right place at the right time.

And with Sydenham and Paine crossing to him or popping it 'over the top', for him to use his pace, Reeves was likely to get more chances to miss than most. What's more, if he wasn't getting on to the end of this supply-line, that could be because O'Brien was thriving on it. The chairman's analysis had failed to take account of the rate at which these *two* strikers were hitting the target: a conversion rate of 1.33 goals a game between them was not at all bad.

Anyhow, Reeves responded with 10 goals, including two hat-tricks, in the next four games, to set up four wins on the trot. That did not, however, prevent a major inquest by the Board, which recorded that this was 'not a promotion side.' Amid concerns about a lack of co-ordination between centre-half Page and his goalkeeper, the injured Godfrey now gave way to Charles and the focus of anxiety switched to Mulgrew, so much so that the Board 'instructed the team manager to search for a good inside-forward.' Not that the word 'instruct' meant a lot to a manager minded to follow the advice of Matt Busby. The Youth Cup-tie against United in 1957 had given Saints' young manager a chance to discuss 'every aspect' of the game with Busby, but he especially valued his thoughts on relationships with directors: 'let them have their say – and do what you want.'

There can be no gainsaying that Bates heeded that advice in 1959-60. Before long, the players with whom he had kept faith were lying second and, from 20 February, they would be a fixture at the top. The away win, at Bury, that installed them in pole position was their 30th League game of the season and, despite the Board's instructions, Mulgrew had played in all of them. From here on in, though, he would have to share the No.10 shirt with Brian Clifton and Gordon Brown. The ever-dependable Clifton weighed in with eight goals in seven games. Brown was an odd signing, just before the transfer deadline, from Derby, where he had made nine Second Division appearances, that season, for one goal. He delivered for Southampton, though, in that his two goals earned a 1-1 draw and a 1-0 win. Having justified his transfer fee, he would hardly play, and never score, for the club again.

The only other problem position was the goalkeeper. Bob Charles had a wobble in March, conceding nine goals in two games. So, just beating the transfer deadline, Ted Bates signed Ron Reynolds from Spurs. He was now set for a run-in that would vindicate his faith in the side the Board had doubted, albeit tweaked at the last with two signings.

Amid this hectic March activity, Terry was twice released for representative games. On 16 March, the third anniversary of his first-team debut, he won his first England Under-23 cap against Holland at Hillsborough. His dad was there to see him score in a 5-2 win. The club had paid for Alec Paine's trip to Sheffield, where Mr Chaplin, the genial director, looked after him: 'the club were family-orientated in those days,' Terry reflects with feeling. A week later, he was in Amsterdam, celebrating his 21st birthday by representing the Football Combination against a Dutch XI. Selection for the Combination side did not depend upon currently being in your Reserves; but having played in it only four times at that point, Terry must have been one of the least eligible players ever to represent that league.

Although four of them missed only five games between them in 1959-60,
Ted Bates called upon nine forwards that season.
(*Left to right*): Harrison, Mulgrew, Maughan, Brown, Clifton,
Reeves, Paine, O'Brien, Sydenham.

None of this caused him to miss a single game, as promotion loomed. It was all but secured on Easter Monday, with a 1-0 home win over Reading, the goal coming from another of Clifton's classic headers. O'Brien rightly predicted that it was a goal we fans would 'always remember' – to the embarrassment of the modest Clifton, who feels that nothing should detract from the achievement of Derek Reeves, who bettered even his 1957-58 scoring ratio: his tally of 39 League goals remains a club record for a season and a divisional record to boot. He had proved the chairman so woefully wrong and had demonstrated that he was more than comfortable with his new strike-partner.

For his part, O'Brien was not totally enamoured of his new team-mates, feeling that the side had 'come good' in the run-in, *despite* 'those who were just happy to jog along' in Division III. Yet he had thrived on his partnership with Paine, to score 23 League goals. The two of them clicked, Terry reckons, from their very first practice session – 'it was telepathy: it just worked!'

All of which helps to explain why the side topped the 100-mark, as they had in 1958. Even though they fell six short, on 106, of their 1958 tally and conceded three more goals (75), they won the Third Division championship, the only side ever to do so after letting in more than 70 goals. There were no seven-goal hauls this time, but they ran up five or more five times in the League and twice in the FA Cup.

With Ron Reynolds (*right*), Ted Bates and the band in attendance, Cliff Huxford receives the Third Division Championship trophy.

Distance is no object as Paine beats Southend's Threadgold from the touchline.

Having beaten Coventry 5-1 in a First Round replay, the Saints made short work of Southend in the next round, when Paine scored from way out on the touchline to set up a 3-0 win and a visit to First Division Manchester City.

As they leave Southampton for a seaside break before their engagement at Maine Road, Sydenham (*left*), Huxford and Paine oblige the photographer in time-honoured fashion.

Some of the players may have affected a jaunty air for the usual photo-call at the station, but just entering such 'a massive place' as Maine Road, an awestruck Bob Charles feared 'a cricket score'. Inside 20 minutes, he was 'picking the ball out' and dreading the worst. Even when Reeves completed his hat-trick with three-quarters of the game gone to make it 4-1 to the visitors – O'Brien had scored the other one – Charles remained nervous. But Reeves's fourth settled it at 5-1 with four minutes to go.

Although he found Bert Trautmann, City's veteran goalkeeper, at fault with three of those goals, Charles was most impressed with the way Saints' wingers 'ran riot: Terry absolutely skinned his left-back.' Paine agrees that it was 'one of those days when things went for you' and he was, indeed, able to turn Cliff Sear, later capped by Wales, 'inside out'.

In collaboration with Sydenham, Terry had introduced short corners to his repertoire that afternoon – not as part of the manager's tactical plans, but as a reprise of something they had got up to, when larking around on the beach at Blackpool, where they had been preparing for the match.

Sydenham's verdict was that 'Derek Reeves's performance was incredible. Terry Paine had a wonderful day. I had quite a good one.'

The Good, The Wonderful and The Incredible.

Sydenham (*left*), Paine and Reeves warm-up for the 1959-60 season, under the watchful eye of Jimmy Gallagher.

If few would argue with that assessment, George O'Brien was not pleased with what he saw as the outside left's failure to cut out balls thrown by Trautmann to right-half Ken Barnes. O'Brien was not one to let the newness of his arrival stop him issuing instructions to team-mates he found less tactically aware, whether it was to avert danger or to hurry the ball to the side's main strength, its right-wing pair. He remains disappointed that Sydenham did not take his advice: 'if you'd told Mulgrew to do that, he'd have done it. But we won 5-1 anyhow, so what do I know?'

That rhetorical question does not, by definition, require an answer but I shall return, in the next chapter, to how much O'Brien did indeed know about tactics and how Paine admired him for being so outspoken about it. Meanwhile, I need to explain the reference to Mulgrew. As O'Brien saw it,

> Tommy was an honest player: he knew what he could do and what he couldn't do. You could play with him, so long as you could tell him what to do… Painie and I were strong personalities, I suppose, and we could tell him what to do and get the ball off him.

Mulgrew had no problem with such attitudes: as far as he was concerned, 'there was a good camaraderie' in that 1959-60 side, with 'no disputes'. He has fond memories of Reeves's four goals at Maine Road – 'wonderful stuff' – as befits an inside-forward who considered Reeves a better centre-forward than the one he had played with at Newcastle – Jackie Milburn.

Reluctant to single out Reeves for his 'four fine goals', the *Echo*'s 'Nomad' paid tribute to 'a team win.' But he felt he had a 'duty' to 'hand a large bouquet to Terry Paine… I am positive that he has never played better than on Saturday.'

Manchester City were impressed, too, and wanted Terry to know that. Not only did they 'phone him to that end, but Jimmy Meadows, recently appointed to their training staff, stopped by at Highcliffe in the summer: 'just passing through on holiday,' he assured Terry. That's all right, then: heaven forbid that they might have been tapping him up.

The incentive to move to a higher-ranking club would be increased, of course, were the maximum wage to be abolished. Discussing that prospect as the season neared its climax, the *Mirror*'s Peter Wilson, a passionate abolitionist, cited Southampton – on what evidence it is not clear – as a 'notable' objector: 'they have two England Under-23 wingers, John Sydenham and Terry Paine [and] they feel it would make it difficult to prevent players of this calibre asking for transfers if they knew the only way to get a £10 weekly increase on Third Division wages was to move to a First Division club.'

The main transfer looming for the two young wingers, though, was into National Service. That prospect apart, Terry Paine was going nowhere that summer – unless you count an early date at Highbury, representing Young England v England on the eve of the Cup Final, soon followed by winning his second U-23 cap, against East Germany in Berlin. Then, before starting his Second Division career with some juicy August fixtures, there would be time for a few weeks of cricket with Hyde Ramblers.

He had left the YMCA for the Ramblers in 1958, so that home games now involved a stroll down to King George's Field. Terry's old mate, Colin Holmes, had put in a word for him at the Ramblers, whose regulars also included Don Marks, who had played in Terry's debut for Winchester City, and Dick Collins, another Ramblers-cum-City all-rounder. Although Terry's 'agility' suited him to fielding in the covers, Collins reckons, Terry fancied his chances behind the stumps. The Ramblers had had a very good young 'keeper in Bryan Timms, another Spearman protégé who had been two years behind Terry at Romsey Road. He was so good, though, that he joined the

Hampshire ground staff in 1958, at the age of 17, *en route* to succeeding Leo Harrison and playing more than 200 times for the county's 1st XI.

So Terry took his chance with the gloves. Don Marks rated him 'a very, very good wicket-keeper – a safe pair of hands.' And, as Les Elms had discovered when he first encouraged him to take up the game, Terry's 'wonderful eye, where he could pick the ball up,' made him a more than useful batsman. 'He wasn't a *stylist,*' Marks explains. 'He wasn't a technically correct batsman, but he struck the ball well.'

That seems to have stood him in especially good stead, opening the batting in the Tichborne Trophy, a limited-overs competition, played on midweek evenings. Terry was invariably prominent in the *Chronicle*'s reports of these games – as for his 'bright knock' (45 not out) that contributed to a nine-wicket trouncing of Flowerdown in 1958 and his undefeated 36, as the same opponents succumbed by 10 wickets in July 1959.

With the *Chronicle* enthusing about his 'good form' that month, he got a game for the Winchester and District Cricket XI. Neither his wicket-keeping nor his batting was needed: Bryan Timms rather put Terry's summer stardom into perspective with an undefeated 107. But Terry was opening – and again top-scoring – for the Ramblers, the following week, as they won the Tichborne Trophy for the seventh time (albeit shared on this occasion, after a tied final with Eastgate).

If his free-scoring style suited that competition, Dick Collins recalls how the captain, John Macey, would enjoin young Paine to curb his impetuosity in the longer, Saturday or Sunday game and play himself in. 'Pick your balls,' he would say as Terry prepared to go out to bat. 'Pick your balls.' Sniggers all round from team-mates within earshot.

All such fun. But, then, Terry's 'times at The Ramblers were always *fun,*' Dick recalls. 'He got on with everybody all right and we had some fun. It was fun-cricket in those days, before the leagues.' The problem was that his season was getting even shorter. It had been bad enough when he had to stop playing in August in order to focus on football; but if he was going to be touring with England sides, there was going to be a front-end squeeze, as well.

His first U-23 tour in 1960 was over on 22 May, so Terry was available, in early June, to play *against* a Winchester XI – for a Hampshire XI, selected by Jimmy Gray as part of his benefit season. With Leo Harrison going in at No.3, Terry's batting was again not needed, but Harrison tended not to keep wicket in benefit matches. Steve White, who opened the bowling in that game, insists that Terry was behind the stumps, but the scorebook shows that he had a bowl – a solitary over, but it was the only maiden of the match.

Whatever, this was surely as good a cricket XI as he would ever play in.

Chapter 6

Out On His Ears

Ted Bates was back in the Second Division, where he had played all of his peace-time football. He was in no apparent hurry to tinker with the personnel that had got him there – although, with no Livesey-style windfall to assist him, he didn't have much option.

But maybe a fresh injection of high-quality local lads might help the club to get into Division I for the first time? Bates allowed himself this thought in a close-season letter to John Walls who, you will recall, had recommended his young British Rail work-mate: perhaps John 'could help to produce a few more Terry Paines and I don't see any reason why we shall not get into the First Division.'

For the moment, though, Bates was in danger of losing Paine, whether permanently to a First Division predator or temporarily to the Ministry of Labour and National Service. West Bromwich Albion's manager, Gordon Clark, had watched him seven times during the promotion campaign and, with the new season about to start, Bill Holden of the *Mirror* had him as the front-runner to sign Terry, valued at £30,000. Alternatively, Holden suggested, Spurs needed a winger and Southampton owed them a favour for 'letting them have goalkeeper Ron Reynolds last season.'

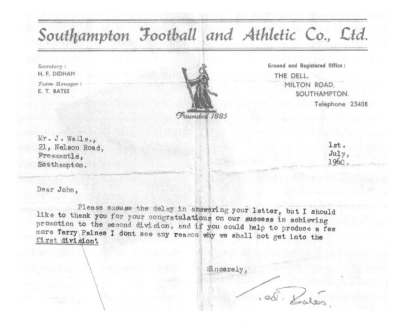

Southampton Football and Athletic Co., Ltd.

Secretary :
H. F. DIDHAM

Team Manager :
E. T. BATES

Founded 1885

Ground and Registered Office :
THE DELL.
MILTON ROAD.
SOUTHAMPTON.
Telephone 23408

Mr. J. Walls.,
21, Nelson Road,
Freemantle,
Southampton.

1st.
July,
1960.

Dear John,

Please excuse the delay in answering your letter, but I should like to thank you for your congratulations on our success in achieving promotion to the second division, and if you could help to produce a few more Terry Paines I dont see any reason why we shall not get into the first division!

Sincerely,

Ted. Bates.

The speculation would continue, but Terry was staying put – unless the men from the ministry could sign him up. National Service beckoned. Here, Bates was under threat on both flanks. Although the legislation provided that men were liable, from the age of 18, to be conscripted, the average age was nearer 20. In the summer of 1960, Paine, now 21, and Sydenham, who would be 21 come September, were both liable to be called up.

Bates had long developed a damage-limitation policy: he had an understanding whereby his young men would serve at RAMC, Crookham, confident that they would often be available to him on a Saturday. The shortcoming of that arrangement was that square-bashing and army drills may have kept young men fit for their military duties but such exercise did not make them fit to play football. Moreover, they could be required to play too often during the week. As John Sydenham recalls,

> you have to play for *everybody*. You have to play for your HQ company, your depot team, the Corps team, the British Army team. And then I could be playing for Southampton on a Saturday: they'd send a cab up for me. Sometimes, I was just crawling out to play: I could hardly walk. But in order to play on the Saturday, I had to play in all those other games. And not only play, but you couldn't go out and stroll about – or they could always stop you playing for your club. But when I was playing for Southampton, I was getting paid £12.50. I couldn't afford to not play. That was a lot of money.

Which is why Bates needed some wing-cover. David Chadwick, who had become the youngest-ever Reserves debutant the previous season – a record beaten a few times since, of course, latterly by Theo Walcott – was now almost 17, but not yet ready for first-team action. Bates's solution was to

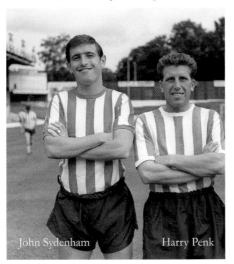

John Sydenham   Harry Penk

sign Harry Penk, who boasted 'two good feet' and had played on both flanks, from Plymouth.

It was a perfect solution all-round. Penk had come down from Wigan to Portsmouth in 1955 but, having seldom made the first team, had joined Argyle. Now, 104 League games later, he was more than happy to return to Hampshire and be near his wife's parents, even though he could hardly expect to keep out Paine or Sydenham, once they had served their time.

As it turned out, he would be needed as a stand-in for Sydenham alone: Paine would dodge the draft. National Service was coming to an end in 1960 and the government had announced that men born in 1940 or later 'need not expect to be called up.' The pivotal year would be 1939: if you'd been born, like Terry, in the first half of that year, you would be conscripted; the prospects for those born in the third quarter, like John, was 'uncertain'; while those from the last quarter were 'unlikely' to be required.

John Sydenham, born right at the end of the third quarter, was, as expected, called up in July and, by the start of the season, was an angry young man at Crookham: with the government treading water as it allowed recruitment to peter out – the last draft would be on 17 November – John resented being involved in what seemed to be 'a waste of time.' The first few weeks were especially demoralising, but 'the one thing that kept me going was the fact that I thought Painie was coming in with me – but the little so-and-so got out of it!'

The best way of 'getting out of it' was to fail your medical examination. In his fascinating study, *The Call-Up*, Tom Hickman lists some of the ingenious methods adopted to fool the examiners and explains why few of them were likely to succeed.

He omits a condition that was hard to refute: enuresis. It worked for Pat Crerand, who'd just signed for Celtic and was desperate for an escape route. When an acquaintance advised him to put bed-wetting on his form, he thought 'they're not going to fall for that, surely.' But when called for examination, he told the doctor that his incontinence was driving his mother to despair. And fall for it they did.

Terry had no such need to lie outright: exaggeration did the trick. He had been having a spot of ear-trouble: some painful boils that had been 'sorted out' by the club doctor. When he reported for his medical, he 'was street-wise enough to lay it on a bit' and not to hear some of the words in the test, 'though I reckon I could hear a pin drop and still can.' Referred to his local hospital, Terry was recognised by the specialist, who declared him unfit: 'whether he was a Saints fan or not, I don't know. I was out of the place and down the road doing handsprings.'

Maybe that Winchester doctor was unduly relaxed but, as Hickman explains, the medical threshold had been raised, as recruitment was being run down: if fewer men were needed, so fewer men would be passed fit.

Not that iffy ears were merely a late-order reason for medical exemption. Harry Penk had, ironically, been passed unfit with a perforated ear-drum when examined in Liverpool in the summer of 1955. Like Paine, he had had problems that he found it convenient to exaggerate, when the examiner discovered wax and he was referred to a consultant:

He tried to get this wax out and the fluid that they use was starting to drip down my nose. The consultant said 'you've obviously got a perforation there. It'll probably heal up.' Portsmouth were after me. They said 'we'll sign you on [from Wigan Athletic], but we'd sooner sign you on if you weren't going into the Forces.' When I realised that if I just blew my nose, it whistled, I thought 'if I do that, it's not going to heal up as quickly as they seem to think.' After a few weeks, I had to go back and it was still like that, so I didn't get passed. So I signed for Portsmouth more or less straightaway, then. It's never troubled me since.

Looking back on that lucky break, 50 years later, Harry says he had no idea that examinees were sticking knitting needles in their ears in the hope of achieving the effect his consultant did. And you might not even have needed to exaggerate your condition if you turned up for your medical to be passed unfit with an ear problem of which you were totally unaware. That happened, for instance, to another winger, Stewart Imlach, a Scottish international in the making.

This must have been the experience, though, of many a young man, whose ears had never been adequately examined before. Wax? Wasn't that something our mothers removed with a hairgrip wrapped in a hankie?

One way or another, then, Sydenham could count himself most unfortunate to be drafted. He was born in the last few weeks of the crucial quarter of 1939; and both his fellow-winger and replacement-winger would be exempted, when surprised to find they had ear problems that they could play up. He would come to value his time at Crookham as 'really the greatest thing that ever happened to me. It just gave me discipline… although, at the time, it was devastating to have two years taken away from what is a very short career.'

Not that Sydenham lost much first-team action in the first half of that 1960-61 season, when he was allowed leave to play in all but two of the 21 League games and all bar one of the six matches it took the side to reach the quarter-finals of the new League Cup competition. Which meant that he participated in three wins over Liverpool, the first two of them sandwiching a 5-1 trouncing of Portsmouth.

The *Football Echo* headline of 27 August had been a long time coming:

AFTER 33 YEARS SNAPPY SAINTS OUTCLASS POMPEY

Quite simply, Pompey had been promoted to Division I in 1927 – literally out of the Saints' league – and had stayed there until 1959, twice winning the Championship in the process. Their narrow escape from further relegation in 1960 set up this first meeting in the League for 33 years.

In Portsmouth's 12 post-war seasons in the First Division, Jimmy Dickinson had been a near-fixture at left-half. But he had become a left-back in Division II, which meant that he was marking, at the age of 35, the 21 year-old winger who would one day overtake his appearances record. It was not his fault that Saints led 4-0 at half-time. He had kept the young pretender fairly quiet until Terry 'opened up the Pompey defence' and fed Reeves. His powerful shot spun back off the post into the path of Paine, who threaded the ball in for the third goal.

Having 'opened up the Pompey defence,' Paine completes the move to make it 3-0.

The hapless Dickinson obliged with an own goal in the second half, but that was the least of his problems: it was a 'tragedy', Archie Quick of the *Sunday Pictorial* reckoned, to see a player of his 'calibre in this planless, near-to-third-division standard Pompey side,' in contrast with the 'class' of the home side, whose wingers 'looked as though they were going to be potent factors in Second Division football this season.' It was 'rather a hollow win' for the *Echo*, too, since the visitors looked inferior to 'half the sides Saints met in the Third Division last season.'

Liverpool, whom Southampton had never met in the League, were a rather different proposition. Bill Shankly had taken over at Anfield midway through the previous season and they had finished third. Not that this guaranteed them an easy ride against the division's new boys: as their right-back, Gerry Byrne, reminds us, 'it's still 11 against 11; and anything can

In his first home game in the Second Division (v Liverpool), Terry Paine gives an immediate demonstration of how he is going to get behind defences at this level and get his crosses in.

happen.' Some of his team-mates did not subscribe, however, to that old adage. Inside-right Roger Hunt confesses that Liverpool 'were very confident of beating Southampton.' And that confidence was boosted by an early goal: 'we were so full of ourselves,' visiting inside-left Jimmy Melia recalls. But the Saints stormed back to win 4-1, the fourth goal coming when Paine rounded his marker and beat the 'keeper. A chastened Hunt remembers it well:

> They just played us off the park: they played fantastic football. I just remember these forwards of Southampton. There were two wingers, Terry and John Sydenham, Reeves centre-forward – and was it O'Brien and Mulgrew? [indeed, it was] They just murdered us. Shankly went mad in the dressing room.

We shall find that Liverpool's manager developed a particular disdain for Southampton, but he would not instantly find a way of beating them. Having sorted out Pompey, Ted Bates's unchanged side would head for Anfield the next week, win 1-0 and go second in the table. They would not sustain that form but by the time they returned to Liverpool in November for the Third Round of the League Cup, Terry Paine had good cause to swagger into Anfield. Hunt happened to be standing at the door with Shankly's then assistant, Bob Paisley:

> You know what Terry's like – all cocky, isn't he? – and he had this pork-pie hat on, a little trilby thing… I remember Bob Paisley saying 'Look! We're going to beat that Southampton. That Terry Paine! Cocky little bugger, walking in here as though he owns the place.' Anyhow, they beat us 2-1. Terry got both goals and I scored for Liverpool.

CONSTANT PAINE

Paine had scored in every round of this new competition so far. And he was rattling them in in the Second Division, too. Having found the net in each of the first four home games, he was level with O'Brien, in the goal-stakes, when Brighton came to The Dell in mid-September. George popped in all of Saints' goals in a 4-2 win, which won him a 'Player-of-the-Week' award from one of the nationals. He had to share the limelight with Paine, even so, as Terry was returning, that week, to Maine Road – not to negotiate with Jimmy Meadows and his boss, but to play in a 5-1 win by England Under-23s against a Danish XI.

That sharing of the honours is reflected in the cartoon (*below*) by Don Osmond (aka 'Oz'), for whom Terry Paine would give good value: Oz would intermittently exploit his weekly spot in the *Echo* effectively to

conduct a dual campaign – that Paine must play for England; and that he must play for no other club but Southampton. A good example of the latter followed (*opposite*) the next month when the forwards turned it on in the First Round of the League Cup. There was a degree of hype here – the opponents, Newport County, were in the Third Division and it had taken Saints three attempts to progress 5-3 – but when it came to Terry Paine, Oz was a man on a mission.

It is ironic that he should draw attention, in his October cartoon, to the 'telepathy' between Paine and O'Brien. Their brilliant on-field understanding will be a recurrent theme of the next few chapters, yet George – whose remarkable memory enables him to recount, in minute detail, when and how he was slighted by whom – will tell you of Terry's non-sharing moments, on and off the field. That week in September is a case in point: the 'Player-of-the-Week' feels that the Young Englander begrudged him the attention and the award that his four goals had earned him.

And Terry might even behave in this way, O'Brien argues, on the field. This telepathic pair had soon developed 'certain tricks', George explains. For instance, Terry would be 'on the ball; I'd come up to him; he'd run over it; and I'd take it away from him; things like that.' But if Terry was in a hogging-the-limelight mood, then 'we didn't do that: he'd see me coming and he'd pull it back.' To those Saints fans old enough to have enjoyed that prolific partnership and to be aware of Paine's assist-rate in it – not to mention their friendship off the field – this accusation will surely come as a shock. Yet we will hear further charges of this order from O'Brien.

Meanwhile, come the Saturday, Paine was taking his turn as the goalscorer, grabbing two in a 3-3 draw at Ipswich. The right-wing pair was revelling in Second Division football – it was a matter, O'Brien reckons, of being able to 'find space' at this level – so that when they won 3-1 at Plymouth on 22 October, exactly one-third of the way through the League season, the pair of them had scored 20 goals (O'Brien 11; Paine 9), while Reeves, who was having trouble scoring in this higher division, had only three.

Terry's goal at Plymouth was his 50th in the League. But he was restless. His two League Cup goals, the following week – in the game against Newport County that provoked Oz's hyperbole – stimulated his second transfer request of the month. Having just made his third appearance for the Under-23 side, he could argue, in one of the Sundays, that 'the time has come for First Division football, for I believe that only that way can I catch the eye of the England selectors.' Conversely, his manager could reason, in the *Echo*, that he had been capped, at U-23 level, as a Third Division player, so why could he not win a full cap as a Division II player? And, anyhow, First Division football was 'well within [Saints'] scope next season,' given that 'Terry is playing,' Bates claimed, 'in one of the best forward lines in the country and that gives a lift to his football.'

Well, Roger Hunt had been impressed with those forwards and had reason to be especially impressed with Paine, following his two-goal riposte to Bob Paisley in that November Cup-tie. Manchester United, who were represented at that game, now expressed an interest in him – and not for the first time, apparently. Matt Busby reportedly had £50,000 to spend on a two-item shopping list: Paine and West Ham's Noel Cantwell. He would get his Hammer.

Bates's description of his forward line was surely exaggerated, in so far as Reeves had not been scoring at this level. He went into December with only five League goals to his name, but then hit five in one game – a remarkable 5-4 win over Leeds United in the Fourth Round of the League Cup. Enough has already been written about the floodlight failures in this match that meant the final whistle going two hours and 40 minutes after the first. So let's take that as read and focus on two features of this game for Terry Paine.

First, he ought, by rights, to have played much of this League Cup-tie in goal. When Ron Reynolds was stretchered off in the first-half, with Saints leading 1-0 – a Reeves header from a Paine cross – Terry should have taken over between the posts: substitutes were still five seasons away. Instead, Cliff Huxford, who had never played there before, assumed the jersey, even though he considered himself 'a bit short for a goalkeeper – it's a big area, you know. I was only 5ft 8½ins – but I had a reputation of being brave, so I suppose that was it.' His supposition at the time, as put to the *Echo*, was that the manager wanted to keep 'the regular deputy goalkeeper' in the attack. The need for Terry, who was even shorter than Huxford, to remain upfront was all the greater, as O'Brien was hobbling from early on.

So, with O'Brien unfit to take advantage of the space he had been finding, there was only one thing for it: Paine would somehow have to keep putting Reeves in. Terry obliged, in 'another of his outstanding games,' with what 'Observer' called 'an important share' in all five of Reeves's goals.

Deputy Paine would soon get his chance in goal, however, when Reynolds went off in a New Year Eve's match at Fratton Park with a burst blood vessel in his throat. The repairs took only 26 minutes, during which Terry kept a clean sheet and gave Oz a thrill. Ron was fit for the following Saturday when Alf Ramsey's Ipswich came to The Dell for the Third Round of the FA Cup. Reynolds had been involved in Ted Bates's plotting to

combat the way Ramsey had his side playing 'a totally new form of attack,' a system that was about to win them the Second Division Championship – and the First Division the following season.

It was appropriate in my biography of Ted Bates to scrutinise his counter-strategy in some detail. There is no need to re-examine it here. Let's just say that it seemed to work that January afternoon, as the Saints raced to a 5-0 lead inside the first half-hour. Then Paine ran through, unchallenged, to make it six before half-time. It finished 7-1. The manager deemed the

Terry Paine (part-hidden) completes his run through the Ipswich defence by hitting Saints' sixth goal.

first-half display 'even better' than the performance, a year earlier, at Maine Road; and 'Observer' applauded 'a forward line that on its first-half form must be as good as any in the country' – which is what Oz had been trying to say, I suppose, in September.

All of the forwards scored bar Reeves, who would add but three more League goals by the end of the season. There would be no more Cup goals for anybody: Saints would go out in the next round of the two competitions – to Leyton Orient in the FA Cup and Burnley in the League Cup.

Notwithstanding that they had just beaten the Champions-designate 7-1, the Saints' 4-2 home defeat by Burnley, the reigning League Champions, perhaps underlined how far short they yet were of First Division standards. And they disappointed against Orient, rather more modest Division II opponents than Ipswich. It illustrated, for Paine, the anti-climactic 'shame of Cup football.' The team heads off to Barton-on-Sea for a golfing break; they return to a drenched Dell; 'pump all the water off; talk the referee into playing; and we get beat 1-0.'

His marker, Eddie Lewis – like Dickinson a convert to left-back – recalls both the prospect and the performance:

We had drawn Southampton away – which was very difficult for us.
Nobody wanted to go to The Dell and play that lot there… For my sixth
game at left-back, I was playing against the great Terry Paine at The Dell. I
remember one national newspaper describing it as the spider versus the fly,
Terry Paine being the spider and Eddie Lewis the fly – Eddie Lewis
making his sixth appearance at left-back, against Terry Paine who was
easily one of the best right-wingers in the country. I'd obviously known of
Terry and it was quite exciting… We were under the cosh for most of the
game. It was very, very wet – which obviously didn't suit George O'Brien,
Terry Paine and John Sydenham. But we worked hard and, actually, we had
the makings of quite a useful side, which we weren't aware of at the time –
but we won promotion, with Liverpool, the following season.

Paine drives off in the golfing warm-up at Barton-on-Sea, with an audience of
(*left to right*) Brown, Davies, Mulgrew, Page and Traynor.
You may have noticed that he is wearing the hat that upset Bob Paisley

Yes, Liverpool, whom Saints had just beaten three times, would go up the
next season, while Ipswich, soon to be the 1961 Champions, had been
obliterated, 7-1. That result continues to rankle with O'Brien, in that it
proves, for him, that Southampton had the makings of a promotion side,
but were foiled by Ted Bates's failure, as he sees it, to improve his squad:

Ipswich got promoted and they went on and won the First Division. Alf
Ramsey got the England manager's job and then went and won the World
Cup… That could have been Ted, if he'd had promotion [in 1961], if he
had made the signings he had to make when we went into the Second
Division – Ted couldn't buy out-and-out defenders – make the managerial
decisions that mattered, like Ramsey did… It's all hypothetical, I know, but

we were a class above Ipswich… If Ted had done what he should have, if we'd have done even a bit of what Ipswich had done, that would have helped a lot of people, wouldn't it? Me, in particular, I suppose: if we'd have been in the First Division, you're really in the public eye [for international selection]. I think we were a better side than Ipswich. I'm sure Ipswich thought that as well. And Ramsey went on to get the England job. So we used to say Ted would have got that job.

George O'Brien certainly gives you good value, the way he answers a simple question. I count three answers here.

The notion that Ted Bates might have managed England need not detain us, although members of the 'what if?' brigade may wish to ponder what that might have done to Terry Paine's international career. Nor need the prospect of O'Brien for Scotland concern us here, although it does raise the whole issue of exposure to the selectors. It has to be said that playing in the Second Division did not stop Paine being capped – indeed, he would win all of his caps while at that level. But, then, Southampton was much more accessible to Alf Ramsey (and any observer whose advice he might have pretended to consider) than it was to Scotland's management: it could be that geography was a greater impediment to O'Brien's international prospects than the club's status.

Or could it just be that he wasn't quite good enough? Scotland had some tidy forwards in the early 1960s and, if it was a goal-scoring inside-forward you needed, they didn't come a lot better than Denis Law. Nobody has ever scored more for Scotland than Law – 'probably one of the greatest players' that Terry Paine has 'ever seen.' That said, Terry compares his Southampton wing-partner very favourably with the man he would partner in most of his games for England. Jimmy Greaves.

George O'Brien

He considered these two inside-rights to be 'very much on a par – at club level. George never played at international level and you never know if they're going to make that step up. But George was that kind of finisher. Jimmy did all of his work in the box. George did it all in the box. A lethal finisher, George!'

Not one to doubt his own ability, O'Brien nevertheless shrugs off this mantle: 'I'm not classing myself with Jimmy Greaves. He was something else.' But, like Terry, Cliff Huxford was in a position to make comparisons, having played a bit with a young Greaves at Chelsea. Cliff cannot think that he 'ever saw a player – even Jimmy Greaves – who was sharper in the six-yard box than George.'

But enough of international prospects: O'Brien's starting point was a domestic concern – his manager failed to improve his side when he should have. Terry Paine has things to say on both sides of that argument.

On the one hand, he applauds the fact that George had strong views and was prepared to express them: 'not all players think about the game,' Terry points out, but the fact that O'Brien had pondered what was needed 'proves' to him that

> George was thinking about the game. And George was also very expressive about how the game should be played – in his opinion, how it should be played. Now, we're not all going to be right, but at least I believe that it's far better that players think about it and let their thoughts be known than the guy who doesn't give it a second thought. I'm sure there are players, from my day, who wish they'd taken a bit more notice.

On the other hand, Terry cautions that players won't always have enough of the facts to prescribe the ideal action by the manager:

> George felt maybe Ted should have done things in different ways. But we all think that: we're all good managers when we're players – we all think we know everything, though obviously we don't. It's easy for players – and I was one of them – to say 'you go and get so-and-so,' but (a) is he available; and (b) have we got the money? I mean, all of these things have to be taken into consideration. It's *easy* for us to say 'go and get him,' but it's another matter being able to tie him up. Now that I've been on that other [managerial] side, I understand the problems a manager gets, as far as bringing a player to a club is concerned.

To illustrate how he had nudged Ted Bates in ignorance, Terry raises a case from much later when he suggested Ted bid for Peter Rodrigues: 'I thought he'd have done us the world of good.'

Later still, Terry discovered that the manager had been interested in Rodrigues in 1970, but had reported to the Board that buying him would be 'too great' a risk, 'owing to Achilles trouble.' That Peter's Achilles would be good for a few more years does not matter here: the point Terry is making is that, without access to the club's minutes, he was ignorant of that situation. Only when I was permitted to read that minute and report it, in 1998, in *Dell Diamond,* did Terry learn why Ted Bates had failed to 'tie up' Peter Rodrigues.

Not that Terry was too disappointed with Ron Davies, the right-back who had missed very few games over the previous three seasons.

But this was a season that would bring to The Dell, one February afternoon, one of the finest full-backs ever seen there, a left-back who Terry thought was the 'tops' – Huddersfield's Ray Wilson, who had already won the first seven of his 63 England caps.

So it was quite a coup for Terry that he should have 'outwitted and outplayed' Wilson – according to 'Observer' – at this first meeting. He rounded off a good afternoon by scoring the 'best' goal in a 4-2 win, when he 'got possession only just over the halfway line in the middle of the field, and made a terrific individual run right through the Huddersfield defence, to score with a great shot.'

Terry treasures that 'lovely' moment, but does not kid himself that it was at all typical:

You always felt that he dominated you. Ray Wilson was, I think, the ultimate. He was a *quick* player. Obviously, there are other ways of skinning a cat, but you like to get *by* your full-back at some time: you never felt that you ever really mastered Ray.

After that Huddersfield game, the Saints would have a poor March and an even worse April. Taking but four points from their last 10 games, they would finish eighth, 15 points adrift of Ipswich.

Paine, who scored his second Under-23 goal in a March win over West Germany at White Hart Lane, would get more than his share of the goals in the Division II run-in to finish on 18 in the League, second only to O'Brien's 22. Add in seven more in the Cups and you have a winger scoring 25 goals in a season (with O'Brien on 27). Playing in the same division in 1937-38, Harry Osman, the man who would go on to manage Terry at Winchester City, scored 22 goals for the Saints, all of them in the League.

He was mainly an outside-left and this achievement will generally be referred to as a record for a Southampton winger, which his protégé had now broken. Yet you may sometimes see Paine's 18 goals in the League credited with having eclipsed Osman's record League haul. Which is accurate if you deduct the seven goals that Osman scored, that season, from his alternative position of inside-left.

However you do the sums, Paine was easily Saints' second-highest scorer that season. Although he scored eight times in the League Cup, Reeves could manage but 10 goals in his 35 League outings. A replacement looked unlikely from within: it was by now evident that Wes Maughan, the Reserves' top scorer again in 1960-61, was never going to achieve permanent promotion.

In today's game, Maughan could have expected to come off the bench and use his speed, if and when Reeves was failing to make an impression, instead of which he had to make many a trip as 12th man. He liked to join his former Youth-team winger in a habit that would lead to a significant development in Terry's later career – of which more in Chapter 17. Not being 'a great card-man,' Terry found all those long train trips, changing in London, 'very boring' and would often walk the corridors.

Audrey Simpson
Miss Viewer
1959

He was happy to venture forth alone, but Maughan would often accompany him on those explorations. It could be just a matter of nosiness – would they find other footballers they knew? – but the bonus would be to locate a girl or two in need of company. Their greatest coup was happening upon a beauty queen. Wes still has the photo that 'Miss Viewer' gave them.

With no international tours in the summer of 1961, playing for Young England v England on 5 May completed Paine's representative duties for the summer – unless you count turning out for the Winchester & District Cricket XI against a combined President's and Vice-President's XI in July. Such games were usually played at North Walls but, on this occasion, Terry was back at King George's Field for one of his wicket-keeping highlights, flying to his left to catch Dennis Silk down the leg side. A future MCC President, no less, Silk turned to congratulate the young 'keeper on his athleticism. For his encore, Terry completed a stumping later in the innings.

All of which was a good warm-up routine for keeping goal in the first match of the new season.

Chapter 7

Romancing on Ice

O'Brien had had his way. The Saints kicked off the 1961-62 campaign, with replacements for the two defenders of whom he had been especially critical: Tommy Traynor, an attacking left-back whose defending was not up to George's expectations; and John Page, who carried too much weight for his liking.

Roy Patrick, from Forest, would replace Traynor – if only briefly – at No.3 but it had looked as though Page would still be at No.5 – until he injured his back in training. Leicester's Tony Knapp signed just in time to play in the opening match, against Plymouth Argyle at The Dell.

It was quite an afternoon. Brian Clifton, who had replaced the departed Conner at right-half, gave Saints a 1-0 interval lead. But Ron Reynolds did not return for the second half, having gone to hospital with an ankle injury. Paine took over in goal. Having let in two – the first by George Kirby, who will be rampaging through the next chapter on the end of Terry's crosses – he handed the jersey to Huxford for the last 10 minutes, but could not help produce an equaliser.

If fielding three 'keepers in one game was a rarity to be noted, the jersey-swapping between Paine and Huxford had a symbolic irony, in that Cliff had just ceded the captaincy to Terry. Huxford had taken readily to that responsibility in 1959, believing one of his strengths to have been 'organising: I'm not frightened of telling players what to do and what I expect.' But he 'always thought one of the jobs of the captain was to go between players and manager,' a role that was undermined, he increasingly felt, by Paine's too frequent visits to the manager's office: 'Terry was Ted's blue-eyed boy – no doubt about that. I didn't like what was going on, so I packed it in.'

Godfrey now took over in goal for the rest of the campaign – easily his best run, which would continue into the 1962-63 season. And Knapp would be there even longer – for two solid seasons – before he missed a game. A 24 year-old, who had toured with the full England squad, he had commanded a transfer fee of £27,500, more than double the club's previous record outlay. It stood to reason, then, that he might also command a high wage. You may recall – from the earlier discussion of how Livesey joined Paine at the top of Southampton's wage structure in 1959 – that, even with a low maximum wage, there could still be differentials within the first-team dressing room. With the historic lifting, during the 1960-61 season, of that feudal ceiling, a greater *range* of wages obviously became possible. Not that every club was going to have quite the range of Fulham, where the chairman, Tommy Trinder, had publicly promised that he would pay his prime asset, Johnny Haynes, £100-a-week.

It seems that Southampton's top rate was £25 plus £10 an appearance. George O'Brien recalls that Paine and he were on that rate, amid 'a lot of animosity' from their team-mates. But those other players could not be sure, of course, who was getting what. Suspicions fuelled resentment, however, to the extent that there was something of a players' revolt against Ted Bates. The issue, for Ron Reynolds, was that Paine was believed to be getting 'a helluva lot more' than the rest. One reason why this stuck in the collective craw was that Terry was perceived, Ron reasoned, not to be contributing enough in away games: 'There was nobody better than Paine *at home*, but whenever we went away, we knew we were playing with only 10 men: Terry was *gone*! He just didn't want to know. I could throw a ball out to him and he'd just be in a dream.'

Ron Reynolds (*left*) and Tony Godfrey, who formed views, from their goalmouth, on Terry Paine's contribution, away from home

Tony Godfrey also claims to have experienced those 'dream' sequences, but he adopts a more measured stance. He felt that Terry's position was too secure, so that he could afford,

sometimes, away from home, if things went bad, to drift out of the game – and we suffered for it. It wasn't all bad: if we were doing quite well, he'd probably have a brilliant game away from home; but if we were struggling a bit, sometimes you'd throw a ball to him, and he'd have his hands on his hips and let it go by – probably because he was a bit annoyed at some of us. It probably went both ways.

Lest we think that he might be dwelling unduly on an occasional irritant, Godfrey adds that Paine

was a *terrific* player. Nobody had the skill that Terry Paine had – not since Stanley Matthews. He had that ability to hold the ball, to sprint with the ball and also – one of the best abilities he had, I thought – he could cross a ball, ever so slow – a real chip – from running quick. Which is very hard to do and I haven't seen any other player do that as well as he could.

The new season was about to kick-off when Bates succeeded in quelling the rebellion. But now Knapp had been added into the mix. Paine and O'Brien somehow came to understand that Knapp was to get £32 a week. Each of them raised the matter with the manager and the right-wing pair soon joined the new arrival at the top of the wage-pyramid.

The issue of who was top-dog came to the fore in another way, following a 5-1 defeat at Scunthorpe in October, which brought to an end an unbeaten run of eight games that had taken the Saints into second place. They had taken the lead at the Old Showground when O'Brien set up a goal for Paine, but the game was an anti-climax for each of them. By failing to score himself, George ended a record-breaking sequence of scoring in nine consecutive League games, while, late in the game, Terry was sent off, along with Scunthorpe's Howells: 'It was just a scuffle,' he contends. 'The fists went flying. I got sent off. It's not a nice feeling, I assure you. It's not one you're proud of, that's for sure – it's a horrible feeling. Not very nice.'

And there were some not very nice consequences. Five weeks later, Terry was suspended – the disciplinary wheels ground slowly in those days – to end a run of 160 consecutive League games (or 180 if you count the Cups), which included three ever-present seasons. Two replacements were required for the visit of Sunderland: one as captain; one at outside-right

Ted Bates handed the captaincy to Tony Knapp and then dropped a bombshell: Knapp would remain captain. Bates told the *Echo* that he had explained to Terry that he 'felt Tony Knapp was in a better position in defence to command the team.' The manager was 'sure he understood the position,' even if it had 'hit his ego.' But Paine was 'very unhappy,' Bates explained, 'about the loss of money from his suspension.' Not only had he lost his wages, but his team-mates had failed to make up the full deficit in the customary whip-round – hardly a surprising reaction to the unrest over differentials.

Paine slapped in a transfer request and told the *People* that, if turned down, he would 'ask again and again. I will do my utmost to get away.' His display of pique may have been serious, but Terry's indignant statements to the *People* generally need to be taken with a pinch of salt: he would develop a habit of sounding off, after a Saturday game, to that Sunday 'paper and then deny the story on Monday. It was all a game: the *People* had its exclusive; Terry pocketed £50; and the story was buried before it had legs.

'Observer' informed his *Echo* readers that he expected Terry to persist in his request and, what's more, he urged the Board to grant it: the money could be used on 'buying one or two players to strengthen the attack.'

CONSTANT PAINE

The forward line that Ted Bates had been acclaiming a year earlier had become most dependent upon O'Brien's goals. Reeves was hardly scoring and Maughan had had his last chance in September. The only youngster looking capable of breaking into the first team was David Chadwick – a candidate, ironically, for Paine's No.7 shirt.

It was Chadwick who got that shirt against Sunderland. By now 18, he had made his debut in the game before, when Ted Bates had shuffled his forward-line, so that O'Brien went to No.9 and Paine to No.8. His suspension served, Terry would retrieve his No.7 shirt. He would be wearing it for the next home game – a 2-0 win over Liverpool – that was watched by England manager, Walter Winterbottom. But it was Saints' new captain, not the deplaced one, who was duly invited to squad-training at Lilleshall.

Chadwick would get a further 10 run-outs on the right wing before the season was out. Yet Paine would miss none of them. In fact, he would miss only that one game against Sunderland: it was just an odd season of juggling by the manager in which his U-23 winger made only 32 of his 41 appearances at No.7, his other nine games being at inside-forward (three times) or outside-left (six).

That meant he played as many times on the left wing as Sydenham: when John was getting leave from RAMC Crookham, it was mainly to play for the Reserves. Penk got his break with 30 first-team outings, but O'Brien took a liking to the combination of Chadwick on the right and Paine on the left. That would have meant omitting Sydenham, whose crossing wasn't accurate enough for George: 'he just used to fire it across; you just had to try and guess, you know.'

Nobody – certainly not Sydenham himself – would claim that accuracy was his strong suit, but nobody else has ever broached such a radical solution with me. And although O'Brien put it to Paine at the time, he was not canvassing support for it. When Norman Dean told me in 2007 what 'a tremendous player' he thought Chadwick was and how unfortunate he had been to be blocked by Terry, I mentioned the O'Brien solution. Norman could see George's point and wondered what it might have meant to bring in 'another load of skill,' in the form of Chadwick at the expense of a 'flyer'. Not that Dean had ever had cause to complain about the service from the left:

> John Sydenham was fine. He could play football, to my mind. It's only when he got to the by-line that John wasn't as creative as Terry. John's only hope was to hit it – boomph! And it was six and two threes whether you got in the way of it or not. If you didn't get in the way, it was a throw-in the other side. It was always the same old cross. It was never a pull-back, a

chip or whatever. John, to my mind, just seemed to hit it – head down, you know: no looking up, the way Terry did, to see where people were.

What this style of crossing demanded of strikers is a subject to which we shall have cause to return – with Dean in Chapter 10 and with Ron Davies in Chapter 14.

The question of whether Bates might have played two wingers of a kind, rather than provide his strikers with such contrasting wide players, is one to which I shall return in Chapter 19. O'Brien's advocacy of the former model is remarkable, given how famously well his right-wing partnership with Paine operated. But George had calculated that this would give him a better service overall from the wings. In fact, his League scoring rate with Paine at No.11 was 4:6 (or 67%) that season, compared with 22:29 (76%) when the two of them were in their normal right-wing pairing. The numbers are too small, obviously, to warrant a generalisable correlation, but there is no mistaking O'Brien's gut feeling that he would have sacrificed Paine's service from the right in order to have had the benefit of Chadwick as well.

Come January, George had the prospect of losing one Paine, while another was recruited to wait in the wings. On the first score, there was talk, as the New Year approached, of Terry Paine leaving. This had been prompted by another transfer request from Terry, which, on this occasion, the Board had granted. And rightly so, the *Echo* again chanted, with a hint that Terry could have shown more gratitude for 'the skill, patience and thoroughness of the Dell coaching' to which 'he owes much.' And, given that Chadwick's 'satisfactory' performances at outside-right proved that he could 'be developed' for that position, 'the change can be managed without too much difficulty' and the transfer money could be used for positions that 'obviously need strengthening.'

Or might Paine feature in an exchange deal? Bill Holden of the *Daily Mirror* compiled a New Year Eve's list of wingers who were on the transfer list or itching to be so. They included the 22 year-old Paine and Aston Villa's Peter McParland, still only 27 but surplus to requirements. Villa's manager, Joe Mercer, an old buddy of Ted Bates, admitted to Holden that he had 'enquired about Paine,' but there was no question, he said, of an exchange for McParland.

I should think not, indeed. With Chadwick waiting in the wings, Bates hardly needed to trade Paine, now valued at £45,000, for an older winger. A speculation of more substance was that Terry might move to Arsenal, in an exchange for inside-forward, John Barnwell, plus what Holden described as 'an undisclosed amount in cash.' That would have been a move of no little irony, given that Arsenal had failed to sign a 17 year-old Paine when he played in the same trial as Barnwell. But, whatever Southampton's terms,

Arsenal were not impressed: 'we are interested in Paine,' their Secretary, Bob Wall, told Holden, 'but we are not so hard up for wingers that we would let Barnwell go in an exchange. We need him more than we need Paine.' Even so, the *Mirror* was reporting, a week later, that Arsenal had bid almost £40,000 for Terry, which would have broken the record for a winger.

But within a few weeks, Terry was off the list and had been invited to join Knapp for England's next training session at Lilleshall. Contrary to the *Echo*'s let-him-go stance, Oz celebrated the withdrawal of his transfer request by scoffing at the media's speculation. So Cliff Jones was still the most expensive winger in the land – at £35,000 from Swansea to Tottenham – and Terry was still commuting from Highcliffe to The Dell.

He had been bringing his kid-brother with him. Trevor had been allowed to kick around there during his summer holiday but now, having left school, aged 15, at Christmas, he had returned for a trial. If Oz was delighted by the prospect of another Paine on his patch, Trevor himself was under no illusions: 'it was on Terry's recommendation that I went down to

The Dell. I was his brother, for goodness sake, so they gave me a chance.' It was bound to be a tough assignment: 'I was always being compared with Terry Paine of Young England. It was difficult and I didn't like it, to be honest.' It was obviously going to be an open invitation to O'Brien to vent his sarcasm: 'if I'd known this was a kindergarten,' George told Terry, 'I'd have brought my kids down.'

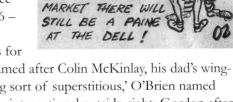

IT'S NICE TO KNOW THAT WHATEVER HAPPENS IN THE TRANSFER MARKET THERE WILL STILL BE A PAINE AT THE DELL!

The irony of that comment is that Colin – the eldest of George's three sons, born in Dunfermline in 1956 – would get to play professionally, making more than 50 appearances for his dad's old club. He had been named after Colin McKinlay, his dad's wing-partner at Dunfermline and, 'being sort of superstitious,' O'Brien named each of his other two sons after an international outside-right: Gordon after Gordon Smith of Hibs and Scotland; and Terry after … need I say more?

Ironic or not, George's ribbing of Terry wasn't going to do Trevor any harm: it would be a different story, though, if the apprehensive young trialist were to encounter directly that barbed O'Brien humour – especially if his big brother failed to come to his support. The incident that encapsulated Trevor's problem is readily recalled by all three of the parties: 'we were playing in the car park,' Trevor recollects,

> and I lost control of the ball and knocked all the milk-bottles over. Well, you can imagine: it was *hysterical*. It could have happened to anyone, but it just happened that I was Terry's brother and he was there with George O'Brien, falling around.

And the two of them were each falling around, 40-odd years later, when reminded of this incident. Once they'd stopped laughing, though, they each apologised for their insensitivity. 'It wasn't very fair to the lad,' O'Brien admits. 'He was only there because he was Terry's brother. It wasn't very nice, really. It was quite funny, but *cruel*.' George feels that his sarcasm 'upset' Terry on this occasion but Terry admits that he was more of a hindrance than a help to Trevor, who remains sore that his brother, having recommended him, wasn't anywhere near upset enough:

> It was horrific… Terry liked to take the mickey – badly, sometimes; too far, sometimes. And it hurt. I didn't like it at all. But that was Terry. I learned that in years to come. That's the way he was. No, it wasn't nice – of course, it wasn't.

It's not that Trevor objects to sarcasm *per se* – 'I'm good at it as well,' he assures us, 'but I'm not *nasty* with it... when you're that age and you're that vulnerable, and you're in that environment with all those professional footballers around you, and you're obviously not as good as they are... George O'Brien and Terry were *terrors,* they really were.'

Terry may apologise – along with his partner-in-terror – today, but Trevor, who would never make it at The Dell, doubts that his brother realises how hurt he was: 'I've never said anything. It's just banter now and it doesn't worry me but, as a youngster, it did.' The question of how much mickey-taking young players should be expected to take, pretty much as a rite of passage, will be another recurring feature of the Terry Paine story.

It could go beyond verbals, of course: roughing up youngsters on the training ground was an institutionalised ritual, in which first-teamers were allowed to engage, without fear of retaliation. According to Tony Heaney, coming through the Youth team a year behind Terry, it was part of the unwritten 'rules' of practice matches that the Reserves must not injure the first-teamers. He recalls wearing plimsolls when practising against the first team, 'so that we didn't cause any injuries,' and having to tolerate booted first-teamers treading on your toes, or worse: 'the niggle came in, now and again, and they're kicking you with studs.' He especially has in mind the occasion when his fellow full-back, Dave Scurr – a Youth team-mate of Terry's, you may recall – had had his full of Terry's niggle,

> but if you did retaliate, the trainer, Jimmy Gallagher, would call you to one side and give you a rollicking for retaliating and upsetting his players. But, this day, Dave Scurr said 'I've had enough of him tapping my ankles: I'm going to have a go at him.' I said to him, 'if you miss him, I'll have him.' We did – and we got pulled to one side. Jim said 'if you two carry on that way, you're in the dressing room.' In other words, you're off, changed, and see Ted the following morning. So we had to abide by the rules.

Trevor's leaving school reduced the opportunities for Terry to play street-games with him and his peer-group. We have established that Terry had mostly rejected the street when he was a young teenager, in favour of being down the fields, alone with a football, or out with mates seven years or so his seniors. But the young professional kicking his heels in Highcliffe of an afternoon had been enjoying the opportunities to come out to play, when Trevor and his mates – some seven or eight years his juniors – got home from school. The game, whether football or cricket, would always be in the road, Trevor recalls:

I can't really remember kicking a ball about with Terry, down at King George's. I can't remember going down the fields to play at all. It was always in the street – always. It was brilliant. You didn't have to worry about cars or anything like that. We'd go out in the street and play cricket: Billy Postle, myself and some of the other lads. Terry would have them fielding somewhere.

Fielding without ever getting an innings, that is. As Bill Postle explains,

it was always Terry *versus* Trevor, with two or three of us younger folk roped in as fielders. It was fiercely competitive between Trevor and Terry and, as a fielder, you were expected to concentrate: remain in position or be told off by Terry – though he used to coach us, as well, so there was some benefit.

This age-group benefited more formally from Terry's footballing guidance. Once Trevor got into the All Saints team, Terry would sometimes go along to coach them and would be regularly seen at their games. Jim Flux, playing in their hero's position on the right wing, recalls the 1958 semi-final in which Terry was shouting instructions to him from the touchline, notably when to cut in and shoot.

He likes to tell people he scored a hat-trick that day, but admits to remembering details of only two goals. He is certain, though, that Terry picked him up at the end of the game and carried him off – a 'claim to fame,' which Jim can guarantee to 'tell everybody I ever meet connected with football.'

Bill Postle can recollect those coaching sessions, but his small group had more privileged access to Terry Paine, the street-cricketer – even if they were not so much players as gofers. 'Eventually,' Bill recalls, 'Terry would get fed up with the game and this was normally signalled by his hitting the tennis ball way up the street or over the roof of a house, leaving us to retrieve it.'

These 'games' were not limited to after-school. Sunday afternoons seem to have been especially memorable for Trevor, in that the street-action formed part of Terry's courting ritual:

He used to bring the odd girl home – always on a Sunday. We used to get a different one every week. Don't ask me to name them. I think Mum gave up in the end – she kept calling them by different names, because she couldn't keep up with him. He'd bring the girl to Sunday tea. Then he'd leave her in there and come out and play cricket or football, out in the road… But it was always someone different – until he met Carol.

Terry met Carol Mackenzie on 5 November 1961 – the Sunday before that Sunderland game for which he was suspended. She was an ice-skater and, although only an amateur, was ahead of the Under-23 international footballer, in so far as she had appeared at Wembley – when she won the Open Junior Free-Skating Championships, aged 14 – and had performed on television, representing the South West in the BBC's *Grandstand Trophy*. Which explains why the 18 year-old Carol was at the ice-rink, practising, that Sunday afternoon.

Terry arrived there from playing golf with Charlie Knott, the rink's managing director. A former Hampshire cricketer – reputed by John Arlott to be 'probably the finest amateur bowler' in the county's history – Charlie had been a childhood-friend of Carol's mother. It naturally followed that, during a break from practice, he introduced Carol to Terry, who was looking 'very sporty', she would later recall for the *Echo*, in his grey mohair sweater. She 'had an idea who he was. Years before, when I was cycling to school, some other girls pointed him out to me. I thought he looked nice.'

From which you will have gathered that Carol was not herself a football fan, even though her parents and grandmother, who lived with them, all followed the Saints. From her home on The Avenue, at the town end of the Common, she had had opportunities to see the players out on their cross-country runs, with Paine and Sydenham – 'the world's worst trainers,' John reckons – forever lagging at the rear and hoping they might yet again get away with catching the bus back.

If that was hardly a way to impress a gal, Terry hung around that Guy Fawkes afternoon and waylaid Carol at the end of her practice. He asked where her boyfriend was, obliging her to admit that she was currently without one. 'Good,' said he. 'Come and have a cup of coffee.' And, from there, it was very soon come home to tea – and sit indoors while I play out in the road. But that was fine with his parents with whom his new girl-friend went down 'brilliantly', Trevor reckons:

> She was giggly, bubbly – a lovely girl. She was as bad as him for taking the mick, to be honest, but she did it in a nicer sort of way and she always backed him up with a giggle or a laugh. She was lovely.

Trevor never minded Carol's brand of mickey-taking – 'deep down, she didn't really mean it as much as he did' – and recalls that she might even take his side occasionally.

Come Terry's 23rd birthday in March, he and Carol were engaged, the Young England footballer and the trophy-winning ice-skater. More than one person has described them to me as the Posh and Becks of their day, although they were, of course, a very long way from attaining such national,

The price for a celebrity footballer becoming engaged to a celebrity ice-skater
was having to get on the ice for the photographer.

let alone international, celebrity. A nearer model, in 1962, would have been
Joy Beverley, of the singing trio, the Beverley Sisters, who had married Billy
Wright of Wolves and England in 1958.

Wright was now managing the Under-23s and brought his squad to
Southampton on the eve of Terry's birthday, for a game against Turkey.
Two future Saints, Joe Kirkup and David Burnside, were in the starting line-
up, but Terry was on the bench. Although substitutes were still four seasons
away in the Football League, they were permitted in a friendly international

WHO CAN BLAME THIS BRILLIANT TURKS' SUBSTITUTE FOR BEING ON TOP OF THE WORLD RIGHT NOW?

THE MAGNIFICENT SEVEN

Oz joins in his protégé's celebrations – and urges his inclusion in the England squad for the World Cup finals in Chile.

such as this. Which was just as well, as Mandy Hill, the Blackpool outside-right, was injured in the first half. Paine came on, to win his fourth and final Under-23 cap (the previous season's game against a Danish XI not counting).

He not only scored in a 4-1 win, but generally starred: 'the evening belonged to Paine,' *Charles Buchan's Football Monthly* applauded.

So this would be the last Under-23 shirt that Terry would be taking home for his mum to wash in that machine he'd bought her – and then put out on the line, next to the pigeon loft.

When Terry was first capped, Bill Postle was 12. And his view, from two doors way, of Ena Paine's clothes line was so good that other kids would join him at his vantage point. 'I could have sold tickets,' Bill claims. 'It's amazing how much pleasure watching an England shirt dry gave to 8-12 year-olds.' But such was the awe in which they held their local hero, with his three lions' worth of fame flapping on the line and a maroon Jaguar parked on the road, their football-cum-cricket pitch.

And neither shirt nor Jag in any danger of being stolen.

That month of March 1962 had begun with a 6-4 home win against Scunthorpe. It was the first of Terry's half-a-dozen games, that season, on the left-wing, from where he was able to cut in and shoot from distance the way he had in his first few games, five years earlier.

He scored twice in that manner that afternoon. It was the fourth time in 1961-62 that the Saints had run up five or more at The Dell. There would be another five-goal haul when Stoke visited on the last day of the season, but a poor run-in saw the side drop out of contention and finish sixth – 17 points behind Liverpool, whom they applauded off the field, as champions, in April, following a 2-0 defeat at Anfield.

Disappointing though it was, the run-in was notable for a significant mid-field switch; for Reeves's last three goals for the club; and for two farewell appearances.

The switch in midfield involved Ken Wimshurst and Brian Clifton. Wimshurst had arrived in the close season from Wolves, where he had never made the first team. Already 23, his League career so far consisted of seven games for Gateshead. After a couple of early-season games at inside-left, he had become Mulgrew's understudy in that position – until January, when he moved to right-half in the Reserves. And it was in that No.4 shirt that he returned to the first team for the last five games.

It was a position he would occupy in spells for the next five seasons. I declare an interest: of all the lustrous images I retain of the Saints in the sixties – Davies salmoning up to meet a Paine cross; or a sprightly young Channon on a run, say – nothing compares with the enduring mind's-eye view of the Wimshurst-Paine-O'Brien triangle so elegantly scything through the opposition's left flank. Even the hypercritical O'Brien appreciated having a right-half who 'had a good idea of the game and he gave me the ball in *my* time… If I get the ball as soon as I can, then I can do something with it.' If anything, Dick Conner had been even better for George, as he would release the ball that bit earlier, but Huxford feels that Ken had 'a bit more vision. He could hit a longer ball. He used to change the play.' And Paine rated him, too, as he explains in Appendix 1.

Brian Clifton

Wimshurst remembers that the 'only instructions' Ted Bates ever gave him for this role 'were "don't have too many touches in your own half and do what you like in their half".' And he soon found that if he 'ever got in trouble', Terry's ability to find space was such that he 'was always available.'

Brian Clifton was not losing his place in the side but switching to inside-forward. I use that old-fashioned nomenclature because, even though the standard formation was by now 4-2-4, the No.10 was still expected to score more goals than the No.4. Clifton made that point, in his typical fashion, by grabbing four goals in those five games. Not that he minded playing deeper and having to time his runs into the box: 'All I did,' he explains, 'was make runs, late-on. We were always taught not to run every time: what you did was you waited and waited and waited, until the guy who was marking you didn't expect you to go; then you just took your chance and went and you could always lose him that way.'

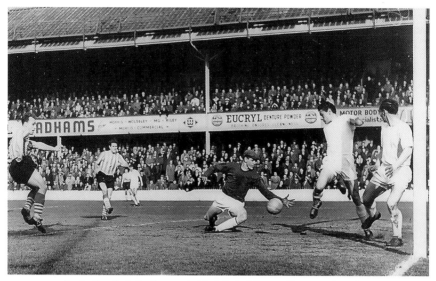

As the Leeds defenders get behind their debutant 'keeper – literally –
this creates plenty of space for Reeves (*left*) to accept a pass from Paine and score.

This was a lesson that Brian and others of his era had learned from
Jimmy Easson and which Ted Bates would pass on. It helped, of course, to
have Terry Paine waiting for you to make your run: 'He could pick you out.
He was so good at looking up and seeing you. You knew it was going to
come across. It was terrific.'

Meanwhile, Derek Reeves, the man Clifton so admired, was scoring his
last three goals for the club. The first of these came when Leeds visited The
Dell in March and Paine found Reeves with room to spare, although – as the
photo shows – this space had been created by the way in which the
defenders had dropped back to cover their novice goalkeeper: fourth-choice
16 year-old, Gary Sprake, had been flown down that morning to make his
debut in Leeds's 4-1 defeat.

And then were the two goals in the season's 5-1 climax against Stoke.
Reeves would never score again for the Saints, although he would at least
start the next season – unlike Tommy Mulgrew and Terry Simpson.

Mulgrew, whom Clifton had replaced at inside-left, had had a good
season in which he'd brought his goal-tally to 100 in 330 appearances. But
he thereupon left for Aldershot, disgruntled – to this day, alas – that Ted
Bates had 'lied' to him about the new wage structure. Simpson was leaving
after only 27 appearances for his home-town club. Paine's inside-right
partner at Youth level had hardly played in that position for the first team: it
might be said that he had suffered from being tried in too many positions in
too few games.

Simpson would flourish, though, in a season at Third Division Peterborough – so much so that he would find himself in the First Division with West Bromwich by May 1963.

In the meantime, in May 1962, Paine made his third, and last, appearance for Young England v England at Highbury, being marked by Ray Wilson – his 'ultimate' opponent – and partnered by John Barnwell, the man whom Arsenal considered too good to swap for him. Then it was off to Lilleshall to train in Walter Winterbottom's 40-strong squad that was preparing for the World Cup.

By the end of the month, Winterbottom's party would be in Chile. Terry had not made the final cut, so he would be able to work as a furniture salesman and even spend some time with his fiancée. His efforts for *Tracys*, the furnishers, would be publicly trumpeted by Mr Tracy, who assured the *Echo* that Terry was 'a highly successful salesman [who] displayed the same amount of energy and verve in the shop as he does on the playing field.' Be warned: as Terry's business career developed in the 1960s – with a foray into politics, too – its progress would often be reported in the local press with superfluous football imagery.

Carol, meanwhile, was working full-time – as secretary to the Managing Director of *Carey & Lambert*, the car-dealers – but she could see Terry at the weekends, although that might mean watching him play cricket, a game that she found 'too slow'. Sunday tea in Highcliffe continued, with Terry out in the road and Carol getting to know her future in-laws. They did have a whole week together, though, for an event to which Terry had been unaccustomed as a child: a holiday. They went with her parents to the Isle of Wight.

Then soon it would be a new football season, in which he and his remaining team-mates of 1957 – Godfrey and Sydenham – would be aiming, in effect, to join Simpson in the top-flight. This would surely require the team consistently to reproduce, in 1962-63, the kind of form they had tantalisingly shown in the autumn of 1961.

Chapter 8

Semi-conscious

The three graduates from 1957 would all start the new season in the first-team, Sydenham having returned from the Army to play almost a full season. Paine would be ever-present, along with Knapp and O'Brien.

Godfrey would be less fortunate, losing his place after the fourth game, a 3-2 defeat at Luton, which left Southampton firmly at the foot of the table with only one point. Although Paine scored an impressive goal with Saints trailing 2-0, it was he who sold his 'keeper short with a weak back-pass from which Luton promptly cancelled out his effort. Knapp, who would acquire a reputation for misdirected back-passes, had already gifted Luton a goal in this manner when they drew 2-2 at The Dell the week before; and his own goal had proved to be Scunthorpe's winner in the opening game of the season. Godfrey feels that he was the fall-guy for the waywardness of a centre-half, who 'had a terrific amount of ability, but he wasn't the steadiest of players. He didn't really give goalkeepers confidence, I don't think. He was always very jittery and excitable. He would do the unexpected.'

To the bemusement of their team-mates, Ted Bates had Knapp practise passing back to Godfrey. Paine roared with laughter, when he recalled that session, while Ron Davies asked rhetorically, 'how can you have *practice* for back-passing?' The fault lay with Knapp, Davies felt, and it was unfair for Godfrey to take the blame.

The trouble was that Knapp's tendency to 'do the unexpected' extended to other areas of his game – like trying 'to take people on in the wrong areas,' Cliff Huxford complains. He had known where he was with Page's basic style of 'stop it, get it and hit it long.' Godfrey concurs: 'I thought John Page was a terrific player. You knew exactly what he was going to do all the time; he was always helpful; and he always wanted to play *with* people.'

So here you had a new captain, no more likely to be dropped by Ted Bates than his previous captain, but coming under criticism from team-mates who felt they couldn't trust his judgment. He had been called into the England squad the previous season, ahead of Paine, and his ability was less in question, it seems, than his temperament. It mattered to Terry that players should believe in their own ability and he admired that quality in Knapp, even if he felt that he was not as good, overall, as he thought he was and 'well below what we needed.' His sympathies were with Godfrey, who appreciated that: 'Terry Paine was very often supportive of me, to want me in the side,' Godfrey recalls, 'Tommy Mulgrew was another one. And Terry never slated me – in a game. Some players slated other players.'

Bates was keeping faith with Knapp, however, even while despairing of his back-passing, thus demonstrating his mantra that, 'in a team, you take a player's strengths and let the team overcome his weaknesses. That gives the team strength.'

If that was a philosophy highly appreciated by Ted's many disciples, it could go against the grain when team-mates felt that a top-paid player was immune to being dropped, whether it was Paine, 'dreaming' on the road (as alleged in the previous chapter), or Knapp, doing the unexpected.

The other player on top wages, George O'Brien, attributes the poor start not so much to unpredictability at the back as to the manager's disturbance of the midfield balance. Bates had gone back to Leicester in the close season to sign Ian White, who took over the No.4 shirt. We have heard from O'Brien – and he's not done yet – on why he expected full-backs to *defend*. The corollary was that the side could then afford to have a right-half bringing the ball out and playing football with the right-wing pair – in the manner to which George had become accustomed, first with Conner and latterly with Wimshurst.

To abandon that format for the more defensively-inclined White – Ian can 'remember Batesie saying "what I'd really like to do is to play you away and to play Ken at home"' – was, in O'Brien's uncompromising opinion, 'a disaster'. With Clifton keeping his place at inside-left, Wimshurst was initially the one squeezed out. But then Paine had another run at No.10, with Chadwick at outside-right.

None of which tinkering lifted the side out of bottom place. Apart from Chadwick, it was not as though the manager had a queue of young forwards knocking at the door, although a strapping 17 year-old amateur had just made his debut for the Reserves and scored a couple of goals. So it was that Ted Bates took himself off to the lad's home, agreed pro' terms with his parents and told him he was in the team for Saturday: Martin Chivers thus made his debut in the Saints' first win of the season – 1-0 against Charlton at The Dell.

He kept his place for a 2-0 defeat at Chelsea, but the youth experiment ended there, as the manager now opted for the alternative: buy experience. And he wasn't messing about, either: he bought three players, two of them forwards. George Kirby arrived from Plymouth, as previously intimated, to assume the No.9 shirt, thus demoting both Chivers, whose time would most demonstrably come, and Reeves, whose first-team career was thereby terminated. And so was Clifton's. David Burnside, signed from West Bromwich to take over the troublesome inside-left spot, would see to that.

David Burnside (*left*) is greeted by Terry Paine and John Sydenham (*right*).

Clifton was such an admirer of Reeves, not just for his goal-scoring feats but for his demeanour: 'Derek was a real gentleman – *why* he was playing football, I don't know.' That doesn't say a lot for this sport but – given that we have already seen how vindictive a dressing room can be and how acidic the humour – you'll know what he means. On a continuum from gentlemanly to barbed, much of football's humour seems to fall, thank goodness, midway between those poles. I'm thinking of the laconic, mildly sardonic jocularity that I associate with the likes of Brian Clifton, whose parting-shot, as he duly left The Dell for Grimsby, was that he was going to a place where they had hair-nets big enough even for Terry Paine's head.

The third signing was a full-back. Ted Bates had been in discussion with Chelsea's Peter Sillett, a member of Ted Drake's Championship-winning side of 1955. Now, at the age of 29, he was out of favour with his new manager, Tommy Docherty, and fancied coming home to Southampton. It would have been a romantic signing for the Saints' manager who had played, in his first season at the Dell (1937-38), with Peter's father, Charlie, and, in his last (1952-53), with Peter himself. But commercial reality routed romance when Sillett asked for 'a few bob under the counter'. The Board wouldn't play ball, so Bates made his move for West Brom's Stuart Williams, who had played for Wales in the 1958 World Cup finals, going out to Brazil but attracting an 'excellent' label from Pelé.

Although essentially a right-back, Williams could – like Sillett – play on the left when need be. Indeed, Southampton's manager, accompanied by his entire first team, had watched him do so the previous November. They had been on their way to The Valley when, learning of their game's postponement, they had diverted to Upton Park to watch the Baggies draw 3-3 with West Ham. George O'Brien cites that occasion as support for his contention that Williams was signed to replace Traynor at left-back, the position in which George was so concerned that better defending was needed.

But Williams settled straight in at No.2, which meant that Roy Patrick had played his last game for the club – the third player to do so with the season still only eight games old. Ron Davies remained, though, to understudy Williams and to provoke a debate, down the right flank, as to whether Stuart or he provided the better balance.

Like many another discussion of tactics in this book, this is a debate in which I had the benefit of some animated views and which I consider relevant to the perennial question of how Terry Paine best fitted into which formations and what these demanded of those around him. If you're less fascinated by such considerations as my informants and I are, you would do well, here, to skip a page or two.

Leading the case for Davies in this matter is that unshrinking advocate, George O'Brien. While he considered Williams 'good on the ball coming forward – he was brilliant,' he felt that Stuart 'couldn't defend.' Davies, on the other hand, 'could mark people out of the game, but he couldn't clear his lines as well as most full-backs' – unless you counted hoofing it into touch: as O'Brien puts it pragmatically, 'you can't score goals from Row Z in the Stand, can you?'

Ron Davies

Paine essentially seconds O'Brien's motion:

> Stuart was a lovely passer of the ball. He would get it and set it up and we had a little triangle going there. But I believe that a defender's got to defend; and whatever they give you after that is a bonus. That's the Old School, if you like, but that's the way I am. Ron Davies was a good right-back, but Stuart couldn't give us that: he couldn't give us defensive stability. But he could give it us *on* the ball. Going forward – Jesus! But defensively, he was a nightmare.

CONSTANT PAINE

If you are old enough to have enjoyed watching that 1962-63 side in full flow, with its exhilarating right-flank triangle – a quadrilateral, even, when Williams ventured forward – then you may find Terry's assessment of Stuart's defending somewhat harsh. But I am interrupting him in philosophical flow:

> People get confused and think that, because we said 'he couldn't do this; he couldn't do that,' we're *criticizing* him. We're not. You've heard from many team-mates that, maybe if I'd trained harder and if I'd done this or that, I might have been a better player: who knows? You are what you are.

Well, yes, but Wimshurst's contribution to this argument is more along the lines of you are what your team-mates enable you to be:

> I think footballers have got to have footballers to play with… Stuart wasn't the greatest defender: that wasn't his strength. But when he got the ball, you could play with him, because he wanted to get it and pass it to me and get it again. Then he'd give it to Terry – he could link up with other people… As long as the ball came over to that right side – Stuart, me, Terry, George – we'd create something. If you've got a non-footballer in that little area, it breaks down.

Williams's own take on all of this echoes what both Paine *and* Wimshurst say. He found the attacking role 'fairly easy because I'd been taught that at West Brom.' The manager, for most of his stay at The Hawthorns, had been Vic Buckingham. He 'wanted defenders to *play* it out' and he had 'encouraged full-backs to go forward,' but it wasn't as simple as that, Stuart explains:

> Obviously, a full-back's main job is to defend – that was my bread-and-butter and anything else is a bonus. I liked to get forward and go on the attack, but you had to balance it and wait for the right opportunities during the game and do it: you couldn't be backwards and forwards all of the time. And it depends on the team you're playing in, how many times you can go forward. I was fortunate when I came to Southampton, in so much as I had Ken Wimshurst and Terry Paine, who were both intelligent footballers and liked to play football. That encouraged me to go forward, because Ken, although he was good at going forward, would also fill in for me if I was caught up-field going on an overlap, for Terry to play a ball to me to get it across.

The notion of Wimshurst dropping back to cover adds a different dimension to the argument but Williams insists that this is how it was:

Yes, Ken would fill in for you. And I'd also got Tony Knapp, who would come across, and Cliff Huxford, who'd then fill in, in the middle. So we had a good formation there and we had a good attacking side. But we also thought that we were quite solid defensively as well. Terry used to come back a bit, though not so much as wingers are expected to do it today. George wasn't a good defender, so he was better left up the field. So it didn't bother us that he didn't come back and defend. We didn't want George defending: we wanted him to save his energy for up front.

In sum, then, the four players who participated in the exciting right flank of 1962-63 all thought the formation worked well going forward; and Williams even thought it was capable of defending, too, with covering, when needed, from Knapp and Huxford.

Ted Bates obviously had faith in this line-up: from the moment of Burnside's debut, Southampton would fulfil 32 League fixtures and play 10 Cup matches. For these 42 games, including all seven in a pulsating FA Cup run, the manager would rely on 11 players, almost unchanged. They would line up, as follows: Reynolds (42 appearances); Williams (39), Traynor (39); Wimshurst (41), Knapp (42), Huxford (38); Paine (42), O'Brien (42), Kirby (39), Burnside (39) and Sydenham (41).

The side that stayed together through the Big Freeze
and the club's best FA Cup-run since 1927.
Back row (*left to right*): Williams, Traynor, Wimshurst, Reynolds, Knapp, Huxford.
Front: Paine, O'Brien, Kirby, Burnside, Sydenham.

CONSTANT PAINE

This consistency may remind you of the side that won promotion three years before. Remarkably, after all the chopping and changing, this settled outfit actually included six of the team that had clinched the Third Division Championship. This was not, however, a promotion side: they would spend the entire season in the bottom half of the table – until the last game, when they climbed into 11th place. *This* was a Cup side, a side that would reach the club's first FA Cup semi-final since 1927.

Before we chart the highlights of that 42-match run that began with Wimshurst's return and Burnside's first game, the joint-debut, two games earlier, of Williams and Kirby deserves a brief mention – as opposed to the fuller treatment this visit of Chelsea received in *Dell Diamond*.

If they needed any reminder of how uncompromising George Kirby could be – leaving his foot in or his elbow out – some of the Southampton players had got it at Fratton Park the week before, watching Plymouth beat Pompey. But Chelsea, having just been relegated, were less familiar with Kirby's style. Their centre-half, John Mortimore, recalls meeting the Southampton party on Waterloo station the Saturday before Chelsea's visit to The Dell, as they returned from a defeat at Stoke and he from defeat at Leeds. Chatting to Knapp about what he might expect from Second Division centre-forwards, he was advised that Kirby was 'the worst bugger'.

We should note, in passing, that the Southampton players would need regularly to pass through Waterloo on an away day and that Mortimore – going home to Farnham – would not be the only Chelsea player they'd meet. One or both of the Sillett brothers – Peter, or more especially his younger brother John, who'd moved with him from Southampton to Chelsea – might be week-ending with their mother and step-father in the New Forest. As we shall see, John Sillett's presence on the Waterloo to Southampton train, of a Saturday evening, would have a crucial significance for Terry Paine's later career.

Neither Sillett brother was in the Chelsea side that came to The Dell on the

The Sillett brothers, John (*left*) and Peter, in their Chelsea days

evening of the Williams/Kirby debuts: John had moved to Coventry in the spring, while Peter was, as I say, surplus to Docherty's requirements. They had a newcomer at left-back, Eddie McCreadie, recently arrived from East Stirling. He was no retiring violet – one Chelsea *Who's Who* describes him as 'a rugged defender whose trademark was a ferocious sliding tackle' – and Paine would come to look upon him as a 'pretty vicious' marker. Kirby was evidently not going to wait and see. As Terry recalls, 'he went straight across and did him.'

This was a new experience for Terry. If you have such a reputation as he acquired for being able to 'look after yourself' – a euphemism for getting your retaliation in first – then, by definition, you don't expect to need a 'minder'. But now here was Kirby volunteering to do Terry's dirty work for him. 'He did me a favour,' says a grateful Paine. 'I had a great game; McCreadie couldn't run. George used to say to me, "leave him to me." He'd say "hey, you're kicking my outside-right." George was brilliant.'

Not everybody, not even among Terry's team-mates, would use that word for Kirby's behaviour: Ron Reynolds, who didn't like George's challenges in that game on Peter Bonetti, either, was especially disapproving: 'it's not good football; it's not nice football; but it can certainly disturb the opposition.' And I'm far from comfortable, myself, with the notion that nobbling a full-back is an acceptable way of easing a winger's path. That said, Terry's appraisal needs to be seen in the wider context of why wingers of that era needed, indeed, 'to look after themselves' and how he, in particular, went about it. We can come back to that in Chapter 23.

For the record, Kirby scored and so did Ian White in a 2-1 win. It took Saints off the bottom for one match, but White – who had been expecting, ironically, to join Chelsea – had been wondering 'what have I let myself in for, here?' The immediate answer was second-team football: two games later, as already noted, Wimshurst would be back for Burnside's debut and was going to bed-in.

The occasion was a 1-1 draw at Elland Road. The Leeds side makes for instructive reading. Peter Lorimer was making his debut at the age of 15. Four games earlier, on the day that Ted Bates was flirting with youth in the form of Martin Chivers, Don Revie had introduced 17 year-old Paul Reaney and Norman Hunter, aged 18, and given a second game to Gary Sprake, following his emergency start at The Dell, the season before. Sprake's biographers have described that switch to youth 'as a watershed in the history of Leeds United' – in contrast, somewhat, to Ted Bates's introduction of purchased experience (though Burnside was still only 23) for this 'watershed' game at Leeds.

As already intimated, this dependence on experience would prove more suited to the FA Cup than to the League – although the Second Division title would be won by Stoke City, whose outside-right Stanley Matthews was crowned Footballer of the Year – for the second time – at the age of 48. Indeed, when Stoke came to The Dell as champions for the last game of the season, the occasion was a triple celebration, courtesy of the *Sunday Mirror*, which had made the Saints its *Giant-Killers of the Year.*

How they went about killing giants is a story of no little drama. There were no giants to be seen in the first two rounds, as they saw off Third Division York City (5-0) and Fourth Division Watford (3-1), both at The Dell, by the end of February. It would normally have been the end of January, of course, but this was no normal winter.

Football was on hold during the 'Big Freeze' of January 1963. It was not until 13 February that the Saints could play their Third Round game and launch a cup-run that benefited in three ways from the frozen standstill. First, there were the 10-a-side matches on the car-park in the afternoons, after the morning work-outs in the gym – matches made possible by the players mucking-in to clear the snow and ice. Ken Wimshurst wonders 'whether players would do that now. I think it created a bit of team-spirit and I'm sure that was reflected in the results when we got started again.'

Having cleared sufficient snow from the car-park,
Wimshurst (*right*) has chipped towards O'Brien (*left*), but he is thwarted by goalkeeper Paine.
The onlookers are (*left to right*) George Horsfall and Tommy Traynor.

Maybe so, although that doesn't explain why the FA Cup results were so much better than those in the League. Secondly, with suspensions still imposed for weeks rather than matches, the suspended Kirby didn't miss a thing. And finally, as the south thawed sooner than the north, Southampton would have less of a back-log than subsequent opponents from the north.

So when they clinched their place in the Fifth Round, their opponents, First Division Sheffield United, had yet to play their Third Round tie. They eventually made it to The Dell, where a Kirby header – from 'a fine run' and centre by Paine, said the *Echo* – was the game's only goal. Southampton were in the quarter-final for the first time since Ted Bates had gone out at that stage, as a player, in 1948. All they now needed to do to establish themselves as 'giant-killers' was to beat Nottingham Forest, another First Division outfit, to whom they'd been drawn away.

They snatched a 1-1 draw with a smart piece of role-reversal, in which George Kirby set Terry Paine free with the '*perfect* ball,' Wimshurst reckons. 'It was the best pass you've ever seen in your life. I'd have been proud of that pass.' Paine 'looked a *mile* offside – *well* out on his own,' to Forest's outside-right, Colin Addison, as he ran on to lob the ball over Peter Grummitt. 'In those days, you didn't get too many people doing the lob,' Forest's goalkeeper generously recalls. And, offside or not, Addison likewise pays tribute to the way in which Terry 'kept his cool. I always thought Painie was good when he was one-on-one with 'keepers. He could go around them and slot it in. But chipping is all the more skilful.'

O'Brien (*left*) and Paine finish training, at Buxton FC's ground, in preparation for their game in Nottingham.

That touch of class set up two of the most memorable matches in the Saints' history. The other three Sixth Round ties had all been settled at the first attempt, with First Division sides Leicester City, Liverpool and Manchester United going through. United were drawn, come the Monday, to meet the winners of Wednesday's replay at The Dell and the *Daily Mail* dispatched Gerald Williams to Southampton to report on the only Second Division side still in with a chance.

He elected to focus on 'the chirpy Paine, 24 now and soon to marry,' reporting that he 'has sold his Jaguar and bought a less ostentatious

As they hear the semi-final draw, Knapp and Paine adopt a 'bring 'em on' attitude, but their team-mates have the expressions of men who fancied facing Liverpool. (*Left to right*): Huxford, Traynor, Knapp, Paine (in his 'less ostentatious Magnette'), Sydenham, Wimshurst.

Magnette. The exchange symbolises his new attitude towards life.' Golly! Fortunately, there was more to this visitation from Fleet Street than the reporter's pseudo-psychology. Williams obtained a few words from Ted Bates, in prescient form: 'I always told Terry he had the ability to play for England and that I thought he could do so as a Southampton player. I think my words will yet be proved true. Terry is capable of brilliant football. He thrives on the big occasion.'

And the replay would be a 'big occasion', all right. Having swiftly sold their own seat-allocation, the Southampton ticket-office had no problem in getting rid of the 850 – of a 1,000-allocation – that Forest returned. And there were additional seats to be had on the night, on the branches of trees in Archers Road, for some of the more intrepid fans locked out of a 29,479-crowd. I was not among them, but goodness knows how many of those spectators have had occasion to relive the experience for me, including three youngsters who would take part, 13 years later, in the Saints' next memorable Cup-run: Mick Channon, by then 14; Paul Bennett (11); and Nick Holmes (8).

But the onlooker offering the most eloquent account of that evening was undoubtedly John Arlott, writing in the *Hampshire Magazine*. When I reproduced a chunk of his report in *Dell Diamond*, 35 years later, Terry was so taken by Arlott's enchanting prose that he gave a reading of it to a TV audience in South Africa, reasoning that his viewers would have known Arlott, as he had, for his spellbinding commentaries on cricket. I do not propose to recycle that excerpt here or, indeed, to cover at length a match that has featured in other Hagiology publications since *Dell Diamond*.

The essentials are these. The Saints were, of course, unchanged, both in personnel and formation: as Ken Wimshurst reminds us, there was only one way 'the team that Ted had accumulated understood how to play. He just let people go and play.' But Forest made positional adjustments, which included half-back Hindley coming in for winger Hockey. Not that there was anything ultra-defensive about the way the visitors went 2-0 up in five minutes. True, they then packed their defence 'so tightly that there seemed barely room,' as Arlott memorably put it, 'for a ferret to have wriggled through it.' They came forward, though, to score again on 54 minutes. Trailing 3-0, with half-an-hour to go, the Saints looked to have clawed one back when Paine ran in to flick-head a Traynor free-kick past Grummitt. Offside! – a decision which, in Arlott's judgment, fired up both fans and players alike.

There were 16 minutes remaining when Kirby, who had been 'needling away' – if you believe Arlott's under-statement – got one back with a header. Forest now

> fell back, rattled by the incessant stream of crosses as Paine, again and again, twisted clear and inwards on the right to search out the hungry heads of his inside-forwards.

Kirby liked to claim that it was his head that made it 3-2 but, according to the referee, Denis Howell, George's mere presence caused Grummitt to take his eye off the ball, whereupon 'the ball hit him and went in the net.' That's certainly the recall of Colin Addison who 'can still see how the ball was cleared and it went high above the bar. And it came down and George Kirby didn't really jump at Peter Grummitt at all. George just looked at him – that's all he needed to do – and Peter took his eye off the ball and went for the punch; it hit his thigh and rolled over the line.'

An account of the last-minute equaliser is best left to the scorer. David Burnside, who had now been at the club for six months, had come to appreciate that, when Terry Paine was seeking to cross, he had a simple, third-man role: if neither of the Georges was available to Terry – O'Brien at the near-post; Kirby at the far – then Burnside knew that he must make himself accessible in the middle.

Never mind a packed defence, a ticking clock and a frenzied crowd, this is how it had to be done:

CONSTANT PAINE

O'Brien (No. 8) has come to the near post, with goalkeeper Grummitt, to watch Burnside's shot 'disappear into the net.'

As Terry comes in the box again… George O'Brien is on the front post [taking the goalkeeper with him, as the photograph shows] and I think George Kirby is at the back somewhere, so I think 'I'll be in the middle'… The ball comes to me, about eight yards from the goal… I always remember a lot of bodies there and the ball arriving to me and it sat there… I can remember concentrating on seeing the ball and striking it as hard as I can between the posts and under the crossbar… just disappearing through one or two players and into the net.

Nothing happened in extra-time to detract from the memories of that 16-minute comeback and nor, of course, was there a penalty shoot-out. The teams would repair to White Hart Lane the following Monday to start anew. Yet again, the Saints' following outnumbered Forest's – as Wimshurst put it, 'Southampton *closed down*' as an estimated 25,000 made for North London – and Forest's manager again shuffled his pack.

This was partly enforced – right-half Jeff Whitefoot was injured – but also tactical: 'they didnae play with an inside-left,' O'Brien explains. 'They played with two left-halves… a normal left-half and somebody behind him.' Donald Saunders of the *Daily Telegraph* perceived this as a 'precaution against undue aggression' by Kirby, but O'Brien saw it as a counter to the threat from Saints' right-wing pair. Acknowledging that Kirby's aggression was indeed a problem for Forest, Addison recalls how this 'old-fashioned centre-forward – and I say that respectfully – had one of the best crossers in the game, in Painie, without a doubt. He had great crossing ability. We all knew his set-plays – his corners and free-kicks. But he could cross a ball on the run, which, in those days, was an *outstanding* quality.'

Whatever their fears and their attempted counter, Forest's approach should remind us – even when we are focusing on the career of an individual star – that football is a *team*-game: if your opponents deploy an extra man to block off your main danger, this should leave a gap for a team-mate, who had better be good enough to exploit it. Wimshurst did not

Jubilation in the dressing room after the 5-0 elimination of Nottingham Forest.
Back row (*left to right*): Kirby, Huxford, Reynolds, Wimshurst.
Front: Sydenham, O'Brien, Traynor, Jimmy Gallagher, Burnside,
Paine, Williams, Knapp, Ted Bates.

disappoint, revelling in the space to produce 'one of the best wing-half
displays' the *Echo* Sports Editor had 'ever seen in a Saints' side.' Ken was
'majestic', the displaced White graciously recalls, as another giant was
brought to earth, 5-0.

So bring on Manchester United! Well, not exactly: it has to be said that
United were a lot more pleased with the draw than their opponents were.
Denis Law thought it 'a piece of luck: you think, with playing a Second
Division team, there wouldn't be such a problem.' He admits that you
shouldn't really think like that – 'in the FA Cup, it's always a battle' – but for
Matt Busby, it was a matter of 'common sense…that when two teams are
playing as well as Liverpool and Leicester are this season, it is best to avoid
them for as long as possible.'

Leicester – the bookies' 2-1 favourite, at this stage, for the Cup – were
riding high and ought, on paper, to have been the side to avoid, but
Liverpool would finish the season with the same number of points as
Sheffield United and Nottingham Forest, the two sides whom Saints had
successively seen off. Busby's side, by comparison, had been having a
dreadful time. Bobby Charlton was wondering whether 'Munich [had]
caught up with us at last? Had we tried to travel too fast since the disaster?'

Charlton talked of a 'slump'. Indeed. United's win against Wolves on the Monday before the semi-final would be only their second in a 12-game run since Boxing Day. The 10th game of that sequence was a 4-3 defeat at Leicester, watched by Ted Bates and three of his team.

One of that trio, George O'Brien, felt that, despite their woeful run and their defeat on the night, United 'were starting to come half-decent.' There was something of a consensus in the Southampton ranks that they would have preferred to meet Liverpool. Notwithstanding that they had applauded Shankly's up-and-coming team off the Anfield pitch only a year ago, the fact remained that, prior to that, the Saints had won all four meetings with Liverpool and fancied their chances against them on neutral territory: 'we knew we'd beat Liverpool,' Wimshurst reasons. 'Saints always beat Liverpool, didn't they?' And the side even fancied their chances, he reckons, against Leicester.

The team they didn't want to meet was Manchester United. They 'had all the best players,' as David Burnside saw it, and, whatever their problems in the League, 'they had individuals that could have beaten anyone in Europe *on the day*.' To orchestrate the two great individual performers, Law and Charlton, moreover, Matt Busby had recently signed Pat Crerand from Celtic.

O'Brien was especially impressed with Crerand's performance when the reconnaissance party went to Filbert Street and noted how he 'got everything from the goalkeeper.' Just as Ken Barnes, Manchester's City right-half, needed to be picked up, in the 1960 cup-tie, when taking a throw-out from his 'keeper, so too would Pat Crerand, United's No.4. You may recall that O'Brien's unheeded recipe in that game against Man City had been for outside-left Sydenham to pick up Barnes. True, given Saints' 5-1 win, George had to chuckle at his anxiety – 'what do I know?' – but he remains deadly serious when he talks of the failure to block off Crerand three seasons later.

The notion of a winger providing defensive cover may not have been as well-established in 1963 as it is today, but it was hardly revolutionary: read any recollections of Southampton's famous FA Cup encounter with Blackpool 10 seasons before and you'll be reminded of the role outside-left John Hoskins played in blocking off Stanley Matthews. But ask John Sydenham whether a similar job might have been required of him when Matthews next visited for the 1959 Cup-tie (relived in Chapter 5) and you'll be told that, 'if they'd expected me to mark Stanley Matthews, then it would have been a pretty sad day, I think, for the club.' In 1961, though, Matthews returned home to Stoke and Tommy Traynor was having his customary 'nightmare' against him. It came natural to Harry Penk to cover for Tommy and even get in a tackle or two on Matthews.

Now, tackling back and cutting off a supply are not the same thing, but Ted Bates undoubtedly had, in Penk, a winger who was more given, generally, to those kinds of donkey-work than the flying Sydenham. And Paine liked sometimes having a grafter on the other flank: it used to give Harry 'all the confidence' he needed, 'that somebody like that wanted you in the side.' So O'Brien's proposition can be restated: should Sydenham have been sacrificed and Penk brought in to block Crerand's supply? We know that the idea of 'horses-for-courses' – should he play the more defensive White away and the attack-minded Wimshurst at home? – appealed to Bates. But, with no substitutes, you could have egg on your face if you gambled on the wrong horse – as Forest's manager had at White Hart Lane.

It wouldn't be too long before Bates was omitting Sydenham and playing with only one winger, but this was a season when he relied on an unchanged side and which 'played exactly the same,' as Wimshurst put it, in every round.

Not that anybody on either side got to play a whole lot of football at Villa Park. As Denis Law says, FA Cup-ties can always be 'a battle' – and this was 'one of the scrappiest matches' he had ever played in.

One reporter, cited by his biographer – the United historian, Brian Hughes – went so far as to claim that, 'in 40 years of watching football, I have never seen a more unpromising semi-final victory.' Law cannot quite explain how many connections he made with which parts of his body to score this dreadful game's only goal, but he does admit it 'really was a fluke, anyway'. The best description that I have read – by which I mean that it confirms my impression at the time, no matter that I was at the opposite end – comes, again, from Hughes. The ball came across from United's right side,

> into the Southampton penalty area. Denis misheaded it and a second of fatal hesitation by the Southampton defence cost them… Instead of going to meet the ball, Reynolds, the Saints goalkeeper, stayed rigid on his line. Denis, on one knee after falling to the ground following his misdirected header, reacted first to the loose ball and prodded it home.

That description equates with Law's autobiographical recall of being on the ground and scoring from 'a second stab at it' and with the headline, DOUBLE-DECKER – LAW STAGES A SIT-DOWN STRIKE. Terry Paine simply admires the way in which 'Denis Law, one of the greatest players I've ever seen,' managed to score from that position.

Law's gymnastics were enough for him to share the plaudits with Crerand who, as predicted by O'Brien, contrived to run the show. But there is a question, even for O'Brien, as to whether it might have been a different game – and a lot better to watch – if the Saints had gone out and 'done our own thing.' Burnside agrees: the side was always capable of conceding two, but scoring three, so Ted Bates should have said

> this day is no different to any other day and if you just go out and do all the things that we've done all year, then you've got a very good chance of winning. If you get beaten, it won't be because you haven't done all the things that you've done all year.

Instead of which they succumbed, as Ken Jones saw it in the *Mirror*, to the 'myth' of Manchester United, 'burdened by the biggest inferiority complex I've seen in a semi-final team. They seemed mesmerised by the magic name Manchester United. And yet they had nothing to fear… But while Southampton believed in the United myth, they never gave themselves a chance.' Paine had assured the *Daily Mail*, in the build-up to the game, that his team-mates and he had no fear of their opponents – only *respect* for them. Maybe they showed United too much respect: John Arlott regretted that the side had not played 'the sweeping attacking football that is its essential character. If they had done that and lost, the blow would not have been so hard.'

If… If… If… If only Ted Bates had changed the winning formation. If only he had better motivated an unchanged team to play the same as ever. If only he could have found a way of satisfying George O'Brien's contention that he might somehow have done both. But, hey, we're talking about losing a semi-final of the FA Cup, where all manner of excuses are to be expected, contradictions notwithstanding.

And there was one other thing: was staying away from it all the best possible preparation? For Stuart Williams, who'd known a bigger stage – those 1958 World Cup finals in Sweden, for instance – the Saints' Droitwich hotel was 'nice and relaxing'. But for most of the side – even if more than half of them had experienced international football travel at some level – this was a massive game.

As Burnside confesses, he 'wanted it so much': his two ambitions were 'to play in the Cup Final and to play for England – in that order!' Getting away 'seemed to be the right thing to do,' but 'the *tension* grew as the days went by' at Droitwich, so much so that he wonders whether 'it may have been better if we had stayed at home and gone through the normal routine.' And perhaps warmed up with a League game on the Monday the way United had?

Huxford is another who found it '*boring*' to be stuck so long 'in the middle of nowhere' and the *Daily Express* sportswriter, Mike Langley, who was allowed access to the hotel's football guests, has confirmed that 'tension was in the air like thunder. Too many of the team could not relax.' To rub it in, there was a Golf Club across the road, but golf was banned after Wednesday. This ban 'was written into the rules,' Paine explains. 'Ted believed it made you heavy-legged. He was probably absolutely right.' Not that that stopped him and O'Brien from sneaking off for nine holes – or as many as they could complete before the manager came looking for them and found them hiding in a bunker.

O'Brien and Burnside both disappointed the unnamed reporter quoted in the autobiography of United's captain, Noel Cantwell: he found them 'erratic when they weren't lethargic.' While Burnside blames his being over-eager to get to Wembley, O'Brien blames Terry Paine: 'he never passed the ball to me all day. He got what he wanted: he got picked for England and went on tour.'

You might have thought that neglecting your inside-forward was a way of *not* impressing the England manager, but Terry feels that Saints' Cup run had indeed helped to put him in the frame after having what Ken Jones of the *Mirror* was describing in March as 'a season in the shadows.' Jones felt that Terry 'did enough' in that woeful semi-final 'to become the game's best winger … and he didn't have to do much to be that.' Whatever it was that clinched it, Terry Paine was on the plane for Alf Ramsey's first England tour.

He would win two caps and be one of the successes of the tour – as discussed in detail in Chapter 11. Noting that Terry thus became the first

Left: Terry surveys the souvenirs of his first full England tour.

Below: His first full cap.

Winchester-born boy to play for England, the *Hampshire Chronicle* took palpable pleasure in recording that this had not gone to his head: 'although a footballing career now promises to take Paine to all corners of the world, it is significant that he has not forgotten the more humble arenas in which he began his career.' Thus he had been spotted at Airlie Road on the eve of his departure for Europe, watching brother Trevor play for King Alfred Boys' Club in the Final of the Colebrook Cup.

It may not have gone to his head, but it certainly went to his bargaining power, as the Southampton directors held a series of close-season meetings about the wage structure, at one of which his pay constituted the agenda. The Board agreed a general policy of rewarding a full international appearance with a payment of £200, if it were for England or Scotland, or £100 for Wales or either of the Irelands. Terry hedged his bets by negotiating a rider with the manager: he would be guaranteed a minimum bonus of £500 for the season ahead, even if Alf Ramsey were to go off him.

As the bride leads the groom a merry dance, he receives half-hearted support from (*left to right*) Traynor, Kirby, Sydenham, O'Brien and Wimshurst.

Carol, by now the secretary in charge of a local secretarial agency, had also been offered an opportunity to tour – if only she would turn pro and globe-trot with *Hollywood On Ice*. Her fiancé wasn't keen on that idea, so she retired instead and married him. On 26 June, his team-mates turned out in force to witness their wedding at St Edmund's Church in The Avenue, Southampton.

Frankie Vaughan accepted an invitation but found his agent had double-booked him. Of Terry's footballing mentors, Henry Spearman, his PE teacher, was among the guests, but Ted Bates wasn't.

He was in Scotland on business. His taste for Scots not having been sated by his two debutants of 1962-63 – Ian White and Denis Hollywood – he would buy two more this summer: David Paton, a 19 year-old centre-half from St Mirren; and John McGuigan, a 30 year-old inside-forward who had long since left St Mirren, latterly to play for Scunthorpe, with whom he had evidently impressed against Southampton in the season just gone.

Chapter 9

Beaten by Butlins

John McGuigan would soon be competing with David Burnside for the No.10 shirt – though not for the first five games in which the team scored 13 goals but contrived to let in 13, as well. It set the tone for another of those crazy seasons in which they would reach 100 goals – for the first, and only, time in a 42-match season – yet, by conceding 73, would again finish well short of promotion.

But the centre-piece of the 1963-64 campaign would be the Third Round of the FA Cup, which brought Manchester United to The Dell. This early opportunity to avenge that semi-final defeat appealed to the Southampton public, who swiftly procured the club's allocation of tickets and another 2,000 the United fans didn't want. I can vouch for the indifference in Manchester, where I was then living. Put it this way: you don't expect to pop along to Old Trafford for a couple of tickets and to be asked won't you, please, take four? I obliged.

In Southampton, though, the scrabble for tickets continued – so the players were glad to escape to a haven at what Mike Langley of the *Daily Express* described as 'the quiet end of Brighton.' But *not* the boring end: Langley, spending time with them as he had for the previous season's encounter with United, found the players training on a dog-track, taking brine baths and golfing on the Dyke course. It was, he reported, a 'freer, more confident' atmosphere than he had experienced at Droitwich, nine months before: 'Southampton are not a side cast down by fears of unconquerable opponents.'

Indeed, Langley's colleague, Bill Fryer, suggested that United would have worries of their own and predicted that left-half Maurice Setters would be 'doing a pendulum at the rear, helping Noel Cantwell in the huge job of marking Terry Paine.'

Cantwell had arrived at Old Trafford in 1960 when, you may recall from Chapter 6, Matt Busby's shopping list had included Paine. Now the United captain was expected to need assistance in handling Saints' outside-right, whose star was very much in the ascendancy: Terry had played in all three of England's autumn matches, scoring against the Rest of the World and getting a hat-trick against Northern Ireland. He celebrated the latter achievement by buying a beagle pup – a companion for Mimi, Carol's toy poodle – and naming it 'Ireland'.

Those three caps had earned him £600 in bonuses from the club, quickly cancelling out that modest 'guarantee' of £500, but they had added to the transfer speculation. Carol had been sitting next to Tommy Trinder, the Fulham chairman, at Wembley. He had offered her a gold-tapped house – with two bathrooms when Terry's first goal went in, rising to eight and an introduction to the Beatles by the final whistle – if Terry would sign for his club. OK, so he was a professional comedian.

While Paine was obviously the man for United to stop, whatever made the man from the *Express* think that Setters would not have his hands full,

Ireland, named after Terry's hat-trick victims, is introduced to Mimi.

marking Martin Chivers? By now 18, Chivers had captured the No.8 shirt and was filling it well, in both senses of the verb. He attributed his increase in size and weight partly to a 'growth spurt' but also to the rigours of a professional training regime. Either way, he was a powerful proposition, as he demonstrated in the 44th minute, when he strode past Setters, to blast an opener. And then, before the half-time whistle could go, Paine somehow eluded both Setters and Cantwell to pop up in the centre of the goal, to head a second from Sydenham's cross.

So much for the visitors' defensive 'pendulum'. It was the match that swung in the second half, though, as United took over to win 3-2. Which of us who were there would disagree with Ian Carnaby's assessment that this was a 'riveting, never-to-be-forgotten encounter?' He recalls how Setters reflected, in a post-match interview, that 'Saints had let United off the hook.' Isn't that the usual way of things? However spirited the come-back, the inquest so often focuses on the woeful failures of the side that had 'surrendered' its lead. So it was with this particular game of two halves. Among the explanations offered for Saints' succumbing to United yet again, two stand out: a change of tactics; and *Butlins*.

Ted Bates has started the game without either of his midfield play-makers from the previous Cup-run. McGuigan and White were in for Wimshurst and Burnside. He now drew them deeper for the second half:

what we have, we hold. 'That wasn't our game,' Ron Davies reasons. 'Our game was out-and-out attack.' That may well remind you of what Ken Wimshurst said about the 1963 Cup-runners. And the outcome was much the same as when Forest played with men withdrawn in that second replay, nine months before: Crerand was allowed the kind of space in which Wimshurst had revelled at White Hart Lane.

The United No.4 had an unfamiliar forward line in front of him. Denis Law was suspended and Bobby Charlton had recently been featuring at No.9. And Matt Busby kept faith in the teenage wingers he had fielded the Saturday before and who could now boast three appearances between them – George Best on the left; and Willie Anderson on the right.

Ron Davies, in for the injured Williams, would not be unduly troubled by Best. It is Anderson who remains in my mind's eye for giving Tommy Traynor a torrid time in the second half. But let's not blame Traynor's tired legs. Tony Godfrey fears that there were other players who did 'tire a bit after being away and not having a rest.' The reason for their not having rested was that their 'quiet' Brighton hotel was a *Butlins*. The night-life, there, was anything but quiet, especially on New Year's Eve, which fell on the Tuesday of the squad's stay. The drink flowed and, one way or another, it was, Terry Paine recalls, 'a *ball* from start to finish... birds in the rooms... absolute chaos.' And you didn't have to be romping in one of those rooms to go short on sleep. As Godfrey, a 'fanatic' for pre-match discipline, explains, 'the walls were paper thin.' And Martin Chivers, agog at the revelries of some of his elders, remembers the manager packing him off to bed early on New Year's Eve, yet being kept awake by the noise.

Chivers nowadays likes to joke, on the after-dinner circuit, that '*Butlins* caught up with us in the second half.' If you've paid money to hear an ex-player's post-prandial reminiscences, then that line will doubtless be good for a laugh. But if you've paid to watch your side knock United out of the Cup for the first time in their history, then this was no laughing matter. When I put that to Terry Paine, he was not impressed: 'Bah! At the time, you don't think it's going to make any difference to you. It's human nature in many ways.'

Well, yes, but don't we fans have a right to expect professional athletes to judge when at least some of those 'ways' need to be resisted? 'Maybe,' says Terry, shifting onto the defensive, but 'we were well beat, on the day, by a better side, second half. Then again, you could say what went on, that week, contributed to that – sure!'

Indeed, we could say that. And, 40-odd years later, this fan is still inclined to say it with feeling. But, then, how pallid football history would be if we whitewashed out the frailties, the recriminations and the consequent 'what ifs?'

Anyhow, there was still a possibility of promotion. The Saints were lying seventh, having lost only one game since October. The start of that good run had coincided with Chivers taking over O'Brien's No.8 shirt. O'Brien had started well enough, with seven goals in the first nine games, keeping him abreast of Kirby, who had scored four on the opening day, a 6-1 win over Charlton.

After five games – for an aggregate, as I say, of 13-13 – the 1963 side experienced its first change, when Mike Hennigan came in for the injured Knapp, ahead of David Paton. The side flew – a first for a League game – to Newcastle. It seems, although there are some contradictions in the evidence, that this may have been the occasion when George O'Brien was tapped up by a representative of the home side. George says the conversation was overheard by his right-wing partner, who then 'never passed one ball' to him, all evening. We have heard that complaint before from O'Brien – think back to the semi-final of the previous season – but he came away with both of Saints' goals in a 2-2 draw, the first from a Sydenham cross, the second from a penalty. He mischievously suggests that Paine's alleged reaction to Newcastle's approach could have been 'a compliment – he didn't want me to go.'

The Saints party boards for the club's first-ever flight to a League match
– at Newcastle, a club interested in signing O'Brien.
Kirby leads the way, followed, on the steps, by Burnside (*left*) and Traynor.
The others, on the tarmac, are (*left to right*) Ted Bates, Williams, Jimmy Gallagher,
McGuigan, Reynolds, Sydenham, Hennigan, White, Huxford, Paine and O'Brien.

That may be so, yet Ted Bates was prepared to let George go when Newcastle promptly came in for him. Ever the pragmatist, the manager told the Board that the club 'had had the best' of a player with an arthritic knee and hoped that Chivers might be ready 'to take over,' should they agree to sell to Newcastle or whomsoever. O'Brien's creaking knee had long been nursed by his manager: George had been excused training, week after week, so that he might lie on the treatment table and get ready, that way, for scoring goals galore come Saturday.

John McGuigan, Ted Bates's latest attempt to fill the No.10 shirt, talks things over with some of his team-mates. (*Left to right*): Traynor, Williams, McGuigan, Paine, O'Brien.

But now it was November, Chivers was in and getting a goal or two and so were the rest of the forwards, despite the repeated shuffling in midfield between permutations of Wimshurst, White, Burnside and McGuigan. And there was a change of goalkeeper in October, after Ron Reynolds injured his shoulder so badly at Fratton Park that he would never play again. This time, with Saints trailing 2-0, Huxford deputised in goal. He kept a clean sheet, but the score remained unchanged. Come February, Pompey would complete the 'double' by winning 3-2 at The Dell. Ken Wimshurst, not long back from breaking his jaw at Sunderland in November, had the misfortune, late in the game, to go off injured again.

If there is nothing remarkable about that, it should be observed that his assailant was Roy Lunniss; and the crippling tackle substantiated Ken's contention that, when Lunniss despaired of catching Terry Paine, he would kick somebody else, instead. The issue of full-backs keen, but unable, to kick Terry is worthy of separate coverage in Chapter 23, in which fuller consideration must be given to the legendary Lunniss-Paine duels.

Wimshurst would recover from Lunniss's lunge in time to play in Kirby's last game for the club. Ted Bates brought his high-scoring combination of Chivers and Kirby to an abrupt halt by selling George to Coventry. Bates now turned to a combination that he had used when Chivers first came into

the side: Martin would move to No.9 and
O'Brien, who had not been sold, would resume
at No.8. In the 10 remaining games, the two of
them would play unchanged, with Paine at
outside-right – save when he took a Saturday
off to win his sixth cap in Glasgow – and score
a remarkable 28 goals between them: Paine, 8;
O'Brien, 9; and Chivers, 11.

Paine's eight included a hat-trick – albeit
aided by two penalties – in a 6-4 win over
Derby County. It was his second of the season.
Chivers and O'Brien grabbed a hat-trick each,
as the last four matches produced 20 goals and
four wins for the Saints. It took them to fifth
place, their highest finish in the Football
League since 1950. The final game brought the
season's goal-tally to 100. A 6-1 home win
against Rotherham, a score-line identical to the
opening day against Charlton, gave the season
a strange symmetry.

Martin Chivers,
who was scoring for fun.

But never mind the pattern from August to April. The point, surely, was
that Ted Bates had ended the season with a formation in which his Nos.7-9
were settled and scoring for fun. And Terry might even learn a close-season
trick or two on tour with England, culminating in the 'Little World Cup'
tournament in Brazil.

He came home, however, with questions on his mind as to his England
future. Of England's 14 games under Ramsey in the last year, Terry had
played in nine of them, with Peter Thompson of Liverpool now the only
competitor in sight for the No. 7 shirt. But that was assuming Ramsey
would continue to deploy wingers, even if he were to depart from 4-2-4:
we can consider in Chapter 13 why Terry felt he had seen the 4-3-3 future
when the squad watched a wingless Argentina humiliate Brazil in São Paulo
to win that four-nation tournament.

But might his international chances yet be bettered by a move to a First
Division club? Having enjoyed partnering Jimmy Greaves in six of his nine
games, to date, for England, Terry would have favoured a move to
Tottenham, if anywhere. With 'Budgie' Byrne in the England squad of late,
Bobby Moore had been rooming with his West Ham team-mate, instead of
Greaves, who had therefore been sharing with Paine.

Greaves remembers Terry as 'a good room-mate' with whom he 'had a bit of fun,' but that begs the obvious question: did he chat up Terry on behalf of Spurs? He would have had good reason to: whereas the Wales outside left, Cliff Jones, had long been a fixture on Tottenham's left wing, Terry Medwin and Terry Dyson had been playing 'musical chairs with the number seven shirt,' the problem being, in Greaves's opinion, that, 'like most wingers, both were subject to inconsistency.'

Medwin had retired in 1963, leaving Dyson unchallenged at No.7, compensating for his lack of skill, in Greavsie's book, with an impressive work-rate. While rejecting any suggestion that he might have discussed, with Terry Paine, how Spurs might use his skills, Greaves recalls that the Tottenham manager, Bill Nicholson,

> used occasionally to say 'who do you think the club could do with?' Terry was an obvious candidate. Terry would have been a great asset at White Hart Lane – there's no question about that.

But, then, Nicholson probably didn't need Greaves to report from the England camp: his assistant, Harry Evans, a war-time team-mate of Ted Bates at The Dell, was forever sniffing around, Terry reckons.

So would he go? Or would he once again settle for Southampton, with their latest red-hot scoring combo? The problem was, he pointed out to the

Coventry manager Jimmy Hill (*right*) admires the fleece of Jimmy Greaves, while Terry Paine, more modestly sheepskin-lined, looks on.

Echo, even as he unpacked his souvenirs from Brazil, not the quality of his team-mates but that of his opponents: he was 'worried that playing against Second Division opponents is spoiling my chances of doing well against world class players,' so much so that he was 'wondering whether I dare spend another season here.' If Ray Wilson had been having a similar problem with Huddersfield, it hadn't shown. Yet he was about to upgrade to Everton, leaving Terry as the only second-tier player among Ramsey's rotating regulars.

On the other hand, neither he nor Carol wanted to leave Southampton – 'we have so much here,' Carol explained to the *Echo* – but just how many bonus schemes could Terry prise from Ted Bates and the Board? Well, maybe they could give him a house? The Board was selling its club-houses to players, but Terry suggested alternative terms: they could sign his house in Bitterne over to him at no charge. It is not unambiguously clear how soon this deal was completed, but Terry signed a new contract before his old one ran out at the end of June.

His summer highlights otherwise consisted of taking Carol to a French chateau to celebrate her 21st birthday-cum-first wedding anniversary and playing for the Winchester & District Cricket XI against a Hampshire XI. The occasion was a benefit match for 40 year-old Henry Horton who, having finished playing football for Southampton in 1954, would still be

As his international career flourished, the *Echo* was keen for new solo shots of Terry, whether The Dell was full (1963-64, *left*) or empty (1964-65).

playing cricket for Hampshire in 1967. Not needed behind the stumps, Terry got to bowl a single over, in which he took one wicket for eight runs, most of them scored by the beneficiary himself.

The wicket, ironically, was of Horton's Portsmouth equivalent, all-rounder Mike Barnard. Coming after a season in which Pompey had completed the first derby 'double' since 1927, Terry Paine had contrived to find a slither of compensation with a cricket ball.

As it turned out, the Paine-O'Brien-Chivers strike-force would play largely unchanged in 1964-65, with the three players missing only four games between them. Terry was ever-present, thanks to a quirk in the Second Division fixture list. Saints' scheduled visit to Cardiff in October was postponed, because Wales were playing Scotland at Ninian Park – a 40th cap for Stuart Williams and a £100 bonus from the club – while Terry was in Belfast, winning his 10th England cap, more highly-valued at £200.

In fact, it would be another of those seasons when nine of the outfield players made at least 35 appearances. The exceptions would yet again be in goal and at inside-left. The season began with another ex-Spurs 'keeper between the posts: John Hollowbread, signed on the recommendation of Ron Reynolds. When he was injured in February, Godfrey was, as ever, available. He remained for the duration, even after Hollowbread had recovered. At inside-left, the McGuigan-Burnside see-saw continued.

I have been taking an optimistic stance in respect of this degree of continuity from the season before: if you end a long campaign with your big guns firing spectacularly and finish higher in the League than you have for 15 years, then it surely makes sense to keep faith in those players. The alternative view is that finishing fifth after four seasons back in Division II represented a failure; and how could the club possibly justify not strengthening the squad that remained incapable of achieving promotion?

That was the gist of the fans' letters that featured in the *Football Echo*, starting after three defeats in four games. The exchanges continued for the next two Saturdays, even though an almost unchanged side had now embarked on a run of six consecutive wins. The most consistent theme was that the club had three 'first-class' home-grown forwards in Paine, Chivers and Sydenham, but needed to buy 'at least another three good players… and blow the expense.' These bank-busting purchases should include 'two really first-class inside-forwards.'

With the manager ringing the changes at No.10, you can see why dissatisfied fans might want *one* new inside-forward, but O'Brien was delivering – and not only by finding the net, either. He had a fine game in a 3-0 win at Portsmouth in September, when the goals came from the Saints' three 'first-class' natives – so much so that a Pompey fan, joining in the *Football Echo* correspondence, commended him on a 'display [that] was the best from an inside-forward I have seen at Fratton Park for many seasons.' The *Echo* certainly liked the way he set up Sydenham's goal with a 'great pass' and how he 'cracked' a quick corner into the penalty area, where Paine ran in to score with his head.

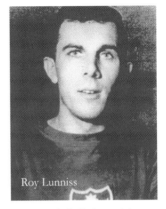

Roy Lunniss

To say that the Pompey defence was caught napping by that corner-kick would be an under-statement. 'That really pissed me off,' Roy Lunniss remembers. 'For some reason, Terry didn't take the corner. I'm on the left post. The ball comes across and he just nips in and nods the ball into the net. I've thought about that over the years and why he never took that corner.'

If that makes it sound as though the surprise element left Paine with little work to do, that's not how it was seen by that out-spoken correspondent to the *Echo*, lamenting the failure of his fellow-Fratton fans to 'appreciate a brilliant winger such as Paine. His headed goal was one of the best goals I have ever seen in League football.' And it was quite unfair, he felt, that the crowd should have shouted 'Dirty Paine'. How 'utterly stupid' of them, given that 'Paine didn't commit one foul throughout the game.' Really? Terry Paine commended for his fair play, even when on the same pitch as Roy Lunniss!

After the winning run came too many draws, but the side had climbed to third by the beginning of November. This didn't halt the letters about the need to find 'two class players' to replace 'the weak links'. Positions not specified but, come the next Saturday, O'Brien scored both goals in a 2-2 draw at Norwich, whose goals came from the head of a striker who would win his second Wales cap at Wembley the following week. Terry Paine would not be there: he was currently out of the England set-up and Peter Thompson was in for a four-match run.

The Welshman was, of course, Ron Davies, but Ted Bates was not in the market for a goal-scorer, so much as a play-maker at inside-left. He found his man in time for Christmas.

When last encountered in Chapter 6, Jimmy Melia was a Liverpool player. He had moved on to Wolves, where he found their 'long stuff' unsuited to his game. So he was willing to come and play some short stuff at The Dell.

He readily settled in, playing every game until the end of the season, with Sydenham outside him, having seen off a December flurry of competition from Chadwick. You may recall a flirtation, in 1961-62, with a formation in which Paine switched to No.11 to accommodate his young understudy on the right. In this season's variation, however, Terry kept his place on the right, while Chadwick came in at outside-left, a position he had tried out in a couple of games for the Reserves. With Sydenham's return, Chadwick would have a further run at No.11 in the Football Combination, as if he was now under-studying for this flank. But he was due to have just one more first-team game in that position – by which time O'Brien, the team-mate championing his inclusion, would himself have left.

In an eight-game spell from the end of February to early April, O'Brien scored 10 times and Chivers seven. Paine 'rammed' in the only other goal, the *Echo* recorded, but nobody else needed to score, as the Saints climbed to fourth in the table. Despite a poor last few games, they hung on to that spot.

The last day of the season was significant for several reasons. The Saints beat Swindon 2-1 at The Dell, with Paine scoring the winner – a goal which, it could be said, sent Swindon down and kept Portsmouth up. Pompey had an evening kick-off at Northampton – where Paine had had two penalties saved in a 2-2 draw in January – and knew that a draw would suffice.

Their hosts had already clinched promotion to Division I, as runners-up to Newcastle, and had nothing to play for. The match ended 1-1 and

The 750th game in Jimmy Dickinson's record number of appearances had taken place at The Dell earlier in the season.

He is welcomed by (*left to right*) Knapp, Hollowbread, Wimshurst, O'Brien, Melia (peeping), Sydenham and Hollywood.

Pompey escaped. But whereas the Saints had finished in the spot they had last achieved in 1950, their neighbours were very far adrift from their position of that year, when they had been League Champions for the second season running.

For Jimmy Dickinson, the regular left-half in those Championship seasons, that game at Northampton was his 764th, and last, League appearance. Nobody had played more games in the Football League than that. It was a remarkable way to celebrate his 40th birthday. Thanks to the War, he was 21 before he made his League debut. So Paine, having started at 17, had quite a start on Dickinson. And, having then kept free of injury and the army – he had just completed another ever-present season to bring his League appearances to 353 – Terry was on schedule to break Dickinson's record in his late 30s.

First of all, though, he had a busy May in store, winning four more England caps in the space of 12 days. And, then, returning to The Dell for pre-season training, he posed for a photograph (*below*) that must count as one of the most unusual in the Terry Paine gallery.

Paine obliges the Empics photographer, with the help of Stuart Williams's legs.

Chapter 10

Change Here for Promotion

The side that started the 1965-66 season included a debutant: David Walker, another, more defensive, replacement for Wimshurst, from Burnley. But the other nine outfield players had turned out, almost unchanged, for the second half of the previous season.

This settled look would be short-lived. Bates would use 24 players, with nine of them making their League debut for the club and nine (including three of the debutants) playing their last game. That hardly sounds like a promotion formula – certainly not in comparison with the stable side of 1960 – but this would indeed prove to be *the* season.

The first casualty was Hollowbread in only the sixth game, when, like Reynolds before him, he sustained a career-ending injury. This was the inaugural season for substitutes in the Football League. Wimshurst became the Saints' first player to come off the bench, as Huxford took over in goal for the last hour of Coventry's visit and, as the chairman remarked in the next home programme, 'kept his charge in a really competent manner.' Who needs goalkeeper Paine?

The side hung on to win 1-0 – which might have been tough with only 10 men – to bag two points that would be so vital come May. Godfrey now returned yet again. It was an interesting welcome-back, as the side scored 14 and conceded 11 in the next three games. A 4-3 win at Norwich took them to the top of the table. A Paine penalty hit the post at 3-3, but Terry was spared embarrassment when Norman Dean, on his League debut, scored the winner.

Despite a midweek set-back, 5-1 at Coventry, the Saints were still leading the table when the next game began in a familiar fashion, Knapp putting the ball past his 'keeper to give Wolverhampton Wanderers a first-minute lead at The Dell. Whereupon the Saints rattled in five before half-time, sandwiching another from Wolves.

On the hour, Paine completed the scoring at 9-3, when he left the visiting goalkeeper stranded to replicate precisely what he had done for the third goal – a double reminder of Colin Addison's tribute, in Chapter 8, to Terry's prowess in slipping round a 'keeper to tuck it away. It could so easily

Paine leaves Wolves' MacLaren stranded and beats the covering defenders,
to slot in Saints' third goal. Uncannily, he would replicate this trick for the ninth.

have been 10, but Sydenham and he each hit the woodwork in the remaining half-hour. Still, this was the first time Southampton had ever run up nine in a League match. Each of the forwards scored, bar Melia, but his performance was one of the main talking points from the match.

The issue was the wearing of the No.9 shirt. Chivers had begun the season in possession but when O'Brien was injured, he took over at No.8, with debutant Dean at No.9. With O'Brien fit to return for the visit of Wolves and Chivers not keen to revert to No.9, the manager asked Melia if he'd mind wearing it. 'It makes no difference to me,' said Jimmy, but it made a huge difference to Woodfield, the visiting centre-half, who 'marked me all over the field,' Melia recalls, leaving 'a big gap, right through the middle,' for the other forwards to exploit. All that stood in their way, apart from the woodwork, was goalkeeper Dave MacLaren, who was acclaimed by the *Echo* for a 'magnificent' display in which he made 'several superb saves.'

The goal-spree would now dry up: over the next nine games, the side would manage only six goals, shared between Chivers and O'Brien. Chadwick would be at No.7 for three of these games – his last chance in this position. On one of those occasions – a 2-1 home defeat by Ipswich – Paine took over the dreaded No.9 shirt from Melia. It would be the only time in his Southampton career that he wore that number.

For Chadwick's other two appearances, Paine was absent – and breaking a long sequence each time. First, in early October, for a top-of-the-table clash that ended in Manchester City winning 1-0 at The Dell, Terry was winning his 15th England cap against Wales in Cardiff. Which meant that he missed only his second game in almost four years, the previous time being when he was winning his sixth cap in Glasgow in April 1964.

The second absence – a 1-0 win over Orient, four weeks later – was even more historic: it was the first time in eight-and-a-half seasons that Terry had ever missed playing on account of injury. In this game, partnered by Chadwick, O'Brien scored his 11th goal of the season – in only 13 matches. The *Echo* calculated that he had thereby overtaken Bill Rawlings as the club's top scorer in League football (counting one peace-time season in the Southern League in Rawlings's case). The *Echo* accordingly brought the 69 year-old Rawlings to The Dell to celebrate O'Brien's achievement with him. But the records show that the 1918-28 centre-forward had scored 156 goals to George's 154. The player who would overtake Rawlings would be Terry Paine in 1971.

O'Brien, you see, would never score for the club again. Indeed, nobody would score at all in his three remaining games for the Saints. George caught hepatitis from one of his sons. With him sidelined, it was Chivers's turn to go on a crazy scoring run – of 18 goals in 11 League games. With Dean chipping in his share of goals, the side was running up some big scores, once getting four and four times getting five, without ever getting back into a promotion slot.

The 4-1 win over Plymouth Argyle in early December was a debut for goalkeeper Campbell Forsyth from Kilmarnock, the Scottish title-holders. Ted Bates had been after the Scottish international for some time but had to wait until Real Madrid ended his participation in the European Cup. Tony Godfrey was not going to wait around for Forsyth to get injured, like Reynolds and Hollowbread before. He moved to Aldershot. Since breaking into the first team seven years before, he had played a part in every season, only to be repeatedly displaced upon the arrival of an older 'keeper.

Campbell Forsyth

That said, the 451 games that he would play in the Football League puts him second – way behind Paine, of course, but ahead of Sydenham – in the appearance records of those Youths of 1957. Disappointed though he is not to have had more than 141 of those outings for Southampton, Tony professes himself 'proud to have played so long in the same team' as his two team-mates from 1957. 'I don't think there's been any side who had any better wide players than Terry Paine and John Sydenham. I think they were the best, possibly, in the Football League, then.'

In the first of the five-goal wins, Preston came back late to halve Saints' 4-0 lead to 4-2. Chivers headed in Paine's cross to settle it at 5-2, but Ted Bates was unhappy to have conceded at a free-kick. He was 'having a go' at Tommy Hare, whose third game this was, when 'Terry said "No. It was my fault",' Tommy recalls. 'He was in the wall and jumped out of the way. He could have kept quiet, him being the big man at the club, but he owned up. I admire him for that.'

The next nap-hands came in successive games at the turn of the year: a 5-3 win at Cardiff, followed by a 5-1 triumph over Bolton at home. The chip that set up Norman Dean for the opening goal against Bolton demonstrates Paine's adaptability. He no longer had a tall guy hovering at the back stick, because, as Dean explains, the flow of a movement would often take the towering Chivers to the near post and himself, at only 5ft 10½ ins, to the far. None of which mattered to Paine, who 'would pick out which one he thought was the best option,' says Dean, approvingly. 'Terry picked me out delightfully for the first goal. He got to the by-line and, from 18 yards, how he chipped it up to the far post!' And the photograph shows how many defenders he took out.

A 'delightful' Paine chip has come over the Bolton defence.
Dean has timed his run to be on the end of it and score.

Despite that moment of vintage Paine, this was not his greatest game: in fact, the *People* gave him and Sydenham the Saints' lowest scores of '6' each. Dean was their top man on '9', while Hartle was Bolton's on '8'. Fans of a certain age will recall that Bolton's full-back partnership of Roy Hartle and Tommy Banks was renowned for its toughness, left-back Banks being celebrated for his warning to opposing wingers: 'tha'd better not try to get past me unless th' wants gravel rash.' The camber at Burnden Park helped to ensure that a winger would experience a 'drop' onto the perimeter track if he ventured to take on his marker.

Syd Farrimond had now inherited the No.3 shirt and was marking Terry Paine. The *Echo* blandly recorded that, with the Saints leading 4-0, he 'clashed with Paine' and was instantly ordered off. Farrimond's recall of the incident is more graphic:

The pitch was muddy – not the best surface for turning on, obviously. Terry had gone past me a few times; I'd whacked him a few times. On this particular occasion, he got the ball; came up to me; dropped his shoulder; knocked it past me; and I slid in to him. Sometimes, it happened like this: you went for him with your right and, if you missed, you got him with your left. So I finished up on the floor, legs splayed apart, and he's above. He's half-down, as well. The referee has blown for a free-kick. So I'm coming to get up and, as I am starting to get up, this boot came down the side of my head. I got a handful of mud and threw it at him: into his face – well, towards his face. It was only a reaction to him bringing the boot down my face, which I thought was deliberate. If it hadn't been muddy, it probably wouldn't have happened – you know, me just grabbing a handful of mud and… phwoosh! It was just an instant-reaction.

Having 'maybe clattered him more than once,' Farrimond expected retribution – even if a boot dragged down the face was out of the usual range. What rankled – and does to this day – is that he did not consider mud-throwing a sending-off offence. 'The referee came up, straightaway, and said "Now, off!" I said "I didn't hit him. I threw mud at him," but, in his opinion, I had hit him, so off I went.' His manager persuaded him not to seek a personal hearing – 'he said he thought I'd hit him' – but Farrimond later 'learned that the club had had letters from Southampton fans who'd been near to the incident, saying that, in their opinion, I hadn't hit him.'

The following month, Saints rattled in five more at Fratton Park. Don Woodward, of the *Daily Express*, enjoyed some 'good, thumping local derby stuff, with enough bite to satisfy those who insist: "It's a man's game".' The *Echo* remarked, in more urbane language, on the game's 'sporting spirit.'

As hinted in the previous chapter, 'sporting' was not a label that you would readily attach to the derby clashes between Terry Paine and Roy Lunniss but, on this occasion, Paine was faced by Ron Tindall. The former Chelsea centre-forward had played at left-back in the First Division when his place was threatened by the arrival of Livesey from Southampton and his manager required him to cover for another ex-Saint, Peter Sillett, who was injured. Having marked Stanley Matthews during that spell, Tindall nevertheless had problems with Paine, partly because he was struggling with an injury but also because he was facing 'a magnificent player [whose] judgment of when he would release the ball was second to none. That's where he did me in that match, a few times.'

There is much more where that came from, but it can wait until Chapter 23, when we can consider which left-backs marked Terry Paine how. When he wasn't bewildering Tindall, Terry even found time to track back, the *Echo* noted: thus, when Pompey's inside-left, Albert McCann, set off on a run, Terry 'raced shoulder-to-shoulder' with him. Although he kept up with him, he failed to dispossess him and McCann went on to 'slam' his side's second goal.

While I mention that as if it was an unusual occurrence, Paine's reluctance to tackle back has perhaps been exaggerated. I call three witnesses.

First, Stuart Williams, giving evidence in Chapter 8, that 'Terry used to come back a bit,' even if he did that less often than is expected today. Next, Tony Godfrey, claiming that not only did Paine – and Sydenham, too – 'come back and defend quite a bit,' but, provided Terry wasn't in the 'dream'-mode explained earlier, both Siddie and he 'used to pick up really good positions,' Godfrey reckons, for him 'to throw the ball to them.' And, finally, we'll come to the testimony of Gerry Gurr in Chapter 16, adducing a photographic exhibit in support.

Terry was certainly doing his bit that day at Fratton Park, being involved in three of the goals. And not just from a wide position. As previously noted, Dean was impressed with Paine's flexible approach: 'Terry didn't always stay on the wing. Terry could come inside and act as a bloody good inside-forward – a play-maker.' And so it was that Terry stepped inside and put Norman 'through from the half-way line, with a nice little, astute ball,' for the young striker to complete his hat-trick.

That move was an exception to Don Woodward's assessment that Saints' goals were 'fluked, blundered and thundered.' The thunder came from Chivers, who scored twice. The flukes and blunders seemingly referred to the way in which the ball ricocheted around for Dean's first two goals, although Norman considers that a misinformed assessment of what it could require to convert a Sydenham cross into a goal. He described this art in Chapter 7 and feels that he demonstrated it with his first goal, that afternoon at Fratton Park, when 'John got to the by-line again and just *hammered* it into a crowded goalmouth. Instinctively, I just stuck my knee up because it was coming that fast. I put my knee up purposely to try and deflect it in. It wasn't a fluke: I knew what I was doing.'

It was now the end of February. March began with a home defeat – 1-0 by Birmingham City – but Saints thereupon went on an undefeated 12-match run-in. It began with a 1-1 draw at Molineux, with a goal by debutant right-back, David Webb, who had come from Leyton Orient in a deal that involved George O'Brien going in the opposite direction – from top post-war scorer to a dispensable chattel in less than four months.

Saints were having to get their goals not only without O'Brien but without any more from Chivers. After an outlandish 30 goals in the first 29 games, Martin had stopped scoring. The problem was his back, although he managed, with manipulation and cortisone from a London specialist, to miss only three games.

His deputy was Mick Channon, by now 17. He made his debut on Easter Monday, the climax to a crucial weekend. Saints were fortunate to play only twice – on Good Friday and Easter Monday – their Saturday game at Brisbane Road being called off. So Easter's traditional three fixtures came down to Friday at Ashton Gate and a 'return' encounter with Bristol City at The Dell on the Monday. You might wish simply to note that the Saints took three points, by dint of a 1-0 away win and a 2-2 home draw, and move on – but not if you have associated these past several years, as I have, with pained City historians and have read the writings on that Easter by the City's celebrated centre-forward, John Atyeo.

This was his last season and his last chance to take the Robins into Division I. Writing in the City's programme, nine months later, when the Saints visited Ashton Gate in the FA Cup, he drew attention to 'an old score to settle with the Saints.' It wasn't that old, but he continued to go on about it in a 1970 article in the Bristol *Evening Post*. His beef, as spelled out in that 1967 programme by the editor, was that City 'were the better side in both games' and, had they taken those three points, then they, rather than Saints, would have been promoted.

That City deserved to win both games seems not to be in dispute. A fluke own goal settled Friday's game, as the Saints kept their first clean sheet for five months. On the Monday, Ted Bates put out a scratch strike-force. With Dean also injured, Tommy Spencer was making his third and last appearance at centre-forward. Channon opened the scoring, but the visitors came back to lead 2-1 late into stoppage time. Whereupon 'Terry Paine burst through to score a spectacular equaliser,' as Bristol City's *Complete History* generously acknowledges.

It was one of nine goals that he contributed in the 12-match run-in, exactly half of the goals the side managed. The two most dramatic came in the last home game and the penultimate away game. When Charlton came to The Dell on 30 April, the game was goalless and 89 minutes old when, bad back or not, Chivers made a memorable run down the right touch-line, his huge stride deceptively making him look slower than the defender giving hopeless chase. 'It was tough to keep up with him,' Terry reckons, but he it was who got himself into the danger zone, bursting into the six-yard box and throwing his body forward to meet Martin's cross, ahead of the advancing goalkeeper. Paine and the ball somehow connected and two more points were secure. What followed was described by the man from *The Times*:

> Paine was chaired from the pitch, and the glow of optimism matched
> the sun. It had been a long time in setting, but for all their over-eagerness,
> punctuated at times by the opposite quality of extraordinary casualness,
> Southampton had done enough to suggest that they were worthy of
> higher things.

Above: Chivers is still standing at the end of his long run,
while Paine has thrown himself at the ball to score a vital goal.

Below: His appreciative admirers chair him from the pitch.

They still had to prove their worth over the three remaining games, all of them away. Paine's availability for the next due game was an issue. It had been predictable, from the start of the season, that Alf Ramsey's World Cup preparations would clash with end-of-season fixtures; and postponed games had made matters worse. Saints had arranged to play their game at Brisbane Road, postponed from Easter Saturday, on Monday 2 May, but Ramsey was unwilling to release his outside-right – even though his selection to win his

17th cap against Yugoslavia on 4 May would be a late one. Leyton Orient sportingly agreed to hold the game over until the following Monday.

This gave Saints a considerable advantage over their promotion rivals. While they were winning 3-2 at Plymouth on 7 May, to bring their points total to 52, Huddersfield and Coventry, who'd started the day on 51 points each, were meeting at Leeds Road. Coventry won 2-0 to put them in second place, on 53 points, behind Manchester City who had pulled clear of the pack to be champions. This should have been the last day of the season, but while that was so for Coventry and Huddersfield, Southampton still had two games to play – not only at Orient but also at Maine Road, where their March fixture had had to give way to City's Sixth Round FA Cup-tie. To add to the fixture congestion, City had taken three games to lose that tie. So now both Saints and they were playing post-season catch-up.

With a superior goal average to Coventry's, Southampton knew that, in order to clinch promotion, they needed to gain one point and avoid a silly goal deficit. They looked good for at least a point at Brisbane Road, where their hosts had not won since November. But, then, Orient were already relegated and might expect to be less tense than their visitors.

Their gates had dropped to under 3,000 by April, but their two most recent visitors, Man City and Coventry, had each attracted around 6,000. The Saints somewhat bettered that: the attendance, that May evening, was 19,839. As for that 1963 Cup match at White Hart Lane, Southampton had once again emptied into the far side of London.

Tense it was. Orient, with O'Brien sidelined, took a seventh-minute lead and an equaliser was a long time coming. But then, in the 52nd minute, Terry Paine headed what he describes as a 'fluke' goal:

Paine has judged the bounce and runs in to head the historic equaliser at Brisbane Road.

> It was a punt from Campbell Forsyth. And, as it's coming, I read it – everybody might miss it. I've got on my bike early and it's bounced. It's bounced over the top of them and I just head it and stick it into the back of the net.

Just like that. Terry is surely being too modest here. OK, so he didn't have to be as brave as for his goal against Charlton nine days earlier, but he had to show the same anticipation as to what *might* be on and go for it.

All they had to do now was hang on for a 1-1 draw and we jubilant fans could invade the pitch, confident that our team could avoid losing 6-0 at Maine Road in a further nine days' time – which is what it would take to throw away that superior goal average.

The team was also celebrating in the dressing room, even though Ted Bates was hedging his bets: 'I'm drinking champagne,' he famously told Terry, 'but I'm not celebrating.' Once bitten, twice shy. Ted had been a member of the 1949 side that had blown a seemingly unassailable lead to miss promotion; and when they went to Gigg Lane in February, Ted had reminisced about the defeat at Bury that had been part of that 1949 slide. Terry can remember the details: 'Ted had a goal disallowed. They went straight down the other end and scored.' Indeed.

Terry thinks he may have provoked these memories by teasing Ted about the folklore explanation for the demise of 1949: *they didn't want to go up.* If you haven't done so recently, I suggest you watch the Saints' *Official History* video: you'll find it includes the manager's post-match interview at Brisbane Road, in which he was still referring to that 17 year-old myth.

While Terry admired Ted Bates's 'professional' conduct, the chairman was less circumspect. 'The Manchester match will be just a case of champions v runners-up,' George Reader told the Portsmouth *Evening News*. 'It's as simple as that.' The Southampton public was collectively of a similar mind, it would seem. John Sydenham found 'everybody celebrating around the town… everyone wanted to give you a drink and celebrate,' yet he still 'had this nagging feeling that it would all be over,' should they lose 6-0 at Maine Road.

Well, Man City never looked like scoring six and, as the game progressed, 'it didn't look' to Sydenham 'as if any team was going to score any goals… The last half-hour of that game, everybody's got a smile on their face.'

But not in Coventry, surely. It would eventually dawn on the football authorities, of course, that allowing a promotion contender to play two of its games in an 11-day epilogue to the season, the way Saints had, was not exactly fair; so all the sides in any given division must now kick-off at the same time, on the designated last day.

But never mind that. Terry Paine had reached the First Division without needing to transfer to Spurs or whomsoever. He will tell you that Ted Bates could always talk him out of moving:

> He was such a nice, persuasive, gentle, kind man. I felt I was letting him down – that's how he made you feel! You felt 'how can you want to leave this club with Ted Bates here?' It was as simple as that, really.

Except that it was not remotely simple, as each man played his cards close to his chest. Ted, who liked his young players to marry a local girl and 'settle down', would periodically ring Carol to invoke her help in keeping Terry in Southampton. So long as her husband was succeeding in extracting weird and wonderful bonuses from the Board, she was hardly going to undermine his bargaining power by letting on how much they both wanted to stay in Southampton, where they not only had their families but had started something of a family business.

Such was the *Black Swan* café in Winchester, which Terry had taken over in 1964, with his brother Tony, a qualified chef, running it, Carol doing the books and other Paines involved from time to time. In the summer of 1966, it was due a rehab', a hiccup with which made the national sports pages: 'Southampton's colours, red and white, just won't go with our new décor,' Tony explained to the 'Sportlight' columnist of the *Mirror*. 'So we've chosen blue and white.' Whoops!

Terry had to leave that embarrassment to Tony. He was needed at Lilleshall, where Alf Ramsey had a decision to make: who would be in his squad of 22 that would tour Europe and then return to England for the World Cup finals?

In occasionally noting, in the last few chapters, how Terry's international career was developing, I have not gone into any great detail. That's because that particular story is worthy of three chapters in its own right. These follow next. This arrangement will suit those readers who welcome an occasional departure from the chronology. But if you don't fancy such a break, then please skip to Chapter 14, where you will find Terry Paine and Southampton installed in the First Division.

Chapter 11

Your Country Needs You...

Having been capped for England at 17 – for that Boys Clubs game against Scotland – Terry Paine had missed out, as his Southampton peers were being capped at Youth level. He continued to take a back seat, in this regard, during Saints' promotion season of 1959-60, as John Sydenham won two Under-23 caps.

In congratulating Sydenham on the second of those caps – against Scotland on 2 March – Southampton's vice-chairman, John Barber, asked, in his next programme notes, 'when is Terry Paine going to receive recognition?' The answer was the very next game on 16 March, the third anniversary of his Southampton debut and a week before his 21st birthday. Paine scored in a 5-2 win against Holland at Hillsborough. His armchair fans were denied seeing his goal, thanks to a loss of TV picture, but the ITV commentator's tribute to his 'very excellent evening' was seized upon by his boardroom champion, who was clamouring in his next match-day column for Terry to be awarded his first full England cap.

If that appears premature, the *Daily Mirror*, whose columnists would become considerable supporters of Paine's international cause, ventured that 'his bursts of speed, with plenty of skill' had guaranteed him 'higher honours in the not too distant future.' It was a question for *The Times* of his having shown that 'he has the temperament and the class for the big occasion,' while the *Daily Herald* envisaged 'great possibilities' for his right-wing partnership with George Eastham.

The *Daily Telegraph* thought him 'surprisingly confident' and the *Daily Express*, too, was surprised by his performance. Maybe they didn't expect a Third Division player to step up so easily to the international stage, although they had already seen John Sydenham do it. Or had he? Sydenham was omitted from this game and, not helped by the call to National Service later in the year, would never be capped again – although he would get to represent the Army.

Terry, on the other hand, was now in the frame. On the eve of the FA Cup Final – just six days after the Saints had clinched promotion – he was in the Young England side that lost to an England XI at Highbury. In fact, he would continue to feature in this fixture every year until 1965. If it sounds like a meaningless friendly, let it be said that it was taken seriously: the side fielded in England's next full international would include eight players from the senior XI in that 1960 game, plus three who had been ineligible by dint of playing in the Cup Final itself. In short, this was, without doubt, the most illustrious company Terry had so far kept – and a significant opportunity to show whether he belonged in it.

He would now be on the U-23 summer tour, playing in the first match, as England beat East Germany 4-1 in Berlin's Olympic Stadium. But while the other 10 players retained their places for the next two games, Paine was

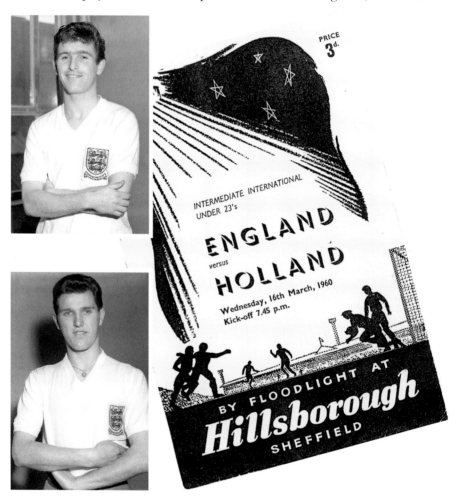

This Under-23 match was a watershed in the international careers
of Southampton's young wingers.
John Sydenham (*top*) was omitted, never to play for his country again,
while it was Terry Paine's first step on the England ladder.

replaced by Wolves' Gerry Mannion. He might have faced the East Germans again, though, come September, but the team was grounded by a leadership struggle in the German Democratic Republic. So new opponents had to be found for the match at Maine Road. The Danish champions, Vejle, filled the breach, which meant that the game would no longer be a cap-worthy event. Terry scored in a 5-1 win, but would play in only one of that season's U-23 internationals, scoring in a 4-1 win against West Germany at White Hart Lane. And, although he made his annual appearance for Young England v England, he would not start in any of the four U-23 fixtures in 1961-62, when Mandy Hill of Blackpool would monopolise the No.7 shirt.

But then came the March evening in 1962 – at The Dell of all places – when, as *The Times* put it, the U-23 side 'stumbled upon success by accident.' The accident was to Hill after 30 minutes; the success was Terry Paine's as he came off the bench to transform the game against Turkey. 'After 30 minutes of incoherent and exasperating play,' his arrival meant that 'almost at once the England attack began to move with more rhythm and menace.' Centre-forward Johnny Byrne was the main beneficiary, in that Paine's 'probing runs and timed passes finally made a new man' of him. As the rejuvenated England romped to yet another 4-1 win, Paine set up a goal for Byrne and scored himself from a flick-on by future team-mate, David Burnside. All of which led *Football Monthly* to declare that 'the evening belonged to Terry Paine.'

The Under-23 squad that practised at the White City for the game at The Dell against Turkey.
It includes substitute Paine and stand-by goalkeeper West,
but Robson would be replaced, on the night, by Burnside.
Back (*left to right*): Billy Wright, Kirkup, Paine, Deakin, Jones, Bonetti, West, Hinton, Moore.
Front: Mandy Hill, Freddie Hill, Byrne, Robson, Harrison.

CONSTANT PAINE

This was the end of U-23 business, though, both for the team's manager, Billy Wright, and the evening's super-sub. Wright had already agreed to manage Arsenal, while Terry Paine, 23 the next day, would now have to wait and hope to break into the full England team.

This would depend upon the selectors: the manager, Walter Winterbottom, was not free to pick his team unaided. After England's second humiliation by Hungary in 1954, the question had been asked: 'do we really need a panel of nine to pick a team of eleven?' So the FA Council had decreed that only two of its members would be selectors, but the number had been allowed to creep back up by the early 1960s. One way or another, it could be a recipe for chopping and changing, as and when a selector might secure a place for a particular fancy of his. Yet, at the time in question – March 1962 – Bobby Charlton had had 17 consecutive games at No 11, stretching over the last two years. The issue was whether and when the selectors might care to make changes on the right. Blackburn's Bryan Douglas had commandeered the No 7 shirt for most of this time, with Burnley's John Connelly occasionally taking over.

Connelly got the nod for two of the three games that Winterbottom's side played at the end of that 1961-62 season, as they prepared for the World Cup finals in Chile, but with Connelly involved in the Cup Final against Spurs, the respective outside-rights for the England v Young England match were Douglas and Paine.

While there was little shuffling of the pack during this World Cup warm-up period, Winterbottom nevertheless had a squad of 40 working-out at Lilleshall. Paine was among them, along with his Southampton team-mate, Tony Knapp, and future team-mate, Jimmy Melia, then of Liverpool. None of them was on the plane, though, that left for South America on 17 May. Douglas still reigned at No 7, with Connelly the travelling reserve.

The 12 players used in Chile were all that much older than Terry, with two notable exceptions: the precocious Jimmy Greaves, who had won his first cap three years before, and Bobby Moore, who had arrived in South America uncapped. An ageing side lost to Brazil in the quarter-finals. England's next competitive engagement would soon be upon them: the qualifying rounds for the 1964 European Nations' Cup finals would begin in October; and England, who had missed the inaugural tournament in 1960, would this time be involved – albeit briefly.

The question now facing the selectors was which other younger players – and this effectively meant under 25 – might now get their chance. Their cause would be helped both by Johnny Haynes terminating his international career in a car crash and Charlton undergoing a hernia operation. And, with Winterbottom resigning, the selectors would suddenly have a flutter with debutants, as the FA fumbled to find a successor.

So it was that England played their first-ever game in this European competition, a 1-1 draw with France at Hillsborough, with no fewer than four debutant forwards, including two new wingers. Three weeks later, the FA revealed the name of their new manager: Alf Ramsey, who had had the success with Ipswich, you may recall from Chapter 6, that George O'Brien felt should have been Ted Bates's with Southampton. But he would be part-time for the remaining five internationals of the season, after which he would become full-time. Meanwhile, the selectors remained in business.

Terry Paine was evidently not to their fancy. Mike Hellawell – with no Under-23 pedigree – came in on the right for a couple of games, while Alan Hinton, Mike O'Grady and Bobby Tambling made their debuts on the left. When they lost the return fixture with France in Paris, England and their new manager could now focus on preparing for the 1966 World Cup – which would necessitate experiments in friendlies, as the host nation had no need, of course, to qualify.

The first new cap of lasting significance would go to Gordon Banks, with the only forward debutants being at No 10, where Jimmy Melia came in, to be replaced, when injured, by George Eastham. Both would go on the three-match summer tour, the 19-man party for which would include three

The England Players			The Football League Players	
SPRINGETT	1	GOAL 1	BONETTI	
ARMFIELD	2	FULL-BACKS 2	SHELLITO	
WILSON	3	3	SHAW	
MOORE	4	HALF-BACKS 4	FLOWERS	
NORMAN	5	5	LABONE	
MILNE	6	6	KAY	
DOUGLAS	7	FORWARDS 7	PAINE	
GREAVES	8	8	HUNT	
SMITH	9	9	BYRNE	
EASTHAM	10	10	MELIA	
HINTON	11	11	DOBSON	

Referee: Mr. A. E. Moore (Lowestoft, Suffolk)

Linesmen: Mr. D. W. Copp (Hemel Hempstead, Herts.) Mr. S. Fautley (Romford, Essex)

RESERVES (for both Teams): Macedo (Fulham), Crawford (Ipswich Town) and Barnwell (Arsenal)

uncapped players: Chelsea's Ken Shellito; Tony Kay of Everton; and Terry Paine. The three of them would get a warm-up in the Football League XI that faced an England XI on Cup Final eve at Highbury, a variation on the annual fixture in order to mark the FA's centenary.

And then they would tour, with a manager free of selectors. With the first two fixtures being against quality opposition, Terry was envisaging that Alf Ramsey might give him 'a consolation game' against the inferior Swiss.

CONSTANT PAINE

Cap 1: Bratislava, 29 May 1963 – Czechoslovakia 2 England 4

Czechoslovakia had not lost at home for five years. And, the previous summer, eight of their side had played in the World Cup Final in Santiago, when they were beaten 3-1 by Brazil. This included the half-back line of Pluskal, Popluhar and European Player of the Year, Josef Masopust, that would represent the Rest of the World at Wembley come October. It might be said that this was a side in decline – the Czechs would not win a match in 1963 – but Bobby Moore, captaining England for the first time in the absence of the injured Armfield, insisted that they 'were still a great side… the stars were all there: Popluhar, Novak, that magical man, Masopust.'

When the match-day programme went to press, Terry Paine was not expected to share the pitch with the star-studded hosts. But then Alf Ramsey leaned over the lunch table at their Bratislava hotel to surprise him with the news that he would be making his debut. This was, for *The Times*, 'an honour he has deserved. There is creative instinct in him and ball control, too. He merits his chance and we hope he will take it.'

There would appear to be no gainsaying that he took it well – helped, surely, by his having ideal targets for his creativity in the Tottenham duo, at inside-right and centre-forward, of Jimmy Greaves and Bobby Smith, with 28 and 10 caps, respectively.

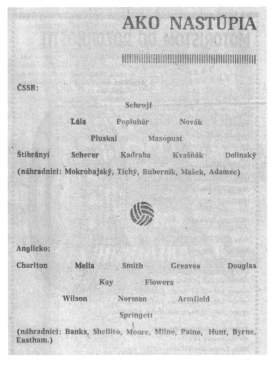

AKO NASTÚPIA

ČSSR:

Schroif

Lála   Popluhár   Novák

Pluskal   Masopust

Štibrányi   Scherer   Kadraba   Kvašňák   Dolinský

(náhradníci: Mokrohajský, Tichý, Bubernik, Mašek, Adamec)

Anglicko:

Charlton   Melia   Smith   Greaves   Douglas

Kay   Flowers

Wilson   Norman   Armfield

Springett

(náhradníci: Banks, Shellito, Moore, Milne, Paine, Hunt, Byrne, Eastham.)

His partner at No.8 – and we were still talking of wing 'partners' in 1963 – was Greaves. Terry had played with him only once before – on his Under-23 debut in 1960 – but had by now been partnering George O'Brien for four seasons. As noted in Chapter 6, not even the self-assured O'Brien would claim to be Greaves's equal – 'he was something else,' George reckons – but speak to anybody who played with O'Brien in that period and they'll rank him in Greaves's league, when it came to getting onto, and converting, a Paine cross. The difference, Terry reckons, is that Greaves was special in running on to a ball 'over the top.' Indeed, it seems to be agreed that, when it came to approaching the 'keeper one-on-one, there was nobody better than Greaves at beating him.

And, at No.9, there was Bobby Smith, a centre-forward of the 'on me 'ead, son' school of soccer science. While lacking the height of George Kirby, Terry's latest target at Southampton, Smith appreciated a winger who could cross to his head. He was accustomed to such international service from Charlton, the incumbent on the left, but found Paine to be an improvement on Douglas: 'Terry was a good crosser of a ball. He knew where to put it and you had to climb up and get it. Bryan Douglas was more of a dribbler. He *passed* the ball over and it didn't come over so strong.'

Both Greaves (2) and Smith were among the scorers in Bratislava. The three of them combined for England's fourth, as Smith fed Paine, who beat his full-back and crossed from the by-line for Greaves to score. By which time, a Paine pull-back from the by-line had set up Charlton for England's third. Greaves felt his new right-wing partner played 'with pace and poise' in what struck him as 'one of the most impressive performances by any England team on foreign soil.' Interviewed by *Ceskoslovensky Sport*, the Czechoslovak coach, Rudolf Vytlačil, had to 'admit that the English were better. They played in a manner that was quicker and more modern... above all, I admired Greaves with his striker's imagination and the two wingers with their impressive sweep towards goal.' Trainer Harold Shepherdson considered six of the side 'outstanding', including Paine, but reserved his 'man of the match' award for the other debutant, Shellito, at right-back.

Yet, as Jimmy Armfield came back for the rest of the tour, Shellito, dogged by injury, was destined to become a one-cap wonder. Paine, in contrast, had staked his claim to succeed Douglas.

Cap 2: Leipzig, 2 June 1963 – East Germany 1 England 2
After a bumpy flight to Leipzig, seven players, including Paine, went down with a stomach disorder. They had time to recover – unlike Greaves, who was abed with tonsillitis. So Liverpool's Roger Hunt came in to partner Paine, an early re-creation of their pairing in May's centenary match. Like Greaves, Hunt liked to play with a partner – he had Ian Callaghan at Anfield – who could get the ball over for him to score: 'I considered myself an inside-forward, linking up with the winger.' And he soon had cause to appreciate his winger, when Paine pulled an inviting ball back to him, 20 yards out, and 'it was one of those you just hit and it went straight in the top corner.' Paine was also involved in the winner, when he cut in, to be felled by the 'keeper taking his legs from under him, leaving Charlton with a tap-in.

All of which earned him headline status – PAINE OUTSTANDING – in *The Times,* whose reporter revelled in the performance of a player whose recent debut had been so 'impressive', and who now had 'another splendid match,' in which he was 'often prominent with his fast runs and accurate centres. He was complete master of the German left-back, whom he beat almost at will.'

And Laurie Pignon of the *Daily Sketch* concluded that 'Terry Paine is learning fast. He has even mastered the continental way of shielding the ball.'

For the final game of the tour, Ramsey made wholesale changes, with Bryan Douglas returning to score in an 8-1 win in Basle. According to Armfield, Douglas 'absolutely tore Switzerland to pieces,' but, then, Armfield, who'd played behind Douglas in the 1962 World Cup, considered him 'a terrific… real, top-class player.' Yet this would be his last game for England. As Douglas put it to Leo McKinstry, 'Alf was a thinking sort of guy… He thought me out of the game. Frankly, I don't think I did the job that he wanted.'

We can ponder, in Chapter 13, what it might have been that Ramsey wanted and consider whether Terry Paine ever succeeded in finding it. For the moment, though, the manager and his debutant winger were in the ascendancy: it had been, Brian Moore concluded, 'a tour without a failure. We all have our own ideas of the outstanding successes. Ramsey was one, of course; Paine was another and so was Charlton.'

Praise, indeed. Terry's reward would be a place in the five games that England played on British soil in 1963-64, beginning in Cardiff.

Cap 3: Cardiff, 12 October 1963 – Wales 0 England 4

As Ken Jones of the *Mirror* put it, when speculating on the likely line-up at Ninian Park, 'wingers Bobby Charlton and Terry Paine [were] virtually picking themselves' and he did not expect Ramsey to 'stray far from the men who brought England success in the summer.'

The programme notes were similarly approving of Terry's selection for a position that 'has been a trouble spot for England for a long time. But Paine could solve it.' This seems hard on Bryan Douglas, who had inherited Stanley Matthews's shirt six seasons ago and had worn it in a way that impressed his team-mates. Jimmy Armfield's star-rating of him has already been noted. If that's not good enough for you, pick up a handful of the various autobiographies churned out by Jimmy Greaves, who played with Douglas 19 times for England and enjoyed his 'wonderful skill'. You'll find that he not only picks Bryan for his Select England XI, but mischievously nominates him in his Top 20 of the many players he rated more skilful than Kevin Keegan.

The wingers who succeeded Douglas likewise admired him. John Connelly, his under-study in the 1962 finals, considered him an 'excellent out-and-out winger' whose 'dribble was quite fantastic,' while Paine himself 'would have thought he'd been a success. He was a very good player. I know a lot of players rated him, in terms of his performances, so I can't see where the problem was.'

Whatever the diagnosis, the next two games would confirm that Paine was, at least for the moment, Ramsey's remedy.

Cap 4: Wembley, 23 October 1963 – England 2 Rest of the World 1

Terry's fourth full international was 'a little bit special', he recollects. While the first game for the FA's centenary had been a parochial affair at Highbury, England were now entertaining, for the second celebratory game, a 16-man squad from around the world. The FA did its best to take the gloss off the occasion by taking a pompous stand against FIFA's proposal that all 16 guests might actually make an appearance. On the eve of the match, the FA Secretary surrendered, while claiming the moral high ground: 'while accepting it, we regret it. It has not been done with our approval. But FIFA are our guests and we are not going to enter into any dispute with this. England will not be doing the same thing.'

So the honour of playing hosts would be confined to 11 Englishmen. It may have been an exhibition match, but the sumptuousness of the opposition made it 'a massive game' not just for Paine, the newest member

of the team, delighted to be 'on the same stage with such a remarkable gathering of world-class players,' but even for the likes of Jimmy Greaves and Scotland's Denis Law, each a year younger than Terry, but with 52 caps already between them.

Reliving the game for me 40-odd years later, Law was still in awe of the Rest of the World forwards with whom he lined up: 'To think I was in a forward line with my hero – Di Stefano from Real Madrid – and Gento from Real Madrid; and Kopa from Real Madrid; and Eusebio from Benfica. Hey! Excuse me!' And that was only in the first-half: Ferenc Puskas came off the bench at half-time and Uwe Seeler joined him in time to be part of the build-up for Law's equalising goal.

Law was much involved, too, in England's opener. A landmark in Paine's career, it merits a detailed account. When Law lost the ball in the England half, it was played up to Paine, just past the half-way line. His duel with his marker, West Germany's Karl-Heinz Schnellinger, struck Bob Ferrier as 'a fascinating little *obligato* within the wider context of the match, Paine challenging boldly with his close dribbling a positive, boisterous full-back.' Those challenges had mainly entailed taking the ball up to Schnellinger and trying to pass him on the outside; but now, in the 65th minute, Terry varied the routine to memorable effect. He cut inside, carried the ball forward and then played it to the feet of Bobby Smith at the edge of the penalty area. The centre-forward spun into the inside-right channel and looped the ball

Amid the debris that remains of the Rest of the World defence,
Terry Paine (No.7) turns to celebrate his goal.
The other players are (*left to right*): Soskic, Schnellinger (part-hidden), Eyzaguirre, Greaves, Popluhar, Smith (coming to join the celebration of his cross), Pluskal and Law (supine).

back into the middle of the goal, in the direction of Greaves, hovering near the six-yard line, but closely attended. At this point, Law, who had hared back to redeem himself, leapt, all arms and legs, to intercept. He failed to connect but seemed to create a distraction for Greaves and his escort. The ball ricocheted back off Greaves's toe and Paine, who had continued his diagonal run, was in prime poaching position to score – a magical moment, diminished only by the fact that there had been a change of goalkeeper at half-time:

> Unfortunately, it wasn't Lev Yashin in goal – you'd like to beat the great Man-in-Black, wouldn't you? It was Soskic, the Yugoslav goalkeeper; but, nevertheless, to open the scoring was great.

The legendary Russian 'keeper was not, as it happened, wearing his famous all-black strip that day, but you know what Terry means. Then, 'minutes later', as Greaves recalled in 2003, 'a series of seductive passes between Uwe Seeler, Denis Law and Puskas' brought about the equaliser. Forty years on, Jimmy was still 'in awe of making mention of a move involving Seeler, Law, Puskas… in the same team.' In the dying minutes, Greaves's own 'dream came true', as he scored the winner.

All of which tells us why, exhibition match or not, the hosts raised their game – playing, their trainer reckoned, 'as well as I have ever seen an England eleven play.'

Terry Paine had reason to be pleased, not just with his first full international goal but with his acclaimed performance against Schnellinger. All in all, the match was, in his estimation, the first (chronologically) of the top three highlights in his England career. The third would be his 19th and last. The second was only four weeks away…

Cap 5: Wembley, 20 November 1963 – England 8 Northern Ireland 3

This was an evening of Wembley firsts: the first full international to be staged under its floodlights; and the first hat-trick to be scored, there, by an England No.7 (Stanley Matthews's three against Czechoslovakia in 1937 having been at White Hart Lane).

Terry Paine not only contributed that historic hat-trick; he had a hand in four of the other goals, including three of Greaves's four. While applauding the way in which the right-wing pair 'did almost as they liked,' Harold Shepherdson rated Gordon Milne, their supply-line, 'the best player on the field.' Inevitably, the seven goals from Paine and Greaves grabbed the headlines: GREAVES AND PAINE A SUPERB RIGHT WING, said *The Times*. Paine's second goal again demonstrated, as against the Rest of the World, his sense of when to pop into the box, the way he felt Ramsey appreciated. As *The Times* described it, 'Eastham flowed up to the left by-line and now it was Paine, at the near post, to volley in the cross. The positional switching was bewildering and the finishing on the mark. Another great goal in fact.'

Ken Jones of the *Daily Mirror* described the goals by the Paine-Greaves partnership as 'the jewels that will sparkle in the memory,' while 'Observer' went further in the *Echo*:

> The question many of the 55,000 spectators were asking after the game was: have England ever fielded a better right-wing pair than Paine and Jimmy Greaves, who between them scored seven of the goals?

The FA *Year Book* answered that question: this was 'one of the most devastating partnerships in international football since the War.' Impressed by 'the deadliness' of Paine's finishing, 'Observer' also rejoiced that 'his speed, ball control and accurate centring were of the highest order.' This might, he feared, be double-edged: it would 'almost certainly keep him in the national side for some time to come [but would] undoubtedly make many First Division sides anxious to secure his services.' Tottenham was the most talked-about prospect. Given how well he had been playing with Greaves and Smith, that is hardly surprising, although, as noted in Chapter 9, Greaves denies ever 'tapping up' his right-wing partner on Spurs' behalf.

With Terry on such a high, there would now be a five-month hiatus in the international calendar, but he would be called, for the first time, to Football League duty: a 2-2 draw with the Scottish League, come March, at Roker Park.

Cap 6: Hampden Park, 11 April 1964 – Scotland 1 England 0

With his future club-mate, Campbell Forsyth, making his debut in the home goal, Paine now played before the biggest crowd he had ever known: 133,245 at Hampden Park. Whoever was compiling the 'Programme Notes' on the England line-ups was at it again: Paine, 'a strong raider with a powerful shot,' was acclaimed as the 'fleet-footed, all-action forager' who had 'solved a perplexing problem for England.'

If that sounds like a job description for a Ramsey winger, the manager had an additional task in mind, on this occasion, for his outside right: he could help to stop the left-sided progress of Jim Baxter, the Scottish play-maker. Terry well remembers that assignment: 'the idea – moving, I suppose, more into that 4-3-3 mode, even then – was that, if I could just tuck-in while the play was on the other side, then, if he got it, I could confront him and try to hold him up.'

So would this confrontation require him to tackle Baxter?

No, just get my body in between him and wherever he was trying to go with the ball. That's what they say: you 'confront' players – you position yourself so that you're the next obstacle; then the man who's supposed to be picking him up can do the job. I can remember that, on at least two occasions, I did it very successfully. Unfortunately, he rolled the ball through my legs – *twice*. Even though I kept my knees together, he seemed to have that tremendous ability to be able to roll it through your legs. That was a little bit embarrassing.

Even so, Ken Jones told his *Mirror* readers that Paine had stuck so well to his task that he had forced Baxter 'into error and finally into ineffectiveness.' Jones was, however, disappointed that, going forward, 'Terry Paine still takes his man on too late and where there is no space into which he can run.' Yet Mike Payne, in his *Complete Record,* suggests that some 'telling' crosses from Paine, late on, might have saved it for England. In sum, Payne rated Terry one of Ramsey's better players in what was generally a 'poor' show by England.

Other observers were less impressed with Paine's achievements at either end of the field: *The Times* felt that the link-up between Baxter and Law was the key to Scotland's superiority, while the *FA Yearbook* named Terry among the England players who had been 'well below their best.' As *The Times* saw it, neither Paine nor Charlton was managing 'to pass their full-backs on the outside or make for dangerous positions near the by-line' – until midway through the second half, when Paine did get to the danger zone and crossed to Charlton, whose shot was blocked.

Cap 7: Wembley, 6 May 1964 – England 2 Uruguay 1

Having played in his fifth successive eve-of-Cup-Final match – promoted to the 'England' XI for the first time – Paine now rounded off a season in which he had featured in all of England's five matches. Although he helped to set up England's 1-0 interval lead in this game – flicking a pass from Greaves onward to Johnny Byrne, who duly scored – *The Times* could hardly have been more disappointed: 'if there was an English failure, it was Paine, who, with the impetuousness of youth, tried to overdo his dribbling against Pavoni, who read his cards cleverly to block him time after time when a more quickly released ball would have paid England and Paine better.'

Three days later, Paine was at outside-right in the Football League side that lost 1-0 to the Italian League in the San Siro. Peter Thompson was on the left, but switched to the right, to the exclusion of Paine, for England's next two games that month: away wins against Portugal and the Republic of Ireland. Although he was playing on the left for Liverpool, with Ian Callaghan on the right, Thompson would be capped, like Connelly,

*on both flanks. He would continue to demonstrate that versatility on the summer tour to
the Americas, alternating between playing on the left, with Paine on the right, and on the
right, with Charlton on the left.*

Cap 8: New York, 27 May 1964 – USA 0 England 10

It was Terry's turn at No.7, with Roger Hunt inside him. As in that romp,
six months before, against Northern Ireland, the right flank dominated the
scoring: Paine got two, while Hunt scored four, making him what the
'American Football Correspondent' of *The Times* described as the 'chief
net-bender', as the home defence struggled 'to keep the English forwards
from taking up permanent residence in front of the American citadel in a
shoot-for-goal spree.'

This spree was watched by a gathering of 5,062, which included a dozen
sailors from Liverpool, who horrified the *Times* correspondent by sporting
their Union Flag upside-down, and by Nicky Nickson, a mentor from
Terry's Corinthian days of Chapter 2, who had emigrated to America:
'I heard he was coming, so I called him at his hotel. *Guess* who answered the
'phone! Jimmy Greaves! He was his room-mate.'

Terry duly met Nicky before the game, to deliver some complimentary
tickets and appreciative remarks: upon being introduced to Nicky's party, he
'said something like "this is the guy who taught me a lot of things when I
was a nipper".' The seats were near the tunnel, which enabled Terry to make
a promise to his guests as he came out for the second half: 'he came over to
us and said "I'm going to score a goal for you".' Inside five minutes of what
the Reuters report called a 'dazzling 25-minute spell' by him, Paine beat two
men and netted from the edge of the area – although it was deflected by the
left-back, Andy Racz, whom he had 'kept in a daze.' Reuters initially chalked
this up as an own goal, but it was eventually credited to Paine. He added
another, with a lob from a narrow angle, before Fred Pickering, a debutant
at No.9, completed his hat-trick with the 10th goal. All that remained was
for Terry to remove his shirt at the end, hand it to Nicky and make sure that
Reuters knew that.

*The party now moved on to Brazil, to participate in a four-team tournament, with
Argentina, Portugal and the host nation, that was branded as the 'Little World Cup'.
Switching to the right for England's opening game in Rio, a 5-1 drubbing by Brazil,
Thompson alone distinguished himself, running at his opponents 'with tremendous
confidence and strength' in what George Cohen rated 'the game of his life.'*

*Next stop São Paulo, where the squad watched Argentina beat Brazil 3-0.
Declaring the game a 'tactical disaster' for Brazil, the Rio sports daily, Jornal dos
Sports, concluded that the home nation had been confounded by a 4-4-2 formation,
although various reports of the tournament have suggested that Argentina went through*

three different formations in their three games, this being the occasion for 5-3-2. However you do the numbers, the fact is that Argentina fielded a defender, Messiano, in the No.11 shirt, his 'mission' being, in the eyes of the Jornal dos Sports, *to 'strengthen the Argentine midfield, where the game was won, by marking Pelé out of the game.'*

Pelé's head-butting of his marker and other hot-headedness, on and off the field, have been well-documented and need not retain us here. Gordon Banks has suggested that having to duck and dive to avoid being hit by fruit thrown by the Brazilian fans prevented the England party from learning much about either team, but the Jornal dos Sports *reporter was surely nearer the mark in his assessment that 'the English party watched the disaster of the Brazilian team with amazement, as if they were witnessing the flood or the Day of Judgment. They could not believe that this was the same [Brazilian] team that had put on a show' against them.*

George Cohen told David Miller that it was 'one of the best displays I had yet seen… There was a lot Alf learned from that visit.' That was doubtless the case, but just what those lessons were with respect to Ramsey's future formations has remained a debatable question, which can be addressed in Chapter 13. Meanwhile, England and Portugal had a game to play.

Cap 9: São Paulo, 4 June 1964 – Portugal 1 England 1

Frank McGhee predicted, in the *Mirror,* that Charlton 'would be replaced by Terry Paine, a man who will obey orders to stay out on the wing.' He was right. Thompson switched to the left, with Paine coming in on the right. As the Portuguese reporter, José Valente, saw it in *Mundo Desportivo,* Terry 'played a lot on the halfway line, the English preferring to put up front the four men with greater finishing power' – Greaves, Byrne, Hunt and Thompson.

If that seems an unusual description of Thompson, who would never score for England, this reporter found him 'the most enterprising' of the English forwards 'and also the most dangerous, with his speed and fighting spirit.' But whereas Thompson had played in Lisbon the previous month – his debut at outside-right – Paine was the surprise package for the Portuguese press, with the 'skills to deceive our defence,' as Alfredo Farinha put it in *A Bola,* 'and create danger for our goal.' Terry told the *Echo* that a stubbed toe didn't handicap him but blamed 'the very bumpy state of the pitch' for a poor showing by England, generally.

Although his marker, Pedro Gomes, gradually 'got to grips' with him, Farinha felt, that didn't stop Terry hitting the bar. Greaves was similarly denied. Hunt succeeded in scoring and the only other incident of note seems to have been the dismissal of José Torres for man-handling the Brazilian referee, after a Portuguese 'goal' had been disallowed. As Greaves has laconically summed up, 'both Terry Paine and I hit the bar, Torres hit the referee.'

The England side that drew in São Paulo.
Back row (*left to right*): Thomson, Norman, Banks, Flowers, Wilson, Moore.
Front: Paine, Greaves, Byrne, Hunt, Thompson.

That was Terry's only game of the tournament. It seems generally to have been agreed that Thompson – his rival for the No.7 shirt, so long as Charlton remained a fixture at No.11 – was the success of the tour, to the extent that he was nick-named, in the home media, 'The White Pelé'.

England completed a humbling tournament by losing 1-0 to Argentina, but they would have an unbeaten 1964-65 campaign: a five-match season, followed by a three-game European tour. Paine would be back for the first match.

Cap 10: Belfast, 3 October 1964 – Northern Ireland 3 England 4

As in his previous appearance, Paine had the No.7 shirt, while Thompson was at No.11, with Charlton moving inside. Paine laid on the cross for Pickering to open the scoring and then helped Greaves to the third goal of a first-half hat-trick. A second-half fight-back was not quite enough for the Irish to level it.

Paine was back in Belfast at the end of the month, scoring for the Football League in a 4-0 win against the Irish League. And come March, he would be partnering Greaves at Hampden in a 2-2 draw with the Scottish League. But he was out of the England reckoning for four games, as Thompson now had a run at No.7. Nor is it clear that Ramsey was planning to bring him back for the end-of-season fixtures. But having been a late replacement for Connelly in the annual eve-of-Final match, he returned to the

England line-up five days later, with Charlton injured and Thompson having played the evening before, when Liverpool took a 3-1 lead against Inter Milan in the first leg of the European Cup semi-final.

Cap 11: Wembley, 5 May 1965 – England 1 Hungary 0

Since Paine's previous appearance, Jack Charlton and Stiles had made their debuts and the 'back six' (in shirt-number order) of Banks, Cohen, Wilson, Stiles, Charlton J and Moore was now establishing itself. Indeed, this was a watershed game, in that it was the last time this defence would appear with a 'front five' that included no player who would appear in the World Cup Final the following summer.

Taking advantage of Ramsey's sudden shortage of wingers, Paine laid on the game's only goal for Greaves. It was a triumph, as Alan Bennett recorded it for the *FA News,* for forwards switching positions to outwit the Hungarians' off-side tactics: centre-forward Barry Bridges drew his marker out to the right wing, leaving Paine, who'd slotted into the inside-right channel, to thread a diagonal ball through the Hungarian rearguard for Greaves to score.

Terry told the *Mirror* that he 'knew that a reasonable game against Hungary would get me a match on tour. I always knew I was good enough, but I got into a bit of a rut after a disappointing season.' Statistically, he had had a good enough season with Southampton – ever-present and averaging

The watershed line-up against Hungary, consisting of the 'back six' who were about to become established, and a 'front five', none of whom would play in the World Cup Final. Back row (*left to right*): Stiles, Charlton J, Banks, Wilson, Moore, Cohen, Harold Shepherdson. Front: Paine, Bridges, Greaves, Eastham, Connelly.

a goal every three games – but, in end-of-season reflections for the *Echo,* he described it as 'a patchy season for me…. Something went wrong somewhere.' Be that as it may, he had lost his England place, in this patchy season, to Thompson. It was ironic, then, that Thompson was now paying the price for Liverpool's success in Europe.

Indeed, Paine would get to play in all three matches on England's European tour. The injured Charlton would not be travelling, while Thompson and Connelly would both be making side-trips, across Europe, for their clubs that would clash with the second game in Nuremberg.

Cap 12: Belgrade, 9 May 1965 – Yugoslavia 1 England 1
Alan Ball made his debut at No.10, as England became the first-ever foreign side to avoid defeat in a full international in Belgrade. As Max Marquis saw it, the debutant 'did well, although not as well as Paine, who gave the great Jusufi an uncomfortable game.'

But the *Daily Mirror*'s Frank McGhee blamed Paine for allowing Popovic to set up the home side's opener, as he 'made no more than a feeble flourish… in a situation that screamed for a crunching tackle.' Terry redeemed himself in McGhee's eyes, however, when he implemented the manager's stratagem for corner-kicks. Having directed his first corner towards Jack Charlton, he watched three defenders move to guard Charlton at the far post as he prepared for his next attempt. Then he 'hit a short, fast ball' to the near post where Barry Bridges rounded off Ramsey's plan with 'a masterly glancing header.'

That did not mollify *The Times,* which continued to lament the absence of Thompson, who had been taken ill, and Charlton. *Football Monthly* was impressed, however, by the way in which Paine and Connelly created 'endless problems' for the Yugoslav defence.

Cap 13: Nuremberg, 12 May 1965 – West Germany 0 England 1
With Thompson recovered but now in Milan for Liverpool's second leg, while Connelly was in Strasbourg for Manchester United, Everton's outside left, Derek Temple, was one of two debutants, the other being Mick Jones of Sheffield United at No.9. Ramsey 'drilled' his makeshift team 'to play 4-3-3 in this game,' Harold Shepherdson has recalled, 'and finally proved that this type of formation was best suited to our style.'

Many an account of this game has Paine in the midfield threesome, with Ball in the front three. Neither Ball nor Paine has remembered it that way. In their versions, Ball was in midfield, sharing the play-making work with Eastham, while Paine was on the right of the front three, with Temple on the left and Jones between them. In other words, the front three included two orthodox wingers, albeit with scoring reputations. True, this particular variation might never have been tried in Nuremberg, had Greaves not been injured in Belgrade, but here was an extreme demonstration that a 4-3-3 line-up need not mean that a side is 'wingless'.

I shall return, in Chapter 13, to the issue of how and why a winger – usually only one, though – was an option in this formation. The point about the line-up, in Nuremberg – and elsewhere on that tour – is that it predated, by 40 years, the system that Chelsea were using in 2005, which Alan Ball saw as a replica: 'it makes me laugh,' he told me at the start of the 2005-06 season,

> that people talk of this *new* formation and new systems that are being played now. Chelsea play 4-5-1. *Do* they play 4-5-1? They play Robben on one wing and they play Duff on the other. So when they've got the ball they play 4-3-3. And they play with two [midfielders who can then join the attack] and Makelele sits. Right! Now let's go back to 1965, England playing with a flat back-four, five in midfield – Connelly, or Temple it was in Germany; Paine; Ball; Eastham; and Stiles sitting [Stiles was, in fact, with his club in Strasbourg, so Ron Flowers was temporarily in the sitting role]. But the two up-and-down wingers made it three in midfield: We [Ball and Eastham] played as a two and [Flowers] sat. Chelsea are playing *exactly* the same – with this 'new' formation that is taking English football by storm. We played that system in Nuremberg in 1965 – and won! And Terry Paine got the goal.

Indeed, he did – and the other winger set it up. Neither Paine nor Temple can recollect being 'drilled' as to his role. Terry doesn't recall this variation on 4-3-3 as being 'a particular ploy: we were just two wide players in that particular formation. I can't remember any particular plan.' It seems to have been a case of the two wide men doing, naturally, what the formation demanded of them. Temple, playing like a real winger, 'managed', as he modestly recollects,

> to get down the wing – which wingers are supposed to do and get crosses in for people to score in front of the goal. I got down to the by-line and pulled it across, low. And Terry had come in off the other line and it was a good poacher's goal, really: it came to him and he whacked it in.'

Just like that. All very workman-like. Yet Max Marquis saw it as proof of 'the value of wingers… emphasised by Paine's brilliance, who scored the only goal, laid on by the other winger, Temple.' The *Times* described it as 'a superbly executed goal,' while the *Mirror*'s Frank McGhee admired the way in which 'Terry Paine, always the coolest, cleverest, most menacing England attacker, was there. He checked, aimed, fired right-footed, and we had won.'

And it certainly impressed the injured Greaves, who can 'remember sitting on the touch-line, watching Terry score the winner. I can see him scoring it now: he just drove in at the near post.'

The 1-0 win, which retained England's record of never having lost to West Germany, generally excited the English press. The only dissentient voice came from the *Sun,* whose Steve Richards objected to some of the tourists' unsavoury tactics. These included a moment of what he called 'unarmed combat' – this was England v Germany and you couldn't expect the *Sun*'s metaphors to be subtle – by Paine, which had Höttges, his marker, 'sinking into the turf in agony.'

Terry's goal would achieve an unwelcome status in the record-books: it would remain the last winning goal scored by an England player on German soil until Michael Owen's hat-trick in the 5-1 win in Munich in 2001.

Cap 14: Gothenburg, 16 May 1965 – Sweden 1 England 2

Arriving in Sweden, Frank McGhee wondered how Ramsey could possibly 'leave out Terry Paine, … who has blossomed into the outstanding individual star of the attack,' so as to accommodate Thompson, returning from European duty with Liverpool. The manager resolved it by declaring Thompson 'worn out', although Connelly, flying in from Strasbourg, was deemed fresh enough to play.

Ramsey was rewarded when his two wide men produced what McGhee described as 'the expected mixture of guile, grace, guts and graft' and 'a great through ball' by Paine put Connelly in to score.

So thanks to Thompson's triple whammy – illness, Liverpool's European success and fatigue – Paine had played in all three tour matches at his expense. Marquis considered him 'the great revelation of the tour' and even the hard-to-please *Times* acknowledged his 'successful tour.' While not doubting that Peter Thompson would be playing in the World Cup finals in 14 months' time, the *Times* correspondent nevertheless conceded that Paine might 'yet maintain a challenge next season at outside-right.'

That was to miss a trick: the one to watch would henceforth be Alan Ball, who had scored England's opener in Gothenburg – his first for his country. This would be the last time Paine and he played together for England: they would henceforth be competing, effectively, for the No.7 shirt, as Thompson drifted out of the reckoning.

Chapter 12

...Or Does It?

Alf Ramsey's England had now had 23 games on their road to the World Cup finals of 1966. Terry Paine had played in 14 of them.

Ramsey now had a further 15 games in which to prepare for the final tournament: 12 full internationals; two Football League representative matches; and the annual fixture against Young England, all of which would effectively be public 'trials' in a nine-month build-up to the tournament.

Ken Jones reasoned, in the *Mirror*, that there could 'be no argument about the choice of wingers Terry Paine and John Connelly because no-one has produced the form to suggest a change.' And that's how it would be for the first two of the 15 'trials', with Charlton at No.10.

Cap 15: Cardiff, 2 October 1965 – Wales 0 England 0
Paine's quick throw almost set up Greaves in the first minute, but this would be, for *The Times,* 'one of his few good acts of the day.'

Cap 16: Wembley, 20 October 1965 – England 2 Austria 3
The same formation again. And the same tune from *The Times*, for whom Paine did 'his one really good deed of the night' when he intercepted an Austrian miscue and hit 'a beautiful central through-pass [which] found Charlton on the move' and striding through to 'crack' an early opener. Puzzled by the way in which Terry subsequently spent more time helping George Cohen to defend the right flank than 'in the role of a thrusting winger,' *The Times* predicted that heads would roll and especially nominated Paine, Stiles and Bridges for the chop.

The fall-out was far worse than that. The next 'England' game was three weeks away, but the team for the third game in Ramsey's 'trials' – the Football League against the League of Ireland – was announced the day after the defeat by Austria. It showed nine changes, 'ample enough commentary,' The Times *reasoned, on Ramsey's view of 'the sad Austrian affair'. Bridges was gone for good. Stiles, who was not winning over* The Times, *was replaced by a future Saint, Burnley's Brian O'Neil, who was welcomed as perhaps 'the man England need urgently in midfield instead of Stiles.'*

Paine made way for Thompson, who remained in favour for the next England game, a fortnight later, against Northern Ireland. The Daily Mail *now conducted a forensic analysis of the respective merits of Paine and Thompson, based on games played at the end of November 1965. Their results will be better discussed in the next chapter, but the analysts were continuing to miss the point: the player who would wear No.7 in England's next four games was Alan Ball, starting with a 2-0 win in Madrid in December, the major significance of which is also explored in the next chapter.*

Cap 17: Wembley, 4 May 1966 – England 2 Yugoslavia 0

With Liverpool due to play Borussia Dortmund in the European Cup-Winners' Cup, the following evening, there were places available. As Martin Peters made his debut at No.4, this was due to be the first time Ramsey played both Ball and him in the same line-up. But an injury to Ball meant a return for Paine. It also meant that there would be only two men in midfield – Peters and Charlton, playing his second successive game in the No.9 shirt – to the joy of those journalists who had not taken to 4-3-3. Thus *The Times* rejoiced that, 'on this occasion at least,' Ramsey had 'largely shelved his 4-3-3 – "bingo" football, as it is now called – for the more orthodox 4-2-4.' Such was his preference for orthodoxy that the man from *The Times* even welcomed back Paine, as this meant 'the return of working wingers in Paine and Tambling, both goal-scorers.'

The fact that both of them played well 'was probably a mixed blessing,' Marquis has mischievously suggested, for Ramsey. But *The Times* was less ambivalent: never mind that Paine had set up a headed goal for Greaves – Charlton got the other – he hereupon slid down their man's list of wingers for the preferred 4-2-4 formation, with Ian Callaghan now being championed for a first cap at No.7. But, then, this correspondent also felt the need for 'a sharper finisher at this level than Hurst.'

This rare peep into the Wembley dressing room shows some of the team changing for the game against Yugoslavia.

(*Left to right*): Wilson, Peters, Charlton J, Hunter, Paine, Greaves and Charlton R.

Terry now had three games in which to clinch promotion with Southampton, before reporting for the final phase of England's World Cup build-up. Two outside-lefts – Derek Temple and Gordon Harris, one-cap wonders each – were among those unceremoniously discarded from Ramsey's long-list of 40: Temple recalls reading of his de-selection in the press. With Bobby Charlton now establishing himself as a deep-lying No.9, the squad of 27 that assembled at Lilleshall on 6 June included four wingers and arguably a fifth. Two of the five – Connelly and Thompson – had played on both wings for England; Paine and the uncapped Callaghan were in consideration only on the right; while Tambling's three caps had all been at No.11, although he had long since forsaken Chelsea's left-wing to become a goal-scoring phenomenon at inside-forward.

After a fortnight at Lilleshall, the party had to be reduced to 22. Tambling was omitted and so, to considerable amazement, was Thompson, who had thought he was 'bound to be in the 22.' Yet Callaghan was in. Their Liverpool team-mate, Roger Hunt, was 'made up for Ian, but on that tour to South America in '64, Peter had been England's best player and looked a definite not only to make the squad but the team. Two years is a long time in football, though.' Indeed. Their surprise was shared by Callaghan himself, who had not expected to be ahead of his Liverpool wing-mate in Ramsey's reckoning.

Armfield – a considerable admirer of Douglas, as we have seen – had played behind his successors long enough to be able to weigh them up. He feels that Thompson had given Ramsey 'something different, but Alf went for the more purposeful type of player, like Callaghan or Paine, as opposed to Peter who was a flyer – and clever.'

The 22 were not only identified at this point; they were numbered. The 'back six', who by now almost picked themselves, were Nos.1-6. With Greaves and Charlton equally

Terry Paine leads the 27-man squad out for training at Lilleshall. Following just behind him are three of the other wingers waiting to see which of them will remain in the 22: Thompson and Connelly on the left of the photo, alongside right-half Milne; and Callaghan, far right.

automatic at Nos. 8 and 9, the only question was who would get the remaining three 'prime' numbers. The answers were Ball 7; Hurst 10; and Connelly 11. Peters, whose only cap to date had been in midfield, would wear No.16, while the other three players who would get an outing in the final tournament – Paine, Callaghan and Hunt – were numbered 19-21.

There were those who took this numbering to mean that Ramsey was flagging up his 1st XI – his 'World Cup team' as Moore saw it – and his 11 reserves. Peters certainly saw it that way: 'you didn't need to be a genius to work out that the first 11 numbers went to Alf's proposed first-choice team, and I wasn't in it.' And so did a disappointed Hunt, who thought his two recent goals at Hampden might have got him the No.10 shirt ahead of Hurst. But Ramsey was not going to unpack the meaning of the numbers for Hunt or anybody else: 'that wasn't Alf's way,' Roger reflected. 'He probably thought I'd be delighted just to be there.'

Perhaps the truth is that Ramsey was hoping to fool people. Leo McKinstry sees it as 'just another example of Alf's campaign of disinformation, designed to leave everyone – press, opposition and his own team alike – guessing about his intentions.' That guessing would continue when the team that lined up in Helsinki, for the first game of a four-match tour, included five of the also-rans, with Callaghan making a successful debut on the right wing, as England beat Finland 3-0. Having assumed that the Nos.1-11 indicated Ramsey's 'strongest team', Callaghan nevertheless wondered, after this performance, whether he 'might have a chance.' But he would stand down for the rest of the tour, as the Paine v Ball contest resumed.

Cap 18: Oslo, 29 June 1966 – Norway 1 England 6

For the second time in his England career, Greaves scored four. But Paine was not on the score-sheet this time, although he did combine with Connelly to set up Jimmy's fourth.

Ball now came in for the games against Denmark and Poland. Shepherdson's view of the latter game in Chorzow was that 'the time for experiments was over. Alf fielded his strongest team.' It excluded Nos.10 and 11 – Hurst and Connelly – in favour of Hunt and Peters. That 'was a bit of choker' for Connelly, who 'was feeling really confident, buzzing,' and hoping that the man wearing No.11 was, indeed, in the 1st XI. But having watched a 'brilliant' 1-0 win over Poland, Connelly thought 'that's it': England would be starting wingless at Wembley in six days' time.

It was not that simple. All 22 players had had a run-out in a highly successful tour: all four matches had been won, with just that one goal in Oslo conceded. And however his trainer might label the line-up in Chorzow, Ramsey was not to be double-guessed.

Upon returning to England, the players were allowed a day at home, before reporting to Hendon Hall – a switch, as McKinstry describes it, from what Jack Charlton called the 'gulag' at Lilleshall to the 'oak-beamed tranquility' of a North London hotel. Tranquil, maybe; but the management team was keen, according to Shepherdson, to avoid too much relaxation indoors – good news for those like Terry Paine who didn't fancy card-schools. The players could relax in outdoor activities. Like cricket.

It wasn't serious cricket, Jack Charlton explains. The pitch was only the length of his living room and the game was played 'with a tennis ball and it was a case of somebody spinning balls at you and you playing shots. Everybody surrounds the batter and you weren't to hit the ball too far, because it would go out onto the main road or it would go out of the garden. It was quite a big garden but not that big that you would slog anything.' They had more room at their Roehampton training headquarters, but the game still involved encircling the batsman, more like French Cricket than the real thing.

With four days to go before the World Cup opener against Uruguay,
it's time for cricket at the squad's Roehampton training ground.
As Bobby Charlton bats, the fielders are (*left to right*) Paine, Stiles and Springett.

Ray Wilson reckoned to play cards but not cricket – 'I come from a mining village, where everybody thought cricket was a fairy's game' – but there is photographic evidence that he was roped in, proof perhaps of Geoff Hurst's contention that Ramsey would brook no exemptions from group activities. 'Alf wouldn't allow anybody to do their own thing,' Hurst explains. 'If the squad was playing cricket, then there'd be nobody doing something completely different.' If that is a slight exaggeration, it seems that, by and large, 'everybody conformed to what the group was doing, whether it was eating, drinking, playing cricket or going to the cinema. Everybody did everything together and that was one of the organisational and discipline things that Alf was famous for' – all of which, Hurst reckons, 'was important for the squad.'

Ramsey was determined to prevent cliques and to stop club-mates always hanging out together – Gerry Byrne recalls how 'Alf told us [Liverpool players] off for being together' – and extended this to rotating who roomed with whom. This was potentially to the advantage of those like Paine and Cohen, who had no club-mates in the squad. Even so, Alan Ball, himself so quick to settle in among his elders, soon noticed that Terry 'was very much a loner. He kept himself to himself quite a lot. In the thick of things – the card-schools and that – he wasn't really a member of what goes on within a squad of players, where cards are concerned and the banter and what-have-you.' Terry participated fully, though, in an activity run by Ball and Eastham, the self-appointed Hendon Hall 'bookies' who chalked up the racing odds on a big black-board.

One way or another, the various memoirs vouch for the camaraderie that Ramsey thereby achieved. And the 'good harmony' extended across the entire squad, Eastham insists: 'It was a good set-up. Alf had got 22 of the best players he could possibly get and there were no arguments at all. He achieved a 'family' team: it was together. It didn't matter whether you played or you didn't play – you still were supportive of the people who played.' Jimmy Armfield, who was effectively the captain of the 11 not chosen for a particular game – 'my lot' as he calls them – believes passionately that England's strength lay in having 22 men who were ready to play and to acquit themselves well.

Contrary to Connelly's assumption after Chorzow, Ramsey did not go wingless into the opening game against Uruguay. Ball kept his place on the right because, he reasoned, Ramsey felt that this

was a typical Alan Ball game – that it was going to be tough game, that it was going to be a hard-working game, that it was going to be a typical opening game of most World Cup finals – that it's 0-0 or 1-1. You're terrified to lose in the first game of a round-robin and so he played me, tucked-in a little bit, on the right side. He was a little bit cautious on that one.

But that doesn't explain why he brought in Connelly for Peters on the left. Perhaps it meant that, for all of his experimenting, the manager still felt the need for at least one winger? As George Cohen has put it, 'the old full-back still couldn't find it in himself' to accept that 'the deeply established idea' that you must have 'a specialist winger, despite all the possible compensations, had been dismembered.'

Brian Glanville's complaint was that Ramsey should have used two wingers, so as to stretch the Uruguayan rearguard. Callaghan would have been his choice on the right, in place of Ball, 'who will never be a winger if he lives to a hundred.'

Playing in this game, and then narrowly failing to score, did not help Connelly's chances of participating in the later stages of the tournament. 'It was such a drab game,' he recalls. 'They never came out at all. It was the first time we'd ever experienced a really tight defence like that. The 4-3-3 formation suited my style, really. But there was nowhere to run – no channels – because they just marked zones. You'd just run into players. We just couldn't break them down.' As a wide man selected to find a way through, Connelly feels that, 'if I hadn't played in the first game, I think I'd have been on the road.' Even so, this might not have been his last game for England if he had scored: 'a couple of chances fell to me – not sitters, but slight chances.'

When the manager asked him how he felt about his omission for the next game, John told Ramsey "'to be honest with you, I feel sick. But, in all fairness, you've always been very, very fair with me." His words were: "I'm not being fair with you now because, if we had come away with a result, I'd not have changed the team".'

As it was, Ramsey left out not only Connelly – for Peters – but also Ball: for Paine. As Ball saw it, the change on the right was a logical corollary of the 'caution' that had achieved the draw against Uruguay: now 'they had to win the next one, so then the best way to win games – and you can lose them – would be to open it out. So he left me out.' But how was this formation any less 'cautious' than the one used against Uruguay if the wide-player was being forgone on the left? The only logical explanation could be that Paine was a better attacking option than Connelly, which is what Ken Jones implied in welcoming the introduction of Paine, whose 'all-round appetite for the game and [whose] ability to go beyond the full-backs along the touchline suggest an improvement in England's ultimate aggression.'

Cap 19: Wembley, 16 July 1966 – England 2 Mexico 0

Reporting for the *Sunday Express*, Alan Hoby applauded the two changes, whereby England were 'lifted to new levels by two newcomers, the gifted Martin Peters and the intelligent Terry Paine.' Apart from a description of how 'Paine jinked in and beautifully beat a lunging Mexican before passing,' Hoby makes no further reference, however, to the contribution of the 'intelligent' wide man on the right. But his report is appended by the

The team for the game against Mexico.
Back row (*left to right*): Cohen, Peters, Banks, Stiles, Moore.
Front: Greaves, Charlton J, Paine, Wilson, Hunt, Charlton R.

manager's post-match statement, which includes a bulletin on the injuries incurred. Thus, 'Terry Paine was concussed from a blow in the face in the first minute, which set his nose bleeding. He was hurt again 20 minutes from the end.'

This is the only reference I have ever seen to the injury in the game's last quarter. And there's no prospect of Paine's recalling what happened and how, as his first-minute bang means that he has no memories at all of a game in which a goal by Roger Hunt and a classic by Bobby Charlton won it for England. Substitutes, introduced into the British game in 1965-66, were yet to be extended to competitive internationals. So Terry could not be replaced by somebody who knew what he was doing.

A substitution would at least have made it obvious to onlookers that he was not fit to play an adequate part in proceedings, but this explanation had to await the Sunday newspapers. Thus Hugh McIlvanney noted in *The Observer* that Paine 'used the ball to so little effect that it was no surprise to learn, at the finish, that he had been concussed for much of the hour and half,' while Brian Glanville, also recording Paine's concussion from that first-minute blow, reported, without further fuss, how Terry later 'chased and caught a pass from Stiles and centred admirably' and, as Charlton moved out to the right, got on the end of his cross to head 'narrowly and acrobatically over.'

As I say, Terry remembers none of this: his recall of that visit to Wembley is of waking up on the dressing-room table. He 'was groggy for a few days after that,' he explained to McKinstry, 'and Alf was one of those managers who ruled you out if there was a suspicion of an injury.' If anybody thought he had sufficiently recovered soon enough to play against France, four days later, it was not the *Times* correspondent, who reported, in a matter-of-fact way, that Callaghan was in for Paine, 'who suffered from concussion… against Mexico.'

I say 'matter-of-fact', although this elementary fact has largely been airbrushed out of World Cup history. Trainer Shepherdson thought not to mention it in his World Cup diary and I have not come across any player's memoirs that refer to Paine's early injury against Mexico and consequent unavailability for the game with France. Bobby Charlton is especially dismissive of a performance in which 'Paine had his moments… but it had to be doubtful if they had been numerous enough or sufficiently menacing.'

True, two or three team-mates have remembered Terry's concussion when I have jogged their memory. One of them, Alan Ball, remarked that 'it didn't stop him from carrying on' – which might strike you as an oddly unsympathetic reaction to an injured player staying on the pitch when no subs were allowed. On the other hand, Ray Wilson imagines that, 'if it hadn't been for that, he would have probably stayed in, wouldn't he?'

Terry has consistently been less determinist than that when interviewed on this matter. 'It would have been interesting,' he told Jeremy Wilson, 'to see, if I had stayed 100 per cent, what would have happened... He might have had the idea to bring Alan back, anyway.' And nor would he speculate for McKinstry: 'I suppose if I hadn't had that injury, things might have been different. That is something I would never know and Alf would never tell.'

Fair enough, but we might surely have expected such a disabling injury to have been properly acknowledged in the published recollections of the tournament. At least McIlvanney's *Observer* account was reproduced in the FA's official report of the tournament, but it has otherwise been left to Ramsey's biographers – like McKinstry, Bowler mentions it – and to other non-playing chroniclers of the 1966 World Cup to record that Paine took that early blow and so became, as Roger Hutchinson puts it, 'little more than a passenger on the right wing.'

The implications for Ramsey's subsequent formations are addressed in the next chapter. Suffice it to say, for now, that when England duly beat France to go though to a quarter-final match with Argentina, there seems to have been no question of whether Callaghan had done enough or whether Paine was fit to return. According to Ball, Ramsey told him he was back in, with a job to do:

> *He said 'you will play against Argentina. They've got a very attacking left full-back called Marzolini who, if not stopped, will cause us problems; and you're the best person in this squad to stop him and turn it round him.' He said 'I will change a winning team and you will play against Marzolini. You will stop him going that way and then you will, with your energy, go the other way and sort his weaknesses out, because he's not the best of defenders.' And I couldn't believe it. But that's how perceptive this man was – and what a fantastic manager he was: so when I thought my World Cup was over, he knew there was another role for me to play, even if it meant changing a winning team. That was so brave of him.*

Ramsey would have had to change the team, *anyhow, of course, as Greaves had been injured against France, but the key change, here, was in the* formation: *the manager had reverted to the wingless system that he had adopted in Poland, now justified with an assignment to block the runs of a dangerous opponent. Yet we have previously seen that Ramsey was prepared to use a winger in that role – as when Paine was pitched against Baxter at Hampden – while Armfield has argued that Callaghan and Paine were both 'purposive' players who could fill a hole in the way Ramsey liked. And Ball has even suggested that Callaghan could have looked after Marzolini. Cohen valued, however, 'the whirring energy of Ball,' deployed in front of him.*

But, then, having opted for horses-for-courses to beat Argentina, Ramsey resorted, for the rest of the tournament, to the alternative philosophy of never-change-a-winning-team. He continued to emphasise that he had a 'team' of 22 and he was determined that all of them would be together at the final whistle against West Germany, to celebrate the victory he had so confidently predicted long since. Armfield was deputed to get his lot down from their seats in the stand a few minutes before the end, so that they could all participate in the on-pitch celebrations. All was going to plan until they had trouble with the lifts and most of them missed the late equaliser by Wolfgang Weber.

Now they had a new problem: the match would last another half-hour, but there was nowhere for most of them to sit. Hence the bizarre photo of Terry and a few others crouching or sitting on the carpeted pathway leading to the Royal Box.

With there being no seats in extra-time for some of the reserves,
they had to make do with the carpet.
Back row (*left to right*): Bonetti, Springett, Hunter.
Front: Eastham, Connelly, Paine.

But then the Cup was won and the reserves were on the pitch. In the chaos of the moment, Callaghan forgot that he had Stiles's false teeth in his pocket, so Nobby would have to flash his gummy gap for the cameras. As the photographers took their shots of the 11 men with their trophy, various reserves were identifiable in the background, showing varying degrees of interest. Terry picked an especially prominent spot.

And he later did so again on the balcony at the Royal Garden Hotel *for the evening's celebrations. The expression on his face is surely that of a man who, far from being envious of those who had played in this match of a life-time, was proud to have been part of it all. Playing in the World Cup finals was the third highlight of his international career to go with those two games in the autumn of 1963.*

He was not to know that he would never play for England again. An outcast from Ramsey's Wingless Wonderland – or is that a simplification too far?

The reserves join the World Cup-winners on the pitch.
Several of them are in shot, but Paine (*left*) has the prime slot.
The 10 winners in view are (*left to right*) Stiles, Peters (bending), Charlton J (waving),
Ball, Banks, Hurst, Moore (aloft), Wilson, Cohen and Charlton R.
Hunt is almost totally obscured by Hurst.

As Alf Ramsey parades
the Jules Rimet trophy
on the balcony of the
Royal Garden Hotel,
George Cohen may
be camera-gazing but
Terry Paine (*left*) has his
eyes on the prize.

Eight years after he made his debut for Winchester City Reserves,
Terry Paine was playing for England.
Having kept in touch with John Philpott, a mentor in that inaugural season,
he accepted an invitation to visit his studio, wearing his 'Centenary Year' England shirt.

Chapter 13

Wingless Wondering

If not having to qualify for the World Cup finals meant that Alf Ramsey lacked the opportunity to test his selections competitively – unless you believe that *everybody* wanted to beat England, especially at Wembley – it also meant that he was freer than other international managers to test personnel and formations in friendly fixtures.

He was not able, though, to shuffle his pack during a match, as substitutes were not normally allowed, even in friendlies. We saw that the Rest of the World were granted a special dispensation to use 16 players at Wembley in 1963, but the FA was not generally given to such departures from Victorian mores. In their 35 build-up matches, from Bratislava in 1963 to Chorzow in 1966, England deployed only three substitutes.

It is against that background that this chapter revisits the question of how and why Ramsey came to win the World Cup with 'wingless wonders'. That alliterative label has been much used as a sufficient explanation in its own right: having run the gamut of alternative formations, Ramsey eventually concluded that, for reasons of tactics and/or available personnel, this was the winning formula.

A compelling exception to that simplistic approach is Leo McKinstry's biography of Sir Alf, which offers an original appraisal of Ramsey's thinking and the mind-games he played with both players and press. While not wishing to replicate his efforts – my focus is not on Ramsey but on Terry Paine and why he made but one appearance in the 1966 finals and then never played for his country again – I shall nevertheless go down some of the same avenues as McKinstry. And I shall necessarily rely upon some of the same sources – although I have conducted fresh interviews with several of his witnesses.

All of which will entail an examination of what seemed to some of the press to be a series of baffling experiments, especially in arriving at his 'front five'. Various reasons have been advanced, however, as to why Ramsey was justified in keeping his options open. I shall consider three of these, before noting a few complicating factors that bedevil any attempt at analysis and explanation.

First, there is the argument that Ramsey had made up his mind, long before the 1966 quarter-finals, that he would dispense with wingers, yet he kept bringing them back – one, or even two, at a time – in order not to show his hand to opponents. Exponents of that view differ as to which event, in 1964-65, persuaded Ramsey that he had found his winning formula.

Terry Paine is convinced that the death knell of 4-2-4 was rung in São Paulo in 1964, when Ramsey and his squad watched Brazil lose 3-0 to Argentina. Listening to Ramsey talking, afterwards, about what they had witnessed and what he liked about it, Terry foresaw England playing 4-3-3. He did not infer, however, that there would necessarily be no role for him in such a formation. In this regard, he would, of course, be proved right, to the extent that the manager juggled his personnel in that and other systems, even to the extent of playing 4-3-3 with two wide front men.

That juggling might sometimes be in private. McKinstry has pointed us to the significance of a practice session at Lilleshall in February 1965, when Ramsey pitted his seniors against the Under-23 side. Playing 4-2-4 and unaware of the manager's machinations, the juniors were baffled by the seniors' 4-3-3 formation. As Ramsey explained,

> the seniors… ran riot with the young lads. They didn't know what it was all about… Contrary to some opinions, I was not influenced by the tactics of the Argentinians during the Little World Cup in Brazil in 1964. The Argentines, for me, played with five players, sometimes more, in the middle of the field. Their object seemed mainly to avoid defeat. Mine has always been to win.

And win he did with 4-3-3 on that summer's tour when, as we saw in Chapter 11, Paine revelled in that formation, operating in a front three that twice included two wide players, scoring from Temple's cross in Nuremberg and putting Connelly in to score in Gothenburg.

Then, in December 1965, when England beat Spain 2-0, playing 4-3-3 in Madrid, this was, for Harold Shepherdson, the game that 'showed up the new style, the first experiments of which had been made in Nuremberg.' It seems to be agreed that the Spaniards were as baffled as the U-23 lads had been at Lilleshall, as their full-backs stood 'picking their noses and scratching their arses,' as Ray Wilson irreverently puts it, while they pondered when they might have somebody to mark. Bobby Charlton had now come into central midfield. It was 4-3-3 with a considerable shift in personnel. It lacked any of the wingers Ramsey had deployed in this formation during the summer and was, he later said, '4-3-3 in all its thoroughness and finest. … I think really this was when it first registered firmly in my mind as a system that could win the World Cup.'

This did not mean, however, that Ramsey would never again play 4-2-4. As he explained to Brian James of the *Daily Mail*, the week after the win in Madrid,

> I think it would be quite wrong to let the rest of the world, our rivals, see what we are doing. I think it is my duty to protect certain players until we need them most… My job will be to produce the right team at the right time and that does not always mean pressing ahead with a particular combination just because it has been successful.

Harold Shepherdson has recalled what happened, in the three years from Bratislava to Chorzow, when 'the time for experiments was over.' It involved a process in which Ramsey

> had shown the world his own form of 4-2-4, had gradually built the formation up to 4-3-3, exposed it in one blinding brilliant fashion before the world's most critical observers in Madrid. Then shadowed it to fox the same observers, before once again settling his team into the 4-3-3 rhythm.

If that's how the manager and trainer saw it, perhaps we should accept that the wingers were pawns in a prolonged game of bluff, at least from the summer tour of 1965. Yet the above facts fit a second theory: that, as he whittled his squad down to the final 22, the manager wanted to be sure that they could play in several formations, suited to the opponents and/or the stage in a match. Ball's take on Ramsey's plans was that 'he wanted us to be able to play *four* systems. We adapted to every single one and, when he wanted to change his team, we played all these systems for a year before the World Cup.'

With no substitutes permitted, this explanation supposes that Ramsey could find players capable of adapting, even during a game, to different strategies. The most obvious adaptors would have to be wingers capable of duties beyond beating the full-back and getting in a deadly cross; or midfielders capable of doing at least some of the things that wingers had always done.

That choice is also the essential feature of the third explanation: that Ramsey wanted to play at least one winger, for all the advantages that would give him, but needed his wide man (or men) to be able to play in a formation other than the 4-2-4 he had inherited. I have stressed the case for multi-tasking wingers, to distinguish this explanation from the well-peddled contention that Ramsey was desperate to play with at least one traditional winger, but none of those he tried, notably during the group stage of the 1966 tournament, was good enough.

Pursuing the latter argument, McKinstry cites Ramsey's contention that 'a vital requisite for 4-2-4 is two attacking wingers with the ability and speed to take on defenders, to get past them, take the ball to the goal line and pull it back… It became apparent that we hadn't got the wingers who could give us this service we wanted.'

That explanation has been relied upon in some of the memoirs, with Bobby Charlton, Greaves and Moore among its keenest advocates. Charlton, who is in 'no doubt' that Ramsey wanted to continue playing wingers after the qualifying games, reasons that he needed them to have 'the ability to undermine seriously the world-class defences of Argentina… and West Germany.' So how does this sit with Ball's explanation that stopping Marzolini was Ramsey's priority in the first of those matches?

Bobby Moore

Greaves likewise insists that 'Alf wanted to play wingers. It's all a myth that Alf developed 4-3-3 with this grand scheme of things: he played three wingers in the first three games [of the finals] and he desperately wanted to play with a winger. He couldn't find anything quite right to suit him, so he finished up playing the system we now know.' If that begs the question of just how his three wide men failed to 'suit' Ramsey, Moore was most outspoken on the matter:

The sad part for Alf… is that he wanted to play wingers but he was crucified for doing away with them. Paine, Connelly, Callaghan… Thompson… all had their opportunities but Alf got no success with any of them. He wanted wingers because they give you a way to get round behind defences, create chances and win games. But the ones who were available didn't have the right attitude, the right temperament… the right something.

Martin Peters offers a subtle variation on this theme. Despite being brought in for the last warm-up game in Poland, he still 'thought that Alf's intention was to play with a conventional winger and nothing has changed my mind on that score…I'm sure that Alf wanted to play with wingers because they provided an invaluable attacking option, but he knew something was *not quite right about the shape of the team.* So he took the radical option and abandoned wingers altogether (emphasis added).

Note how Peters has shifted the emphasis from the quality of the available wingers to the 'shape' of the team. That is a position that takes account of two factors that are not considered in the 'not-good-enough' argument: the variety of ways in which Ramsey had deployed his wingers; and the manner in which the 'balance' of the side was affected, first by Charlton moving to a central position and then by Hurst's coming in, with West Ham habits, for Greaves.

In a 1978 interview for the *News of the World*, Ramsey declared that he did 'not favour old-fashioned wingers, the type who were stationed out on the touchline and waited for the ball to be served up to them. To have two players stuck out on the flanks is a luxury, which can virtually leave a side with nine men when the game is going against them.'

Paine and Ramsey discuss tactics
for the Rest of the World game

Yet if you watch the video of the 1963 game against the Rest of the World, you will surely notice how each of his wide men – Paine and Charlton – remains in 'station' – until each has the audacity to cut inside and create a goal. One of Ramsey's biographers has described this as a game in which 'Alf chose to give Bobby Charlton an opportunity in a free role, coming through from deep.' That certainly describes the run that set up Greaves's winner, but it is otherwise at odds with the video evidence. And it is at odds with the wing-play for which the press would continue to clamour. Tellingly, when Charlton gave way, in São Paulo six months later, to Paine, Frank McGhee described Terry, as we saw, as somebody 'who will obey orders to stay out on the wing.'

That is surely to over-simplify, though, if we consider how Paine was used, at Hampden Park, in the interim, to tuck in and hold up Jim Baxter. And then, as previously stressed, came the 1965 tour, when the 4-3-3 formation twice included two orthodox wingers, combining each time to score the winning goal.

At Hampden in 1966, it was John Connelly's turn to help out defensively, blocking the runs of right-back, Greig. Staying wide to baulk an overlapping full-back is, of course, a different role from stepping inside to 'confront' the midfield play-maker. But there's the point: the jargon of 'tucking in' and 'tracking back' masks a variety of ways in which wide men could be used defensively. And these ways were far from being the inventions of a revolutionary Ramsey: we have seen how Ted Bates was requiring Harry Penk to perform defensive duties that he would not have expected of John Sydenham; and George Cohen's expectations of an England outside-right had been shaped, he says, by the kind of cover he had received, at Fulham, from his Scottish team-mate, Graham Leggatt.

Ian Callaghan

What Ramsey demanded of Connelly at Hampden and what Cohen generally expected of his No.7 for England was what, of course, Ramsey asked of Ball in the quarter-final, when he assigned him to block off the runs of Marzolini. He dropped Callaghan and brought in Ball for that task. Ball told David Miller that 'a winger couldn't have done it. A winger wants the ball and then to go with it. As a midfield player, I knew all about "filling in" in defence.' Yet he added that 'Callie could have done it as well as me.' Jimmy Armfield agrees that not all of the wingers of that era could adapt to the varying demands of 4-2-4 and 4-3-3 but reminds us that Paine, like Callaghan, was 'an all-purpose player: he could tackle back; and he would do his share; and he didn't get tired; and he could pass.'

An 'all-purpose' Terry Paine would not have been instantly recognizable to one or two of his Southampton team-mates. Cliff Huxford believes that the Paine he knew was never going to satisfy Ramsey's demands that his wingers

work up and down… Terry didn't work for us. He hardly trained. He was there, but he went through the motions. If he was really fit, he could have been in the England squad for a long, long time – I'm sure of that. When you play for England, you can't, all of a sudden, start going up and down like a train.

Other team-mates have countered, though, that Terry was naturally fit. And he claims that Ramsey told him, in 1966, that Bobby Charlton and he 'were the fittest players he'd ever seen.' Armfield, who played behind him six times for England, liked the fact that

> he never looked *tired*. I like players who never look tired: I can't do with them when they're gasping. I can never understand players being tired. I used to look at him and think 'he never looks tired.' He'd keep running up and down: no problem. If Terry Paine were playing today, he'd be picked for more than 19 caps on the right-wing, wouldn't he? I think the modern game would suit him. I don't think it would suit some other good players I can think of… Terry liked to be mobile; he liked things to be going on around him. I think he'd do well in the modern game. I don't think he'd have what I call the dribbling skills of Matthews or Douglas, but his was a very purposeful style – and always a threat. He was shrewd and he was strong; and he could look after himself.

Not that any of this means, necessarily, that he could match Callaghan when it came to supporting his full-back. Jimmy Melia, who played with each of these wingers at club level, considered his Liverpool team-mate superior in that regard: 'Ian Callaghan's work-rate was unbelievable,' Melia reckons. 'As a team-player, you couldn't look for a better player than Ian. He'd come back and defend like a full-back.' Mind you, Jimmy feels that Paine otherwise had 'more ability than Ian Callaghan. He was a better crosser of the ball than Callaghan. His knowledge of the game was better than Callaghan's and he scored more goals than Callaghan.'

Jimmy Melia, who had views on the pros and cons of Paine v Callaghan.

As Connelly saw it, Paine was 'a different winger' than either he or Callaghan was, in the way that he would come inside and 'thread balls through. Well, I never threaded balls through for anybody: people were threading balls through for me, because I was farther upfront than Terry was: Terry was always a bit deeper.' That describes, of course, how Paine liked to put Greaves through with a ball 'over the top' – a technique he would come to hone, at club level, for the galloping Channon. For David Miller, Paine was 'the thinking man's winger,' in contrast to Thompson, the 'darting dragonfly.'

In sum, Ramsey expected multi-tasking wingers and there is support from their team-mates for the view that Paine and Callaghan each offered Ramsey that in a way that Thompson didn't, with Paine capable of the greater variety of contributions, but with Callaghan edging it when it came to defensive duties.

The issue remaining, then, is whether Ball brought more to the right flank than either of those two wingers Ramsey had used there in the group stages. Cohen swore by Alan's 'whirring energy', while Ball himself reasoned that what was needed was his ability – which Paine, Callaghan and Connelly lacked – to play what he called 'inside-to-go-out.' From his tucked-in position, he

> could go out wide and I had enough legs – enough energy and everything – to work up that right-hand side and at times, when needed, to do a defensive thing in front of George Cohen. And also, because Alf wanted Bobby Charlton to be allowed the freedom to go forward, he needed legs in the middle of the pitch to come and support Nobby. To my way of thinking, that's why Alf plumped for my high work-rate and energy level, which meant that I could do all of those things, whereas the other lads – Connelly, Callaghan and Terry – were basically wide men.

I have used the phrase 'tucked-in' in this context, to convey the defensive formation that would become a feature of how Terry Paine would be used by Ted Bates in the First Division (as we shall see in the next few chapters), when Southampton would increasingly play 4-2-4 at home and 4-3-3 away, with Paine as the flexible man, who could, of course, be expected to switch during a game as the score-line demanded. Callaghan would make a similar shift for Liverpool – as late as 1976, he was the midfield dynamo, setting up the only goal in the League Champions' Charity Shield win against Cup-winning Southampton – and Ray Wilson feels that both players were more effective spraying balls from deep than they had been as wingers. That's an extreme view, perhaps, but it does underline the *attacking* value of using such skilled ball-players tucked in – especially if they are capable of going wide, when needed, to put in a quality cross.

All of which brings us back to the contention that the four main wingers Ramsey had tried (other than Bobby Charlton) had somehow failed him. Peter Thompson had many admirers in the squad and it clearly came as a surprise that he did not make the final 22. But whatever formation he was playing, Ramsey liked his wide men to drift in to a scoring position when an attack was mounted on the opposite flank. While Paine scored seven times in his 19 appearances for Ramsey – and Connelly was seven for 20, going back to Winterbottom's days – Thompson can't have helped his cause by failing ever to score for England. That is a 'very fair comment,' he accepts. 'I loved beating men and crossing the ball: I wasn't goal-minded. It never crossed my mind. I should have been more goal-minded, but I wasn't bothered about that.'

That is perhaps an under-statement of how Thompson, who had been a centre-forward at Preston, performed at club level – his record of 41 goals in 322 League games for Liverpool compares favourably with Callaghan's 50 in 640, if not with Connelly's 108 in 294 for Burnley and Manchester United or even Paine's 160 in 713 for Southampton. True, these bare statistics mask which division goals were scored in and who dropped deep late in their careers, but the bold facts are that neither of the Liverpool wingers was an obvious goal-scorer. As Hunt, who thrived for Liverpool on crosses from Callaghan and Thompson, observes of the latter's problem with Ramsey, 'Peter didn't score goals. He was a fantastic player but he wasn't a goal-scorer. To play in the kind of system that Alf wanted to play, you needed to be a goal-scorer like John Connelly and Terry Paine.' While each of them would pop up in the box from time to time, 'Peter would be out there, on the wing, getting to the by-line and whipping it back.'

As noted in Chapter 11, Thompson performed that role especially well in the 1964 tournament in Brazil. Yet there, surely, lies the irony of that event. Argentina dazzled everybody with their variety of wingless systems, while England's star was an out-and-out winger. But England could manage only two goals in their three games. Whatever this said about systems and the players leading the attack, it didn't say that England lacked old-fashioned crossing.

Max Marquis has suggested that Thompson's successful tour would 'help to lead Ramsey down a false trail for some time to come.' This is perhaps the wrong metaphor. It was surely more a case of Ramsey's wanting to have his cake and eat it – where the 'cake' is defined as a winger's ability to reach, and cross from, the by-line, while the 'eating' required him to do that much more than had perhaps been expected of him at club level. As we have seen, Jimmy Armfield was an admirer of Thompson but wondered whether he was 'purposeful' enough for Ramsey's liking: 'the more purposeful type of player,' like Callaghan or Paine, was more generally 'in the game, more or less filling in – so that when something breaks down, they go and fill a hole.'

Apart from popping up to score a reasonable quota of goals, Connelly was encouraged by Ramsey to 'do the two wings, just floating.' That brought him a couple of chances against Uruguay, but he hit the woodwork each time. Connelly found, however, that he could not get behind the massed ranks of Uruguayans to cross – to which extent he failed Ramsey. Yet he recalls the manager's telling him that he would have been retained had

England won: as he would demonstrate in the later stages, Ramsey was capable of not changing a winning side, even when the rationale for selecting that particular team had changed.

But out went Connelly and in came Paine, albeit on the other flank, for the game against Mexico. Such is the received wisdom – as repeated in one autobiography after another – that he, too, failed to deliver that it feels tantamount to special pleading on my part again to mention that he was concussed in the first minute. Although he was reported to have made some notable contributions during this game, it was also observed that his performance suffered from his concussion. As we saw, Ray Wilson thinks that, 'if it hadn't been for that, he would have probably stayed in, wouldn't he?'

If Ball was indeed brought in for the quarter-final to hound Marzolini, then it would seem that Callaghan had no chance of keeping his place – unless Ramsey were to have been persuaded of Ball's own view that 'Callie could have done the job'. But, then, as Wilson surmises, Callaghan might never have played against France had Paine not been concussed against Mexico. We shall never know, of course, what would have happened next if a clear-headed Paine had persistently penetrated the Mexican defence, kept his place and had a blinder against France. Would Ramsey have recalled Ball for the Marzolini assignment or would he have stood by the side (with the exception of the injured Greaves) that had come through the last two games of the group stages? The ultimate 'what if?' question is whether Paine would then have stayed in all the way to the Final and a rematch with Schnellinger.

If that's a legitimate question for his biographer to pose, it's ridiculously superfluous in terms both of what Ball achieved, not least in his outstanding performance in the Final, and of England actually winning the World Cup. One person who is not complaining is Terry Paine, an unstinting admirer of Ball:

> Bally was brilliant. You couldn't fault him in that formation. In all the time I played football, if you had wanted a midfield player who had an absolutely magic first touch, and could play the ball early, it had to be Alan Ball: there was no doubt about that. Again, like me, he wasn't blessed with a lot of speed – but, goodness me, he had a soccer brain that was second to none. He could sum up situations and his one-touch play was probably as good as I've ever seen from any international.

And he also recognises the futility of the ifs-and-buts when the end result – and it's not as though England has won anything since – so demonstrably justified the means. As he put it to Jeremy Wilson, Alf Ramsey had 'got it right because they won the World Cup.' What's more, Terry assured Wilson, he has 'never complained about my time with England. I really appreciate the fact that [Ramsey] brought me on board when I was a Second Division player.'

Whichever way we look at it, the repeated argument about failing wingers is not, surely, a sufficient explanation. But nor is the above analysis the full extent of the story, ignoring, as it does, the Charlton and West Ham factors and the issue of 'balance' on the flanks.

First, Ramsey's decision to bring Bobby Charlton in from the wing – belatedly, United fans might say – was bound to affect the forward formation. The immediate victim was George Eastham, who effectively made way for what might have been described in the previous decade as 'a deep-lying centre-forward.' Eastham is today laconic about his 'bad luck' and chuckles heartily at his misfortune, as he echoes Paine's recognition that the outcome justified the means: 'when success comes, you can't say, "I should have been there" – because you shouldn't have been.'

But playing Charlton centrally also affected, surely, the case for wingers. Whereas England's midfielders had traditionally been required to play simple balls wide for wingers – Charlton on the left and whoever was in favour on the right – to do their stuff, the main danger-man was now sitting deep centrally, wanting the ball with which to run at the defence – if 'run' is not too prosaic a word for what has been variously described as 'gliding' or 'floating'. Moreover, a formation in which Charlton was cocooned by Ball, Stiles and Peters meant, as Peters has reasoned, that the side's 'finest creative player' could be spared tracking-back duties.

Geoff Hurst, who brought the West Ham style to Ramsey's Final formation

Secondly, Hurst made demands of, and contributions to, the formation that differed from those of Greaves. It was not just a question of build. Roger Hunt perceived himself, like Greaves, to be 'an inside-forward, linking up with the winger,' a role he performed with Paine in Leipzig and when they shared six goals in New York. But Hurst was a centre-forward, albeit of a distinct style that differed from that of Bobby Smith and the other No.9s whom Ramsey had since tried.

That style was the West Ham style developed by Ron Greenwood. Both Hurst and Peters have described it in their respective autobiographies, but that astute tactician, Alan Ball, has explained especially well its origins and advantages:

> West Ham brought in the near-post ball, where everyone made near-post runs and you didn't have to over-hit the ball. Let's take the Ron Davies-ball, right to the far post, where you've got this fantastic header of the ball [Ball brackets into this category his Everton team-mate, Joe Royle]. He'd just peel to the far post and you knock it up to the back stick and these big lads come in on it and score goals. Then, as they always do, football coaches started to combat that – which they had to – and they made it harder for that man to make those runs into the box. So the near-post ball came in, which was expertly worked by the West Ham lads to start with, for people to come across people – a lot of glanced headers into the goal – just meeting the ball on the near post.

Hurst enthuses to this day about the virtues of the tactic: 'when you do it well, with the timing from the wide player, it's virtually unstoppable, even when people know you're going to do it. We still scored goals against people who knew we did it and who knew we were going to do it and tried to stop it and still couldn't.' Who needs reminding how he demonstrated the ploy majestically in the quarter-final, beating Argentina from a cross in open play, and again in the Final, flicking in England's first goal from a quickly-taken free-kick? If you remember those goals, you'll also recall, no doubt, that the suppliers were his West Ham team-mates, Peters and Moore, respectively.

Martin Peters

The late introduction of Peters into Ramsey's permutations, with his ability to 'cross the ball early,' was 'crucial', Hurst reckons, to what England then achieved. Perhaps it would be more accurate to say that Hurst benefited from having practised early balls so often with Peters and from having thereby developed the kind of 'telepathy' that Paine had had with George O'Brien when the latter made his near-post runs to bullet home a rather different kind of cross. In other words, England may have been helped, in this regard, by having three players from the same club, although it might alternatively be argued that Ramsey had had plenty of time with his players to get them used to each other's better habits. Ball reasoned that Paine could play near-posts floaters, if the occasion arose, although he rated Channon 'the best at that,' while Armfield argues that 'it seemed logical when Alf put Hurst in at centre-forward, hardly having played him at all, that you're going to need somebody who's going to get the ball into him.'

He saw that as a job for a winger, but how well Peters delivered! And maybe that club-honed understanding was, indeed, 'crucial': as Peters recalls his cross in the quarter-final, 'I didn't know precisely where Geoff Hurst was at the time but I suspected that he'd be waiting for me to deliver the ball into his path at the near post, because we'd done the same thing so many times on Saturday afternoons up and down the country.'

And yet to argue that Hurst needed this or that kind of cross is to do his versatility an injustice. He scored his Final hat-trick in three quite different ways. The first may have been a West Ham special, as he drifted to the near post to meet Moore's free-kick, but the second – awarded by an out-of-position Russian linesman, blessed with unbelievable peripheral vision – came when Ball got to the by-line and squared the ball back in the manner expected of Paine and Callaghan. And the third, signalling that it was, indeed, 'all over', required him to plough down the inside-left channel and bury Moore's through-ball.

Finally, that question of 'balance'. On its left flank, the side that played the last three games of the tournament had Ray Wilson, perhaps the greatest left-back in the world and capable of overlapping to effect, and Martin Peters, a decent crosser of a ball – notably in the West Ham style that especially suited Hurst.

On the right, though, you had Ball and Cohen. If Terry rated Alan an outstanding one-touch footballer, Ball, for his part, admired Paine as

> a wonderful crosser of the ball – not as pacy a crosser of the ball as the Beckhams and that, but he was a centre-forward's dream, because they *knew* that he was going to produce; and he produced really telling crosses for people to finish with… He was a real out-and-out winger. That was Terry's *forte* and he was *miles* better than me at it, if I may say so: if you want an out-and-out winger, you'd pick Paine before Ball, without a shadow of a doubt, because he had more [in his repertoire] to go and create stuff from there.

Behind Ball, Ramsey had Cohen, a formidable defender but, by all accounts, an inferior overlapper to Armfield, the star of England's 1962 World Cup expedition, whom he had replaced. It seems to be agreed that Cohen could not be expected to cross a ball with any great hope of accuracy: as Paine put it, 'George could hit the guy in the crowd behind the goal, regularly.' Or, as Ray Wilson artfully assures us, 'whenever George crossed the half-way line, we all ran back the other way.'

All of which might prompt an objective observer to raise the possibility that the right flank appeared unbalanced: mightn't it have been comprised, ideally, of an overlapping full-back (Armfield), along with a tucked-in non-crosser (Ball, his Blackpool club-mate), *or* of a less menacing overlapper (Cohen), behind an expert crosser (take your pick from Callaghan, Connelly and Paine)?

When I put that 'logic' to Armfield, he agreed with its sense, but the pragmatism of his follow-up took me by surprise: 'there was no logic in that Final side when you look at it, right through. The logic went out when he put Geoff Hurst in for the quarter-final. In a tournament, you chop and change: things do happen that are unaccountable. In a way, they stumble into it.'

But, then, Armfield concluded that England's victory may have owed more to venue than to formation:

> The thing that Ramsey had was home advantage: it makes a helluva difference. We never had to travel – not even as far as Watford. Everything was played on our own pitch in our own conditions. I always thought that was a big issue.

And a big swindle, too, so that those of us who'd bought tickets, months in advance, for what should have been the England v Portugal semi-final at Goodison Park, fell victim to the skulduggery that saw that game switched to Wembley.

Perhaps that shameful switch is one of the reasons why the question of venue has been seldom raised, as commentators – from the lazy labellers to such a serious analyst as McKinstry – have focused on formation. I make no apology for devoting a chapter to the latter explanation, in arguing that the tag of 'wingless wonders' has been too aimlessly used to describe Ramsey's manoeuvres – and, following therefrom, the termination of Terry Paine's England career.

Not that this exploration was ever likely to produce a definitive conclusion: the evidence adduced could support more than one explanation. And however much we sift the variables, I am impressed by Armfield's emphasis on serendipity – how much the acclaimed formation may have owed to the injury to Greaves. None of which alters the fact that Paine's concussion has been airbrushed out of the story of 1966.

Not that Terry Paine is complaining that his 19th cap proved to be his last: 'Blimey! That's 19 more than I ever thought.'

Chapter 14

Head Master

So Terry Paine returned to Southampton as a World Cup-winner. After an almost unbroken eight weeks with the England party, he needed a break and was excused the three-match tour of Germany and Holland, on which his team-mates were about to embark.

They included a newcomer in David Thompson, Ted Bates's latest attempt to find a winger who could tackle back, as David Chadwick, Paine's perpetual understudy, departed for Middlesbrough. Tommy Spencer, after a brief contribution to the promotion run-in, moved to York. And Stuart Williams retired – to coach at his former club, West Bromwich Albion.

Like other arrivals from Molineux, Thompson was shocked by attitudes and facilities at The Dell, starting with the standard visit to Chilworth to take tea with Ted and Mary Bates: 'What an experience that was! Ted gave me a piece of cream-cake. That was something different.' Not among the dietary recommendations at Wolverhampton, you gather. But, then, Thompson found it

> an entirely different set-up at Southampton to Wolves. They were that poor. They had a lot of talented players, but the training facilities were very poor. The field we used to train on! It had mole-hills and stuff: you couldn't control anything; it used to bounce all over the place. That probably improved the ball control, you know.

Like Melia before him, he was glad to be leaving Wolves' long-ball game for Southampton, where he found 'more of a passing game. For me, it was like going to, say, Arsenal now, where they *pass* the ball.' As Thompson recovered, on tour, from his initial shock and became 'blooded', as he puts it, into the Southampton passing game, his new manager stayed at home, hoping to complete his shopping.

He had a reported £100,000 to spend and had been prepared to splash 90 per cent of it on Cardiff's Barry Hole, a central defender with 18 (of his eventual 30) Welsh caps to his name, and Middlesbrough's Ian Gibson, a goal-scoring midfielder, boasting a couple of Scotland U-23 caps. But neither player fancied playing for the First Division's unfashionable new boys. Each opted for Second Division football: Hole with Blackburn, just relegated from Division I; and Gibson at Coventry, the side Saints had pipped for promotion.

So with his budget all but intact – Thompson had cost only £7,500 – Bates still had the option of buying a striker. Two 24 year-olds were in his sights. He could have shelled out £80,000 for Chelsea's Bobby Tambling, whose last appearance (of three) for England had been in May, in the same forward line as Paine. Baulking at that tab, Bates switched his attention to a lower-priced No.9 from the Second Division: Ron Davies was available from Norwich City for a mere £55,000. He had won five Welsh caps but, unlike Tambling, had no experience of the top flight. Then, again, while Tambling was a lethal finisher who could play wide (as he had for England) or upfront, Davies was built like a true centre-forward.

You will perhaps recognise here a variation on the summer of 1959 when, having been rejected by Cardiff's Hewitt, Ted Bates had bought the lesser-known George O'Brien, who proved to be the perfect near-post target for Paine's crosses. Now, priced out of the Tambling market, Bates had bought somebody tall enough for Terry to hang it up to at the far post.

Not that many of his players had formed a positive impression of Ron Davies as *any* sort of goalscorer. Paine has no recall of Davies performing during Saints' four meetings with Norwich in 1964-65-66. He scored a couple of goals, but Wimshurst remembers him dropping so deep that he found himself marking him. Davies would see that as a compliment: he disliked being renowned for his heading ability, because he wished to be acknowledged as the *leader* of the line, who could do it on the deck.

Ted Bates had noted, however, that Ron was 'particularly good in the air' and told the *Echo* so. Paine gives 'great credit' to his manager for having foreseen how Davies would fit in: 'he knew what he wanted; he knew how he wanted his teams to play. And when he bought him, that was a stroke of genius.' A stroke not to be wasted by having Davies drop back too far when he was needed, upfront, getting on to the end of a Paine cross – and sometimes capitalising on Sydenham's less accurate, less floated crosses.

Sydenham appreciated Davies's 'great ability' to make less than '100 per cent accurate crosses into good ones.' This helped to make him, in Sydenham's book, 'the greatest header of the ball The Dell's ever seen.' O'Brien may have wanted more predictable crosses, but the beauty of Davies, from Sydenham's point of view, was that he could time his run and his leap, and then twist his neck, to turn a miscued cross into another scoring opportunity. That knack was appreciated even by the more precise Paine: 'You could lay the ball into areas and know that he was going to contest the ball. You didn't have to pick him out.'

It would take a while, though, for Davies to start heading in crosses. It fell to Paine – rated 'the most skilful man on the field' by the *Sunday Express* – to open Southampton's First Division account, with a goal of 'World Cup class' that helped them to an opening day draw, 1-1 at home to Manchester

Paine opens Southampton's First Division account with a goal of 'World Cup class'.

City, their companions in promotion. And it would be the third game, at Blackpool, before Davies got on to the score-sheet – with a lob – and the seventh game, at Leicester, before he succeeded with his head, beating Gordon Banks from a Paine free-kick.

This 'rocket', said the *Echo*, 'particularly pleased' the manager, 'because one of the factors which influenced him in signing Davies was… that he was a specially useful header of the ball.' Davies was now on a run of scoring in 10 consecutive League games, sandwiching a hat-trick against Plymouth in the League Cup, when the *Echo* acclaimed the contribution of 'Paine's deadly accuracy in placing the ball' on Davies's head.

And so it went on, with Davies scoring three League hat-tricks to finish the season with 37 League goals, the highest tally not only in the division but in the entire Football League. Six more in the Cups gave him a total of 43, making him the top scorer, overall, pipping Geoff Hurst by scoring four on the last day of the season. Ron had gone into that game with his head leading his feet 20-19, but four goals with his right foot, including a penalty, meant a win for the Davies boots, 23-20.

If those statistics contradict the image of Davies, the ultimate header of the ball, they support Ron's protests that he could do it on the ground and did not deserve to be remembered for his heading alone. That said, he acknowledges how Paine and Sydenham helped him to appreciate, in that first season together, what he could achieve with 'a system that suited me:

I never even thought I was so good in the air.' Ask Ron to describe how it all 'blossomed' and you can guarantee that he'll always include the supply from Sydenham, even though he forever talks of Paine as 'the best crosser of the ball – the best winger – I've ever played with in my life.'

Those sentiments are mutual. Paine insists that Davies was 'the best I've ever seen in the air. You can take your Tommy Lawtons – you can take whoever you want. I mean, the height that he could get!' And, as already noted, Terry appreciated that Ron's timing and positioning were so good that 'you didn't have to pick him out.'

The matter of whom Terry might 'pick out', whereabouts, had changed somewhat from the options described by David Burnside in Chapter 8. After six-and-a-bit seasons of hitting George O'Brien at the near post, Paine now had Martin Chivers at No.8. Martin interpreted his role as being 'more of a near-post merchant' than he had been hitherto, 'because Ron was dynamic on the far post,' whence he would often 'knock the ball down to me. They were frightened out of their life of Ron Davies. They couldn't mark both of us. It gave me a lot of space.'

Which explains how, even as second fiddle, Chivers came to score 18 League and Cup goals that season. So it didn't matter too much that Melia – an ever-present, along with Paine – was not getting into the third-man position that Burnside had identified: that was not part of Jimmy's role as what Paine dubs a 'linker'. While Melia consequently contributed only four goals, Paine chipped in with a dozen, 11 of them in the League. No matter that he was now in the First Division, this was the fifth consecutive season that his League tally was in double figures – though it helped that he took six penalties (plus another in the League Cup), two of which were saved, although he followed up, in one of those cases, to convert the rebound.

Two of his League penalties were scored in one match, when West Ham United came to The Dell in February. It was a chance for the Southampton

Paine takes the penalty, against Fulham, that would bring him his 10th League goal of the season – but only from the rebound, after Macedo had saved the initial attempt.

On an afternoon when he was 'baffled and beaten' by Terry Paine (second left),
Bobby Moore (No.6) watches Ron Davies outjump Ken Brown.

fans to see the trio of recent World Cup fame – Moore, Hurst and Peters –
and they seized it in record numbers: the gates were shut on the first Dell
crowd to exceed 30,000 since the epic promotion battle with West Brom in
1949. There was less immediately at stake this time, as the struggling Saints
entertained the mid-table Hammers. The division's top goalscorers, Davies
and Hurst, had a comparatively quiet afternoon, with a goal apiece, as the
Saints' forwards laid the foundations for the belief – folklore, even – that
they enjoyed playing against Bobby Moore: 'Chivers used to *roast* him,'
Ken Wimshurst assures us.

On this occasion, it was a 'top-form' Paine, as the *Echo* saw it, who so
'tormented and teased' Burkett, his marker, that Moore had to cover for
him, only to 'finish this testing, self-imposed penance as baffled and beaten
as Burkett.' With the score at 2-0, Paine went on a run that had reporters
competing for the appropriate superlative: the *Echo* opted for 'devastating'.
It took him past Burkett and Boyce before it was 'ruthlessly ended by
Moore's wild tackle' in the box. Terry got up to make it 3-0 from the spot.
A few minutes later, he lobbed the ball over Moore for Chivers to head a
fourth. Soon after half-time, it was five, when another Paine run was ended
by a Bovington foul. This time he planted his penalty past Standen, on the
opposite side from the first. It finished 6-2.

Heady stuff. But surviving their first season in the top flight depended less
upon Paine-inspired goal-fests at The Dell than on Saints' keeping a clean
sheet away from home – especially if they could nick the odd 1-0 win.
They did that three times, at Villa, Leeds and Everton, in that order. I saw

them all, but especially remember the last two for the performances of new signings.

Let's go first to Elland Road in October, where they told us, on the PA, that this was the 23rd birthday of one of Terry's World Cup squad-mates: Norman Hunter. But the man with most to celebrate at the end of this game was Dave MacLaren. If you were keeping up with the excitement in Chapter 10, you'll remember that he was the goalkeeper whose heroics kept the Saints' tally down to nine – with a little help from the woodwork –

Dave MacLaren

against Wolves. He had moved on to Plymouth when, after only eight games of this season, Campbell Forsyth broke his leg against Liverpool. Never mind that MacLaren was not to blame for the Wolves debacle, the laugh would long be on Ted Bates for signing him a year later. That afternoon at Elland Road, however, the laugh was on the birthday boy and his team-mates, as MacLaren stopped everything they threw at him. As Ken Jones, revelling in such a performance in his native back-yard, recalls it, 'a fair result would have been 10-1. No matter what MacLaren did, he did it right. It hit his arms, legs, crossbar, post… It was unbelievable. We just absolutely got annihilated and how ever we won 1-0…'

The goal came when Davies salmoned up above Jack Charlton to head in a corner delivered by another player returning home to West Yorkshire: David Thompson. Taking corner-kicks was about as near as Thompson needed to come to attacking. This close-season signing could play on either wing. But like Harry Penk, another of that ilk, he soon learned that Ted Bates 'wanted me – because I were a bit of a workhorse – to play on the left wing and then tuck in and fortify the midfield.' Indeed, he believes that this was one reason why Jimmy Melia, who had been good to him at Molineux, had recommended him to Bates. If such a deployment of 'wingers' was inevitably going to be tried more widely in the domestic game after Ramsey's success, it was not exactly novel to the Saints' manager: as I say, we have only to remind ourselves that Penk had been that kind of No.11 during Sydenham's National Service.

Yet Ted Bates had continually reverted to 4-2-4 with the flying Siddie on his left flank – although he had sometimes been playing Paine in midfield, this season, with Sydenham more advanced in a 4-3-3 formation. If this was understandable away from home, as the side struggled to adjust to First Division football, Terry was even being deployed in this way at home. The introduction of Thompson increased those options. Bates could now withdraw Thompson to tuck-in and even man-mark, while Paine could drop back and hit more of those through balls that Connelly had admired when Terry did that for England.

All of which was of no avail when Thompson made his debut, against Everton at The Dell, in the week that culminated in that win at Elland Road. The letters to the *Echo*, following the Saints' 3-1 defeat, were headed ARE PAINE'S TALENTS PROPERLY USED? While conceding that 'Paine is highly efficient in passing the ball, particularly the long cross-field ball and through ball to his striking forwards, and also has a reasonable "work rate", all attributes necessary to perform this [midfield] role,' Mr J Pragnell of London SW19 believed that 'statistics prove that he achieves more when playing a more "orthodox" wingman's game... Put him back on the wing where he is, always has been and always will be, most effective.'

Another way of expressing this problem would have been to ask what Ron Davies was supposed to do, however good he was on the ground, when deprived of Paine's crosses – not to mention those of Sydenham. Rather

Terry Paine and Tornado,
with stable lad, Raymond Davies.

like Penk before, Thompson was pleasantly surprised to be nurtured by Paine, who 'was different to what I'd thought he'd be. I'd never seen him play – except possibly on the television – but I'd always got the impression he were a flying winger. But he weren't; it was Siddie who was the flyer, wasn't it?'

And then Terry rather took the young lad under his wing, not least in respect of horses. David was invited out to Toby Balding's stables to see Terry's first horse – Tornado, a three year-old steeplechaser that he'd bought with his World Cup bonus – and he recalls a trip to Newton Abbot races, where Tornado 'ran like a donkey.' (We can spend a while with Terry Paine, the race-horse owner, in Chapter 16).

Thompson's chance as a man-marker came with the November visit to The Dell of Manchester United, when Ted Bates decided that his No.11 might need to stifle Pat Crerand. This was, you may recall, what George O'Brien was advocating four seasons earlier. But, whereas this role was not part of Sydenham's game, it came easily to Thompson.

The strategy got off to a dodgy start against United, when Bobby Charlton scored in the first minute. But by using a winger in this way – like Penk before – Bates had more options than he'd have in a system with which he would begin to experiment towards the end of this season, using a defender as a spoiler at No.11. Not only did he have the obvious option of pushing Thompson forward, but he might even swap him with Paine, if the latter was having a tough time and fancied a change: a good option to have when you had two men who could play on either flank. Against United, Thompson was able to demonstrate the flexibility of the system when he crossed for Davies to head an equaliser.

OK, so they eventually lost 2-1, but experiments with withdrawn wingers were very much of their time. The rueful assessment of the Football League's Secretary, Alan Hardaker, that, after Ramsey's World Cup triumph, 'nearly everybody in the English game immediately copied 4-3-3,' may be an exaggeration, but there must have been a considerable temptation to adopt the ultimate winning formula and to field one winger at the most; and if you were newly arrived in the top-flight and leaking at the back, then such an adjustment must have seemed especially prudent. Paine was a fixture; so would Sydenham have to go?

The immediate answer was 'No'. Thompson's autumn run lasted only six games, ending in a 5-3 defeat at White Hart Lane that underlined the issue of how best to deploy Paine's talents. Wherever he was playing, he could still take the free-kicks and place them unerringly on Davies's head, as he did to brilliant effect in the game's third minute. Yet Spurs led 4-1 at half-time, with the Saints' formation wasting Davies who, as one reporter put it, 'is currently a better striker even than Greaves coming back to form.' As the visitors rallied in the second half, with Melia setting up goals for Davies and Paine, it was apparent to 'Observer' that, 'instead of being largely engaged in defence,' Paine 'was able to do more in attack [where] he caused a good many gaps in Spurs' defence.'

There was, alas, only one Terry Paine. But now Sydenham returned from injury and mainly remained at No.11 until Thompson started a spring run in the March visit to Everton. The side at Goodison Park included two new signings: Eric Martin and Hugh Fisher. Scottish goalkeeping may have been laughable to Jimmy Greaves, but Martin became the third Scot in Ted Bates's goal in a single season. Spoiling Norman Hunter's birthday was not enough to make MacLaren a long-term prospect, so Bates had been to Scotland in search of a replacement.

He might not have needed to do so, had he been able to call upon a fit home-grown product. He had given a debut in January to 20 year-old Gerry Gurr, who had saved a penalty but let in four at home to Leicester City. But, then, so had Gordon Banks at the other end. A 4-4 draw. Given that he was carrying a torn muscle and had been 'shot full of cortisone,' Gurr had nothing to be ashamed of. He was assured that he was in for the next game at Liverpool. But by then he 'could hardly walk.' He would have to wait a season-and-a-half for his next chance. Ted Bates failed to sign his Scottish target, Dundee United's Sandy Davie, but brought back Dunfermline's Eric Martin, instead.

Fisher was likewise a second pick. He had starred in a bizarre New Year's Eve game at The Dell, when Blackpool, who would be relegated, had won 5-1. If that made him a potential target, Ted Bates especially fancied Preston's Howard Kendall, but – a familiar story – he couldn't afford North End's asking price. So he bought Fisher for £35,000, while Kendall went to Everton for £85,000 and made his debut in this match against the Saints. But neither he nor

Fisher (*left*) is welcomed to The Dell by Tony Knapp, watched by (*left to right*) Ted Bates, Davies, Forsyth and Jimmy Gallagher.

Fisher could steal the show from Eric Martin, who was likened by Brian Stanley to Frank Swift and awarded 10 out of 10. That's four points more than Martin's outfield hero, Alex Young, whom Everton had brought south from Hearts. Some of the credit for Young's low score must go to Thompson, who had been deputed by his manager to 'stop him playing.' It was a role he enjoyed: 'the easiest job in football, if you're fairly fit, is to mark a player out of the game.'

Easy, yes. Enduring, no. After a run of five games, Thompson was out – hardly ever to make the first team again – and Sydenham was now at the mercy of the other experiment at which I hinted: it was time for the No.11 shirt to be worn by an out-and-out defender. Again, the opponents were Manchester United, this time at Old Trafford. The player was 20 year-old Tony Byrne, making his League debut. He would come to acquire a reputation for his man-marking jobs on George Best, but on this occasion he was just an additional defender, with Paine, according to the *Echo*, 'virtually an extra half-back.' It worked well enough until half-time, but the League leaders, on the verge of winning their first post-Munich Championship, ran out 3-0 winners. Thompson feels that the use of a defender, rather than a tuck-in winger, was, quite simply, 'wrong'. Maybe so, although once Charlton had opened the scoring – following a slack midfield pass from Paine that set up a flowing exchange between Charlton and Law – Ted Bates still had the option of moving Terry forward. He had Sydenham waiting on the bench, but in this second season of substitutes, it remained the law that they could be used only when a player was injured.

Two more defeats followed and it looked as though it could go down to the last game against fellow-strugglers Aston Villa. But Terry Paine completed the escape in the penultimate match against second-placed

Above: As Paine prepares to take the vital penalty, Sydenham (No.11) is poised to snap up any rebound, but other team-mates are not sure where to look.

Below: Referee Pye has come close to take a very good look, though, ensuring that Grummitt has not moved before his dive that failed to keep out Paine's kick.

Nottingham Forest, hitting the winner with yet another penalty. As he faced his memorable adversary of 1963 – goalkeeper Grummitt, returning to The Dell for the first time since that famous FA Cup evening – some of his team-mates could not bear to watch. Referee Pye added to the tension by coming into the six-yard box to motion Grummitt back to his line. Amid all this, Paine kept his nerve and the Saints were safe.

Which meant that Terry could relax and let Davies clinch his fourth hat-trick of the season, when he took the last-day penalty against Villa. The 6-2 score-line brought the side's League total to 74, a remarkable haul for a struggling side. But, then, Hurst had helped West Ham, who ended up only two points above Saints, to total 80. The key to finishing at the top of the table was not about scoring massively more goals than the battlers at the bottom – runners-up Forest managed a mere 64 – so much as conceding fewer than 50. Saints shipped 92, by far the worst in the division and second-worst in the entire Football League.

A sensational season for Ron Davies, then, but an odd one for Terry Paine, strutting his stuff in the First Division – where quite a few managers had for so long wanted him to play – yet not getting another cap. Ramsey had now gone wingless with a vengeance: not a single wide man played for England that season. Two of his World Cup wingers – Paine and Connelly – did get a final representative run-out in September, though, scoring twice each, when the Football League beat the Irish League 12-0 at Home Park.

Chapter 15

Who Needs Coaches?

The summer tour of Malaya and Singapore was an act bordering on the vindictive, in so far as Ron Davies, scourge of the First Division defences, was now marked by players who were mostly far too short for the task.

That didn't stop Terry Paine from putting crosses on to his head, for Ron to chalk up hat-tricks against two select XIs, Malaysian and Asian, respectively. And nor did it stop Terry from being 'typically competitive' in the first game – to the extent that, although he was diplomatically removed at half-time, he still caused a full-time riot.

Longstanding Saints fan, Rob Holley, was then teaching in Malaya, along with his wife, Diane. They managed to get themselves imprisoned on the team coach at the end of the 7-1 win, with a police guard. The siege lasted an hour – not a pleasant experience, Rob assures us, with the windows closed, on police orders, and with the players unshowered. Martin Chivers's solution for a hastened end to this purgatory – throw Terry Paine to the mob: 'he started it!' – was not taken up.

The journey to the second game took the party past the Holleys' home, so they arranged to stop off for refreshments. Expecting the players to 'have massive thirsts in the oppressive

Terry Paine (standing) and Mick Channon are joined by some of their young fans at the pool.
The Holley children are Ruth (seated, left); Lisa, in front of Terry; and David, the smaller of the two boys with her.

heat,' Rob 'had bought in quite a few crates of *Tiger* beer, but all they wanted was cup after cup of good old-fashioned tea.' The Holleys followed them to their next venue, where they hosted them at the local swimming pool, along with a party of children – their own three, plus some from their school. Lounging in the pool, the players were a huge hit with the kids. The Holleys' other child was absent. Duncan was back at Peter Symonds. The Saints historian still talks with envy about this family event that he had to miss.

But Ted Bates, feeling more relaxed about his summer shopping than in the previous close season, was able to be in the party and still have time, on his return, for some pre-season wheeler-dealing. Kendall's move to Everton had given him a new target: Jimmy Gabriel, the man displaced. The two-cap Scot was reluctant to come south. He hoped he'd be moving to Stoke, an expectation encouraged by his team-mate, Alan Ball, whose father was the assistant manager at the Victoria Ground.

When Stoke failed to make a move, Jimmy signed for Southampton. Ball wondered if he was going mad – 'you'll win nothing, there' – but having agreed to come for talks, Gabriel had warmed to Bates's way of thinking. Not positionally – he would find himself at No.5, not his favourite spot, replacing Tony Knapp – but strategically. Knapp had taken over the captaincy from Paine and seemingly shared his immunity to omission by Ted Bates; and I rather assumed that the fans would generally have perceived Tony, as I did, as a sophisticated replacement for the more basic Page. So I was surprised to discover how little some of his team-mates trusted him – for reasons discussed in Chapter 8 – consistently to make the right decisions. True, we also saw, in that chapter, that Stuart Williams valued his covering qualities, while Brian Clifton likes to fantasise about how easy it would have been to play as sweeper to a player who 'attacked the ball brilliantly,' the way Knapp did.

A patient Bates has got his man. Jimmy Gabriel has eventually agreed to come south.

Whatever Ted Bates and fans like me may have thought of him, the point, here, is that Knapp was never going to be trusted, by his team-mates, in the kind of decision-making role that Gabriel felt Ted Bates was according him from the start:

It was everything I wanted. At my age – I was 26 [Knapp was by then coming 31] – I think you need to be trusted to go on that park and kind of work it out for some of the players and work it out for yourself and see what you had to do *on that day* to make it happen for your team. And he trusted me with that and he trusted Terry Paine with that.

As Jimmy saw it, it was accepted that he would organise the defence, while Terry sorted things out upfront. Terry agrees with that recall of a kind of dual captaincy, a prerequisite of which was that he demonstrated to Jimmy that warnings about his shortcomings as a team-mate were unjustified. Gabriel had 'heard all these rumours about Terry this and Terry that: "Terry rules everything; watch your back; he's in cahoots with the manager; he's the boss of the team," and all that sort of stuff. He'd been with the England team and he was kind of selfish – this sort of thing. I'd heard all that from outside sources: it wasn't coming from Southampton.'

Gabriel had two reactions. One was 'let's see what I find: I go down there and I played with him for five years and got on great with him and found him to be a smashing lad.' The other was to dismiss the very idea that any one player could 'boss' the team:

I'd heard that and I felt that it was *nothing,* because I knew that, on the field, there were several captains – and I was one of them. So, when I went on the field, whether I was tossing the coin or not tossing the coin, I was going to be a captain in that game, because I could read what was happening in the game and how we needed to change it to win the game. And Terry did the same. He thought about the game; he'd talk about it at half-time. Quite often, we'd try to convince Ted to make a change or two, because we felt that that change would help us.

And they didn't always wait until half-time: the manager 'trusted' the likes of Gabriel and Paine 'to make decisions for the team and we could go on that field and say "we've got to change a wee bit of this or a little bit of that." Ted was magnificent. Ted gave us licence, up to a point, to get things happening. He made us feel a much bigger part of the team.'

I wonder whether such a dominating presence as Gabriel, playing either at the back or in midfield, might have been in a better position to captain the side than Paine was, if and when he was playing wide. Jimmy is having none of that: 'Not really. I think you captain the team through your personality. I don't think there's ever one captain in a team. There's one guy who tosses the coin but there are three or four guys,' – Jimmy cites Melia, Fisher and, later, McGrath – 'who have their finger on the pulse of the game and any one of them can change it a bit and say "hey, we need to do this" or "we need to do that." I felt that Terry and I had that.'

Paine was not leading by example, though, in the opening-day defeat, 3-0, at Newcastle. This was his 492nd competitive game for Southampton. But by adding in non-competitive matches – including his latest close-season appearances, on tour and in pre-season friendlies – the *Echo* calculated that this was his 514th game for the club, overtaking Tommy Traynor's 513.

His response was far from fitting. He should have given Saints the lead but under-hit a penalty when a goal-bound Davies header was punched out by Frank Clark. There was no question of the full-back's being sent off for that: this was 1967, when five players – including the visitors' Paine, Gabriel and Webb – might have been dismissed in the closing minutes, according to John Dunn in one of the Sundays, but none was even booked. The *Echo* took a dim view of 'the large number of fouls that certain Saints' players committed,' with Paine, 'whose only real contributions to the match were flashes of temper,' a notable culprit.

It was the same in the next match – a 3-2 win over Manchester City – when Terry was 'in one of his niggly and petulant moods,' though it took him another four games to get himself booked – for arguing with the ref at Coventry. In the meantime, he had laid on four of the goals, two each for Chivers and Davies, in a 6-2 win at Stamford Bridge, where he was able persistently to get the better of Eddie McCreadie, without needing his centre-forward to nobble him.

If you do not yet have a sense of Terry Paine's mixed start to this campaign, it is perhaps captured in the opening words of a report on the 10th game of the season, a 2-1 win over Nottingham Forest, assessing 'Southampton's debt to the fitful genius of Terry Paine.' He had given Saints the lead, rounding Peter Grummitt, who must have been getting sick of him, but it was his contribution to Davies's winner that had this reporter drooling as 'Paine jinked down the right, leaving the hapless Winfield stranded yet again.' Whereupon centre-half McKinlay came to cover and 'Paine nonchalantly slipped by him, put his foot on the ball, looked up, motioned Davies into position and centred' for Ron to 'bullet' his header past Grummitt.

Should you be wondering whether Terry could really find so much time and space against such a strong side as Forest, he confirms the above account: 'once I had got past McKinlay, I had all the time in the world: time to signal to Ron and time to decide how to cross it. And once I saw Ron start moving in, I knew it was a goal.' Just like that.

Gabriel had been making a go of his centre-half duties, which included coming up for corners and hovering for a knock-down from Davies or, less often, from Chivers. Which is how Jimmy came to score his first Southampton goal, a very late equaliser when Leeds visited The Dell in September. Norman Hunter describes, in his autobiography, how and why he was blamed – and got it 'with both barrels' from Don Revie – for the careless throw-in that led to the Paine corner from which Gabriel scored. Younger Saints fans may think of Portsmouth as *the* 'rivals', but talk to men from the top teams of the day – Leeds, Liverpool and Manchester United, say – and they'll tell you why they disliked playing Southampton away. It was a triple whammy: a difficult destination to reach; the crowd on top of you; and, then, as Hunter points out, some dangerous forwards to contend with. The perceived 'tightness' of The Dell added, Hunter feels, to the challenge of facing Terry Paine:

> At Southampton, it was so tight and he used to come at you with that right peg of his; and he was quick and all and he could go outside. A great crosser of the ball. Picked the ball up, had a look – not very often did he just whack it in there; he tried to play it; tried to work it; and then knock it in. You were always wary before the game. If you're telling each other, 'get close to him; get stuck into him; try and put him off his game,' then you know he's a good player. And down there [at The Dell], he did what Strachan did for Leeds: he was wide right, but he had *such* an influence on the game.

And he could take a good corner, too. Which is why Hunter shouldn't have ruined Revie's planning by letting him have that corner-kick, from which Gabriel registered his first success as the third man at Paine corners.

Jimmy's spell at No.5 ended in October, following his return to Goodison Park for a 4-2 defeat and a 5-1 humiliation by Leicester City at The Dell. The latter match will be remembered for how Campbell Forsyth came to let a clearance from Peter Shilton bounce over his head and into the goal. Even so, the *Leicester Mercury*'s Jimmy Martin found space to congratulate Terry Paine on pleading with referee Gow not to book his marker, Richie Norman, for a foul on him. 'It was an accident,' Paine wanted the ref to know: after all, his reputation depended upon left-backs being unable to do him intentionally.

Gabriel would not now be wearing the No.5 shirt for a while. David Webb took over at centre-half, as he had done a few times in the 1966 run-in. This freed Gabriel for a midfield role, initially in the No.11 shirt, as Bates again sacrificed Sydenham.

Paine would sometimes join Gabriel in midfield. The pros and cons of this arrangement were identified in the accounts of two successive November matches: a 3-2 defeat at Old Trafford and a 3-2 home win against Sunderland. The result against Manchester United notwithstanding, 'much of the [Saints'] increased effectiveness' in this game was attributed to Paine's 'use in a midfield role where his incisive distribution gave Saints a more penetrative build-up than we have seen recently.' As Saints reverted to 4-2-4 for Sunderland's visit, however, the same reporter commented on the contrast: the corollary of Paine's deeper role at Old Trafford had been 'the non-stop running' of Mick Channon, starting for the first time with Davies and Chivers, in a front three supported by Paine, Melia and Gabriel; but now, as Paine reverted to his wide role at home, 'magnificently' so, 'young Channon seemed uncertain of his duties.'

This problem of who needed to adjust how to different formations and personnel was not going to go away. Lying deep and hitting Channon on the run was a different ploy from going wide to hit Chivers or Davies on the head. Ted Bates felt 'there was no way' this front three was going to work, long-term. He was soon presented with two solutions, one of which would be permanent.

The permanent solution resulted from a transfer request by Chivers. The saga of where he would go has been recounted at some length in *Dell Diamond* and need not be rehearsed here.

Suffice it to summarise. Bates rated Chivers 'the only *good* player I ever let go' and insisted that he would not have sold him to Tottenham – begging the question of what further adjustments would be needed of whom – if Chivers had shown him the 'aggression' that he developed at White Hart Lane. As Paine puts it, why did an athlete of such 'magnificent' physique always leave you doubting 'whether he really wanted it enough?' Terry recalls the Spurs manager asking him, soon after signing Chivers, 'how do you get this fellow to run towards his opponents' goal?' But Bill Nicholson found a way and Chivers became 'a terrific player,' by Ted Bates's reckoning, greatly admired by him and Paine alike (and, of course, by the England manager). Frank Saul, the makeweight in the transfer deal, was but a stop-gap while the 20 year-old Channon was still 'sort of feeling his way,' Bates explained: Saul 'plodded around a bit' for him until Micky was ready.

The departure of Chivers pretty much coincided with a knee injury to Jimmy Melia, which forced Bates into a temporary arrangement, whereby Paine would play midfield with Gabriel and Fisher. Ted decided that Terry, who'd proved himself capable, on the wing, of 'looking after himself' (a footballers' euphemism that will be unpacked in Chapter 23), needed to practise coping with the tighter marking that he would experience in midfield. Which is why he took aside two of his young reserves, Ray Ames and Bobby Stokes, and briefed them to make life difficult for Terry on the practice pitch. There was nothing new about this managerial ploy: Gerry Gurr recalls his trial in 1964, when Paine, evidently acting on orders, 'came and whacked me a couple of times from behind,' so that Bates could see if the 17 year-old had 'got the stuff.' Now, in 1968, Paine was the one on trial. As Ames recalls,

> Ted said to me and Stokesie, 'just sit with Terry. Wherever Terry goes, don't let him get the ball. Just stop him from playing.' That's all we had to do. I remember tackling him and I ran away with the ball. He tried to hack me down. I stumbled on and he hacked me down again and I went sprawling. By the time I got up, there were three or four Reserve-team players grabbing hold of him. Ken Jones. David Paton. I think because we were youngsters, Terry thought he could take advantage of us. We nippers wouldn't have done anything about it. Dave was captain of the Reserves and Ken always stuck up for us.

That's the way Ken Jones, who'd 'never seen owt like it,' remembers it, too. We have seen how first-teamers had a certain licence to rough up young reserves on the training ground, but this incident breached the unwritten rules of that licence. Yet the 'nippers' would have treated it as part of their day's work, Ames assures us, the more so perhaps because he felt 'Terry looked after me quite a few times.' He describes how Terry helped him out, later in 1968. Ray had married and had a daughter while still only 18. Terry and Carol had recently adopted twin girls and, seeing Ray's difficulties, 'Terry said "I'll bring some stuff in for you" and he brought in a load of gear that was near-nigh brand new – but it wasn't one, it was two, of everything. He really looked after us that way.' And that arrangement lasted a while, as the twins grew out of their clothing ahead of Ray's daughter.

Meanwhile, back on the pitch, Paine's 11-match spell at No.10 turned out well enough, even though the Saints contrived to exit the FA Cup, in a Dell replay against a West Brom team that had a full-back in goal for the second half. League-wise, the side pulled themselves up from 20th in the table to 16th – helped, seemingly, by a change of personnel at the back. David Webb wanted a move to London and Ted Bates had been trying to swap him for Chelsea's Marvin Hinton, who had played with Paine at Under-23 level and who was capable, like Webb, of operating both at No.2 and No.5. When that plan fell through, Bates signed *two* of Terry's U-23 team-mates, one for each position: full-back Joe Kirkup, in exchange for Webb, from Chelsea; and centre-half John McGrath from Newcastle.

Gabriel now dropped back to play alongside McGrath, a centre-back pairing that older Saints fans will surely rank as one of the best they remember at the club. The full-backs weren't bad, either, though Gabriel feels that the First Division wingers of that era – survivors of the Ramsey-inspired culls – could still get behind their markers, unless the latter were of the quality he had known at Everton, with Tommy Wright and Terry's hero,

In the days before a new signing held up a scarf or a newly-named shirt
for the cameras, the *Echo* photographers liked to snap a handshake from the manager
or captain. McGrath and Paine oblige, while Walker and Saul mock this traditional pose.
(*Left to right*): Gabriel, McGrath, Webb, Jones, Paine, Forsyth, Walker, Saul.

Ray Wilson. Whereas those Everton backs had forced wingers to cross the
ball *into* the centre-backs, it was so much harder for the likes of Gabriel
when the wide men were getting to the by-line and crossing, so now

> that ball's going *away* from you. Now it's the forwards who are going to be
> heading the ball and you have to do something special to defend that type
> of cross, to get that type of cross away. I felt we were vulnerable a bit in
> that area. That's not to say the guys who were playing there weren't good
> players, but I looked at Southampton and thought 'well, we could be a
> Championship-winning team if we could have tightened up in that area.'

Upfront, the manager not only played both Channon (however unready he
might have been) *and* Saul, but he also brought back Sydenham. Paine
continued at No.10 and responded to those who considered him wasted in
midfield with a match-winning performance when Sheffield Wednesday
came to The Dell in March, a week after his 29th birthday. In what
'Observer' considered 'one of his best games since he undertook the work
of a No.10 linkman,' Terry's contributions to both goals in a 2-0 win again
demonstrated the range of his ability. First, he broke down the left wing
and crossed for Ron Davies to score. Then, picking up the ball from a

John Sydenham raises his arms triumphantly as Paine, who started the move, finishes it off.
The white-coated steward in the upper stand seems pretty pleased about it, too.

Wednesday corner, he spread the play with 'one of his many good passes to Sydenham' and raced goalwards – to score when the 'keeper failed to gather Sydenham's cross.

Finding that 'Wednesday had no-one to match the consistency of Paine,' Trevor Williamson of the *Telegraph* ventured the opinion that Terry was 'a better player in midfield than he was on the wing,' a view supported enthusiastically by a spectator in international transit – Tony Knapp, whose stint at Coventry was already over and who was flying out, the next day, to join Los Angeles Wolves.

Be that as it may, Melia was fit, two games later, to reclaim his No.10 shirt and Paine reverted to No.7. Bates had another trick up his sleeve, though, when an Easter Saturday injury to Ron Davies meant that he needed another No.9 for the Monday visit to Highbury. In the party and promised his full debut, 19 year-old Mick Judd 'thought the boss would throw me the 11-shirt: keep wide; run up and down; and look pretty.' Although he always expected to establish himself as a winger – more of which in Chapter 19 – it was the No.9 shirt that Bates 'threw' him that day. Channon, who had scored on his Easter Monday debut two seasons before, pulled one back for Judd to do the same. In the absence of Davies, Paine had to vary his game. Deprived of his principal place-kick target – and Gabriel was also out, injured – he rolled a short free-kick into the stride of Kirkup, whose intended cross floated over a surprised Bob Wilson. And when Simpson fisted away his shot, Terry, who'd ceded penalty-taking to Davies after his opening-day miss, had to step up to the spot. He scored to seal a 3-0 win, which completed an Easter 'double' over Arsenal and meant that Southampton were safe, with four games to go.

Their run since the introduction of Kirkup and McGrath had involved only two defeats, including a 6-1 hammering at White Hart Lane, with two assists and a goal from Chivers. Watching the game was Southampton's new assistant manager. The club had advertised for somebody who would 'take charge of the coaching, training and discipline of the players.' From an impressive shortlist that included Harry Gregg, Lawrie McMenemy and Jimmy Scoular, the Board appointed John Mortimore. Last encountered in Chapter 8, as Chelsea's centre-half discussing George Kirby's robustness, Mortimore had most recently been coaching at Sunderland. Hampshire-born and bred, he had been a schoolteacher and amateur international, while playing for Woking, before going to Stamford Bridge.

Recite that *c.v* to Terry Paine and you can guarantee that he'll focus on Mortimore's classroom years: 'a schoolteacher among seasoned profess-ionals!' The very idea! Remind him that John was a well-seasoned pro – 279 games for Chelsea, nearly all of them in the top flight – and it will cut no ice: 'I know it came over that he was a schoolteacher. And when he walked out!' Then follows Terry's imitation of Mortimore's first-day instructions, refined teacher's accent and all: 'he got off to the worst possible start.' Terry is not alone with such initial memories. Eric Martin reacted to the new man's dress and deportment: 'John looked like a ballet dancer to me... I thought "this guy's in the wrong business." But he did his job. He was good.'

In other words, Eric let the evidence of what Mortimore *did* – a shift from 'sit-ups and a medicine ball' to one of 'dance around the track' and,

Terry Paine's head drops as John Mortimore 'gets off to the worst possible start.'
(*Left to right*) Thompson, Mortimore, Gabriel (part-hidden),
Saul, Paine, Gurr, Kirkup, Channon.

all in all, 'a sort of European thing' – contradict his first impression. But Terry didn't. No matter that Mortimore had had so much more First Division experience than he – and 'hadn't been in a classroom for quite some time,' he points out – Terry still has him down as a schoolteacher. John Sydenham never took, either, to the introduction of 'a clip-board man.' The problem, as Jimmy Gabriel sees it, is that the players didn't respect their new coach (or his successor, as we shall see), 'because it was a new thing, something breaking in, and there was no need to get a coach in there – nothing against coaches because I think the guys gave it their best shot and did reasonably well, but I don't think it was the time at Southampton for coaches.' That time might have come, he reasons, after Terry and he, who were running the show in the way described above, had gone and there happened to be

nobody to step into our places; and maybe a coach would have been needed *then*. And it could have been either me or Terry that could have taken over the coaching, because we knew the players, we knew what they were good at; but at that time, the coach was stepping on the ground that belonged to Terry and me. Part of our job, which had been assumed by Terry and me, was to do the coaching, to make sure everything was right. We'd taken responsibility for what went on on that park. That was sensible and it was the way things were done in those days. The older players did that sort of thing; and getting a coach was new stuff. They tried to influence our performances with ideas: some were ridiculous and some were good. It was a difficult beginning for the players and for the coaches. The players would listen to the older players, like myself. *Now* they come to coaches: they use the coaches. But at that time, they wouldn't do it: they'd come to me or Terry – or John McGrath or Hughie Fisher – and ask us. They'd come to us for advice; you'd give them that advice and then the coach wouldn't like you, because you'd given the players advice. They wouldn't go to the coaches because they didn't have their finger on the pulse, because they'd left the game and we hadn't.

Mick Channon, who was still only 19 when Mortimore arrived, has a less sweeping view of coaching but agrees that older players can have an important teaching role. He cites how he initially learned what was needed of him more from Terry Paine than from Ted Bates:

Mick Channon, at the end of the 1967-68 season.

When you're young, you don't listen to anyone, do you? You're that wrapped up in yourself. The world's passing you by at 100 mph, so you never really see the picture. It was hard to understand Ted Bates; it was easier to understand Terry Paine, cos I played with him. When he put the ball down and looked at me, I *knew* what to do: it was instinct. Painie understood Ted, but that was experience. So, really, he was handing his experience down to me; and, hopefully, I handed it on to some others. Painie had a great football brain. So did Ted Bates, but Ted wasn't the easiest to understand when you were young.

Channon distinguishes two types of discipline – on the field; and more generally. The problem of the Southampton side in which he was just finding his feet was, he reckons, of the former variety: 'if we had a fault, we weren't disciplined enough, as a *team*. We had great skill and great flair. And we had some great characters – and match-winners! Individuals, you know.' Talking to me in the run-up to the 2003 Cup Final, he contrasted Gordon Strachan's squad with that of Ted Bates: 'what's different now is that, as a unit, they're far more disciplined.'

The trickier issue facing the Board and their new assistant in 1968 was discipline in general, including personal life-style. But how do you begin to instil a change of attitude in a group of players who were quite happy with their manager's notion of discipline? It wasn't broke and didn't need fixin'. Channon holds Alf Ramsey responsible. The England manager had disciplined some notorious drinkers and there were now club directors who figured that this was the way to go. But they would find 'player power' a considerable obstacle at this level.

Young Channon was able to put that theory to the test in the last away game of the season at Craven Cottage. With the Saints trailing 1-0 at half-time to already-relegated Fulham, Mortimore, who was in charge, instructed Mick to change his boots. He refused: 'nobody tells me what boots to wear!' Whereupon, he came out, ran on to a Paine pass and equalised – and celebrated with 'an offensive gesture' to the bench. The Board fined him £20. So what? Such a sanction 'wasn't going to change our lives that much, was it?' Yet even this angry young man found that he came to terms with this new approach to discipline: 'it was unheard of you, you know. But we got through it. I survived. John Mortimore survived… I think John's a good bloke, but you don't change things overnight.'

But, then, this would not be the last time that this strong-minded dressing room would have to adjust to change. Ted Bates, now 50, had had almost 13 seasons in charge and two of his squad had come through from the Youth team with him.

Chapter 16

Minding His Business

Discipline remained a problem in the 1968-69 season, with the Board twice having to debate sanctions for broken curfews on the road.

An incident in October was straightforward enough: nine players found cause to celebrate, beyond midnight, after a 4-0 League Cup win at Norwich. Four were out until 2.00 a.m and were fined £25 each. The other occasion involved a weekend break in Harrogate between the team's first two away games of the season: defeats at Sunderland and Burnley. What was different was that all 13 players – including low-frequency drinkers, Paine and Melia – made a concerted effort to break the 11 o'clock curfew.

Perhaps that is why the Board rejected the manager's request for fines all round. Or maybe they weren't impressed that Ted Bates's Sunday morning inquest had been abandoned in uproar, after Mick Channon clumsily attempted to have his say. In his autobiography, *Man on the Run,* Channon recounts his 'fumbled' effort, in which he 'got more and more tongue-tied.' It didn't help that his tongue was tied to what would become his trademark exclamation: effing and blinding may be the first language of the dressing room, but it was not the way to respond to a managerial dressing-down.

Given their declared intention to improve discipline, the Board might have been expected to back the manager against such a bold display of 'player-power'. By now, Mortimore reasons, the directors had come to realise why it would be 'difficult to enforce' their intended policy of relying upon an assistant to raise standards of discipline. He explains why this arrangement was doomed to fail:

> It was very difficult to put the discipline side onto the No.2, when the No.1 was in control. If I'd come in and been *in charge* of it all, I think it would have been easier. I'd had *some* problems at Sunderland – with Jim Baxter and people like that – but they hadn't been at the club as long as some of the established players – Sydenham, Paine and all those – had been at Southampton. I had to respect the way Ted had been doing things with the players. Terry was probably more in Ted's office than I was. That was the way things had been, over the years, and they had worked well: the team had come up with players who had been there a long time and they'd done well.

They weren't starting this season too well, though. They ended August with another away defeat, but achieved their first away point, on their next trip, against Manchester City. The line-up at Maine Road illustrates a side in transition. Eric Martin had just been dropped in favour of Gerry Gurr, whose debut appearance, during that 1966-67 season of the three Scottish 'keepers, you may recall. When Gerry left the field that day, Gordon Banks, his counterpart at the other end, had talked of 'having to watch out for my England place.'

The side in transition that won its first away point of the season at Maine Road. Back row (*left to right*): McGrath, Walker, Kemp, Hollywood, Gurr, Gabriel. Front: Kirkup, Channon, Paine, Davies, Melia.

He may have been joking but, amid glowing write-ups, Gurr would soon be attracting serious predictions that he could be among Banks's understudies in the 1970 World Cup finals. He would keep his Southampton place for the rest of the season, being dazzled but not fazed by all the internationals on the field with him: 'I was the only one in the programme,' he chuckles, 'that I'd never heard of.'

The back four of Kirkup, McGrath, Gabriel and Hollywood was the one that had come together six months earlier. Ken Jones would be called up to replace each full-back in turn, but the centre-back pairing of Jimmy Gabriel and John McGrath was consolidating at centre-back. McGrath would be ever-present in League and Cups. And so would Paine be, although he came off after scoring against Burnley on Easter Monday, the first time he had ever been substituted. The substitute law had been changed, the previous season, so that an injury was no longer a necessity:

a player could be removed for tactical reasons. Ted Bates had welcomed this change in his *Echo* column, but hardly ever exploited it. He shuffled his starting line-ups, but his basic strategic switch during a game was to move Terry Paine from midfield in a 4-3-3 formation to his more accustomed wide role.

It was in the matter of tactics that John Mortimore felt he played a role. And it was one in which he felt Bates and he had the players' full support. Terry Paine's cooperation, in adopting to the 4-3-3 away from home, but playing wide at home, was especially important. Mortimore reasons that Terry thereby performed, on the road, with more *involvement* in the game. If you're playing wide, away from home,

> and you're under a bit of pressure, you're not going to get in the game very much. But Terry sat in the centre of midfield and did a *great* job for us. He could *pass* the ball – he was such an excellent passer of the ball.

Actually, the 4-3-3 was often 4-1-2-3, with David Walker playing what he called a 'marauding' role in front of the back four. And there was a replacement engine in midfield, whether in the home or the away formation, in Freddie Kemp, coming in for Fisher. Another import from Molineux, Kemp had played in the 1966 promotion side, wearing No.10, and even No.9. Like any midfielder who likes to burst forward with the ball, Freddie was always likely to be a crowd-pleaser. But that pleasure wasn't universally shared by those who had to play with him.

As a full-back, Ken Jones felt that Kemp left him exposed, especially when the formation allowed Freddie to go forward with Terry. 'Consequently, we had two players,' Jones explains,

> that weren't picking people up. Freddie used to go wandering off and he wasn't a particularly good marker. If you put Hughie in the same position, Hughie would concentrate more on who he had to mark. Freddie had a lot of skill and, from the crowd's point of view, he looked good. But when you lost the ball, you'd got two players in the team out of the game; and then it's very easy for them to get at our defence.

Joe Kirkup shared Jones's preference for Fisher, whose 'phenomenal' work-rate and intelligent covering meant that Joe didn't have to worry unduly if Paine didn't track back: he was happy for Terry to concentrate on doing 'a fantastic job, going forward.' For his part, Paine felt that Kemp's runs 'could be infectious': not only could they thrill the fans, but they 'could rub off on other players.' The problem was that the 'end-product didn't warrant all that energy.' At the end of the day, though, the manager and his assistant were at one with Freddie's fans.

Where to play Paine was just one of Ted Bates's problems as to width: the other was whether to play Sydenham *at all*. But, then, if you've stuck with the plot, you'll know that Bates had for long wrestled with this dilemma and that Sydenham had kept bouncing back. After a lengthy spell in the Reserves, John would be back in the spring – to the delight of Gurr.

As Tony Godfrey explained, in Chapter 10, a 'keeper likes a wide man to whom he can clear the ball and Gurr felt that 'Terry and John gave us so many "outs" in so many different ways – with Big Ron in the middle and people feeding off them.' And he discounted the argument that Paine failed to get back enough: 'I've got a picture of him stood next to my goalpost, in

the snow at Hillsborough [in the last game of 1968], so I don't think that can be quite right.' All of which explains why Gerry felt that 'we were so lucky to have Terry Paine and John Sydenham, who, for me, had to be probably the best *pair* in the country – though you could probably argue it with the Liverpool lads: Callaghan and Thompson were a good pairing.'

'Argue it', if you will, but I've contrasted Paine's style and achievements with each of the Liverpool wingers, in turn (in the England chapters), and feel no need to debate the respective merits of Gurr's two pairs. For Ted Bates, the issue was perhaps not so much the quality of his

Hillsborough in the snow
– the winter scene with which Gerry Gurr likes to confront those who say Terry Paine didn't come back far enough.
Gurr remains focused as Kirkup (No.2) and Paine prepare to race the referee.

wingers, now each in his 30th year, as the strength of the defensive cover he had elsewhere in the side, if he was going to play with one of them wide, let alone both.

The pros and cons of using Paine in midfield were demonstrated in consecutive games in October. First, Saints chalked up their first away win of the season, playing 4-3-3 at Old Trafford. With the score at 1-1, Paine hit a through-ball from his own half, for Davies to run on and score the winner. The next Saturday, at home to Sheffield Wednesday, Ted Bates decided to stick with what one sceptical reporter called his 'defensively-weighted formula.' Yet that decision was not to blame, this sceptic felt, for the way Saints struggled to draw 1-1: the system 'depends on 100 per cent effort,' he reasoned; and, while this had been shown on the road, it was lacking in this home game.

Paine then worked harder, reportedly, than he had all season, at White Hart Lane in midweek, as the Saints went out of the League Cup, 1-0 to Spurs, leaving Brian Hayward to voice his preferences in the *Echo*:

> Terry Paine's great ability makes him a valuable player whether on the wing or in midfield, but the further he goes forward at home makes me happier and must increase the scoring power. Paine has the great gift of snatching goals when none looks likely, but if he moves up only for the last ten minutes or so, then his chances are greatly restricted. I suppose it is a question of making the best use of players available. If Saints could find another player able to work effectively from midfield, then Paine would be freed for an attacking role.

Well, yes, but even supposing Ted Bates could find such a midfield man, the 'best use' of his squad might then be to rest a midfielder at home and an attacker away, with Paine alternating between his two positions. And Bates would still have the option – were he to make fuller use of the amended substitution rule – of switching Paine, if need be, during the game. Hayward had his way when Saints completed a double over Manchester United in December, with Paine 'playing more on the right touchline than in most of the recent games.'

Whichever position he was in, Terry was always going to be making goals from set-pieces. Indeed, my best-remembered Davies goal came from a Paine free-kick in the 1-0 win against Leicester City in March. I was standing under the East Stand, level with Terry's back as he bent to place the ball for a free-kick. My lasting image is that he seemed to take the kick before he had fully straightened up, catching the Leicester defence flat-footed, as Davies rose to put a 'majestic' header past Peter Shilton. Or so said the *Echo* of this 'flash of brilliance from the Old Firm.'

In the few remaining games, the Paine-Davies firm shared the goals with two youngsters, Micky Judd and Bobby Stokes. You may recall that Judd had scored on his full debut at Highbury, the previous season, wearing No.9. But he considered himself a wide player and in March took over the No.11 shirt that had been alternating between Saul and Sydenham. A self-confident 20 year-old, he believed that everyone had seen it coming:

> John Sydenham knew that I would take his place. People like David Thompson knew that I had more skills. Frankie Saul said 'you're *there*!'...
> It was no question that I was going to take Terry Paine's place. That was the way Ted was thinking... all my development was for No.7.

'The Old Firm', together in 1968-69.

For the moment, he would have to be content with swapping wings, from time to time, with Paine – if only when Terry came across to take a left-wing corner and stayed that side for a while. Judd had studied from on high Paine's corner-kick repertoire. Looking down from the gantry on the West Stand roof, from where some of the reserves liked to watch, he was impressed by what he saw:

> Terry was fantastic. He could put them on a sixpence, basically. As you grew up, you took corners and you hopefully got them in the air and somewhere around the penalty area; but when you saw Terry, he had so many types of corner. There was the out-swinger; the in-swinger; there was the near-post ball for the man running and suddenly coming through; there was the hanger, with so much back-spin on it that the goalkeeper would come, thinking it was an ordinary corner, and he'd be caught underneath it, because it's holding there, and then it would just drop like a stone and you see the goalkeeper floundering under this ball which has held; and Ron Davies has just buried it. It was beautiful to watch.

Judd felt that he proved, over Easter 1969, what he could achieve by changing wings. With Saints trailing 2-0 to QPR at The Dell on the Saturday, Paine and he exchanged positions. It worked. In a four-minute spell, Davies headed home two crosses: from Paine on the left; and then from Judd, dribbling past two men to cross from the right. An own goal sealed the win for the Saints and Judd was on a high. As he later explained in an extensive *Echo* interview, his 'confidence began to grow after this game… Playing on the right in a 4-2-4 formation, I began to feel I was the equal of anyone else on the field.'

Two days later, Judd popped up on the right, early in the game against Burnley, to cross for Stokes to score on his debut. That made it three seasons in the last four that a debutant had scored on Easter Monday. Stokes added a second, in a 5-1 romp, and kept his place, with Channon seeing out the seasons in the Reserves.

Judd has popped up on the right to cross for Stokes to duck low and score.

That high-scoring Easter, with new kids buzzing on the block, belied a season of tightening up. Saints' tally of 57 was their lowest since the war, but this was the first season in which they had scored more top-flight goals than they conceded (47). A triumph for the input of a defensively-experienced coach? Or for the way Jimmy Gabriel was marshalling the troops at the back?

Either way, it was enough to clinch seventh place in the First Division – Southampton's highest-ever placing, to date, in the Football League – and to book them their first taste of European competition.

The players warmed up for Europe with two summer tours: to Bermuda in May and June; and to Holland and Germany in July. Their matches in Bermuda included a 4-2 win over West Ham, a success for a variation on 4-3-3, with Paine in midfield, alongside Kemp and Gabriel, while Judd was on the right, up front, with Channon and Davies. Paine knew, from his England days, that you could play wide in such a front three, yet still be expected to pop up and score – as he had done, most famously, in Nuremberg. If such was expected of Judd, he was up to it – with a hat-trick. Mick might have had all four goals, but Billy Bonds cleared from him off the line. Midfielder Paine was following up, to score.

Judd felt he had proved that this was his position:

> That was really where, I think, *everybody* in the club realised was quite a strong place for me. Chronologically, it was relatively weak on the left. We still didn't have anybody to sit in there: we'd tried several different moves from there but I think, overall, that playing on the right was my strength.

He would, however, start the season on the left. After defeats in the first two games, though, he was among those dropped for the visit to Old Trafford. John Sydenham recalls overhearing Bates and Mortimore discussing whether to attack United on their own patch. They did – with Saul and Davies upfront and with Paine and Sydenham wide.

Having contributed a cross-field pass which sent Sydenham on his way past Shay Brennan, the Republic of Ireland international, to set up Davies's first goal, Paine had no need to do a lot more: Sydenham could do as he liked against Brennan, while Davies was towering above Foulkes and Sadler, with Rimmer rooted on his line. The outcome was a 4-1 away win, with all four goals scored by Davies: a hat-trick from Sydenham crosses and a fourth as Ron showed off his skills on the deck.

And accolades all round for Davies, notably from Matt Busby, who had just moved upstairs, making Ted Bates the longest-serving manager in the Football League. Davies recalls the occasion as

the biggest thrill of my life…
The mighty United! Busby said to me 'Ron, I've been after you for years. They won't let you go.' Ted Bates never let on. I would have gone at a heart-beat. I would have relished the opportunity of winning a few medals. But maybe I wouldn't have done so well – cos I think Painie was a better player than Willie Morgan [the Scotland international winger who scored for United that afternoon] and on the left-hand side, I had Sydenham.

Ron Davies soars above Sadler and Rimmer is stranded yet again.

Unfortunately for Davies and Southampton, Ron's 'biggest thrill' was also his goal-scoring peak. He would stab in his 100th goal for the Saints in his next game, but he would never again get a hat-trick for them. Indeed, he would score only eight more times in 26 more League games this season, surrendering the top-scoring spot to Mick Channon. And so it would remain until Ron left The Dell.

There were two tactical reasons for this, both exploiting Channon's speed. First, Ted Bates needed Davies to lie up, flicking in Channon on the run. Secondly, Paine had shown that he was capable, from deep midfield, of hitting Mick's runs. While very different from targeting George O'Brien at the near post, this relied on a similar 'telepathy', Terry feels: 'I *knew* that there were areas where I could hit the ball and I knew that he'd be on his bike. He *knew* when I was going to release it and he knew when to run.'

Davies was far from happy with this development. And Channon disliked having to start his runs from further forward than he fancied – and 'used to say so,' according to his manager. But the system suited Paine – 'luckily for me, I had the ability to read it from those angles, as well' – as he lost 'that half a yard.' And if he could no longer get to the by-line so regularly, he had become a keen admirer of 'the *pace*' that enabled Channon to do so.

How fortunate we Southampton fans were to witness two of our own getting to the by-line so often, as the jinking genius of Paine was followed by the exhilarating speed of Channon. We shall never know whether Micky Judd might have done that down the right-flank. Those two games at the start of this 1969-70 season would be his last in the first-team: come October, an injury in the Reserves ended his career.

And nor did his 'incredible day out' at Old Trafford, as he remembers it, leave Sydenham with much to celebrate. Little more than three months, to be precise. By the end of November, he had started in most of Saints' League outings and had played in two rounds of the Fairs Cup. When Rosenborg of Norway came to The Dell in September, as Southampton's first competitive visitors from Europe, John managed to pick up his first-ever booking: what a difference in temperament from his longstanding team-mate on the other wing!

Then, just before the Third Round of this competition in December, Ted Bates brought in a new signing from Reading. Perhaps surprisingly, it was not another tackler-back in the Thompson mode but an orthodox outside-left. Tommy Jenkins was not a flyer like Sydenham, though: Ted Bates called him 'The Weaver.'

If Jenkins's weaving would thrill the media and the fans – and guarantee him a long run at No.11 – it would sometimes prove to be another setback for Ron Davies. As previously noted, both Davies and

Sydenham knew that the former could capitalise on the latter's crosses, even when they were less than ideal. Ron was aware that the cross was coming – if not exactly where – and had some idea when to make his run, because Sydenham's skill lay in hitting the ball, left-footed, on the run: checking back was not his style. Davies struggled from time to time, though, to predict whether Jenkins was going to cross or duck back and beat his man again.

By the time Sydenham moved on to Aldershot in March 1970, Ted Bates had signed another winger as cover – and as a replacement, sooner or later? – for Terry Paine. Terry could surely claim to have proved himself at each new level he attained and to have maintained that record in Saints' inaugural European adventure. In their six games – culminating in defeat by the holders, Newcastle United, on a Third Round away goal – Terry managed a couple of smartly-taken goals and three assists. The latter included a 50-yard dash to set up Channon in the 5-1 trouncing of Vitoria Guimareas (for an 8-4 aggregate) at The Dell. True, Harry Miller suggested, in the *Mirror*, that the Portuguese visitors afforded 'Paine and Sydenham… the sort of room they would relish in League combat,' but who was going to knock that kind of effort from two 30 year-olds?

Having lost Judd, however, Ted Bates was looking for another heir to the Paine shirt – not so much somebody of Judd's pace but, according to his Scottish scout, a jinker in the Paine 'mould'.

Thus briefed, that scout – former 'keeper, Campbell Forsyth – came up with Gerry O'Brien, a part-timer at Clydebank. Bates took the plunge and told the Board that, once he was training full-time, O'Brien 'could become a younger edition of Paine.'

O'Brien's opportunity to justify that testament of faith was premature:

'A younger edition of Paine' is welcomed to The Dell.
(*Left to right*): O'Brien, Ted Bates, Channon, Gabriel.

DISCIPLINARY COMMITTEE

MINUTES OF A MEETING

HELD AT THE HOTEL CAVENDISH, LANCASTER GATE, LONDON, W.2
ON MONDAY, 23RD FEBRUARY, 1970

Present: Messrs. E. M. Gliksten (in the Chair), R. H. Speake and G. C. Sanderson.
Messrs. H. N. Bird and P. Slater.

121.—PLAYERS INSTRUCTED TO ATTEND BEFORE THE COMMITTEE IN RESPECT OF
HAVING THREE CAUTIONS ADMINISTERED TO THEM WITHIN 12 MONTHS.

    (a) D. WALKER OF CAMBRIDGE UNITED F.C. was suspended for 14 days from Monday, 2nd
March, 1970 and fined £10.

    (b) T. PAINE OF SOUTHAMPTON F.C. was suspended for 21 days from Monday, 2nd March,
1970 and fined £25.

    (c) D. FRANCIS OF AVELEY F.C. was suspended for 21 days. The operation of the suspen-
sion was suspended for 12 months.

122.—CLUB OFFICIAL INSTRUCTED TO ATTEND BEFORE THE COMMITTEE.

    MARGATE RES. v. TUNNEL SPORTS, KENT LEAGUE, 20TH DECEMBER, 1969.

       Mr. T. J. R. Morris, Team Manager of Margate F.C., was suspended from all foot-

---

after three bookings and an FA hearing (*above*) in February, Terry would sit
out four matches. He had missed a game in February through a rare injury
and would miss another in March, so that he would end the season having
played only 36 League games. I say 'only', but mark that statistic well: since
August 1957, Terry had now played 13 full seasons and this was the first in
which he had made fewer than 40 League appearances.

That February-March of 1970 had also been a watershed in Terry's life
outside football. He had by then become a father, successful businessman,
race-horse owner, freemason and politician – but in February, Carol left the
marital home.

Married life had been good to the young footballer. Carol initially
continued working full-time, while devoting her 'spare' time to being the
secretary both to Terry's fan club, which she had started for younger
supporters, and his various businesses, and accompanying her husband to
the functions to which a local celebrity was inevitably invited. Terry's
business activities increasingly expanded their social circle and the two of
them didn't socialize a lot with his team-mates. There was a period, though,
when they would sometimes join the gang of players, after a home game,
who headed for Trant's night-club, the *After Eight*, to listen to *The Sunsets*.
This group included Gerry Gurr on guitar and Mick Judd on drums. If
you've ever heard Dave Paton's Scots brogue, you may wonder, as I did, how

he could possibly have been their singer. 'He was more comprehensible when singing,' Gurr assures us, 'than when he was speaking.' Like Roy Orbison, Gerry insists.

Terry's first business venture was a development from his close-season activities, previously noted, selling furniture for *Tracys*. In June 1963, he became a director of the company, with responsibility for their newest branches at Romsey and Totton. Then, in February 1964, he took over the tenancy of the *Black Swan* café in Winchester, trading as the *Paine and Mackenzie* catering company. As noted in Chapter 10, his brother Tony, a qualified chef, ran it for him. Carol did the books. She would also open up on a Sunday and get her hands dirty, while Terry chatted to the customers. The business thrived on its proximity to the Law Courts, which had no refreshment facilities. This not only kept the café busy at lunch-time, but Tony would also send in food ordered by closeted jurors. So when the courts acquired their own restaurant, the café suffered seriously. Business continued for a while, until Terry sold up.

Meanwhile, in February 1969, he had started another enterprise with Eddy Penfold, who delivered fruit to the café. Terry suggested they go into business together and they duly opened the *Terry Paine Fruit and Vegetable Centre* in Shirley. The shop was initially on Shirley High Street but soon moved just around the corner into Howard Road – about 300 yards from The Dell. Again, Carol did the books. Eddy's wife, Mary, worked in the shop and Terry's principal role was to pick her up of a morning – Eddy would long since have left for

Eddy Penfold embraces his wife and his business partner at the *Terry Paine Fruit and Vegetable Centre*.

the fruit market – and drive her to the shop on the way to training. Some days, Mary recalls, 'he'd come back from The Dell when he'd finished his training. He might serve a couple of customers and have a laugh with them – that way, he kept everyone happy.' Ron Allison – Terry's fan at the BBC, to whom you were introduced in Chapter 3 – will vouch for that: when visiting his parents, just off Howard Road, he would sometimes spot Terry serving. And genuinely so: 'it wasn't only for a photo-call.'

CONSTANT PAINE

Not that Terry needed to put in much of an appearance for the shop to become a landmark. The name TERRY PAINE was emblazoned above the window and the public image of a footballer serving fruit and veg' was bound to attract attention. And it could be good for business to exaggerate his role, as Terry tried to explain to Mary when he invited the press, or even the TV cameras, along. She recalls his going to a nearby garage to borrow a garage-hand's coat, 'to put on, as if he worked in the shop.' She still chuckles affectionately at the image of Terry talking to the interviewer, while 'holding a big cauliflower in his hand, pretending he's working in the shop.'

He would genuinely work there, though, of a Sunday morning, when Eddy and he opened up, hoping to dispose of Saturday stock that might be past its sell-by date come Monday. Charlie Knott, who could never have imagined that he was introducing Carol to a wannabe greengrocer – even if Terry's paternal grandfather had been in this trade in Portsmouth – was among their Sunday regulars. When they'd done, Eddy and Terry would head off to meet their friend, Wally Stoner, at the *Waterloo Arms,* often taking a basket of left-over fruit for the landlord to include in his Sunday raffle. The landlord was Terry's former right-wing partner, George O'Brien.

Significantly, in a Q & A profile for *Shoot!* magazine in 1973, Terry would list his 'best friends' as Eddy, Wally and George. He enjoyed those Sunday lunch-times, playing 'spoof' with his best buddies. He was astonished that not only had I never played spoof, I'd never heard of it. He tells me it's a guessing game about the number of matches held in a clenched fist and that it can determine, by a process of elimination, who buys the next round.

Harmless fun, but Eddy and Terry 'had some riotous times,' Mary recalls. Not that Carol and she were excluded: the two couples socialized a lot together. It might be an evening out, playing ten-pin bowling; it might be a black-tie affair.

The Penfolds were among the many friends and associates whom Terry introduced to his racing circles. His first horse

Terry, during his brief moustachioed phase, with Eddy (*second left*) and Mary (*second right*) at a black-tie occasion.

appeared in Chapter 14. Terry and Tornado were photographed at Toby Balding's Weyhill stables. Balding looks upon racing as 'one of the greatest bringers-together of every corner of the social spectrum' and was committed to generating, at his stables, 'team-spirit and team-involvement at all levels.'

There was a stables football team, in which Terry liked to play when the opportunity arose. No photos of this exist. Cameras were banned, lest evidence reach Ted Bates that Terry was risking injury – even if he did take the precaution of playing in goal. Beyond the football, though, Terry thrived, Toby feels, on the whole '*ambience* of a racing stable and its "team".'

Beyond the team, however, Terry became one of Balding's '*special* people,' with whom he has 'much more than just a racing relationship… I would consider him to be my very best friend.' Terry was also close to Caro, Toby's late wife. In fact, she was for Terry, Toby feels, a guide to unknown territory:

> I think a lot of the intrigue for him was suddenly meeting a totally different social setting from that to which he had been brought up and was used to. He was extremely fond of my wife and had enormous respect for her baggage: the daughter of a smart stock-broker type, extremely well-educated, well-read and always quite prepared to cope with his inquisitiveness; and he'd never be embarrassed to ask anything. She was very involved in helping him with – for lack of a better word – social graces. You can take him anywhere, but he very much looked on Caro, in particular, as a role-model on how to behave. He was always naturally good-mannered, but he was inquisitive about what was appropriate in this new social setting.

Others have remarked on Terry's inquisitiveness. After spending time with Terry for his book on *Cult Heroes*, Jeremy Wilson told me that he had never known a footballer so interested in the whys and wherefores of who his interviewer was. Had I noticed that, Jeremy wondered? Indeed I had. Nothing about my private affairs, but plenty about my occupational history and where my values came from. Another journalist fears that Terry's desire to learn – his 'engaging naivety', as he puts it – has sometimes led him to accept too many challenges, to bite off more than he had the time to chew.

The principal example, for him, was Terry's entry into politics. This brings us to the Deacon connection.

The Deacon building and property dynasty in Southampton essentially consisted of the father, John, and his two sons: David on the building side of the business; and Clive on the estate-management side.

John's ambitions included a directorship at The Dell. He would never achieve this, but would settle for Fratton Park, instead, becoming chairman in 1973. David would later become the Portsmouth chairman. It was Clive Deacon who featured largest in Terry's life. He helped in the purchase – and conversion, where necessary, into flats – of two houses in Shirley, roughly equi-distant between the grocery shop and The Dell. More work for Carol, then, furnishing the flats, finding the tenants, setting up the tenancy agreements and all the rest of the bookwork expected of a super-woman secretary.

Still an active mason 40-odd years on, Clive recalls the time in the mid-sixties, when there were at least five freemasons at The Dell: his father-in-law, Gordon Baker, the club secretary; Ted Bates, then his neighbour at Chilworth; Campbell Forsyth, 'visiting' from a Scottish lodge; Terry Paine; and Stuart Williams. Enough to prompt Ron Davies – a rival for the right-back spot with Williams, as discussed earlier in some detail – to remark, allegedly, that you had to be a freemason to get into the team.

It was Gordon Baker who suggested freemasonry to Terry. An invitation to join the Buffaloes had been sent to Terry at the club. Opening the letter in the secretary's office, Terry asked him what he knew of this outfit. Baker advised him to join the freemasons, instead. Arthur Simmonds, printer to Southampton FC and a social friend, was Terry's promoter when he duly joined the William Rufus Lodge at Totton. Ted Bates was at another lodge and Terry has only one recollection of ever discussing freemasonry with him – when the team was staying at a Blackpool hotel that houses a local lodge.

Clive Deacon was the broker in arranging for Terry to become a Conservative-Ratepayer candidate for the Bargate ward in the 1969 local elections. Terry recalls being at Southampton Central station, awaiting the train to an away game, when Clive appeared on the platform: would Terry step outside and have a word with his dad? Terry obliged and found himself being invited into the back of the Deacon Rolls-Royce. Having confirmed his suspicion that Terry was a Tory, John Deacon asked him to be his running partner in the forthcoming elections.

So what was Terry doing voting Conservative? This was three seasons before Hunter Davies conducted his famous survey of Tottenham's dressing room and Steve Perryman came up with his memorable rhetorical question: 'aren't all the players Labour?'

Apparently not: the Spurs squad consisted mainly of what Davies called 'apathetic Tories', with only two of Perryman's team-mates leaning leftwards, faithful to their background rather than with the conviction that he had – Perryman couldn't countenance that any of his team-mates were planning to pay for their kids' schooling.

Although I knew of Davies's findings by the time I first met Terry in 1997, almost my opening question to him was: 'why Tory?' He referred me back to his upbringing in the terms voiced in Chapter 2: people shouldn't have to grow up in such privation. Coming from such a similar background to his, I ventured that this is precisely why people like us vote Labour. A bit simplistic, I grant you. Terry is entitled, however incredible it seems to me, to reject Perryman's notion of loyalty to our roots: 'I may have come from a working background,' Terry explains, 'but it was just something about the Labour Party that I couldn't handle.' And his belief that Conservatism offers a remedy for the inadequate resources his parents had always known – what Peter Hennessy has called 'never-again Conservatism' – was, of course, the philosophy of Harold Macmillan, the having-it-so-good Prime Minister during Terry's teens.

However you care to label his Tory beliefs, his father was not impressed. As noted in Chapter 2, Alec Paine was a paid-up member of the Labour Party and Trevor recalls that Terry's becoming a Conservative candidate 'didn't go down very well.' Not that he can 'remember much being said between them' at that time, so much as recall political bantering over a longer period:

I can remember Terry taking the mickey: 'It's all you Reds' fault.' That's all he used to say to Dad and, of course, that riled Dad. I can't say they ever came to an argument, at all, but it was always Terry saying 'You Reds!' And May Day: 'that's a Red Day', he said; 'that's a Communist holiday.' So he used to wind him up.

And then there were the Election campaigns when, Terry confesses, he might tear down the Labour posters that his parents had put up, toss them into the garden and blame vandals unknown. Most of the time, though, father and son knew that it was better to keep off politics.

Having agreed to stand and told the *Echo* that he welcomed the 'chance to help Southampton, which has helped me considerably over the years,' Terry topped the poll in May, ahead of Deacon, inevitably attracting the headline, PAINE SCORES FOR THE TORIES.

BARGATE (TWO SEATS)

T. L. Paine (Con.-RP)	..	1,228
B. J. Deacon (Con.-RP)		1,192
R. Burns (Lab.)	....	650
R. W. Russell (Lab.)	....	549
G. A. W. Cleverley (Lib.)		166
Majority	....	507

Two Con.-RP gains.

He was duly elected, at the first meeting of the new council, to serve on its Entertainments and Publicity Committee – which had a reputation for using celebrity councillors, from the

The new councillor for Bargate
with the new mayor, Alderman Mrs H.K. Johnson

world of sport and elsewhere, to fulfil public engagements – and to be the council's representative on the Southern Sports Council. So far, so good. And three months later, he was assuring the *Echo* that he had the time to do more for his adopted city than was being asked of him: as he trained in the morning, he had the afternoon free for committee meetings and the monthly council meeting. In fact, he had 'enough spare time', he ventured, 'for even more council work,' especially for the residents of Bargate Ward, if only they would come and tell him their problems.

There is no disputing that Councillor Paine was attentive to those who reported their tribulations to him, but he failed to 'represent' the people of Bargate, in so far as he neglected to participate sufficiently in meetings of the council and its committees.

In his first year, he attended only two of the council's 10 meetings – at one of which he spoke on the residents' parking problems in the Polygon area of his ward – and only six committee meetings, so that opposition councillors were questioning whether he should cease to hold office under the rule that non-attendance at council meetings over a period of six months can result in expulsion.

That record represented, for the third member for the Bargate ward, Alan Reynard (Lab), an 'opportunity squandered'. It was the price the Southampton Conservatives paid, he argues, for the way in which they selected their candidates: whereas a wannabe Labour councillor must be a party member for at least two years, 'the Tories literally pick people off the streets' – or off railway platforms in the case of Terry Paine. 'As a result,' Reynard reasons, 'a lot of them were loose cannons.'

Cllr Paine was so loose that he was hardly there at all. And when he was, his contribution to debates left Cllr Reynard saddened by a sense of waste:

> Nobody could have come on the council with more appeal, more opportunity. Most of us would have given our hind legs to have been able to influence people like he could have. He didn't. And that really was sad. He arrived as a famous person and left the council as a nonentity. Basically, that's it: opportunities lost.

Reynard was basing this assessment not only on Paine's many absences from the chamber, but on his being unversed, when he did put in an appearance, in political speech-making. When told that this allegedly inarticulate politician had become an accomplished TV sportscaster, Cllr Reynard was unfazed. He'd known others get onto the council, of whom he'd thought, 'there's nothing there: what the hell are they wasting their time for? Ten years later, they're quite different people – articulate, know what it's all about. They've found their niche and, once they've found their niche, they're OK. It's while they're looking for it that they're less than helpful.'

Being a helpful councillor is about more than speaking at council meetings, of course. Terry could handle the kind of speech-making required of him at public engagements – provided Carol didn't make him laugh and miss his lines, he explained to the *Echo* – and he was very much in demand. And then there was the job of handling enquiries from the residents of Bargate, the part that Terry enjoyed – unseen by those who would have had him removed – and in which, as I say, his record was not being challenged.

Councillor Paine fulfils another public engagement, presenting prizes to Mark Cain and Paul Page.

It was his absence from the chamber that continued to vex his opponents. When his attendance record was being questioned by them in May 1970, Terry had just left for the Saints' tour in the Far East. To explain to the press that a member of the council was thus engaged in the cause of the city was an easy defence for the Leader of the Council, Alderman Walter Head, to enter on behalf of his absent colleague. But he added that there were other 'extenuating circumstances', which were 'very personal and private.' He would convey the details to the Leader of the Opposition.

Which poses the question: how much, if any, of those matters are any of our business in this biography of Terry Paine, the footballer?

In order to explain whether I intend answering or evading that question, let me first sum up where Terry Paine stood in that spring of 1970. He had played his part, as goal-scorer and goal-maker, in the Saints' first adventure in Europe. He was a councillor and businessman and had two year-old twin daughters. I alluded, in the previous chapter, to the girls, Karen and Tracey, of whom Terry and Carol had taken possession, at five weeks-old, in January 1968 and had legally adopted in the May.

Determined to be a full-time Mum, Carol had not only given up work but had withdrawn from the evenings out – although there were still the books to be done, for the shop and the flats, once the girls were in bed.

Terry and Carol with the twins, Karen (*left*) and Tracey.

That was her preference and was not a problem, she later explained to a posse of court reporters, until 'Terry started staying out at night.' This disruption led to her removing herself and the twins from the marital home in February 1970 and to her filing for divorce on the grounds of his adultery with Mrs Patricia Smith, who was, by the time of the court hearing, living with Terry, along with her two young children.

Judge David Pennant not only granted Carol's application, come October 1970, but, in the absence of Terry, who had opted not to defend the petition, made so bold as to deliver a judgment not just on the facts but upon the respondent. He found it 'most regrettable' that an adoptive father

> should start to allow his marriage to break up such a short time after the adoption – leaving these two little babies without the parent figures they should expect.

Terry had frequently and freely exposed his domestic life to the media, posing with Carol for photographers not just out and about but in their own home. *Echo* readers had seen him and Carol relaxing with the twins and the dogs. We even knew the dogs' names.

And yet, when all is said and done, Terry Paine is one of the most 'private' people I have ever met and I have never considered it any of my business – or, it follows, yours – to ask a whole load of questions about his marital relationships.

But his headline-making divorce had put his private actions into the public domain and the judge had roundly cast him as the wicked father. At the risk of appearing to contravene my non-inquisitorial stance, I shall venture five observations.

First, this adverse publicity appears to have done Terry no lasting harm: in my 10 years of talking to people about him, nobody has ever portrayed him in the way that Judge David Pennant chose gratuitously to do. This probably owes much to Carol's restraint: after her statement to the press at the door of the court, she has declined opportunities to shame-and-blame. Moreover, as Pat, the co-respondent, has reminded me, the 'other woman' is invariably more likely to be cast – as, indeed, she feels she was – as the scarlet culprit, no matter what a divorce-court judge might have to say about the errant male.

Secondly, Terry would marry Pat Smith in 1972 and help to raise her two young children, Debbie and Darren, along with Teresa, their biological child. When I met Pat and her two daughters in 2006, Debbie referred to herself as 'Terry Paine's daughter' – any notion of 'step' didn't enter into it – while her mother was unstinting in her praise of Terry's performance in the role of the acquired father whom her children 'loved'.

The new Mrs Paine gets carried away.

Thirdly, although it caused some upset at the time, none of this had a lasting affect on Terry's relationships within his family. His brother, Tony, expressed his disapproval by declining an invitation to the wedding of Terry and Pat. Tony died in 1987, but his widow, Thelma, claims that he was 'shocked' by his younger brother's behaviour – 'he couldn't understand Terry taking on those two children,' yet failing, as he saw it, to 'knuckle-down and be a family-man. Although he was a celebrity, he still had duties at home.'

Thelma acknowledges that, 'as you get older' and think more objectively about the social lives of young celebrities, you can put those events of the late 1960s into perspective, 'but at the time, when it's actually part of your family and happening round you, you just get cross about it.' Cross enough to boycott a wedding although, in time, Tony came to accept the changes of personnel in his extended family.

If Tony's disappointment was overt, it seems that Terry's father had especially good cause to harbour some misgivings: 'Alec *worshipped* Carol,' Thelma reckons. 'He really did: he thought the world of Carol.' And Trevor feels that his father's experience of losing both parents by the age of 15 affected his attitude to the twins' being deprived of their adoptive father. Terry acknowledges that that 'could well have been' the case,

but he never let on to me. He wouldn't have said to me 'why did you do it?'
He was never one to speak to you about any problem: he just got on with
it. He never made any comment about my games: he never said, 'you were
crap/good/indifferent.'

Terry's mother could be more outspoken, but she 'never really interfered in
any way, shape or form – whether it was about my football or whether it was
about my private life. You know how mothers are: they're more *understanding*,
probably. I think they take things on board a lot better, probably, than
fathers do.'

Fourthly, while it may have affected his attendance record in the council
chamber, Terry's performance on the field appears to have been unaffected
by the domestic upheaval. 'Trouble at home' seems so often to be cited,
today, as a reason for a player's loss of form, but nobody has ever put it to
me that Terry Paine *ever* lost form – for domestic, or any other, reasons. And
nor would anybody suggest, surely, that his suspension, at this time, had
anything to do with his marital situation: we have seen ample evidence that
he needed no such external provocation to rile referees.

Finally, as Terry was excelling in his role of step-father, the downside
was that, after a few visits to their non-custodial father, the twins would not
see him again for the best part of 16 years. His reunion with them, when he
came to the Saints' centenary celebrations in 1986, was again in the public
domain, in so far as the *Echo* reported and photographed their meeting at
The Dell. I shall return to that moment in Chapter 28 but, in the meantime,
I shall have little else to say on these matters – as little as Terry has had to
say to me, over our 10 years of chatting, on-and-off-the-record, about
events and relationships that he protects as private.

Meanwhile, as I say, Terry was leaving behind his domestic reorgan-
isation and political shenanigans to tour in the Far East.

Chapter 17

Alehouse Whines

For the seven-match tour of the Far East – playing against select XIs in Colombo, Bangkok and three Japanese cities – Terry had a new team-mate: Brian O'Neil from Burnley.

O'Neil liked to travel light, soon making it obvious that he expected to 'borrow' everyday clothing and match-day kit. Without permission, of course. Rooming with the new boy, Paine was to become a victim of this habit when the party reached Kobe for the third of their Japanese games.

Asked to look after the visitors from Southampton, the Vice-Consul in Kobe, Brian Walder, a native of the Isle of Wight who had seen his first game at The Dell in 1948, was only too pleased to do so. He took his official guests to *The Double Top,* a mock-English pub of a kind that was 'just beginning to make a show in Japan.' He got to partner Terry Paine in beating Channon and Stokes at darts: 'Terry was not a bad player,' he recalls: 'he was certainly better than Bobby Stokes, although Bobby won the competition for who could drink the fastest glass of beer.'

Elsewhere in the bar, though, O'Neil entered into another kind of drinking competition – of the last-man-standing variety – with Ken Jones.

The captain receives a bouquet from the team's Japanese hosts.
(*Left to right*): Jones, Walker, Channon, Gabriel, Fisher, Davies,
O'Neil, Martin, Paine, Mortimore.

It ended with Brian wetting his trousers. Except that they weren't, of course, *his* trousers: he'd helped himself from Terry's wardrobe. As Mick Channon recounts, in *Man on the Run*, it added to the hilarity of the occasion that the laugh was on the dressing room's great mickey-taker. Terry chuckles about it today, albeit with a degree of indignation: 'it was not just a pair of trousers; they were my *best* trousers.'

Of the two competitions – the speed of drinking a single glass and the O'Neil v Jones test of endurance – the former was a lot more consistent with the manager's much-quoted injunction to 'have a drink, but don't bathe your feet in it.' That jocular mantra expressed just one of Ted Bates's codes on drinking, on which I have touched in recent chapters. The others were to ease off on the days before a match; respect any curfews; and watch your weight. Denis Hollywood discovered just how seriously his manager took the last rule, when he was excluded from the tour and ordered to report daily for training and to be weighed.

Hollywood, who would have loved to go to Japan, tells this story with considerable regret, but he will assure you that he found Bates 'very fair'. This was the season, though, when Bill Shankly, Liverpool's manager, complained about the 'ale house' behaviour of the Southampton players, in terms that they – not to mention opponents who've weighed in on the matter – considered far from fair.

It was the way in which the Saints beat Liverpool at The Dell, at the end of September, that provoked Shankly's remark. Two incidents had upset him. Paine nudged his marker, Alec Lindsay, causing him to head past his 'keeper for the game's only goal; and John McGrath caught Alun Evans so

Paine follows in, as the involuntary header from Lindsay loops over Clemence's head.

heavily in a clash of heads that Evans was knocked out and swallowed his tongue. He recovered but had to be substituted. Nigel Clarke suggested, in the *Mirror,* that the referee 'must have been the only person in the ground not to see' Paine's push, which seems to have received more media attention, initially, than the injury to Evans.

Thus, Brian Hayward simply noted, in the *Echo*, that, as McGrath and he went up for a cross, they 'collided in mid-air and Evans fell awkwardly.' Which is how Denis Hollywood, who was near the incident, judged it: 'John clattered into him, all right, but it was a perfectly good challenge. They both went up for the ball. You couldn't *mean* to head somebody on the back of his head, could you?' Probably not. McGrath acknowledged that he hit Evans 'that hard, he hit his head on the ground,' but little more would have been heard of this incident, surely, had not Shankly issued his famous verdict, quoted at length in the *Mirror*:

> It was the worst foul I have seen in 10 years. I thought the boy had broken his neck. McGrath should certainly have been sent off. Southampton played alehouse football throughout this game. One of their players personally gave away 10 fouls. They were pushing and shoving around and their goal should never have been allowed. Alec Lindsay was not just pushed – he was spun around. And instead of heading the ball away, he put it into his own net. It's not nice to get beaten like that. If Evans had not gone off, we'd have skinned them.

It was by now, of course, 10 years since Paine first put Liverpool's noses out of joint – we have Roger Hunt's testimony for that in Chapter 6 – but Shankly was casting his net much wider here. In his *Man on the Run* chapter on 'The Ale House Lads,' Channon treats the label as referring to the squad's drink culture, an interpretation that I pursued in *Dell Diamond.* It is surely clear from the context, though, that Shankly was alluding to their style of play. Channon is unfazed by that: the side had 'a lot of good players who could score goals,' he reasons, but Bates had had to bring in a few who could 'scratch, bollock and bite... players who could handle themselves. We had to *get* the ball to let Painie play, to get me in or to knock a cross in for Ron to score. It was all *there.*'

Such a view was put to the *Echo*, when Hayward conducted an immediate survey on the Shanklyism, asking a dozen First Division managers whether Saints were 'a dirty side'. Coventry City's Noel Cantwell reckoned that they had, until recently, been 'a bit soft' and that they were a better side for having become 'competitive and aggressive'. Such a distinction between being hard and being dirty dominated the responses, essentially endorsing Channon's appraisal of the *balance* that has always been needed in a team of 11 footballers. Even so, it would be fair to say that this Southampton side had its share of players – Paine, Gabriel, Hollywood and O'Neil – appearing at Lancaster Gate on disciplinary charges.

The Saturday before the Liverpool game, Gabriel had been sent off – for the first time in his career – at Elland Road. Having had enough, after 80 minutes, of Allan Clarke's niggling, Gabriel tried to head-butt him. Clarke swayed out of the way but went to ground, as if pole-axed, and stayed down. Gabriel joined in the charade and followed him down, holding his face. He was dismissed – on a stretcher. Clarke, the better actor, stayed on.

Jimmy complained to the *Echo* that 'player after player gets sent off against' Leeds, an allegation which Hayward supported with statistics. Such was their skill in 'codding referees', as Brian Clough put it. I shall return, in Chapter 23, to such issues of cheating by 'dirty Leeds'.

Gabriel had only just appeared as a witness in the successful defence of Manchester City's Mike Summerbee, who had been dismissed on the season's opening day at The Dell. Summerbee, in his turn, defends Southampton's style, as being similar to City's:

> They weren't *Ale House Lads*. They worked hard, trained hard and played hard… We were the same. We were physically a very strong side and physically fit – but we used to enjoy ourselves. I know Bill Shankly was a great manager, but he was also a great person at saying things – clichés.

So there was honour among the hard men. Summerbee's manager, Joe Mercer, responded to Hayward's survey in a similar vein: Southampton had 'hard' players like McGrath and Walker, while Fisher was 'tough', but 'all three of them tackle face-on. They are not late and they are not over-the-ball experts.'

Hayward would surely have seen that last comment as a cheeky side-swipe, by the ever-jovial Joe, at Terry Paine. When we return to these matters in Chapter 23, we shall need to consider Terry's standing among the knockers, nudgers and nigglers.

Whatever might have been said about their style in 1970-71, the side finished seventh, as in 1969, and so qualified again for the Fairs Cup. Paine missed one game with a groin strain – allowing Thompson a rare run-out at No.7, in what would be his final appearance for the club – but there were four ever-present players. Had this barely-changed side maintained its March form, it could have finished even higher, although Paine's April goal against Arsenal, in a 2-1 home defeat, was of statistical significance in two ways.

Paine slides in to defy the entire Arsenal defence
and score his record-breaking 157th League goal.

First, it was his 157th League goal, thus making him the club's highest-ever scorer, until overtaken by Channon, in League football. And it was the only goal conceded by the Gunners in a nine-game run that took them to a League and Cup double.

Arsenal's *Official History* concedes that Saints might have had a late penalty. But, then, would they have converted it? We have it on good authority, from Bob Wilson himself, that the Arsenal 'keeper had a poor record on penalties, but the home side had long been queuing up to miss them. After his failure against Ipswich in August 1969, Paine had been relieved of the job. Hollywood and Davies had then missed, before Channon succeeded, only for Davies to be reprieved and to score.

Which is why Ron Davies started this 1970-71 campaign as the penalty-taker. An initial success was followed by two failures. So Paine got the job back come November – and blew it, firing wide against Newcastle. Channon now volunteered, but did no better. Over to Gabriel. He made no mistake from the spot at Ipswich, the Saturday before Arsenal's visit, but it would surely have been asking too much of him to repeat his success so soon – even against Wilson.

The penalty misses continued in 1971-72, contributing to an instant end to Saints' second European adventure. The first leg of the First Round tie against Bilbao was only five minutes-old at The Dell when Gabriel's penalty was saved. When they were awarded a second penalty with the score at 1-1,

Channon stepped up to the spot to give the Saints a 2-1 lead to take to Spain, but it was not enough. They went out 3-2 on aggregate.

Yet there were domestic 'adventures' aplenty – most of them negative – in a season that the club began with neither their centre-forward nor an assistant manager.

Ron Davies missed the first eight League games of the season, having fallen foul of a plot that misfired. The intended victim was Steve Middleton, an 18 year-old third-choice goalkeeper, who had become the principal butt of the first-team mickey-taking. If Middleton has any idea why this should have been the case, he doesn't want to talk about it today, but the general view is that his hound-dog reaction to his baiters only made matters worse – so much so that it could sometimes take on a physical shape in the gym.

With four days to go to the start of this season, it seems that word got out, among the younger players – Middleton included – that he was being targeted in the next 11-a-side practice 'match', the ritualistic end-of-training encounter, in which, as we have seen, teaching the kids a lesson was a first-teamer's prerogative. So some of the 16 year-olds, who weren't yet eligible to participate in such a learning exercise, sat in the stand, waiting to see what would happen when, as expected, Ron Davies zoomed in on a Paine cross and clattered the young 'keeper. According to Pat Earles, one of those spectators, what happened was that Middleton ducked out of the way and Davies, thus denied a buffer, went flying over on his ankle and did eight matches' worth of ligament damage.

If Terry Paine had the reputation of being Middleton's chief tormentor, Nick Holmes, a contemporary of Earles, claims that most of the senior pros, at that time, were as bad as one another in this regard. Don Taylor – who was, as physio, in a good position to observe the dressing-room dynamics and training-pitch antics – agrees with that assessment: 'there were a lot of players doing that. There was nothing abnormal about that. It's all part of character-building: there's no argument about that.'

Holmes wagers that this would then have been going on at every club in the Football League, no matter what division. There would be the occasional senior pro who did not participate: he cites Hughie Fisher, as a player who could be relied upon to put his arm around a young victim and offer words of reassurance. And yet, Nick argues, this tradition would soon be modulated: in the Southampton dressing room of the early eighties, for instance, the likes of Mick Mills and Chris Nicholl would be actively encouraging the kids.

Looking back, Terry Paine admits that what he and others did to Middleton 'was *wrong* – we shouldn't have done it' – and that 'maybe I could have encouraged young players a little bit more. I wouldn't deny that.' He does points out, though, that Ted Bates asked him to help out with the

CONSTANT PAINE

1968-69 Youth team: 'I never got paid. I just used to go in and help. They got Bobby Stokes to come and say that the players really appreciated what I had done.'

It's a side of Terry Paine that would later come to the fore, as he gained a reputation, wherever he went, for bringing on youngsters, but not one that you'll hear much of in memories from The Dell.

There was no assistant manager because John Mortimore had left to manage Ethnikos in Greece and would not be replaced until late August. The eventual appointee was Stuart Williams, whose last four seasons as a player had, of course, been spent at The Dell. He would last only two seasons, but this is where a most tantalising 'what if?' deserves to be aired. A candidate who was twice interviewed for the post was John Sillett, who was already a very good friend of Terry Paine's and who remains, unquestionably, his biggest friend in the game.

Their friendship had been formed, as intimated in Chapter 8, on Saturday evening train journeys from Waterloo to Southampton, when Sillett, then at Chelsea, was going home to his mother, for a weekend in the New Forest:

> I'd get on the train at Waterloo and there would be the Southampton team, on occasions, travelling back home after a match. So Terry always invited me into the carriage where the boys were dining, and to have a drink. If I was on that train, he'd find me. He would walk down the train: he'd want to know who was on the train. He wouldn't want to miss anybody, would he? So, therefore, he was either being nosy or he was genuinely wondering if I was on board. And I would take the first: who's on; who can I talk to?

Stuart Williams returns to be the new coach.
(*Left to right*): Gabriel, Davies, Paine, Jenkins, Stuart Williams, George Horsfall, Walker, Ted Bates, Martin, Fry.

As and when Sillett afforded Terry company on that train from Waterloo, Terry would invariably give him a lift home to his mother's. 'We really became good mates that way,' Sillett recalls. 'That was how our friendship started. We had a great shared interest – which was horses – because I was hoping, in my younger days, to be a jockey; not a footballer. I used to ride pony-racing in the New Forest, but a thing called height-and-weight took its toll and that was it. Terry also had a love of horses. We used to talk about it and how one day we'd own one – and it happened!'

All of which sets the scene for one of the biggest 'what if?' moments in the Terry Paine story. Just suppose that Sillett had been appointed in 1971 and made a go of it? Might he then have been promoted to manager when Ted Bates was ready to retire in 1973-74? And how many guesses do you need to figure out who would then have joined his coaching staff, perhaps initially as player-coach? We wouldn't have had Lawrie McMenemy to take us to Wembley and to sign all those superstars, but how different the post-1974 chapters of this book would have been.

But back to reality – and an eventful October-November. This two-month period began with Hugh Fisher breaking his leg when he collided with Arsenal's Bob Wilson at The Dell. I perhaps overdid my inquest, in *Dell Diamond*, into this accident, examining too many perspectives and then failing to exonerate Wilson as unambiguously as I had intended.

Recalling the incident in his 1975 memoirs, the referee, Gordon Hill, made a similar mistake, I feel, as he rambled ambiguously. Having deemed the collision 'a complete accident' – which is how it appeared to me, standing under the East Stand, near enough to hear the crack – Hill alluded to his subsequent realisation that 'Wilson had a reputation in the game for being perhaps too physical in these types of situations [and that] when he came out for a ball, *he really didn't care* who was in his way' (emphasis added).

The italicised phrase is disturbingly ambiguous: while it is doubtless intended to convey that Wilson was careless as to his own safety – which the catalogue of injuries he incurred in this way would suggest – it could also suggest that he was reckless as to the injury he might inflict on an opponent. Hugh Fisher puts it rather better, when he describes Wilson's action as 'a bit kamikaze, but goalkeepers did that in those days. He was brave.' Wilson modelled his approach on his 'boyhood idol', Bert Trautmann, who had, of course, broken his neck this way in the 1956 Cup Final. It is probably fair to say that when a goalkeeper comes out and throws himself at the ball, the oncoming player will more often than not have time to judge whether to keep going or to hurdle the 'keeper. But Fisher didn't have that option, because the angle of the pass meant that he couldn't see Wilson.

The angle mightn't have mattered so much had the weight of the pass been right. So says the man who played the ball through, as Fisher broke towards the Archers Road penalty area: 'if I'd given him a better pass,' Paine volunteers, 'poor Hughie wouldn't have been blind to him coming out.' Fisher agrees that the pass 'was a little bit long and a little bit wide. So I couldn't see Wilson.' And he recalls that 'Terry was almost crying, when he came to see me in hospital, because he blamed himself.'

I hope that appraisal is fair to all the parties but, in the heat of the moment, some of Fisher's team-mates were less rational. Brian O'Neil, for one, 'went stupid,' he recalls. 'It was a bad break. It was horrible to see. I thought he'd done Hughie – at the time.' Paine didn't help matters either. He admits to arriving early on the scene, witnessing the leg 'flapping about in the wind' and remonstrating with the Arsenal 'keeper. Wilson blames that reaction for the stick he received from the Archers Road end, although he felt the fans along the sides were kinder to him. As I say, that included me and it never struck me, until I was researching *Dell Diamond*, that there had been any adverse crowd reaction – although, checking the *Echo* report, I see that it was deemed 'an accident and the chant of "animals" from a section of the crowd was quite pointless.'

Whether or not he helped to inflame the crowd behind Wilson's goal, Paine is suspected of having then set about conning the referee. Here is Gordon Hill's charge-sheet:

> As Fisher was carried off, Southampton's captain Terry Paine said to me: 'Don't worry about it, Gordon, we know it was an accident.' However, I've often been misled by Terry. He's a good friend of mine, and I have respect for him in many ways, but in moments of doubt I don't think I would rely on him 100 per cent to be on my side. Maybe at that moment Terry was disarming me, was really trying to suggest: 'Gordon, don't start looking for trouble now, there won't be any,' so as to make it easier to exact some of his own retribution.

If Terry was going to be vengeful, and had he had eyes in the back of his head, he might have targeted the Arsenal player who, according to the *Echo,* punched him in the back as the referee was having a deflationary word with the captains, 'but this went unnoticed.' O'Neil suspected that there would, indeed, be 'a vendetta' of some kind, but he became preoccupied with an argument with Charlie George and the mood passed.

The thought of George soothing a pumped-up O'Neil should be allowed, perhaps, to draw a most unlikely line under an incident for which

Terry Paine wishes it to be known that he was to blame, by virtue of a slightly over-weighted pass.

November was a most interesting month. It began with a new venture for the club: playing in the *Daily Express* Five-a-Sides. 'We only went up as a rag-bag outfit,' Mick Channon claims. 'We just got in a couple of cars and went up to Wembley. We thought we had no chance.' The *Express* reporters, Steve Curry and John Davies, agreed with that assessment. But the team they rated as 'rank outsiders' won the thing. With the benefit of hindsight, these reporters reflected that the rag-bag's victory 'made a lot of sense,' as they were 'five soccer stars [Martin, Gabriel, Paine, Stokes and Channon] with a wide range of differing skills, who blended together into a winning combination.' A combination that had given the lie, however modestly, to Alan Ball's warning to Jimmy Gabriel that he'd 'win nothing' at Southampton.

The Five-a-Side Cup-Winners
Left to right: Martin, Stokes, Paine, Channon, Gabriel.

Ten days later, in a serious 11-a-side engagement at The Dell, Southampton beat Leeds 2-1. Mick Channon, who had just won his first England cap, left Jack Charlton sitting on the halfway line, to score the most exciting goal that I can remember of his. Charlton remembers it well, too: he 'felt ashamed' that he failed to get close enough to stop Channon's burst.

Significantly, he refers to Mick as being the 'centre-forward' whom it was his responsibility, rather than Norman Hunter's, to pick up. Perhaps that says something about how far forward Channon was by now playing, even with Ron Davies still in the side. You could say it was a rehearsal for what Channon describes as Bates's *'fantastic* 1-9-1 system' that would become more the norm as Ron Davies faded out the following season.

However you explain it, there was not a lot for Charlton to be 'ashamed' of. Indeed, given what would happen when Leeds hosted the 'return' fixture come March – more of which in a moment – it was remarkably generous of him to bring up this November game, spontaneously, when I asked him, 30-odd years on, to relive matches against Southampton.

Because that 7-0 game at Elland Road in March 1972 has become such a favourite *Match of the Day* replay, it can easily be forgotten that, on the Saturday after they beat Leeds at home, Saints lost 8-0 at Goodison Park. Not only was Ted Bates without Fisher in midfield; he had lost O'Neil to injury during the win over Leeds. An ever-present up to that point, O'Neil would now be out until the end of February, as his recovery from a cartilage operation would coincide with a nine-week suspension in December. Hollywood, who would be suspended at the same time, in his case for seven weeks, also missed the Everton game as Jimmy Gabriel returned to his old club in the unaccustomed position of right back. He had coped at No.2 against Leeds, but struggled at Goodison, he recalls:

> Everton had a fantastic game that day. One of the reasons it was a fantastic game was because Ted played me again at right-back and I got this little flying winger [Alan Whittle] playing against me. With me playing at right-back, that was a *hole* that Everton used. They got it to the winger and the winger came flying at me and I didn't have the speed, as a full-back, to be playing against wingers like that; and there were holes created because of that. To be fair, everything they hit went in. We'd just beat Leeds 2-1, but we went up there and we didn't play very well. And if you have an off-day and they have an on-day, the score could be anything.

Alan Ball, who scored one of Everton's eight goals, 'can remember feeling really sorry for Jimmy Gabriel, to go back to his old club and get the biggest run-around. He was just losing his legs and I was in my prime at that time and it was as painful for me – but, being me, you have to *destroy* people.' Fair enough, but as John McGrath put it, when the *Mirror* conducted an inquest, the 'result was a complete freak: no two teams in the First Division are eight goals apart.' Indeed, the Saints had beaten a not-too-dissimilar Everton line-up 2-1 in the League Cup, in September, when Paine opted, with no Davies to aim at, to score direct from a free-kick. But 8-0 it was at Goodison Park, as the scoreboard behind Eric Martin clearly records.

Nobody seems to have blamed Martin. So many 'weaknesses' in the team had been 'ruthlessly exposed,' Brian Hayward reasoned, that, 'even allowing for the brilliance of Everton,' he had 'never seen a Saints' side give a worse display.' Yet McGrath felt justified in making a laughing matter of Saints' humiliation: 'it was so ridiculous,' he reasoned, 'that we didn't take it seriously. There were a lot of laughs on the train going home.' But the players were singing *Auld Lang Syne,* Paine recalls, with a degree of concern to match Hayward's: 'we *knew* that was the end of that team. It was going to be broken up.'

Not yet awhile, though. Ted Bates kept an unchanged side for the next game, Manchester United's visit to The Dell. Which meant that the hapless Gabriel was now facing George Best – who ran riot and scored a hat-trick in United's 5-2 win – although Jimmy did score

Eric Martin leaves the tell-tale scoreboard behind him.
The row of numbers indicates the order in which the goals were scored by David Johnson (No.7), Joe Royle (9) and Alan Ball (8).

one of Saints' goals and cross for Davies to get the other. Gabriel was making a habit of popping up to score against Man Utd – this was the third game in three that he had done so; and he would have a chance to make it four, come January, in the FA Cup.

Before that, though, West Ham were due at The Dell for another episode of 'Let's take on Bobby Moore,' while Terry Paine was about to become embroiled in another row about his dereliction of political duties.

West Ham's visit didn't go according to plan, as they went 3-0 up inside the first half-hour. But then, inevitably, they felled a runner in the box – Jenkins on this occasion – and, far from inevitably, Gabriel scored from the spot. Now Paine and Channon turned it on. Terry beat Trevor Brooking near the by-line and Mick headed in his near-post cross. Then, for their next trick, they combined, at the expense of Moore, for a goal of consummate skill, made to look beguilingly simple. Paine put Channon away on the diagonal – a better-weighted version of the pass that had done for Fisher – but Moore kept pace with Micky. And then Channon checked in that unpredictable way that could wrong-foot even world-class defenders; looked up; and rolled the ball back to the edge of the penalty area, where Paine was arriving. As he took the ball in his stride, Terry seemed to have a barricade of Hammers blocking his way forward. Yet he swayed left and slotted the ball left-footed past Ferguson, as if his path were totally clear.

Well, that's how it looked to me on the Southampton FC version of the *Match of the Day* highlights. The still photo doesn't do justice to the action. It shows that Paine was firing though a gap: what it cannot convey is that his body-movement had created it for him.

With Channon having taken Moore literally out of the picture,
Paine fires through the man-made gap in the West Ham defence,
to score an exquisitely-worked goal – his penultimate top-flight goal, alas.

But now he had to deal with an off-the-field gap that he had less cleverly created – in his attendance record at meetings of the council. It had become woeful enough to be the subject of an *Echo* leader in December 1971, woeful enough to be condemned as 'bad for the reputation and effectiveness of local government.' Whereupon Terry issued a statement, explaining that he would not be seeking re-election in 1972, 'basically because I have not got time for it.' He again protested that his work on problems in the ward was more important than debates in the chamber and provoked letters to the *Echo,* praising his visits, especially on Christmas Eve, to the Children's Hospital. This was the kind of appearance that doesn't feature in any records, wrote one of those correspondents, 'and anyhow it is not front page news.'

Even so, Terry confessed to 'being disappointed in myself' for giving so much less time to his council obligations than he had intended: perhaps he should have 'waited three or more years,' he told the *Echo*, 'until I could have devoted more time to it.' So he was expecting to remain in Southampton when he'd finished playing? Interesting.

In sum, he was 'not sorry that I became a councillor.' Even though he had performed poorly, the fact that he made the effort won the approval of a Labour minister. Asked how he found Paine on the field, Denis Howell, the referee who would become the inaugural Minister for Sport, joked that, while he 'never had any trouble with him in any matches I refereed, the only trouble I had with Terry Paine was that he became a Conservative councillor.' Becoming serious, though, Howell added that he was 'pleased to see he went into politics – I think sportspeople should be in politics.'

But Councillor Paine was about to come out of politics – and stay out.

For the moment, though, Manchester United were again at The Dell for the Third Round of the FA Cup. Gabriel got his goal, all right. A Gabriel classic: a Paine free-kick on to the head of Davies; a nod-down from Ron; and Jimmy was in for the kill. It was enough to equalise a Charlton goal, but Ted Bates now had to take some raw recruits to Old Trafford for the replay. The *Echo* post-mortem on the Everton debacle in November had been headed SAINTS MUST BUY NEW MEN NOW. But, having had no luck in the market, the manager had brought in two home-grown full-backs, Bob McCarthy and Roger Fry, and was giving O'Brien an extended run at No.10.

Ted Bates (*right*) and trainer George Horsfall (*seated*) head for Old Trafford with their raw recruits. The players in the doorway are (*from top*) Jenkins, Gabriel and Talkes. Yet to board are (*left to right*) Fry, McCarthy, Byrne, Paine, O'Brien and Channon.

This young side took the game to their hosts and Davies hit the woodwork from a Paine corner. Two minutes later, though, it all came together as O'Brien 'ghosted his way past two lunging tackles,' in the words of the *Echo*, 'and found Paine with an exquisite pass. The Saints' skipper, belying his years, rounded Francis Burns on the outside and crossed from the by-line. Up went Mike Channon to score with a header.'

Having proved he could still hack it, Terry had a chance, early in the second half, of an encore. O'Brien again put him through but, with Davies hovering, he fired his cross into the crowd. He explained to a baffled Brian Hayward that he had been trying to cross too early. Fallibility, indeed. George Best promptly 'galloped' through for an equaliser, but Paine almost won it with a quick free-kick, which Alex Stepney, taken by surprise – wondering where Davies and Gabriel were, perhaps? – managed to push onto his post.

And that was that. The home side hit three goals in extra-time and Terry Paine had suffered his third FA Cup defeat by Manchester United. Yet he would later tell the *Echo* that this was the best Cup-tie he had ever played in.

Before January was out, Bates had brought another Forsyth-find south from Scotland: Dundee's Jim Steele. He was initially allowed to ease his way into English football in midfield, but when Southampton went to Leeds in early March, he slotted in at centre-back, alongside Gabriel, with McCarthy and Fry at full-back. This was a callow defence to take to Elland Road, where the home side, yet to lose this season, was flying high. Yet, notwith-

Jim Steele was deemed
ready for defensive duties
at Elland Road.

Southampton have chance of a League "Double"

That thrilling and memorable 5—1 victory over our old rivals Manchester United two weeks ago gave us a double-double over the two Manchester clubs but today we welcome Southampton to Elland Road with the knowledge that they are one of four clubs who have a chance of completing a League double over us.

To achieve that at our expense the Saints will have to succeed where all other sides have failed on visiting Elland Road in the League this season.

We have, of course, been beaten twice on our own pitch this time but those defeats were in cup matches, first when the little-known Belgian side, Lierse triumphed 4—0 in the first round of the new U.E.F.A. Cup and then when West Ham United knocked our League Cup hopes with an extra time goal from Clyde Best. In the League, however, we have prevented any of our visitors returning home with maximum points.

Out of 11 matches played at Elland Road only two sides, West Ham United and Ipswich Town have returned home with anything to show for their efforts, although in two of the four early season home games which were played on neutral grounds, Wolves and Tottenham Hotspur, won a point.

NO SURRENDER

Nevertheless our record at Elland Road this season is one of

> **COVER PICTURE**
> **LEEDS UNITED v. MANCHESTER UNITED**
> **SATURDAY, 19th FEBRUARY**
> at ELLAND ROAD
>
> Leeds forward Mick Jones beating Manchester United 'keeper Stepney to score Leeds 4th goal and his hat-trick.

The programme alerted Leeds fans to the threat from Southampton, while reminding them that the front cover illustrated a 5-1 win over Manchester United.

standing their 5-1 trouncing of Manchester United in their previous home game, the match-day programme alerted the fans to the possibility that the visitors were in the unusual position of being able to complete a 'double'. If that smacks of kidology by the superstitious Revie, there is an extent to which his team did indeed respect Southampton. What Norman Hunter admired about their visits to Elland Road is that 'they used to come to us and, really, they had *no fear* of Leeds United. They had no fear of us and they tried to play football.'

They managed to live up to that reputation for the first quarter or so of the game, that March afternoon: 'there was nothing in the game, early doors,' Hunter recalls. 'it was battled; it was what we expected.' And Channon even had a chance to put his side 1-0 up. But then, in a stunning 38-minute spell, Leeds scored seven times without reply, before relaxing for a game of keep-ball, a sequence which the BBC tends to replay *ad nauseum*.

Various Leeds players have since dissociated themselves from this exhibition, Peter Lorimer explaining that it came about by accident and that he, for one, had not wanted to 'embarrass fellow-pros'. Hunter 'loves to watch it' and will gleefully recall the highlights for you if you have the time – even though he feels 'it was quite cruel, with Johnny Giles.' And he wonders 'how the Southampton lads let us do that, because I'd have gone and launched somebody – or somebody would have done.'

Now there's a surprise! But more of 'dirty Leeds' in Chapter 23. This was not a day for complaining about Leeds's cheating, but rather for admiring their football. 'It was as if we had gone to another world and found superior beings,' Jimmy Gabriel reflected. But, then, he feels that Southampton 'weren't a *team* at that time: we were a mix-and-match situation; and something had to be done at the end of the season.' That 'something' would include him leaving for Bournemouth, while Hollywood went to Blackpool.

Terry Paine hung in there. He had gone 'wittering' to the dug-out to get himself taken off at Leeds, but he would experience substitution – and even starting on the bench – less voluntarily, before the season's end. This sequence began on 25 March, two days after his 33rd birthday, when Liverpool, a team he had loved to tantalise, came to The Dell. Terry was removed with half-an-hour remaining to make way for Paul Gilchrist, a striker signed from Doncaster. Brian Hayward was horrified that 'a certain section of the crowd' had cheered when Terry departed: 'how short their memories must be!'

They needed only to recall the moment that Hayward had enthusiastic-ally reported the previous Saturday, when Paine 'pin-pointed a superb pass' from all of 30 yards inside his own half to put Bobby Stokes through to score against Ipswich, away. Terry had undone that good, though, when he beat a tackle by Robertson and got his pass in, yet nevertheless went back to express his disapproval – with a head-butt. He was sent off. Not clever: the 10 men surrendered the 1-0 lead that Stokes had given them.

So he had consecutive early baths. Then, three days after the Liverpool game, he was on the bench for the first time ever, coming on for Gilchrist at Highbury. In the remaining eight matches, he would make only four starts, missing two games, injured, and coming off the bench in the other two.

This was not how Terry Paine was used to ending a season.

Channon climbs high above Arsenal's Simpson on a significant occasion:
Gilchrist (No.9) is making his first start, pending substitution by Paine,
who was on the bench for the first time.
Charlie George (*right*) has the air of a man who is still wondering what
the October altercation with O'Neil had been all about.

Chapter 18

Nemesis

For the only time since 1957, Terry Paine was not starting the season in the first team. For 15 consecutive seasons, he had lined up on the opening day, but now he was missing.

His moment of madness at Ipswich on 18 March was to blame: such was the deliberate pace of the FA's due process that only now was he suspended. This would result in two notable rarities.

First, Mike Channon's opening-day goal – in a 1-1 home draw with League Champions, Derby County – came from a Hugh Fisher free-kick. Fisher had taken most of the free-kicks at Blackpool, but when he first shaped to do so at Southampton, he heard a command: '*le-e-e-eave it!*' Set-pieces belonged to Terry Paine.

Secondly, before Terry could resume first-team action, Ted Bates would give him a post-suspension run-out in the Reserves. Bristol City Reserves were made to pay, as Terry laid it on in a 7-1 romp. Bill Ellerington, who was with the team that afternoon, still marvels at the way in which 'Terry was the catalyst for Terry Spinner,' a centre-forward 'who wanted a little bit of something,' but who got all he needed from Paine, in this game, and helped himself to five goals.

Pat Earles, who also scored, cherishes the memory of the one occasion he played in a competitive match with Paine: 'He made this awful difference to the whole side. He was up a level. He saw things before other players. There are players who are like that. Alan Ball was like that' – as Pat would later observe, playing for Reading against Blackpool.

Terry's good friend, John Sillett, was appalled by the way his Bristol City charges folded in the mid-August sun. There was no chance of Terry's being troubled that way, Sillett reckons, given that he swapped wings at half-time, so that he played the entire game, hugging the touchline in the shade of the West Stand – and baiting Sillett in the dug-out when the mood took him. You may think that an embellishment, but Terry's stroll on the park clearly made an impact. As a self-assured affirmation of his stature, it could hardly have been bettered.

Returning to the first team, he was brought back down to size, with a couple of away games as substitute, once coming off the bench. Whereupon he settled in for the rest of the season, starting 36 League games and another five in the Cups, never being substituted. His goal against Notts

County in the League Cup was his only goal of the season. Never before had he failed to score in the League. But, then, he was playing deeper, he explains, and seldom likely to venture within scoring range.

One of his principal objectives from that position was to create scoring opportunities for Mick Channon, the more so after Ron Davies ceased to play: having appeared in the first 20 league games and four League Cup matches, Ron would miss most of December and reappear briefly in January; and then, save for one appearance as sub' in March, his Southampton career was over.

Indeed, the highlights opposite, as recorded in the *Echo,* tell the story of this season.

Davies was playing in two of those games, but we were now seeing what Channon always describes as the 1-9-1 formation. It hinged on Paine's ability to thread through-balls to him. In the late 1960s, as Channon was breaking into the team, Terry 'was more or less angling,' Mick reckons, 'to be a midfield player. He was always going that way. But he could do everything. He was brilliant. He could play wide. He could play in the middle of the park. He *was* Southampton.'

Stuart Williams had left The Dell in 1966, as Terry was beginning to tuck in when necessary, mainly away from home. That strategy had evolved during John Mortimore's three seasons of formation-plotting with Ted Bates – when, as we saw, the assistant manager welcomed Paine's willingness to vary his role as the circumstances demanded. Williams, now back there in a coaching capacity and having an input, reasoned that the system needed Terry to

> become more of a permanent midfielder. Terry was good enough, in there, to just make enough space; look up; see Mick Channon; and he was accurate with his delivery. He used to play some great balls to Mick and off Mick would go.

As already noted, Terry was comfortable, as he lost 'that half a yard,' in a position from which he felt he could still 'read the angles.' And Channon felt able to read Paine. Their understanding had long relied upon Mick's catching Terry's expressive eyes: 'those eyes of his told me exactly what he was going to do,' Mick told Peter Batt, his biographer, 'but the defenders marking me didn't know, so I could invariably steal that vital yard on them.'

If and when Terry dropped deeper, so that eye-contact became more difficult to achieve, Mick still felt he could read Terry's body language:

Saints did not deserve to be behind and with Paine playing with great skill in midfield they mounted many attacks... Paine took the corner and Channon darted in to steer his header inside Clemence's left-hand post *(14 October v Liverpool (H) 1-1)*

Paine whipped a long through pass, which saw Channon race away from Jefferson and, as Parkes came off his line, Channon slipped the ball into goal *(6 January v Wolves (A) 1-0)*

Paine... caught the Ipswich defence out with a precision 30-yard through pass and Channon, quickly into overdrive, flashed past Beattie and was then faced by Best who had raced outside his penalty area. Channon, keeping his cool, went round him and with his left foot put the ball into the empty net. It was a fine equaliser, brilliantly engineered by Paine *(27 January v Ipswich (A) 2-2)*

Paine took the free kick swiftly and Channon darted in to steer his header well out of David Latchford's reach *(17 March v Birmingham C (H) 2-0)*

Paine judged a through pass to perfection, its flight taking the ball over the top of the defence, and Channon burst clear to control the ball and put it into goal *(7 April v Spurs (A) 2-1)*

Mike Channon (second right, stripes) watches his header beat Ray Clemence for Saints equaliser against Liverpool

Owen Barnes Photograph

Mike Channon scores his second goal in the match against Tottenham at White Hart Lane

Given the programme editor's liking for a cover that showed a goal being scored, Channon had now taken over from Davies as the cover pin-up.
These covers show the goals – against Liverpool *(left)* and Spurs – as described above.

You can certainly do it over 40 yards. It's a *look*. You'd be looking that way; and then you look there; and then you go back that way – and you're *gone*! It's a look, rather than just eyes, you know. It's the whole way you set yourself up. If Terry saw a space, you could see him going… [mimics facial movements, not just of the eyes, but of the mouth, too]. So, in certain situations – you can't say in every situation, but say eight times out of 10 – once he got it, I *knew* what he was going to do: I knew what he was going to look for; and it was invariably me. And his delivery was so good. He only had to hit me and I was quick enough to get on to it. I probably prolonged his career by two or three – or four – years by being such a great outlet.

It should also be noted that, apart from the quick free-kick against Birmingham, which brought a first-minute goal, all of the Channon goals recorded above were scored in the last half-hour or so, two of them in the last five minutes, reminding us that, even if Paine had been having a quiet game, you always hoped, so long as he was on the pitch, that he might conjure a late goal for you, whether to snatch an equaliser or a winner.

One way or another, it added up, for Brian Hayward, to 'a remarkable season' for the captain, 'playing with creative genius in midfield.' Even Bill Shankly joined in the tributes after Saints' visit to Anfield in March. That was in contrast to his more typical reaction when Channon headed in Paine's corner in October – as highlighted above – to clinch that 1-1 draw at The Dell: he complained, to Steve Curry, of the *Express,* that negative Southampton had played 4-4-2 at home. Curry agreed with Ted Bates, however, that his side had done enough attacking to win and had 'provided the game with its star player in the seemingly ageless Terry Paine.' But, then, as Curry saw it, 'Shankly rarely has a good word for the Saints.'

Indeed. But he could afford to make an exception in March, when a very late goal by Kevin Keegan secured Liverpool a 3-2 win. Shankly, gracious in victory, confided in Brian Hayward that 'Paine has one of the best brains in football and he is the complete master of his role.'

Two matches in Mauritius in early June afforded Terry his favourite tour: he found it such 'a magnificent place to be' that he's been back several times, from South Africa.

The party travelled without an assistant manager: Stuart Williams had resigned in April. He had not had an entirely happy time as the coach who, in Jimmy Gabriel's estimation, wasn't needed.

Stuart has no argument with Jimmy's belief that senior players, notably Terry and he, could pass on their knowledge, 'but what about when they've finished training: what's he going to do with them then?' How, in other

Paine leads out the tourists in Mauritius.
The five front Saints are (*left to right*): Fisher, O'Neil, Stokes (mostly hidden), Paine and Martin.

words, are they going to discharge the disciplinarian duties that the Board expected of their coach? 'Coaching is a full-time job,' Williams argues:

> *You've got to have players who respect you* and what you're saying: make them realise you're doing what's best for them and that it's in their interest. I used to tell them that. I said 'it makes no difference to me what you do. I'm paid to help you and make you a better player than what you are now. *It's up to you whether you accept what I say* and do as I tell you' (emphases added).

That word 'respect' again. If Williams got that from any of the 1971-73 squad, I have yet to meet them. It didn't help that he was back with Paine, who had rated him as a team-mate. As a coach, 'Stuart just didn't *have* it,' Terry reckons. 'He didn't have the respect of the players – I think that's what it boiled down to.'

It followed that he couldn't get some of his charges to accept his suggestions as to what was good for them. Again, the drinkers were the main headache. Once the players left the training ground, Williams had to

> trust them to look after their bodies and not go out drinking. Everybody likes to go out drinking. There's nothing wrong with having a couple of

halves of beer and that. They could all drink. Some were doing it at the right time; but there were too many who were doing it at the wrong time. Some of them had got deep-rooted problems and they couldn't change to the way I wanted them to be.

Despite that *impasse*, Williams had reason to be satisfied with a tightening-up defensively – in December, the side had the best goals-against record in the First Division and their final deficit of 52 was a marked improvement on the previous season's 80 goals – but he was keen to improve their attacking options.

He presented Ted Bates with a shopping list of three players he had watched: a striker – Hull City's Stuart Pearson – and two midfielders, Burnley's Alan West and West Bromwich's Asa Hartford. Williams had known Hartford, at West Brom, from when he was 16. Now 22, the Scottish midfielder had been rejected by Leeds in 1971, after a medical examination revealed a hole in his heart. Williams scoffs at that finding: 'I don't know where they found that hole in the heart. He could go on forever, Asa. And he proved me right' – by adding another 44 Scotland caps to the six he had already won and playing League football until he was 40.

His initial move from The Hawthorns, in 1974, would be to First Division Manchester City, but Williams's other targets would each opt for Second Division football, each then winning promotion in his first season: West with Luton in 1974, swapping with relegated Southampton; and Pearson with Manchester United in 1975. Pearson would also win 15 England caps – and it won't take you long to figure out who partnered him, upfront, in most of those games. Channon, of course.

Williams had had enough. The Board now decided to advertise for an 'Assistant to the Manager/Team Manager Designate.' Two candidates for the 1968 Assistantship – John Mortimore and Lawrie McMenemy – had no need to apply: each would be courted independently.

Mortimore, the successful applicant in 1968, was ready to return from Greece and discussed the latest vacancy with the chairman, George Reader. But he was also being wooed by John Deacon, the Portsmouth chairman. Deacon – whom we met in Chapter 16, as a multi-tasking associate of Terry Paine's – had failed, you may recall, to get on to the board of Southampton FC, so had got himself on to the Portsmouth board, which he was now chairing. Mortimore was not enamoured of the job-title at The Dell, where he felt he'd already served his apprenticeship, so opted to become Pompey's 'Team Manager'.

Which left the way open for McMenemy. Since 1968, he had graduated from coaching at Hillsborough to a couple of managerial posts, winning Fourth Division championships with Doncaster Rovers and Grimsby Town, in turn. The story of how he came to be formally appointed Southampton's Team Manager Designate on 21 June – with the job-title to be reviewed 'at Christmas' – and of how the Board couldn't wait for Christmas to appoint him Manager, has been told in detail in *Dell Diamond*.

Yet however painstakingly those details are spelled out and however often they are repeated, the myth resiliently remains that McMenemy took over from Ted Bates in December, with the team lying fifth in the table, and duly took them down to Division II. Not so. The Southampton board had appointed him manager on 15 November, when the Saints were in ninth place and the *Echo* headline was optimistically proclaiming that they were ON COURSE FOR BEST PLACING. It certainly looked that way as they then climbed to fifth in mid-December, only to slide inexorably down the table and out of the top flight.

Moreover, the formal details disguise the fact that McMenemy had taken over as manager, in all but name, from the moment, on 26 July 1973, when Bates introduced him to the players: 'that was it!' Channon reckons. 'He took it all. Ted was gone.'

As you can see from the photograph of McMenemy's first day, he was directing training, complete with clip-board, while Bates was in the back-

As Lawrie McMenemy takes over, Terry Paine looks as comfortable
as he did when John Mortimore arrived.
(*Left to right*): Gilchrist, O'Brien, Fisher, Walker, O'Neil, Paine, Bennett, Steele,
Lawrie McMenemy, Ted Bates (mostly hidden), MacLeod.

ground. As when Mortimore arrived, first impressions were interesting. With Mortimore, it had been about dress and deportment; with McMenemy, it was his size. 'The first thing I saw,' says Eric Martin, 'the guy was so *big*. Booming voice.' But just as he had with Mortimore, he thought 'let's wait and see what he does.' Terry Paine's reaction was more instantaneous:

> I made the most stupid remark I've ever made… He walked into the dressing room with Ted, to be introduced to the players, and I've never seen a bigger head on a guy in my life. It was huge – or *appeared* to be at the time. I said 'Christ! We'll call him "Elephant Head".' It just, physically, looked like a big head. I look at it now and he's such a big man, it's *normal*.

In this instance, then – as distinct from his life-time labelling of Mortimore as a school-teacher – Terry was prepared to reconsider McMenemy's build and to regret his hasty – literally disproportionate – assessment. But it was too late to prevent the name sticking – to special merriment in the dressing room, it seems, when Gerry O'Brien referred, in broad Glaswegian, to 'Elephant Heed'. It was all behind the manager's back and unknown to him, but I learned, from a then BBC journalist, that the diminutive, 'E-Head', was in circulation. And all because of Paine's urge to articulate his hasty impression in the dressing room.

You get an idea of how fully McMenemy had taken over from the way in which he was, from the start, speaking to the press about how pre-season training had gone. Then, in September, when John McGrath was substituted at Coventry, it was Lawrie, who was picking the team and bringing on the subs, who told him to throw his boots in the bucket – dramatically symbolizing the end of his playing career – and who duly appointed him Youth-team coach.

There are essentially two dominant questions about this season: what went wrong – having risen to fifth in December, how did the Saints come to be relegated in April? – and was Paine's departure, at the end of the season, really necessary?

A chapter of *Dell Diamond* was devoted to a detailed consideration of these two riddles. There is no reason to rehearse, in depth, the various answers that have been suggested to the former question, but the issue of Terry Paine's leaving The Dell obviously needs to be raised again, here.

Terry started the season as he had played the previous one, floating a free-kick for Channon to head a near-post equalizer: QPR 1 Saints 1. He continued to attract good notices and even got on the score-sheet against

Stoke in October – his only League goal of the season, although he would double his tally by scoring in the FA Cup, also. So impressively was Terry performing in the autumn that Brian O'Neil told *Goal* that he had been 'playing almost better than I can ever remember him doing.'

It's Official! Chief Executive Ted Bates (*left*) unscrews the 'Team Manager Designate' door sign. McMenemy is now the manager.

And then it was November and McMenemy was formally being appointed the manager. No matter that Lawrie had been in charge of just about everything since July, the record books will tell us that Ted Bates was the manager up to and including a 1-1 draw at St Andrews on 10 November. What they won't reveal is that this was Paine's 782nd start for Bates (League 683; Cups 84; Europe 8; Others 7), plus four more League appearances, coming on as sub'.

If you deduct those early-season matches (15 in the League and three in the League Cup) when McMenemy was the *de facto* manager, that would still leave Paine on 764 appearances for Ted Bates. Games played for one manager don't feature in any book of football stats that I'm aware of, but whether you make it 782 or only 764, this must surely be some kind of record. At the time of writing – as the 2008-09 season begins to unfold – maybe Ryan Giggs stands a chance of making more appearances than that for one manager, but only if he continues to be brought on for the 10-minute cameos that have swelled his number of 'games' played for Sir Alex Ferguson. Paine, by contrast, was starting every game in 1973-74 and would continue to do so, missing only the last game of the season.

Come 15 December and McMenemy's men were mounting a late charge to beat Ipswich 2-0 at The Dell. Channon and Gilchrist, who had been ever-present as a replacement for Davies, got one each. That brought their goals, at this half-way stage of the season, to 12 and five, respectively, reflecting the fact that Gilchrist was being played as a target man, whose role including putting Channon in. He had no problem with that and accepted that he would be by-passed when Paine was able to play Channon in directly:

> Terry Paine was so good for Mick Channon: his passing was fantastic. He could put a ball wherever he wanted to. He used to look for Mick, making runs across the back of the defence, putting balls into space. Mick

Channon's pace was so strong that he could make a lot of goals from that.
Terry made a great supplier to Mick – more for Mick than for me, because
Mick had so much more pace than I had.

Gilchrist also accepted that, as 'Terry's legs started to go a little bit, he was
getting a lot of youngsters to use their legs, doing the work-rate – getting
back and helping out – so you always did it: you always respected him and
his career and always looked up to him.' Ally Macleod, another Forsyth-find
who was getting very few chances to contribute his legs to this cause,
observes that the energetic presence of those who were 'running about after
him, working hard' – the likes of Fisher, O'Neil and Stokes – meant that the
team could still 'afford' Terry: 'if he hadn't had those types of players, he
might have been more of a luxury.'

Indeed. Yet there was still enough in Paine's legs to afford his manager
the 'luxury' of being able to push him wide when the situation required –
as happened, indeed, in this watershed game against Ipswich. McMenemy
told the *Sunday Mirror* why he had switched Paine, in the second half, from 'a
cluttered' midfield 'to the left
wing to widen our attack.'

The Sundays agreed that
the move worked, with Paine
having what the *Echo* described
as 'a considerable influence on
Southampton's fortunes.'

This was, however, where
those fortunes went into
cataclysmic decline: having now
climbed as high as fifth (*right*),
the Saints were about to slide
down the table.

		HOME					AWAY					
					Goals					Goals		
	P	W	D	L	F	A	W	D	L	F	A	Pts
Leeds	20	6	3	0	21	6	8	3	0	18	5	34
Liverpool	20	9	0	0	16	5	2	5	4	9	11	27
Burnley	19	6	5	0	15	7	4	1	3	12	10	26
Everton	20	5	5	1	12	6	3	2	4	11	13	23
Southampton	20	6	3	1	19	8	2	4	4	7	17	23
Newcastle	19	6	1	3	16	11	3	3	3	12	10	22
Derby	20	6	3	1	18	9	2	3	5	4	11	22
Coventry	21	7	1	3	14	8	2	3	5	9	17	22
Q.P.R.	20	2	7	0	14	9	4	2	5	16	17	21
Leicester	20	5	3	2	13	7	2	4	4	11	14	21
Ipswich	19	5	2	2	14	11	3	3	4	15	19	21
Arsenal	21	4	4	3	13	12	3	2	5	12	16	20
Chelsea	19	6	1	3	23	13	1	3	5	9	13	18
Sheffield Utd	19	3	3	2	13	7	3	3	5	10	16	18
Manchester City	19	5	1	2	12	8	2	3	6	9	14	18
Tottenham	20	4	0	6	11	17	2	5	3	10	13	17
Wolves	20	3	3	3	10	11	2	2	7	13	21	15
Stoke	19	4	3	2	17	9	0	3	7	8	17	14
Manchester Utd	19	4	4	3	12	10	0	2	6	5	13	14
Birmingham	19	4	3	4	14	15	0	2	6	7	19	13
Norwich	19	2	5	3	8	12	0	3	6	5	15	12
West Ham	20	1	4	5	12	17	1	3	6	6	16	11

By the time Ian Turner arrived as goalkeeper-cover at the end of
February, the side had won only once since that Ipswich peak and had
dropped to 15th in the table. But that still left seven clubs below them and
the team didn't feel to Turner like a team in trouble: 'Far from it. The lads
were very close and they stuck together. Everything about it seemed right.
The club was so friendly – it was like coming into an extended family.
Everyone made you welcome. Brilliant! Absolutely brilliant!'

They would soon be in the bottom five, but would not drop into a
relegation place until the last week of the season. They can count
themselves unlucky: they were the first victims of the three-down rule and
their 36 points exceeded totals on which Southampton had survived in three
of the past seven seasons.

Paine feels that 'someone with more experience, like Ted Bates,' would have averted the slide down the table: 'he would have closed up at the back and pinched points.' The most consistent criticism, though, is less about tactics than personnel: McMenemy was in too much of a hurry, the argument goes, to change the squad that he had inherited. Paul Bennett believed that the back four, himself included, was too inexperienced. Paine feels Bennett is being too hard on himself – 'for two seasons, I thought he was as good as any centre-half playing in the First Division.' Paul not only doubts the wisdom, though, of releasing the 34 year-old Kirkup, but questions whether McMenemy's first signing, David Peach, a 23 year-old full-back from Gillingham, was ready to be plunged into the First Division fray, effectively as Kirkup's replacement. And Peach, in his turn, queries the decision to buy Peter Osgood, which meant having 'to change the way we played to accommodate him.' Or, as Ian Turner puts it, Ossie 'was *special* – at times, he was a little bit too special for us.'

Never mind what these signings would contribute to winning the FA Cup two seasons later: the general view seems to be that McMenemy 'wanted to change too much too quick,' as director (later chairman) Guy Askham saw it, 'and we got caught out'. Paine not only shares that view, but feels that McMenemy was

> bringing in players to make change for change's sake, not making changes to keep us in the First Division. He wanted change for change's sake; he didn't want change for the *better*. Lawrie was so anxious to make his mark that he disregarded players purely for the sake of disregarding them. And he brought in players who weren't ready and certainly couldn't cut it. There was no doubt about that: that's why we slumped like we did. You can't change a club too quickly. You can make one or two changes and gradually blend in other players over a period of time: you look at teams that turn over players quickly and invariably they fail.

Some might argue, though, that seasoned professionals – of which the squad still had its share, despite Bennett's concerns – should be able to adjust not only to a change of manager but to the changes in the playing personnel that this invariably brings about. That view was put to me by the youngest member of the squad, Mike Earls, then a 19 year-old centre-half, who would make his debut this season.

As he sees it, McMenemy had shown from the start that, not being handicapped, the way Williams had been, by having previously played with several of the senior pros, 'he knew what he wanted and he was going to sort it out in his own way.' And players who 'were used to Ted's ways, and who were comfortable with those ways, didn't take kindly to change,' especially once it accelerated, when 'a few of them let Lawrie down.' Nor does he exempt Paine from that charge. Mike thinks back to his debut at Anfield at the end of February. Liverpool had dropped only one point at home all season and were lying second, so this was always going to be a tough assignment. John McGrath went out of his way to brief Mike for it, but the debutant would have welcomed, also, a few words of encouragement from his captain. The side battled well that afternoon, only to succumb to a late, and controversial, goal. But Earls's lasting memory of the team's fruitless struggle at Anfield is of a shortfall in 'Terry's commitment to the game.'

That disappointment in a captain who had been such a professional role-model to him, as he came through the ranks, continued in Mike's home debut, when West Ham came to The Dell at Easter. When Clyde Best scored, on the stroke of half-time, from a corner that he had conceded, Earls again felt a word of encouragement was needed, rather than a reprimand, from the captain.

Hurt though he was by this lack of support from Paine and others, as their season crumbled about them, he is sympathetic to Terry's position: he had become a First Division footballer 'the hard way,' and had 'played a major part to get Southampton where it was,' so it was understandable to Mike if Terry's suspicion of change was manifesting itself in what he, the squad's junior member, perceived as inadequate leadership on the park.

With the benefit of hindsight, it is an oddity that, amid all the changes, Paine continued to start every game, reaching in January/February, two more milestones: his 700th League game (counting four appearances as sub); and his 800th competitive fixture.

To honour those two landmarks, the club presented him with a commemorative silver salver before the kick-off of his 51st FA Cup match: a Fifth Round tie at home to Third Division Wrexham. It was the visitors' first appearance at this stage. It was Terry Paine's third – and last – in what had been, despite some spectacular exploits, a disappointing FA Cup career. Manchester United had seen to that. There would be no second appearance in the Sixth Round. Wrexham saw to that, 1-0.

Terry gave a revealing interview, the month before this ceremony, to the *Echo*'s Brian Hayward. Asked about the prospects of his overtaking Jimmy Dickinson's record of 764 League appearances, Terry indicated that, 'this time last year,' he would have had his 'doubts'; but now, he told Hayward, he was feeling 'in really top shape and I… certainly anticipate playing all next season.' Hayward shared his optimism: 'the way he's playing just now makes

Top left: For their January 1974 assessment of whether and when Paine might overtake
Dickinson's record, the *Echo* brought the two of them together.
Dickinson brought along a photo, to show Paine, of a Pompey team of old.

Top right: January 1974. Feeling in 'really top shape', Paine discusses form with McMenemy.

Below: Paine acknowledges applause for the salver
he has received from the chairman, George Reader.

him look good for some time yet' – and, should he remain free of injury, Terry would reach 765 appearances early in the 1975-76 season.

In an ambitious conclusion to the interview that would come to acquire a considerable irony, Terry expressed the hope that playing on into 1975-76 would enable him to 'play my part in bringing a major trophy to The Dell.' So there you have it: as his 35th birthday neared, Paine was ever-present and hoping to keep it that way, for quite a while yet, under the new manager.

He was being substituted a few times, though. After coming off early a couple of times towards the end of the 1971-72 season – the first time by request on that humiliating afternoon at Elland Road – Terry had, as already noted, finished every game he started in 1972-73. But he would be subbed six times in 1973-74. The last occasion would be in the penultimate game of the season – a 3-0 defeat at Burnley – when he was replaced by Nick Holmes. The 19 year-old, who had made his debut at Highbury the previous month, was disappointed to come bouncing off the bench at Turf Moor and not to have his hand shaken by the departing Paine. If it is understandable that Holmes should remember Paine's breach of convention, the real significance of the occasion, which would not have been obvious at the time, was that Terry Paine had just played his last game for Southampton. He would miss the last game – with a bad back – and prepare himself, at 35, for a second spell in Division II.

That never happened, of course. McMenemy made him available for transfer. Opinion is divided as to whether Terry was yet capable of Second Division football. Despite reckoning him to be 'still a great passer of the ball,' Hugh Fisher thinks that, 'with hindsight', McMenemy was right. Paul Bennett disagrees: Terry was still 'doing it on the field.' Despite starting him consistently, McMenemy felt that Terry had not delivered for him: 'he'd been a great, great player – an *outstanding* player – who didn't impress me because, when I got there, he was past his best.'

For many of the squad, however, Terry's on-field contribution was not the issue. More to the point was whether or not McMenemy needed his influence in the dressing room. Bennett reasons that a manager coming up from the lower divisions needed all the help he could get from his experienced players: he should never have released Kirkup; now he needed to hang on to a player who knew more about the game than he did. The converse view, espoused by Eric Martin, is that Paine was so much 'part of the community [and] so loyal to Ted' as to make it difficult for Lawrie.

It would be easy, but not necessarily helpful, to label Paine 'a Ted Bates man'. Mick Channon described himself that way in his first autobiography, but was keen to stress that this did not inhibit him from performing for McMenemy and getting on 'very well' with him. The point is that the divided loyalties, if any, of the players he has inherited may matter less for an upwardly-mobile young manager than his own credibility: he may have earned his spurs, winning a couple of lower-division championships, but could Lawrie McMenemy hack it among the internationals in the Southampton dressing room?

We know that the answer to that question would very soon be an emphatic 'yes'. But it was far from obvious in 1974. Lew Chatterley, following McMenemy down from Grimsby in the February, was in a good position to contrast the control Lawrie had exercised at Blundell Park, where 'the players were just grateful to be in the side,' with his 'struggle' at The Dell to handle the likes of Paine and Channon and even some of the lesser stars:

> Terry Paine was Top Man. He'd always been Top Man. He liked his way. Channon was an up-and-coming star and he liked *his* way. Lawrie'd got to come in and 'Lawrie Who?' was the word. He'd then got to instil his way of doing this and doing that. Lawrie had to prove to them that he could manage *them*.

Which meant, as Channon expressed it in *Man on the Run*, that 'Top Man' Paine had to go in order for McMenemy to assume that title. Fisher has arrived at a similar conclusion: 'Lawrie was a strong character. He obviously wanted to be his own man. I think one of the quickest ways was to break up the Paine-Bates relationship.'

Hugh Fisher

Not that Fisher is suggesting that Bates was still associating in any significant way with Paine. Terry confirms that Ted was out of it, although he does recall an occasional chat, notably following his early departure at Turf Moor: 'Ted said something to me afterwards – one of the few times – "Don't worry, son".'

Which turned out to be inappropriate advice. Yet, even if McMenemy had cause to be rid of Paine *the player*, might he not have used him on the coaching staff? Lawrie did not consider that a possibility: 'if he wasn't going to be playing, and playing well, there wasn't any place for him.'

He echoes what others have said about Terry being 'a very strong fellow and a strong influence. He just had a habit of dropping little pearls in and stirring things up.'

Chatterley was suspected, by some of his new team-mates, of being McMenemy's source of information as to what was being said by his doubters in the dressing room, not least by Paine, with his provocative 'little pearls'. There is no evidence of that. I have it on good authority that

McGrath was McMenemy's eyes and ears in such matters. Although no longer a member of the first-team dressing room, he was around the place as Youth coach and well-placed to keep the manager informed.

Not that McMenemy needed a deal of ongoing feedback if, as he says, it was evident from the start that Paine would not last long: the two of them 'were always going to be on a collision course,' he reasons, 'because Terry was coming to the end of his career and probably thought he'd be there forever.' Terry confirms that he had indeed hoped to 'get a job there' once he hung up his boots,

> but, obviously, it wasn't to be. He wanted to sweep clean. The Old Guard was going to be swept away – the likes of me. He wanted me out. I still think he saw me as a danger to his position. He could see that I had such popularity at the club: on the terraces; and I always got on well with the Board. He needed to nip it.

No matter that Terry had no coaching qualifications, there seems to have been a widespread impression that he would sooner or later succeed Ted Bates. Younger players, especially, were queuing up to offer their views. Paul Bennett had expected Terry 'to go onto the coaching staff and eventually finish up as manager. And he would have done it. He would have been brilliant at it.' Bob McCarthy had likewise assumed that Terry was in line to become 'Ted's Second-in-Command', who would 'take over' when Bates retired. Ally MacLeod had the same idea, but he has given some mature thought to the problems of any player becoming a coach at his own club: 'I always think that, if you're going to go into coaching, you go away somewhere and have a break from those players. It's very difficult to go straight from the dressing room,' he argues. 'It's hard to think of anybody who's done it successfully.'

Indeed. And even if the Board had wanted to retain and nurture their longest-serving player in some such way, that sequence of events needed to have been set in motion in 1973. Once McMenemy had been appointed manager-designate, let alone full manager, that option no longer existed. Recruiting Terry to McMenemy's boot-room was a different proposition altogether. McCarthy feels that 'he could have contributed a lot more to the club by staying.' That said, Bob can quite see why Lawrie would want to be rid of somebody who had become so 'strong at The Dell,' in favour of bringing in his own coaching team.

In fact, by the time of Paine's release, that team already included not only McGrath but Jim Clunie, another import from Grimsby, in succession to Bill Ellerington, who switched to scouting duties. Bill had been, and would continue to be, an acclaimed talent-spotter, but his removal from the coaching staff represented another break with the Bates era. Bill Stroud, who had played with Bates and Ellerington, continued to work with the Youth team, assisting McGrath.

McMenemy had known McGrath from his Newcastle days and it was soon apparent to Terry that John was 'McMenemy's man. That was made pretty clear upfront, when Lawrie arrived.' I don't generally associate him with conspiracy theory, but Terry saw the McMenemy-McGrath axis as just the beginning of a northern plot against Bates's legacy and, in particular, himself: 'the perception was that all northern players were *strong* and good; and southern players were soft and weak.'

That sounds far-fetched to me, especially given the early signings of Peach and Osgood, but Terry is insistent:

> That was most certainly how it came over to us, anyhow, from the people he got on board. That was when the attempt was made to change whatever they wanted to change – it became obvious then that they were trying to undermine *me;* and by doing that, they were trying to let everybody else know.

Whether you buy that explanation or not, the fact remains that Lawrie McMenemy had quickly filled his boot-room with friends from the north and there was going to be no place, there, for a local lad who'd been around the place for 18 seasons.

Chapter 19

Pretenders and Contenders

In charting Terry Paine's Southampton career, I have pointed, from time to time, to two reasons he was able to play so many games: his natural fitness and freedom from serious injuries; and Ted Bates's allegedly blind faith in his protégé's ability – to the extent that he was criticised for bringing Terry in too soon; for not dropping him when he should have; and for not replacing him sooner, preferring to leave it to Lawrie McMenemy to pull that plug in 1974.

I have alluded, in previous chapters, to murmurings on each of those three charges against his doting manager. There is a school of thought that says those mutterings were just typical of any football squad and quite simply unjustified. 'Painie was supreme,' Paul Bennett attests. 'It's as simple as that. That's what it was about.' Next chapter, please!

To prove their point, those who think that way may well invite you, as Bennett does, to consider the number of games Terry played: doesn't that show how 'supreme' he was? Well, you don't have to convince me, but the counter-argument is that nobody should play that many games, without deserving an occasional 'rest'. Ken Jones may rate him, as we shall see in Chapter 23, the best winger he ever tried to defend against, but there were days, inevitably, when, he claims, Terry was 'a waste of space, but he knew he'd be picked the next week. We used to call him "The Rubber Stamp". He was stamped up: 42 games a season.'

That didn't matter to an admirer like Bennett, for whom it was right and proper that 'Painie didn't get chosen: he was just *there*.' What irks Jones, though, is that setbacks demanded changes – what he calls 'a little shuffle' – and others who had played no worse than Paine would be left out. He purports to speak for team-mates in this regard; and listening to him on this point, you have to wonder whether it might occasionally have helped team morale if Ted Bates could have done something to convince Ken, and other doubters, that he considered his supreme player to be fallible.

An occasional under-performance is one thing; needing to make way for a permanent replacement is quite another. It has been argued, though, that one or two of the pretenders to his No.7 shirt were serious contenders. The rest of this chapter is devoted mainly to the ways in which such claims surfaced from time to time; but the prior question, addressed in Chapter 5, was whether Terry was brought in too soon.

When he came into the first team in March 1957, the teenage Paine was effectively keeping the No.11 shirt aired until John Hoskins resumed it. While Hoskins then largely succeeded, over the next two seasons, in fighting off competition from John Sydenham, Paine was making the No.7 shirt his own.

Dickie Dowsett

I recorded in Chapter 5 how **Eric Day** and **Dickie Dowsett** both departed in the summer of 1957, essentially leaving **John Flood** to contest the outside-right slot with Terry. And we heard, in that chapter, from **Peter Brown**, who had the speed to play there – and had done so a few times for the first team – but who saw himself as an inside-forward, dashing through the inside-right channel to take advantage of 'the ball over the top' and so top-score for the Reserves both in 1956-57 and 1957-58.

Peter Brown

He nurses no grievance about Paine's early promotion. As he saw it, Terry was already capable, at 18, of exceptional crossing, even 'with those old balls we used to play with, with the leather lace. It takes its toll, I think, on a player trying to cross it.' Never mind the old joke about which side the centre-forward wanted the lace: with Terry, it was a question, Peter reckoned, of 'which panel do you want? Just mark it! The ball he sent across to the far post was immaculate.'

In 1957-58, with Paine missing only two first-team games, Flood and Brown formed a regular right-wing pair for the Reserves, in a forward-line that always included one or more of the four forwards who'd played with Terry for the Youth team. So there was plenty of scope in the Reserves' dressing room, for 'underlying comment' – of which we heard, in Chapter 5, from Terry Simpson and Brian Flood, John's younger brother – to the effect that Paine had been promoted prematurely. But, then, 'who was right?' Simpson asked. 'Ted was, wasn't he?'

John Flood

Ted Bates felt he had good reason to advance Terry: 'John Flood was quite a neat, tricky little player but he wasn't in the same class as Paine.' So is he saying that Terry was already in that upper class at 18? Yes, Ted 'always thought so.' Whether Flood thought differently and resented Paine's rapid preferment is a matter he has refused to discuss, either for Bates's biography or this one. While acknowledging that his brother was bound to feel a bit resentful, Brian Flood feels that 'Terry deserved to be in there,' for the reasons he outlined in Chapter 5.

John Flood departed for Bournemouth at the end of that season, leaving a motley collection of forwards to share his Reserves shirt in 1958-59, while Paine was ever-present at outside-right for the first team.

Bernard Harrison

With the League season finished, he then turned out for the Reserves' final game, scoring in a 6-6 draw at Norwich. He was replacing **Roy Littlejohn**, a former Pompey amateur, who'd become an England amateur international and had impressed for Woking, earlier in the season, in an FA Cup-tie at The Dell.

Littlejohn would be overtaken for the 1959-60 season by another Pompey reject. **Bernard Harrison** had been good enough, however, to make it at Crystal Palace – so convincingly that, in 1957, *Soccer Star* predicted that, once Palace's fortunes improved, he would become 'one of the most talked about wingers in the game.' But Palace were going down and Bernard decided – as a Hampshire 2nd XI-opener, understudying Jimmy Gray and Roy Marshall – to come to The Dell as understudy to Terry Paine.

This all-rounder never ousted those who were in his way at either of these two sports, 'perhaps,' his biographer has argued, because he was 'too talented for his own good' – or, as Harrison himself put it, he 'was doing too many things: I didn't even have time to train.' Mind you, he felt that he was 'really fit' and had no more need than Paine to take training seriously. But, according to his biographer, he had the additional problem of being misunderstood by managers who were 'insular and narrow-minded' and suspicious of 'individuality, skill and flair.'

That's pretty much how Harrison viewed the waste of his talents at The Dell. His run of three appearances at outside-right in October 1959 – when Paine switched, as injury-cover for Sydenham and O'Brien, in turn – certainly got him 'talked about' rather favourably by the *Echo*. Thus, after his 'assist' for one of Derek Reeves's four goals in a 5-1 win over Swindon – when Paine was at No.8 – the *Echo* reported that Terry 'made a success of his new position, inside-right. With Bernard Harrison doing well on the right wing, the new set-up in the Saints forward line might solve some problems.'

It is far from clear what those problems were, with the forwards having been unchanged for 13 games, pending Harrison's first start, unless it be that O'Brien had stopped scoring for four games and Reeves for three. Harrison felt the problem spot was at no.10 – which, as you can see from the statistics in Chapter 5, was indubitably the case – and 'couldn't understand, to be honest,' why Ted Bates failed to switch Paine to inside-left to accommodate him on the right wing.

That would surely have compromised prematurely the production from Paine, the wide player, whom Harrison rated 'the best crosser of a ball, with both feet, I've ever seen – even now [2005]. If you go through all the England right-wingers, I think you'd put Painie pretty high. He was very unlucky to have only 19 caps.' The point is that Bernard felt he was good enough on the right wing to justify shifting such an outstanding winger.

That was not an opinion shared within the squad. However under-valued his biographer might feel he was, the general view seems to be that Harrison was not as accomplished as he believed. Bob Charles, who played in all three of Bernard's run-outs for the first team, puts it especially witheringly: 'I didn't think Bernard was up to it, really. Everyone thinks he's "best player" and so they have to be there. And every "best player" is sat in the stand – that's the way I look at it.'

Not that Harrison was going to sit in the stand at The Dell – when the season ended, he was off to Exeter for one final season of under-achieving in League football, while Ted Bates focused on the development of his

David Chadwick

latest home-grown winger. Born in India but raised in Lymington, **David Chadwick** had first played for the Reserves in October 1959 – becoming the then youngest-ever Reserves debutant at 16 years, two months – and had had made several appearances at No.7, obliging Harrison to switch to the left-wing.

Over the next few seasons, Chadwick would become a regular as the Reserves outside-right, until he broke his leg, in a practice-match clash with Cliff Huxford, halfway through the 1962-63 season, when Ted Bates ordered a no-frills warm-up to get his players back into the swing of things after the Big Freeze. Talk to those who played in the Reserves with him and you will be assured that he would have been a serious contender for a first-team place, had he not suffered that broken leg and had he not been under-studying Terry Paine.

It seems to be agreed that he was similar in style to Paine and, although lacking Terry's two-footedness, otherwise had some of his skills. Not least, he crossed the ball well. He 'was as clever as Painie,' Channon reckons, although Terry 'probably had just a little bit more pace than him.' He didn't have Paine's *vision*; but, then, who did? In Ian White's estimation, 'half the team that was playing with him couldn't see things that Painie could see.' And nor, Ian suggests, did Chadwick have Paine's 'guile'. Or, as Channon puts it, Chadwick 'wasn't as *cute* as Terry. Painie had a brain on him – he was light years ahead of anybody else.'

That sounds like a big enough challenge for an understudy, without breaking your leg. David was still on crutches when Stoke City came to The Dell for the last game of that 1962-63 season. Ted Bates introduced him to Stanley Matthews and told the Footballer of the Year what 'a great player' his young reserve was going to be. While Matthews was his hero and model, Chadwick was quite an admirer, also, of Paine's ability not only to play in the Matthews mode, but to offer an added extra: 'Terry could go both ways – he could go inside. I could as well, but I wasn't so good with the left foot. And Stan didn't have a left foot, either.'

Terry's accomplished left foot is a recurrent topic of comment by his team-mates. Johnny Walker, his inside-left partner on two of his debuts, as you may recall from Chapter 4, rates Terry 'the best winger I played with' and brackets him with Tom Finney and former Wolverhampton team-mate, Johnny Hancocks, as outside-rights who had a superior left foot to Stanley Matthews's.

Not that this mattered to Matthews, of course, when defenders who *knew* he was going down the outside couldn't tell when. Whatever, the message of Chadwick's comparisons is that he was conscious of having 'a great player in front of me' in the queue for the No.7 shirt and a player who was hardly ever injured.

Ted Bates made three attempts to square this circle. The first of these, in 1961-62, was discussed in some detail in Chapter 7. It involved switching Paine to outside-left, the position in which he had played for Winchester City and started for Southampton. He was more comfortable on the left than Chadwick – who, as we have just seen, admired Terry's ability to use his left foot – and with Sydenham in the Army, it was worth a shot.

George O'Brien felt it worked so well that it should have survived Sydenham's return from National Service. But John was back in force the next season, playing in what became, after 10 games, an almost unchanged forward-line. For half of the disastrous 10-match start to the season, Chadwick had again been tried at outside right, with Paine at No.10. But then Bates bought David Burnside, a *real* No.10, and Paine went back to his wing. Chadwick has no argument with that: 'Burnside was a good player. Ted was a *master* at being able to buy players to fit roles.'

And then came the broken leg and a two-year wait for another run in the first-team – as replacement for Sydenham at outside-left. It lasted only a few games, but Ted Bates took the experiment seriously enough to keep playing Chadwick on the left for the Reserves. And Sydenham took it seriously enough to demand a transfer. He got his place back, though, and eventually it was Chadwick who left, in 1966, for another nine seasons of League football.

It is a measure of his ability, surely, that Ted Bates should ever have contemplated sacrificing the flying Sydenham and forgoing the *contrast* in wing-play that he offered.

Ian White would have been interested to see O'Brien's idea given a longer run, reasoning that Paine cutting in on his right foot would have provided some variety, but questions whether it would have been worth losing the 'big advantage' that Sydenham's pace provided on the counter-attack: 'just give him the ball – knock it in behind his full-back and the whole defence was turning. Probably the reason George is saying that is because he couldn't get up there quick enough when Siddie set off.'

Ouch! Perhaps only a Glaswegian would dare to take George on like that. I'm staying out of it.

David had asked for a transfer before 1966, but there were two reasons why he was tolerably content to wait around: he kept expecting one of the First Division bids for Paine's services to succeed; and he was happy living with his parents in Lymington, where he was a youth minister in his local church. That was not, of course, the kind of detail that you wanted known to a dressing room containing Paine and O'Brien: 'they used to call me "The Reverend",' Chadwick reveals. 'They could be really cruel. It *hurt* you deep down, but you had to learn to overcome that. Terry wasn't a bad person to me, though. I think he felt frustrated for me sometimes.' And the cynical O'Brien was, we have seen, a doubty champion of his cause.

While Bates was experimenting with Chadwick, **Harry Penk** was playing on the right for the Reserves. Bought as a cover for Sydenham on the left, Penk was realistic about his chances of replacing Sydenham, let alone getting into the first team on his preferred right: 'I was always right wing at Portsmouth and then finished up playing in their first team on the left wing. I could never get in on the right wing here, because Terry never got injured, never missed matches – unbelievable, really.' So did anybody stand a chance of replacing Paine? Penk thinks not:

> There was nobody, was there? Terry was just something else. He was such a phenomenal player and could read the game so well. I was at Portsmouth with Peter Harris and other internationals. And Gordon Dale was good, but nobody could compare with Terry.

Arriving in 1966, **David Thompson** was very much in the Penk mould and with similar expectations. Southampton were now in the First Division and he was happy in a tucked-in role on the left, sometimes man-marking. He was less happy when Ted Bates felt he could no longer afford a defence-minded winger and needed to play an extra defender in the No.11 shirt.

As we saw in Chapter 14, Sydenham kept getting his place back but, as Ted Bates told Tony Pawson in the early seventies, 'you must have depth as well as width.

David Thompson

Two wingers give you the width, but leave you exposed. One is essential, two a luxury you cannot afford.' And if there were to be only one winger, it had to be Paine, although he was increasingly tucking in when Bates felt the need, especially away from home, to play 4-3-3.

So by 1969, when Terry became 30, it was a question of how soon might he be replaced by a young winger.

Mick Judd

Mick Judd fancied that he was the solution. That presupposes that right-wing was his position. In 1965-66, as a 17 year-old breaking into the Reserves, he wore every forward's shirt bar No.11 and, if he had a position at all, he was looking more like third choice at No.8, behind Chivers and Channon, who was by a few months his junior, than a future No.7.

Judd was bold enough to challenge Channon's getting an Easter 1966 debut ahead of him, but accepted Ted Bates's explanation that "'a good big 'un will always beat a good little 'un." And, of course, he was absolutely right. It was the Second Division and it was pretty hard out there. I was 5ft 7ins, nine stone, wet-through.'

Chadwick's departure, that summer, gave him the Reserves' No.7 shirt, but he soon came in from the wing again to accommodate another young winger, **Ray Ames**, who'd broken into the side at 15. A left-footed player, who could play on either wing, he would never make the first team. He did not see Judd as threatening Paine's position, as he 'seemed to play better when he moved inside. He was a good goalscorer.' As Paine had proved, being able to find the net should not disqualify you from playing on the wing, but the dilemma increases for a manager, surely, if a player has Judd's added pace.

Whatever, Judd finished that 1967-68 season scoring freely at No.9 – and making his full debut in that position. He had to be patient the following season, but he ended it with a sustained run at No.11, taking authorised opportunities sometimes to swap wings with Paine. He was still on the left at the start of the 1969-70 season – although he had looked the part at No.7 on the summer tour of Bermuda. But then an injury in the Reserves ended his career, without his ever having worn that coveted No.7 shirt in a proper first team game.

A fortnight after that career-ending injury, he gave an interview to the *Echo* – which I drew upon in Chapter 16 – explaining why the right flank was his rightful position. He remains convinced of that:

> I just thought that was the opening. I think my strengths were from the right-hand side. So I always *believed*, myself, that I would take the No.7 shirt. Now, whether that would have happened, I don't know. Only time would have told. I didn't feel uncomfortable at all in the First Division. Once you've got that comfort and you've got the ability to start scoring and you get the confidence in yourself – and the *belief*, both from other people and yourself – then you can do all sorts of things. You've got to push yourself to the highest level and Terry Paine was probably the finest footballer I've ever seen – without a doubt. As a dead-ball kicker, he was magnificent. He made Ron Davies; he made a lot of players. A great player, but I was going to take his shirt – there's nothing wrong with that.

Nobody seems to have doubted Judd's ability, but nobody appears to think that he was a serious candidate, by 1969, for Paine's shirt. Ken Jones, who had had 'a few battles with him in the gym, but couldn't catch him,' feels that Judd was, at that stage, 'better than Micky Channon' and that 'he had a fantastic future.' That future would have been at inside-forward, Jones fancies: 'I don't think he was a right-winger.' On the other hand, Denis Hollywood, who also got to mark him in training, shared Judd's belief that 'they were grooming him to take over Paine's position.'

Channon rolls those piercing eyes of his at the suggestion that Judd was a contender for either his shirt or Paine's: 'Micky Judd was a very good player, but I never considered him a *threat* to me – and *certainly not* to Terry. Never in a million years!' That statement nicely encapsulates Channon's attitude to his standing in the game: he was good enough to keep out a 'very good' contender, but Paine was, he believes, in a class beyond that.

As I say, though, Paine was now 30 and the 21 year-old Judd had his sights trained on that No.7 shirt. We shall never know whether he might have got it, and how soon. Paine certainly rated him:

> Micky Judd was a sharp little boy. He was no fool. If he could have gone on, and not had the injury, he may have been an excellent player – and a bloody good finisher. If he had stayed sound, I think he would have been an asset – whether he played upfront, wide, wherever he was.

With Judd out of the equation and Thompson just an occasional cover once Tommy Jenkins had arrived in mid-season to replace Sydenham on the left, Ted Bates was still looking for a right-sided player, who would cover for Paine and maybe eventually replace him. As we saw in Chapter 16, he believed he had found, in **Gerry O'Brien**, a player who 'could become a younger edition of Terry Paine.' His arrival was timely in that he could fill in for the suspended Paine but, over the next four seasons, Gerry would never get the No.7 shirt.

Although he'd sometimes played on the left for Clydebank, O'Brien saw himself as an outside-right. He had known

who Terry Paine was, but I didn't know how good he was till I got there. He was such a great player. He was probably getting on in football terms [about to be 31] but he was so fit and a fantastic professional: it was very hard to replace him. He was one of the old-time good wingers, who could cross a ball and put a ball on somebody's head, without even thinking about it, and he did that all the time. It was really hard for me, as a winger, to replace him, because he was such a good winger. Terry Paine was just too good to replace. And that's it – I could nae get by him.

Gerry O'Brien

There are those who will tell you that Gerry would fume about that obstacle, but his philosophical take is that 'you'd like to be playing, but you *don't* resent if it somebody's playing well and doing a good job. I think Ron Davies was quite happy that Terry Paine was there.' By this time, though, Terry was less often playing as an 'old-time winger', crossing to Ron. Although still wearing No.7, he would often be in midfield – perhaps, even, alongside O'Brien, who'd be wearing No.10. The question of whether and when Southampton might replace Terry Paine on the right wing had become redundant.

Yet we have seen how that was, for many years, a question being posed by pretenders to his shirt, from those who overstated their claim, like Bernard Harrison, to more realistic challengers like David Chadwick and Mick Judd. 'But they were not Painies,' Mick Channon shrugs. 'Painie was different class. He was in a different league.' Jimmy Gabriel agrees:

You couldn't have stopped Terry being in that spot: there was nobody good enough to knock him out. Whoever they played in there wasn't good enough: Terry Paine was the Top Man; he was a good player; and he got better with age. He didn't lose anything with age: he never had blinding pace and he was more skilful and artful because of his experiences. His technique was fantastic, he could do a lot of great things and age didn't affect him.

CONSTANT PAINE

The last word should perhaps be left to the manager who kept faith with Terry. Asked whether his 1957 protégé always did his best for him, Ted Bates said he

> would think so. Obviously, if you play the number of games he did, there must have been times he played when he was a bit sluggish or tired. *But I would still have preferred him on one foot to anybody else.* (emphasis added).

That final sentence is so double-edged. On the one hand, it is a measure of what Bates thought of a player who had made 782 appearances for him. On the other, it provides ironic backing for the various complaints against him, from when he allegedly promoted the teenage Paine too soon, through the times when he might have left him out now and again, until he handed him over, at 34, to a sceptical Lawrie McMenemy.

The evidence adduced in previous chapters, and summarised in this, seems largely to support Ted Bates's judgment. But now there was a new question: at what level, if any, was the 35 year-old Paine capable of playing?

Chapter 20

Land of Hype and Glory

They don't do statues of heroes at Hereford United.

But if you go past the club's Edgar Street ground, heading out of town along the A49, you'll soon come to a monument in the form of a street sign. ADDISON COURT – named after United's most-celebrated manager, Colin Addison.

You'll find no such tribute, though, to the man who succeeded Addison in 1974 and who took the club, two seasons later, into the second tier of English football – for the first, and so far only, time in their history. That is quite simply because what Addison achieved, in the space of two rounds of the FA Cup in 1972, so put Hereford on the map that, in the words of a principal curator of the Addison legacy, 'nothing was ever likely to be quite the same again.' Successors beware!

Hereford United had been a Southern League club since 1939, never threatening to become a household name in the manner of, say, Yeovil Town, although they had attracted a couple of Welsh internationals – Ray Daniel and, latterly, John Charles – as player-managers in the 1960s. It was Charles whom Addison succeeded in October 1971.

A former York City, Nottingham Forest, Arsenal and Sheffield United midfielder, Addison had scored for Forest at The Dell in that epic FA Cup replay in 1963. Three months after his arrival at Edgar Street, he scored what would prove a rather more significant Third Round equaliser at St James' Park. It took First Division Newcastle back to Hereford. The replay – with the Ronnie Radford goal that must have been repeated by the BBC even more often than Leeds United's keep-ball sequence against Southampton that same season – is the stuff of legend. And rightly so: Hereford's 2-1 win was the competition's first non-league victory against First Division opponents since Yeovil put out Sunderland in 1949. In a 2007 *Observer* poll, it was voted the best-ever FA Cup-tie. And, for good measure, Hereford took West Ham, also of the First Division, to a replay in the next round.

This giant-killing episode remains the treasure in the Addison legacy, despite his having been the only United player, of the 12 used in that celebrated replay, whom he had *not* signed: he had acquired the others from his predecessor. Chris Moore, who was one of the *Hereford Times* reporters on the Cup run, can disabuse anyone who sees a contradiction here: Addison had taken over a 'close-knit' band of players, but what he had 'installed in them,' he reasons, 'was all-for-one and one-for-all: everyone was together.' And nor should we forget that Addison 'was a very hard-working, aggressive midfielder, who got stuck in' and generally 'led by example.'

In short, Addison had amply succeeded in shaking off the mantle he had inherited from John Charles. A hero wherever he had previously played – from Swansea to Turin – Charles's popularity at Edgar Street had survived his having to issue a grovelling apology in the *Hereford Times*, after being quoted – but distorted, he argued – in one of the Sundays as dubbing Hereford 'a soccer backwater,' where 'the cows are better known than the people.'

His superstar status had not been enough, though, to get United elected to the Football League in 1971. In 1972, when they tried again, Hereford were one of 12 non-league applicants for a place in Division IV, competing with the bottom four clubs in that division, who were seeking re-election. Until 1987, when promotion from, and demotion to, the Conference was introduced, that was how it was: The Football League's failures would hope to be reprieved by their fellow-members, while non-league upstarts would lobby to be allowed in.

This time around, Hereford had something greater than the charisma of John Charles: the glamour of their giant-killing in the Cup. They had finished only second in the Southern League, but the champions, Chelmsford City, hadn't taken any League scalps in the Cup since 1939, when they humiliated Second Division Southampton. It seems generally to be assumed that Hereford's 1972 Cup exploits played a major part in their being voted aboard. Barrow, the club they replaced, had already been reprieved 10 times. That's how hard it was to break into this closed shop and why, indeed, it probably needed the Cup run to clinch it for Hereford.

Having replaced some of Charles's signings, Addison immediately won promotion from Division IV, as runners-up. In 1973-74, a late run secured Division III safety, but the highlight was another Third Round replay in the FA Cup, this time avenging West Ham's bubble-bursting act of 1972. Hereford again exited in the Fourth Round, however, when Bristol City beat them 1-0 on an Edgar Street 'paddy field'.

The visitors had encamped at the *Brockhampton Court Hotel*, south of Hereford, and their coach had them playing a practice match on a muddy field. The hotelier reported this to Peter Hill, a Hereford United director. The Board was impressed by such preparation, 'to get them used to Edgar Street,' as Hill saw it. 'We thought "that chap's a bit shrewd".'

That chap was John Sillett, whom we last encountered, in Chapter 18, managing Bristol City Reserves at The Dell. His Brockhampton practice session meant that he had a head-start when he decided to apply for the vacancy at Edgar Street, that was suddenly created in June 1974 by Addison's resignation. Frank Miles, the chairman, had fallen out, over contractual matters, with Addison; the Board had backed the chairman; and Hereford were looking for a new manager.

Indignation that Addison – 'the best thing that has ever happened for football in this county' – had been pushed out swelled up in the local sports editor's June postbag, where the irate correspondent feared that 'the prevailing uncertainty' might discourage applicants for the post at 'this now internationally famous club.'

You may be puzzled, as I was, by this notion of global fame. I am assured by the letter-writer, Malcolm Whyatt, that it was a reference to the way in which the clip of Radford's screamer, with John Motson excitedly commentating, had been seen by audiences across the world. So that explains it.

Addison himself is more measured, although he does talk of the Newcastle replay as 'that one game [that] will never go away. That one day just turned this club upside-down. I think that turned it all round for us. I think that had a lot to do with getting us in the League.' Add to that his instant success in Division IV and you can see why Addison feels it was going to be harder for anybody to follow him than he had found it following Charles – who had, after all is said and done, won nothing.

The hyperbole of the 1974 postbag has been maintained not just by Whyatt himself, but by Roger Townley, another postbag regular and sometime chairman of the Giant Killers Reunion Committee. In a loving souvenir brochure to the Giant Killers of 1972, Whyatt claimed that their 'glorious FA Cup exploits can never be overstated.' That may come as news to some outside observers.

In March 2005, when John Motson hurried from commentating on Southampton's FA Cup exit – a 4-0 home defeat by Man Utd – to be at yet another Giant Killers Reunion Dinner in Hereford, the brochure for the evening included this claim from Whyatt:

> Never on the field of football has a team given so much, to so many, for so long. In a different era like now, the chairman would probably have received a knighthood, the manager an MBE and the entire team, and their trainer, the Freedom of the City. They certainly deserved it!

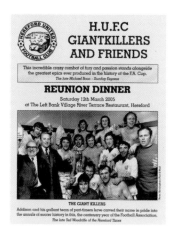

H.U.F.C GIANTKILLERS AND FRIENDS

This incredible crazy combat of fury and passion stands alongside the greatest epics ever produced in the history of the F.A. Cup.
The late Michael Bean - Sunday Express

REUNION DINNER

Saturday 12th March 2005
at The Left Bank Village River Terrace Restaurant, Hereford

THE GIANT KILLERS

Addison and his gallant team of part-timers have carved their name in pride into the annals of soccer history in this, the centenary year of the Football Association.
The late Ted Woodcliffe of the Hereford Times

This welcome to the 2005 celebration for the heroes of 1972 provides a continuing reminder of the 'helluva big hill' that Sillett and his men had to climb.

If that counts as under-statement, it may give you some idea as to why Townley believed that *any* successor to Addison was going to have 'a helluva big hill to climb,' just in order to overcome the crucial handicap of not being Colin Addison.

It was Townley who told me that things could never be the same after Addison, but that view was not confined to the nostalgists for 1972. The club trainer, Peter Isaac, had kept goal for Hereford in the 1960s and had seen a few managers come and go.

The problem, as he saw it, for anyone taking over in 1974 was that Addison had been not only '*very* successful – non-league, giant-killers, into the League and promotion – but so popular: Colin lived in Hereford; knew everybody; *great* PR man; out meeting the supporters; any charities, a match-ball; signed autographs; and everything.' Such was the hill to be climbed, 'but it would have been the same,' Isaac reasons, 'for anybody who took over from Colin.'

None of which seemed to deter aspirants to the vacancy at 'this now internationally famous club.' While we might assume that showings of Radford's goal across continental Europe did not attract applications from Serie 'A' or La Liga, it seems a safe bet that it would have helped, domestically, to make Hereford better-known among job-seekers who might otherwise have thought of this small cathedral city, somewhere in the direction of Wales, in Charles's cow-country terms.

As it was, there were 50-odd applicants, with Sillett a front-runner ahead of John McGrath, who came recommended by Lawrie McMenemy. By this time, Sillett had left Ashton Gate, following a wage dispute. When he was explaining that decision to Graham Russell of the *People*, Russell suggested he apply for the Hereford job.

Indeed, the Bristol-placed journalist, being well-known to the Edgar Street board – not only as a post-match visitor to the boardroom, but as a fellow well-met on race-courses by Hill and other directors – was ideally situated virtually to broker Sillett's appointment. Russell 'prompted and prodded' the Board, Hill recalls, although his Brockhampton practice session had already put him in the frame.

Sillett had been content to be a No.2 – you may recall, from Chapter 17, that he applied to be Ted Bates's assistant in 1971 – where he could focus on coaching, rather than administration. Until cajoled by Russell, he had 'never, really and truly, thought about management – never given it a thought. I loved coaching and thought I'd get another job coaching.' And he'd certainly not thought about where he might find an assistant.

The Hereford board liked the idea of a first-time manager having an assistant – Frank Miles had questioned Addison's judgment in the market and so had taken some of his ideas for team-building to assistant manager, John Barnwell, Addison's former team-mate both at Forest and Sheffield United. Barnwell is one of those people who keeps making an appearance in the Terry Paine story – latterly, you may recall, as a player Arsenal valued too highly to swap for Paine.

He had quit Edgar Street early in the 1972-73 season, leaving Addison to run things with trainer, Peter Isaac, alone. But the Board wanted Sillett to have an assistant. Having sealed his appointment as Hereford's manager on Sunday 7 July, Sillett was sitting in his office, the next day, never dreaming that his good friend Terry Paine might be the answer to his problem. But then the two friends had a telephone conversation. Memories have blurred as to which of them rang the other and as to which of them started the banter about Paine joining Hereford as player-coach. What is agreed is that Sillett was protesting that he'd 'like to be able to afford you,' while Terry was insisting that he'd come cheap enough.

Wanting to believe that, Sillett took a contract with him when he met Terry the next day at *The Swan*, near Newbury. Although he'd had a quick word with his chairman and had been urged to sign his old pal at any cost, Sillett still felt that Hereford would be unable to meet the demands of 'a class act' like Terry Paine. But such was Terry's trust in John that – subject to Lawrie McMenemy, who was in Spain on holiday, agreeing this free transfer – he signed a blank contract, leaving Sillett and his chairman to fill in the numbers. Sillett couldn't believe his luck:

> It just amazed me. Driving back, I thought 'I don't believe this. I've signed Terry Paine and there's not a pound mentioned in the contract.' I had his signature on a form, with no agreement on bonuses; no agreement on wages; but signed. I got back to the chairman and he said 'what do you think is a fair wage?' We discussed it and I think you'll find it was £120 a week – but with bonuses, a signing-on fee and removal, things like that. We did everything very fairly and when he saw the contract, he was chuffed. He *wanted* to play: that was the important thing for me. He still had this lovely will to win. And he wanted to beat the record [number of appearances, held by Pompey's Jimmy Dickinson].

Which begs the question as to why Sillett felt that his 35 year-old friend would be able not only to play Third Division football, but to *coach*. Terry had no formal qualifications. That did not worry Sillett:

> We'd talked, as youngsters, about football and he was always coming up with points and I'd think 'I don't know about that. I'll have to think about that.' He thought deeply about things and his answer was spot-on, I found. I wanted somebody who was sharp, because I think I think that way: I'm very quick. I wanted somebody who was sharp, somebody who was doing what we wanted on the field.

Before the month was out, Hereford would have three new signings. The priority was a striker who could take advantage of Paine's crosses. Sillett made a bee-line for Lincoln City's Dixie McNeil, a player he had fancied taking to Ashton Gate. After a faltering start to his football career, McNeil had done well at Sincil Bank, with 53 goals in 97 League games. He was feeling ready for a change and was certainly ready to be flattered: he confesses that Sillett 'sold' him the club by dwelling on why he'd wanted to sign him for Bristol City and how he now needed him to spearhead Hereford's next promotion. That gambit worked so well, in fact, that Sillett had no need to mention to Dixie that he'd just brought in a winger capable of helping him to maintain his goal-scoring ratio:

Dixie McNeil

> He didn't at the time but, as soon as I got down there and Terry was there, I knew – to play with somebody who'd played that many times for England! Terry was putting a lot of his reputation at stake to come and play in that League and show what he could do. I think it was a brilliant and brave thing to do. You wouldn't get many international players who would do that – because I think there were a lot of full-backs in that League who were saying 'I'm going to have you. You can be Terry Paine. You can play for England. You can play 800 games with Southampton, but I'm going to nail you.' But they never did. They never got near him. He just had so much skill. He was so *whippy* – those two or three yards at the beginning, when he sprinted off the ball, that they couldn't get near him.

Dixie recalls how simple his orders from his new player-coach were. All Terry said was 'you make your runs forward, behind the defence and down the side of the defenders, you show me that '0' of the '10" – like Chivers, McNeil didn't want the '9' – 'and I'll drop it over your shoulder.'

The other July acquisitions were both from Southampton. Peter Trevivian, a 19 year-old who'd been released by McMenemy after half-a-season's worth of games at right-back for Saints Reserves, was surprised to get a 'phone call, 'right out of the blue,' from Terry Paine, inviting him to become Sillett's first signing. He couldn't wait to get to Edgar Street and sign what amounted to a trial-contract: 'obviously, with Terry being the big name he was and the reputation that he had at Southampton, it was an opportunity too good to miss. You really did feel it was an honour – that a player of his status remembered bits and pieces that he'd come across and then thought about it.'

His chances to impress Terry with his 'bits and pieces' had been limited to practice matches at The Dell. He recalls Terry saying that

> he liked the way that I got forward... With him playing as a wide player, he said to me, one day after a practice match with the first team, that, from his point of view, it's a big bonus if you've got a full-back who's prepared to come forward and help. When somebody of that status, and stature within the club, says something to you, as a young kid you take it on board. I thought 'if that's a positive to Terry Paine, that's something I've got to really grab hold of and work with.'

Unfortunately, Trevivian would spend most of his brief stay at Edgar Street being treated, in vain, for a back injury, and would never get to play League football.

The second arrival from The Dell was Tony Byrne, for a fee of £18,000 – some £3,000 more than Sillett had paid for McNeil, although the deal was that 20 goals from Dixie would cost Hereford a further £5,000. If McNeil was ready for a change, Byrne was desperate – desperate 'to get away from Lawrie: I couldn't improve under him.' So he 'jumped at' the chance to rejoin Terry: 'Lawrie could handle the old players, but he didn't have a clue how to coach the young ones.'

Yet he saw the badgeless Paine 'as a coach – because of all his experience, for crying out loud!' And he rated Terry as a tactician, crediting him with the idea of using him as a man-marker, notably against George Best. For his part, Terry thought Tony would be 'ideal' for Hereford, although he warned Sillett that he was a chirper:

> I said to John, 'he'll chirp: he'll stand at the back of the crowd and you can hear him chirping away at the back. He'll never come up and confront you, face-to-face, but you can hear the little chirps in the background. He was always that way, but you're going to get a player who's going to do us the world of good.'

Another ex-Saint was already at Edgar Street. Freddie Kemp had arrived from Halifax in June. We saw in Chapter 16 that Paine was no fan of Kemp, so it is not surprising that, on hearing of Terry's imminent arrival, Freddie apparently told his new club-mate, Tommy Hughes, 'That's it, then. It's been nice knowing you. Terry and I go back a long way; and I won't be here much longer.' Terry makes no bones about it: 'he had to go.' Yet, no matter that his comments on Freddie's limitations are as damning as any I have heard from Terry of a team-mate, he feels sorry that Kemp should have sensed he was about to be ousted from his new club: 'That was unfortunate for him. He goes to a place for a new start. Who arrives but me?'

Actually, it would be March before Freddie left for Durban, to rejoin Addison, the manager who had signed him. For the moment, though, Hereford United had four ex-Saints, all of whom played in the 2-2 draw in

The new player-coach comes out for pre-season training. Freddie Kemp (*right*) had reason to believe that his days at Edgar Street were numbered.

the opening pre-season game at Exeter, where 'Paine, without a doubt, was easily the most outstanding player on the field.' That was the verdict of Chris Moore, one of the three journalists reporting on United's games for the *Hereford Times* or its sister newspaper, the *Evening News*.

In the space of the next four days, it was apparent that the new player-coach had an instant fan club among all three of them.

In the second friendly, a 4-0 win against Veendam of Holland, Sports Editor Ted Woodriffe found Paine's 'ball control and distribution… immaculate.'

And when they lost their third warm-up 4-1 at Shrewsbury, Laurie Teague reported that 'a vital factor … was the absence of … Terry Paine and that there was no doubt that United missed his precision passing.'

John Sillett (*left*) and his short-lived physio appointee, Lew Clayton,
line up with the squad for 1974-75.
Back row (*left to right*) Kemp, Gregory, Tyler;
Middle: Naylor, McNeil, Hughes, Tilsed, Tucker, Redrobe, Evans.
Front: Rudge, Ritchie J, Paine, Gane, Lee. Inset: Byrne.

Such appreciative write-ups continued, match after match, but the
report on the sixth game of the season – a 1-0 home defeat by
Bournemouth – gives a clue to a problem: 'there were at least half-a-dozen
passes from Terry Paine that could have been match-winners,' Woodriffe
lamented, 'if the other players had been able to take advantage of the
situations he created.' That may have been obvious from the press-box, but
there was impatience on some sections of the terraces that an England
international seemed unable to pass the ball to a Hereford player.

They were rather more patient with Terry in the Vice-Presidents' Club,
an organisation of local businessmen and others who liked to pay a
premium to watch the game in style. Andrew Reed, the club doctor and an
honorary member of this elite, felt that Paine's barrackers initially

> didn't understand clever football and a good footballer. They expected the
> ball to be booted up the middle: they were used to Southern League
> football. It was said that we'd kicked our way out of the Fourth Division –
> which we probably had – and suddenly we were playing sophisticated
> football; and we did play bloody good football in that [Third] Division.'

To say that Addison's 1972-73 side 'kicked their way' to promotion perhaps
fails to do justice to what Ron Parrott, author of the *Complete Record* of
Hereford's first spell in the Football League, prefers to call 'solid defence':
to concede only 12 goals in 23 home games and to keep 22 clean sheets in

a 46-game season was something to be proud of, even if that approach lacked the quality and entertainment value that Sillett was soon offering.

The downside was that its success in 1973 encouraged 'a certain section' of those who stood on the terraces, as Ron did, to believe that the kind of football they had watched in the Southern League – 'players who'd run through a brick wall for you, chase anything and who, basically, didn't play any constructive football'– worked just fine in the Football League and didn't need changing.

Paine was appreciated in the directors' box, too. Enjoying such an 'amazing signing', Peter Hill feels that

> it was a question of hoping the crowd would get to appreciate the delicacies of a world-class player suddenly playing for the club. They'd always been used to old bread-and-butter players, who would get stuck in on anything. And, of course, Terry was very delicate, the way he played – stayed out of trouble. In the 90 minutes, you know how often he would quietly drift out of the game, whereas they had been used to kick-and-running, up-and-down. They couldn't see, for a while, what he was doing but, as soon as he got a ball, he always did *something* with it: there was never a wasted ball.

Save when the intended target misread it, that is. But, then, John Charles had had a similar problem when he arrived at Southern League Hereford in 1966, giving Ted Woodriffe cause to defend him, in the *Hereford Times*, against his barrackers. Charles answered them for himself, within the month, by scoring five times in a 6-1 thrashing of Folkestone, but that kind of crowd-pleasing response was not, of course, available to Terry Paine. Recalling how Charles kept on heading goals for Hereford, Chris Moore muses that, 'if John Charles had signed Terry and had him crossing for him, God knows how many goals he'd have scored then.'

In the real world, though, it was going to take a play-maker longer than a towering centre-forward to pacify his critics. In his *Complete Record,* Parrott suggested that Paine's 'vintage show of precision passing and close control' against Blackburn Rovers in December – when the Third Division leaders were seen off 6-3 – 'won over those few fans still sceptical about his worth to the side.' But that doesn't explain why the manager was still feeling it necessary to take issue with Terry's barrackers after a 3-2 home win over Grimsby in February. He knew that those supporters had wanted him 'to bring off Terry Paine,' Sillett told Woodriffe, even though Terry 'had a hand in all three of our goals and also had one disallowed. He's there to create openings and that's what he did.' Woodriffe concurred, crediting Paine with 'a particularly good game in the second half,' as Hereford came back from

2-1 down, when he 'always looked the player most likely to prize open the tough-tackling Grimsby defence.'

A party from the Vice-Presidents' Club put this all into perspective when they travelled down to The Dell at the end of the season for Terry's testimonial against Ipswich. In a letter to the *Evening News*, they reported not only on the beneficiary's 'superb display', but on the adulatory reaction of the Dell crowd: 'that he should receive such worship from the Southampton fans makes one realise what a tremendous asset he is to us here at Hereford United,' the V-Ps wrote. 'How long before he is appreciated as such?'

The 'worship' that the Hereford visitors observed
(*Left*) Paine acknowledges some of his worshippers.
(*Right*) John Hannam presents him with a silver salver from the Isle of Wight Saints, whose president he had been.
Hannam is accompanied by (*left to right*) Denys Rayner, Dave Pitts and Tony Butt.

As O'Brien (*left*) and Steele make themselves available, Paine works the ball out from deep.

As you'd expect, the tributes in the programme were mainly to his collection of records and to the combination of skills that made him, for Ted Bates, 'one of the most accurate and devastating passers of the ball in the game.' Those skills included his 'perception on the field which is second to none' – or, as chairman, George Reader, put it, his 'perceptive vision, equal to any.' Team-mates were queuing up, in *Dell Diamond*, to marvel at Terry's vision. Ted Bates had a special way of expressing this: Terry could have 'seen a train coming out of the tunnel before it had gone in at the other end.'

But we come back to the point that, in order to capitalise on that vision, a team needs other players, especially in positions where they are expecting to receive the ball from Terry, who can sense what he has picked out. At its best, that kind of understanding was described, in previous chapters, as 'telepathy'. Which is why Bob Brunskell was musing nostalgically, in his *Echo* report on the testimonial match, on how Terry had an outlet – in Mick Channon, 'loping in space' – for 'that telepathic ability of his to find the right man at the right time with typical, inch-perfect passes.'

Resuming his relationship with Mick Channon was one thing; establishing any such understanding with his Hereford team-mates was quite another. As Clive Joyce, who had replaced Chris Moore at the *Hereford Times,* has observed, even at the end of that first season, Sillett was still getting his 'building-blocks into place.' In the meantime, Terry had inevitably been 'left a bit exposed in our play, because he was a skilful player, but not a worker.'

In a variation on that theme, two players who *had* developed an early telepathy with Terry – Dixie McNeil and Steve Emery – both point out that it wasn't just a question of which of their team-mates could read his passes, but of how long a side with so many new players needed to settle in as a team. Whereas Addison had bided his time before signing supplements to Charles's acquisitions, Sillett had fielded five new signings in the opening game of the season and had kept on buying bargains – notably Forest's John Galley, who had been with him at Bristol City, come December.

All of which made it an honourable achievement, McNeil reasons, to finish 12th, with 46 points from the 46 games: 'you need to gel together as a side… When you get all those people coming in in one season, you're not going to get it together in the first season, that's for sure.'

Which is why Emery thought it 'impressive' that Hereford's most successful-ever side 'came together within a season-and-a-half. We *knew* each other.'

Never having played in a higher division than the Third, McNeil sympathised with the dumbing-down problems that Paine had experienced: 'we had a lot of – dare I say it? – journeymen in that side, including myself. I think once you drop down to a lower League, you will not sometimes understand the wave-lengths of other players. Perhaps they don't react to how you play: they don't read you.' Journeyman or not, Dixie 'liked to think that I could read Terry. I wasn't the quickest, but what people say about a lot of goalscorers is that you have to be alert in the penalty area. And I like to think that I was alert and I could *read* a game within the penalty area.'

Hat-trick man, Dixie McNeil, is congratulated by Terry Paine on scoring against Chesterfield.

His reading ability was good enough to bring him 31 goals that season – 30 of them in the League, to make him the top-scorer in the entire Football League. His haul included two hat-tricks: against Chesterfield in September, which was Hereford's first in the Football League; and in that 6-3 win against Blackburn in December.

His telepathy with Paine worked especially well at free-kicks, when a lot depended, a drooling Sillett recalls, on 'eye contact: he was superb at that. He'd put it down; look; weigh up; and deliver. And his delivery was brilliant. The weight of the pass – the precision of it – was tremendous. I've never seen it bettered.' McNeil reckoned to be able to read Paine, though, even without eye contact:

If we had anything around the edge of the penalty area, I never looked at him and Terry never looked at me but I knew, when he was putting the ball down, he would deliver it in the right spot. The goals we scored from those set-plays! And that was because of his quick thinking and mind. You didn't look at him: you just knew that you would have to make a run to the near-post or the penalty spot and the ball would be there. If you were there, the ball was there. You never ever got there and the ball wasn't delivered in. So you could never turn round to Terry and moan at him for not getting the ball in the right area. He would moan at you if you weren't there, that's for sure: thankfully, we got it right most of the time.'

CONSTANT PAINE

Team-mates knew to keep clear of Dixie's runs on to Terry's free-kicks. Roy Carter, who arrived, late in the season, from Falmouth Town, has explained the rationale:

> Terry would just put his hand on the ball. Dixie would be in the box, minding his own business; and, all of a sudden, you'd see Dixie get to the near post and Terry would put the ball right on his head. They *knew* what was happening between them and *no-one* was allowed to go near that near post. John Sillett would slaughter you if you were there. So you just left it open and everybody was talking to each other, just minding their own business. Once Terry put his hand on the ball, Dixie was gone – because he knew Terry would take one step back and just flick it in and Dixie would head it.

Even so, there were variations to this routine. Reckoning that he 'had a pretty good shot on' him, Steve Emery would stand alongside Paine, when a shot was a possibility. Terry would sometimes roll the ball to him, or maybe skip over it, with instructions, as Emery recalls, 'just to hit the target': if you don't score, somebody may get the rebound.

In fact, the side developed a handful of free-kicks, all choreographed by Terry on the training ground. Centre-back John Layton, another Sillett debutant, was deployed in the variation in which McNeil and his fellow-striker would peel away, taking their markers with them. Layton would then run from outside the box, towards the penalty spot. 'As soon as I got to the "D",' he recalls, 'Painie would start his run-up and deliver the ball to the penalty spot; and by that time, I'd accelerated onto there and often I'd have a free header.' He knew that the ball would arrive 'at *pace*. And the best part about it was that you knew, within a one- or two-yard area, that ball was coming in, there.'

With Paine wont to take such quick free-kicks, there was often neither time nor need for the elaborate semaphore deployed by place-kickers today. If he did need to signal his intent, he could do so with the digits of one hand, so long as he was content with only five varieties. But there came the day, Layton recollects, when Terry had them practising a sixth play

> on the edge of the box: we were getting more free-kicks there, where Dixie was being fouled. We said 'what do we call this one?' He said 'call it 99.' Painie was taking a free-kick, sometime after, and he shouts out '99'. One of the opposition said 'Bloody hell! You've got some free-kicks, haven't you?'

Six options or not, McNeil expected most of Terry's free-kicks to be on his head – to an extent he had never previously known: 'I hadn't had anybody who gave service like that off free-kicks. I'm only 5ft 10ins, but if you start moving around in the penalty area, then you just need the ball to be *delivered* – and Terry Paine's delivery was 100 per cent.'

There was more to Paine's repertoire, of course, than taking free-kicks: as goalkeeper Tommy Hughes saw it, he was 'fantastic at taking corners,' too. Hughes's concern was that Terry's 'work-rate, away from home, wasn't the best' – though 'to be fair,' Tommy adds, 'that was because of his years.' Indeed, he feels that the veteran Paine personified the case for an innovation from the USA:

> When you were under pressure and you were up to your neck in muck and whatever, I always used to say that Terry should have been the first guy to do what they do in American Football: the kicker who just comes on to take the penalties. Terry should have been the first footballer to do that [with set-plays]. He'd have been great in that role, because he wouldn't even have been tired taking the free-kicks.

Bob Dixon was generally too busy scouting for youngsters – and doing 'a super job', Sillett reckons – to watch many first-team matches. But when those duties allowed, he enjoyed watching Terry's 'brilliant' set-pieces – so much that he felt the side could 'afford' to have him on the pitch for those alone and 'carry' him for those tasks his legs could no longer perform. Clive Joyce was not so sure. He found himself threatened with exclusion from the team bus, after he appeared to attribute to Sillett his thought that 'Paine is a midfield luxury United cannot afford away from home.' That happened in March when Joyce was praising Terry's 'brilliant' display, as sweeper, in a 1-1 draw at Peterborough. It was a performance that thrilled the Sundays: BRILLIANT PAINE SWEEPS THEM UP trumpeted one headline, while John Ross made Terry his 9-out-of-10 man-of-the-match.

So he kept the position for the next game, a 0-0 draw at Grimsby. It was Laurie Teague's turn to enthuse. This was, for him, 'a role ideally suited to [Paine's] experience and ability to read the game, [which] took him into the right position to mop up the Mariners' attacks time after time.' This proved to be a lasting impression: when I met Teague, almost exactly 30 years later, he instantly volunteered that this was 'the best game I saw Terry Paine play.'

All of which meant that the manager needed to explain, in the next match-day programme, why there had been such a gap between his first experiment with Paine as sweeper – at Watford in October – and the March revival. Sillett pointed to his team's good autumn results on the road, with Paine restored to midfield: 'I have always believed in attacking football,' he concluded, 'and Terry can be a match-winner in midfield.'

As Tony Byrne points out, though, a Third Division midfield was a different proposition than that which Terry and he had known in the top flight: 'What people don't realise is that you don't get time on the ball. And fair dos: Terry was getting on and it didn't give him a lot of time. It was very difficult.' It was easier, Byrne reasons, with his younger legs, especially if you were playing facing the ball, as he invariably was – as, of course, Paine was when sweeping.

Which raises the question as to when Sillett's 'block-building' might get to complement his veteran play-maker with competent young runners around him. By the end of the season, Terry was able to take advantage of two such pairs of younger legs. First, there was Steve Emery, converted to right-back by Sillett. He liked to overlap and was encouraged to do so by the kind of service he received from Paine:

> He always knew that I was coming down the right wing, so it was just a matter of putting it in place and I would be there. He knew that if there was space outside him, then I would be going. And more often than not, his pass was there. I'd always had that in my game, anyway, but now I *knew* that, if I went on a run, I had somebody there whose pass wasn't going to be very far away from me. Before that, we probably didn't have that, but now you knew that you were running onto a decent ball.

Secondly, with the arrival of Roy Carter, Terry had a reserve-tank: 'I was his legs,' Carter reckons, 'and he was the brains. That's what he used to say to me: "You do the running, Roy, and I'll do the passing".'

In one position or another, Terry chugged along – missing only six League games and a Welsh Cup-tie, all season. As ever, he suffered more from suspensions than injuries.

Hereford's Assistant Secretary, Jim Finney, despaired of Terry's indiscipline. A former World Cup referee, who would come out of retirement to referee Terry's testimonial, Finney felt that

Jim Finney (*left*) applauds Terry onto the pitch at his Dell testimonial.

> Terry's basic problem was just petulance: silly little things. A lot of it was *mouth,* more than anything: it wasn't a case of tripping or use of the arms. John Sillett was a very hard disciplinarian, but he couldn't handle that side of him. They were very dear friends, but I know John would fine him. But the next match, he'd do the same again. Whether he thought that, by virtue of being the coach, it was his prerogative to have a go at referees and query decisions, I don't really know, but a lot of it was just silliness, quite honestly.

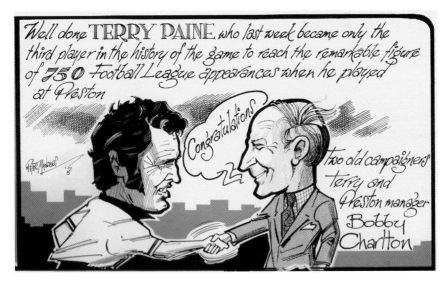

Well done TERRY PAINE *who last week became only the third player in the history of the game to reach the remarkable figure of* 750 *Football League appearances when he played at Preston*

Congratulations

two old campaigners terry and Preston manager Bobby Charlton

Sillett would, indeed, fine his player-coach for his bookings and had done so as early as August. None of which stopped Terry making his 750th appearance in the Football League in April – in a 2-2 draw at Deepdale. Preston's player-manager, Bobby Charlton, left himself out, but appeared for the benefit of Peter Manders (*above*). Terry Paine, just turned 36, thrilled Joyce with 'one of his best away performances of the campaign.'

The season over, Terry had that testimonial to savour, followed by a remarkable continental adventure with the Youth team. Bob Dixon, who'd found so many of Hereford's apprentices, was impressed by Sillett's interest not only in their development but in talking to their parents, a form of PR at which Dixon found Sillett an improvement on Addison. But Sillett attributes much of the successful parent-liaison to Paine:

> He was great with parents, which is very important. The kids get tempting offers. You get the big clubs – Aston Villa – coming in and they say 'Right! We'll nick that one.' But Terry had all the parents lined up. Not many kids got away: I'll tell you that!

Peter Isaac saw the two of them as giving United 'the best set-up we ever had with the Youths – and I was there for 30-odd years. The set-up was down to those two.' Terry's part in this set-up involved extra afternoon training for the younger players. He continued in that role, even after Sillett brought in Tony Ford, another Bristol City old boy, in October, as Youth Development Officer. Ford and Paine went way back: Tony scored in that landmark Easter Monday game in 1966, when Terry's late goal helped to rob City of the promotion they felt they deserved – the whinge you'll surely remember from Chapter 10.

CONSTANT PAINE

You might wonder – I certainly did – whether Ford might now have another grievance: if he was in charge of the youngsters, wasn't he in danger of being upstaged by Terry's afternoons? He is having none of that: 'because of what Terry was – an international and all the rest of it – the young players looked up to him. For him just to come out and do a little bit of work with young players made them feel good.' And it offered them variety: 'it was a different *voice* – and they were able to do something different – because I was with them all day, every day, almost.'

The players expected to attend the afternoon sessions ranged from Kevin Sheedy – given half-day release from school to train with United – to first-teamers like Steve Emery and Roy Carter. Sheedy found it 'a great education' to have somebody 'with such experience and knowledge' to watch and learn from, especially in dead-ball situations. And the fact that Terry 'had good habits' and so kept himself fit made him something of a role model.

It wasn't a fault-free model. We have seen how much Emery learned from, and admired, Paine, but he was not impressed by the way in which Terry lived up to 'his reputation of being a "topper", leaving his foot there, which you didn't need in the game… If I had a bad thing to say about Terry, it would be that.' John Galley objected to a different kicking-habit of Terry's – the one I disliked, as a fan of his, but which I've seldom heard mentioned by other players: 'he tackled people from behind. I didn't like people like that: I'd sooner have somebody who hits you up the front and will face you. I don't like people who do it from behind.'

Yet nobody seemed to mind that Terry might rough up a young player during a practice match. As Peter Trevivian, coming from The Dell, puts it,

> If there was a youth player there who needed the real world to be painted, or needed a reminder that they weren't as good as they thought they might have been, the senior players at Southampton – the Terry Paines; the John McGraths; the Hugh Fishers and Brian O'Neils – weren't slow in giving you a physical reminder of what it was all about. That was, at the time, quite commonplace, I think. If it was for the good of the youngster to learn a lesson, if it was a physical lesson, then so long as it wasn't dangerous, the senior players weren't slow to give you a little kick or a little nudge, or whatever, just to show you what the game's about.

As a senior player at Hereford, Tommy Hughes wasn't enamoured of this rite of passage but accepted that this 'was the way football was. You used to get young lads and knock them into shape. You saw it happen, no matter what club you were at.' And, in this regard, Terry was no worse, Hughes reckons, than other established pros at Hereford.

Tommy draws a clear distinction, though, between rough-handling a youngster and teaching him how to commit an over-the-top tackle: 'it's things like that which, when you're an old pro, leave a taste.' Which is why it rankled with him – and it still does – when he overheard Terry coaching a young winger called Timmy Davies in this art.

Timmy had been sent off, in a Youth-team game, Kevin Sheedy recalls, 'for elbowing an opponent. The next day, Terry pulled him aside and taught him the art of going over the top of the ball.' Kevin acknowledges that this 'was when the game was full of hard men and you had to look after yourself,' but he is uncomfortable with the idea that, if you're going to risk the wrath of the ref, you should avoid blatant fouls like elbowing and instead develop the crafty, but nasty, habit that some wingers were using to get their own back on hefty full-backs, even if it meant retaliating first.

It seems that this incident, like the Ames incident at The Dell (as recounted in Chapter 15) has left a nasty taste with a team-mate or two, for Terry's work with young players and their parents was, overall, very well regarded. As I say, even a regular first-teamer like Emery had to stay behind, after morning training, for the sessions with Terry. But only when specifically asked to do so.

Steve Emery

One afternoon, when Terry had neglected to invite him to linger a while, Steve got as far as the station, for the train home to Ledbury. But then, 'all of sudden, Terry comes racing along the platform. He'd come to the station in his car to get me off the train and take me back to training.'

Serious stuff, then. But worth the effort: 'you train with a full international and it's got to be beneficial,' Emery reflects – although he especially valued what he learned from Terry *during* a match:

> There are times when you know you've done something wrong during a game and the old eyes would open up and tell you, without actually saying anything. Obviously, when you got *bad* eye contact, you knew you'd done something wrong. But, on the other side of the coin, when you'd done something right, he would always congratulate you. Basically, it was just such a privilege to play alongside him. It was great.

Emery won't be the last youngster from whom we hear this kind of testimony to Terry's non-verbal tuition on the field.

Steve's reward for being a good student was to captain the Youth team when it played, that summer, in the Blauw Wit Youth tournament in Holland. What's more, he rode there in style – along with other young players who had already made the first team. Carter recalls what it was like to be first among equals, travelling not with their less-experienced team-mates but in

> Mr Paine's wonderful Jaguar. A *massive* car – and it caused quite a stir in Holland. Everybody looked at it because it was that big and unusual. The younger pros – the ones who'd played in the first team – went in that and the younger lads went in the minibus. It was great in the car, because we *flew* there.

Hereford were in for a double surprise: they would win the tournament, but lose a player. Their Dutch guide turned out to be scouting for some of Holland's top teams. Roy Carter was in a party of four youngsters taken by him to Ajax and feels that he was 'tapped up to go and sign for Ajax. Mr Paine and Mr Sillett never knew that.' But his room-mate, Nick Deacy, signed for PSV Eindhoven. This caused an embarrassment to Dixie McNeil, who saw the news, on TV,

> '*Hereford to sell striker to PSV Eindhoven*. I thought 'Phwoor! I'm off! Nobody's told me about this.' Five minutes later, the door-bell rang – and Terry was at the door. He said 'we've sold a player to PSV Eindhoven.' I was all smug: what a move for me! 'You'll never believe it,' he said: 'it's Nick Deacy.' I think I went from 7ft 2ins to 4ft 7ins. Terry had come to tell me, because they were so pleased that they'd made some money.

Indeed, they were: bought for £1,300 from Merthyr Tydfil, Deacy fetched £20,000. Enough to fill Terry's gas-guzzling Jag – both tanks – and still leave Sillett with sufficient change to invest in a strike-partner for McNeil. The problem with Dixie's record-breaking 30 goals had been that Galley, in his half-a-season, had been the next highest scorer on six, just pipping Paine on four (plus one in the League Cup).

McNeil was staying put, although it hadn't taken long for his goalscoring to attract other clubs. As early as October, Hereford had rejected an offer for him of £50,000 from Cardiff. In that same month, Sillett was linked with the managerial vacancy at Stamford Bridge, after Dave Sexton had been sacked. Chairman Miles told the *Hereford Times* that any move for Sillett would be resisted: 'he is the best manager we have ever had.'

Had Sillett gone, it is clear that Paine would have accompanied him. Come January, the pair of them were discussing a couple of vacancies elsewhere. One was at Dean Court. Paine recalls Sillett telling him 'we've got it if we want it.' But why would they want it? After a good start to the season, Third Division Bournemouth were lying 20th at the turn of the year, 10 places behind Hereford. So, apart from the challenge of maybe rescuing them from relegation, Bournemouth seemingly offered nothing more than a return, for the two Hampshire lads, to their native county (although the town of Bournemouth had just been transferred to Dorset under the local government reforms of 1974).

The other opening was at the City Ground. Nottingham Forest had been relegated to Division II in 1972 and were in need of a manager to get them back up. George O'Brien, who was doing some scouting for Hereford (more of which in the next chapter), remembers a call from Terry, advising him that there'd be a proper scouting post for him, were Sillett to land the Forest job.

Paine had no doubts that Sillett was amply capable, with a decent budget, of managing at the top. He was never going to be able, at impoverished Hereford, to achieve what he was capable of and

deserved better than that, because he was an outstanding coach. He came out with so many things that we did, which were way above what even the First Division clubs were doing. That's why we said we would cream it if we ever got a First Division side. We thought we'd be First Division stuff – the pair of us. There was no doubt about that. We saw the things that were going on above us. We thought how differently we would have handled it. We looked on that as a doddle, compared with what we were trying to do at Hereford. We had no fear – we could have run Man United and done a great job.

They would not get the chance, however, to prove their potential at the City Ground. The Forest board opted for the rather more experienced duo of Brian Clough and Peter Taylor.

Chapter 21

Champions and other Milestones

Sillett's summer funds were sufficient for him to buy not only a strike-partner for McNeil, but a goalkeeper, a full-back and a midfielder, to boot. Each signing represented a return for networking: one way or another, Paine or Sillett exploited a connection from the past.

The striker, Plymouth-born Steve Davey, had signed for his home-town club, aged 17, in July 1966, the month in which Sillett had himself joined Argyle from Coventry. With 47 goals from 224 League games, Davey could hardly be classed as a goalscorer. But he'd had spells playing deep at Plymouth, even at full-back, and insists that he came to Hereford as 'an out-and-out striker,' while happy for McNeil to remain the main man.

Davey's claim that he 'was better than Dixie in the air' has yet to be disputed in my presence, but it was accepted that McNeil's head would still be the principal target for Paine's free-kicks. In open play, though, it wouldn't matter which of the pair went to the near post and which to the far: 'either way,' Davey reckoned, 'Terry would pick one of us out. He was so good at what he could do – the *best* crosser I ever played with.' And as John Galley, the man displaced by Davey, points out, Steve provided more pace upfront. Sillett found an alternative niche for Galley – at centre-back, where he had once seen him deputise for Bristol City in an emergency.

The new 'keeper was Kevin Charlton, who came recommended both by his Boxing Day performance for Bournemouth, when they had beaten Hereford 2-1, and in scouting reports from George O'Brien. Sillett had been under pressure from Paine to find some competition for Hughes, so when George fancied the 20 year-old Charlton, Terry was prepared to back his judgment: 'Hey! George O'Brien is the hardest bastard in the world to please – a right miserable bastard. You've got to be something if George recommends you.'

Charlton played in the Blauw Wit tournament, effectively as a trialist, and convinced Sillett that he was, indeed, good enough. Terry would go back to Southampton not just for O'Brien's advice, but for the thoughts of Bill Ellerington. That suited Sillett, who 'respected Bill as much as any scout I've ever met. An excellent judge – *hard* to please!'

The incoming full-back was Morton's Steve Ritchie. The younger brother of Tom, the Bristol City striker, Steve had been an apprentice in Sillett's time at Ashton Gate. The midfield signing was Jimmy Lindsay from Colchester. The former West Ham player came recommended by Sillett's brother, Peter.

Both Ritchie and Lindsay would be ever-presents this season, but Ted Woodriffe's man-of-the-match on the opening day – a 0-0 home draw with Port Vale – was the midfielder Sillett had coveted: Vale's Brian Horton. But, then, Lindsay had cost £15,000; Horton had been unavailable at £25,000.

Woodriffe was also impressed by the centres coming in from Paine and Emery, but McNeil could not capitalise on them: he had to be content with being the only player in the Football League to have scored on the first days of the previous three seasons.

If that was a quirky item of pub-quiz trivia to launch Dixie's season, he would end it with a far more important one, in which Paine could justly claim an historically significant role. In fact, this was a season that can be charted as a series of milestones, oddities and record-breaking moments for Hereford United and, most especially, for Terry Paine. Permit me to be your chronological guide through 10 of them.

1 Paine's 900th: The League Cup-tie on 10 September was billed as Terry's 900th first-class game (but that included almost 30 non-competitive matches not incorporated in the records at Appendix 2). For the only time for Hereford, he wore the No.9 shirt. The hosts' No.9 was Mike Summerbee. The two old combatants managed to stay on the pitch as First Division Burnley romped to a 4-1 win.

Terry told Roger Malone, of the *Daily Telegraph*, that he did not train hard the next day. 'But, then,' he confessed, 'I've never been a hard trainer. I like to leave a bit in me for when it matters – on the field.' Indeed! Terry Paine must have uttered, at least 900 times, that justification for regular midweek football: playing is much more fulfilling than training.

2 Paine overtakes Sproson: The 2-0 home win against Wrexham on 11 October was Terry's 762nd League game, overtaking Roy Sproson's League appearances – all for Port Vale. The *Hereford Times* was counting-down the matches to Paine's equalling the League appearance record of 764 – held by another one-club man: Pompey's Jimmy Dickinson.

3 Paine catches Dickinson: In Terry's 764th League game on 21 October, second-placed Hereford draw 2-2 away to the divisions' leaders, Crystal Palace. Clive Joyce, who had once dared to question his contribution on the road, recorded that Terry 'flighted a perfect corner' for Layton to head United's first goal and, as late as the 79th minute, when the poor old chap should surely have been at home with his cocoa, 'he pierced the home defence with a through-ball of slide-rule precision,' to set up Dudley Tyler's equaliser.

4 Paine breaks Dickinson's record: Having read his telegrams – including congratulations from the Chief Executive of Southampton FC and the Secretary of Portsmouth FC: Ted Bates and Jimmy Dickinson, respectively, of course – Terry ran out, for his 765th League game on 25 October, to a standing ovation. The 4-2 home defeat by Peterborough would be a considerable anti-climax to the build-up features in the nationals.

Continuing to follow Terry's career, Mike Langley of the *People* had ventured that anybody could smash Dickinson's record, just by observing a few 'simple rules':

- Win a first-team place at 17 and give the manager no cause to drop you for the following 18 seasons.
- Avoid injury. Don't put on weight. Go easy on the drink.
- And never cry off with anything less trivial than double pneumonia or a broken leg.

A reasonable summary, surely, of how Terry had remained injury-free and maintained a healthy life-style. It was about 'looking after himself' not only on the park – the euphemistic description of his jousts with full-backs to which I shall return in Chapter 23 – but also off it. He was fortunate that his body was not injury-prone. He couldn't touch his toes on account of his short hamstrings. 'If you've got very short hamstrings, then you are inclined to tear them,' Andrew Reed explained to me. That was John Sydenham's misfortune, so how come Terry never had any trouble with his hamstrings? The club doctor's biology lesson continued:

> It must have been the type of muscles he had. People now realize that muscles vary. I can see him stretching his quadriceps. But if it was a quadriceps problem that he had, it never stopped him playing. I can see him now in the bath, stretching because of one muscle or another that was troubling him: 'I'll be all right by Saturday,' he'd say, 'don't you worry.'

Langley noted how little Terry had changed. Despite his career-long antipathy to training, he had put on hardly any weight and was still only 10st 10lb. He would have broken the record sooner, of course, had it not been for the suspensions. But when Frank McGhee of the *Mirror* asked him about his disciplinary record, Terry referred him to the game that the two of

Terry's 765th League game

(Clockwise from top left)
On the morning of his big day, Terry poses
with Pat and Teresa.

The mascots join in the build-up.

Paine celebrates his record-breaking
achievement by causing mayhem and
protestations among his opponents.

John Sillett (*left*) and chairman Frank Miles
celebrate with Terry after the match.

them watched in São Paulo in 1964 (details in Chapter 11, if it's slipped your memory), when Pelé head-butted Argentina's Messiano. 'The point is,' he suggested to McGhee, 'that the vast majority of players who were anything had a bit of devil in them. They wouldn't allow themselves to be trampled on. I never would and still won't.'

He talked to Langley about discipline of a different order: 'the essential difference' between this division and the First was that the players 'can't concentrate for 90 minutes on organisation. You rehearse dead-balls, then shout out the drill numbers in a match – only to find out half of them have forgotten what they mean.' It's perhaps as well, then, that he didn't really have 99 set-pieces in his repertoire.

It had taken him time to adjust to such 'limitations', he said, not helped by the added responsibilities of coaching and by the impatience of the crowd. By way of illustration, he referred Langley to the spectator they all still talk about at Hereford, 'always bellowing "kick it, you camel".'

John Sillett was still having to contend with the barrackers and had fulminated against them to Woodriffe the previous month, after a 'downright ignorant' section of the crowd – 'the worst I have come across during my 20 years in the game' – had booed his bringing on Steve Davey for Barry Silkman, a crowd-pleasing winger who 'talked a better game than he played,' Sillett recalls. Davey had responded by scoring, but how was Sillett meant to satisfy these fans, he wondered, if they were still jeering when his team had lost only one home match in the last 12 months?

The manager let his players know what he thought of the 'yokels' who were barracking him. One day, having sounded off like this at training, he turned to one of the home-products in his squad: 'You're one of them,' he said. 'You're from this village.' This was not too clever: it was an open invitation for a bunch of mickey-taking footballers to nick-name the local lad 'Village' – implying 'village idiot', of course. Not that this stayed among the players: Andrew Reed revealed, entirely unsolicited, that he had heard Terry Paine use the term.

Old habits die hard, but you would hope that the player-coach might have detached himself from such name-calling. The player in question, who succeeded in getting Sillett to put a stop to it after a couple of weeks, does not, however, blame Terry or, indeed, any of the players. As far as he is concerned, the guilty party was Sillett, who had insulted not him but the supporters: 'He was saying "the people around here don't know anything about football" – that, basically, they're village idiots. I didn't say anything to any of the supporters – or to the press: I thought it would go away.'

At least the manager was not having to defend Paine so far this season. The 'evergreen Terry Paine' had been getting regular accolades from Woodriffe and others, such as 'masterly', outstanding' and 'an inspiration'.

And even as the side struggled against Peterborough, Paine still impressed Laurie Teague with 'the subtlety and accuracy of his passing, which are the hallmark of his game.'

Which explains why Sillett told Langley that he didn't want Terry to stop at the record – 'not while he's in such terrific form.'

5 Hereford top the table: A 4-1 win over Cardiff City on 4 February took Hereford to the top of Division III – the highest position yet in their history – where they would remain for the rest of the season. Paine had a chance to demonstrate his set-piece repertoire outlined in the previous chapter. The first of McNeil's two goals came from Terry's 'perfectly placed free-kick' onto his head, beating the cover of the former Wales international, Mike England. Then Emery 'blasted an unstoppable shot' for the third goal, after Terry had stepped over a free-kick.

You might have thought that England would have been wise to Paine's placement, but Terry treasures this particular kick as one that was taken so quickly that 'people didn't even know I'd taken it and Dixie had scored. There was a stunned silence.' In further defence, moreover, of Mike England and other thwarted markers, Roy Carter – arriving from Western League football and in some awe at the spectacle of the Paine-McNeil free-kicks – would

Roy Carter

bet you that, after a while, when they'd scored a few goals, managers would have picked that up and would have told their defenders to be aware of Terry Paine on the ball; but Dixie was still that little bit quicker and Dixie only needed a yard; and Terry was so accurate, it was *there*.

6 Another record for McNeil: In a 5-0 win over Chester on 10 March, Dixie became the first Hereford player to score four in the Football League. His season's tally was now 26 goals in the 27 League games he had played.

7 Season's first for Paine: On 31 March, Terry scored his first League goal of the season. He'd not been used to waiting that long, of course. Indeed, he was the last of United's outfield players to open his account this season.

8 Paine's freak injury: Terry missed the game at Gillingham on 6 April, with a back injury sustained in a Gravesend park the evening before. A knock-about game of cricket may have been just the thing for team-spirit on the road, but the player-coach should have known better than to apply the roller single-handed. He was able to take training the next morning but had to sit out a thriller, as United came back, from 3-1 down with 25 minutes left, to win 4-3.

It was, Terry told a local reporter, 'a fight-back second to none in all the years I have been involved in professional football.' And there were all those Saints fans – me included – thinking that the 1963 come-back against Nottingham Forest (of Chapter 8 fame) would not be so easily eclipsed for him.

9 Promotion: a 0-0 draw at Walsall on 17 April clinched promotion. The previous record for rising from election to the League to the Second Division was Oxford United's six seasons. Hereford had taken only four. They would secure the championship, two days later, with a 3-1 home win over Shrewsbury.

That would be the start of a busy week for Terry who had to attend the annual dinner of the Football Writers' Association in London. This is, of course, the occasion when the scribes name their Footballer of the Year. They had invited Terry to sit at the top table – an honour traditionally reserved for past winners of that accolade. That was an apt recognition of his record-breaking and he even picked up votes for this season's award. The clear winner, though, was Kevin Keegan.

Flanked by Peter Isaac (*left*) and John Sillett, the Hereford players celebrate promotion, in their Walsall dressing room, with the help of two champagne-minders.
Back (*left to right*): Redrobe, Paine. Standing: Galley, Carter, Tyler, Walker.
Seated: Ritchie S, Davey, Charlton, Lindsay (obscured by bottle), McNeil. On floor: Tucker.

Terry would, however, win one of the six annual Rothmans Awards for his contribution to the game in 1975-76 – a recognition, the citation said, for the way in which 'the advancing years have been borne lightly by this sprightly performer,' as he overtook Dickinson's record and helped Hereford to promotion.

10 Last-day records: Going into the last game of the season on 26 April, Dixie McNeil needed two more goals to catch Ronnie Moore of Tranmere, whose season has already finished. Dixie went out in style with a hat-trick, pipping Moore to finish as top-scorer in the Football League with 35 goals. Which meant, of course, that he had topped the League's charts in successive seasons. It wasn't something that McNeil had ever expected to achieve, once even: 'to do it two seasons on the trot was absolutely fabulous.' Indeed, it was – and *very* rare.

Ted MacDougall had done it with Bournemouth, both in 1970-71 and 1971-72, and the only other player previously to have done this particular double, since the War, was Ron Davies in 1966-67 and 1967-68. Both McNeil and Davies had achieved this in their first two seasons of playing with Terry Paine. Dixie reflects that this must 'tell you something, doesn't it? You don't get *coincidences* like that, do you? It doesn't matter how good you are at heading it, you need the service to do it.' There can be no arguing with that, surely.

The evening also produced Hereford's youngest-ever League debutant – Kevin Sheedy, at 16 years, 190 days. He had had a bit of a run-out with the first team in January, coming off the bench when Second Division Chelsea came to Edgar Street for a friendly: Terry Paine made way for him after only 33 minutes. Sheedy welcomed the chance to have

> a run-out for a good period of time – an hour. I was grateful to get on and I loved every minute of it. They obviously knew I had the ability, but sometimes they need to see you playing against good opposition. Chelsea were a big team.

Some 20-odd years later, Sheedy would hear Ron Harris's after-dinner story about his quest to avenge an over-the-top challenge by Terry Paine. What Kevin hadn't realised is that Harris was seeking vengeance in that friendly. When Tommy Hughes had met 'Chopper' – a friend from Tommy's Chelsea days – before the game, he had agreed to convey Harris's agenda to Terry. A friendly was the perfect opportunity to follow Terry wherever he went so that, after only half-an-hour of being pursued, Terry came off – feigning an injury, the club doctor reckoned. 'And there's me thinking that the manager wanted to have a good look at me,' says a rueful Sheedy.

That said, Terry had been pushing for Kevin to make his full debut and sat out the 3-1 win over Preston, coming off the bench for just the last three minutes, in place of Peter Spiring.

The status of the games played by Spiring was about to become a most controversial issue. Another associate from Sillett's Bristol City days, he had not made it at Liverpool and had arrived at Edgar Street on loan from Luton, before signing a permanent contract on 16 April. So he appeared to be one day short of the Welsh FA's 14-day qualifying period when he scored both of Hereford's away goals against Cardiff City, in the 1st leg of the Welsh Cup Final on 29 April. But the number of games played could supersede the 14-day rule and Spiring's games on loan would hence qualify him – or so Sillett told Woodriffe he had been assured. His chairman was not so sure and told him so in the boardroom at Ninian Park.

Terry had been worrying about the possible impact, in the manager's dealings with Frank Miles, of Sillett's self-confessed 'short fuse' and had told him that he must avoid winding-up his chairman. Recognising that this advice might not be heeded, he had undertaken to stand by Sillett – literally – when he was with the chairman. As Sillett recalls, Terry had said 'there's going to be a big bust-up one day. When you two get together, I'll come and stand by you and, if I see a problem – if I think you should pull out; you're going too far – I'll tap you on your toe.'

This strategy was needed when Miles challenged Sillett's understanding of the Spiring ruling:

> At that point, I'm gone. Painie stands on my toe. I said 'Painie, you stand on my toe once more and I'll sort the bloody pair of you out.' And poor old Painie had just been trying to get me out of trouble. The signal didn't work.

Nor had Sillett's calculations. The second leg, due to be played at Edgar Street the next week, was put on hold while the Welsh FA conducted an enquiry.

Which rather complicated matters for Terry who had just received an invitation to 'guest' for Crook Town on a tour of India, leaving on 2 May. I have referred previously – in Chapter 4, when the teenage Paine was a participant in the competition – to the particular glamour of the FA Amateur Cup. Well, Crook had won it five times, including four Wembley appearances between 1954 and 1964. I grant you that may not seem like a pedigree sufficient to warrant a two-week visit to Calcutta, but that is to reckon without the connections and clout of the Northern League club's doctor, Arun Banerjee.

A native of Calcutta and a life-member of that city's Mohun Magan Athletic Club – a multi-sport organisation that included one of India's top football teams, for whom his father, Haradhan, had played in the 1930s – it was he who negotiated for Mohun Magan to host the first footballing tour of India by a British side since Independence. The hosts imposed two terms: the referee for the latest Cup Final, in 1975, should come along to officiate at every game; and the squad should include a member of the 1966 World Cup-winning squad, their first choice being indicated in the title of Steven Chaytor's whimsical book of the tour, *Can You Get Bobby Charlton?*

The refereeing requirement was easily met: Pat Partridge lived just down the road from Crook and readily accepted. Hedging his bets on the other condition, Dr Banerjee went beyond the Charlton brief, approaching not only Jimmy Greaves, who was committed to his summer job, but even George Best – not so much a 1966 winner as one of the greatest players never to play in a World Cup final tournament. Banerjee was advised that 'India could not afford George Best,' but it didn't matter: Bobby Charlton, who had resigned as Preston's manager at the end of the previous season, said 'yes'.

It proved, however, to be a retractable yes. A fortnight before the party was due to leave Heathrow, Charlton withdrew. Just how grievously he had been injured guesting for Shay Brennan at Waterford remains a topic for debate in County Durham but, hoping that he'd at least be able to walk onto the pitch, a mortified Mohun Magan modified their expectations: would Bobby be willing to turn up just for the final match – a major event, as we shall see – and wave to the crowd? Negative. A distraught Banerjee now welcolmed a managerial intervention.

To complement the club doctor's contacts and knowledge of India, the party needed a manager who knew what was involved in a foreign football tour. Banerjee approached the former manager of neighbouring Bishop Auckland, but Lawrie McMenemy was otherwise engaged in winning the FA Cup. Gordon Jones, the former Middlesbrough full-back – who had just resigned as assistant manager at Darlington and who was an experienced traveller, both with Boro and England Under-23s – took the job. It was he who assured both Banerjee and Charlton that he would find a replacement from the 1966 squad.

His first thought was Terry Paine, with whom he had played at U-23 level – photographic evidence of which was produced in Chapter 11 – and had had some testing duels at club level (more of which in Chapter 23). Terry was willing to be Charlton's stand-in, but was in no position to accept for the whole tour: it was still unclear when he might be needed to play in the Welsh Cup Final – over however many legs the Welsh FA might yet decree it should be played.

It was agreed that he would fly in for the last game on 15 May. Meanwhile, he had an engagement with his own club doctor – as arm-chair fans watching, together, the FA Cup Final on TV.

For the first time since that disappointment of 1963, Southampton had reached the semi-final of the Cup and had this time avoided Manchester United. Now they met them at Wembley on 1 May. You won't need me to dwell on details of a match decided by Bobby Stokes, whom you may recall being deputed, as a lively juvenile, to rough up Terry in practice eight seasons before.

The following week, skipper Paine received a Player of the Year award on behalf of the Hereford team. And then came a ludicrously busy six days. On Friday 14 May, he flew to Bombay and changed planes for Calcutta. Arriving at 9.00 a.m on Saturday, he had time for a sleep, in the luxury of the *Grand Hotel*, before the team departed for Eden Gardens' Ranji Stadium, the Test Match cricket ground where Crook had opened their tour before a crowd of 100,000. The squad had become accustomed, from the moment of their being enthusiastically received and garlanded on arrival at Calcutta airport, to plenty of rituals and ceremonies. But there were new pre-match treats in store, both on their way to, and at, the ground. First, they travelled to the stadium with an armed escort: they were playing the Chief Minister's XI; the chief minister was the President of India; and, as they promised on the match-day tickets, 'the President of India will grace the occasion with his presence.'

On the strength of several eye-witness accounts, Chaytor has been able to capture what happened at the stadium, as a helicopter landed on the pitch:

> The President of India, Fakhruddin Ali Ahmed, had… arrived in some style. The crowd gave respectful applause to their leader as he milked the moment… and it was then that the two teams… entered the arena to a familiar but no less remarkable ovation and lined up to be introduced to the [President]. However, there was one final introduction. Terry Paine was given the PA treatment and hailed as the England World Cup star that he was. Any lingering fears that the disappointment of Bobby Charlton's non-appearance would overshadow Terry's arrival were instantly quashed by a reception to remember. He ran, waving, onto the field to a rapturous and appreciative ovation. Bobby might not be there but Terry had made the effort and the Indian public was grateful.

Gordon Jones concurs with that account, in so far as words can convey the magnitude of what the Crook party witnessed: 'you had to be there,' he

Accompanied by mascot Aninder Banerjee and club captain Charlie Gott,
and supervised by referee Pat Partridge, Terry Paine exchanges pennants
with the captain of the Chief Minister's XI.

insists, 'to see the tremendous ovation that Terry got… It had been well-
publicised that he was coming out *specially* for this game. You had to be there
in India, at that particular time, to realise what it meant to these people.
It really was something special to them.'

If it followed that an international-class performance was expected
of him, then the crowd stood to be disappointed: the jet-lagged and non-
acclimatised Paine had just completed, at the age of 37, a season in which he
had played in all bar two of Hereford's 54 games in the League and the two
English Cups – not to mention that leg of the Welsh Cup Final that would
be expunged from the records – and had barely met, let alone practised
with, his team-mates.

Not that this cut any ice with the reporter from the local *Amrita Bazar
Patrika* newspaper. Having expected a World Cup star to distinguish himself
– even in the afternoon heat that had been affecting much younger players –
he regretted that, 'if we had not known who the international player was, we
would never have picked him out.' Dismissing that verdict as 'bollocks',
Chaytor prefers to focus on the way that Terry 'was treated as an honoured
guest,' alongside whom the Crook players were proud to have played.

And Jones was glad to have him along, not least when their connecting
flight from Hong Kong was so delayed that the homeward-bound party had
an overnight wait in Bombay:

> Terry came up to me and said 'Gordon, go and tell them we want to be in a hotel – now!' To be honest, I hadn't thought about it. So I just went up and said 'we want a hotel.' They were a bit grumpy about it, but I insisted – and I had Terry with me – and they fixed us up with a hotel for the night.

Having been appointed for his savvy abroad – which he had needed in order to avert a diplomatic incident, threatening the rest of the tour, when responsibility for the players' drinks tab was disputed – Jones was grateful, on this occasion, for the company of an international traveller who 'was even more street-wise than I was.'

A bed in Bombay or not, it still meant that it was late on Monday 17 May when Terry landed at Heathrow. Hardly the ideal preparation for a revival of the Welsh Cup Final, the two legs of which would now be played over the next two days, a 3-3 draw at Edgar Street, in which Terry scored, being followed by a 3-2 defeat at Ninian Park. A 6-5 aggregate defeat to climax his 56-game season, with a whirlwind trip to Calcutta as ambassador for Crook, thrown in.

The extent of the gratitude still felt in Crook is considerable. Banerjee, who just *had* to conjure up a stand-in for Charlton or let down his father and his Calcutta club, remains indebted to this day and will 'never forget' how Terry rescued him. And Jones feels that Terry did him 'a great favour: he helped me out tremendously well. That's the nature of Terry. That's the sort of lad he was.'

Chapter 22

Retiring – Twice!

So Terry Paine was back in the Second Division – the tier at which he had excelled for Ted Bates, while winning all his full England caps and being coveted by First Division managers.

It was also, of course the division for which Lawrie McMenemy had deemed him unfit for purpose in 1974. McMenemy had managed not only to hang onto his younger international stars, Channon and Osgood, but to bring in others – Rodrigues and McCalliog – as he fashioned a side fit to lift the FA Cup. He would need to spend 1976-77, though, in the further rebuilding needed for promotion.

So Southampton were far from being the biggest threat facing Sillett's new kids on the block. Of the three sides just relegated, Wolves had the most fire-power. Chelsea, relegated the season before, had failed to score enough goals in their first season down but had a likely side, orchestrated by Ray Wilkins, who had just won his first England cap. And then there was Nottingham Forest, where master-builder Brian Clough was assembling a side that would win, within the next three seasons, not only the First Division Championship but the European Cup.

In contrast, Hereford United, whose manager had welded bargain buys and home-grown talent into a promotion side, 'didn't have two pennies to rub together,' Paine regretted. 'You couldn't improve the squad in any shape or form.' So John Sillett's most notable summer splash-out was a personal one: on getting married, with Terry as his best man.

The best man reads the telegram messages to the boss

His club spending was restricted to bringing in Les Briley from Chelsea and Phil Burrows from Plymouth. There was talk of signing George Best from Los Angeles but, like Crook Town's travelling show in May, Hereford could not afford him. Best opted to join Bobby Moore at Craven Cottage, along with Rodney Marsh, another repatriate from the USA. This might not guarantee Fulham a place among the con-tenders but might produce some flamboyant football when those ageing entertainers felt like it – as United would soon discover to their embarrassment.

I say 'ageing' but, while Moore was 35, Marsh, 31 and Best only 30, Terry Paine was 37. Yet, after three games of this season, with United undefeated, Sillett was telling the local 'paper that, 'the way he played this afternoon he could go on for ever.' The occasion was a 3-0 home win over relegated Burnley, when Paine, making his 800th League appearance, had a hand in all three of McNeil's goals and was acclaimed by the *Mirror* as 'the mastermind behind an emphatic victory.'

All was going well in the next game, as Hereford led 2-0 at the City Ground, but Forest came back to win 4-3. Whereupon United went into free-fall, failing to win in their next nine matches. Four successive games in this run, which took them to the foot of the table, featured a televised humiliation at Fulham, a mauling at home by Wolves, an interesting debut at Luton and a sentimental afternoon at The Dell.

Dixie McNeil had got off to a flyer, with six goals in the first four games, so when the team arrived at Craven Cottage for their seventh game, and met up with John Sillett's brother Peter, much was expected of him:

> Terry, Peter and John got hold of me and tried to get me hyped up that Fulham were so worried about me, because I'd been scoring on a regular basis. I had the most fantastic warm-up where I couldn't miss the goal but, once the game started, I never saw the ball. We just got utterly and completely played off the field by Rodney Marsh and George Best. Every other move, it was high-fives to each other and, after that, it was almost 'Well, George, I'm going to upstage you.' 'Well, Rodney, I'm going to upstage you.' They were just like two magicians on the field that day. We never got a smell, the whole game. I don't even think Terry got a touch. We never saw the ball – it was as simple as that. As a forward, if I don't get the service from Terry Paine, I can't do anything; and Terry Paine didn't get any service either. So that was the end of it.

The end of it was a 4-1 defeat, an own goal having kept Hereford in the game for a while. The Best-and-Marsh exhibition was preserved for the nation by the ITV cameras. You may have seen the clip in which Paine fouls Best and, while he's still berating the referee, the free-kick has been taken and the ball is in the net. Sillett remembers this shameful episode:

> He was arguing with the ref and if anybody else had been doing that, he'd have gone potty. He was *so* disciplined with other players, yet there he is, setting the example: some example! They went boomph! – and it was in the net. You see him [on TV] turn round and look and say 'what's happened there?' The opposite way, he was as sharp as a razor: he would

love to see somebody arguing with the referee because he'd be the first to take the free-kick and get on with it. Everything in that incident was *anti* to what Terry Paine preached: arguing with the referee; them taking the quick free-kick.

The job of marking Best should, of course, have been Tony Byrne's by rights, but he had been out injured for a while. Dudley Tyler got the job and kept it for the visit of Wolves. He could not stop Steve Kindon running riot. Nor could anybody else. The visitors romped home 6-1, after Paine and Spiring had missed early chances. There was perhaps little hope of Terry missing the afternoon's great novelty: on the day that red and yellow cards were introduced, he picked up a yellow.

George Best contrived to be red-carded, that afternoon, in Fulham's 4-1 defeat at The Dell. The Saints then won 6-2 at Molineux, so they awaited their next visitors, Hereford, on the back of some starkly contrasting results against Fulham and Wolves. In the meantime, United were at Luton, where Sillett rested Paine and gave a debut to Colin Sinclair. The 28 year-old striker had been among a handful of players from Darlington or Hartlepool with whom Gordon Jones had boosted his Crook Town party on their Indian tour. Paine had been sufficiently impressed by his performance in the Calcutta sun to recommend signing him from Darlington.

McMenemy sent Ted Bates to Kenilworth Road to watch Hereford lose 2-0. Bates can't have been too thrown by Terry's absence – he should have had a fairly good idea of what he would hope to do the following Saturday at Southampton – but what he wasn't to know was that this game at The Dell would suddenly be billed as Terry's swansong. This news broke after Sillett and Paine had taken a walk in the New Forest.

The Hereford party was staying at the *Balmer Lawn Hotel*, that edifice that you can't possibly miss as you enter Brockenhurst from the north. After dinner on the Thursday evening, manager and coach went for a stroll. Only six weeks after Sillett had boasted that Terry 'could go on forever,' he ventured a contrary view:

> I said 'D'you know, I think it's time – your legs have gone – I think it's time for you to go full-time coaching, now. But I don't want to be the one to stop you playing.' He was so pleased that I'd told him. He'd beaten the record, which was very important to him. He'd well and truly beaten the record, so therefore I felt that I needed him more to be talking longer hours with me. As a player, he'd have to go away, Friday lunch-time, to rest up ready for Saturday; but he'd still be sitting around at the club, instead. I was putting a lot more work his way. I should have helped him a bit more, possibly, but I just felt that his game was starting to deteriorate a little and felt it was time he just got into the other side of the job.

Terry agreed: he'd gone to Hereford, as player-coach – 'as a stepping stone to get into the coaching. It was a logical time.'

There was time to alert the media. The *Mirror* even sent a photographer to stage Terry doing press-ups on the cricket pitch that fronts the hotel. You can imagine the mirth this image caused: no team-mate had ever seen him do one of those before, etc. One wag wondered if he was looking for 10p that he'd mislaid.

Everything about the Saturday afternoon was a celebration of Terry Paine. Apart, that is, from the result: Nick Holmes scored the only goal of the game. It could have been the 'ideal' setting, Terry feels, for him to bow out, but it didn't work out that way:

A demob-happy Paine does press-ups in the rain on the eve of his 'retirement'.

> I never enjoyed that game, going back to play against Southampton. That did nothing for me in terms of playing. It was so strange. And, of course, there were so many accolades coming in – people sending me cakes and best wishes.

One distinguished visitor to the dressing room brought a unique retirement present: Herbert Blagrave, the Southampton FC President, announced that he would be naming a yearling at his stables, TERRY PAINE.

But that was not quite that. After two more games, and two more defeats, Sillett recalled Paine for the visit of Chelsea, 'after one of the shortest retirements on record,' Ted Woodriffe laconically reflected. The 2-2 draw halted a run of seven straight defeats and Paine was 'tremendous', his manager reckoned: '*outstanding!*' Sillett remembers why he had second thoughts: 'I said to Terry "We're getting worse – purely because your passing is not there; your distribution; your laying on the ball. You just *stand* there to pass and you improve us" – which he could do, brilliantly. The goals weren't coming for Dixie McNeil and Steve Davey. So I said "Go on! Have a go!"'

It got better – well, for the next game, at least: a 3-2 win away to Bristol Rovers. The *Hereford Times* rejoiced that Paine's 'experience, and his ability to

'Retirement' Day at The Dell

(Clockwise from top left)

Terry Paine stands at the Milton Road end, surveying what might have been the 'ideal' site for his last match. But it wasn't ideal. And nor, as it happened, would it be his last match.

With Lawrie McMenemy barring his way, Terry body-swerves around him to make his final entrance at The Dell.

He runs the welcoming gauntlet of *(left to right)* Channon, Middleton and Fisher.

As Sillett *(left)* applauds his Last Exit from The Dell, Terry is escorted through a group of young admirers.

slow the game down when it was needed, proved to be a vital factor.' That was, however, a false dawn. Hereford would not win again until February.

If sitting at the bottom of the table wasn't enough to make it a miserable Christmas, Terry had to contend with the sudden loss of his father. The nearest thing to a holiday his mum and dad had ever had was when Terry drove to Winchester to fetch them up to Hereford for a break. Alec and Ena had come for Christmas. On Christmas Day, Alec, who'd long suffered from angina and 'had been having some very bad turns,' died of a heart attack. Andrew Reed came over to help out and Terry decided that he should play in Hereford's only holiday fixture on the 27th at Cardiff. It would be his 100th League game for Hereford. He scored in a 3-1 defeat and can 'remember saying "that one's for you, Dad".' For good measure, he scored on New Year's Day, too – in a 5-1 trouncing at Chelsea.

Alec had lived long enough to learn that his son would be made MBE in the New Year's Honours List. 'That was,' Terry feels, 'the crowning moment for him – most certainly.'

Pat, Terry and Ena at Buckingham Palace

Ena and Pat would accompany him to the Palace in March to collect his award – another recognition of his record-breaking service to the game. Although he was no longer pursuing the appearances record, the *Hereford Times* continued to keep count. On 23 March, his 38th birthday, he played his 820th League game. The 2-2 draw at home to Sheffield United was Kevin Sheedy's first full game in Division II. Laurie Teague noted how he 'frequently found Terry Paine with some raking cross-field passes,' to which Paine 'responded with a series of made-to-measure crosses.'

The next due fixture was the home game against Southampton, but this was postponed because Mick Channon was winning his 39th cap for England – and scoring twice in a 5-0 romp against Luxembourg. The re-arranged fixture brought the Saints to Edgar Street for the penultimate game of the season. Sillett attributes Hereford's opening goal to his assistant's plotting. The blunt description of the goal – a Paine throw-in to Ritchie, who crossed 'for Lindsay to nip in between two defenders' and head past goalkeeper Wells – disguises the fact that Jimmy Lindsay's far-post run had been posited on Terry's scouting report on what he considered to be deficient covering of that post by Southampton's left-back, David Peach.

A 2-0 win – only their sixth home win of this woeful season – was not enough to keep Hereford up. So they had nothing to play for in their final match – at Brisbane Road, the ground where the Saints had virtually clinched promotion, thanks to Paine's header, in 1966. Terry was spared the trip, which meant that his second retirement was also against Southampton.

This time, there would be no retraction. Six weeks later, he was released by Hereford. The chairman told the *Hereford Times* that 'Terry is now keen to get into football management and did not think it was fair to remain on our payroll while waiting for the right job to come along.'

The 'paper reported that he had been linked with the managerial vacancy at Reading. Maurice Evans, who'd played over 400 times for the Royals, had been appointed caretaker-manager in February and an expectation that he would get the permanent position probably accounts for the very few applications received. The Reading FC minutes make no mention of an application from Terry Paine but, on 25 April, the Reading *Evening Post* gave extensive coverage to what purported to be a statement to their man from Terry, to the effect that he had 'officially applied for the job and, if offered it, I'd jump at the chance... I am tremendously interested in the job.' Yet he dismisses all this as 'paper talk': he was not an applicant, he insists, and we should give no credence to John Galley's story that he had declined an approach by John Sillett, on Terry's behalf, as to whether he might fancy assisting Terry at Elm Park, if he were to be appointed.

Press fabrication? Players' confused memories? Whatever, Evans duly got the job in May. And it is not disputed that, a month later, Paine gave an exit-interview to the *People*'s Graham Russell, who, as noted at the start of Chapter 20, had a special interest in Hereford United's affairs. 'For the first time,' Terry told him, 'I am free to speak.' What he chose to speak about was the

> disgraceful... activities of a few people around the town... What is it they want? This is a super little club, which came from nowhere to the Second Division in five years [four, actually]. Yet it's a town of many jealousies.

The Supporters Action Group of Hereford United had been formed – with a change of management and a re-establishment of 'good public relations' with supporters its main demands – and 4,000 leaflets had been distributed, advertising a meeting the following week. But Terry told Russell that he had 'been aware of under-currents ever since I came here three years ago to join John Sillett. They've been having a go at him all along. He had to win promotion to silence them for a time but now they are after him.'

They were not 'after' his retired player-coach, though. In the opinion of Malcolm Whyatt, a principal convenor of the meeting, 'nobody was jumping at Terry Paine.' And yet Terry had focused, in his interview for a Sunday newspaper, on a defence of Sillett *versus* the Group. That rather elevated the meeting to a serious climax to three years of baiting Sillett, as if the organising foursome, including Whyatt and Townley, were representative of United's fans. I tend to the view that only those who fill a newspaper postbag believe themselves to be representing majority opinion. But ask Whyatt, 30 years on, whether he believed that the instigators of the Action Group were representative and he is unabashed: 'Very much so! What we did was take on board what the *town* knew; what the town felt.'

Well, the Group's petition was signed by 600 fans, a quarter of whom then attended the meeting. The joke in the Boardroom, attributed to Frank Miles, was that the Group gathered in a phone-box. But it was no laughing matter for John Sillett, who was apoplectic when told that I'd spoken to Whyatt and Townley. Despite the passing of the years, the wounds remain raw. It doesn't matter whether or not they were representative: they were vocal and persistent and they had clearly left their mark on Sillett.

But not on Terry Paine. His defence of Sillett might have been expected, however, to rebound on him. Far from it. Opening the meeting, the Group's Chair cited Terry with approval: 'he states that in his opinion our complaints go back three years or more and how right he is. This I trust will therefore dismiss the idea that we have only been formed due to relegation. Nothing could be further from the truth.'

That decoupling of Paine from the complaints against Sillett is consistent with all of the testimonies I have gathered in Hereford. If this book were a biography of John Sillett – or even a contribution to a history of Hereford United's managerial politics – I would be able to draw upon plenty of evidence that I have accumulated, mostly inadvertently. I need, however, to focus here on Terry Paine.

The 'Sillett-Out' protesters may insist that they had no beef with Paine, but Whyatt believes that he might have been 'tarnished unfairly', in some quarters, by being associated with an unpopular manager. Townley wonders, though, whether some people felt that Terry consider himself 'a bit superior to Hereford.' He acknowledges that 'that sort of attitude is very parochial but, then, Hereford can be pretty parochial – like lots of smaller places, I imagine.' According to Russell, Ted Woodriffe had often made similar comments about Paine and Sillett, as being two misfits in town: 'he explained that "they don't quite fit in with a market-town",' Russell recalls. 'And when you think of it, of course, they didn't.'

Terry readily acknowledges that Hereford was not his kind of town:

> I didn't particularly like it. I suppose living in a big town like Southampton, and knowing everybody, it was just different. I liked Southampton – and the area: the New Forest and the other bits and pieces. Hereford was a cattle-town. It wasn't a soccer town.

Having hailed, like Terry, from Winchester, Pat's attitude to Hereford was so different from his:

> I loved it. Oh yes! Did I love Hereford! I really, really loved it. It was maybe getting out of Southampton – I don't know – but it was lovely. I was never that happy in Southampton: it was just the hustle and bustle, I suppose. Hereford was laid-back. I loved Winchester and I loved Hereford – very similar kind of places. It was good.

Although she had not liked living in Southampton, she had been pleasantly surprised to find that she enjoyed being associated with Terry's football there: she 'could *never* understand, for the life of me, why 22 men wanted to kick a ball up and down a field. But then I met Terry, went to a couple of games and I thoroughly enjoyed it. And I've loved it ever since.'

She'd valued the friendship of people at the club, especially Mick Channon's first wife, Jane: 'she really was a lovely person. They all were. They were all very nice people that I came across.' But life with Hereford United suited her even better:

> It was more family-orientated. Southampton was a big club and very sort of distant, really – whereas Hereford was very family-orientated and I'm a very family-orientated person, which was maybe why I enjoyed it. *Everybody* got on with each other. It was amazing.

So everybody got on with each other, did they? Was Pat not aware that there had been people at Hereford who liked her but not her husband? 'Are you serious? Oh! Well, I never! No! Good heavens! I loved the people. They were such lovely people.'

Terry shared some of Pat's sentiments about the club. He rather liked the way in which directors, the businessmen in the Vice-Presidents Club and the ordinary fans 'all seemed to be clumped in together. There was no separation at all. It was one of the things that I found quite strange when I went there.' In contrast with Southampton, whose 'directors you hardly ever saw, Hereford was such a small town and everybody had a business within the town – whether it was an estate agent's; or a pub; or whatever it was. The directors weren't what you'd call *big* business men in terms of Sir George Meyrick [a substantial land-owner serving on the Southampton FC board] or that kind of stature. And I think that was part of the fun of the place – the fact that they were all thrown in together.'

There is an irony, here, in that Sillett discontinued some of those traditions. As Hughes puts it, 'he didn't want us drinking with the supporters: he didn't think we were being professional enough.' Even so, the set-up at the club remained one that Terry enjoyed more than he enjoyed the city of Hereford. That said, the informal environment at Edgar Street inevitably left room for some people in the mix to dislike others. Yet Pat insists that she had not encountered any antipathy towards Terry. 'No, I didn't know [of any]. He can be a funny bugger. People either take to him or they don't take to him: he's one of those people. *You either like him or you don't.*'

Indeed. Middling views of Terry Paine were not a regular feature of my interviews. But, as with so many of the appraisals of his Hereford years, Terry is fully aware of the criticisms and has developed, I would say, that thickness of skin that must be a necessary shield for any truly talented *competitor.* as Andrew Reed, a huge admirer and good friend of his, put it,

> he was so *sharp* – sharp in every way. I think this about all really good players, people with flair – people like Stan Bowles and Rodney Marsh. They're odd characters: they're not ordinary people. There's something in their personality *off* the field that shows up; and it may not be necessarily very nice.

To go with the thick skin, Terry has adopted as a mantra the dictum that 'you cannot please all the people all the time.' This corruption of Abraham Lincoln's observation that 'you cannot *fool* all the people all the time' may have become a cliché, but it must surely have become a motto for many a dedicated footballer, who has made enemies in his ascent of the game's greasy pole.

And if you want to find a niche in football where being popular is especially difficult, then try being a player-coach .

So who'd be a player-coach? There are, essentially, two questions here for us: what are the general difficulties, regardless of personalities, of this role; and did either Sillett or Paine do anything to exacerbate the problems of Terry's position at Hereford?

The basic problem of the role is obvious: the player-coach comes off the field for the *post mortem* in the dressing room. The manager will be there at first, but is likely then to leave him to shower and change with his team-mates, until such time as he's ready to join the manager and directors in the boardroom. Dare the players continue their inquest in front of the player-coach: can he be trusted not to feed their sentiments back to the manager?

I say 'obvious', but this was one of those issues that initially came up spontaneously, rather than from my questioning, and which Terry, who has considered – and considerable – views on the role, had somehow never thought to introduce into the first 20-odd hours of our on-the-record conversations.

The problem was first put to me by Clive Joyce, the travelling reporter:

> You're seen as the eyes and ears of the manager in the dressing room and, although I've got no recollection of players saying to me overtly that Terry was a bit of a snitch in the dressing room, I got the impression that one or two players – before, perhaps, they realised the set-up – may have said things in the dressing room that got back to John Sillett, probably through Terry, and that they regretted it. I've got no examples of that – it was just a feeling you got that people were a bit guarded in the dressing room after a while.

This was generally a matter which the players perceived as inevitable and not a question of personalities. And dropping down a few tiers would not protect you: Tony Byrne would have this problem at Trowbridge Town and he is sympathetic to the difficulties Terry experienced.

The position is to be distinguished from that of the player-*manager*. As John Layton, who would later player-manage, sees it, if you complain to the manager, whether or not he's still playing, 'you know what you've said to him, but we didn't know if Terry would turn things round a little bit, so people used to keep a little bit quiet.'

Peter Isaac, who would expect, as trainer, to remain in the dressing room after Terry had left it, recalls how 'the players used to talk in front of me, but maybe they wouldn't say the same thing in front of Terry because then he's going into the boardroom to talk to the manager. I never used to go into the boardroom but I always talked to the manager, obviously.' So did that mean the players trusted Isaac? He 'would like to think so, yes,' but he warned them that their trust should not, and could not, be absolute:

> I'd tell them straight: 'you'll let me down before I let you down, but if there's anything I think the manager should know, I'll tell him.' But there were a lot of things the manager didn't know, because I wouldn't tell him,

because I didn't think they were relevant. I thought 'we can get away with
that; I can handle that.' But there were things that I thought the manager
should know and they knew I'd tell him, because I'd tell them I would. I'd
say 'hey, if you've got anything like that to say, you should tell the manager
– or I will tell him.'

Terry has no argument with the above sentiments:

You're changing with the players in the dressing room. They talk and you
pick up bits and pieces. And, obviously, they thought I'd be the *spy*: if they
said something, they thought I was going to tell John. On occasion, they
were probably right: I probably did. I make no bones about it: my loyalty
was to John Sillett; not Hereford United.

So the players were bound to be mistrustful, he feels, especially 'the old
brigade – the Tommy Hugheses and the Dudley Tylers [a survivor from the
giant-killers]. Peter Isaac had been there a while with them. They trusted
him more then they trusted me. I can understand that.' John Galley, arriving
after Terry, felt that the mistrust extended beyond that: 'there was just
something about the guy, that players didn't trust him – *as a person*.' The
emphasis is his – even though he expressed especially well why he felt Terry
had 'an impossible job… I think it's a nightmare. I wouldn't even consider
it.' And, what's more, he shared Terry's view of where a player-coach's
loyalty ought to lie: he *should* inform the manager 'who's said this or that,
because he is, first and foremost, the manager's right-hand man – not the
players' right-hand man.'

The Trappist tendency extended to the press. A journalist will expect to
talk to a player, with each party confident that the other will not report any
of the conversation to the manager. But could a journalist trust a player-
coach in the same way? Clive Joyce thought not: 'I was always a bit careful
with what I talked about with Terry, because you couldn't talk to Terry
without knowing that John Sillett was probably going to know about the
conversation if it was something that was a bit critical of somebody. He was
his No.2, really, so I suppose, to be fair, there were some things he'd have to
tell him.'

Again, Terry takes the point: 'I probably would have passed on some
tittle-tattle – so-and-so was out last night – yeah.' If all of this wasn't
enough to create what he viewed as a 'no-win situation', Terry adds a further
consideration:

As a *player,* you've still got to perform when you go out on a Saturday
afternoon – and I can have a bad game as well as anybody else. And the
first thing the other players do, of course, is point at you. Yet on the

Monday morning, you've got to get them back in and go out and coach and say 'Look! This is what we did wrong.' And they'll be looking at you and saying 'Well, you were as much at fault as I was' and that's quite true: you *were*! That's why it's very, very difficult to do that job.

So did Paine or Sillett do anything to make matters any worse? I wondered whether they might have got too close to the Board in respect of race-going? They part-owned a horse, with Peter Hill and an auctioneer-colleague of his. This didn't cause any problems with the players – unless, of course, they backed it.

There was, however, a way in which Terry stands accused of making the job harder for himself. Galley argues that the 'spy' in the dressing room could easily become, if he so wished, an *agent provocateur*: 'He could have a little listen, have a little dig and see what reactions come back. And, if the reactions come back against John, then Terry will pass 'em on. I think this is why people don't like player-coaches.' What's more, he felt that Terry 'was very good at it – with certain people. He'd only do it with certain people.'

If that charge is a little vague, there were two specific ways in which Sillett created difficulties for his coach. For a start, Terry was his pub spy. One of Addison's most popular signings was reputed to be a drinker, Terry recalls,

John Galley

and we heard one or two rumours that he was on the rounds during the week. John sent me to different pubs to try and catch him in them. So that would get back to [the player under surveillance]; of course, it would. The landlord's going to say 'Hey, Terry Paine was in looking for you.' All I'm saying is that you get the blame for a lot of things, but all you were doing, basically, was carrying out orders and doing whatever job John wanted me to do – which I made no secret of: I was there for John Sillett; I wasn't there for Hereford United.

And then there was the task-master role that Sillett delegated to Terry: making the players run – and run *again* – in training. Isaac was conscious of the persistent complaint that 'he's not bloody running like we're running.' And Sillett could add to their moaning, if he was giving them a half-time 'bollocking about not being fit,' as Layton puts it:

You'd hear a bit of muttering: 'that's because we did all that running on Tuesday' – or whatever. And Sill might say 'Painie's still looking sharp.' And, of course, everybody's going 'we know bloody well why Painie's looking sharp: he wasn't running round, there, like we were.'

This is to suggest that the running had made them knackered, rather than fitter. Layton takes the point: 'We were fit, to be fair, but it was just mental: when things aren't going well, you look for anything to grab hold of. And it's difficult for John Sillett to start having a go at Painie; but, to be fair to him, he used to have a go, sometimes. Terry would sit up: '*me*, gaffer?'

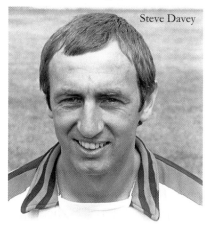
Steve Davey

The scapegoating when 'things aren't going well' was a concern of Steve Davey, too. In the relegation season, he feels it 'got to a point where John decided that we were losing because we weren't fit enough.' He disagrees with that reasoning and the consequent emphasis on more fitness-training: 'so we're working our cobs off and Terry's telling us to do it. I think that caused a bit of resentment in the club, because he didn't do the training that we did. It didn't bother me, but I know players who were very upset. I'm not prepared to say who. If we'd been successful that year, I don't think it would have been an issue. But when things go wrong, people look for excuses.'

Galley admits to being one of those who were upset, even though he recognises that it wasn't Paine's fault that he was running the players,

> while John's sitting in his office, probably making a 'phone call somewhere – or probably putting a bet on a horse somewhere – so Terry has to take the brunt of it. Really, John should have come out himself [when he decided more physical work was needed] and had Terry doing it with us. But it was nearly always Terry who was doing that physical side of the training, which obviously meant that Terry wasn't doing it. If you could have seen Terry doing what he was telling us to do, then it might have been a different tale.

But it was never likely to be 'a different tale' so long as players were 'looking for excuses', as Davey put it. Some hope! Galley agrees that 'footballers are always looking to blame somebody' and that, in the relegation season, the player-coach was an easy target.

Again, Terry accepts that this was inevitable: 'if I'm going to say "Right! 15 minutes sprinting" – or whatever it is – I can't do it. But, at the same time, I've got to do enough to keep me fit: very difficult!'

And in terms of which exercises Terry could and couldn't do, this was shown up even more when Sillett was barking the orders and Terry was one of the players. Back-track to the second away game of the first season – a 3-1 defeat at Walsall. It still rankles with Tommy Hughes, who had planned to stay over for a family weekend in the West Midlands, that Sillett ordered the team to report for training, back at Edgar Street, on the Sunday morning. Tommy thought Terry was especially culpable for his lack of effort and told him so: 'I said "Well, Terry, we were playing with 10 men" – which basically we were. I still honestly believe we were.'

To make matters worse, Terry was physically incapable, he freely admits, of doing extra work on a Sunday: 'I couldn't do it. We were doing doggies: sprint five yards; check; come back 10 yards; sprint 15 yards; come back; and so on. I just wasn't capable of doing it, after playing on the Saturday.' In his role as a player, needing to share the blame and the punishment, he felt he had to make an extra effort so, at the end of the session, he 'stayed behind and tried to do it. But I couldn't.'

A 'no-win situation,' indeed – except that it seems to be generally agreed that there were at least two 'wins' to his role. The first was explained by Sillett in the club publication, *The Record-Breakers*: 'Usually, it takes about 10 minutes to make an instruction from the touchline take effect; it takes that long to spread through the team. But with Terry on the pitch it takes effect immediately.' It seems to be agreed that, however well a tuned-in captain might implement touchline instructions, communication between Hereford's manager and his on-pitch coach worked especially well – to the extent that arch-critic, Roger Townley, felt that the '*fantastic* football' the Sillett-Paine coaching team produced owed so much to Terry's presence on the field: 'if you wanted to alter any system on the field, you could just tell Terry and it would be done. They had a close understanding – which showed with the way the Hereford team responded, how it played.'

Secondly, even in the dressing room, there was a positive role for Terry to play: he could be a calming influence whenever Sillett lambasted the team and then departed, with Terry still sitting there.

Isaac was in a position to observe how this left Terry with a choice: he 'either backs the manager up – he might say 'Dixie, well, come on, the boss is right' – or he might say "Well done!"' Emery and McNeil both feel that it worked well when Terry opted for the latter approach: 'he used to come round,' Emery recalls, 'after Sill had had a blast, and say "Right. We could have done better than that, lads." It was a double act. It worked well.'

McNeil likewise saw this as a feature of how Sillett and Paine functioned beneficially as

> a good managerial team. I thought they were great. John was a lot more volatile than Terry: he would come out and be fiery and make everybody get on their toes. Terry would put his arm round your shoulder and perhaps cajole you: 'Come on! We can be a lot better than what we are.' They always say one good one; one bad one – and that's what they were.

Terry acknowledges that, 'up to a point,' he was indeed obliged to play 'good cop' to the boss's 'bad cop': this 'was a role both John and I understood. I had to do what I felt was right; and there were no restrictions on that kind of thing. Obviously, he and I would have our Monday morning inquest and John would probably say 'how did it go after I left?' I'd say I had a word with them – 'try and look at it from the governor's point of view' – you know, try to take the *heat* out of it. And it *must* have worked; otherwise, we wouldn't have had the success that we did.'

Indeed! And if it hadn't worked, Dixie McNeil would hardly have chosen to team up with this odd couple of cops, later on (as in Chapter 26).

But, then, if a club reaches the highest point ever in its history, you'd expect to conclude that the managerial arrangements had 'worked', even if it took only one season in the Second Division to prove that it had risen beyond its means.

We have seen that the story of Terry Paine's three seasons at Hereford was a lot more complicated than that, even when that story is separated from the even more complex tale of how John Sillett found it impossible to rid himself of the stigma of not being Colin Addison.

Having considered at length the question of how Terry fared as a player-coach, I need, in conclusion, to sum up in respect of the two aspects of his role: Paine the player; and Paine the coach.

In his valedictory comments to Graham Russell, Sillett claimed that, as a player, Terry 'was in a class by himself. Hereford have been lucky to have had two really great players in recent years in John Charles and Terry.' Yet he felt that 'Terry was never really appreciated by the crowd here.'

That is surely too pessimistic a conclusion. The evidence of the last three chapters is that Terry pleased several sections of the crowd from the start and that his barrackers had been silenced during the promotion season. Goalkeeper Tommy Hughes, his main critic in the dressing room, questioned his contribution away from home, but made allowance for

Terry's age. Yet there is an extent to which age had nothing to do with it:
Terry had provoked such negative comments from a young age – especially,
it seems, from goalkeepers. What is it about the view from the goalmouth?
Do 'keepers just have a better perspective, plus the time available, from
which to judge who is or is not running around to effect?

But, then, as director Peter Hill observed, Terry's game entailed taking
quiet time-outs, before bursting into such effective action. Such players
will never satisfy those critics who demand non-stop action. Ask Matthew
Le Tissier.

If Sillett had a problem with Paine, it was surely less about his
limitations, than about how to make the most of his range of skills. Over
and above his dead-ball kicking, we have seen that he offered Sillett
unparalleled crossing from wide; exquisitely weighted through-balls from
midfield; and such wily reading of the game that he could play behind a
back four. Despite the accolades to his sweeping, it meant sacrificing both
of the first two attributes. The issue, then, was where to play him in
midfield: wide right and sometimes cutting in to hit through-balls; or tucked
in and going wide when the opportunity arose, as an alternative to sending
Steve Emery through on the overlap. The latter role worked well in the
promotion season when Terry could rely upon the engine not only of
Emery but of Carter.

His relationship with those younger players seems to have been the
highlight of his coaching. While delegating the fitness training to his
assistant – to Terry's undoubted detriment, we have seen – Sillett took
charge of the first-team coaching, especially with the defence. Sillett even
wondered aloud how things might have been had Terry been the manager
and he the coach: 'I think he would have made an excellent manager
because, with detail, he was as good as any I ever met and his awareness of
every part of the football club was excellent.'

That awareness was such that all parties expected him to brief Sillett on
issues he felt should be raised at Board meetings: as Peter Hill recalls,

> You'd say 'Excuse me: has Terry been giving you the bullets to fire?' John
> would start laughing, because this was exactly what Terry would do – 'you
> bloody well go and tell them this; you tell them that.'

He would have delivered as a manager, Sillett argues, had he been 'given his
head, and if it was something he really believed in. But he would need a
strong coach, because he would just bark at players and get their backs up.'

And there you have the dilemma: the loud manager, who delegated
much of the 'barking' to Terry on the training ground, perceived Terry
as somebody who would himself have needed, as manager, a mollifying

assistant – precisely the role that Terry needed to play for Sillett when he lost his rag in the dressing room: 'I wasn't the easiest to work with, I promise you,' Sillett confesses: 'I could be a little bit quick-tempered.'

For those reasons, there is a view that Terry was perhaps the better man-manager of the two, but this maybe derived from the way in which he played good cop to Sillett's bad cop. As we have seen in respect of the third season, Steve Davey feels that Sillett was found wanting when things were not 'going particularly well and he got upset. Then he was quite aggressive and he reverted too much to *physical* training to put it right, rather than his vast experience as a player.'

I am in danger here of playing, once more, to the 'what if?' school of football theorising: if John Sillett and he had reversed roles, might Terry Paine have made it as a manager at this level? We shall never know. We can but conclude that he came through a tricky assignment as a player-coach, being at his best as a coaxer, especially of the kids. He did that so well that the youngsters forgave his tendency occasionally to leave stud-marks down their legs in practice matches.

It seems widely to have been accepted that many a senior pro will do that to the younger players, as part of their toughening-up process. But, then, this was an era when it was accepted that 'leaving your foot in' was a way of testing out your opponent and that this approach might especially be needed by slightly-built wingers hoping to indicate that they were not going to be intimidated by hulking full-backs.

That is an issue of some import in any appraisal of Terry Paine's career, which is why the next chapter is partly devoted to it.

Chapter 23

Defenders and Offenders

Terry Paine's Football League career was now over, after 20 seasons and a bit.

Along our journey through those seasons, a number of issues have been raised about a player who seemed seldom to attract middle-of-the-road comments. It was appropriate to address some of those opinions as and when they arose, but I have postponed until now a broader discussion of how he was viewed by defenders – mostly, but not entirely, left-backs – whom he played against over those 20 years.

There are two issues here: the success or otherwise of his efforts to evade defenders; and why he often needed to evade their reprisals, as well. Clearly, they are often inter-related, but it will make sense to consider them separately.

For full-backs of the Paine era, there were essentially two challenges: to stop the opposing winger going past you, whether down the line or by cutting inside; and if and when he did get to the by-line, to block his cross.

There was photographic evidence, in Chapter 4, of Terry, on debut, cutting in against Brentford. His marker, Wally Bragg, had failed to achieve the target of 'getting the winger [to go] down the line.' Apart from 'drawing the centre-half,' as Bragg explained, the winger who cut in was likely to be moving onto his marker's weaker side.

Gordon Jones, the Middlesbrough and England Under-23 left-back who took Terry to Calcutta (in Chapter 21), gave me the most comprehensive account of what this all meant. As 'a very strong, left-footed sort of a player, I liked to show people the line,' he explained. So, when he first marked Paine, he 'basically tried to push Terry that way, but Terry was such a good player that he was cutting in on my weak side all the time and causing all kind of problems.'

His illustrious predecessor at Ayresome Park, the former England full-back, George Hardwick, had advised Jones, when he was a very young reserve, to keep a notebook, recording the problems presented by different wingers.

So Gordon was ready for his second encounter with Terry and 'counter-acted a bit,' but he soon realised that 'it was difficult to put anything down,' in the notebook, for Terry:

GEORGE HARDWICK
MIDDLESBROUGH & ENGLAND

> it was no good having a game-plan to play against him, because he would do something completely different against you. That was Terry Paine, for me. You push him down the line and he goes the other way on you. Whatever he did, it seemed to come as a surprise to me. That's what made Terry such a good player.

West Ham's Frank Lampard, almost 10 years Terry's junior, can remember what it was like, as

Gordon Jones's mentor, whose advice was of no avail when it came to stopping Terry Paine

> a young lad, playing against a player of that experience. Terry was one of the hardest players to mark. I think he was very clever in what he did. He had very good control of the ball – very tight control. He wasn't one of those wingers who ran up and down the wing like a madman: he was a thinker. I always found it hard playing against him. He didn't always have to beat you: he could run at you, put it to the side and just clip it in [sway of the hips to convey how Terry did that] So, next time, you got so tight to him to block him off, he'd come inside you. He was clever, very clever: I didn't like playing against him. Terry Paine was a great winger.

Pompey's Roy Lunniss likewise found that 'you couldn't get close to him. You had to be tight on him, all the time.' This problem for the full-back was exacerbated by the lack, in that era, of zonal marking: 'in those days, it was man-to-man marking, so if your outside-right was better than you, you had problems. If you play zones, you've got some help.' Terry added to that problem, Lunniss recalls, in that he would 'always be running across-field and that's why you'd get confusion, because if you're playing man-to-man, you get to a point where it's "do I follow him all the way or where do I stop?"' It all reminded Roy of being beaten 4-1 in an FA Cup Third Round tie at Stoke, when Stanley Matthews 'dragged me all over the field.' That was January 1964, when Matthews was almost 49 and Portsmouth had headed north early, spending New Year's Eve away in the manner of their foolhardy neighbours who were partying in Brighton – as you may recollect from that woeful episode in Chapter 9.

Ron Tindall also evokes comparisons with Matthews. Lunniss marked Paine five times for Portsmouth, but on the occasion of Saints' 5-2 win at

Fratton Park in 1966, Tindall had the honour. Although normally a centre-forward, Tindall had turned out for Chelsea at left-back and especially remembers marking Matthews. When the Saints went to Portsmouth in 1966, Ron was returning from injury, injected to dull the residual pain, and found himself 'against a magnificent player, so I just used common sense and I just knew he was going to get the better of me. Defending against him I found very, very difficult.'

Ron Tindall

What he especially remembers – and here we come to the full-back's second problem – is how difficult it was to cope with Paine on the by-line:

> I could hold him off in certain positions – to try and make him make the decision, rather then me make the decision as to what's going to happen – but he had the ability to take the ball, get virtually along the by-line and – perhaps five metres away from the goalpost – get the ball up in the air very quickly, when most of the team's defence would be at the near post. Normally, with people who don't have that ability to get the ball up in the air very quickly, the ball comes in at the near post. What he was able to do was to get into that position and, as a player comes to him to block, he was able to get the ball up into the air, over the goalkeeper, and to the far post and people like Ron Davies scored.

And you didn't have to be as tall as Davies, or as exceptional in the air, to take advantage of such a delivery. Consider the photo in Chapter 10, of Norman Dean scoring against Bolton, a month before the romp at Portsmouth. It illustrates so well how a Paine cross could take out so many defenders at once and leave the man arriving at the far-post with so much room. It was, as Tindall testifies,

> a *fantastic* thing that he did. I can't say it's unstoppable, but his judgment of when he would release the ball was second to none. That's where he did me in that match, a few times. I misjudged when he was going to do that. I'd get him into a position where I felt 'I've got him now,' because he was probably less than a yard away, so I thought 'well, he can't get the ball up now' – but he could. So then that made me have to push in a little bit closer and so disrupt our defence; and then he would knock the ball *not* up in the air, but just knock it back for someone to shoot.

So how did his torrid afternoon at Fratton Park compare with marking Matthews? 'Terry couldn't dribble like Stanley,' Tindall reckons, 'but Stanley couldn't cross the ball like he could. I haven't played against – or really seen – anybody who managed to get it *up* so quickly and accurately.'

To underline that point, Ron wonders how he might have fared – as a centre-forward whose 'major strength for goal-scoring was in the air, from crosses' – had Paine been outside him: 'if I'd played games for long periods with him, putting in the crosses, I'd would have scored a lot more goals – and that's the same for every striker.' So is he saying that his two England wingers at Chelsea – Peter Brabrook and Frank Blunstone – were not as good at crossing as Terry? 'Nothing like!'

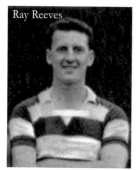

Ray Reeves

Not every left-back was queuing up to tell me how devastating Terry Paine was. Reading's Ray Reeves 'always used to enjoy playing against him. I very rarely tackled him, you know. He was always moving the ball before he got to me. They say he used to get rid of the ball before he got over the half-way line, because he didn't want to face me. I had every respect for him as a player: he was a good player, but I never found him a difficulty.'

Reeves was a big man. In reliving his debut in Chapter 4, Terry talked of a 'lumbering full-back.' He would come up against many more of those in the Third Division and – in the likes of Lunniss, described in the Portsmouth *Who's Who* as 'big and beefy' – in Division II, as well. But a 'new breed' of full-backs was emerging in the 1960s – shorter, nippier players who would hope to master a winger not by fear and dread but by speed and guile.

The exemplar was Terry's 'ultimate' opponent, Ray Wilson, for whom marking Paine was a case of once bitten, twice dominant. Having been stranded by Terry on his first visit to The Dell in 1960 (as described in Chapter 6), Ray had the better – both men agree – of their subsequent exchanges. Wilson feels that Paine and Callaghan each 'had a little bit more than most wingers had: I think they were more fiery' – which is why he considered both of them more effective when they moved to midfield:

> After playing against them as wingers, I just got the feeling that they were more suited to midfield, because they were involved in the game more, all the time, not just standing there, waiting for 20 minutes for the ball to come. I bet that Terry enjoyed being *involved* as a mid-fielder.

You begin to wonder whether anybody troubled Wilson. Garrincha, maybe – although Ray feels he 'didn't do too bad against him, to be honest.' Lesser full-backs can name a few who troubled them. Gerry Byrne, Wilson's understudy in 1966, had some difficulty with Bryan Douglas's trickery, but even greater problems with the speed of Harry Redknapp. Eddie Lewis and Gordon Jones each applies the test of who 'gave them a chasing,' as old full-backs like to say. Lewis found that Paine never gave him

> a hard time. I'm quite surprised, because he had the ability to take me on. I wasn't the quickest but I was a little bit intelligent and it didn't worry me playing against him. Terry was a great player but I think, on the whole, I did very well against him. He's chased far better players than me. The one who really gave me a chasing – and I dreaded playing against him – was George Armstrong.

Few gave Gordon Jones a 'chasing', either – not even George Best. Then there were Bryan Douglas and John Connelly: 'you could virtually set your stall out to play against these fellas,' Jones claims, 'and not get a chasing off them; but you had to be on your guard all the time against Terry. I think he probably came out on top of me more than I came out on top of him.'

Which explains why Jones ranks Paine in his top few opposing wingers, along with Helmut Rahn, hero of Germany's 1954 World Cup win, QPR's Mark Lazarus and Ipswich's Joe Broadfoot, who 'was the most unorthodox winger.' Lunniss, whose knowledge of Broadfoot went back to the winger's Millwall days, also lists him among his more difficult customers.

Giving your full-back a 'chasing' was, however, only the first part of the winger's job. It wouldn't help the cause if he couldn't then deliver a quality cross. Ken Jones, so often tormented by Terry in practice matches, makes that point:

> His balance was superb: when you thought you'd won the ball, somehow he could lift it over your tackling foot. And he wouldn't just get it over your foot: somehow, he would pick somebody out. There are no two ways about it: I think he was the best player I ever played against, I really do, and I played against most of them.

So highly did Ken rate Terry's crossing that he argues, like Jimmy Armfield in Chapter 13, that, 'if he were playing today, he'd be in the England team:

> it would be a rubber-stamp job – just like he was down The Dell – because there's nobody in the country at the moment that can cross a ball like he could.'

Jones would put Paine ahead of Callaghan, as Melia did in Chapter 13, because 'Terry created more.' And Byrne, another of Callaghan's Liverpool team-mates, agrees that Terry was the superior crosser: 'he had more time,' Gerry reckons. Like me, you'll doubtless have asked yourself how Terry ever made all that time. 'It's born in you,' Byrne believes. 'You make the room and you make the time. It's not something you can learn. He was good.'

So good that Ron Tindall rated him, in this regard, better even than Stanley Matthews.

Despite the tributes to Terry Paine recorded in the first half of this chapter – and, indeed, throughout this book – my personal memories of him, as the greatest Southampton player I have ever seen, were tarnished by an enduring image of him chasing after an opponent, after he had lost the ball to him, to tap his ankles.

Ray Wilson had a problem with this. 'Terry was *unusual* for a winger,' he explains. 'If you nicked the ball of most wingers, you knew you were OK. Now, Terry would come and have a look at you – and clip your ankle or what-have-you.' Colin Addison takes a broader view of Terry's reaction to losing the ball:

> He was a nasty little bastard – and I say that respectfully, because he could defend. He was a scrapper: if he lost possession, he used to get his arse back. He tracked back; he tackled back; he could get his foot in.

Note that Addison said '*get* his foot in' – a compliment accorded to forwards who make some attempt to tackle back – as opposed to '*leave* his foot in,' one of the game's cardinal sins, usually associated with forwards coming on to defenders or, more deviously, cutting across them late.

George Best named four 'masters' of this illicit 'front-tackle', as he called it – Terry Paine, Peter Osgood, Mike Summerbee and, 'most especially,' Johnny Giles – whose 'skill... enabled them to get away with subtle fouls that the referee couldn't spot.'

'Subtle' is a euphemism for what others would call 'sneaky'. The sneaky front-tackler would come in over-the-top, leaving his foot in, on the opponent's ankle or shin, as he played the ball. Defenders clearing their lines were especially vulnerable, the more so if the referee's eyes were following the ball. Putting the case for the victim, Jack Charlton has complained that 'the referee might not know what's happened, but you do... When you follow through [with your clearance] and you hit six studs [of the late-tackler], it doesn't half hurt.' In this regard, he mentions Paine as 'being one of the ones you kept an eye on when you played,' although he seems to have reserved the 'sneaky' label for his Leeds team-mate, Allan Clarke. The 'sly' Paine and Clarke headed Tommy Smith's list of foulers who were 'sneaky'.

That's opposed to 'honest cloggers', a label attached by referee Gordon Hill to Smith and Norman Hunter. Emlyn Hughes made another distinction – between those, including Paine, who were 'cute', and the blatant Eric Cantona, who was so 'stupid' as to commit fouls that referees couldn't miss.

But, then, Matt Le Tissier has complained that referees should be aware of who the late-tacklers are and should avoid 'following the ball' when those cute guys are around. I'd settle for assistant referees who did a better job of assisting when the ref's back is turned, but I can see, with hindsight, why I have no recall of Paine's ever doing anything to earn a reputation for leaving his foot in: I, too, was doubtless following the ball.

The ingenuity required of a referee when both he and his assistants miss such a tackle was illustrated for me by Jim Finney, recounting a game in which Terry

> did a naughty little thing, which I didn't see, because it was done behind my back. The ball had been cleared up the field and, all of a sudden, I heard a shout from the left full-back. I won't repeat the words. The boy was hobbling. So I stopped the game and went back to this boy. He showed me the stud-marks up his leg and he said that Terry had back-kicked him. I think if I'd seen it, it would have been a sending-off offence. I checked with both linesmen but, like myself, they'd followed the ball. I went back and said 'I'm booking you for the offence. Although I haven't seen it, it's obvious what you've done and, if there's any more, Terry, I'm afraid you'll be going off.' I think that was the one and only time I did book him. Otherwise, I got on quite well with Terry.

So well that Finney, who had by then retired and was assistant secretary at Hereford, came out of retirement, as noted previously, to referee Terry's testimonial. We saw, in Chapter 17, that another referee, Gordon Hill, considered Terry 'a good friend' but was wary of being conned by him during a game. Gerry Byrne, who never had a problem with Paine leaving his foot in – the way he did with Bremner and Giles or even with his 'best mate', Morrissey – believes that Terry could fool referees by the way he manipulated his face: 'his mouth used to go up a little bit [mimics Terry's hurt expression]. He winces. He moves his face up. I think the referees took pity on him.'

Gerry Byrne

Nowadays, of course, referees get a chance, after the game, to see what they've missed or how they've been conned – and players who think they've got away with it may yet be suspended –

thanks to relentless TV replays. Ask Roy Lunniss why his derby clashes with Paine were so infamous, given that they'd opposed each other only five times, and you'll get a blunt answer:

> In them days, you didn't have 20 or 30 television cameras on you. So the ball's down the other end of the field and nobody knows what's going on down the far end of the field, do you? They run up behind you and kick you up in the air - and stuff like that – don't they? So that's just the way the game was in them days. There was nothing malicious about it. It was a lot of fun.

Lunniss introduces, here, another element: full-backs expected to have a dig at wingers and, if the latter kicked back – or even 'retaliated first', as the saying goes – then good for them. This gives rise to another euphemism: such a winger 'could look after himself.' Actually, that phrase covers a range of wingers – from, let's say, John Connelly and Ian Callaghan to John Morrissey and Johnny Giles (although Giles would come in from the wing, after moving from Manchester United to Leeds United).

When lists of tough-nut wingers are being compiled, neither Connelly nor Callaghan is going to get top billing. But let's hear from their Manchester United and Liverpool team-mates, respectively. Pat Crerand is still in awe of the way Connelly responded when Bobby Collins, 'a dirty little sod' whom Crerand blames for 'corrupting' Giles, 'went over the top to tackle Connelly, but John went higher. Nobody had done Bobby Collins. John was a nasty, nasty so-and-so on the pitch.' Connelly agrees that that was true, 'a little bit, from time to time. I could look after myself.' Yet he believes he didn't have Paine's reputation for being 'an over-the-top man – though, having said that, most players, if somebody's had a go at them, they've got to be looking to save themselves.'

Bobby Charlton, in a general exoneration of self-defending wingers, groups Connelly with Paine and Morrissey:

> In those days, there was a small group of talented wingers who had learned that in an increasingly physical game, they could not afford just to take knocks, brush themselves down and return to the action. They had to make their presence felt as ruthlessly as they could and Connelly elected himself to this tough group of survivors, which included Terry Paine of Southampton and Johnny Morrissey of Everton. In my view, though, Connelly was the best in this category. He wasn't afraid of leaving his foot in and this was never a secret; it produced instant respect in any marker.

But ask Roger Hunt whether he'd bracket Callaghan, his Liverpool team-mate, with Paine and Morrissey and he'll assure you that 'you could never put Ian Callaghan in that group… He was a tough little fellow but he was never dirty. He was tough: to play so many games of professional football, you've got to be able to look after yourself.'

I have suggested that 'looking after yourself' is a euphemism, but Crerand thinks not. As he sees it, big guys are out to intimidate small guys and the latter need an answer: 'you can understand little fellows, like Terry Paine. There was nothing of him. You know he's going to get clattered. I think wingers had to protect themselves, to a certain degree. Terry was like that.' Jimmy Armfield makes a similar point, with the felicitous phrase that Terry 'could play his weight. He could stand up for himself. You had to in those days: he was a tough little devil.' So was he the worst when it came to self-protecting wingers? Good gracious, no! 'He was an amateur,' Crerand insists, 'by comparison with Johnny Giles and Johnny Morrissey. Dear me!'

But here Crerand introduces an interesting distinction: while Paine was one of those 'little fellows' whom he 'can understand doing it to protect himself, Johnny Morrissey didn't have to do it. I think he just did it because he enjoyed doing it. He was well-built – a very well-made lad.' What, more like Summerbee? 'Yes. An exact replica of Michael's build… Mike was dreadful, as well.'

Summerbee can speak for himself on this. Indeed, he has done so, rather forcibly, in his 2008 autobiography, where he takes a swipe at Terry Paine, as having been 'a fantastic player [who] could be a sneaky and dirty player.' In a previous discussion of his style and Terry's, Mike had explained to me how aggression was an essential part of his own game, but Terry 'was too slight,' he reasoned,

> to be an aggressive type of player. He was in a different league, when it comes to beating people with trickery. He was more of a Stanley Matthews, Finney, type of player, that could get past people. He looked after himself, but *he could take the knocks, as well* (emphasis added).

Denis Hollywood,
the 'baby-faced assassin',
who couldn't intimidate
Terry Paine

The last point deserves emphasising because it rarely gets a mention when Terry's ability to *avoid* crunching tackles – and hence injury – is being repeatedly commented upon. Denis Hollywood, the baby-faced assassin who took no prisoners, marked Terry enough in training to conclude that 'you couldn't intimidate him.' And Mick Channon argues that it was part of Terry's gamesmanship actually to entice foul challenges:

Terry didn't mind getting kicked, you know. He didn't *want* to get kicked – he jumped out of the way quick enough – but if he was getting a free-kick on the edge of the box, he didn't mind that. He played to get you mad, so that you would lose your cool and give something away.

That is a significant qualification of Channon's comment in *Man on the Run*, that Terry 'wasn't the bravest of players.' That's the sort of remark you expect from opponents who complained of Terry kicking them and not hanging about to take the pay-back. Like Ron Harris, who didn't

think Terry Paine was the bravest of people. He made out he was, but Eddie McCreadie and I used to give him some stick: if I missed him, Eddie would catch him. He wasn't our flavour of the month. There were a few people who tried to get at Painie, but he was shrewd enough either to just jump out of the way or go on the other wing.

Younger readers of this chapter may be wondering how on earth we older fans saw all the exciting wing play so often recalled in this book, if the wingers were spending so much time kicking or avoiding full-backs. Terry has his own take on this. He is pleased that this type of duel

doesn't happen nowadays – and quite rightly so. The skill factor's allowed to develop now. Think of the skill we produced in those days and yet defenders used to tackle anywhere and anything. Anything that moved, they used to kick it.

It followed – to come back to Bobby Charlton's defence of wingers who could 'make their presence felt' – that wingers might feel the need to prove that they didn't 'have peas for a heart,' as Summerbee puts it. Paine strongly agrees with those accounts of their era:

In those days, the winger was always looked on as a little bit of the airy-fairy kind of player, wasn't he? You know, a little jinker who would go by people but, if you got on top of him physically, he'd disappear. That was the way. So a little bit of retaliation, a little bit of getting your own back – *first!* – never used to go down too well. The full-backs found it difficult to accept and then *you* had become the dirty player. Yet they were doing exactly that, all their playing career, coming in at all angles and in all shapes and sizes. I always smile at the thought that *they* could kick you; but, my goodness, if you retaliated and kicked them, that was unheard of.

Strangely, the most striking account put to me of the winger's need to develop such counter-measures came from Roger Fry, describing an incident in training. It was a regular part of the challenge of marking Terry that you would 'maybe try to go through him – not to hurt him but shake him up a bit.' One day, though, when Roger was miffed at being dropped and suspected Terry of having influenced the manager's decision, he was

> looking for a chance to have a go at Terry: I would try to get into a 50:50 situation, where I was going to marmalise him – *legally*! He saw me coming and he probably knew that I meant business. He got rid of the ball, but he put his studs up. He did me right down the thigh. I was carried off – in a practice match, this is! That was the *nasty* bit about Terry. He had that nasty streak in him.'

You could say that this criticism of his behaviour rather makes the case that Terry was trying to put: he spots that he is about to be whacked; so he goes on to the offensive; now *he* is the 'nasty' one. Fry preferred it when Terry anticipated a challenge and 'jumped – he was certainly better than any of his horses.'

Let's leave it at that, but I do want to assure younger readers that there were matches in the sixties and seventies – even matches involving Terry Paine – in which a full-back and winger might actually refrain from kicking each other.

Thus, Gordon Jones, who acknowledges that 'we all left our little boots there, now and again,' felt he had no reason to do that to Paine, who never did that to him, in the way that Mike Summerbee – 'the worst I played against' – was wont to do. Indeed, Gordon sympathised with Terry:

> In those days, a lot of full-backs would go out to kick wingers to put them off – especially Terry, because Terry had a lot of skill. Nine times out of 10, the full-back would try to kick the winger; and I think that wingers such as Terry would come wise to it and had to be ready to jump or to give them one back and say 'you're not getting it all your own way.' I think it was more self-protection than anything else. It's as simple as that. I can't remember having a kicking-match with Terry Paine, at all. We had some fair tussles and some hard games, but if you didn't kick him, Terry wouldn't be looking to kick you.

With Eddie Lewis, there was almost a no-kicking contract, revolving around a trade in complimentary tickets. Terry and he developed a habit of exchanging their complimentary ration. When the Saints visited Orient, Eddie would expect to receive the tickets that Terry had from the visitors' allocation – and *vice versa* at The Dell. When the two of them met for the hand-over, Eddie recalls, 'Terry used to say "don't kick me tonight." I never kicked him.'

CONSTANT PAINE

It seems that neither Jones nor Lewis would have joined the 'left-back union' that Arsenal's Bob McNab apparently told Ian White he was thinking of starting, with the object of ganging up to catch Terry Paine.

There is much more that could be said, but if you wish to explore the above themes any further, there are plenty more examples in Phil Thompson's compendium on the game's 'hard men'.

There are two good reasons for not taking it a lot further here. The first is practical: in order to evaluate Terry Paine's reputation as a 'topper', it seemed appropriate to

Oz comes out in sympathy with McNab's proposed union

compare his attitude and approach with those of other wingers of his day – but I don't want to get bogged down in the minutiae of who should be placed where on a continuum of such wingers. The second is ethical. I have discussed these matters with four of the wingers I have named – Paine, Callaghan, Connelly and Summerbee – but I have not sought out Giles and Morrissey, so as to ask them how they feel about being persistently cited among the naughtier 'front-tacklers'.

Naughty enough, perhaps, to be in Jack Charlton's 'little black book'? Never mind that the 'book' was a bunch of names in Jack's mind – dressed up as a notebook for dramatic effect on the after-dinner circuit – the names most often reputed to be in it seem to be Paine and Morrissey. Charlton confirms that Morrissey is in the 'book', but insists that he 'never looked at Terry as an *enemy*. He wasn't on my list.' That's not because Terry never left his foot in on Jack, but because when he did, Jack wrought his revenge, or got a team-mate to do so, and so there is no need for Terry to feature in the 'little black book'.

There are two tales to be told here: one I find hilarious; the other somewhat disturbing. I have heard the first story from both Charlton and the referee, Jim Finney, although I cannot trace the game. Charlton, who reckons that 'it's never the big ones that get you; it's always the little ones,' had been caught by Paine, he says,

> with an over-the-top tackle. He'd got me a beauty. I went after him. I
> caught up with him and hit him on the back of his head. I knocked him

down and I went for him and, as I was going for him to get a grip on him, Jim Finney came running across and he got me by the neck and pulled me off. He turned me round, he put his hand on my chest and looked up at me and he said 'You, you big sod. I should send you off for that, but that little bastard got exactly what he deserved.' That's what I call an understanding referee.

'Understanding'? What the likes of Finney perhaps understood is that a 'little bastard' would sometimes get his retaliation in first against a 'big sod' and that the big guy might hope for a little licence to exact retribution.

But Jack didn't trust all referees to be that accommodating. At Leeds, he reveals – in another glimpse of the side's chilling approach to collective disruption – there was an understanding that retaliation should ideally be entrusted to a team-mate or two:

> It was like 'don't you get him; we'll all get him.' Leeds had a helluva reputation for that: we looked after each other. If the referee knew that somebody had got me and I went and got him back, you would automatically get your name taken. So you didn't: you left it to somebody else – and Gilesie was good at that.

Getting Paine had to be left to Giles, Hunter reckons, because 'Jack had been trying to get him for years, but couldn't get him. The only person who got him was Johnny Giles.' It happened at The Dell after Norman had been nutmegged by Terry. But then Giles intervened, Hunter recalls, 'got really close to him and he just turned sideways and – I know it's not funny – but he caught him an absolute beauty, right down his shins. Brilliant! Clever! Controlled it with one; over the top with the other; took the ball away.'

The irony of all this, from Charlton's point of view, is that he disliked Giles's fouling and told him so: 'I fell out with John, during games, many times because he would do things that were *totally* unnecessary. Then the rest of the team that you were playing against would be wanting to get you back, but they didn't always get *him* back: he would sometimes disappear out of it – or they were frightened to go near him – and then you had to take the repercussions of what he had created in the first place.'

Charlton has talked also of such 'aggravation' when Allan Clarke opted to 'leave the boot in just a bit longer than he should have done.' Ken Wimshurst makes a similar point – though far

Ken Wimshurst, who expected to be clattered by Lunniss, as a proxy for Paine.

more light-heartedly – about the way Paine 'used to goad' Lunniss: 'he used to speak to him on the field, tell him how *bad* he was – like he couldn't run.' Then, as illustrated in Chapter 9, Ken – not being 'as clever as Terry to get out of the way' – might be 'clattered' by Lunniss, as a hapless proxy for the elusive Paine.

The other way in which Paine's feuds could affect the team was when his efforts to escape his assailants took him out of the game. Ken Jones – such a huge admirer of Terry's skills, as noted earlier in this chapter – feels that Terry sometimes 'didn't put himself about' away from home and that this could be explained by his knowing that 'one or two people wanted to have a go at him and he didn't seem to pull his weight, sometimes, in difficult games. I'm not saying he wasn't trying – that's a bit cruel – but I thought he could have done better in some games, when we went up north.' Or even to Stamford Bridge, where Harris and McCreadie were waiting to put him off his game and perhaps even force him onto the other wing.

We previously saw how Harris took advantage of a friendly at Hereford to pursue Terry wherever he went. But a defender can't always do that in a competitive fixture, no matter that he might be expected, the way Lunniss explained, to man-mark. And, as Channon noted, the niggling Paine might be hoping to buy a reprisal in a good position for a free-kick. Even if the defenders didn't fall for that, Mick reasoned that, if they 'were trying to kick him, and not play, what an advantage!'

Whether his ding-dongs with full-backs were ultimately a benefit or a burden to them, most of his Southampton team-mates seem to have accepted that Terry's 'topping' tackles were just part of his game.

As for Hereford, we saw that Steve Emery was uncomfortable with this side of his mentor's game. Exactly. Wasn't this a bad example, and quite inappropriate behaviour, from a player-coach? Dixie McNeil, while acknowledging that Terry was forever arguing the toss – 'I know better than you, referee' – and still going in 'a little bit too high,' is nevertheless surprised at that question:

> I've got to be honest and say that, as a player, I never even thought about it like that. You didn't: it's what we came to expect of Terry. He never got himself sent off [with Hereford]. You can keep kicking people or knocking people: if you don't get sent off, that's fine. It's when you get sent off and you're down to 10 men, you're letting people down.

Perhaps the last word can be left to one of Terry's most-admiring of team-mates. Having been blunt about how 'nasty' his hero could be, Mick Channon reasons that 'having that rotten streak in him made him the player and competitor he was.'

Chapter 24

Kuwait a Moment

On the way home from Mauritius in 1973, the Southampton party landed in Kuwait. It was midnight as they stepped off the plane, yet oppressively hot.

'Who'd ever come and live and work here?' asked Terry of his team-mates. Four summers later, the answer was Terry Paine. Having 'learned a lot under John Sillett, as far as the managerial side was concerned – how you go about things and what you have to do, etc' – he fancied a coach-and-manager position on his own, at a suitable 'apprenticeship' level, as he puts it.

It hadn't been part of his plan to serve that apprenticeship abroad, but he answered an advert' in the *Daily Express* for a vacancy, managing Kazma in Kuwait. He got the job, perhaps helped by the presence, in the Kazma board-room, of an Engineering graduate from the then Portsmouth Polytechnic, who had watched him at The Dell.

He wouldn't have to be in Kuwait until late September, so it looked as though he had the summer free, with no pre-season training for the first time since 1955. He did have a football engagement in July, though, when he returned to the Empire Pool, Wembley, to play in – and again win –

England win the World Cup at Wembley – again!
Seven of England's winning squad of nine line-up with their manager and trainer of 1966.
(*Left to right*): Greaves, Hurst, Springett, Paine, Alf Ramsey, Stiles,
Harold Shepherdson, Moore.

a Five-a-Side tournament. This time, he was representing England in a competition between World Cup squads for the Alf Ramsey Trophy.

After that, two courses of action appeared to be available to him for the next two months: the golf-course and the race-course.

That changed when he went to Salisbury Races on 10 August and met up with a footballing contemporary – Denis Allen, who had played a few games each for Charlton and Bournemouth, book-ending a substantial career with Reading. After managing in Ostend, he had joined Cheltenham Town in 1974 as player-manager, although he had by now abandoned the playing side. Terry and he had talked football at race meetings before, but this time they had an appointment and Allen was carrying a contract – for Paine to join Cheltenham on match-by-match terms, pending his departure for Kuwait.

So it was that on the day the domestic transfer record reached £400,000 – the fortune that Liverpool paid Celtic for Kenny Dalglish – Terry Paine, who had never commanded a transfer fee – other than the £25 token of appreciation that Southampton had sent Winchester City – interrupted a day at the races to sign for the 'Robins'.

You might consider that a misleading nickname if you think of Cheltenham as a club who play, like Winchester and Southampton, in red-and-white stripes. The fact is that their strip has fluctuated, over the years, between those cherry stripes and plain red. Terry had signed up for a stripeless period.

Not that there was any marketing potential in this fickleness: replica shirts of many colours had yet to be thought of. In fact, the Board was desperately looking for ways of making money under their new chairman, Colin Badger, after a period of financial and administrative disarray. Despite these problems off the field, 1976-77 had been a good playing season. Having been in various sections and divisions of the Southern League since 1935, the first team had won promotion back to its Premier Division, while the Youth team had finished second in their regional league, behind the Hereford side that Paine had assisted to its championship.

They took their Youth team seriously at Whaddon Road – sufficiently to have a Youth Development Officer in Dennis Mitchell, while the first team's right-back, John Murphy, acted as their manager. The size of the squad was such that the fastest-developing youngsters could expect to double up, playing for the Reserves under their part-time manager, former right-back, Roger Thorndale, who had recently retired after a record-breaking 702 games for the first team.

If he personifies the club's development of home-grown talent, Thorndale feels that the Robins had become unduly dependent upon local lads, because they were too 'skint' to buy in. That's not to say that none of the first-teamers had sampled higher things. Tetbury-born Dave Dangerfield had played League football, over the county border with Swindon, while Jeff Miles, from just across the Severn, had kept goal a handful of times for Newport County. But the born-and-bred local hero was centre-forward Dave Lewis, who'd come up through the local leagues, getting into the Robins' first team at 16 and making his Southern League debut, aged 19, in 1970, on his way to becoming the club's record goal-scorer.

The first-team coach was part-timer Tony Passey, a former Robins reserve and long-time local PE teacher. Allen was the only full-time member of the management team, even though he continued to live in Reading, where he was a business partner of Badger, the new chairman. Indeed, the club's bank account was with a Reading bank.

That anomalous arrangement apart, this was, evidently, a very local club, with extremely limited resources, to which Terry Paine had agreed to commute from Hereford. He was not available when the season kicked off: while Cheltenham were entertaining Gloucester City in the first leg of a Southern League Cup-tie, Terry was in Scotland, playing in a Pro-Am golf tournament.

On Tuesday 23 August, however, the Cheltenham team that took a 5-0 lead to Gloucester for the second leg included their new signing.

The hosts had been left behind by their neighbours' promotion to the Southern League's Premier Division.

Their chairman attributed this to Cheltenham's superior organisation – all is relative – to which he drew attention in the

GLOUCESTER CITY -v- CHELTENHAM TOWN - 23RD AUGUST 1977

GLOUCESTER	CHELTENHAM
1. Stow.	1. Miles.
2. Allan.	2. Murphy.
3. Mortimer.	3. Dangerfield.
4. Gough.	4. Foster.
5. Boots.	5. Dean.
6. Eaves.	6. Chalkin.
7. Pocock.	7. Paine.
8. Turner.	8. Rice.
9. Wood.	9. Lewis.
10. Evans.	10. Hehir.
11. Gardiner.	11. White,
Sub. Moulsdale.	Sub. Davies.

Referee: J. Roost (Bath)
Linesmen: P. Harneman (Red flag)
            R.N. Rosser (Orange flag)

Good evening everyone, and welcome to the second leg of the Southern League Cup. The Robins have had the better of the City on very many occasions in recent years and our now in the Premier Division of the League

Why is this? I think for two reasons. 1. They are a better organised club both on and off the field and 2. which is the most important they have a strong band of people who work for the club to raise money by the way of pools promotions to enable them to afford players like Terry Paine.

                    Dick Etheridge (Chairman)

match-day programme: how he envied the Robins' fund-raising, which had 'enable[d] them to afford players like Terry Paine.'

The 38 year-old debutant needed no time at all to respond to this covetous welcome and to make an impression on Derek Goddard of the Cheltenham-based *Gloucestershire Echo*:

> The game's first move showed what Paine can do. His opening pass,
> beautifully weighted and sent long towards a corner flag for Wayne
> Thomas to chase, brought a corner inside 10 seconds.

Wow! It was but a corner and Cheltenham scored only once in the first half,
before he was substituted at half-time, but Terry clearly had an instant fan in
the press-box. And nor has that admiration faded with the years. Recalling
that first impression, 30 years on, Goddard enthused about Terry Paine,

> as a player and as a man. He was clearly a much better footballer than you'd
> normally get in the Southern League, as it was then. And as a man, too: he
> was very extrovert and pleasant… he was a very nice man when he came
> here. He was nice to me, as he was nice to everybody.

The home fans would now have three games at Whaddon Road whereby to
judge why Goddard had been so excited by the first full international to play
for the Robins. They had better not get too used to it, though: he was now
needed in Kuwait. Which meant that, after just four games, he would be
gone until April.

Once Terry had got going in Kuwait, Pat and Teresa joined him. Pat liked
Kuwait, even though she found it 'a weird experience; it was very different.'
It was certainly very different from a footballing point of view, too. Kazma
was not just a football club but a whole recreation and entertainment
complex, with not only indoor pitches and basketball courts, but cinemas,
too. Basketball, and several other sports, got a far better coverage than
football – well, in the English-speaking press at least. So if you were hoping
to follow Terry Paine's season in Kuwait through the press reports, the way
we have been doing in previous chapters, you are going to be disappointed.

Although he was succeeding a Scot – Billy Hodgson, the former
Sheffield United player – the predominant international influence in Kuwaiti
football, at this time, was Brazilian. Mario Zagalo, the first man both to play
in, and manage in, a World Cup Final, was now managing Kuwait's national
side, as it attempted to qualify for the 1978 finals in Argentina. He was
assisted by Carlos Alberto Parriera, the manager of Kuwait City, the side
that would win the 1977-78 league title, with Paine's Kazma in second place.

None of which was going to get Terry or his team a single mention in
Kuwait's English-speaking press. The football news in the *Kuwait Times,* the
self-styled 'Leading Independent Daily in Arabian Gulf', focused heavily on
England, so Terry could keep abreast of developments in the First Division,

with the progress of record-signing Dalglish exciting the Associated Press reporters who contributed this news from England.

Towards the end of the season, he could even read of the Second Division promotion race, involving Southampton, described as 'the team with former England World Cup star Alan Ball.' You might expect a link to have been made with the resident ex-Saint from the 1966 squad, but this was another syndicated report from London. In fact, the football news was coming in from across the world, as the qualifying groups for Argentina reached their climax. Yet, as far as I can see, the domestic game in Kuwait received less than a handful of mentions during Terry's stay, not one of them involving him.

I make that claim cautiously because, although I have consulted the sports page for every day of that stay, the compositors at the *Kuwait Times* seemed to slip in sports items wherever a space took their fancy; and reading every page of this turgid newspaper was beyond reasonable expectation. Kuwait's own World Cup qualifiers occasionally made the front page but, even when the build-up to their show-down qualifier with Iran was featured under the heading of SOCCER SPECTACLE OF THE YEAR TODAY, it occupied fewer column inches than the domestic cricket news alongside it.

So big was Wimpey League cricket, in fact, that, when its fixture list became available, it occupied an entire page of this newspaper. If cricket was by far the fullest-reported domestic sport, basketball and tennis also fared well, compared with the minuscule mentions of football.

If the last few paragraphs demonstrate what newspaper research has *not* revealed, rather than what it has, then perhaps this fairly conveys the kind of footballing country that Terry had come to. If the Cheltenham he had left was a footballing backwater, Kuwait was a veritable desert.

The backwater's football reporter accorded Terry a hero's return in April, reasoning that his four appearances at the start of the season had remained 'a regular talking point.' And rightly so, Goddard still enthuses:

> The fans weren't used to having players of his quality playing for Cheltenham. They just didn't get ex-stars – not of his stature. And he gave it what he could – he didn't just go out there and waste his time; he played properly. It was one of the best things that had happened to Cheltenham Town for many years. He was a stand-out. The rest were just harbourers of the rest of the game, you know. He was a different level. They could do with him now [2007], in fact – as he was then – very much so.

John Davies, a local lad who'd seen ex-League players come and go – a few 'who came for a few quid and didn't want to do anything,' but several who were good players – agrees that Terry had brought something 'different' from the others, not least in enabling him to be a better striker. He contrasts himself, in this regard, with the 'instinctive' Dave Lewis. While Lewis seemed to know where a through-ball was coming, Davies knew no better, he confesses, than just

> running into the space where I wanted the ball to come… But then, all of a sudden, Terry came and there were situations where I just made the runs I'd been making always and the ball would appear where I wanted it. That was his ability to see where you were running: rather than me being able to tell him where I was running, he could *see* what was going on. I would be running into a space and Terry would hit the space – whereas, at a lower level, people didn't have the vision, perhaps, to see where people were going. And so, by the time they got their head up, you'd gone, you were offside or they blocked your run. Terry was good at hitting the ball early – he wouldn't wait until everybody compacted – and I was quite quick. That was Terry's *gift*, whereas my run was, as much as anything else, a case of see a hole and go for it. And Terry would hit it. I don't say that happened every game, but that's how I perceived Terry and what he did for me.

The set-up to which Terry returned showed few changes from that which he had left in September. That's because the club's money-raising efforts, however superior they might be to those of their envious neighbours, had foundered. The local brewers, Whitbread, had agreed to make an interest-free loan of £5,000, in return for being the sole supplier to the club's bars, but this had been delayed.

Which meant that the transfer budget had been capped at £750, all of which – and more – Allen had spent on Barnet's Denis Brown. Allen had told the Board that his best hope of close-season bargains lay in recruiting part-timers from Scotland's Second Division, but this depended upon two inputs: lottery money from a proposed deal with Littlewoods was essential, while the directors would have to help find local jobs for their Scottish immigrants.

The latter consideration had been rendered redundant when the Littlewoods deal collapsed and Allen had already informed the Board that he had no option but to retain his existing contract players, bar two. He'd have been able to shed a few more, but, after some discussion, the Board decided not to abandon its Reserve team.

Meanwhile, he had Terry Paine back for the last game of the Southern League season. While obviously far from match-fit, he was able 'to taunt Hastings United with his talents,' Goddard rejoiced. Indeed, his *Echo* match report bubbled with mentions of moves started by Paine; and when Terry's shot was cleared off the line, Tim Bayliffe followed in to score the only goal of the game.

Having graduated through local football and Cheltenham's youth team, Bayliffe had been only 17 when Paine arrived at Whaddon Road. He recalls being 'excited' that a member of England's 1966 World Cup squad – who'd then 'become the highest-appearance player' – was joining his club. And although he soon realised, for reasons I'll come to, that he was not Terry Paine's type of footballer, Bayliffe continued to admire a veteran who 'still had a good touch on the ball; he could pick out a pass and get a cross in; and he had a good shot.'

Which is why Goddard wondered 'what might Cheltenham Town have done if they had had Terry Paine all season?' True, Terry seems to have been helped by an end-of-season approach to this game, in which 'there was little marking,' so that he had 'every chance to express himself, a chance he took to give 668 people and 21 other players a last-match treat.'

I can't think that I've ever read another match report in which a player is credited with laying on a 'treat' for all the other players involved. No wonder the manager told Goddard, the next week, that he hoped Paine would again play on a match-basis the following season, although he feared this was a default-option, as Terry was 'looking for a job in League football and has applied for a couple.' That was speculation on Allen's part, Terry insists: 'I never ever applied for a job in English football.'

The Cheltenham Town line-up, 1978-79
Back row (*left to right*): Tony Passey, Davies, Murphy, Foster, Miles, Deans, Ireland, Dangerfield, Denis Allen.
Front: Bryant, Edwards, Slattery, Lewis, Paine.

The 1978-79 season began, like the previous one, with a two-legged tie against Gloucester City in the Southern League Cup. Terry again missed the first leg, a 2-1 defeat away, but started his season with the second leg, a 4-2 defeat at Whaddon Road. While still lacking match-fitness, he impressed his mentor at the *Echo* by lasting 90 minutes: he surely 'knows enough about the game,' Goddard reflected, 'to look after himself in the Premier Division of the Southern League. The influence of such a man is desperately needed.'

Terry Paine's 'desperately needed influence' on show at Bath.

Denis Allen clearly thought so. He would play Terry six times in the next four weeks, with away defeats at Bath and Maidstone sandwiching four home wins – an interesting run of games in which he twice came up against team-mates from the 1966 World Cup and he achieved two 'firsts' in the FA Cup.

His first reunion was with Geoff Hurst, the player-manager of Telford United. Cheltenham's 2-1 win in this game coincided with the news that Terry would no longer be commuting from Hereford: he was about to take the *Prince of Wales* pub in Portland Street and so would be coming 'to live in the town and be associated with the Robins.'

Ten days later, Jimmy Greaves arrived with Barnet for a 'poignant' reunion, Goddard observed, as Terry and he 'embraced in front of 688 onlookers.' Paine won the game with its only goal – his first for the Robins – in the 83rd minute, although his intent was open to question as 'a cross from the by-line went in and out of the clutching hands of [the] goalkeeper.'

He followed up, a week later, with a notable hat-trick. In the First Qualifying Round of the FA Cup, Cheltenham entertained Clevedon Town of the Western League. Centre-forward Dave Lewis and Paine each scored three in the Robins' 6-1 win – although an inquest cast doubt on the provenance of one of the goals attributed to Terry.

This was his 60th appearance in the FA Cup, but the first time he had ever played in a qualifying round. He had 11 FA Cup goals to his name, but this was his first hat-trick in the competition.

Or was it? Steve Foster was required to disown Cheltenham's fourth goal, swearing that he'd never got a touch. So it remained credited to Paine, direct from a corner.

The defeat at Maidstone would be Terry's last start of the season, as Allen brought in three new players. One of them, Keith Hardcastle – a winger, less than half Terry's age, from Bristol City – soon 'created quite a stir' and Paine dropped off Goddard's radar. The next time he made the sports pages was on 12 October, when his arrival at the *Prince of Wales* was announced.

Terry had now been back from Kuwait for six months, with no waged income other than the odd match-fee – a source that had just dried up. This was 1978, when a 39 year-old ex-footballer 'couldn't save enough money,' Terry reminds us, 'to say "I'm retiring." We had to earn a living.' Even if you'd made a few bob from business ventures along the way, you still needed a regular source of income.

So he opted for the ex-player's stand-by: take a pub and let your name and fame draw people to your door. Having adapted both to football and to Hereford, Pat wasn't too keen on this move – especially since she had more than an inkling of what the publican's lot could be like. Her sister, Elaine, had been in the trade a while. So Pat and Terry spent a week with Elaine and her husband, Steve, at the *Coach and Horses* in Chichester. Elaine remembers warning Terry 'that it's not just turning up behind the bar' and it's apparent that he went into the business with his eyes open.

But, then, what were his options? 'Quite honestly,' he reflects, 'I didn't know anything different.' All he knew was how to exploit his wits, his name, his contacts and the willingness of his family members to muck in. Welcome to the *Prince of Wales*!

He had been there only a week when the *Echo* was advocating a new role in the game for him. Reporting that he had 'decided to leave football alone' while he settled in at the pub, Goddard noted that there were two vacancies on the board: surely 'somebody with [Terry's] enormous experience of the game should be able to make a contribution to the running of a Southern League club.'

Nothing came of that idea. The pub job that Goddard had heralded as a way of Terry Paine doing more for the Robins had – at least for the time being – taken him away from

Welcome to the *Prince of Wales*!

the club. He was back in Goddard's Cheltenham Town column, however, come the departure, in April, of the manager. Allen's business associate and chairman, Colin Badger, had resigned and a sub-committee of the Board had been set up, following issues raised by Allen about his expenses. Its brief would extend to the terms of Allen's contract and – with the staff wage-bill now running at £580 a week – to those of other staff.

Its findings were not reported to the Board – or, if they were, they were not recorded – but Allen's resignation was accepted by the directors at their next meeting on 4 April. A caretaker had already been lined up: as the minutes record, 'it was decided to accept the offer of Mr Terry Paine to look after the team to the end of season 1978/9, free of emoluments, but that reasonable expenses be paid.'

Along with the affordability of a Reserve team, managerial expenses were a recurrent issue for the Cheltenham board at this time. Not that the directors had been presenting audited accounts to the shareholders: the club's upcoming AGM in July 1979 would be its first since 1976.

While it is clear, from the minutes, that at least one director must have discussed the manager's job with Paine before the Board accepted Allen's resignation, there is nothing, here, to suggest that Paine was a part of a conspiracy to get rid of Allen. Yet that is what some of the players thought at the time – to the extent that they convened a meeting to discuss it, as Davies recalls:

> Just heat-of-the-moment stuff. But, at the time, when you're young and you're having what you consider to be the best time of your life – when you're playing in a good League and all that sort of stuff – and all of a sudden, the bloke who took me to Cheltenham is ousted and Terry, who he'd brought in and who had gone away, comes back, two and two don't take long to make four. It was almost 'Well! So Terry's got rid of him, then.' That sort of stuff was floating around and it was never said that that didn't happen. It was just said that Terry was going to take over. I think there were a few of us who thought that Terry had had a part in Denis leaving.

And that thought clearly still nags away at Davies, today. Grateful as he is to Terry for improving him as a player, he confesses that the suspicions about the change of management changed his 'attitude to Terry, because Denis had been a friend as well as an employer... I've never really spoken to Terry about it and Denis, in fairness, never told me – and I saw Denis many times after he'd finished at Cheltenham. He never accused Terry of anything.'

In contrast with Hereford, where Sillett and Paine had been perceived as the flash immigrants, Terry was taking over from a man with whom he had some similarities. Born three weeks before him in Dagenham, Denis Allen had inevitably come across as 'a bit brash', Goddard reckons, 'in comparison with Bob Etheridge,' the former Bristol City player and 'down-to-earth Gloucester boy,' whom he succeeded. Davies looked upon Paine and Allen as two of a kind: 'very much Jack-the-lads,' especially in their betting behaviour. And, as for 'the two of them together: you never knew where they were going to turn up next – and who with; and why.'

Two ways in which Paine differed, as a manager, from Allen should be noted. The first, which became apparent 'as soon as he took over,' Davies recalls, was that he

> was more aloof. Denis would have had a game of cards with us. He would have had a drink. Terry then came in as a *manager,* rather than being part of it as a player. He separated from it. He was more professional. No, 'professional' is not the right word: he was just *different* as a manager – 'I'm in charge, so I can't be drinking with you.'

Secondly, he lacked his predecessor's coaching qualifications. Allen had a full FA coaching badge and so did his part-time coach, Tony Passey. Upon Paine's appointment, Passey joined the roll-call of resignations. There was nothing personal about this. He had 'got on very well' with Allen and, although he had no reason to think he wouldn't get on with his successor, this seemed 'a good time to go,' if only so that he might spend more time with his other coaching responsibilities, both for the FA and his school.

It all exposed the badgeless Paine, however, to the obvious question from his longstanding admirer at the *Echo*: what was his coaching 'philosophy'? 'To be honest,' Terry confessed, 'I'm not a great believer. You can't get it all from manuals.' He had a philosophy on discipline, however, and he warned Goddard to expect 'a completely new complexion' in this regard.

As an example, he took drinking. Not only did he withdraw from drinking with the players: he felt that some of their drinking should be restrained. 'I don't accept shorts and wine,' he told the *Echo*, 'but I do accept that everybody has to have a pint or two of beer' – an apt philosophy, you might feel, for a publican-cum-football manager. 'But they are sensible lads,' he assured Goddard, 'and if you treat them like grown-ups they will knuckle down and get on with the job.' Recollecting his experience of travelling to away games with the team, when he was much the same age as most of the players, Goddard questions just how 'sensible' the club's drinking culture was at that time: 'we always stopped on the way back from games. How we ever took until midnight to get back from places like Redditch on a Saturday afternoon, I don't know – but we did.'

Tim Bayliffe agrees that 'there was definitely that culture, there; there's no hiding that.' Moreover, it was not confined to the old sweats of the first team. He recalls how 'the youngsters – three or four of us – were always out, drinking, clubbing and stuff like that.' And he volunteers, with hindsight, that this was inappropriate behaviour with which Paine was right to take issue: 'he'd come from a professional set-up' and greater discipline 'was the way to go.'

And Terry was getting straight down to it, compared with Geoff Hurst, his counterpart at Telford, who learned the hard way from his initial 'mistake of accepting part-time attitudes,' such as players arriving late for training after a day's work.

This would not be the last time, though, that Terry Paine would encounter that awkward question: how much professional discipline can you hope to instil in a group of footballers who, as Bayliffe puts it, had 'not been brought up' that way?

It was truly a culture-shock for Tim, who admits that, 'at the time, I didn't cope with it, because I couldn't change the way I was. I carried on doing what I was doing and I got left aside,' when the new manager promptly made him available for transfer. So what needed to change: his habits or Paine's expectations? Bayliffe has no doubts:

> I needed to change. It was my responsibility to change. That's the way he saw the club going forward. And that's what had to happen. I've got no problems: you look back on it and he was dead right. He had to change the culture to try and move the club on and that's what he tried to do. I understand that totally and I was one of the victims of that.

Dave Lewis, who survived the new discipline, shares Bayliffe's recall of being in a team that 'played to enjoy the game and, obviously, there was a fair bit of drinking on Saturday nights.' No shorts or wine, though: if his memory serves, the team-tipple was lager.

The notion of playing for pleasure permeates a conversation with Lewis, but he was able to adapt to the expectations of a man who, whether as a team-mate or the manager,

> was always wanting to win. He was a winner. He had a League attitude. We were just playing part-time and it was a *sport*, really, to us. To get somebody like Terry Paine in – who'd played all those games and had that attitude – was quite a change for us.

So did that matter to players whose way of life had been disturbed by this injection of professionalism? When pressed, Lewis concedes that Paine's 'League attitude' may have ruffled a few feathers: 'but I was a bit naïve. I just wanted to play football. If the Queen had been in charge, it wouldn't have made any difference to me.' As he recalls, 'you get a lot of League footballers dropping down into the Southern League and probably not earning their money.' But Paine was different: he was 'a winner'.

Not that he was going to win much as a manager. His views on drinking featured in the *Echo* on the day of his first game in charge: a 2-0 defeat at Barnet. You will appreciate the irony of this if you recall that the home side's squad included Jimmy Greaves, surely one of the most publicised examples of a footballer damaged by drink. And this was his first appearance – coming on as a second-half substitute – since the recent publication of his book, *This One's On Me*, in which he had paid tribute to the Barnet chairman who had 'gently coaxed' him 'back into the game' as a cure for his drinking. Who scripts these twists?

Three more defeats followed, all at home. Paine named himself as sub' a few times and came off the bench in the last two games of a season in which his managerial record had been P10 W2 D2 L6.

It had been such a dismal campaign that his four-goal burst in September left him as the team's fourth-highest scorer. Things could only get better. Maybe.

Chapter 25

For Pub and Club

**By now, Terry had been appointed manager for the 1979-80 season –
at a salary of £30 a week, plus £30 expenses. Well, that's one way
of capping expenses – even if the taxman might have had cause to
question its legality.**

Two directors had voted to advertise for a new manager, but Paine's
appointment was eventually unanimous. Conducting their business in a
strange order, the Board had by then agreed the retained list with their
caretaker-manager. Out went Brown, Allen's big buy, and both centre-backs,
Dean and Foster: it looked as though Paine would be giving youth its
chance. But, as previously intimated, 19 year-old Bayliffe was surplus to his
requirements. Tim was not at all surprised. He knew that Paine objected not
only to his drinking, but also to his style of tackling. He had been made
aware of this when Terry arrived as a player:

> He didn't like the way I played: he made that quite clear. I was a get-stuck-
> in type of player. He accused me of going over the top to people – and
> stuff like that. He obviously didn't approve of my style of play.

Bayliffe was clearly unaware, until I told him, of his manager's reputation,
in the professional game, for leaving his foot in. He had never known him
do that in a Robins shirt and was surprised that I should raise the matter:
'he was basically playing wide,' he says, oblivious to the way in which so
many top-class wingers of the 1960s and '70s had reckoned to 'look after
themselves'. John Davies was not so ingenuous. He cites the instance when
Terry went in higher than an opponent and then justified himself in the
dressing room. John can picture him grinning,

> with that unique set of teeth, and saying, 'he tried to do me, but I went a
> yard over him.' That was how Terry was: you don't play all those games
> without being able to take care of yourself. When he came down to our
> level, and people weren't quite so cute, Terry could see it coming and he
> would always be gone; or he'd have done him first.

Even so, Davies could see why Terry was concerned about Bayliffe's
tendency to 'jump-tackle.' It was not so much over-the-top as 'a two-footed
tackle: nobody around liked the way he did it.'

The top tiers of non-league football were being reorganised for 1979-80 and, by finishing 18th in the 22-team Southern League, Cheltenham had failed to qualify for the inaugural season of the new Alliance Premier League (which would later become the Conference). So they would be playing in the newly-regionalised Southern League (Midland Division).

With no money to spend and faced with the prospect of smaller crowds, Paine took his solution to his first Board meeting as the permanent manager: he would scrap the Reserve team and rely on a first-team squad of 16 and the Youth team. His faith in the youngsters was well-founded: they were good enough to have been entered in the summer tournament in Holland, which you may recall Hereford winning, and the Board even agreed, at this same meeting, to chip in £100 towards their expenses, the young lads having already raised most of the funding themselves.

As already noted, many of these teenagers could expect to turn out both for the Youth team and the Reserves, so scrapping the latter side had a certain logic to it. We have seen that this possibility had been aired more than once at Board meetings: indeed, the directors had agreed, at their December meeting to withdraw the side from the West Midlands League, while postponing a decision on whether the club needed a Reserve team at all. So the new manager was pushing at an open door.

Perhaps if the Board's protracted discussions of a side it couldn't afford – and arguably didn't need – had been known to the media and the players and had Terry not enthused so openly about his plans, he would not have been taken to task by Goddard at the time – and still blamed, to this day – for this 'controversial' decision.

The question of what this might all mean for the Reserves' manager was solved by his resignation. Roger Thorndale felt that he had been making a go of the change of management: 'I used to go in and see Terry – at the *Prince of Wales,* more often than not – to see what players he might need' for the first team, so that a Reserve team could then be picked; this was 1979, remember, when both teams would still be playing simultaneously most of the time. 'It was easier for both of us to meet over a glass of shandy, or whatever. That was OK for a while, but it wasn't that clever, really: we just didn't *get on.* It's as simple as that, really.'

If their general relationship was a bubble waiting to burst, the big bang came with the agreement to abolish the Reserves. Thorndale, who 'had an inkling that was going to happen, just went to the Chairman and said I'd rather not carry on.' This forced Terry to announce his plan sooner than he had intended. Goddard denounced his 'shabby' treatment of Thorndale, but the club would be better-off, Paine reasoned, concentrating on its successful Youth side. He reminded Goddard that, while still playing in the Youth team, he had made his first-team debut for Southampton.

The traditionalist Lewis (*left*) and Davies (*right*), at training with Terry Paine.

And he stands by that decision, still: 'you have to take on board the financial situation. I wanted to try and produce the youth within the area but there was only one way I could get that. I couldn't have both: I couldn't have a Reserve side *and* a Youth team – economically.'

The either/or element in the manager's rationale seems not to have impressed the traditionalists for whom the Reserve team was part of the process for 'bringing a lot of local youngsters through,' as Dave Lewis reasons. That's what Roger Thorndale had been doing, in partnership with whoever was managing the Youth team. So here, for Lewis, was another disturbance of the local way of doing things:

> I don't know what influence Terry had on the Board, but they decided to scrap the Reserves. From the local point of view – because we were a lot of local players – it was a bit controversial, really, because Roger was getting all the best talent around this area... It was a friendly little club and along came this big man with big ideas. Terry was imposing himself on the club. Change is hard to take when you've been there a few years. I'd been there 10 years [and the rest – in more than one spell]; the Reserves had always been there and a lot of players in the first team had come through the Reserves. So it was pretty controversial – because, if they didn't play, they liked to drop down to the Reserves.

By August, Paine would have in place a scheme for dealing with the problem of those members of the first-team squad who were not getting a game and who were ineligible for the Youth team. Meanwhile, he had signed up for a life-changing trip.

He had gone to Salisbury Races to look at a young hopeful called Terry Paine – not a footballer but the horse. You may recall, from Chapter 22, that when Terry retired (temporarily), Herbert Blagrave, the Southampton FC president, had named one of his yearlings after him. And Terry had gone to Salisbury to watch the horse run. His plan was interrupted, however, by an announcement, over the tannoy, that he was wanted on the 'phone.

When Terry got to the Secretary's office and picked up the 'phone, it was Bobby Charlton on the line:

> It was a case of trying to listen to Bobby with one ear and listen to the race that actually went off as I got to the 'phone. We got beat by a short-head, but I was trying to listen to Bobby at the same time: it was an invitation to go to South Africa with an ex-internationals XI.

Actually, a couple of the 16-man squad in which Terry toured South Africa in July – Geoff Strong and Ron Wilson – were not internationals. But the members of the party were certainly 'ex': their average age was 38½, with two Republic of Ireland internationals, Eoin Hand and Ray Treacy, the juniors at 33.

Far from being a retirement 'jolly', this four-match tour would be a rehearsal, in Terry's case, for a whole new life. That being so, it makes sense to postpone discussion of it to the next chapter, when we can venture to South Africa with the emigrant Paine.

By the time he returned to Cheltenham, the players had begun their pre-season training. Terry was in time for the AGM, where the Board apologised for the chaos that had prevented them reporting to the shareholders for three years. They attributed this 'traumatic time' to executive power: the previous chairman had been 'running everything'.

Terry was soon raving to the *Echo* about his players' performances in friendlies against League opponents – Newport County, Wrexham and Swindon – and was counting the number of scouts who were watching two of the youngsters he had introduced: local lad Rich Caudle and John Williams, from Abergavenny, whom he had spotted in the Holland tournament.

Cheltenham's results were less impressive once the Southern League season got under way, but the *Echo* reported 'an early start', on 18 August, for Terry's strategy for occupying those players who, because there was now no Reserve team, were being denied a game: Colin MacDonald turned out for Swindon Town's Reserves. Although the Board never discussed this arrangement, Terry spelled it out for the *Echo*. Third Division Swindon had had problems fielding a Reserve team in 1978-79, needing to borrow a

Cheltenham player more than once. So they had agreed with Paine that, in 1979-80, any player not in his first-team squad would be available for Swindon's Football Combination side. 'It's a great outlet for me,' Terry enthused, and it would be good for the players: 'the Combination is the best reserve league in the world.' A rash claim, perhaps, from a man who had hardly ever been asked to play in that league, but he insists that 'it was full of good players.'

Before the month was out, he was being approached about a managerial position in the Third Division. Mick Channon was 'sliding down the glass mountain,' as he puts it, at Manchester City and contemplating an offer to manage Blackpool. Having obtained approval to bring Terry Paine with him as assistant manager, Mick sounded him out. Terry turned him down and told Goddard that 'I had to tell him I now have some loyalties to Cheltenham, now that I have the pub.' Pub before club, then. It all became academic when Channon rejected Blackpool's offer, explaining to the *Echo* in his turn that he felt he still had something to offer in the First Division – a point he would promptly prove by re-signing for Southampton.

The following week, Terry was at Bath Races – for another adventure involving his equine namesake. The two of them appeared in the winners' enclosure together, when Herbert Blagrave's horse won the Be Hopeful Memorial Handicap Stakes at 8-1. That was its first – and, it would prove,

Herbert Blagrave, the owner of Terry Paine, the winning horse, is joined for the victory celebrations by Terry Paine, the football manager-cum-publican.

only – win, but Terry couldn't hang about to share the champers: he had a home game against Alvechurch that evening.

So far, he had not been playing. He was reserving himself for the FA Cup. On 1 September, he turned out in the Preliminary Round – a stage of the competition he had never before experienced – in a 1-0 win over Devizes Town. He played sweeper, a position from which he 'talked his team through the difficult times,' as Goddard put it, and 'instilled more tightness.' In the next round, away to Paulton Rovers, he played himself at right-back in place of Rich Caudle, one of his young hopefuls.

By showing that he could adapt to that position at the age of 40, 'he proved a point,' Dave Lewis reckons, 'by getting everybody going.' So how could he do that? 'Well, you've got a great man, who's played 700 games at right-wing, suddenly imposing himself at right-back. Obviously, his legs had gone, but he was still using his mouth a lot,' Lewis explains, chuckling at his own audacity.

He would never play in the FA Cup again, but Terry was now on a roll, announcing to the Board, on 25 September, that he had signed both his first apprentice professional and Bobby Stokes on loan. His former Saints team-mate was back in England from the States, where he was playing for the Washington Diplomats, and available until February. By way of a change from talking terms at a racecourse, Terry opened negotiations at a wedding in Portsmouth, where a friend's daughter was marrying Bobby's cousin. 'I was quite thrilled,' Terry recalls. 'It was a bit of a coup.' He saved his corniest line, though, for the *Echo*: 'I came away with the best man,' he told them.

Stokes made an impact on and off the pitch. He would turn up with merchandise for sale, most memorably a consignment of 'about half-a-dozen sheepskin coats,' Davies recalls. 'He'd sell them for 20 quid a piece – or whatever it was in those days. Every week, he'd come in with something different.' Terry remembers buying a coat: 'Del Boy style, you know. Bobby probably got more out of selling those coats than he got from being on the pitch.'

That's as maybe, but his on-pitch contribution was appreciated by Mark Buckland, an 18 year-old debutant, when Enderby Town came to Cheltenham in Stokes's first month:

> When you look at him, you think 'Oh! He's nothing.' But when he had the ball, he passed it and moved and his movement was so smooth. Normally, someone passes it and they don't move. You turned and did your own thing. Bobby was already moving: as he's passed it, he's moved. He expected to get a one-two going. I thought I could do that already, but he made me a better player.

Davies confirms that Buckland – who would go on to make 50 League appearances for Wolves – did, indeed, have an instinctive understanding of how to play 'give-and-go,' an art that he, himself, needed to learn from Paine. The lesson, which has clearly left a lasting impression on John, confirms Terry's acumen as an on-pitch teacher. It came about for Davies one day when, facing his own goal, he turned, half-circle, to play a ball down the wing. Terry, standing facing him, gently pointed out the error of his ways:

> He looked at me and said 'I could have done that for you, John.' Obviously, it was better for him to make the pass, because he didn't have to turn round. It was just a lay-it-and-go. I'd have been involved in the play again; he'd have been facing the play. It's dead simple, yet I was 26, 27, and still didn't understand it. But he said it in a way that made it stick. That might sound absolutely ridiculous but I think, even now, a lot of local footballers don't understand.

So, with the exception of talents like Buckland and the 'instinctive' Lewis, players at that level needed lessons from Paine in how to keep it simple? 'Yes,' says Davies,

> it's the simple things: lots of things. As a kid growing up without coaching, you don't give it and go – you tend to want to be the player to beat. Playing with Terry helped me. He made some real good, solid statements, which haven't just helped me in football; they've helped me in life, to be honest. You learn little lessons, like it's not always about you having to do it all yourself. When you learn that sort of thing, they're good lessons – things that stick in your cranium.

And even the precocious Buckland can remember benefiting from on-pitch tuition, on debut: 'I did something and I thought I'd done well, but as I turned round, all I could see was the anger in his face.' Mark mimics Paine's grimace, as formed by what Davies described as 'that unique set of teeth.' The accompanying oral message was 'Get stuck in! Get the ball!'

Whereupon, the young debutant 'sort of realised "I'm in the first team here and I've got to do my job if I want to stay here." I honestly thought that, at half-time, he might take me off. But he kept me on and I scored the third and fourth goals. You learn by these things. It's not all pretty and nice: he's had a right go at me; I thought I'd done something right but, obviously, it was wrong. It lifted me up and I got stuck in a bit more and got more aggressive and I think that's what made me score two goals.'

Mark refers to the photographic evidence of his first goal, demonstrating 'the aggressiveness' he needed 'to get there and hit the ball before

Doing as he'd been told, Buckland (*right*) asserts himself against two Enderby Town defenders to score the first of his debut goals. Stokes is on hand, just in case.

the big lad came across, and with the lad behind me trying to kick me from behind. I caught it sweet and it went in the top corner.' His second was from a rebound, after Paine had hit the bar.

Terry was certainly putting his faith in youth, having just given starts to a 16 year-old goalkeeper (Les White) and an 18 year-old centre-half (Wayne Hams). And then, in the week after Buckland's debut, he presented to the Board his plans for youth development, that he had negotiated with Coventry City's manager, Gordon Milne, his former England team-mate. The eight terms of the agreement, whereby Cheltenham's Youth team would be a kind of 'feeder' to the First Division club, included Coventry's helping out with kit and balls, Terry explained to the *Echo*. In exchange, they would have first claim (at the appropriate transfer fee) on any young Robin who looked 'capable of making the grade.' Cheltenham had been finding and developing its own youngsters – and still would – but now Coventry would hold youth trials from which Cheltenham could 'get the pickings': Terry was 'over the moon about it.'

The Youth team manager also liked the idea. Gordon ('Jasper') Cook, another part-time member of the Whaddon Road boot-room, had been offered full-time terms by Denis Allen but had decided not to give up his day-job at the estate agency of club director Don Perry. He enjoyed working under Terry Paine – 'he left the management totally to me' – but admired the way Terry threw his managerial weight about when the occasion demanded, as during a match when the Youth team was 'playing very badly,' so much so that Jasper

> was wondering what I was going to say, at half-time, in order to lift the players and try to get a better performance in the second half. Terry, who had given me complete control and who was a very amiable fellow at times, didn't suffer fools gladly; and on this occasion, he certainly wasn't going to. As the players were entering the dressing room at half-time and I was ready to begin my criticisms, or support, or do whatever I had to do to try and improve their second-half performance, Terry *burst* through the door and, in a most unusual manner – strictly non-technical – launched into the players with a terrific broadside which I think might have flattened one or two of the less experienced youngsters among our players but generally had the effect of lifting them; and certainly the second-half performance was much, much better.

Buckland vouches for Paine's 'lifting effect':

> Who he was – you know, your ex-professional – commanded a lot of respect. If he said something, you did it. Nothing against Jasper at the time: starting off in management, it's hard – especially with local lads who knew him – to get respect. When Terry came down to the dressing room, people stood up and listened. Once or twice, he came into the changing room and talked to individuals – 'go out there; do this; do that' – especially people he wanted to look at [for possible promotion to the first team].

The early signs for the Coventry link-up were good: Terry still goes so far as to describe it as 'brilliant'. In the *Football Weekly News* for the first week of October, he defended the scheme as being 'the only protection I have to stop bigger clubs poaching my best young players.'

It all fitted into his view of football supply and demand, with Cheltenham an especially tough case: 'The people here are not really football minded,' he explained. 'We have to compete with rugby and West Brom are only three-quarters-of-an-hour away.' And the manager-cum-publican certainly couldn't afford to be buying players, as transfer fees were spiralling out of control – along with beer prices:

> Every one is concerned at the escalating fees for players but, there again, I deal in beer and that's costing 36 pence a pint now. Some sanity has got to come back into the game…Even at my level, players are being talked about around the £2,000 mark. The spiral continues right the way down the line from the top League clubs to the small non-league clubs – it's just incredible the way it's going.

It was not going especially well for Terry. He didn't have £2,000 to spend and the team he'd inherited was not delivering. What's more, the Thorndale resignation remained capable of creating further tension. While managing the Reserves, Thorndale had seldom been free to watch the first team, but now he could. He had kept his counsel, but sensed that his presence at first-team games was creating a problem for the manager:

> I think 'disruptive influence' were the words that were used at the time. Terry thought I was a little bit of a disruptive influence, because I knew all the players. That didn't bother me, but things weren't going that well and I think Terry thought I was a little bit of a problem. You know what football's like.

The possibility of an atmosphere is not difficult to imagine. Roger Thorndale had been to Cheltenham Town what Terry Paine had been to Southampton. It could only increase any tension – and bring it out into the open – when, in the November, Thorndale talked to Derek Goddard about his resignation six months earlier. This became a catalyst, if not perhaps the entire reason, for Terry to quit, in turn.

Thorndale didn't go into details, but his statement to Goddard, that he 'couldn't see Terry Paine's policies working and I still can't,' was sufficient to light the tinder-box. The story appeared on the day of a home game against Kidderminster Harriers. Goddard reported that Paine was 'obviously upset' by the comments and that he 'declined to speak' to him at the game.

Terry blamed both men and asked the Board to ban them from the ground. In Thorndale's case that was a tall order: Roger recalls the chairman, by now Frank Tuohy, telling him that there was 'no way he was barring a person that had played 700 games for the club.' Not surprisingly, the Board refused the request and Terry resigned.

Not only had he clashed with a local hero; he had succeeded, at a stroke, in alienating two local football reporters, in Cheltenham and Hereford, who had been such huge admirers. Back at the *Hereford Times,* Ted Woodriffe weighed in on the side of the directors who had 'turned down his dictatorial demand' and generally railed against managers who seek to 'gag the press.'

Derek Goddard bears no grudges, though:

> As a manager he was fine. I was always welcome: ring him up, any time; rang me up, any time – and he spoke very pleasantly – until he went. In many ways, it's a pity it didn't last, but he didn't quite make the same manager as he made a player… The end of his tenure was a bit of a shock to me – and possibly to everybody else – because there hadn't been a row and I got a feeling he was probably looking for a way out, anyway, by then, because things weren't going too well on the pitch. I might be wrong, but it

was rather a manufactured end to it. There was always the feeling that perhaps he wanted to go anyway and this was a little peg to hang it on.

Terry doesn't demur from that conclusion. Cheltenham were lying 18th in a 22-team league, with only three wins from 12 matches. He has no regrets at abandoning the futile task the Board had set him: 'they were hopeless. They had no chance, with what they were trying to run it on.' Which would perhaps explain why they finished the season one place lower, even, than when he walked out.

It seems that the most immediate casualty of his departure was the nurturing of young players. Mark Buckland, eternally grateful for the way in which Terry 'set me on the way to going here, there and everywhere,' feels that 'there were seven or eight lads in the Youth team who could easily have got into the first team if Terry would have stayed longer.'

But Terry had now retired from managing in England. Although he had been linked, without needing formally to apply, with management posts in the Football League, his 22 games in charge of Southern League Cheltenham would be his lot. His future in management would be in South Africa.

More of that in the next chapter. Meanwhile, he had a pub to run – even as beer prices rocketed to 36p a pint.

Terry Paine, now out of football, still had his memories on the walls of his pub – like his famous goal against the Rest of the World.

With that knack he had of finding a works-team to play for – from the BR Body Shop to Toby Balding's stables – it is perhaps not surprising that running the *Prince of Wales* got Terry involved in not just one football team, but two. Billy Burke, a regular at the *Prince of Wales*, ran the pub's football team that played in the Cheltenham Premier Sunday League. Turning out for them was quite like Sundays of old for Terry, in that they played their home games on the King George V fields – save that the sides were restricted to 11 players at a time. That gave him space in midfield to 'knock a great ball,' Billy recalls, to the 'fast lads' that he had upfront.

And then, in December 1980, came another shot at management. The announcement that he was to player-manage for a local brewery caused quite a splash in the *Whitbread News*. Apart from the Whitbread brewery in the centre of town, the company's regional office was also in Cheltenham. This gave them ample men – with a few outsiders inevitably recruited over the years – to run a decent team or two, including the Saturday side that played, under the name of Whitbread Flowers, in the Cheltenham League.

TERRY-FIC!

Former England star helps to revive Flowers' flagging football fortunes

TERRY PAINE has been called in to revive Flowers' flagging football teams.
The former England star, who played on Southampton's right wing in more than 700 matches "I approached Terry because I thought if he was interested in becoming involved. be able to encourage people that we have better facilities than other local teams. Whitbread...

Captain Geoff Parker can remember the revolution that now occurred at Whitbread's Brockworth sports ground: 'We had floodlights set up – the ones that you can move around. Terry came up with ideas to help us train – the fitness side of it – and, obviously, he came up with ideas on how we should play. He still wanted to *win*.'

That sounds familiar. Wasn't this another chance, even though they were training only one night a week, for the consummate professional to expect too much of an amateur set-up? Parker won't have that:

Whitbread's sales director, Harry Moffett, and captain, Geoff Parker, welcome the new manager.

> Everybody used to enjoy it. We had 20 or 30 people turning up for training – they wouldn't turn up if they didn't enjoy it. It was *refreshing* that you had somebody who was willing to give his time to help people who were way below his standard. He helped us enormously.

When the team played in Whitbread's inter-regional competition, for the Brussels Trophy, only employees of the company were eligible to play. Their player-manager was excluded, by virtue of being a *tenant* of Whitbread at the *Prince of Wales,* not an employee. So he had to be content with managing the side to the Final, played on a snow-threatened Sunday at Whitbread's Sports and Social Club in Luton. Much heavier snow in the Cotswolds trapped the coach-loads of employees, expected at Luton in support. Fortunately, the team had travelled on the Saturday, stopping off for racing at Sandown, where 'Terry came up with one or two tips,' Parker recalls, 'and we all lost a few bob on them.' But, even without the support of their work-mates, Whitbread Flowers won the Cup.

Captain Geoff Parker holds the Brussels Trophy,
while the manager pours in the Whitbread's.

It was now 1981 and the Paines, the publicans, were on the move – out into the Cotswolds at Frampton Mansell. Running the *White Horse* was harder work than the *Prince of Wales*, because it involved a high quantity of food. But Pat enjoyed it a lot more: 'it was nicer having a country pub. We had a huge garden and people flocked there in the summer. I enjoyed it a lot more than Cheltenham: I didn't like the big-town pub.'

If you are surprised to hear Cheltenham described as a 'big-town', remember that Pat was a small-town gal, at home in Winchester and Hereford, compared with Terry, the small-town lad who had become a big-city guy. Terry seems to have adapted well, though, to life among the country gentry: 'just down the road was Princess Anne, just down the bottom of my lane. I was a member at Lord Bathurst's polo club. That's where I first had a drink with Prince Charles.' So from serving drinks at the *Prince of Wales* to drinking with the Prince of Wales: Terry Paine had seemingly arrived as a Cotswold squire.

The landlord (*left*) welcomes Eddy Penfold (*right*) and friends to the *White Horse*.

He rejects that label, but confesses that the hunt assembled outside his pub and that, 'if you're going to have a pub, that was the place to be. But, unfortunately, it was a summer pub.'

His ideal summer had long since included a good deal of golf and racing: John Sillett and he had a horse stabled nearby, with trainer, David Nicholson. Since 1980, though, his summers had been put on hold until he'd got Robertsham's season under way in the Transvaal League.

This annual experience had given him the taste for his biggest move of all – from the Cotswolds to Johannesburg.

Chapter 26

Missionary

When Terry rang Pat from South Africa in the spring of 1984, to ask whether she fancied emigrating, he was on his fifth visit and had a sense of what she – and a child or two – would be coming to.

She had never accompanied him on those trips – she had a pub to run – but felt no need of a reconnaissance visit. She was recovering from a cancer operation in the January and felt ready to get out of pub-life. By November, Terry, Teresa and she had emigrated to South Africa. Debbie, who was working, stayed with some friends in Frampton Mansell, but would join them later. Darren had joined the Five Signal Regiment and was stationed in Germany. He married a German girl and has stayed there. Pat is impressed with her daughter-in-law's English, which 'is far better than anybody's who… definitely better than Terry, my little 'ampshire boy.'

How sweet! But what was this Hampshire boy doing, anyhow, bringing this small-town Hampshire girl – sight, unseen – to South Africa, the troubled land to which Bobby Charlton had brought him five years earlier?

Unlike some of his squad-mates, Terry had himself been travelling to an unknown country in 1979. Charlton had previously guested in South Africa for Arcadia United in Pretoria, a departure from the tendency of fellow-Boys of '66 to head for Cape Town. The magnet there was George Eastham, who was managing Hellenic, for whom he had first played in 1971-72 and where he had successfully succeeded his father as manager. Two of his recruits – Roger Hunt and Bobby Moore – were in Charlton's party, along with two other members of the 1966 squad: Jack Charlton and Ron Springett, who was sharing the gloves with Bob Wilson.

Football was, at this time, in a strange position in South Africa. The crushing of the uprising in Soweto in 1976 had reminded the world of this country's oppressive regime, while Steve Biko's death in custody in 1977 spoke of the brutal force of apartheid. Yet there had been recent relaxations in the application to sport of apartheid's rule, in ways of special significance to football – or 'soccer' as it was sometimes called, and still is, pretty much interchangeably.

Whatever you like to call it, this was predominantly the black person's game, in contrast with the white person's team sports of rugby and cricket, as symbolised in the 'Springbok'. Non-black footballers had their separate leagues that reflected South Africa's four-fold racial classification, as decreed in the apartheid legislation: black (or 'African'); white; Indian; and 'coloured' (or 'Cape-coloured') This is not the place to enter into the sociology or politics of these legal classifications: readers seeking a simple introduction could do worse than consult the autobiography, or Peter Oborne's penetrating biography, of that celebrated 'Cape-coloured', Basil D'Oliveira.

Nor, for the purposes of this beginner's attempt to paint a background to the football environment that Terry Paine was entering, do I need to account for these relaxations: were they a response to events in Soweto or to other considerations of global economics? Such questions have been addressed by Peter Alegi and Douglas Booth, visiting scholars whose analysis could take us way beyond what is needed here. Suffice it to acknowledge their reservations: I take Booth's point that what happened, especially in football and boxing, in the 1970s – first, under Prime Minister Vorster and then, from 1978, under P.W.Botha – was 'a process of racial contraction rather than retraction' and I can appreciate why these 'cosmetic changes', as Alegi describes them, have been dismissed as 'apartheid in drag'.

Segregated football had experienced a British invasion long before 1979. In the previous two decades, ex-players like Eastham, along with other internationals like 'Budgie' Byrne and Scotland's Alex Forbes – and a good number of former journeymen from the English and Scottish Leagues, besides – had come out to play, had stayed to manage and had then brought out numerous 'guest' players during the British close season.

This neo-colonial presence seems not to have been controversial and it was still possible, in 1979, for a touring party of ex-footballers to visit from the UK, without the 'rebel' label that would be attached to visiting sports teams, following the establishment, in 1981, of the United Nations 'blacklist'. Perhaps, like me, you associate the notion of a 'rebel tour' more with cricketers, notably Mike Gatting, than footballers. But Mick Channon has pinned that label on the tour he joined in 1982 and has opted to address the question that could be asked of visiting footballers, even in the 1970s: were they mercenaries or missionaries?

The former charge would be levelled by those who argued that it was in the interest of South African government and business to pay a seductive ransom to British stars – or, in Charlton's case, former stars – not to mention an also-ran or two, to come and legitimise what was happening in a nation desperate to free itself from the slogan of 'no normal sport in an abnormal society.' The counter-argument was that such representatives of British football could help to bring on the South African game by holding football 'clinics', notably in the townships. As Channon reasoned, he had 'trained barefoot kids in Soweto,' which gave him 'a stronger platform to talk about South Africa than the people who condemn the way things are run there when they haven't been within five thousand miles of the place.'

Charlton's party had the additional counter that it had been invited at a time of increasing multi-racialism in football, both to forward that cause and to hold training clinics. Their tour was the brainchild of George Thabe, who had brought the four racial groups together, under an integrated Football Council of South Africa, in 1976. This multi-racial effort was sponsored by *Mainstay,* a name derived from a cane spirit, whose producers, the Stellenbosch Farmers Winery, unashamedly admitted that it was seeking, through its sponsorship, 'a definite spin-off from black consumers.'

Having sponsored the Mainstay Cup, won by Wits (a white team originating from Witwatersrand University in Johannesburg) in 1978, when they defeated Kaizer Chiefs from Soweto, the Winery was a natural sponsor of the first touring party to meet a multi-racial football team.

Charlton's party at Johannesburg airport. (*Left to right*): Paine; anonymous man, hiding behind sunglasses; Hunt; Lawler; Charlton; Yeats (tall man, hiding behind his captain); Strong; Newton.

That was the third game for Charlton's party, following a 1-0 win against a Transvaal XI and a 1-0 defeat by Natal. The tourists lost 2-1 to a multi-racial South Africa XI, after Bobby Moore had managed to get himself sent off. Terry Paine thereupon got himself into the local *Citizen* newspaper with the gratuitous observation that 'your chaps have no idea of how to penetrate a defence and they shirk responsibility by passing the buck – the ball – to someone else.'

The four-match programme climaxed, the following day, against Kaizer Chiefs. Playing against an all-black team – before a crowd of 40,000 in Soweto's Orlando Stadium, compared with the 8,000 who had turned up for the multi-racial effort – was 'the eye-opener' for Roger Hunt. He had seen 'a lot of south Africa,' jetting across the country for Eastham's Hellenic in 1971, yet had only ever faced white teams.

Despite losing 2-0, some of the tourists again offered advice to their hosts. Ian Storey-Moore pointed out to the *Star,* most ungraciously, that the Chiefs had 'managed only two goals against a team whose average age is 38 and-a-half, and who had played a hard game against the national team the day before. In our prime, we would have thrashed them 10- or 15-nil.' Arfon Griffiths was at least constructive: he 'would like… to take several of them back to Wales,' he said, so that he might add some 'discipline' to 'their natural flair… And then what superb players they would be.'

Maybe so, but Terry Paine would do it differently: he would be returning to South Africa to coach. When the tourists' itinerary had taken them to coaching clinics in Soweto, Terry had got to know Lenny Ross, the manager of nearby Robertsham, a white side playing amateur football in the Transvaal League. Ross had introduced him to the club chairman, Harold Gordon, who had invited Terry to return for a short spell, in the close season, to help equip his players for the season ahead.

It wasn't a difficult contract for Terry to agree – he had 'probably never been to a club with so much talent in all my life' – and he would be back, each close season, from 1980 until 1984.

Kenny Sadler, then the captain at Robertsham, confirms that they were indeed a talented side. They would become something of a 'nursery' team for nearby PG Rangers, a leading professional club, managed, in several stints, by Alex Forbes. But that didn't mean that Robertsham were bursting with players, in the early 1980s, who were keen to make the professional grade: most of them 'played because they wanted to play,' Sadler reckons, 'and they weren't too keen to maybe play for a professional club.'

Now that set-up – an abundance of talent, coupled with a lack of personal ambition – sounds like a recipe for players' resisting the input of a visiting coach. Far from it: Sadler believes that Terry's visits, starting in the close-season and continuing for a few weeks of Transvaal League Division I fixtures, 'helped us a little bit more on the "professional" side of it. He just got a bit more out of the players, because they were very keen.'

Shane MacGregor endorses that assessment. He had just quit Robertsham, his local club, for Rangers, when Terry first came out to coach, but he would come along to watch the lads and generally remained very close to the club. Although he concluded that 'Terry was too advanced for local football,' he feels that the injection of a 'professional attitude' was 'like a revolution' for the good: 'Terry changed the look of the club, just by doing that. When you're playing at the amateur level and you feel a bit more professional than opposing teams, it does make a difference.'

Helping the seniors was only part of the job: Robertsham had a junior section and Terry made an impact with the kids. There is an extent to which he didn't need to do a lot to inspire them: as at Hereford and Cheltenham, there were those he could impress just by being there. 'When a guy of Terry's status came to coach,' Sadler explains, the youngsters 'were very keen to learn. With somebody like that, you just went the extra mile for him.'

Whatever it was Terry achieved with them, it certainly went down well with the Johannesburg press. When he was appointed coach at Bedfordview, a club in the same league as Robertsham, with one of the biggest junior sections in the country, *The Citizen* acclaimed it as a 'major coup' for them, given that 'his efforts that went into encouraging [Robertsham's] youngsters were incredible.'

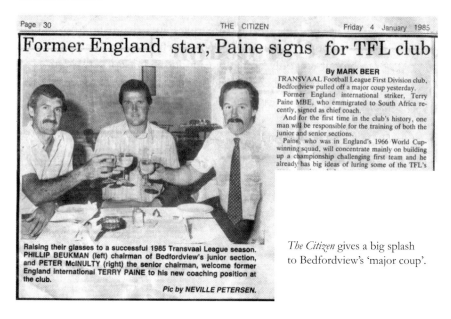

Page 30   THE CITIZEN   Friday 4 January 1985

Former England star, Paine signs for TFL club

By MARK BEER

TRANSVAAL Football League First Division club, Bedfordview pulled off a major coup yesterday.

Former England international striker, Terry Paine MBE, who emmigrated to South Africa recently, signed as chief coach.

And for the first time in the club's history, one man will be responsible for the training of both the junior and senior sections.

Paine, who was in England's 1966 World Cup-winning squad, will concentrate mainly on building up a championship challenging first team and he already has big ideas of luring some of the TFL's

Raising their glasses to a successful 1985 Transvaal League season. PHILLIP BEUKMAN (left) chairman of Bedfordview's junior section, and PETER McINULTY (right) the senior chairman, welcome former England international TERRY PAINE to his new coaching position at the club.

Pic by NEVILLE PETERSEN.

The Citizen gives a big splash to Bedfordview's 'major coup'.

The notion of a newspaper reflecting, in this way, on a part-time managerial appointment at an amateur club, let alone enthusing about a 'major coup', may strike the British reader as odd. It reflects not only the strength of the Transvaal League, which *The Citizen* covered on Tuesdays and Saturdays, but also the high profile of Terry Paine. This was partly a function of reputation, Billy Cooper of *The Citizen* explains, but also of his media-friendliness. That is to say that the press enjoyed having a World Cup player among them and that Cooper liked the way Terry would talk to him about what was going on – just as he always had, even as a player, with the press in England. And it helped that Cooper had captained Bedfordview's Reserves and had been chairman of the club in the late 1970s.

It was the first time Bedfordview had had one coach in charge of both its senior and junior sections, but it was not a full-time job. Terry had emigrated to South Africa in the autumn of 1984 to take a job not in football but in Kenny Sadler's office supplies business. When he got the Bedfordview post in January 1985, he could continue to work for Sadler and be a football coach in the evenings: the club had floodlights and training sessions ran from 7.30 to 9.30 pm.

So Terry Paine, who had dabbled in business while playing full-time professional football in England, even selling furniture for *Tracys*, was now doubling up, with a day-time job in office supplies and an evening job as a football coach. This saddened Peter Harvey. A former Southampton Schoolboy player – in the same side as Paul Bennett – Harvey had worked at the *Echo* before emigrating to South Africa, as a 25 year-old, in 1977.

He took with him an image of his Southampton hero. He had been having treatment at The Dell for the hamstring injury that had removed him from the English Schools Cup-run of 1966-67, when Terry Paine wandered in and *spoke* to him: it was only 'something along the lines of "all right, nipper? How're you doing?"' but the teenager was 'gob-smacked: it was like God walking in,' Peter recalls. 'I just remember the sheep-skin coat and the whole image.'

Which explains why Harvey was distressed – as the chief sports sub-editor at *The Citizen* who was turning out as an amateur for Bedfordview – to find his hero not only coaching at a level that he considered unworthy of his talents, but working in office supplies in order, as Peter saw it, to scrape together a living:

He was being paid to coach, but obviously not enough and that was the sad part of it – I keep coming back to it – to see this idol, who always had the lovely clothes and the Jags, but who, when he arrived in South Africa, where's it all gone? *Where* has it all gone? Sure, at that time, the ex-pros weren't the multi-millionaires they are today, but he'd been on a pretty good whack, from what I'd gathered, at The Dell and I thought he'd invested it well, in businesses and properties, so it comes back to having this vision of this man and how did he end up *here*, trying to make a living wherever he could – by coaching and doing whatever else?

Peter Harvey's hero, remembered for his 'lovely clothes and the Jags'.

But isn't this missing the point? Whereas a journalist could leave a Southampton newspaper and obtain full-time employment on a Johannesburg 'paper, a British footballer could not expect to retire into a comparable living, coaching, even at a professional club, in South Africa.

Playing for Bedfordview's 'Juniors', Peter had limited opportunities to experience Terry's coaching methods, but he did get the occasional chance, outside the club, to play with him.

One was for *The Citizen*'s team. Harvey remembers, from his days at the *Echo*, that Terry 'always fancied himself as a columnist. He put the *Echo*'s nose out of joint: they didn't take him up on an offer to write a column there, so he went to the *Southern Sentinel,* which was a sort of knock-and-drop 'paper – a give-away, a freebie – in Eastleigh and he wrote a column there.' So Peter wasn't surprised when Terry landed himself a column at *The Citizen.*

Looking back at his 'British Soccer Snippets', 20-odd years on, you would find them rather tedious, I'm sure – but in those days, a column peddling transfer gossip from the UK was about as good as it got for a Johannesburg football audience. It wasn't until the late 1980s that the South African Broadcasting Company (SABC) began to feature British football matches.

As a columnist for *The Citizen,* Terry, now in his late 40s, was asked by Billy Cooper to play for their football team – against other newspapers and in various charity matches. He just couldn't kick the habit of turning out for works' sides. Cooper's team was integrated, occupationally, in that it 'had the guys from the sports department to the guys in distribution and the van-drivers.' Which meant that it was also integrated racially: and how those white guys in editorial appreciated the black van-drivers! 'They were the best players, man – not like us old farts,' Peter Harvey recalls. 'We let them do all the running around.' Not that Terry needed to do any running at all: 'he used to play in goal,' Harvey explains, 'and he wasn't a bad goalkeeper. But it was just great to be playing in the same team as Terry Paine.'

And then there was the 'Over-35s' tournament in Durban, for which Peter had just become eligible in 1986. The 47 year-old Paine was again in goal,

> but he just came up for this free-kick – it must have been about 30 yards out – and it was unbelievable. Such precision! Top right-hand corner. The goalkeeper didn't even move. It just brought it all back: how precise; and the vision.

For somebody who'd admired that precision from the terraces, 'it was,' for Peter, 'just a unique occasion to see it up close.'

He was not the only Old Sotonian at Bedfordview with Terry. Mike Barfoot was initially playing in the Juniors, another 'old hand', along with Harvey, nursing the youngsters coming through. But the squad soon expanded – 'the whole club was buzzing at that time,' Barfoot explains. 'Everybody wanted to play for Bedfordview, with its very professional set-up, lovely grounds and a big club-house.' So, while Harvey carried on playing for a while, Terry asked Mike to turn his hand to coaching the kids. This would not be the last time that the formally unqualified Paine would suggest to a kindred spirit that he had it in him to coach. I say 'kindred spirit' because Barfoot

> liked Terry's methods. He had his own methods of training: he didn't necessarily go by the coaching manual. He doesn't like lazy players and he can spot a lazy player. He knows weaknesses and strengths – he's very good at picking that up in a player – and you could see, when you look at him coaching, the way he picks and highlights somebody and gets them homing in on their weaknesses.

And there were plenty of weaknesses in a club that Barfoot considered to be nearer Hampshire League standard than Southern League – more like Winchester City, then, than Cheltenham Town. But Terry 'immediately turned round' Bedfordview's football, Barfoot reckons, partly by attracting some better players but mainly by his approach to the squad he had inherited: 'he actually took it on just like he would a professional club. Just because they weren't the best team around, he still handled it as though they were.'

Those sentiments will be familiar to you: isn't this just what players said at Cheltenham about the injection of 'professional' standards? Barfoot is in no doubt that players benefited from this approach:

> I saw players vastly improve. There was a player there called Goodie Bentley, on the wing. Terry concentrated on him – and the improvement in two or three months! He was crossing the ball, working to instructions that Terry had coached him on. A vast improvement! Terry got a lot of enjoyment out of seeing that team improve so much – and then he was snapped up, obviously, by the professional game.

His first professional club was Witbank Black Aces. He joined them at the start of the 1986 season, at what Sy Lerman of *The Citizen* described as a 'critical period' for a struggling side. Paine turned their fortunes around, with a run in which the side went unbeaten for 16 games. Witbank, a mining town north of Johannesburg, involved a long journey back and forth for their new manager. And he was needed there most days – certainly for more than just the couple of evenings a week that had sufficed at Bedfordview. He brought in some white players, including his protégé, Goodie Bentley from Bedfordview. And Lerman contended that 'no-one could dispute the commendably thorough way in which he stabilised a club that was riddled with internal dissent and languishing at the bottom of the log.'

A chance to end the tiring commute to Witbanks came when Wits University's manager, Brian Goldrick, was shunted into an administrative position at the club. Wits had invited their recently departed manager, Joe Frickleton, to return. He told Lerman that the offer 'was difficult to refuse.' But he did. Terry Paine didn't: it was 'an offer I could not refuse,' he assured another reporter, Bafana Shezi.

Despite Lerman's saluting Paine's achievements at Witbank, the reports of this appointment generally focused on his status *as a player*. Thus, both Lerman and Shezi referred to his membership of the 1966 World Cup squad, as if that was a unique distinction in South Africa. Yet Terry shared that honour with George Eastham, who had, like him, 19 England caps to his name. So Raymond Hack, the Wits chairman, was exaggerating when he told Lerman that Paine's 'experience as a player extends into a dimension that no other coach in South Africa has approached' – unless you are inclined to argue that actually *playing* once in the 1966 finals was a dimension beyond Eastham.

This kind of coverage was a reflection, though, of Billy Cooper's point made earlier: Terry Paine was 'charismatic' and 'media-friendly' and a special friend of *The Citizen*. That said, Lerman was not getting carried away with Terry's playing achievements of 20 years before: 'playing acumen cannot always be equated with coaching skills,' he reasoned. 'And the dedicated Paine, who surprisingly found it difficult breaking into the big-time in coaching in South Africa, does not yet have the tried and tested credentials of managers like [the Chilean] Mario Tuani, [the Scot] Joe Frickleton and Alex Forbes.'

Hack was very soon assured, however, that his new coach could achieve at this level. In their opening game of the 1987 season, Wits beat League Champions, Rangers, 3-1. Billy Cooper reported that 'Paine's 4-4-2 tactics were spot on' and felt he had 'installed a new lease of life into the side.' Terry promised him that 'the days of Wits playing kick and run football are over. We are pledged to play entertaining, open soccer.' His chairman 'was ecstatic,' Cooper reported. 'We outplayed the champions with virtually a team of youngsters,' Hack told him.

Even at this level, Hack explains, Terry's standards exceeded what Wits had been used to:

He'd come from a very professional set-up [in England]. Because of the fact that we were isolated and we weren't part of FIFA, we had our own version of what an interest in soccer would be – and maybe it wasn't up to his standards. I think Terry, in fairness, may have been before his time for South African football. He certainly changed it around and he certainly changed our fortunes around: he made our players more professional; and a lot of their ability to read the game I would certainly attribute to him.

The message is becoming repetitive: at club after club, Paine's standards were more 'professional' than his players were used to. The then Wits president, Ronald Schloss, has explained what this entailed:

He was a hard task-master. The players weren't used to it at first. But he would call a spade a spade. He insisted that he got the best out of the players and he was a very good motivator. Terry wasn't shy at screaming at the players and telling them straight what he thought about them. You can only do that with certain players; you can't do it with all the players. Terry was an old-style, English manager: it worked well with most of the players that we had, but one or two weren't up to it.

Terry's old-fashioned, 'English' style of management will be a recurrent theme of this and the next chapter. Schloss, nowadays the Chief Operations Manager at the Premier Soccer League, has defined this style for us:

I think the coaches today aren't as vocal as the older coaches in England used to be. Terry, on the bench, would play an *active* role. He would be *pushing*, as if he was going to play the ball, going this way, then that way – knocking his assistant coach and things like that. He was *playing* the game with his body: he wasn't on the park, but he was playing the game. And then he'd jump up and he'd be telling the players what to do and telling the referee what to do. He let everybody know – but in fairness to Terry, he used to read a game fantastically well.

This blunt, vocal approach didn't work with every player. Schloss feels that this was a 'cultural thing. If Terry swore at a player, the white players would laugh about it, just ignore it and basically tell him what to do, under their breath, whereas, if a black player was sworn at, he would take offence.'

A white player might even venture a sarcastic response to the inveterate mickey-taker. Terry chuckles at an example, as he tells a story against himself. Wits had equalised late in a game and Terry felt the need for his full-back, Neil Van Ryan, to get tighter on his opponent. He made this abundantly clear, pacing the touchline and screaming, 'Neil, for … [expletives withheld],' and repeating this enjoinder when Van Ryan was slow to respond.

Wits hung on to draw, but the full-back felt justified, as he came off, in asking his manager, 'Boss, what's my name?' 'Neil.' 'No, my full name.' 'Neil Van Ryan.' 'Exactly! So why do you keep calling me "Neil Forfuxake"?'

Very droll. And confirmation that the arch mickey-taker could handle being on the receiving end. But black players were likely to be less comfortable, Schloss is telling us, with this managerial abrasiveness and dressing-room back-chat. Shane MacGregor argues that this 'cultural' argument is two-staged. First of all, many of his compatriots, black or white, were generally resistant to professional standards being brought in from the British game. For whatever reasons – notably, perhaps, a lack of resources – the influx of British coaches had made limited inroads, he argues, into the 'amateur set-up' that existed in South Africa's First Division.

It is a second-stage argument, for MacGregor, that a black player might be more sensitive to the hectoring, 'English' style of management. Whatever difficulties Terry Paine and other exponents of that style may have had with their African charges, though, Schloss wants us to appreciate the significant contribution that Terry Paine made to racial integration at Wits:

> You must remember that when Terry brought a couple of white players to the club, as youngsters, they'd never played with a black player; they'd never had a drink with a black person. As far as Terry was concerned, 'you're all equal. You're my players and I couldn't care whether you're pink or yellow: I'm going to play the *best* team. And I want you to live as a team, to socialise as a team.' And that's what happened.

Billy Cooper agrees with that assessment – with Terry, 'it was very much a case of best-player-for-the-job.' Not that he's suggesting that Terry was unique, in this regard, among the British coaches: Eddie Lewis was 'very big', Cooper claims, in the early development of multi-racial sides.

Paul Evans, a white novice whom Terry brought to Wits in his second spell at the club, has a lot to say about Paine's contribution to multi-racial football. We can get a flavour of it in the next chapter.

Terry's first spell at Wits was short-lived. In 1988, John Sillett summoned him once again.

Sillett was now managing Coventry City. The Sky Blues were on something of a high, having beaten Spurs, in one of Wembley's more thrilling Finals, to win the FA Cup in 1987. What's more, their youngsters had won the FA Youth Cup that season, managed by Mick Coop, a stalwart of over 350 League games for the club. But now, a year on, he was taking over the Reserves; so would Terry like to return to England, Sillett wondered, and manage the Youths? He would and he did.

In Terry's first season, his lads won one of the regional competitions, the Purity Youth League title, and reached the final of the other, the Purity Youth League Cup. I say 'his lads' but it is especially difficult, as players become ineligible for the Youth team and managers come and go, to apportion credit, when the team does well, to this or the other manager. What we do know is that this was a purple period for Coventry, with eight of the lads turning pro, of whom forward Lee Hurst and goalkeeper Dean Kiely made it in the top flight. Hurst would play almost 50 League games for Coventry, while Kiely has topped 600 League games elsewhere, having found Steve Ogrizovic immovable at Highfield Road.

Hurst, who had played under Coop in 1987-88, gives him plenty of residual credit for the success of the 1988-89 side and points out that Sillett, who'd previously had a spell as Coventry's Youth coach, was also taking a keen interest in the young lads. Neil Sillett, the boss's son, was involved, as well, as the assistant physio. As far as Hurst is concerned, Terry Paine was in charge, everybody pulled together and it worked. And he cannot praise Terry enough for what he did for him, personally: 'Terry was a lovely man. He was very good to me. He brought things out in me.'

Terry did that, Lee explains, by making him not only captain, but 'Head Lad', the youngster responsible for ensuring that his peers did all their jobs properly – cleaning everything from boots to showers – and taking the can, and a rocket from Paine, for any short-comings: 'that helped me to be the person who I am today, self-confident and able to accept responsibility.'

Well, that makes it sound like a job worth coming home for. It was a job that allowed Terry the time to develop another activity for which his playing responsibilities had left him insufficient time at Hereford – spying on the first-team's next opponents.

It was about more than reporting on how sides played, how they used set-

A few of the Coventry City Youth squad of 1988-89.
Goalkeeper Kiely stands behind
(*left to right*) Terry Paine, Neil Sillett and Lee Hurst.

plays and how they defended them; if he was spying on a home side Coventry were due to visit, he would note which brand of ball they used, so that Sillett could have the team practising with it the following week. If that all sounds rather routine to you, the revel was in the detail for Terry Paine. He still talks with some passion, today, about the minutiae of his reports, which made Sillett rate them the 'most thorough he had ever seen.'

Elsewhere on the scouting front, Terry was again using George O'Brien to sniff out young talent. O'Brien came up with a young winger whose game had been explicitly modelled on Paine's. Keith Guppy, one of Terry's mentors at Winchester City, had taken his young son, Steve, out on to Littleton Rec', where he 'passed on', he reckons,

> a lot of Terry's skills. I'd say 'Now, this is one of Terry Paine's tricks. Work at it.' That's how we used to do it. Terry's favourite one was down the right wing, feint to cross the ball, get the opponent to put his leg up, then just dip it over.

Steve confirms that this was, indeed, 'a trick I did work on and, every now and then, it got me out of a bit of trouble.' Guppy's style – 'his gait and everything' – reminded George O'Brien less of Terry Paine than of Chris Waddle. Having watched him twice one weekend in 1989 – playing for Colden Common on Saturday and the *Arrow* pub on Sunday, George was keen to get Steve up to Coventry for a trial.

That never worked out. In March 1989, Guppy went to Southampton, instead, played half-a-dozen games for the Reserves – 'a jump that was just too big' for him, he feels – and was released. He signed for Wycombe Wanderers and became a devoted acolyte of Martin O'Neill. It might have been Terry Paine.

By way of a change from spying on opponents, Sillett sent Terry to spy on a coach. He wanted to know how Dixie McNeil was shaping up on the training ground. McNeil had been the manager at the Racecourse Ground since 1985. In 1989, he had taken Wrexham to the Final of the Fourth Division play-offs. Having lost to Leyton Orient, they were doing less well the following season when, McNeil explains, 'Terry asked me if he could come to some training sessions: it was out of the blue, but he said he was in the area. I said "Of course, you can." So he came and watched me take training for a couple of days.'

It was only when he lost the Wrexham job and was invited to join the coaching team at Highfield Road that it dawned on Dixie that Sillett might have 'sent Terry to see what I was like as a coach.' When Paine confessed that this had been the case, McNeil was flattered that Sillett and he, the scheming pair, should have gone to that trouble.

McNeil was duly installed as first-team coach at Highfield Road, with Paine now in charge of the Reserves.

So Sillett's back-room staff now consisted of people from three parts of his life: his family; Coventry City; and Hereford United. You might perhaps surmise that this could have created a degree of tension between cliques. Steve Ogrizovic, who was then about to start his fifth season in Coventry's goal, was surprised that I should entertain any such notion and dismisses what clearly came across as an insult to Sillett's skills in assembling a coaching *team*:

> Sill knew how to create the right atmosphere around the place and you knew that anybody who walked into the club was the right person, who was going to fit in.

It helped Terry to 'fit in' that he came with a pedigree for which Steve had 'the utmost respect: it was great that somebody like Terry, with the career that he'd had and the things that he'd done, had come to Coventry City.' It further helped Terry's cause, as far as Ogrizovic was concerned, that 'he was a very amenable person – always willing to talk.'

Terry would not have long at Highfield Road, however, in which to enhance his reputation. In the autumn of 1990, Sillett was sacked. He had been off, ill, and Paine had been in charge, picking the side for a few games, when – as Coventry's *Complete Record* dramatically puts it – Sillett 'learn[ed] of his dismissal from his sick-bed.'

Paine soon followed him out of the door, with his old job at Wits waiting for him.

Although Terry had a job to return to, it looked as though he might no longer have a wife. Pat talks of how 'our marriage went downhill, when he took the job at Coventry,' in a way that suggests she blames herself. There was a period of coming and going between England and South Africa, but they 'had drifted apart, really. We'd changed. Very sad.' That's all I know and all I feel I need to know. End of.

He was back at Wits, but it was of as much, if not more, significance to his subsequent career in South Africa that he was recruited to an expert panel, commenting upon Italia '90.

The architect of this arrangement was Barry Lambert. A former Crystal Palace reserve, who had quit pro football to become a detective – playing for the Metropolitan Police at The Dell – he had emigrated in 1969 and had landed a job with the SABC.

The Italia 90 panel.
(*Left to right*): Lambert, Bailey, Paine, Sono.

The panelists who joined Lambert for the 1990 World Cup finals in Italy were Terry Paine, Gary Bailey and Jomo Sono. Bailey had returned to South Africa, from his impressive stint in Manchester United's goal, in 1988 and had recently retired, after a short spell with Kaizer Chiefs. He had already done some work for the SABC but, as intimated earlier, coverage of British football had been slow to develop.

Sono, *aka* 'The Black Panther' and 'Troublemaker', and a former Footballer of the Year and Sportsman of the Year, had also returned from a foreign adventure – with New York Cosmos. In 1983, he had bought Dion Highlands Park, a white football club of repute and had renamed it Dion Cosmos – and later Jomo Cosmos.

Lambert was sufficiently impressed with his two recruits from British football that when he moved to M-Net and won the contract for showing live Premier League matches, it was '*natural*', he reasons, 'to take Terry and Gary with me.'

So Terry was embarking, in his mid-fifties, upon a busy new career, combining football management with TV punditry – not to mention a major interlude as ambassador for South Africa's bid to host the 2006 World Cup finals.

Chapter 27

Ambassador

The story of Terry Paine's second stint at Wits was one of continuing where he had left off: bringing on youngsters and integrating them into a multi-racial club.

Paul Evans, from the Natal town of Newcastle, provides an instructive illustration of what this involved. His first – and lasting – love was rugby, but his mother had made him convert to a safer sport. By the age of 16, he had become a goalkeeper. There was only one white football team in Newcastle, so Paul had to develop his understanding of his mother's preferred code in the local Indian League.

He developed it well enough for his father to approach Roy Bailey, who referred him to Terry Paine. A brief trial later, Terry had signed him.

Now, after having associated with no black footballers other than the family's gardener – 'a pretty decent footballer' whom he could not take with him to his local club in Newcastle – the 18 year-old Evans was in

Paul Evans signs for Wits.

a multi-racial Wits squad. Resident in an Afrikaans-speaking area of the East Rand, he would give lifts to players living in a neighbouring black township. He took not only to the novelty of multi-culturalism, but to his manager's brash style:

> There are very few football managers I respect as people and he's one of them. I just thought he was a fantastic person – a wonderful man, I would say. He called a spade a spade. I like that in people. I don't like people who beat around the bush. If he wanted something from you – on the pitch – he'd tell you. If you didn't do it, he'd lambaste you. That's good coaching.

Evans confirms what Schloss has said about the manager's behaviour during a game: 'He used to go crazy, sometimes. The language was a bit choice, sometimes. Some guys don't respond well to that. To people like myself, it's water off a duck's back; other people take it personally.' And, like Schloss, Evans regrets that his black team-mates were more likely to be offended by Terry's bluntness and ripe language: 'you don't call a black man every name under the sun. Swearing at him will not get the best out of him.'

That comment could, of course, be perceived as racial stereotyping in its own right, but I am repeating what I have heard from Terry Paine's admirers at Wits, in boardroom and dressing room alike. What I am hearing is that Terry was a significant force for integration, *despite* the unease of at least some of his black players with his 'English' style.

I should perhaps interject, at this point – after these comments on his managerial lexicon – that I do not associate Terry with industrial language of the Channon variety. I have heard him use the F-word a lot, but the word is 'friggin' – as in 'it's friggin freezin,' when the Johannesburg temperature drops below 75°F. And one of the strangest compliments I have heard him paid came, out of the blue, from Geraldine Evans, Paul's mum: 'He could swear in front of a woman,' she assured me, 'and she would still feel like a lady – which is not very often done by a man, is it?' Well, maybe not, although the example she cited, as to why Terry wouldn't buy her an effing cold drink in the Wits bar, but would buy her a whisky – whether she liked it or not – struck me as anything but gallant. But who am I to judge? Geraldine Evans had been

> a little bit in awe of him at the beginning, but he just made you feel so comfortable. He was a person who had us all in awe - *all* his achievements, all his money and he'd had an MBE. Yet he was so down to earth. It was like talking to the man next door. That's what I respected him for.

Which rather brings us back, albeit in an extreme form, to what John Sillett had found at Hereford: part of Terry's talent for bringing on the kids had been his patter with the parents. It may have been helped in the Evanses' case, Paul suggests, by the fact that his father was a freemason and recognised a fellow-handshaker, albeit a lapsed one, in Terry.

One way or another, this was another club at which Terry enhanced his reputation for nurturing young players. Hack talks of his 'keen eye for youngsters,' while Schloss, who likewise admired his knack for 'picking a good youngster and developing him,' credits Terry with bringing on Bradley Carnell, the youngest footballer ever to play in South Africa's top flight.

Evans would prove good enough to be taken to England by Leeds United. He would not make it there and, after a second spell in England with Sheffield Wednesday, he would eventually settle for non-league football with Bath City. But that does not diminish his gratitude to Terry Paine for enabling him to achieve anything at all in the sport he never really wanted to play. He recalls how his team-mates at Wits told him that he was 'rubbish' when he arrived, so that they wondered why the returning coach had signed him. It follows, for Paul, that it was Paine's training regime that made him the goalkeeper he became:

> I thought Terry was a very good coach. He didn't have a lot of patience, but I thought his input, and the training routines that we went through, were very good – probably better than some of the stuff I got into with Sheffield Wednesday. I always enjoyed his training methods. I loved his sessions. A lot of it was geared to incorporating the goalkeepers. There was always a lot of shooting; a lot of crossing; a lot of small-sided games, which always had the goalkeepers involved. The pitches would be tiny, so you had shots flying in from everywhere. The 'keepers would sometimes crawl off the pitch: you'd be that tired. But it benefited us and made us so much better 'keepers. It must be through his training methods that I improved endlessly. He must have done something right in those early years.

It will not have escaped your notice that Paine had his players practising with *a ball,* an object he felt he saw too little of in his training sessions at The Dell. Evans also valued, though, the individual sessions, in which Terry would make him

> dive everywhere; chase this; chase that, swearing at me constantly – 'you lazy this, that and everything else.' He used to drill me into the ground. But, after that was finished, I felt like he was my father-figure: he really did look after me.

By the time Evans departed for Leeds, his mentor had himself moved on to a new career, combining TV work with running a football club.

M-Net developed a sports channel, Supersport, whose management decided they wanted not just to be bringing English football to living rooms across Africa – or, at least, to those households that subscribed – but to have a team playing in South Africa's own top flight.

During the 1994 season, Terry was sent out to buy a football team. He picked upon the impoverished Pretoria City, which had been playing under the name of Albany City, after the bakeries that owned the club. They could not change their name until the end of the season, by which time they had been relegated. Only then could they become known as Supersport United.

CONSTANT PAINE

Stan Lapot, another Scot who had been in South African football –
as a player, then manager – since the late sixties, was already in place as
coach. Terry became the general manager/managing director. It was he who
brought in Robertsham old boy, Shane MacGregor, from Kaizer Chiefs. A
former Footballer of the Year and Players' Player of the Year, MacGregor
had been capped by South Africa.

Moving from the Chiefs to Pretoria was a shock to Shane's professional
system. He promptly took his complaints of poor discipline and resources
to Terry and was impressed by the response: balls galore arrived, plus all the
bibs and cones that organised training required. 'That was Terry,' Shane
explains. 'If we're going to do this, let's do it properly – *professionally*. Pretoria
City had been training out of the back of a boot but, within a week or two,
he'd changed everything. That's the way he was, you know.'

In a bid to stave off relegation, Paine took over from Lapot for the
last half-a-dozen games. And with that way he had of spotting a coach,
he installed MacGregor as his assistant. Their improved results were not
enough to prevent them dropping into the regionalized Second Division.
Supersport United would play their first full season in that division's Inland
Stream, with Paine soon moving back upstairs and MacGregor promoted
to coach. Shane was still playing, though, for much of the season, and
enjoying Second Division football – even if the visits to some of the Inland
Stream's rural outposts meant that you had to overcome the rulings of local
referees: 'you know you're going to have to score six or seven,' he explains,
'to win 1-0.'

The wily Paine amply got his own back for home games, though. The
host club was expected to book the refs and to determine when, over the
weekend, the game would be played. With Supersport's wealth, their
managing director could afford to pay a premium to have First Division
referees and hope to get fairer decision-making than was generally to be
expected at this level. And opting for Friday night home games could give
Supersport two advantages: several teams in this division were unused to
playing under lights; and, if they could afford neither to fly nor to have two
nights away, they might have to travel a long distance, by road, on the day of
the game. 'That's where Terry was very professional and very clever,' Shane
reckons. 'Every little advantage he could get, he got for us.'

The managerial set-up suited MacGregor. Although the two of them
would discuss potential signings, he 'didn't want to get involved in the
purchasing of players. The final decision was always in Terry's hands. That's
where he was brilliant: he could spot talent.' On matchdays, though, Shane
was in sole charge – and not only for an away game that Terry was giving a
miss. For home games, Terry would sit in the stand, not on the bench, and
take good care to demonstrate to the players that he was not interfering.

If he did want a word at half-time, to advise the coach on what he'd seen from on high, he would make sure it was in the corridor. 'He would pick up a lot of things,' MacGregor recalls:

> He was very professional and *brilliant* at picking up where we were going wrong – but he said he didn't want the players to see that he was talking to me and it looking as if I'm not knowing what I was doing.

So Terry avoided going into the dressing room, unless invited in by Shane to 'have a chat with the guys.' This all worked out well and the side won their league, going undefeated all season, until they lost in the Final of the *Bob Save* Super Bowl to Cape Town Spurs, having beaten First Division Orlando Pirates in the semi-final.

Before they could get back to top-flight football, they had to play a transitional half-season of knock-out matches. South Africa needed to fall in line with FIFA's international weekends in Europe, so their domestic season would follow a more European calendar for 1996-97. And the First Division now became the Premier League.

MacGregor continued as coach, grateful for the 'professionalism' that his managing director had brought to the club: not just the improved training facilities and discipline, already mentioned, but two 'firsts' that MacGregor claims for the innovative Paine: bringing in Medical Aid (a form of health insurance); and the appointment of a *full-time* physio: 'even the Chiefs had a part-time guy,' Shane adds, underlining his point.

'Professionalism' is a recurrent theme when people talk about Terry Paine's way of doing things, usually when he is exhibiting plenty of it in a less than welcoming environment. The problem arises when his quest to support players, to get them to play to their potential, clashes with an individual's desire for plenty of amateur fun. You may recall that Terry encountered this barrier with one or two players at Cheltenham, but it could be a factor in South Africa, MacGregor argues, even in the top-flight: here was 'an amateur set-up,' he claims,

> masquerading as professional. Terry used to get on the players' backs too often. They would get upset, because they weren't used to his professional way of running things. Terry has to win at everything and our guys weren't used to that, because they were playing more for fun than anything else, even though they were so-called professionals. And for them to change has taken a long while: I think he was just too advanced, at that stage, for the country and for the club.

Thomas Madigage, the South Africa international whom Paine brought to Supersport, endorses that assessment: Terry was a 'pioneer, who put many club officials to shame and a lot were forced to follow his lead. Because of him, the mindset of many clubs was changed.' The particular example Madigage cites is Terry's introduction of proper contracts – to the extent, he argues, that 'a lot of players' at other clubs 'hoped that Terry would sign them, so that they could have the security of a contract.'

As far as Thomas is concerned, then, Terry fulfilled the promise he had made him – that, if he signed for Supersport, he could help Terry in his 'plan to transform South African soccer.' It is a measure of how successful Madigage feels Paine was in that quest that he wishes Terry were still at the club, where Thomas is today assistant coach. 'If Terry Paine were still running Supersport United, the club would be in an even stronger position,' Thomas believes, 'than it is today.'

Even stronger? At the time Madidage made that statement (October 2008), Supersport, the 2007-08 champions, were top of the Premier League.

It was central to Paine's 'plan', Madigage argues, that he 'brought in people in crucial positions.' Terry's most innovative recruit, his full-time physio, is still at Supersport, 14 years on.

Jacqui McCord had already worked with rugby players, but she was the first female physio to work with footballers. She encountered no resistance to this innovation – 'the players were so grateful to have some proper physio' – and, by way of a variation on a theme, she found the black players even 'more appreciative' than the white players: 'they had had so little medical care in their lives,' she explains, 'compared with the private health care that the white players took for granted.'

Jacqui maintains that 'every team needs a mother around – somebody who can be a little more sensitive than the coach,' especially when the coach is as 'strict' as Terry, who was 'so adamant about what he wanted and who was always telling the players what that was in his colourful language.' McCord found Terry 'interesting to work with,' though, and remains grateful to him for starting her off in a sport she hadn't been following.

Another beneficiary of Paine's innovative hunches was the assistant coach-cum-occasional goalkeeper whom he brought to Supersport that season. Perry Suckling had retired, aged only 29, from the English game, with 10 Under-21 caps and a dodgy back – which he sardonically attributes to bending down to pick the ball out of the net eight times when Coventry City came to The Dell in 1984. When Paul Evans left for Leeds in 1995, Suckling came out of retirement, and out to South Africa, to join Wits, expecting his back to be good enough. Having appeared on TV with Terry – and found him so knowledgeable as to be 'intimidating' – he was surprised to get a call from him, asking whether he would be interested in coaching.

Yes, Paine was at it again. On the strength of a beginner's performance as a pundit, Paine the coach-maker was offering him the first rung of what would be a coaching career.

Supersport's second Premiership season proved to be a difficult one for MacGregor and, with the side struggling, Paine stepped downstairs for the run-in, assuming the coaching duties. That was fine with Shane, who had decided he was more interested in managing than coaching. Relegation was avoided and, for the next season, it suited all parties for Terry to concentrate more on the TV side of Supersport's affairs, with MacGregor becoming general manager and a new coach being brought in.

Although he didn't see his future in coaching, MacGregor remains grateful to Terry Paine for the hunch that he had it in him to coach: 'I don't think I would have got the opportunity if Terry hadn't given me the opportunity. I think maybe *he saw something in me that he could nurture*' (emphasis added).

As I say, this uncanny ability to 'see something' in a younger person, without the supporting evidence of formal qualifications, was becoming a habit. Now, though, Terry Paine was stepping upstairs and leaving his two acolytes with a new coach, an Englishman of his own age.

Roy Matthews, a former Charlton Athletic player, had been in South Africa for more than 30 years, initially as a player, but as a manager for the last 20, including a recent spell at Bedfordview. Whenever my South African witnesses mentioned the hectoring 'English style' of management, they would invariably cite Matthews as the great exception: 'he would go with the flow,' as Suckling puts it. 'He was very laid-back; very quiet; very quietly-spoken.' In a word, Billy Cooper assures us, 'Roy Matthews is a gentleman – for me, one of the greatest gentlemen, ever.'

With a gentleman installed below stairs – and winning the Cup in that 1998-99 season, before moving on – Paine could focus on his TV work.

I have lost count of how many stories I've heard told, often in interviews for this book, of the person concerned being somewhere in Africa – or even in Europe – and seeing Terry broadcasting from Johannesburg. And he was good, they all tell me.

M-Net is the largest TV sportscaster in the world, expecting to be received in over 50 African countries, but being picked up, as I say, beyond that continent. There are reasons for Terry being good. Based on talking to his colleagues, seeing him at work and meeting people who watch him regularly, I'd say these reasons boil down to his store of knowledge; careful research; speed of thought; and being 'natural'.

He does carry a store – or a whole warehouse, more like – of sporting information in his head – not just about football, but about golf and horse-racing, too. This versatility came in handy on *Super Saturday*, a live 90-minute show that ran from 1999 to April 2008, with Terry as a resident panelist, spurred on by Neil Andrews, a quick-witted anchorman originating from Farnham in Surrey. Terry and he had previously been tipsters on a show called *Super Bet*.

Terry does not rely solely, though, on that enviable ability to pluck facts and stories from his memory-box. Far from it: he is hugely respected by his colleagues for the thoroughness of his research. There is the general updating – Gary Bailey is impressed by how much Terry absorbs from watching Sky Sports – and there is the match-specific preparation. I experienced the latter at first-hand, while staying with him during the 2006 World Cup finals, when he would go to the BBC website and download information on the relevant squads. And just in case he needs to look something up in the studio, a copy of the current edition of the *Sky Sports Football Yearbook* resides in the small hold-all that he always carries to work.

I also witnessed the way in which he 'calls the matches' when Mario Lacueva, the producer of *Super Saturday,* 'phoned him on Friday morning to ask which incidents Terry would like to be shown the following day. Out the top of his head, Terry rattled off two or three controversial moments from games shown in the past week: this would normally be from the Premiership but, while I was there, they were all from World Cup matches. And when Lacueva played these on the Saturday, Terry talked the viewer, totally unscripted, through the incident. Not a note in sight.

When I mentioned to John Clingen – his Executive Producer for those weekend programmes for which Super-sport takes a live 'feed' of Premiership games – how impressed I had been with Terry's off-the-cuff listing of incidents to which he then spoke without notes, his response was rather grand: 'That's how revered Terry is. If you want to know something about football, Terry's the one – he's our man.'

Paine of Supersport
'He's our man'

Terry also 'calls the highlights' for Clingen, during those Premiership matches – incidents that he will then discuss at half-time or full-time. You may be forming an impression – I certainly did – of a gifted, unscripted performer. This all requires speed of thought and an ability to make instant connections. Not everybody has that skill. In my former trade, you were expected, with your 'trained academic mind', to do that. Terry does it without the benefit of any such training and, what's more, in the pressure-cooker setting of a live studio.

Wearing an ear-piece, moreover. Presenters have to be able to do this, of course, but this is rare for a pundit, Clingen explains:

> Of the non-presenters, he's the only one who can handle it, who can actually talk and *listen*, without it upsetting him. Others have tried and it's been a disaster. With Terry's experience as an analyst, he can listen to me and he knows what's coming up. He can talk about a goal that happened last week, say the goal is ready and he will link to it – 'let's have a look at that incident' – and I will roll the incident in and it makes the whole process so smooth. Then he'll talk over it.

And then, come Saturday morning, he would get his chance to inject another ingredient into the unscripted exchanges: sarcasm. The format for *Super Saturday* was simple: Neil Andrews chaired an expert host-panel, which was joined by three guests in turn, with a few commercial breaks and an interlude where Terry would take the viewer through the highlights Lacueva had lined up at his behest.

I don't know about you, but when I watch a British panel show – *Have I Got News for You?*, say – I wonder, suspiciously, how much of the point-scoring between panelists has been scripted, or even separately recorded at the end of the show. But *Super Saturday* went out live, relying upon razor-sharp wit from the chair and some quick-fire ripostes from the panelists to maintain the entertainment, without any of the seemingly staged nonsense of *They Think It's All Over*.

I can vouch for how it worked, having been a guest on the show. Come in and talk about the biography – and whether it will *ever* be finished – said Terry. Sensing that that would not fill my 25-minute slot, I asked him how we'd occupy our time: 'we'll take the piss out of you,' he said. That's all the preparation I had – no warning, whatsoever, of the question with which Andrews was going to test my initial response-rate: how was my hernia? Terry knew that my hernia, overdue for surgery, had been playing me up. Being asked about it on live TV was straight out of the Paine-O'Brien School of Send-Up. I can't remember my answer or much else about the show, save that I inadvertently made Terry the butt of Andrews's sarcasm.

All I did was volunteer the story, explained earlier, of how Terry would leak a rumour to a Sunday 'paper, pocket £50 and deny it on Monday. For the rest of the programme, Andrews rounded off every item by assuring Terry that 'we'll deny it on Monday, Terry.' His colleagues had not heard of this chicanery before and revelled in the moment.

OK, so it wasn't uproariously funny. And even if it had been, it would be difficult to convey, here, the buzz of this happening on live TV – which is the entire point of my reporting the incident. As if Terry cared, though: he'd had another successful show, holding his own with guests from boxing and rugby.

All in all, I am reminded of what Cllr Reynard said – in Chapter 16 – about an untrained performer finding his niche. Working with Terry that morning, as he bantered his way through a 90-minute show, and then watching him the next day as a live pundit on the England v Ecuador game, I was left in no doubt that Terry had found his on TV in Johannesburg.

As Mick Channon would say, the Lad Done Brilliant. It seems to be a badge of honour among footballers-turned-pundits that they use adjectives as adverbs. Terry is no exception, I discovered, as I watched a World Cup game with his partner, Hilly – to whom you can be introduced properly in a moment. 'He did that comfortable,' said Terry, as he took us viewers through the highlights he had 'called' for Clingen. In my usual manner of talking at the set, I corrected him aloud, but Hilly told me, with a sigh, that she had abandoned the English lessons. As Peter Harvey says, Terry is 'a natural as a broadcaster.' Although he might 'cringe a bit at some of his pronunciations,' Peter enjoys how well Terry comes across – 'and so natural.'

The question is how long can a white male, now in his 70th year, hope to keep on entertaining admirers of his knowledge and natural style, given the legislative requirements, under the Black Economic Empowerment Act, for opportunities to be opened up to people of colour? It was a question I put to his colleagues at Supersport. Clingen assured me that the company is 'very aware' of the need to bring on black role models, but was blunt about the fact that his viewers

> still love and respect people like Gary and Terry. They don't really worry about the colour: in fact, they couldn't give a damn, basically. They just want a person who knows their soccer and who can tell them out there – the viewers – what the team's doing wrong and why. They just want to see, and hear from, qualified people. Terry has the knowledge. He's played at a high level and he's really *revered* by viewers across the continent of Africa – highly respected because of his qualifications. People love him and we continue to use him.

Bailey captures the dilemma: 'we have to reflect our society, but not many people of colour have played in England.' Among those who have, Andre Arendse, a South African international who kept goal a few times for Fulham and Oxford United in the late 1990s, sometimes appears as a Supersport pundit. Otherwise, Supersport have tried to square the circle by nurturing a black presenter. It's essential, Bailey argues, that the presenter knows less about the subject than the pundits: his job is to know how to get the best out of the experts in the studio with him.

Gary Bailey, in the Supersport studio with Terry Paine

Thomas Mlambo performed that role extremely well when I was watching. His approach certainly convinced me that he was pleased to be in the presence of experts who have played the game at the top and to have the chance of tapping into their knowledge and insights. Thomas had played for Wits colts under Terry, but had not made it; so, naturally, he had to survive some dressing room-style humour before he could start learning, from his former coach, how to be a TV presenter: 'Terry said "I remember you. You were crap".' Nothing new there, then. His account of how he learned his trade is that of a most appreciative apprentice:

> I watched what Gary and Terry were doing. They set a really high standard. Even Terry, who's got *massive* experience in the game, does a lot of research before a match and, in order for me to be at that level, I had then to do even more research than him and go to more websites and watch more football, in order even to be close. So that was something they taught me and you've got to respect that, after all that time in the game, a man like Terry Paine is still a *student* of the game, still going to check out what the latest is. And the thing that blew me away was when we'd be watching a game and he'd see a player and he'd say 'Oh! That boy came up from Gillingham, three seasons ago.' I'd be: 'how the hell does he know that?' He just keeps up-to-date with *everything* – even players who aren't in the Premiership – and that showed me that, OK, you need to know a little bit of that, too. He always has that [*Sky Sports*] book with him.

It is a nice observation – don't you think? – that Terry remains a 'student of the game,' even while teaching the next generation. Hilly believes that Mario Lacueva has likewise been '*drawn* out' by Terry, who 'teases him and gives him such a hard time. I think Mario has just thrived on it and has come out of himself.'

It is noticeable that, in the world of TV, as in football, Terry has been nurturing young learners with his customary combination of ridiculing them and setting them demanding standards. This has become a hackneyed theme of this story, I know, but the evidence is there to behold. Anybody who met Mario in England in November 2007 would surely have found him 'thriving', as Hilly puts it: the young producer had summoned up the energy to spend a week with Terry in Southampton and thereabouts, filming his hectic involvement in various reunion activities.

I mention advisedly the need for energy. I first met Mario when he was 25, and Terry 67, and he was telling me about his Supersport 'away-weeks' at the Fancourt golf estate: 'Terry has just got more energy than me,' he complained, 'and he doesn't stop. After five days, you just want to throttle him.' Hilly feels sorry for his younger colleagues, the way he thrashed them at snooker when they'd gone away to relax – 'and he has such a *style* about himself: he just seems to be good at everything.'

That includes, of course, his golf – at 69, he is playing off a handicap of 6. And, in a recent twist to his sporting versatility, he has obtained an Assistant Trainer's licence. That's to train horses. He is working, when he can find the time, at the stables of Penny Kimberley, who has been training his horses since the late 1990s. Penny and he go back a long way, to the days when she was working with Michael (later Sir Michael) Stoute at Newmarket. She has become so impressed by Terry's knowledge of, and passion for, horse-racing that she talks of him – unprompted, I assure you – as 'a great ambassador for racing. He loves it almost as much as he loves football. Well, maybe not.'

Playing off a handicap of 6 at The Wanderers Golf Club in Johannesburg.

What Penny indubitably wants to impress upon us is that, just as in football, Terry Paine doesn't need a formal qualification to sound off a great deal of sense, when it comes to preparing for action: 'there's a lot of stuff he can impart to me,' she volunteers, going on to explain how Terry will extrapolate from his knowledge of post-match recovery from tweaks and injuries to footballers, to advise her on the likely post-race recovery of horses. 'We talk about it a lot,' she says: 'racehorses can't talk to you about their injuries.' So she listens earnestly to her licensee's extrapolations: 'you can never stop learning.'

And I shall never stop being surprised by Terry Paine's range of talents.

I have been referring, in recent paragraphs, to Hilly Goffe-Wood. She has been part of Terry's life since 1995, when they met at her friend's 40th birthday party. The friend was dating Murray Medcalf, a sometime business partner of Terry's, who has since married Debbie.

Hilly is not much into sport herself, but she had to learn a little bit about football when she began to edit Terry's latest series of articles for *The Citizen*. Gradually, she became more of a ghost than an editor, but she blew her cover when she used the word 'epiphany'. The lads on *Super Saturday* decided this was not a Terry Paine word and would subsequently ask, on air, 'what's Hilly said this week?' in her football column.

She initially enjoyed the buzz of accompanying Terry to events where she met famous sportspeople, but began to limit her attendance when she came to feel that she was inhibiting his fans and admirers who 'want to come up and talk to him, but if I'm standing there, they stand back a bit.' That said, she names two events in England that she did enjoy: the 100 Legends evening – of which more in the next chapter – and the last game at The Dell, which she found 'tremendously exciting, because then I realised just how popular he was over there.'

She has long since got accustomed to his popularity on the streets of Johannesburg and admires 'the way he stops to talk to people, even if it can be quite irritating for him at times, when they go on and on, asking him questions.' And yet, if she spots 'a little boy just looking at him,' she'll point him out to Terry and 'he'll always go over and sign autographs or just have a chat to him.'

Jeremy Wilson has described what it is like trying to accompany Terry to a restaurant and the banter with the owner that has to be endured before you can eat. Being there during the 2006 World Cup meant, I found, that the food would have to wait while Terry gave the staff his latest tips on which teams would progress how far and the owner went off to 'phone his bookie. When the food eventually arrived, there was always too much: when I think of that massive bowl of king prawns we had for my first lunch, I appreciate why he mocks, at every opportunity, my serving him cheese sandwiches when I first entertained him for lunch in 1997.

And then he has his own special fan-club in the form of South Africa Saints. The ex-president of the Isle of Wight Saints is now the president of the Johannesburg-based branch of the Southampton Supporters Club. You may wonder how there can be so many Saints fans there – don't they all support Manchester United? – but an ad' in the Johannesburg *Star* in 1996 attracted 53 replies. Terry's 'input has been terrific,' the club officials tell me: generally helping with their PR, finding their guest-speakers and invariably fetching them Saints souvenirs – signed shirts and whatever – from his visits to Southampton.

The South Africa Saints assemble with their president and his biographer.

Back row (*left to right*): Alan Jones, David Yeo. Middle: Rodger Butt, Helen Butt, Symon Vokes, Tony Ford, Peter Harvey, David Bull. Front: Terry Paine, Ethan, Nicola and Dave MacLeod.

It is no exaggeration, then, to say that, one way or another, Terry Paine is a roving ambassador, in South Africa, for British football. I have tried to convey how that is an everyday, informal aspect of his life. At a more formal level, he has been commissioned, from time to time, by the British Consulate to visit rural areas, presenting football kits.

When it came to bidding to host the 2006 World Cup, though, the South Africa Football Association (SAFA) decided that he and Gary Bailey would be powerful ambassadors for South Africa, bidding *against* England.

No matter that Morocco was also bidding, South Africa's was a pan-Africa bid. Roger Milla of the Cameroons and Abedi Pelé of Ghana were ambassadors for the South African bid – along with Supersport's Bailey and Paine.

Terry distributes kit, on behalf of the British consulate, to a community on the Swaziland border.

Two reasons were put to me for choosing these two Britons. The first came from Raymond Hack, Terry's chairman at Wits, where Bailey had played. Hack is nowadays the CEO at SAFA. He felt that both Terry and Gary were well-placed to 'convey a perception of South Africa' for the benefit of foreigners who feared for their safety: 'it was a question of somebody who had adopted this country as their home and could go out to the outside world and say "Hey, this is what we have in South Africa. Don't listen to all those stories you hear: I live there; I am happy there; and this is what I'm telling you".'

The second reason, advanced by Bailey, is that it was a question of their knowing the enemy: their role was 'specifically to deal with the England threat.' England fielded as ambassadors Sir Bobby Charlton and Sir Geoff Hurst. But their bid was never a 'threat' to anybody and the vote came down to Germany v South Africa. The story of how England paid the price for its arrogance has been told, in some detail, by Leo McKinstry in *Jack and Bobby*, his biography of the Charlton brothers. He cites the 2001 proceedings of the House of Commons Culture Committee, before which Charlton appeared, when it examined the reasons for England's failure.

The essential issues were whether the FA was generally seen, in world football, as being too arrogant, and, specifically, whether they had reneged on an oral understanding. Germany had backed 'football coming come' to England in 1996 and it was being said that the FA had promised, in exchange, to support Germany's bid for the 2006 World Cup. All of which was tangential to the South African bid, so you may be relieved to know that the Committee's report is not compulsory reading.

There was, however, a serious side issue between the England bid-team and the South African representatives. Maurice Lipton of the *Mirror* told McKinstry that Charlton was avoiding Paine, who reported, in turn, 'a bit of frostiness in their relationship.' Both Bailey and Paine have confirmed that there were problems with Charlton. Yet Terry enjoyed, as ever, chatting to Lady Norma Charlton and got on fine with Hurst. 'It was not a question of rivalry at all,' Sir Geoff reasons:

> There was some rivalry in naturally wanting to do your best for your country, but it's like playing against each other: you play against somebody; you want to beat them; you want to tackle them hard; and you want to wallop them. But, after the game, you respect them and you get on with them. You don't take any grievances from the field off the field, afterwards.

We can treat as unconscious irony the reference to 'your country': there is no suggestion, from anyone, that Hurst had any issues with his two compatriots turning out for the opposition. The trouble was, in Lipton's view, that Charlton 'took any opposition to England's bid very personally' and, in Bailey's opinion, that Sir Bobby did not appreciate that the South African team was outraged not by him but by Tony Banks MP.

A former Minister for Sport, Banks had been appointed to a lead-role in the bid and Bailey blames him, in particular, for

> the way England's bid came across as *so* incredibly arrogant and anti-African. I'd always, through my dad, believed that, as English, we stood up for a certain code of conduct. The Germans were wonderful. Everybody we competed against was wonderful. Of course, they would put forward their point of view, of how good they were, but they wouldn't trash us in the process. But the English, for some reason, had a right go at us – that we couldn't organise it; we weren't secure; we didn't have good stadiums; we didn't have this; didn't have that. Tony Banks dragged people like Bobby Charlton into it. That annoyed me, because Bobby's got a great name and, next thing, he was being linked to some of these comments about Africa. Tony Banks was saying 'we', but Bobby has been a good friend of South Africa. So we had a go at him. Both Terry and myself had a go in the press and I know a few people in England were taken aback by what we said. Tony Banks dragged England down. A lot of people here asked me how England could do that and I didn't have an answer.

Sir Geoff shares Bailey's views on proper behaviour:

> Protocol in any sports-selling is to sell what you've got and not knock the opposition. I think that's the general good manners – or professionalism – of good selling: to sell your product – be it a tin of beans or a World Cup bid – and not knock the opposition. It's a very poor way of being an ambassador.

Hurst found Banks 'quite a lively character, to say the least,' but who knows whether he thought Banks had breached that code of conduct? I certainly never expected him to tell me. And Charlton did not consider himself 'an appropriate person to talk about Terry Paine.'

It seems that Sir Bobby continued to take it personally, though. Bailey recalls that, when 'he came out here afterwards, he was a bit cold towards me. We've since seen each other a few times and he's fine. The proof of the pudding for me was that, within six months, the Sports Council of the UK started trying to help South Africa. The Sports Minister's been out here a few times and there was a lot of Government input into building bridges, because I think they knew that they'd overstepped the mark, big-time.'

The issue, for Bailey and Paine, was that South Africa had impressed the FIFA inspection team more than England had and that the England team – well, Tony Banks – had 'tried to hide this by trashing us.'

The four ambassadors join the Minister of Sport, Ngconde Balfour, and two represent-atives of SAFA – Kaizer Motaung and Dr Irvin Khoza, owners of Kaizer Chiefs and Orlando Pirates, respectively – to welcome FIFA's Alan Rothenburg.

Back row (*left to right*): Milla, Bailey, Paine, Pelé, Motaung. Front: Balfour, Rothenburg, Khoza.

Terry is passionate about the South African bid in general and about the site inspection by FIFA, in particular. The inspection was conducted by a specialist team, as opposed to the 24 delegates who would be voting in Zurich. Their four-day visit is best left to Ambassador Paine to describe:

We obviously had problems with the conception of what South Africa was all about – especially the security issues – and Danny Joordan, who headed the bid-team, left no stone unturned, as far as proving our worth was concerned. He really was absolutely brilliant. He brought in the ministers at different functions, to let the inspectors see that the government were very much behind the bid; and he had back-up teams that were second-to-none. Starting in Johannesburg with a big banquet, we moved on from there. We did some coaching clinics in Soweto, which they came to view, and went to the telecommunication centres in other areas that they wished to visit, in and around Johannesburg. We conducted more clinics in Durban, prior to one of the big games of the season – Orlando Pirates and Sundowns – which, again, the delegation visited. Then we moved from there down to Cape Town where we met all the

parliamentarians. Nelson Mandela was there. They were absolutely gob-smacked at how warm the Big Man is and how he holds no bitterness about his time as a political prisoner.

When the FIFA delegation went to watch a game in Durban, Ambassador Paine sat with the Minister of Culture, Eileen Shandu.

Well, if that smacked the inspectorate in the gob, the hosts now went for the solar plexus. They took the team out to Robben Island to see where Mandela has been imprisoned. Terry recalls the visit to what had been Mandela's cell:

> Believe me, you'd be hard pushed to lie down in there, such was the size of his home for 18 of his 27 years in prison. It was that small. We looked out of his window, such as it was. Straight in front of him was another brick wall. That was his view for 18 years. Then we had the final press conference, where the Inspection Team summarised what they had seen. And, although they don't say yea or nay right there, they said that they had been satisfied. And then, to finish up their visit, the bid-ambassadors played a five-a-side on the patch where Nelson Mandela used to exercise – which went down extremely well.

I bet it did. So how come Germany got the 2006 World Cup? Amid all the complex politicking, the answer seems to come down to two key players: Sepp Blatter and Charles Dempsey.

Invited to the 2006 World Cup finals in Germany, as a guest of FIFA,
Terry Paine met up with Sepp Blatter (*left*), who had supported the South African cause,
and Franz Beckenbaeur, ambassador for the German bid.

Sepp Blatter, the FIFA president, who had openly backed the idea of taking the World Cup finals to Africa – Europe had held them nine times already – had apparently upset the Asians in 2002, by denying them an additional place in the final tournament in Japan and Korea. Which was enough, it seems, to hand the Asian votes to Germany, along with what amounted to a block vote, Scotland apart, from Europe: whatever the rights and wrongs of the allegations that England had broken a gentleman's agreement with Germany – as I say, you can always make up your own mind by reading the report of the House of Commons Committee – it seems that the mud had stuck.

All of which made the Scottish-born New Zealander, Charles Dempsey, the swing vote. Terry Paine is adamant that when he met the Oceania delegate in Malaysia,

> he made it clear that he would vote for England. He would hope that England would win it but, if they didn't and if England would fall away and not make the final vote, then the vote would come South Africa's way. I can see him now: those were his exact words to me. With England out, it was *mandated* by the Oceania Federation that he had to vote South Africa's way.

But he didn't. He abstained and Germany became the hosts for the 2006 finals of the World Cup. The fact that this gave South Africa four more years to prepare for the 2010 finals is another story.

The vote in Zurich is where we came in – 398 pages ago. As I explained on page 1, Terry thereupon flew to England, where he did two things that he's very good at: he talked authoritatively and passionately to the media about the Dempsey let-down; and he went to reunions, both with some of the ex-team-mates mentioned in previous chapters and with supporters' groups, from Bristol to the Isle of Wight.

Which is why I think of him as a Reunion Man and why the next, and final, chapter is devoted to that theme.

Chapter 28

Reunion Man

Many a reader will have his or her own memories of being at a gathering or two, in the last 20-odd years, when Terry Paine has come over from South Africa to be there.

I have a few such memories, dating back to the centenary dinner of Southampton FC in 1986. Recalling those occasions, and pondering photos of similar events that I'd missed, I came to the conclusion that I should round off this story of Terry's career by capturing a few highlights of homecomings by the 'Reunion Man'.

By way of introduction, though, let's consider a photo of a reunion in the 1960s, when Terry was the host. It shows Terry at his home in Bitterne, with his former classmate, Roy Igglesden, and two former Highcliffe Corinthians – Nicky Nickson, home from America, and Derek Igglesden – all wearing England caps.

Nicky needed a cap to go with the shirt that Terry presented to him in New York on the occasion (recorded in Chapter 11) of England's 10-0 win over the USA. Terry has been generous with his caps, the first of which he presented to the club in 2003 (of which more in a moment).

Nicky Nickson is home from America for a private,
Highcliffe Corinthians reunion at Terry Paine's home.
(*Left to right*): Derek Igglesden, Terry Paine, Nicky Nickson, Roy Igglesden.

Terry is reunited with Tracey (*left*) and Karen.

With Martin Chivers at the
centenary dinner.

On the pitch at the game
against Manchester United.

Having emigrated to the sunshine, Terry returned to a snowy England in February 1986. His purpose was to attend the centenary dinner of Southampton FC. He stayed long enough to watch a 1-0 win over Man Utd. Before the game, though, he had a major reunion – with his twin daughters, Tracey and Karen, whom he had not seen since 1970.

Tracey now decided to join her father in South Africa for a few years. Having met him briefly at the dinner – how long does it take to get a menu autographed? – I would not see him again to speak to, until 1997, when I interviewed him for *Dell Diamond*.

And speak we most certainly did. We had to stop after six hours, because a Winchester City historian was arriving to interview him, after which we had an appointment at the pub with a bunch of older Saints fans. By the time we left the pub, Terry had been with me for 11 hours. I would come to appreciate that this is what he so often does when he's over – generously giving up a whole day to be at the beck and call of fans wanting this, that or the other from him.

In the meantime, he had come over for a players-only gathering at The Dell, on the occasion of Ted Bates's retirement, at the age of 75, from the Board. Terry had so many eras of players with whom to re-unite, but I took a fancy to the shot of him with Arthur Holt, the former Saints and Hampshire all-rounder, who had got Terry playing for the county's Club and Ground XI in the 1960s.

By contrast, his 1998 visit, to celebrate Bates's first 60 seasons with the Saints, was very much an afternoon and evening with the fans. Paul Bennett, the ex-player who organised that event, was determined that it would be open to 'people like my mum.' A long day climaxed with some dream line-ups for the photographers, including a forward-line of Paine, Chivers, Davies, Channon and Sydenham – truly a 'dream' in so far as this line never turned out for the Saints. Terry was here, there and everywhere during dinner, not only re-uniting but introducing himself to men he'd never played with, notably Doug McGibbon, who had made his Saints debut six weeks after Terry was born.

Ted Bates's biographer was allowed to sneak into the fore-ground of this photograph of Ted with a 'dream' forward-line of (*left to right*) Paine, Chivers, Sydenham, Channon and Davies.

With cricketing mentor, Arthur Holt,
at Ted Bates's retirement dinner.

With Doug McGibbon at the 1998
celebration of Ted Bates's first 60 seasons.

Terry Paine and John Sydenham, who played over 600 first-team games, between them,
at The Dell, acknowledge the crowd at the last game there, on 26 May 2001.

The next major event was the leaving of The Dell in 2001. Terry and
John Sydenham felt they had to be there. And the crowd appreciated that.

The two ex-wingers were similarly moved to fly in for the FA Cup Final
in 2003 – Terry from South Africa, as ever, and John from Australia. Terry
brought along his *Super Saturday* colleague, Neil Andrews, and a cameraman.
Having filmed in Cardiff, as the fans arrived at the Millennium Stadium,
Terry and his crew watched the Saints lose 1-0 to Arsenal.

CONSTANT PAINE

Andrews recalls the walk from the stadium back to their car, some 90 minutes or so after the game:

> There were two Southampton fans, sitting on a wall. One guy jumped up off the wall and said 'Excuse me, are you Terry Paine?' And so Terry said 'ooh, yeah, yeah' [funny man Andrews does good impression of Paine's accent]. He says 'what happened, Terry?' Terry says [still in dialect] 'We weren't good enough. Arsenal were just too good.' And then the guy turned to his mate, who was still sitting on the wall, and gave him a friendly whack, with a back-hand. '*Stand up!*' he said. 'You're talking to a legend. It's Terry Paine.' That really put it into perspective. The other guy was miserable because they'd lost and he hadn't been listening, but he leapt up and said 'Terry Paine!' and was straight into the conversation, then. It was a lovely little touch – and when you think of how long Terry's been out of the UK, it's amazing that he hasn't lost that recognition and respect.

Not for some of us, it isn't. The crew moved on to St Mary's, on the Monday, for the presentation to the club of Terry's first England cap. It was a poignant occasion, the last appearance in public of the man for whom Terry had made 782 competitive appearances: club president, Ted Bates.

In his last official function as president of Southampton FC, Ted Bates accepts Terry Paine's first England cap, to be mounted in the Terry Paine Suite.

Above: Terry with Neil Andrews (*right*)
and cameraman, John Bescoby, at St Mary's.

Left: Terry interviews Toby Balding,
who trained his first horses,
sitting on seats retrieved from The Dell.

Their crew's itinerary took them, naturally enough, to the racing stables of Mick Channon and Toby Balding.

It is an indicator of Terry's status at Supersport that they sent a crew over to film him following the Saints to the Cup Final and visiting some horses. They did it again in 2007: we saw, in the previous chapter, how Terry's Saturday morning producer, Mario Lacueva, accompanied him, camera at the ready, to an ex-Saints dinner and other events.

There doesn't have to be an *event* to bring Terry to England. The previous chapter ended with Terry side-tripping from the fateful vote in Zurich in 2000. Even by his standards, he packed in a very full programme. His itinerary invariably entails staying with Trevor and his wife Linda, just up the road from Highcliffe; seeing Carol; visiting John Sillett, or meeting him at a favourite new Forest golfing pub; and often going to see Mary Penfold. And he still left time, on this occasion, to attend meetings of fans' groups, in Bristol and the Isle of Wight, and a Winchester evening, organised by Fred Norris, who had assembled many of the former neighbours and team-mates mentioned in Chapters 2-4.

Once a Saint, always a Saint!, Terry proclaimed, when speaking at the 1998 dinner for Ted Bates. Those sentiments are surely reflected in the occasions I have mentioned and illustrated above: quite simply, Terry expects to come home for just about any relevant reunion involving the Saints. I found the less formal Winchester evening a rewarding addition to the routine.

Return of the Native, Winchester 2000.
(*Left to right*): Ron Cook, Colin Holmes, Trevor Paine, Colin Thorne, Fred Norris,
Robin North, Norman Morris, Cladge Howard, Les Elms, Terry Paine, Keith Guppy,
John Johnson, Reg Grace, Pete Marston, Dick Collins, Phil Bumstead, Bob Collins.
All bar one of the above feature in chapters 2-4.

The Three W(h)ingers
(*Left to right*): Callaghan, Connelly and Paine

As a measure of how far Terry has come from those Winchester beginnings, though, I must mention two gatherings that place him in the pantheon of 20th century stars, whether domestic or international.

I referred in the last chapter to the FIFA event in 2006, to which all surviving members of World Cup-winning squads were invited. In his album of photos of him in Munich, with international stars, I especially liked the shot of the three wingers who played one game each in the final tournament of the 1966 World Cup. They got themselves a badge, saying 'Three Wingers', but somebody added an 'h'. Good for a laugh but, as we saw in Chapter 13, Terry does not whinge about Alf Ramsey's winglessness.

If that decision of Alf Ramsey's restricted him to 19 caps, it didn't stop Terry being invited to an even more exclusive gathering in 1999, when the Football League celebrated its centenary by naming 100 'legends' of the game, across the League's 100 years.

Tony Adams 1983 – 1998	Ivor Allchurch 1948 – 1964
Ossie Ardiles 1978 – 1990	Jimmy Armfield 1954 – 1971
Alan Ball 1962 – 1984	Gordon Banks 1958 – 1973
John Barnes 1981 – 1998	Billy Bassett 1888 – 1900
Cliff Bastin 1927 – 1948	Colin Bell 1963 – 1979
Dennis Bergkamp 1995 – 1998	George Best 1963 – 1983
Danny Blanchflower 1948 – 1964	Steve Bloomer 1892 – 1915
Liam Brady 1973 – 1990	Billy Bremner 1959 – 1982
Charles Buchan 1910 – 1929	George Camsell 1924 – 1939
Eric Cantona 1991 – 1997	John Carey 1937 – 1954
Raich Carter 1932 – 1953	John Charles 1948 – 1966
Bobby Charlton 1956 – 1975	Ray Clemence 1965 – 1988
Alf Common 1900 – 1915	Wilf Copping 1930 – 1939
Bob Crompton 1896 – 1921	Kenny Dalglish 1977 – 1990
Dixie Dean 1923 – 1939	Jim Dickinson 1946 – 1965
Peter Doherty 1933 – 1954	Ted Drake 1931 – 1939
Duncan Edwards 1953 – 1958	Tom Finney 1946 – 1960
Trevor Ford 1946 – 1961	Billy Foulke 1894 – 1908
Trevor Francis 1970 – 1995	Neil Franklin 1946 – 1958
Hughie Gallacher 1925 – 1939	Paul Gascoigne 1984 – 1998
Ryan Giggs 1990 – 1998	Johnny Giles 1959 – 1977
John Goodall 1888 – 1904	Jimmy Greaves 1957 – 1971
Alan Hansen 1977 – 1990	Eddie Hapgood 1927 – 1939
George Hardwick 1937 – 1956	Sam Hardy 1902 – 1926
Johnny Haynes 1952 – 1970	Harry Hibbs 1925 – 1939
Glenn Hoddle 1974 – 1996	Archie Hunter 1888 – 1891
Norman Hunter 1962 – 1983	Geoff Hurst 1959 – 1976
David Jack 1920 – 1935	Alex James 1925 – 1938
Pat Jennings 1962 – 1985	Cliff Jones 1952 – 1970
Kevin Keegan 1968 – 1984	Denis Law 1956 – 1974
Tommy Lawton 1935 – 1957	Billy Liddell 1946 – 1961
Gary Lineker 1978 – 1993	Nat Lofthouse 1946 – 1961
Dave Mackay 1958 – 1972	Wilf Mannion 1936 – 1956
Stanley Matthews 1931 – 1966	Bill McCracken 1904 – 1924
Malcolm MacDonald 1968 – 1977	Paul McGrath 1981 – 1998
Jimmy McIlroy 1950 – 1968	Frank McLintock 1959 – 1977
Joe Mercer 1932 – 1954	Billy Meredith 1893 – 1925
Jackie Milburn 1946 – 1957	Bobby Moore 1958 – 1977
Stan Mortensen 1938 – 1958	Alan Mullery 1958 – 1976
Terry Paine 1956 – 1977	Martin Peters 1960 – 1981
Alf Ramsey 1946 – 1955	Bryan Robson 1974 – 1997
Arthur Rowley 1946 – 1965	Ian Rush 1978 – 1990
Peter Schmeichel 1991 – 1998	Elisha Scott 1912 – 1934
Len Shackleton 1946 – 1958	Alan Shearer 1987 – 1998
Peter Shilton 1965 – 1997	Frank Swift 1933 – 1951
Tommy Smith 1962 – 1979	Graeme Souness 1972 – 1984
Neville Southall 1980 – 1998	Clem Stephenson 1910 – 1930
Nobby Stiles 1959 – 1974	Tommy Taylor 1950 – 1958
Bert Trautmann 1949 – 1964	Viv Woodward 1908 – 1915
Billy Wright 1946 – 1959	Alex Young 1960 – 1969

CONSTANT PAINE

Survivors and widows were invited to an 'Evening of Legends' at the *London Hilton* in Park Lane. I joined Terry for lunch and we were soon talking to Len Shackleton. Terry told Len that he had seen him star for Sunderland at Highbury in 1954 (on the Corries' outing mentioned in Chapter 2). Shackleton remembered the game.

One of my greatest pleasures in the course of football research is seeing an ex-player talking, in the role of a fan, to an older ex-player he'd watched. This conversation must have struck a chord with Shackleton, too. When his famous autobiography, *Clown Prince of Soccer*, was republished, updated, in 2000, he listed nine ex-players he had met at the event, including Paine – who, he added, 'even flew in specially from South Africa.'

Well, yes: as I say, *that* is what he does, flying in to meet ex-players – be it in a Winchester hall or the Park Lane *Hilton* – and invariably making the time to get among his fans. The publication of this biography will trigger a few such events, mainly in Winchester or Southampton, and he will be accosted by so many of those fans wanting to remind him of the pleasure he gave them, of how often they wanted to raise him high like the fans on the cover of this book.

And generally to thank him for being their **Constant Paine**.

Appendix 1

Paine's Pick

One of the standing jokes, among Terry's ex team-mates, is that he helped to pick the team at Southampton.

'Joke,' I hear some of them protest. '*What* joke?' Well, I look at this way: if you've read the chapters on Terry's time at The Dell, you'll have noticed that there were two or three players he didn't rate, but whom Ted Bates picked relentlessly. So much for Terry's opinion, then.

Terry does not deny that he spent more time than most in the manager's office, at what Hugh Fisher mischievously calls 'their own little team-meetings,' and he confirms that Ted would sometimes ask his opinion: 'we've got this problem; what do you think?' And there were times when Terry wouldn't wait to be asked. Especially when he had George O'Brien nudging him to help Ted understand what was needed to improve the service to the right-wing pair. But to suggest that Terry ever 'picked the team' is, as he puts it, 'degrading Ted Bates and what he was all about.'

One of the handicaps to any player venturing his thoughts to the manager is that he won't have spent the club's money on a new player, the way the manager has. If and when that newcomer disappoints, the players may mutter, but the manager, even though he may share at least some of their misgivings, has 'got to play' his acquisition, Terry reasons. 'He's got to justify buying him. If he leaves him out, what does that say about his judgment? We all do that: we all make mistakes.'

All of which explains why I think it's a *joke* – but a good one, at that. I realised that it had spread beyond Southampton when I met up with John Connelly and Roger Hunt. John told me how Roger had asked Terry, very dryly, when the Boys of '66 were FIFA's guests in Germany in 2006, 'Is it true, Terry, that Ted Bates sometimes helped you pick the team?' Connelly later repeated this crack to Brian O'Neil at a Burnley funeral and I was present when Brian recycled it to a group of ex-Saints, who then competed with assessments of how many times Terry had *dropped* them.

I love that kind of gallows humour among ex-players. But it's time to get serious. On this occasion, Terry *has* picked the team – with no help from anybody that I'm aware of. I left the formation to him and stepped aside.

So the next four pages are his alone…

CONSTANT PAINE

Terry Paine writes:

My team would play 4-4-2. This was always our formation: we never came away from that too much. In my time at Southampton, we could always score goals. We couldn't always defend, but we had players who could put the ball in the back of the net. You can call the formation what you want, but the emphasis, at the end of the day, is on having two wide players. That's what it's all about, really. It's the width that you worry about in a formation – whether you can get enough width at the right time.

I wanted to get as close as I could to representing all of the eras I played at Southampton. But trying to get everyone in was, of course, impossible. My selection has a bit of 'Ale House', with a lot of flair. I have seven subs on my bench, reflecting the latest arrangement in the Premiership, where my team would certainly be playing.

Campbell Forsyth came to us with a big reputation. I'd played against him, not long before, for England v Scotland. I was over the moon when he joined us. He was my kind of keeper: big and commanding.

My substitute 'keeper, *John Christie*, was what you might call a continental goalkeeper. He was very much a line 'keeper – very agile – and he could read the game extremely well. I could have picked Eric Martin or Tony Godfrey, but John left a good impression with me, the way he performed.

I like my full backs to be defence-minded. I know the modern aim is to get your full-backs down the line, but you can't tell me any of them crosses a decent ball in the Premiership, from those kinds of position. As far as I'm concerned, **Bob McCarthy** was one of the most brilliant readers of what was happening on the other side of the park and he would be on the cover, to mop up whatever came through. We had better players *on the ball* at right-back – Stuart Williams; Joe Kirkup – but I look for defensive qualities first and Bob's defensive qualities were excellent. He maybe didn't have enough confidence in himself – that may have been his biggest drawback – but, to my mind, he deserved a lot more games at right-back for Southampton.

My centre-backs would be **Jimmy Gabriel** and **David Webb**. Jimmy Gabriel was an absolute class act – an *outstanding* footballer. You could play him centre-forward; you could play him midfield. Wherever you played him, you'd always get a performance from Jim. A very intelligent player. And he *loved* to play – that's what I liked about him: he wanted to play but, more, he wanted to win.

David Webb was a great, strong character, excellent in the air. A good commander, in terms of organisation. He had the personality to organise things and he was a great asset when he came up for dead-ball situations. It was mainly his organisational skills and his big, strong character that I liked. I know he played mostly at right-back for Southampton, but we always said that centre-back was where he was needed most. He played a few games there in the promotion run-in of 1966, which suited those of us who had been on to Ted for ages to play him there, because David was more stable than Tony Knapp when the pressure was on.

Tony trained very hard and kept very fit, so he set a good example from that point of view. But he'd come to us with a reputation – a guy on the fringe of the England team – and I never felt he quite lived up to that. That's not a *criticism*; it's just an observation.

I know my selection means splitting the McGrath-Gabriel pairing that went down well with the fans, but John McGrath wasn't my type of player, overall. He was big and strong, very aggressive and good in the air, but I found him very one-pace; very one-dimensional.

My left-back, **Denis Hollywood**, would contribute to the fear factor, especially at home. You know, 'we don't want to go to The Dell: we know we're going to be in for a hard slog, today.' You need that within a team: you need a reputation for being very hard. Like McCarthy, you wouldn't expect Denis to get forward, but to do the defensive work. I liked his tenacity. I liked his will to win. I liked the fact that he hated losing. And he could certainly mix it with the best of them. You can't all be ball-players and great headers of the ball. The puzzle has to fit.

I guess some would have preferred Tommy Traynor. Tommy had his strengths: a lovely left foot and a great slide tackle – what was it Mick Channon said: that he could slide further than he could run? – and he gave great service. As the game quickened up, though, and players were a lot fitter, Tommy left a little bit to be desired.

Ken Wimshurst was extremely unlucky not to get an England call-up, about the same time as I did. A great passer of the ball, good vision, he always gave me good service and, at the end of the day, that was what was needed. You needed a midfielder who could pull the strings and get the ball in a position where we could go forward. Ken liked to get the ball and get forward and, like a few of us, his strength wasn't in chasing back. And we know he wasn't a great tackler or a good header, with a big engine. The manager is always looking for the perfect player, isn't he? But you don't get all of that in Ken's position – unless it's Duncan Edwards.

Hugh Fisher was, again, a bubbling kind of player. He was a bit more tenacious than Ken, but Ken was a bit smoother, silkier. If I have Ken in right midfield, though, I can't have *David Burnside* as left midfield. Two lovely players, two intelligent footballers, as we saw in the 1963 Cup-run, but too much of a muchness, really. I have to have one midfielder to complement the other. In central midfield, you need a grafter, somebody who can win the ball. Never forget: if you don't win the ball, you can't give it to those who can play. **Brian O'Neil** had the guts and determination to do that. Throughout his career, Brian put his heart on the line. David Burnside would give us a little bit more down the left than Brian but, as I say, I couldn't have him and Ken.

John Sydenham is another modern-day kind of player, with his tremendous pace. It always frightens full-backs, even in today's game. You've seen it with Theo Walcott. I know a lot of people have said that John's final pass was not as good as it should have been, but, again, you can't have everything, can you? His service wasn't as bad, anyhow, as some people said. His final ball may have been a little bit erratic, but he could take you so quickly from a defensive position to an attacking position. Ted Bates tried to vary it on the left, with Harry Penk and David Thompson. They were both decent players. They could certainly do a job, whether it was on the left side or the right side. David Thompson would probably have been a very decent player in today's game, where you need that industry up and down the line. You could see him working well within the team framework and Harry was in the same vein. They were very competent footballers, with good brains.

Mick Channon and **Ron Davies** would probably have been, on form, as good a striking partnership as the country has ever seen. If you can't go through people or round the side, and you have to go over the top, who better to have than Channon and Davies? Mick could get on the end of balls that you knocked over the top and Ron would be able to head them down. You can play pretty football – this, that and the other – but if it doesn't work, you've got to have that alternative, that 'out'; and we certainly had that at Southampton with those two. The magnificent Ron Davies and the very quick and mobile Mick Channon were a brilliant combination. It was an absolute pleasure to play with them when they were at their peak.

George O'Brien is never going to forgive me for starting with him on the bench but, in the modern game, he would have been the absolute *crème de la crème*, as far as substitutes are concerned. You could have brought him on and stuck him in there, particularly if you were on top – because a lot of teams are on top but can't find the finish – and I can assure you George would have found one for you, somewhere. He was magnificent in and around the penalty box, absolutely magnificent.

I always thought *Martin Chivers* was an outstanding player, and he went on to prove that at Spurs. But we had the *best* in Mick Channon and Ron Davies and I wouldn't split those two up. What a combination O'Brien and Chivers would be, though, to have on your bench.

I'd also have *Bobby Stokes* and *Tony Byrne*. Bobby was a brilliant one-touch player. Again, he would have been an ideal substitution, the way that he came off defenders and brought you into the game. And he wasn't a bad goal scorer himself. He obviously had a different physique from Channon, Chivers and Davies, but at times you just need a variation to get a result and I believe he could give us that variation. And he was a tremendous *team*-player, prepared to run his socks off for you – and that was really appreciated by those who played with him. One of the nicest guys you'll ever meet.

Tony Byrne was under-rated. He was quick; he was aggressive. If you needed, as the game went on, to push Jimmy Gabriel forward and bring somebody on at the back, Tony Byrne could deal with that quite comfortably. Again, I'm not looking for his strength on the ball, but his strength *off* the ball: so quick and aggressive.

I've said George O'Brien wouldn't forgive me for not starting him. He wouldn't be the only one, but that's fine by me. If there's anything about them, players are always a bit miffed if they're not in the team. That's a natural reaction: 'I think I'm better than him.' That's human nature and I accept that.

What I always say is that, if you get the chance to come in, do the things that you should do and you hold your place. Managers pick players whom they can trust. They pick those players in front of other players they aren't 100 per cent sure of.

I've picked players that I could trust. I'd go into the trenches with them.

Appendix 2

The Statistics

This appendix, compiled by **Dave Juson with Gary Chalk**, records Terry Paine's appearances and goals in the Football League and those Cup competitions that involve League clubs.

So games for Southampton in the Southern Professional Floodlight Cup, and for Hereford United in the Welsh Cup, are included; but matches for Cheltenham Town in the Southern League or Southern League Cup are not.

Paine did, however, play three games for Cheltenham in the FA Cup. These are included in a final table devoted to his 62 appearances in that competition.

Friendly games, such as testimonials and tour games, are not included.

The FA Cup table has a key of its own. The key to the other tables is as follows:

- *Shading*: League games are shown in standard black-on-white. Cup competitions, of any kind, are in rows, shaded grey.
- *Shirt numbers*: An **X**, in lieu of a shirt number, indicates a missed game.
- *Reason for not playing*: The final column shows whether Paine was on England duty, suspended, 'retired' (for two games) or known to be injured. The remaining 'missed' games are labelled 'omitted', indicating that he was not in the starting line-up and, that if he was on the bench, he did not come on.
- *Milestones:* The final column indicates the main career milestones.

Abbreviations:

SPFC	Southern Professional Floodlight Cup	Rd	Round
ICFC	Inter-Cities Fairs Cup	SF	Semi-Final
Apps	Appearances		

1956-57 Division III South - Southampton

Date	H/A	Opponent			shirt no	goals	
16-Mar	H	Brentford	3	3	11		
23-Mar	A	Aldershot	1	1	11	1	
26-Mar	A	Reading	4	2	11	1	
30-Mar	H	Watford	3	1	11		
04-Apr	A	Newport County	3	2	X		Omitted
06-Apr	A	Shrewsbury Town	0	0	X		Omitted
13-Apr	H	Walsall	3	1	X		Omitted
19-Apr	A	Torquay United	0	2	X		Omitted
20-Apr	A	Swindon Town	0	0	11		
22-Apr	H	Torquay United	1	0	11		
27-Apr	A	Watford	2	4	11		
01-May	H	Ipswich Town	0	2	11		
04-May	H	Newport County	3	0	7		

	Season		Accumulative	
	Apps	**Goals**	**Apps**	**Goals**
League	9	2	9	2

1957-58 Division III South - Southampton

Date	Venue	Opponent			shirt no	goals	Notes
24-Aug	A	Millwall	2	1	7		
28-Aug	H	Walsall	4	1	7		
31-Aug	H	Gillingham	5	1	7	1	
05-Sep	A	Walsall	1	1	7	1	
07-Sep	A	Exeter City	2	2	7		
11-Sep	H	Port Vale	0	3	7		
14-Sep	H	Queen's Park Rangers	5	0	7	1	
16-Sep	A	Port Vale	0	4	7		
21-Sep	A	Southend United	2	3	7		
25-Sep	H	Plymouth Argyle	0	1	7		
28-Sep	H	Brighton & Hove Albion	5	0	7		
30-Sep	A	Plymouth Argyle	0	4	7		
05-Oct	H	Bournemouth & Boscombe Athletic	7	0	7		
09-Oct	H	Swindon Town	1	3	7		
12-Oct	A	Coventry City	0	0	7		
19-Oct	H	Shrewsbury Town	2	2	11	1	
26-Oct	A	Reading	0	1	7		
28-Oct	H	Luton Town	0	2	11		SPFC Rd 1
02-Nov	H	Northampton Town	2	1	7		
09-Nov	A	Watford	0	3	7		
16-Nov	A	Walton & Hersham	6	1	7		FA Cup Rd 1
23-Nov	A	Torquay United	1	1	7		
30-Nov	H	Brentford	4	2	7		
07-Dec	A	Crystal Palace	0	1	7		FA Cup Rd 2
14-Dec	H	Norwich City	7	3	7	2	
21-Dec	H	Millwall	3	2	7		
25-Dec	A	Aldershot	5	1	7	1	
26-Dec	H	Aldershot	2	2	7	1	
28-Dec	A	Gillingham	1	2	7	1	
04-Jan	A	Newport County	1	1	7		
11-Jan	H	Exeter City	6	0	7		
18-Jan	A	Queen's Park Rangers	2	3	7		
25-Jan	H	Crystal Palace	2	1	7	1	
01-Feb	H	Southend United	2	2	7		
08-Feb	A	Brighton & Hove Albion	1	1	7		
15-Feb	A	Bournemouth & Boscombe Athletic	2	5	7		
22-Feb	H	Coventry City	7	1	X		Omitted. Played for Reserves at Coventry
01-Mar	A	Shrewsbury Town	3	1	7		
08-Mar	H	Reading	0	1	7		
15-Mar	A	Northampton Town	3	1	X		Omitted
22-Mar	H	Torquay United	4	2	7	1	
29-Mar	A	Norwich City	2	0	7		
05-Apr	H	Watford	5	0	7		
07-Apr	A	Swindon Town	0	1	7		
12-Apr	A	Brentford	0	0	7		
19-Apr	H	Colchester United	3	2	7		
23-Apr	H	Newport County	2	1	7		
26-Apr	A	Crystal Palace	4	1	7	1	
01-May	A	Colchester United	2	4	7		

	Season		Accumulative	
	Apps	Goals	Apps	Goals
League	44	12	53	14
FA Cup	2		2	
SPFC	1		1	
Total	47	12	56	14

1958-59 Division III - Southampton

Date	H/A	Opponent			shirt no	goals	Notes
23-Aug	A	Mansfield Town	6	1	7	1	
25-Aug	A	Chesterfield	3	3	7	1	
30-Aug	H	Swindon Town	1	1	7		
01-Sep	H	Chesterfield	0	0	7		
06-Sep	A	Brentford	0	2	7		
08-Sep	A	Halifax Town	0	2	7		
13-Sep	H	Hull City	6	1	7	1	
17-Sep	H	Halifax Town	5	0	7		
20-Sep	A	Bradford City	3	2	7	1	
25-Sep	A	Notts County	2	1	7	1	
27-Sep	H	Wrexham	1	2	7		
01-Oct	H	Notts County	3	0	7		
04-Oct	H	Reading	3	3	7		
08-Oct	A	Accrington Stanley	0	0	7		
11-Oct	A	Bournemouth & Boscombe Athletic	1	2	7		
18-Oct	H	Norwich City	1	1	7		
25-Oct	A	Southend United	1	1	7		
27-Oct	H	Watford	0	0	7		SPFC Rd 1
01-Nov	H	Bury	4	2	7		
04-Nov	A	Watford	3	2	7		SPFC Rd 1, replay
08-Nov	A	Queen's Park Rangers	2	2	7		
15-Nov	H	Woking	4	1	7	1	FA Cup Rd 1
22-Nov	A	Tranmere Rovers	0	2	7		
29-Nov	H	Plymouth Argyle	5	1	7	2	
06-Dec	A	Queen's Park Rangers	1	0	7		FA Cup Rd 2
13-Dec	H	Stockport County	2	1	7		
20-Dec	H	Mansfield Town	3	2	7		
25-Dec	A	Newport County	2	4	7		
27-Dec	H	Newport County	3	3	7	2	
03-Jan	A	Swindon Town	1	3	7		
10-Jan	H	Blackpool	1	2	7		FA Cup Rd 3
18-Feb	A	Luton Town	0	4	7		SPFC Rd 2
24-Jan	A	Doncaster Rovers	2	3	7		
31-Jan	A	Hull City	0	3	7		
02-Feb	H	Rochdale	6	1	7		
07-Feb	H	Bradford City	1	2	7	1	
14-Feb	A	Wrexham	3	1	7		
21-Feb	A	Reading	1	4	7		
28-Feb	H	Bournemouth & Boscombe Athletic	0	0	7		
07-Mar	A	Norwich City	1	3	7	1	
09-Mar	H	Brentford	0	6	7		
14-Mar	H	Southend United	3	2	7		
21-Mar	A	Bury	0	1	7		
27-Mar	A	Colchester United	3	1	7	1	100th game - all competitions
28-Mar	H	Queen's Park Rangers	1	0	7		
30-Mar	H	Colchester United	3	0	7		
04-Apr	A	Rochdale	0	1	7		
11-Apr	H	Tranmere Rovers	2	3	7	1	
18-Apr	A	Plymouth Argyle	0	1	7		
22-Apr	H	Accrington Stanley	3	1	7		
25-Apr	A	Doncaster Rovers	1	1	7		
27-Apr	A	Stockport County	0	4	7		

	Season		Accumulative	
	Apps	Goals	Apps	Goals
League	46	13	99	27
FA Cup	3	1	5	1
SPFC	3		4	
Total	52	14	108	28

1959-60 Division III - Southampton

Date	H/A	Opponent			shirt no	goals	Notes
22-Aug	H	Norwich City	2	2	7		100th League game
24-Aug	A	Chesterfield	2	3	7		
29-Aug	A	Brentford	2	2	7	1	
02-Sep	H	Chesterfield	4	3	7		
05-Sep	H	Colchester United	4	2	7	1	
07-Sep	A	Port Vale	1	1	7		
12-Sep	A	Southend United	4	2	7		
16-Sep	H	Port Vale	3	2	7		
19-Sep	H	Mansfield Town	5	2	7		
23-Sep	H	Shrewsbury Town	6	3	7	1	
26-Sep	A	Halifax Town	1	3	7		
28-Sep	A	Shrewsbury Town	1	1	7	1	
03-Oct	H	Bury	0	2	7		
07-Oct	A	Barnsley	0	1	11		
10-Oct	H	Swindon Town	5	1	8	1	
14-Oct	H	Barnsley	2	1	8		
17-Oct	A	York City	2	2	7		
24-Oct	H	Coventry City	5	1	7		
26-Oct	H	Aldershot	3	0	7	2	SPFC Rd 1
31-Oct	A	Accrington Stanley	2	2	7		
07-Nov	H	Queen's Park Rangers	2	1	7		
14-Nov	A	Coventry City	1	1	7		FA Cup Rd 1
18-Nov	H	Coventry City	5	1	7	1	FA Cup Rd 1, replay
21-Nov	H	Wrexham	3	0	7		
28-Nov	A	Tranmere Rovers	4	2	7	1	
05-Dec	H	Southend United	3	0	7	2	FA Cup Rd 2
12-Dec	A	Bradford City	0	2	7		
14-Dec	A	Crystal Palace	2	2	7		SPFC Rd 2
19-Dec	A	Norwich City	2	1	7		
26-Dec	H	Newport County	2	0	7		
02-Jan	H	Brentford	2	0	7		
09-Jan	A	Manchester City	5	1	7		FA Cup Rd 3
18-Jan	H	Crystal Palace	2	1	7		SPFC Rd 2, replay
23-Jan	H	Southend United	3	1	7	1	
30-Jan	H	Watford	2	2	7		FA Cup Rd 4
02-Feb	A	Watford	0	1	7		FA Cup Rd 4, replay
06-Feb	A	Mansfield Town	2	4	7	1	
13-Feb	H	Halifax Town	3	2	7		
20-Feb	A	Bury	2	1	7		
24-Feb	H	Bournemouth & Boscombe Athletic	4	3	7		
27-Feb	A	Swindon Town	3	0	7		
05-Mar	H	York City	3	1	7		
07-Mar	A	Newport County	1	5	7		
12-Mar	A	Coventry City	1	4	7		
19-Mar	H	Tranmere Rovers	1	1	7		
21-Mar	A	Colchester United	1	1	7		
26-Mar	A	Queen's Park Rangers	1	0	7		
28-Mar	A	Coventry City	1	2	X		SPFC SF - omitted
02-Apr	H	Grimsby Town	1	1	7		
09-Apr	A	Wrexham	1	2	7		
15-Apr	A	Reading	0	2	7		
16-Apr	H	Accrington Stanley	5	1	7		
18-Apr	H	Reading	1	0	7		
23-Apr	A	Bournemouth & Boscombe Athletic	3	1	7		
26-Apr	A	Grimsby Town	2	3	7		
30-Apr	H	Bradford City	2	0	7		

	Season		Accumulative	
	Apps	Goals	Apps	Goals
League	46	8	145	35
FA Cup	6	3	11	4
SPFC	3	2	7	2
Total	**55**	**13**	**163**	**41**

1960-61 Division II - Southampton

Date		Opponent			shirt no	goals	
20-Aug	A	Rotherham United	0	1	7		
24-Aug	H	Liverpool	4	1	7	1	
27-Aug	H	Portsmouth	5	1	7	1	
31-Aug	A	Liverpool	1	0	7		
03-Sep	H	Leeds United	2	4	7	1	
07-Sep	H	Derby County	5	1	7	1	
10-Sep	A	Middlesbrough	0	5	7		
14-Sep	H	Derby County	2	2	7	1	
17-Sep	H	Brighton & Hove Albion	4	2	7		
24-Sep	A	Ipswich Town	3	3	7	2	
01-Oct	H	Scunthorpe United	4	2	7	1	
08-Oct	A	Huddersfield Town	1	3	7		
10-Oct	A	Newport County	2	2	7	1	League Cup Rd 1
15-Oct	H	Sunderland	3	2	7		
17-Oct	H	Newport County	2	2	7		League Cup Rd 1, replay
22-Oct	A	Plymouth Argyle	3	1	7	1	
26-Oct	H	Newport County	5	3	7	2	League Cup Rd 1, 2nd replay
29-Oct	H	Norwich City	2	2	7		
31-Oct	A	Colchester United	2	0	7	1	League Cup Rd 2
05-Nov	A	Charlton Athletic	3	1	7		
12-Nov	H	Sheffield United	0	1	7		
16-Nov	A	Liverpool	2	1	7	2	League Cup Rd 3
19-Nov	A	Stoke City	2	1	7		
26-Nov	H	Swansea Town	5	0	7	2	
03-Dec	A	Luton Town	1	4	7		
05-Dec	H	Leeds United	5	4	7		League Cup Rd 4
10-Dec	H	Lincoln City	2	3	7		
17-Dec	H	Rotherham United	3	2	7	1	
26-Dec	H	Bristol Rovers	4	2	7		
31-Dec	A	Portsmouth	1	1	7		
07-Jan	H	Ipswich Town	7	1	7	1	FA Cup Rd 3
14-Jan	A	Leeds United	0	3	7		
21-Jan	H	Middlesbrough	3	2	7	1	
28-Jan	H	Leyton Orient	0	1	7		FA Cup Rd 4
04-Feb	A	Brighton & Hove Albion	1	0	7		
06-Feb	H	Burnley	2	4	7		League Cup Rd 5
11-Feb	H	Ipswich Town	1	1	7		200th game - all competitions
18-Feb	A	Scunthorpe United	0	2	7		
25-Feb	H	Huddersfield Town	4	2	7	1	
11-Mar	H	Plymouth Argyle	1	1	7		
18-Mar	A	Lincoln City	3	0	7	1	
20-Mar	A	Bristol Rovers	2	4	7	1	
25-Mar	H	Charlton Athletic	1	2	7	1	
29-Mar	A	Leyton Orient	1	1	7		
01-Apr	A	Swansea Town	1	4	7		
03-Apr	H	Leyton Orient	1	1	7		
08-Apr	H	Stoke City	0	1	7		
15-Apr	A	Sheffield United	1	2	7		
17-Apr	A	Sunderland	1	3	7		
22-Apr	H	Luton Town	3	2	7	1	
29-Apr	A	Norwich City	0	5	7		

	Season		Accumulative	
	Apps	Goals	Apps	Goals
League	42	18	187	53
FA Cup	2	1	13	5
League Cup	7	6	7	6
SPFC			7	2
Total	**51**	**25**	**214**	**66**

1961-62 Division II - Southampton

Date	H/A	Opponent			shirt no	goals	Notes
19-Aug	H	Plymouth Argyle	1	2	7		
21-Aug	A	Leyton Orient	3	1	7		
26-Aug	A	Huddersfield Town	0	1	7		
30-Aug	H	Leyton Orient	1	2	7		
02-Sep	H	Swansea Town	5	1	7	2	
06-Sep	H	Walsall	1	1	7		
09-Sep	A	Bury	2	0	7		
13-Sep	H	Rochdale	0	0	7		League Cup Rd 1
16-Sep	A	Luton Town	4	1	7		
19-Sep	A	Walsall	2	0	7		
23-Sep	H	Newcastle United	1	0	7		
27-Sep	A	Rochdale	1	2	7		League Cup Rd 1, replay
30-Sep	A	Middlesbrough	1	1	7		
07-Oct	H	Brighton & Hove Albion	6	1	7	2	
13-Oct	A	Scunthorpe United	1	5	7	1	200th League Game
18-Oct	H	Preston North End	0	0	7		
21-Oct	H	Norwich City	2	2	7		
28-Oct	A	Leeds United	1	1	7		
04-Nov	H	Bristol Rovers	0	2	8		
18-Nov	H	Sunderland	2	0	X		Suspended
25-Nov	A	Rotherham United	2	4	7		
02-Dec	H	Liverpool	2	0	7		
09-Dec	A	Stoke City	2	3	7		
16-Dec	A	Plymouth Argyle	0	4	7		
23-Dec	H	Huddersfield Town	3	1	7		
26-Dec	A	Derby County	1	1	7		
30-Dec	H	Derby County	2	1	7		
06-Jan	H	Sunderland	2	2	7		FA Cup Rd 3
10-Jan	A	Sunderland	0	3	7		FA Cup Rd 3, replay
13-Jan	A	Swansea Town	1	0	7		
20-Jan	H	Bury	5	3	7		
03-Feb	H	Luton Town	3	0	7		
10-Feb	A	Newcastle United	2	3	7	1	
21-Feb	H	Middlesbrough	1	3	10		
24-Feb	A	Brighton & Hove Albion	0	0	7		
03-Mar	H	Scunthorpe United	6	4	11	2	
06-Mar	A	Charlton Athletic	0	1	11		
10-Mar	A	Norwich City	1	1	11		
17-Mar	H	Leeds United	4	1	8		
24-Mar	A	Bristol Rovers	0	1	11		
31-Mar	H	Charlton Athletic	1	2	7		
07-Apr	A	Sunderland	0	3	7		
14-Apr	H	Rotherham United	2	1	7		
21-Apr	A	Liverpool	0	2	7		
23-Apr	A	Preston North End	1	1	11		
28-Apr	H	Stoke City	5	1	11		

	Season		Accumulative	
	Apps	Goals	Apps	Goals
League	41	8	228	61
FA Cup	2		15	5
League Cup	2		9	6
SPFC			7	2
Total	**45**	**8**	**259**	**74**

1962-63   Division II - Southampton

Date	H/A	Opponent			shirt no	goals	
18-Aug	A	Scunthorpe United	1	2	7		
22-Aug	H	Luton Town	2	2	7		
25-Aug	H	Bury	0	3	7		
29-Aug	A	Luton Town	2	3	7	1	
01-Sep	A	Rotherham United	0	2	11		
08-Sep	H	Charlton Athletic	1	0	10		
10-Sep	A	Chelsea	0	2	10		
15-Sep	A	Stoke City	1	3	10		
19-Sep	H	Chelsea	2	1	10		
22-Sep	H	Sunderland	2	4	10		
26-Sep	H	Scunthorpe United	1	1	10	1	League Cup Rd 2
29-Sep	A	Leeds United	1	1	7		
02-Oct	A	Scunthorpe United	2	2	7	1	League Cup Rd 2, replay
06-Oct	H	Preston North End	1	0	7		
09-Oct	N	Scunthorpe United	0	3	7		League Cup Rd 2, 2nd replay
13-Oct	A	Portsmouth	1	1	7		
27-Oct	A	Huddersfield Town	3	2	7		
31-Oct	H	Cardiff City	3	5	7		
03-Nov	H	Middlesbrough	6	0	7	1	
10-Nov	A	Derby County	1	3	7	1	
17-Nov	H	Newcastle United	3	0	7		
24-Nov	A	Walsall	1	1	7		
01-Dec	H	Norwich City	3	1	7		
08-Dec	A	Grimsby Town	1	4	7		
15-Dec	H	Scunthorpe United	1	1	7		
26-Dec	A	Swansea Town	1	1	7		
13-Feb	H	York City	5	0	7		FA Cup Rd 3
23-Feb	A	Preston North End	0	1	7		
27-Mar	H	Watford	3	1	7		FA Cup Rd 4
02-Mar	H	Portsmouth	4	2	7	1	
09-Mar	A	Cardiff City	1	3	7		
16-Mar	H	Sheffield United	1	0	7		FA Cup Rd 5
20-Mar	H	Huddersfield Town	3	1	7		
23-Mar	A	Middlesbrough	2	1	7		
30-Mar	A	Nottingham Forest	1	1	7	1	FA Cup Rd 6
06-Apr	A	Newcastle United	1	4	7		
03-Apr	H	Nottingham Forest	3	3	7		FA Cup Rd 6, replay
08-Apr	N	Nottingham Forest	5	0	7		FA Cup Rd 6, 2nd replay
12-Apr	A	Plymouth Argyle	1	2	7		
13-Apr	H	Walsall	2	0	7		
15-Apr	H	Plymouth Argyle	1	1	7		300th game - all competitions
20-Apr	A	Norwich City	0	1	7		
22-Apr	H	Swansea Town	3	0	7	2	
27-Apr	N	Manchester United	0	1	7		FA Cup SF
01-May	H	Derby County	5	0	7		
04-May	A	Sunderland	0	4	7		
07-May	A	Bury	1	1	7		
11-May	H	Rotherham United	1	0	7		
13-May	H	Grimsby Town	4	1	7		
15-May	H	Leeds United	3	1	7	1	
18-May	A	Charlton Athletic	1	2	7	1	
20-May	H	Stoke City	2	0	7	2	

	Season		Accumulative	
	Apps	Goals	Apps	Goals
League	42	10	270	71
FA Cup	7	1	22	6
League Cup	3	2	12	8
SPFC			7	2
Total	**52**	**13**	**311**	**87**

1963-64 Division II - Southampton

Date	H/A	Opponent			shirt no	goals	Notes
24-Aug	H	Charlton Athletic	6	1	7		
28-Aug	H	Huddersfield Town	1	1	7		
31-Aug	A	Grimsby Town	2	2	7		
03-Sep	A	Huddersfield Town	0	4	7		
07-Sep	H	Preston North End	4	5	7		
11-Sep	A	Newcastle United	2	2	7		
14-Sep	A	Leyton Orient	0	1	7		
18-Sep	H	Newcastle United	2	0	7		
21-Sep	H	Swansea Town	4	0	7	1	
25-Sep	A	Tranmere Rovers	0	2	7		League Cup Rd 1
28-Sep	A	Portsmouth	0	2	7		
01-Oct	A	Rotherham United	3	2	7	3	
05-Oct	A	Middlesbrough	0	1	7		
19-Oct	A	Norwich City	1	1	7	1	
26-Oct	H	Leeds United	1	4	7		
02-Nov	A	Swindon Town	2	1	7	1	
09-Nov	H	Manchester City	4	2	7		
23-Nov	H	Northampton Town	3	1	7	2	
30-Nov	A	Sunderland	2	1	7		
07-Dec	H	Cardiff City	3	2	7	1	
14-Dec	A	Charlton Athletic	2	2	7		
21-Dec	H	Grimsby Town	6	0	7		
26-Dec	H	Plymouth Argyle	1	2	7		
28-Dec	A	Plymouth Argyle	1	1	7		
04-Jan	H	Manchester United	2	3	7	1	FA Cup Rd 3
11-Jan	A	Preston North End	1	2	7	1	
18-Jan	H	Leyton Orient	3	0	7	1	
29-Jan	H	Scunthorpe United	7	2	7		
08-Feb	H	Portsmouth	2	3	7	1	100th goal - all competitions
15-Feb	H	Middlesbrough	2	2	7	1	
22-Feb	A	Scunthorpe United	2	1	7		
29-Feb	H	Bury	0	1	7		300th League Game
03-Mar	A	Swansea Town	0	6	7		
07-Mar	A	Leeds United	1	3	7		
21-Mar	A	Manchester City	1	1	7		
28-Mar	H	Norwich City	3	0	7		
30-Mar	A	Derby County	2	3	7		
01-Apr	H	Derby County	6	4	7	3	
04-Apr	A	Northampton Town	0	2	7		
11-Apr	H	Sunderland	0	0	X		England v Scotland
18-Apr	A	Cardiff City	4	2	7		
21-Apr	A	Bury	5	1	7	2	
25-Apr	H	Swindon Town	5	1	7	1	
27-Apr	H	Rotherham United	6	1	7	2	Scores Saints' 100th goal of season

	Season		Accumulative	
	Apps	Goals	Apps	Goals
League	41	21	311	92
FA Cup	1	1	23	7
League Cup	1		13	8
SPFC			7	2
Total	43	22	354	109

1964-65 Division II - Southampton

Date	H/A	Opponent			shirt no	goals	Notes
22-Aug	H	Middlesbrough	0	3	7		
26-Aug	H	Bolton Wanderers	3	2	7	1	
29-Aug	A	Newcastle United	1	2	7		
02-Sep	A	Bolton Wanderers	0	3	7		
05-Sep	H	Northampton Town	2	0	7		
12-Sep	A	Portsmouth	3	0	7	1	
16-Sep	H	Preston North End	3	1	7		
19-Sep	A	Huddersfield Town	3	0	7		
23-Sep	H	Cardiff City	3	2	7	1	League Cup Rd 2
26-Sep	H	Coventry City	4	1	7	2	
10-Oct	H	Manchester City	1	0	7		
13-Oct	A	Swindon Town	1	2	7		
17-Oct	A	Charlton Athletic	5	2	7	1	
24-Oct	H	Leyton Orient	2	2	7		
26-Oct	A	Crystal Palace	0	2	7		League Cup Rd 3
30-Oct	A	Bury	3	3	7	1	
02-Nov	A	Preston North End	0	0	7		
07-Nov	H	Crystal Palace	0	1	7		
14-Nov	A	Norwich City	2	2	7		
21-Nov	H	Rotherham United	6	1	7		
28-Jan	A	Swansea Town	3	3	7	1	
05-Dec	H	Derby County	3	3	7	3	Opener was 100th League goal
12-Dec	A	Middlesbrough	1	4	7	1	
19-Dec	H	Newcastle United	0	1	7		
26-Dec	H	Plymouth Argyle	5	0	7		
02-Jan	A	Northampton Town	2	2	7		
09-Jan	H	Leyton Orient	3	1	7		FA Cup Rd 3
16-Jan	H	Portsmouth	2	2	7		
23-Jan	H	Huddersfield Town	3	3	7	1	
30-Jan	H	Crystal Palace	1	2	7		FA Cup Rd 4
06-Feb	A	Coventry City	1	1	7		
13-Feb	H	Cardiff City	1	1	7		
17-Feb	A	Plymouth Argyle	0	4	7		
20-Feb	H	Manchester City	1	3	7		
27-Feb	H	Charlton Athletic	4	0	7		
06-Mar	A	Derby County	1	2	7		
13-Mar	H	Bury	3	1	7		
20-Mar	A	Crystal Palace	2	0	7		
24-Mar	A	Cardiff City	2	2	7		
27-Mar	H	Norwich City	1	0	7		
04-Apr	A	Rotherham United	3	1	7		
10-Apr	H	Swansea Town	3	1	7	1	
17-Apr	A	Leyton Orient	0	0	7		
19-Apr	A	Ipswich Town	0	2	7		
21-Apr	H	Ipswich Town	1	1	7		
24-Apr	H	Swindon Town	2	1	7	1	400th game - all competitions

	Season		Accumulative	
	Apps	Goals	Apps	Goals
League	42	14	353	106
FA Cup	2		25	7
League Cup	2	1	15	9
SPFC			7	2
Total	46	15	400	124

1965-66 Division II - Southampton

Date		Opponent			shirt no	goals	
21-Aug	A	Derby County	3	0	7		
25-Aug	H	Carlisle United	1	0	7		
28-Aug	H	Portsmouth	2	2	7		
31-Aug	A	Carlisle United	0	1	7		
04-Sep	H	Bury	6	2	7		
08-Sep	H	Coventry City	1	0	7		
11-Sep	A	Norwich City	4	3	7	1	
14-Sep	A	Coventry City	1	5	7	1	
18-Sep	H	Wolverhampton Wanderers	9	3	7	2	
25-Sep	A	Rotherham United	0	1	7		
29-Sep	H	Rochdale	3	0	7		League Cup Rd 2
02-Oct	H	Manchester City	0	1	X		England v Wales
09-Oct	A	Bolton Wanderers	3	2	7		
13-Oct	A	Burnley	2	3	7	1	League Cup Rd 3
16-Oct	H	Ipswich Town	1	2	9		
23-Oct	A	Birmingham City	1	0	7		
30-Oct	H	Leyton Orient	1	0	X		Injured
06-Nov	A	Middlesbrough	0	0	7		
13-Nov	H	Huddersfield Town	0	1	7		
20-Nov	A	Crystal Palace	0	1	7		
27-Nov	H	Preston North End	5	2	7		
04-Dec	A	Charlton Athletic	2	2	7		
11-Dec	H	Plymouth Argyle	4	1	7	1	
18-Dec	A	Ipswich Town	0	3	7		
27-Dec	A	Cardiff City	5	3	7	2	
01-Jan	H	Bolton Wanderers	5	1	7		
08-Jan	A	Huddersfield Town	0	2	7		
22-Jan	A	Hull City	0	1	7		FA Cup Rd 3
29-Jan	H	Derby County	3	1	7		
05-Feb	A	Portsmouth	5	2	7		
19-Feb	A	Bury	3	1	7		
26-Feb	H	Norwich City	2	2	7		
05-Mar	H	Birmingham City	0	1	7		
12-Mar	A	Wolverhampton Wanderers	1	1	7		
19-Mar	H	Rotherham United	1	1	7	1	
02-Apr	H	Middlesbrough	3	1	7	2	
08-Apr	A	Bristol City	1	0	7		
11-Apr	H	Bristol City	2	2	7	1	
16-Nov	H	Crystal Palace	1	0	7		
20-Nov	H	Cardiff City	3	2	7	2	
23-Nov	A	Preston North End	1	1	7		
30-Nov	H	Charlton Athletic	1	0	7	1	
07-May	A	Plymouth Argyle	3	2	7	1	
09-May	A	Leyton Orient	1	1	7	1	
16-May	A	Manchester City	0	0	7		

	Season		Accumulative	
	Apps	Goals	Apps	Goals
League	40	16	393	122
FA Cup	1		26	7
League Cup	2	1	17	10
SPFC			7	2
Total	**43**	**17**	**443**	**141**

1966-67 Division I - Southampton

Date	H/A	Opponent			shirt no	goals	Notes
20-Aug	H	Manchester City	1	1	7	1	
24-Aug	A	Sunderland	0	2	7		
27-Aug	A	Blackpool	3	2	7		
31-Aug	H	Sunderland	3	1	7	1	
03-Sep	H	Chelsea	0	3	7		
05-Sep	A	Aston Villa	1	0	7		
10-Sep	A	Leicester City	1	1	7		400th League Game
14-Sep	H	Plymouth Argyle	4	3	7	1	League Cup Rd 2
17-Sep	H	Liverpool	1	2	7		
24-Sep	A	West Ham United	2	2	7		
01-Oct	H	Sheffield Wednesday	4	2	7		
05-Oct	H	Carlisle United	3	3	7		League Cup Rd 3
08-Oct	H	Sheffield United	2	3	7		
12-Oct	A	Carlisle United	1	2	7		League Cup Rd 3, replay
15-Oct	A	Stoke City	2	3	7		
25-Oct	H	Everton	1	3	7		
29-Oct	A	Leeds United	1	0	7		
05-Nov	H	Stoke City	3	2	7	1	
12-Nov	A	Burnley	1	4	7	1	
19-Nov	H	Manchester United	1	2	7		
26-Nov	A	Tottenham Hotspur	3	5	7	1	
03-Dec	H	Newcastle United	2	0	7		
10-Dec	A	Fulham	1	3	7	1	
17-Dec	H	Manchester City	1	1	7		
26-Dec	A	Arsenal	1	4	7		
27-Dec	H	Arsenal	2	1	7	1	
31-Dec	H	Blackpool	1	5	7		
07-Jan	A	Chelsea	1	4	7		
14-Jan	H	Leicester City	4	4	7		
21-Jan	A	Liverpool	1	2	7		
28-Jan	A	Barrow	2	2	7		FA Cup Rd 3
01-Feb	H	Barrow	3	0	7		FA Cup Rd 3, replay
04-Feb	H	West Ham United	6	2	7	2	
11-Feb	A	Sheffield Wednesday	1	4	7		
18-Feb	A	Bristol City	0	1	7		FA Cup Rd 4
25-Feb	A	Sheffield United	0	2	7		
04-Mar	H	Leeds United	0	2	7		
18-Mar	A	Everton	1	0	7		
25-Mar	H	Fulham	4	2	7	1	
27-Mar	A	West Bromwich Albion	2	3	7		
29-Mar	H	West Bromwich Albion	2	2	7		
01-Apr	A	Nottingham Forest	1	3	7		
08-Apr	H	Burnley	4	0	7		
18-Apr	A	Manchester United	0	3	7		
22-Apr	H	Tottenham Hotspur	0	1	7		
29-Apr	A	Newcastle United	1	3	7		
06-May	H	Nottingham Forest	2	1	7	1	
13-May	H	Aston Villa	6	2	7		

	Season		Accumulative	
	Apps	Goals	Apps	Goals
League	42	11	435	133
FA Cup	3		29	7
League Cup	3	1	20	11
SPFC			7	2
Total	48	12	491	153

1967-68 Division I - Southampton

Date	H/A	Opponent			shirt no	goals	Notes
19-Aug	A	Newcastle United	0	3	7		
23-Aug	H	Manchester City	3	2	7		
26-Aug	H	West Bromwich Albion	4	0	7	1	
30-Aug	A	Manchester City	2	4	7		
02-Sep	A	Chelsea	6	2	7		
05-Sep	A	Coventry City	1	2	7		
09-Sep	H	Leeds United	1	1	7		
16-Sep	H	Liverpool	1	0	7		
12-Sep	A	Ipswich Town	2	5	7		League Cup Rd 2 - 500th game all competitions
23-Sep	A	Stoke City	2	3	7		
30-Sep	H	Nottingham Forest	2	1	7	1	
07-Oct	A	Everton	2	4	7		
14-Oct	H	Leicester City	1	5	7		
23-Oct	A	West Ham United	1	0	7	1	
28-Oct	H	Burnley	2	2	7		
04-Nov	A	Sheffield Wednesday	0	2	7		
11-Nov	H	Tottenham Hotspur	1	2	7		
18-Nov	A	Manchester United	2	3	7		
25-Nov	H	Sunderland	3	2	7	1	
02-Dec	A	Wolverhampton Wanderers	0	2	7		
16-Dec	H	Newcastle United	0	0	7		
23-Dec	A	West Bromwich Albion	0	0	7		
26-Dec	H	Sheffield United	3	3	7	1	
30-Dec	A	Sheffield United	1	4	7		
06-Jan	H	Chelsea	3	5	7		
13-Jan	A	Leeds United	0	5	7		
20-Jan	A	Liverpool	0	2	7		
27-Jan	H	Newport County	1	1	7		FA Cup Rd 3
30-Jan	A	Newport County	3	2	7		FA Cup Rd 3, replay
03-Feb	H	Stoke City	1	2	10		
10-Feb	A	Nottingham Forest	2	2	10		
17-Feb	A	West Bromwich Albion	1	1	10		FA Cup Rd 4
21-Feb	H	West Bromwich Albion	2	3	10		FA Cup Rd 4, replay
26-Feb	H	Everton	3	2	10		
02-Mar	A	Sunderland	3	0	10	1	
08-Mar	H	Fulham	2	1	10		
16-Mar	H	West Ham United	0	0	10		
23-Mar	A	Burnley	0	2	10		
30-Mar	H	Sheffield Wednesday	2	0	10	1	
06-Apr	A	Tottenham Hotspur	1	6	10		
10-Apr	H	Arsenal	2	0	7		
13-Apr	H	Manchester United	2	2	7	1	
15-Apr	A	Arsenal	3	0	7	1	
20-Apr	A	Leicester City	1	4	7		
27-Apr	H	Wolverhampton Wanderers	1	1	7		
04-May	A	Fulham	2	2	7		
11-May	H	Coventry City	0	0	X		Suspended

	Season		Accumulative	
	Apps	Goals	Apps	Goals
League	41	9	476	142
FA Cup	4		33	7
League Cup	1		21	11
SPFC			7	2
Total	46	9	537	162

CONSTANT PAINE

1968-69		Division I - Southampton			shirt no	goals	
10-Aug	H	Leeds United	1	3	7		
14-Aug	H	Liverpool	2	0	7	1	
17-Aug	A	Sunderland	0	1	7		
20-Aug	A	Burnley	1	3	7		
24-Aug	H	Wolverhampton Wanderers	2	1	7	1	
28-Aug	A	Stoke City	2	0	7	1	
31-Aug	H	Leicester City	1	3	7		
04-Sep	H	Crewe Alexandra	3	1	7		League Cup Rd 2
07-Sep	H	Arsenal	1	2	7	1	
14-Sep	A	Manchester City	1	1	7		
21-Sep	H	Ipswich Town	2	2	7		
25-Sep	A	Newcastle United	4	1	7		League Cup Rd 3
28-Sep	A	Queen's Park Rangers	1	1	7	1	
05-Oct	A	West Ham United	0	0	7		
09-Oct	A	Stoke City	0	1	7		
12-Oct	H	Everton	2	5	7		
16-Oct	A	Norwich City	4	0	7		League Cup Rd 4
19-Oct	A	Manchester United	2	1	7		
26-Oct	H	Sheffield Wednesday	1	1	7		
30-Oct	H	Tottenham Hotspur	0	1	7		League Cup Rd 5
02-Nov	A	Coventry City	1	1	7	1	
09-Nov	H	West Bromwich Albion	2	0	7		
16-Nov	A	Chelsea	3	2	7		
23-Nov	H	Tottenham Hotspur	2	1	7		
30-Nov	A	Newcastle United	1	4	7	1	
03-Dec	A	Liverpool	0	1	7		
07-Dec	H	Nottingham Forest	1	1	7		
14-Dec	A	Everton	0	1	7		500th League game
21-Dec	H	Manchester United	2	0	7		
26-Dec	H	West Ham United	2	2	7		
28-Dec	A	Sheffield Wednesday	0	0	7		
04-Jan	A	Oxford United	1	1	7		FA Cup Rd 3
08-Jan	H	Oxford United	2	0	7	2	FA Cup Rd 3, replay
11-Jan	H	Coventry City	1	0	7		
18-Jan	A	West Bromwich Albion	2	1	7		
25-Jan	H	Aston Villa	2	2	7		FA Cup Rd 4
29-Jan	A	Aston Villa	1	2	7		FA Cup Rd 4, replay
01-Feb	H	Chelsea	5	0	7		
15-Feb	A	Newcastle United	0	0	7		
01-Mar	A	Leeds United	2	3	7		
08-Mar	H	Sunderland	1	0	7		
11-Mar	A	Nottingham Forest	0	1	7		
15-Mar	A	Wolverhampton Wanderers	0	0	7		
22-Mar	H	Leicester City	1	0	7		
29-Mar	A	Arsenal	0	0	7		
05-Apr	H	Queen's Park Rangers	3	2	7		
07-Apr	H	Burnley	5	1	7	1	150th League goal
12-Apr	A	Ipswich Town	0	0	7		
19-Apr	H	Manchester City	3	0	7	1	
22-Apr	A	Tottenham Hotspur	1	2	7		

	Season		Accumulative	
	Apps	Goals	Apps	Goals
League	42	9	518	151
FA Cup	4	2	37	9
League Cup	4		25	11
SPFC			7	2
Total	50	11	587	173

426

1969-70 Division I - Southampton

Date		Opponent			shirt no	goals	
09-Aug	H	West Bromwich Albion	0	2	7		
13-Aug	A	Wolverhampton Wanderers	1	2	7		
16-Aug	A	Manchester United	4	1	7		
20-Aug	H	Wolverhampton Wanderers	2	3	7		
23-Aug	H	Chelsea	2	2	7	1	
27-Aug	A	Ipswich Town	4	2	7		
30-Aug	H	Stoke City	1	2	7		
02-Sep	H	Arsenal	1	1	7		League Cup Rd 2
04-Sep	A	Arsenal	0	2	7		League Cup Rd 2, replay
06-Sep	H	Burnley	1	1	7		
10-Sep	A	Derby County	0	3	7		
13-Sep	A	Nottingham Forest	1	2	7	1	
17-Sep	A	Rosenborg	0	1	7		Europe (ICFC) Rd 1, 1st leg
20-Sep	H	Newcastle United	1	1	7		
27-Sep	A	Everton	2	4	7		
01-Oct	H	Rosenborg	2	0	7	1	Europe (ICFC) Rd 1, 2nd leg (agg 2-1)
04-Oct	H	Tottenham Hotspur	2	2	7		
08-Oct	H	Manchester United	0	3	7		
11-Oct	A	Sheffield Wednesday	1	1	7		
18-Oct	H	Coventry City	0	0	7		
25-Oct	A	Liverpool	1	4	7		
01-Nov	H	West Ham United	1	1	7		
04-Nov	A	Vitoria Guimaraes	3	3	7	1	Europe (ICFC) Rd 2, 1st leg
08-Nov	A	Manchester City	0	1	7		
12-Nov	H	Vitoria Guimaraes	5	1	7		Europe (ICFC) Rd 2, 2nd leg (agg 8-4)
15-Nov	H	Leeds United	1	1	7		
22-Nov	A	Sunderland	2	2	7		
29-Nov	H	Crystal Palace	1	1	7		
06-Dec	A	Arsenal	2	2	7		
13-Dec	H	Nottingham Forest	1	2	7		
17-Dec	A	Newcastle United	0	0	7		Europe (ICFC) Rd 3, 1st leg
26-Dec	A	Chelsea	1	3	7		
27-Dec	H	Stoke City	0	0	10		
03-Jan	H	Newcastle United FAC 3	3	0	10		FA Cup Rd 3
14-Jan	H	Newcastle United	1	1	7		Europe (ICFC) Rd 3, 2nd leg (agg 1-1, lost on pens)
17-Jan	H	Everton	2	1	7		
24-Jan	H	Leicester City	1	1	7		FA Cup Rd 4
28-Jan	A	Leicester City	2	4	7	1	FA Cup Rd 4, replay
31-Jan	A	Tottenham Hotspur	1	0	7		
07-Feb	H	Sheffield Wednesday	4	0	7	1	
11-Feb	A	Newcastle United	1	2	X		Injured
20-Feb	A	West Bromwich Albion	0	1	7		
28-Feb	A	West Ham United	0	0	7		
07-Mar	H	Sunderland	1	1	X		Suspended (three weeks)
11-Mar	H	Liverpool	0	1	X		
14-Mar	A	Crystal Palace	0	2	X		
21-Mar	H	Arsenal	0	2	X		
24-Mar	A	Burnley	1	1	7		
28-Mar	A	Leeds United	3	1	X		Injured
31-Mar	A	Coventry City	0	4	7		
04-Apr	A	Ipswich Town	0	2	7		
08-Apr	H	Manchester City	0	0	10		
15-Apr	H	Derby County	1	1	10		

	Season		Accumulative	
	Apps	Goals	Apps	Goals
League	36	3	554	154
FA Cup	3	1	40	10
League Cup	2		27	11
Europe	6	2	6	2
SPFC			7	2
Total	**47**	**6**	**634**	**179**

1970-71 Division I - Southampton

					shirt no	goals	
15-Aug	H	Manchester City	1	1	7		
18-Aug	A	Huddersfield Town	1	3	7		
22-Aug	A	Coventry City	0	1	X		Injured
25-Aug	H	Tottenham Hotspur	0	0	7		
29-Aug	H	Ipswich Town	1	0	7		
31-Aug	A	West Ham United	1	1	7		
05-Sep	A	Blackpool	3	0	7		
09-Sep	A	Leicester City	0	1	7		League Cup Rd 2
12-Sep	H	Derby County	4	0	7		
19-Sep	A	Leeds United	0	1	7		
29-Sep	H	Liverpool	1	0	7		
03-Oct	A	Crystal Palace	1	3	7		
10-Oct	H	Wolverhampton Wanderers	1	2	7		
17-Oct	A	Manchester City	1	1	7		
24-Oct	H	Burnley	2	0	7		
31-Oct	A	Chelsea	2	2	7		
07-Nov	H	Newcastle United	2	0	7		
14-Nov	A	West Bromwich Albion	0	1	7		
21-Nov	H	Manchester United	1	0	7		
28-Nov	A	Stoke City	0	0	7		
05-Dec	H	Nottingham Forest	4	1	7		
12-Dec	A	Everton	1	4	7		
19-Dec	H	Coventry City	3	0	7		
26-Dec	A	Arsenal	0	0	7		
09-Jan	H	Huddersfield Town	1	0	7	1	
11-Jan	H	Bristol City	3	0	7		FA Cup Rd 3
16-Jan	A	Tottenham Hotspur	3	1	7		
23-Jan	A	York City	3	3	7		FA Cup Rd 4
30-Jan	H	Stoke City	2	1	7		
01-Feb	A	York City	3	2	7		FA Cup Rd 4, replay
06-Feb	A	Nottingham Forest	0	2	7		
13-Feb	A	Liverpool	0	1	7		FA Cup Rd 5
16-Feb	H	Everton	2	2	7		
20-Feb	A	Manchester United	1	5	7		
27-Mar	H	Chelsea	0	0	7		
06-Mar	A	Burnley	1	0	7		
13-Mar	H	West Bromwich Albion	1	0	7	1	
20-Mar	A	Newcastle United	2	2	7		
27-Mar	H	Blackpool	1	1	7		
03-Apr	A	Ipswich Town	3	1	7		
10-Apr	H	Arsenal	1	2	7	1	
12-Apr	A	Derby County	0	0	7		
17-Apr	A	Wolverhampton Wanderers	1	0	7		
24-Apr	H	Leeds United	0	3	7		
27-Apr	H	West Ham United	1	2	7		
01-May	A	Liverpool	0	1	7		
04-May	H	Crystal Palace	6	0	7		

	Season		Accumulative	
	Apps	Goals	Apps	Goals
League	41	3	595	157
FA Cup	4		44	10
League Cup	1		28	11
Europe			6	2
SPFC			7	2
Total	**46**	**3**	**680**	**182**

1971-72 Division I - Southampton

Date	H/A	Opponent			shirt no	goals	Notes
14-Aug	A	Sheffield United	1	3	7		
17-Aug	H	Stoke City	3	1	7		
21-Aug	H	Ipswich Town	0	0	7		
24-Aug	A	Nottingham Forest	3	2	7		
28-Aug	A	Derby County	2	2	7		600th League appearance
01-Sep	A	Leicester City	1	0	7		
04-Sep	H	Huddersfield Town	1	2	7		
07-Sep	H	Everton	2	1	7	1	League Cup Rd 2
11-Sep	A	Liverpool	0	1	7		
15-Sep	H	Atletico Bilbao	2	1	7		Europe (UEFA Cup) Rd 1, 1st leg
18-Sep	H	Coventry City	3	1	7	1	
25-Sep	A	Manchester City	0	3	7		
29-Sep	A	Atletico Bilbao	0	2	7		Europe (UEFA Cup) Rd 1, 2nd leg (agg 2-3)
02-Oct	H	Arsenal	0	1	7		
05-Oct	A	Liverpool	0	1	7		League Cup Rd 3
09-Oct	A	Wolverhampton Wanderers	2	4	7		
16-Oct	H	Sheffield United	3	2	7		
23-Oct	A	Chelsea	0	3	7		
30-Oct	H	West Bromwich Albion	1	1	7		
06-Nov	A	Newcastle United	1	3	7		
13-Nov	H	Leeds United	2	1	7		
20-Nov	A	Everton	0	8	7		
27-Nov	H	Manchester United	2	5	7		
04-Dec	A	Tottenham Hotspur	0	1	7		
11-Dec	H	West Ham United	3	3	7	1	
18-Dec	A	Huddersfield Town	2	0	7		
27-Dec	H	Crystal Palace	1	0	7		
01-Jan	A	Coventry City	0	1	7		
08-Jan	H	Derby County	1	2	7		
15-Jan	H	Manchester United	1	1	7		FA Cup Rd 3
19-Jan	A	Manchester United	1	4	7		FA Cup Rd 3, replay
22-Jan	A	Stoke City	1	3	7		
29-Jan	H	Nottingham Forest	4	1	7		
19-Feb	A	West Bromwich Albion	2	3	7		
26-Feb	H	Newcastle United	1	2	7		
04-Mar	A	Leeds United	0	7	7		Substituted
11-Mar	H	Wolverhampton Wanderers	1	2	7		
18-Mar	A	Ipswich Town	1	1	11		
25-Mar	H	Liverpool	0	1	11		Substituted
28-Mar	A	Arsenal	0	1	12		Substitute for Gilchrist
01-Apr	H	Crystal Palace	3	2	12		Substitute for Stokes
04-Apr	A	Manchester City	2	0	X		Injured
08-Apr	H	Everton	0	1	12		Substitute for Gabriel
11-Apr	H	Leicester City	1	0	11		
15-Apr	A	Manchester United	2	3	X		Injured
18-Apr	H	Chelsea	2	2	11		
22-Apr	H	Tottenham Hotspur	0	0	11		
01-May	A	West Ham United	0	1	7		

	Season		Accumulative	
	Apps	Goals	Apps	Goals
League	37 (+3)	2	632 (+3)	159
FA Cup	2		46	10
League Cup	2	1	30	12
Europe	2		8	2
SPFC			7	2
Total	**43 (+3)**	**3**	**723 (+3)**	**185**

CONSTANT PAINE

1972-73		Division I - Southampton	shirt no	goals		
12-Aug	H	Derby County	1	1	X	Suspended
15-Aug	H	Stoke City	1	0	X	Suspended
19-Aug	A	Coventry City	1	1	X	Omitted (captain, Reserves - 7-1 win v Bristol City)
23-Aug	A	Norwich City	0	0	X	Omitted
26-Aug	H	Wolverhampton Wanderers	1	1	7	
30-Aug	A	Leeds United	0	1	11	
02-Sep	A	Sheffield United	1	3	12	Substitute for Stokes
05-Sep	H	Chester City	0	0	7	League Cup Rd 2
09-Sep	H	Ipswich Town	1	2	7	
13-Sep	A	Chester City	2	2	7	League Cup Rd 2, replay
16-Sep	A	Everton	1	0	X	Omitted
20-Sep	N	Chester City	2	0	7	League Cup Rd 2, 2nd replay
23-Sep	H	Crystal Palace	2	0	7	
30-Sep	A	Arsenal	0	1	7	
03-Oct	H	Notts County	1	3	7	1 League Cup Rd 3
07-Oct	A	Leicester City	0	1	7	
14-Oct	H	Liverpool	1	1	7	
21-Oct	A	Birmingham City	1	1	7	
28-Oct	H	West Bromwich Albion	2	1	7	
04-Nov	H	Norwich City	1	0	7	
11-Nov	A	Stoke City	3	3	7	
18-Nov	H	Chelsea	3	1	7	
25-Nov	H	Manchester United	1	2	7	
02-Dec	H	Tottenham Hotspur	1	1	7	
09-Dec	A	Newcastle United	0	0	7	
16-Dec	A	Manchester City	1	2	7	
23-Dec	H	West Ham United	0	0	7	
26-Dec	A	Crystal Palace	0	3	7	
30-Dec	H	Coventry City	2	1	7	
06-Jan	A	Wolverhampton Wanderers	1	0	7	
13-Jan	A	Crystal Palace	0	2	7	FA Cup Rd 3
20-Jan	H	Sheffield United	1	1	7	
27-Jan	A	Ipswich Town	2	2	7	
10-Feb	H	Everton	0	0	7	
17-Feb	A	Derby County	0	4	7	
03-Mar	H	Leicester City	0	0	7	
06-Mar	H	Manchester City	1	1	7	
10-Mar	A	Liverpool	2	3	7	
17-Mar	H	Birmingham City	2	0	7	
24-Mar	A	West Bromwich Albion	1	1	7	
31-Mar	H	Manchester United	0	2	7	
07-Apr	A	Tottenham Hotspur	2	1	7	
14-Apr	H	Newcastle United	1	1	7	
20-Apr	H	West Ham United	3	4	7	
21-Apr	A	Chelsea	1	2	7	
23-Apr	H	Arsenal	2	2	7	
28-Apr	H	Leeds United	3	1	7	

	Season		Accumulative	
	Apps	Goals	Apps	Goals
League	36 (+1)		668 (+4)	159
FA Cup	1		47	10
League Cup	4	1	34	13
Europe			8	2
SPFC			7	2
Total	**41 (+1)**	**1**	**764 (+4)**	**186**

1973-74 Division I - Southampton

			shirt no		goals		
25-Aug	A	Queen's Park Rangers	1	1	7		
29-Aug	A	Newcastle United	1	0	7		
01-Sep	H	Wolverhampton Wanderers	2	1	7		
04-Sep	H	Norwich City	2	2	7		
08-Sep	A	Coventry City	0	2	7		
12-Sep	H	Norwich City	0	2	7		
15-Sep	H	Leeds United	1	2	7		
22-Sep	A	Derby County	2	6	7		
29-Sep	H	Sheffield United	3	0	7		
06-Oct	A	Manchester City	1	1	7		Substituted
08-Oct	H	Charlton Athletic	3	0	7		League Cup Rd 2 - Substituted
13-Oct	H	Liverpool	1	0	7		
20-Oct	H	Stoke City	3	0	7	1	
27-Oct	A	Leicester City	1	0	7		
30-Oct	H	Chesterfield	3	0	7		League Cup Rd 3
03-Nov	H	Burnley	2	2	7		
10-Nov	A	Birmingham City	1	1	7		Final game for Ted Bates (782 +4)
17-Nov	H	Tottenham Hotspur	1	1	7		
21-Nov	H	Norwich City	0	2	7		League Cup Rd 4
24-Nov	A	Chelsea	0	4	7		
01-Dec	H	Everton	2	0	7		Substituted
08-Dec	A	Manchester United	0	0	7		
15-Dec	H	Ipswich Town	2	0	7		Substituted
22-Dec	A	Sheffield United	2	4	7		
26-Dec	H	Arsenal	1	1	7		
29-Dec	H	Coventry City	1	1	7		
01-Jan	A	Wolverhampton Wanderers	1	2	7		
05-Jan	H	Blackpool	2	1	7	1	FA Cup Rd 3
12-Jan	A	Leeds United	1	2	7		
19-Jan	H	Queen's Park Rangers	2	2	7		
26-Jan	H	Bolton Wanderers	3	3	7		FA Cup Rd 4
30-Jan	A	Bolton Wanderers	2	0	7		FA Cup Rd 4, replay. 800th game - all competitions
02-Feb	A	Ipswich Town	0	7	7		
05-Feb	H	Newcastle United	3	1	7		700th League game
16-Feb	H	Wrexham	0	1	7		FA Cup Rd 5
23-Feb	H	Manchester City	0	2	7		
26-Feb	A	Liverpool	0	1	7		
02-Mar	A	Arsenal	0	1	7		
05-Mar	H	Derby County	1	1	7		Substituted
16-Mar	A	Stoke City	1	4	7		
18-Mar	H	Leicester City	1	0	7		
23-Mar	H	Birmingham City	0	2	7		Paine's 35th birthday
06-Apr	H	Chelsea	0	0	7		
12-Apr	A	West Ham United	1	4	7		
13-Apr	A	Tottenham Hotspur	1	3	7		Substituted
15-Apr	H	West Ham United	1	1	7		
20-Apr	H	Manchester United	1	1	7		
22-Apr	A	Burnley	0	3	7		Substituted
27-Apr	A	Everton	3	0	X		Injured

	Season			Accumulative	
	Apps	Goals		Apps	Goals
League	41	1		709 (+4)	160
FA Cup	4	1		51	11
League Cup	3			37	13
Europe				8	2
SPFC				7	2
Total	**48**	**2**	**Southampton Totals >**	**812 (+4)**	**188**

1974-75 Division III - Hereford United

Date	Venue	Opponent			shirt no	goals	Notes
17-Aug	H	Aldershot	2	0	8		
21-Aug	H	Shrewsbury	1	1	8		League Cup Rd 1
24-Aug	A	Charlton Athletic	0	2	8		
27-Aug	A	Shrewsbury	1	0	8	1	League Cup Rd 1, replay
31-Aug	H	Peterborough United	2	0	8		
04-Sep	H	Watford	0	1	8		
07-Sep	A	Walsall	1	3	8		
11-Sep	A	Exeter City	1	0	8		League Cup Rd 2
14-Sep	H	AFC Bournemouth	0	1	8		
18-Sep	H	Crystal Palace	2	0	8		
21-Sep	A	Port Vale	0	3	8		
24-Sep	A	Plymouth Argyle	0	1	X		Omitted
28-Sep	H	Chesterfield	5	0	8	1	
02-Oct	A	Watford	1	1	8		
05-Oct	H	Preston North End	2	2	8		
08-Oct	A	Ipswich Town	1	4	8		League Cup Rd 3
12-Oct	A	Gillingham	3	2	8	1	
19-Oct	H	Halifax Town	0	0	8		
23-Oct	H	Colchester United	3	1	7		
25-Oct	A	Southend United	0	1	7		
02-Nov	H	Huddersfield Town	1	1	7		
06-Nov	A	Colchester United	2	1	7		
09-Nov	A	Wrexham	1	2	7		
13-Nov	H	Barry Town	1	0	X		Welsh Cup Rd 3 - omitted
16-Nov	H	Brighton & Hove Albion	2	0	7		
26-Nov	H	Gillingham	1	0	7		FA Cup Rd 1
29-Nov	A	Tranmere Rovers	1	6	7		
07-Dec	H	Swindon Town	2	1	7		
14-Dec	A	Cambridge United	0	2	7		FA Cup Rd 2
21-Dec	H	Blackburn Rovers	6	3	8		
26-Dec	A	AFC Bournemouth	1	2	7		
28-Dec	H	Bury	1	1	7		
04-Jan	A	Crystal Palace	2	2	8		
11-Jan	A	Swindon Town	0	1	8		
14-Jan	A	Cardiff City	0	2	7		Welsh Cup Rd 4
18-Jan	H	Tranmere Rovers	2	0	8		Substituted
01-Feb	H	Wrexham	1	0	8		
08-Feb	A	Huddersfield Town	1	2	8		
15-Feb	H	Grimsby Town	3	2	8		
22-Feb	A	Brighton & Hove Albion	1	2	8		
01-Mar	A	Peterborough United	1	1	8		
04-Mar	A	Grimsby Town	0	0	8		
08-Mar	H	Plymouth Argyle	1	5	X		Injured
15-Mar	A	Chesterfield	1	4	X		Suspended
19-Mar	A	Aldershot	2	2	X		Suspended
22-Mar	H	Walsall	2	0	7		
28-Mar	A	Bury	0	3	7		
29-Mar	A	Blackburn Rovers	0	1	X		Omitted
31-Mar	H	Port Vale	1	0	X		Omitted
05-Apr	H	Southend United	1	0	8		
12-Apr	A	Preston North End	2	2	7		750th League game
19-Apr	H	Gillingham	1	1	8		
23-Apr	H	Charlton Athletic	2	2	7	1	
26-Apr	A	Halifax Town	2	2	7	1	

	Season		Accumulative (Hereford)		Accumulative Totals	
	Apps	Goals	Apps	Goals	Apps	Goals
League	40	4	40	4	749 (+4)	164
FA Cup	2		2		53	11
League Cup	4	1	4	1	41	14
Welsh Cup	1		1		1	
Europe					8	2
SPFC					7	2
Total	47	5	47	5	859 (+4)	193

1975-76 Division III - Hereford United

Date	H/A	Opponent	shirt no	goals		Notes
16-Aug	H	Port Vale	0	0	7	
18-Aug	A	Port Vale	2	4	7	League Cup Rd 1, 1st leg
23-Aug	A	Rotherham United	1	1	12	Substitute for McNeil
27-Aug	H	Port Vale	2	0	12	League Cup Rd 1, 2nd leg - substitute for Layton
30-Aug	H	Sheffield Wednesday	3	1	X	Omitted
01-Sep	N	Port Vale	1	0	12	1	League Cup Rd 1, replay - substitute for Davey
06-Sep	A	Millwall	0	1	12	Substitute for Redrobe
10-Sep	H	Burnley	1	4	9	League Cup Rd 2
13-Sep	H	Colchester United	0	0	8	
20-Sep	A	Chesterfield	3	2	7	
24-Sep	H	Swindon Town	1	0	7	
27-Sep	H	Gillingham	1	1	7	
04-Oct	A	Chester City	1	0	7	
11-Oct	H	Wrexham	2	0	7	
18-Oct	A	Halifax Town	1	0	7	
21-Oct	A	Crystal Palace	2	2	7	
25-Oct	H	Peterborough United	2	4	7	Beats Dickinson's record
01-Nov	A	Preston North End	4	3	7	
08-Nov	H	Grimsby Town	3	2	7	
12-Nov	A	Stourbridge	2	1	X	Welsh Cup Rd 3 - omitted
22-Nov	H	Torquay United	2	0	7	FA Cup Rd 1 - substituted
29-Nov	H	Bury	2	0	7	
06-Dec	A	Brighton & Hove Albion	2	4	8	
13-Dec	A	Bournemouth	2	2	7	FA Cup Rd 2
17-Dec	H	Bournemouth	2	0	7	FA Cup Rd 2, replay
20-Dec	A	Aldershot	2	0	7	
26-Dec	H	Walsall	1	3	7	
27-Dec	A	Shrewsbury	1	2	7	Substituted
03-Jan	A	York City	1	2	7	FA Cup Rd 3
10-Jan	A	Sheffield Wednesday	2	1	7	
17-Jan	H	Chesterfield	4	2	7	
19-Jan	A	Newport County	2	1	X	Welsh Cup Rd 4 - omitted
24-Jan	A	Colchester United	4	1	7	Substituted
26-Jan	A	Southend United	3	1	7	Substituted
31-Jan	H	Crystal Palace	1	1	7	
04-Feb	H	Cardiff City	4	1	7	Substituted
07-Feb	A	Mansfield Town	2	2	8	Substituted
11-Feb	H	Mansfield Town	1	0	7	
14-Feb	A	Grimsby Town	0	1	7	
18-Feb	H	Porthmadog	4	0	X	Welsh Cup Rd 5 - omitted
21-Feb	H	Southend United	2	1	7	
24-Feb	A	Swindon Town	1	0	7	
27-Feb	A	Peterborough United	3	0	7	
10-Mar	H	Chester City	5	0	7	
13-Mar	A	Wrexham	1	2	7	
17-Mar	H	Halifax Town	1	2	7	Substituted
20-Mar	A	Bury	3	2	7	
23-Mar	H	Shrewsbury	1	1	X	Welsh Cup SF - omitted
27-Mar	H	Brighton & Hove Albion	1	1	7	
31-Mar	H	Aldershot	2	1	7	1	
03-Apr	A	Port Vale	1	1	7	Substituted
06-Apr	H	Gillingham	4	3	X	Injured
08-Apr	A	Shrewsbury	1	1	X	Welsh Cup SF, replay - omitted (5-4 on pens)
10-Apr	H	Millwall	0	0	12	Substitute for Redrobe
14-Apr	A	Cardiff City	0	2	7	Substituted
17-Apr	A	Walsall	0	0	7	
19-Apr	H	Shrewsbury	3	1	7	Substituted
24-Apr	H	Rotherham United	3	2	7	Substituted
28-Apr	H	Preston North End	3	1	12	Substitute for Spiring
18-May	H	Cardiff City	3	3	7	1	Welsh Cup Final, 1st leg
19-May	A	Cardiff City	2	3	7	Welsh Cup Final, 2nd leg

	Season		Accumulative (Hereford)		Accumulative Totals	
	Apps	Goals	Apps	Goals	Apps	Goals
League	40 (+4)	1	80 (+4)	5	789 (+8)	165
FA Cup	4		6		57	11
League Cup	2 (+2)	1	6 (+2)	2	43 (+2)	15
Welsh Cup	2		3		3	
Europe					8	2
SPFC					7	2
Total	48 (+6)	2	95 (+6)	7	907 (+10)	195

1976-77		Division II - Hereford United	shirt no		goals	
14-Aug	A	Chester City	0	2	7	League Cup Rd 1, 1st leg - substituted
18-Aug	H	Chester City	4	3	7	League Cup Rd 1, 2nd leg
21-Aug	H	Hull City	1	0	7	
28-Aug	A	Sheffield United	1	1	7	
04-Sep	H	Burnley	3	0	7	
11-Sep	A	Nottingham Forest	3	4	7	
14-Sep	A	Carlisle United	2	2	7	
18-Sep	H	Charlton Athletic	1	2	7	
25-Sep	A	Fulham	1	4	7	
02-Oct	H	Wolverhampton Wanderers	1	6	7	
09-Oct	A	Luton Town	0	2	X	Omitted
16-Oct	A	Southampton	0	1	7	806th League game. Now retires
23-Oct	H	Notts County	1	4	X	Retired
30-Oct	A	Millwall	2	4	X	Retired
06-Nov	H	Chelsea	2	2	7	Un-retires
13-Nov	A	Bristol Rovers	3	2	7	
20-Nov	H	Oldham Athletic	0	0	7	
27-Nov	A	Blackburn Rovers	0	1	7	
15-Dec	H	Bolton Wanderers	3	3	7	
18-Dec	H	Orient	2	3	7	
27-Dec	A	Cardiff City	1	3	7	1
01-Jan	A	Chelsea	1	5	7	1
08-Jan	H	Reading	1	0	7	FA Cup Rd 3
22-Jan	A	Hull City	1	1	7	
29-Jan	A	Middlesbrough	0	4	7	FA Cup Rd 4 - substituted
09-Feb	H	Plymouth Argyle	1	1	7	
12-Feb	A	Burnley	1	1	X	Omitted
14-Feb	A	Blackpool	1	2	7	Substituted
25-Feb	A	Charlton Athletic	1	1	X	Omitted
02-Mar	H	Nottingham Forest	0	1	7	
05-Mar	H	Fulham	1	0	X	Omitted
12-Mar	A	Wolverhampton Wanderers	1	2	X	Omitted
19-Mar	H	Luton Town	0	1	12	Substitute for Spiring
23-Mar	H	Sheffield United	2	2	7	Substituted
01-Apr	A	Notts County	2	3	X	Omitted
06-Apr	H	Cardiff City	2	2	7	
09-Apr	A	Plymouth Argyle	1	2	X	Omitted
11-Apr	H	Bristol Rovers	1	1	7	1
16-Apr	A	Oldham Athletic	5	3	X	Omitted
20-Apr	H	Millwall	3	1	X	Omitted
23-Apr	H	Blackburn Rovers	1	0	X	Omitted
30-Apr	A	Bolton Wanderers	1	3	X	Omitted
04-May	H	Carlisle United	0	0	7	
07-May	H	Blackpool	1	1	X	Omitted
11-May	H	Southampton	2	0	7	
14-May	A	Orient	1	1	X	Omitted

	Season		Accumulative (Hereford)		Accumulative Totals	
	Apps	Goals	Apps	Goals	Apps	Goals
League	26 (+1)	3	106 (+5)	8	815 (+9)	168
FA Cup	2		8		59	11
League Cup	2		8 (+2)	2	45 (+2)	15
Welsh Cup			3		3	
Europe					8	2
SPFC					7	2
Total	30 (+1)	3	125 (+7)	10	937 (+11)	198

FA Cup appearances

Season	Round	Date	Opponents (+ their league)	Venue	Score	Paine goals
1957-58	1	16.11.57	Walton & Hersham (AL)	A	6-1	
	2	12.12.57	Crystal Palace (3S)	A	0-1	
1958-59	1	15.11.58	Woking (IL)	H	4-1	1
	2	06.12.58	Queens Park Rangers (D3)	A	1-0	
	3	10.01.59	Blackpool (D1)	H	1-2	
1959-60	1	14.11.59	Coventry City (D3)	A	1-1	
	1r	18.11.59	Coventry City	H	5-1	1
	2	05.12.59	Southend United (D3)	H	3-0	2
	3	09.01.60	Manchester City (D1)	A	5-1	
	4	30.01.60	Watford (D4)	H	2-2	
	4r	02.02.60	Watford	A	0-1	
1960-61	3	07.01.61	Ipswich Town (D2)	H	7-1	1
	4	28.01.61	Leyton Orient (D2)	H	0-1	
1961-62	3	06.01.62	Sunderland (D2)	H	2-2	
	3r	10.01.62	Sunderland	A	0-3	
1962-63	3	13.02.63	York City (D4)	H	5-0	
	4	27.02.63	Watford (D3)	H	3-1	
	5	16.03.63	Sheffield United (D1)	H	1-0	
	6	30.03.63	Nottingham Forest (D1)	A	1-1	1
	6r	03.04.63	Nottingham Forest	H	3-3 e	
	6 2r	08.04.63	Nottingham Forest	N	5-0	
	SF	27.04.63	Manchester United (D1)	N	0-1	
1963-64	3	04.01.64	Manchester United (D1)	H	2-3	1
1964-65	3	09.01.65	Leyton Orient (D2)	H	3-1	
	4	30.01.65	Crystal Palace (D2)	H	1-2	
1965-66	3	22.01.66	Hull City (D3)	A	0-1	
1966-67	3	28.01.67	Barrow (D4)	A	2-2	
	3r	01.02.67	Barrow	H	3-0	
	4	18.02.67	Bristol City (D2)	A	0-1	
1967-68	3	27.01.68	Newport County (D4)	H	1-1	
	3r	30.01.68	Newport County	A	3-2	
	4	17.02.68	West Bromwich A (D1)	A	1-1	
	4r	21.02.68	West Bromwich A	H	2-3	
1968-69	3	04.01.69	Oxford United (D2)	A	1-1	
	3r	08.01.69	Oxford United	H	2-0	2
	4	25.01.69	Aston Villa (D2)	H	2-2	
	4r	29.01.69	Aston Villa	A	1-2	
1969-70	3	03.01.70	Newcastle United (D1)	H	3-0	
	4	24.01.70	Leicester City (D2)	H	1-1	
	4r	28.01.70	Leicester City	A	2-4 e	1
1970-71	3	11.01.71	Bristol City (D2)	H	3-0	
	4	23.01.71	York City (D4)	A	3-3	
	4r	01.02.71	York City	H	3-2	
	5	13.02.71	Liverpool (D1)	A	0-1	
1971-72	3	15.01.72	Manchester United (D1)	H	1-1	
	3r	19.01.72	Manchester United	A	1-4 e	
1972-73	3	13.01.73	Crystal Palace (D1)	A	0-2	
1973-74	3	05.01.74	Blackpool (D2)	H	2-1	1
	4	26.01.74	Bolton Wanderers (D2)	H	3-3	
	4r	30.01.74	Bolton Wanderers	A	2-0 e	
	5	16.02.74	Wrexham (D3)	H	0-1	
1974-75	1	26.11.74	Gillingham (D3)	H	1-0	
	2	14.12.74	Cambridge United (D4)	A	0-2	
1975-76	1	22.11.75	Torquay United (D4)	H	2-0*	
	2	13.12.75	Bournemouth (D4)	A	2-2	
	2r	17.12.75	Bournemouth	H	2-0	
	3	03.01.76	York City (D2)	A	1-2	
1976-77	3	08.01.77	Reading (D3)	H	1-0	
	4	29.01.77	Middlesbrough (D1)	A	0-4*	
1978-79	1q	16.09.78	Clevedon Town (WL)	H	6-1	3
1979-80	pre	01.09.79	Devizes Town (WL)	A	1-0	
	1q	15.09.79	Paulton Rovers (WL)	A	2-0	

Abbreviations:

Opponents' league: D1, 2, 3, 4 = Football League division;
3S = Division Three (South);
AL, IL and WL = Athenian, Isthmian and
Western League, respectively.

Rounds:
r   replay;
2r   second replay;
SF   semi-final;
q   qualifying round;
pre   preliminary round.

Score: e = after extra-time.
* this indicates that Paine was substituted (having started in every FA Cup-tie he ever played in).

Sources

These details of sources are in two parts. First – save where the source is obvious in the text, eg. all the references to Channon's autobiography – you are told, chapter by chapter, which published sources (mainly books, but a few articles) were drawn upon. Where a named person is accompanied by an asterisk (*), this means that there are other quotations, or paraphrased information, in the chapter, taken from an interview with that person. There then follows a bibliography, providing, in the conventional manner, fuller details of published sources.

- **Chapter 2: Corinthian** Hennessy's recent histories, of the 1940s and '50s, have helped in painting the background picture. Dalton's prediction of 'football crowds' winning the 1945 election is cited by Howard.

- **Chapter 3: Citizen Paine** Ramsey's account of how Matthews met his requirements is from his 1952 autobiography.

- **Chapter 4: Changing His Stripes** The accounts of how Busby 'cornered' young talent and of how TV first featured youth football are from Connor and Wolstenholme, respectively. Alec and Terry Paine talked to a railway magazine that I have been unable to identify.

- **Chapter 5: Rising Star** The thoughts on Roper's attributes are from Whittaker's autobiography.

- **Chapter 6: Out on his Ears** Details of the law and procedures in respect of National Service are from Hickman. Accounts of medical exemptions are from Imlach* and Crerand.*

- **Chapter 8: Semi-Conscious** Accounts of the 1963 Cup-run are from Arlott, Cantwell, Bobby Charlton (1967), Hughes and Law*. Pelé's tribute to Williams is from his autobiography. McCreadie is described by Lovering. For the 'watershed' game v Leeds, see Sprake and Johnson.

- **Chapter 9: Beaten by Butlins** Greaves's* thoughts on Spurs' No.7s are from his 2006 memoirs. Carnaby's match report is in Juson and Bull.

- **Chapter 10: Change Here for Promotion** For Atyeo's prolonged grievance, see Hopegood. Godsiff wrote the Bristol City history.

- **Chapters 11-13** The three chapters on England have drawn upon autobiographies by Armfield,* Ball,* Cohen,* Hunter,* Hurst,* Banks, Peters, Shepherdson, and Charlton (2008); on biographies of Ramsey by

Bowler, McKinstry and Marquis; and of Moore by Powell. Downing reports press reaction to the win in Nuremberg. Greaves's thoughts* on Douglas are from his 1972, 1979 and 1990 memoirs. Hunt's thoughts* on Thompson's omission are in Massarella and Moynihan (eds.). See also Payne on England internationals and Hutchinson and Miller on 1966. Bennett, Ferrier and Moore reported in FA publications. Connelly and Thompson were interviewed by Moore for Sky.

McKinstry* led me to several of his primary sources, but I have been unable to verify the source of three comments by Ramsey – on the Lilleshall experiment; winning in Spain; and the lack of suitable wingers – each of which I have had to take, unattributed, from *Sir Alf*.

- **Chapter 14: Head Master:** See Hardaker's autobiography.

- **Chapter 15: Who Needs Coaches?** For Hunter's* boob, see his autobiography.

- **Chapter 16: Minding His Business** Hennessy's label is from his 2003 book.

- **Chapter 17: Alehouse Whines** Lorimer explained his embarrassment to Broadbent. The Arsenal history is by Soar and Tyler.

- **Chapter 19: Pretenders and Contenders** Harrison's* biographer is Smallbone. Pawson interviewed Bates about management.

- **Chapter 20: Land of Hype and Glory** See Risoli for Charles's time at Hereford.

- **Chapter 23: Defenders and Offenders** The quotations from Best, Hughes, Smith and Le Tissier are from Thompson's compendium of 'hard men'. Others are from Cooper or the biographies of Channon,* Bobby Charlton (2007), Jack Charlton,* Crerand,* Hill or Summerbee.*

- **Chapter 24: Kuwait a Moment** The Cheltenham chapters have referred to the history by Palmer and Goold and profiles by Matthews and Halliwell. See Hurst's autobiography for thoughts on managing Telford.

- **Chapter 26: Missionary** See the works on South Africa of Alegi, Booth and Raath.* Coventry's *Complete Record* is by Brown.*

- **Chapter 27: Ambassador** See McKinstry's biography of the Charltons.

Bibliography

All Hagiology titles owe a debt of gratitude to the researches, collections and collations of Duncan Holley and Gary Chalk:

Saints: a Complete Record of Southampton FC, 1885–1987, Breedon Books, 1987.
Alphabet of the Saints: a complete who's who of Southampton FC, ACL/Polar, 1992.
In That Number: a post-war chronicle of Southampton FC, Hagiology Publishing, 2003.

The other reference books on which I have constantly drawn have been the relevant seasons of those dependable annuals – the *News Chronicle Football Annual* (succeeded, from 1961-62, by the *News of the World Football Annual*) and the *Rothmans Football Yearbook* (reconstituted as the *Sky Sports Football Yearbook* from 2003-04) – and five other invaluable record books to which any chronicler of British football needs persistently to refer:

Mike Collett, *The Guinness Record of the FA Cup*, Guinness Publishing, 1993 (republished as *The Complete Record of the FA Cup*, Sportsbooks, 2003).
Barry J. Hugman (ed.), *The PFA Premier & Football League Players' Records 1946-2005*, Queen Anne Press, 2005.
Ian Laschke, *Rothmans Book of Football League Records 1988-89 to 1978-79*, Macdonald and Jane's, 1980.
Jack Rollin, *Rothmans Book of Football Records*, Headline, 1998
Dennis Turner & Alex White (eds.), *The Breedon Book of Football Managers*, 1993

For this biography, I have referred, in ways noted on the previous two pages, to the books, articles and videos listed below:

Peter Alegi, *Laduma! Soccer, Politics and Society in South Africa*, University of KwaZulu-Natal Press, 2004.
John Arlott, 'A Southampton Football Epic', *Hampshire: the County Magazine*, June 1963 (reproduced in David Rayern Allen, *Another Word from Arlott*, Pelham, 1985).
Jimmy Armfield, *Right Back to the Beginning: the autobiography*, Headline, 2004.
Alan Ball, *Playing Extra Time*, Sidgwick & Jackson, 2004.
Gordon Banks, *Banksy: my autobiography*, Michael Joseph, 2002.
Peter Batt, *Mick Channon: the authorised biography*, Highdown, 2004.
Alan Bennett, 'The Hungarians Return to Wembley', *FA News*, June 1965.
Douglas Booth, *The Race Game: Sport and Politics in South Africa*, Frank Cass, 1998.
Dave Bowler, *Winning Isn't Everything … : a biography of Sir Alf Ramsey*, Gollancz, 1998.
Rick Broadbent, *Looking for Eric: in search of the Leeds Greats*, Mainstream, 2000.
Jim Brown, *Coventry City: the elite era – a complete record*, Desert Island, 2006.
David Bull, *Dell Diamond: Ted Bates's first 60 seasons with The Saints*, Hagiology, 1998 (rev. pbk edn, 2004).
Noel Cantwell, *United We Stand*, Stanley Paul, 1965.

Mick Channon, *Man on the Run,* Arthur Barker, 1986.

Bobby Charlton, *Forward for England,* Pelham Books, 1967.

Bobby Charlton, *The Autobiography: my Manchester United years,* Headline, 2007.

Bobby Charlton, *The Autobiography: my England years,* Headline, 2008.

Jack Charlton with Peter Byrne, *Jack Charlton: the autobiography,* Partridge, 1996.

Steven Chaytor, *Can you get Bobby Charlton?,* Kipper Publications, 2003.

George Cohen, *My Autobiography,* Greenwater Publishing, 2003.

Jeff Connor, *The Lost Babes: Manchester United and the forgotten victims of Munich,*
    HarperCollins, 2006.

Mick Cooper, *Pompey People: Portsmouth Who's Who, 1899-2000,* Yore, 2000.

Pat Crerand, *Never Turn the Other Cheek,* HarperCollins, 2007.

Hunter Davies, *The Glory Game,* Weidenfeld and Nicolson, 1972.

Basil D'Oliveira, *The D'Oliveira Affair,* Collins, 1969.

David Downing, *The Best of Enemies: England v Germany,* Bloomsbury, 2000.

George Eastham, *Determined to Win,* Stanley Paul, 1964.

Bob Ferrier, 'The Match of the Century', *FA News,* December 1963.

Peter Godsiff, *Bristol City: the complete history of the club,* Wensum Books, 1979.

Jimmy Greaves, *My World of Soccer,* Stanley Paul, 1966.

Jimmy Greaves, *This One's On Me,* Arthur Barker, 1979.

Jimmy Greaves, *It's a Funny Old Life,* Weidenfeld & Nicolson, 1990.

Jimmy Greaves, *The Sixties Revisited,* Queen Anne Press, 1992.

Jimmy Greaves, *Greavsie: the autobiography,* Time Warner, 2003.

Jimmy Greaves, *The Heart of the Game,* Time Warner, 2005.

Jimmy Greaves and Reg Gutteridge, *Let's Be Honest,* Pelham, 1972.

Alan Hardaker with Bryon Butler, *Hardaker of the League,* Pelham, 1977.

Peter Hennessy, *Never Again: Britain 1945-51,* Jonathan Cape, 1992.

Peter Hennessy, *Having It So Good: Britain in the 1950s,* Allen Lane, 2006.

Tom Hickman, *The Call-up: a history of National Service,* Headline, 2004.

Gordon Hill and Jason Thomas, *Give a Little Whistle,* Souvenir Press, 1975.

Tom Hopegood and John Hudson, *Atyeo: the hero next door,* Redcliffe Press, 2005.

Anthony Howard, 'We are the Masters Now', in Michael Sissons and Philip French (eds.),
    Age of Austerity 1945-1951, Penguin, 1964.

Brian Hughes, *The King: Denis Law, hero of the Stretford End,* Empire Publications, 2003.

Norman Hunter, *Biting Talk: my autobiography,* Hodder & Stoughton, 2004.

Geoff Hurst, *1966 And All That: my autobiography,* Headline, 2001.

Roger Hutchinson, *... it is now! The real story of England's 1966 World Cup triumph,*
    Mainstream, 1995.

Gary Imlach, *My Father and Other Working-Class Heroes,* Yellow Jersey Press, 2005.

Dave Juson and David Bull, *Full-Time at The Dell,* Hagiology, 2001.

Peter Lovering, *Chelsea, Player by Player,* Guinness Publishing, 1993.

Denis Law, *Denis Law: an autobiography,* Queen Anne Press, 1979.

Denis Law with Bob Harris, *The King: an autobiography,* Bantam Press, 2003.

Leo McKinstry, *Jack & Bobby,* HarperCollins, 2002.

Leo McKinstry, *Sir Alf,* HarperCollins, 2006.

Max Marquis, *Anatomy of a Football Manager: Sir Alf Ramsey,* Arthur Barker, 1970.

Peter Matthews and Mark Halliwell, *Cheltenham Town: the rise of the Robins,* Tempus, 2002.

Arthur Mee, *The King's England: Hampshire with the Isle of Wight,* Hodder and Stoughton, first edition, 1939.

David Miller, *England's Last Glory: the boys of '66*, Pavilion, 1986.

Brian Moore, 'The England Tour', *FA News,* August 1963.

Peter Oborne, *Basil D'Oliveira – Cricket and Conspiracy: the untold story*, Little, Brown, 2004.

Jon Palmer and Tom Goold, *50 Greats: Cheltenham Town Football Club,* Stadia, 2006.

Ron Parrott, *Hereford United: the League era,* Desert Island Books, 1998.

Pat Partridge and John Gibson, *Oh, Ref!,* Souvenir Press, 1979.

Tony Pawson, *The Football Managers,* Eyre Methuen, 1973 (Readers Union edn, 1984).

Mike Payne, *England: the complete post-war record*, Breedon, 1993.

Pelé, *My Life and the Beautiful Game,* Doubleday, 1977.

Martin Peters with Michael Hart, *The Ghost of '66*, Orion, 2006.

Jeff Powell, *Bobby Moore: the authorised biography,* Everest, 1976 (updated as *Bobby Moore: the life and times of a sporting hero,* Robson Books, 1993).

Peter Raath, *Soccer Through The Years 1862-2002,* www.soccerthroughtheyears.com, 2002.

Alf Ramsey, *Talking Football,* Stanley Paul, 1952.

Mario Risoli, *John Charles: gentle giant,* Mainstream, 2003.

Len Shackleton, *Return of the Crown Prince,* GHKN Publishing, 2000.

Harold Shepherdson, *The Magic Sponge,* Pelham, 1968.

Colin Shindler, *George Best and 21 Others,* Headline, 2004.

Kevin Smallbone, *Brushes with the Greats: the story of a footballer/cricketer,* Sportingmemoriesonline.com, 2001.

Phil Soar and Martin Tyler, *Official History: Arsenal, 1886-1995,* Hamlyn, 1995.

Stuart Sprake and Tim Johnson, *Careless hands: the forgotten truth of Gary Sprake,* Tempus, 2006.

Mike Summerbee, *The Autobiography: the story of a true City hero,* Century, 2008.

Phil Thompson, *Do That Again Son and I'll Break Your Legs: football's hard men,* Virgin, 1996.

Tom Whittaker, *Tom Whittaker's Arsenal Story,* Sportsmans Book Club edn, 1958.

Jeremy Wilson, *Southampton's Cult Heroes,* Know The Score Books, 2006.

Kenneth Wolstenholme, *Young England,* Stanley Paul, 1959.

TV and video: I have drawn upon the *Brian Moore Interviews* (BSkyB, 1999) and three videos:

The Official History of the Saints, Meridian Films, 1990.

John Motson, *Match of the Day: Southampton FC,* BBC Enterprises, 1991.

England v Rest of the World, ICC, 1994.

Index

This index refers only to the 28 chapters and Appendix 1 (pages 1-412 of the text). Where a name occurs only in a caption, especially of a team line-up, it may not have been indexed.

Hagiology Publishing

**"Of all the single-club football histories,
those from the roseate crew
at Southampton are always the ones to relish."**

That is how leading sportswriter, Frank Keating, has described the histories of Southampton FC that have been produced by Hagiology Publishing.

The six books already published are:

DELL DIAMOND – the story of Ted Bates's first 60 seasons with the Saints. Initially published as a 366-page hardback in 1998 at £18.99, it was republished, as a commemorative, paperback edition (£9.99) in 2004, with a special, new chapter honouring Ted's last six seasons.

MATCH of the MILLENNIUM – accounts of the Saints' 100 most memorable matches, a 222-page paperback published in 2000 at £12.99.

FULL-TIME at THE DELL – a 240-page paperback published in 2001 at £16.95, this homage to Saints' 103 seasons at The Dell was included in Frank Keating's *Guardian* selection of "Top Six" sports books of 2001.

IN THAT NUMBER – this 640-page hardback, published in 2003 in full-colour at £35, is a post-war chronicle of the Saints, with reports on over 2,500 games and profiles of almost 400 players. Said by *BBC Sport OnLine* to "transport the mere club history to a new dimension" and to "set the yardstick by which every other club history will by now be judged."

SAINTS v POMPEY – this 288-page paperback, published in 2004 at £18.99, reports on the first 209 games played between these neighbours, from 1899 to 2004, and not only charts the men who have played for both but hears from fans who have followed both.

TIE A YELLOW RIBBON – this 178-page hardback, published in 2006 at £15.99, follows Lawrie McMenemy's team through the rounds of the FA Cup in 1976 to victory at Wembley and then hears from the 15 players in the squad about their subsequent experiences in football and life.

The collective, as photographed at St Mary's during the 2005-06 season.
(*Left to right*.) David Bull, Dave Juson, Gary Chalk, Duncan Holley.

Formed in 1998, Hagiology Publishing is a collective of four Saints fans committed to the collection and dissemination of accurate information on the history of Southampton FC.

This latest venture is Hagiology Publishing's seventh publication – and the sixth within an agreement with Southampton FC and the *Southern Daily Echo* regularly to produce books on aspects of Saints' history.

**To order any of the six previous publications direct –
with at least 20% OFF the hardback price and at least 25% OFF
the paperback prices – please visit *www.hagiologists.com*
or contact us at the address/number below.**
Postage extra – but not if we can arrange a pick-up,
at St Mary's or elsewhere

Enquiries about **CONSTANT PAINE** are welcolmed. Please contact:

David Bull, 170 Westbury Road, Bristol BS9 3AH
Tel: 0117 962 2042
bull.hagiology@blueyonder.co.uk